Paideia: the Ideals of Greek Culture

VOLUME I

Paideia: the Ideals of Greek Culture

By WERNER JAEGER

Translated from the Second German Edition
By GILBERT HIGHET

VOLUME I

Archaic Greece
The Mind of Athens

SECOND EDITION

OXFORD UNIVERSITY PRESS
New York

OXFORD UNIVERSITY PRESS
Oxford   London   Glasgow
New York   Toronto   Melbourne   Wellington
Nairobi   Dar es Salaam   Cape Town
Kuala Lumpur   Singapore   Jakarta   Hong Kong   Tokyo
Delhi   Bombay   Calcutta   Madras   Karachi

Paideia, the title of this work, is not merely a symbolic name, but the only exact designation of the actual historical subject presented in it. Indeed it is a difficult thing to define; like other broad comprehensive concepts (*philosophy*, for instance, or *culture*) it refuses to be confined within an abstract formula. Its full content and meaning become clear to us only when we read its history and follow its attempts to realize itself. By using a Greek word for a Greek thing, I intend to imply that it is seen with the eyes, not of modern men, but of the Greeks. It is impossible to avoid bringing in modern expressions like *civilization, culture, tradition, literature,* or *education.* But none of them really covers what the Greeks meant by paideia. Each of them is confined to one aspect of it: they cannot take in the same field as the Greek concept unless we employ them all together. Yet the very essence of scholarship and scholarly activity is based on the original unity of all these aspects—the unity which is expressed in the Greek word, not the diversity emphasized and completed by modern developments. The ancients were persuaded that education and culture are not a formal art or an abstract theory, distinct from the objective historical structure of a nation's spiritual life. They held them to be embodied in literature, which is the real expression of all higher culture. That is how we must interpret the definition of the cultured man given by Phrynichus (s.v. φιλόλογος, p. 483 Rutherford):

Φιλόλογος ὁ φιλῶν λόγους καὶ σπουδάζων περὶ παιδείαν.

CONTENTS

BOOK TWO

The Mind of Athens

PREFACE

I PRESENT to the public a work of historical research dealing with a subject hitherto unexplored. It treats *paideia*, the shaping of the Greek character, as a basis for a new study of Hellenism as a whole. Although many scholars have undertaken to describe the development of the state, the society, the literature, and religion, and the philosophy of the Greeks, no one seems to have attempted to explain the interaction between the historical process by which their character was formed and the intellectual process by which they constructed their ideal of human personality. I did not, however, take up this subject merely because I happened to observe that it had not yet been approached, but because I believed that a solution to this important historical and intellectual problem would bring a deeper understanding of the unique educational genius which is the secret of the undying influence of Greece on all subsequent ages.

The first volume describes the foundation, growth, and crisis of Greek culture during the periods dominated by the heroic and by the civic or political types of personality, that is, during the archaic and the classical epochs. It ends with the collapse of the Athenian empire. The second volume will record the renaissance of the intellect in the age of Plato, its struggle to master culture and the state, and the transformation of Greek civilization into a world-wide empire. I intend later to show how Rome and early Christianity were drawn into the cultural process which started with Greece.

The book is meant not only for scholars, but for all who seek to rediscover the approach to Greece during our present struggles to maintain our millennial civilization. It was often difficult, in writing it, to strike a balance between the wish to give a broad general survey and the pressing need to rehandle the complex material of each section of the book with the depth and accuracy it deserved. My study of the ancient world from this particular point of view has called my attention to a number of new problems, which have been the chief interest of my teaching and my research for the last ten years. But, rather than spoil the cumulative effect of the whole, I have determined not to publish my results in the form of supplementary volumes, which would have made the whole work disproportionately large. In the main, the proofs of my views are provided by the book itself, which always starts by interpreting the original texts, and puts the facts in a connexion which allows them to explain themselves. Footnotes give references to the passages quoted from classical authors, and to the most important modern literature—especially that which is directly concerned with problems in the history of culture. Where detailed exposition was indispensable, I was seldom able to give it in the form of notes. I have therefore published some of that part of my work in separate monographs, which are briefly cited in the footnotes; and I intend to publish the rest later. My book and my monographs form a whole, and constantly support and explain one another.

In the introduction, I have endeavoured to sketch the position of Greek paideia in history, from a more general point of view. I have also briefly pointed out how our understanding of the Greek type of cultural education affects our relation to the humanism of earlier centuries than our own. This problem is to-day more hotly debated than ever. Obviously, it cannot now be solved by historical research of this type, because it concerns not the Greeks but ourselves. But even to-day, it is impossible to have any educational purpose or knowledge without a thorough and fundamental comprehension of Greek culture. It was that conviction which created my scientific interest in the problem, and through it this book.

October 1933

PREFACE TO THE SECOND GERMAN EDITION

THE fact that a second edition of the first volume of *Paideia* has been called for after eighteen months is an encouraging sign that the book has quickly won friends. The time since its first publication has been too short to allow me to undertake any large changes in the text, but I have taken the opportunity to correct a few slips.

However, the nature of the book is such that most of the criticisms and discussions it has evoked are, as it were, reflections produced by the impact of one definite conception of history on a number of different minds. It has also initiated a discussion on the aim and methods of historical study which I cannot pursue here. It would require a separate book to give a theoretical basis for my attitude to Greek history: I prefer to allow it to be confirmed by the facts which have led me to adopt it. It is hardly necessary to say that the type of history embodied in this work is neither intended nor able to replace history in the traditional sense—the history of events. But it is no less necessary and justified to describe history in a way which explains the life of man through the creative literature which represents his ideals. Apart from the fact that many centuries of Greek history (for example, the archaic period) provide no other type of evidence worth mentioning, literature, even in periods which we know from other sources, is our most direct approach to the spiritual life of the past. For that reason, literature is the chief concern of this book, which is intended to describe the paideia of the Greeks, and, at the same time, the Greeks themselves as the paideia of mankind.

July 1935

PREFACE TO THE SECOND EDITION IN ENGLISH

AFTER the publication of Volumes Two and Three of *Paideia,* a new edition of the first volume has become necessary. Only minor corrections have been made in the text but the notes have been greatly expanded. They have been put at the end of the book in order to give the three volumes a more uniform appearance. The new notes were not translated from the German, as in the other two volumes; rather I have ventured to write them in English. I am indebted to Miss Aileen Ward of Radcliffe College, who has read my manuscript and helped me give my thought its final expression. I wish to thank also Mr. James Walsh of Harvard University, who copied the difficult manuscript, checked the references in the notes, and shared with me the burden of proofreading. Mr. Cedric Whitman of Harvard University has helped me in making the new index of this volume and I wish to thank him for this valuable service.

WERNER JAEGER

Harvard University
Cambridge, Mass.
Easter, 1945

TRANSLATOR'S NOTE

THIS translation has been read and approved by the author; but, if any slips have been overlooked, I should be grateful for notice of them.

References are to the Oxford Classical Texts, or failing them to Teubner. Philosophical fragments are quoted from the 5th Edition (by W. Kranz, 1934-7) of Diels' *Fragmente der Vorsokratiker;* and the lyric, iambic, and elegiac poets from Diehl's *Anthologia Lyrica Graeca* (Leipzig, I 1936, II 1925).

Quotations from classical authors are rendered in verse or prose, and occasionally compressed or simplified, to correspond with the style and scale of the original German version of the Greek. Where there are several possible interpretations of any text, I have of course followed that chosen by Professor Jaeger.

GILBERT HIGHET

INTRODUCTION

THE PLACE OF THE GREEKS IN THE HISTORY OF EDUCATION

EVERY nation which has reached a certain stage of development is instinctively impelled to practise education. Education is the process by which a community preserves and transmits its physical and intellectual character. For the individual passes away, but the type remains. The natural process of transmission from one generation to another ensures the perpetuation of the physical characteristics of animals and men; but men can transmit their social and intellectual nature only by exercising the qualities through which they created it—reason and conscious will. Through the exercise of these qualities man commands a freedom of development which is impossible to other living creatures—if we disregard the theory of prehistoric mutations in species and confine ourselves to the world of experience. By deliberate training even the physical nature of the human race can alter, and can acquire a higher range of abilities. But the human mind has infinitely richer potentialities of development. As man becomes increasingly aware of his own powers, he strives by learning more of the two worlds, the world without him and the world within, to create for himself the best kind of life. His peculiar nature, a combination of body and mind, creates special conditions governing the maintenance and transmission of his type, and imposes on him a special set of formative processes, physical and mental, which we denote as a whole by the name of education. Education, as practised by man, is inspired by the same creative and directive vital force which impels every natural species to maintain and preserve its own type; but it is raised to a far higher power by the deliberate effort of human knowledge and will to attain a known end.

From these facts certain general conclusions follow. To begin with, education is not a practice which concerns the individual alone: it is essentially a function of the community. The character of the community is expressed in the individuals who compose it; and for man, the ζῷον πολιτικόν, far more than for any animal species, the community is the source of all behaviour. The formative influence of the community on its members is most constantly active in its deliberate endeavour to educate each new generation of individuals so as to make them in its own image. The structure of every society is based on the written or unwritten laws which bind it and its members. Therefore, education in any human community (be it a family, a social class, a profession, or some wider complex such as a race or a state) is the direct expression of its active awareness of a *standard*.

Now, education keeps pace with the life and growth of the community, and is altered both by changes imposed on it from without and by transformations in its internal structure and intellectual development. And, since the basis of education is a general consciousness of the values which govern human life, its history is affected by changes in the values current within the community. When these values are stable, education is firmly based; when they are displaced or destroyed, the educational process is weakened until it becomes inoperative. This occurs whenever tradition is violently overthrown or suffers internal collapse. Nevertheless, stability is not a sure symptom of health in education. Educational ideals are often extremely stable in the epoch of senile conservatism which marks the end of a civilization—for example, in pre-revolutionary Confucian China, towards the end of Greco-Roman civilization, at the end of Judaism, and in certain periods of the history of the churches, of art, and of scientific schools. The history of ancient Egypt, which is reckoned not in centuries but in millennia, is marked by a dreadful rigidity which is almost fossilization. But among the Romans also, political and social stability was the highest good, and innovations were little desired or needed.

Greece is in a special category. From the point of view of the present day, the Greeks constitute a fundamental advance on the great peoples of the Orient, a new stage in the development of society. They established an entirely new set of principles for communal life. However highly we may value the artistic, religious, and political achievements of earlier nations, the history of what we can truly call civilization—the deliberate pursuit of an ideal—does not begin until Greece.

In the last hundred years, modern scholarship has immensely extended the horizon of history. The *oecumené,* the 'inhabited' world known to the Greeks and Romans, which for two thousand years was believed to be coterminous with the entire earth, has shrunk to a narrow section at its centre; and hitherto unexplored intellectual domains have been opened to our view. Yet it is even clearer to-day that this expansion of our intellectual horizon has not altered the central fact: in so far as it is not the history of one particular nation but of a group of nations to which, physically and intellectually, we belong, our history still begins with the Greeks. I have therefore called our own group of nations Hellenocentric.[1] By 'begins' I mean not only the temporal commencement, but also the ἀρχή, the spiritual source to which, as we reach every new stage of development, we must constantly revert in order to reorient ourselves. That is why throughout our history we always return to Greece. Yet our return to Greece, our spontaneous renewal of this influence, does not mean that by acknowledging the timeless and ever-present intellectual greatness of the Greeks, we have given them an authority over us which, because it is independent of our own destiny, is fixed and unchallengeable. On the contrary: we always return to Greece because it fulfils some need of our own life, although that need may be very different at different epochs. Of course each of the Hellenocentric nations feels that even Hellas and Rome are in some respects fundamentally alien to herself: the feeling is based partly on blood and sentiment, partly on organization and intellectual outlook, partly on historical distinctions. But there is a gigantic difference between that feeling and the sense of complete estrangement which we have when we confront the Oriental nations, who are both racially and intellectually different from us; and it is undoubtedly a serious mistake in historical perspective to separate, as some modern writers do, the western nations from the Greeks and Romans by a barrier comparable to that which divides us from China, India and Egypt.

Yet our kinship with Greece is not merely racial, however important the racial factor may be in understanding the nature of a people. When we say that our history begins with the Greeks, we must be sure of the meaning which we attach to the word history. History, for example, may connote the exploration of strange half-understood new worlds: that is how Herodotus conceived it. So to-day, when we have a keener perception of the morphology of human life in all its forms, we study even the remotest peoples with closer attention, and try to enter into their minds. But history in this quasi-anthropological sense must be distinguished from the history which is based on a true and active spiritual kinship, whether within one nation or within a small group of nations. Only in this type of history is it possible to achieve true understanding of the inner nature of a race or an epoch, and a creative contact between the observer and the observed. And only through it can we realize our common fund of mature social and intellectual forms and ideals, regardless of the manifold variations and interruptions, the blends and conflicts, disappearances and rebirths, which these forms and ideals must undergo among the many different races which make up one family of nations. Such a community of forms and ideals exists in a special sense between Greece and Rome on the one hand, and the great modern nations of the west, individually and collectively, on the other. If we accept this deeper conception of history—as expressing a community of origin and ideals— we can never make the whole world the object of a historical survey; and however widely our geographical horizon may be extended, the frontiers of our history can never recede beyond those which for the past three thousand years have bounded our historical destiny. It is impossible to say whether at some time in the future the whole human race will be united by a spiritual bond of the kind described here; and the question has no bearing on our present study.

The revolutionary, epoch-making position held by the Greeks in the history of education cannot be explained in a few sentences. The purpose of this book is to give an account of their culture, their *paideia,* and to describe its peculiar character and its historical development. It was not a sum of several abstract ideas; it was Greek history itself, in all its concrete reality. But the facts of Greek history would long ago have sunk into oblivion if the Greeks had not moulded them into a permanent form —the expression of their highest will, of their resistance to change and destiny. At the earliest stage of their development they had no clear conception of the nature of this act of will.

But as they moved into ever clearer vision, along their historical path, the ever present aim of their life came to be more and more vividly defined. It was the creation of a higher type of man. They believed that education embodied the purpose of all human effort. It was, they held, the ultimate justification for the existence of both the individual and the community. At the summit of their development, that was how they interpreted their nature and their task. There is no reasonable ground for the assumption that we could understand them any better through some superior insight, psychological, historical, or social. Even the majestic works of archaic Greece can best be understood in this light, for they were created by the same spirit. And it was ultimately in the form of paideia, 'culture', that the Greeks bequeathed the whole achievement of the Hellenic mind to the other nations of antiquity. Augustus envisaged the task of the Roman empire in terms of Greek culture. Without Greek cultural ideals, Greco-Roman civilization would not have been a historical unity, and the culture of the western world would never have existed.

We are accustomed to use the word culture, not to describe the ideal which only the Hellenocentric world possesses, but in a much more trivial and general sense, to denote something inherent in every nation of the world, even the most primitive. We use it for the entire complex of all the ways and expressions of life which characterize any one nation.[2] Thus the word has sunk to mean a simple anthropological concept, not a concept of value, a consciously pursued *ideal*. In this vague analogical sense it is permissible to talk of Chinese, Indian, Babylonian, Jewish or Egyptian culture, although none of these nations has a word or an ideal which corresponds to real culture. Of course every highly organized nation has an educational system; but the law and the prophets of the Israelites, the Confucian system of the Chinese, the Dharma of the Indians are in their whole intellectual structure fundamentally and essentially different from the Greek ideal of culture. And ultimately the habit of speaking of a number of pre-Hellenic 'cultures' was created by the positivist passion for reducing everything to the same terms: an outlook which applies hereditary European descriptions even to non-European things, and neglects the fact that historical method is falsified by any attempt to apply our conceptions to a world for-

eign to them. The circular reasoning to which almost all historical thought is liable begins with that basic error. It is impossible
to do away with it entirely, because we can never escape from
our own inborn ways of thinking. But we can at least solve the
fundamental problems of history, and one of them is to realize
the cardinal distinction between the pre-Hellenic world and the
world that begins with the Greeks—the world in which a cultural
ideal was first established as a formative principle.

Perhaps it is not great praise to say that the Greeks created
the ideal of culture. In an age which is in many respects tired of
civilization, it may even be a disparagement so to describe them.
But what we call culture to-day is an etiolate thing, the final
metamorphosis of the original Greek ideal. In Greek terms, it
is not so much paideia, as a vast disorganized external apparatus
for living, κατασκευὴ τοῦ βίου. It seems, in fact, that the culture
of the present cannot impart any value to the original Greek
form of culture, but rather needs illumination and transformation by that ideal, in order to establish its true meaning and
direction. And this realization of and return to the archetype
implies a mental attitude closely akin to the Greek—an attitude
which recurs in Goethe's philosophy of nature, though probably
without direct historical descent from Greece. Inevitably, towards the end of a historical period, when thought and custom
have petrified into rigidity, and when the elaborate machinery
of civilization opposes and represses man's heroic qualities, life
stirs again beneath the hard crust. At such times, a deep-seated
historical instinct drives men not only to go back to the resources
of their own national culture, but also to live once more in that
earlier age when the spirit of Greece (with which they have so
much in common) was still fervently alive, and from its ardent
life was creating the forms which eternalized its ardour and its
genius. Greece is much more than a mirror to reflect the civilization of to-day, or a symbol of our rationalist consciousness of
selfhood. The creation of any ideal is surrounded by all the
secrecy and wonder of birth; and, with the increasing danger of
degrading even the highest by daily use, men who realize the
deeper values of the human spirit must turn more and more to
the original forms in which it was first embodied, at the dawn of
historical memory and creative genius.

We have said that the world-wide historical importance of the

Greeks as educators was derived from their new awareness of the position of the individual in the community. When compared with the ancient East, they differ from it so fundamentally that their ideals seem to blend with those of modern Europe. Hence it is easy to conclude that the Greek ideal was the modern one of individualistic freedom. And in fact there could be no sharper contrast than that between the modern man's keen sense of his own individuality, and the self-abnegation of the pre-Hellenic Orient, made manifest in the sombre majesty of Egypt's pyramids and the royal tombs and monuments of the East. As against the Oriental exaltation of one God-king far above all natural proportions (which expresses a metaphysical view of life totally foreign to us) and the Oriental suppression of the great mass of the people (which is a corollary of that quasi-religious exaltation of the monarch), the beginning of Greek history appears to be the beginning of a new conception of the value of the individual. And it is difficult to refrain from identifying that new conception with the belief—which Christianity did most to spread—that each soul is in itself an end of infinite value, and with the ideal proclaimed during and after the Renaissance, that every individual is a law to himself. And how could the individual's claim to value and importance be justified, without the Greek recognition of the value of human character?

Historically it must be admitted that, since at the summit of their philosophical development the Greeks formulated and tried to solve the problem of the individual's place in the community, the history of personality in Europe must start with them. Roman civilization and the Christian religion each made some contribution to the question, and the mingling of these three influences created the modern individual's sense of complete selfhood. But we cannot clearly and fundamentally understand the position of Greek thought in the history of culture by starting from the modern point of view; it is far better to attack the question by considering the peculiar character of the Greek mind.

The variety, spontaneity, versatility, and freedom of individual character, which seem to have been the necessary conditions that allowed the Greek people to develop so rapidly in so many different ways, and which strike us with amazement in every Greek author from the earliest to the latest times, were not deliberately cultivated subjective qualities in the modern sense. They were natural, inborn. And when the Greeks who possessed them consciously realized their own individuality, they did so indirectly—by discovering objective standards and laws which, as soon as recognized, gave them a new certainty of thought and action. From the Oriental standpoint it is impossible to understand how the Greek artists contrived to represent the human body in free untrammelled motions and attitudes, not by the external process of copying a number of casually selected positions, but by learning the universal laws governing its structure, balance, and movement. Similarly, the distinguished and effortless ease of the Greek mind was produced by their lucid realization of the fact (concealed from earlier nations) that the world is governed by definite and comprehensible laws. They had an innate sense of the natural. The concept of 'nature,' which they were the first to work out, was without doubt produced by their peculiar mentality. Long before they conceived it, they had looked at the world with the steady gaze that did not see any part of it as separate and cut off from the rest, but always as an element in a living whole, from which it derived its position and its meaning. We call this the organic point of view, because it sees individual things as elements in a living whole. This sense of the natural, mature, original, and organic structure of life is closely connected with the Greek instinct to discover and formulate the laws governing reality—the instinct which appears in every sphere of Greek life, in their thought, their speech, their action, and all their art.

The characteristic Greek method of constructing and looking at a work of art was first and foremost an aesthetic instinct, based on the simple act of sight, not on the deliberate transference of an idea to the realm of artistic creation. It was relatively late in their history, in the classical period of the fifth and fourth centuries, that they idealized art, and blended an intellectual attitude with a physical and aesthetic act. Of course, when we say that their aesthetic sense was natural and unconscious, we have not explained why the same thing which is true of plastic art is also true of literature, where artistry does not depend on sight, but on the interplay of language and emotion. In Greek literature we find the same principles of form as in Greek sculpture and architecture. We speak of the plastic or the architectonic qualities of a poem or a prose work. Yet the qualities so described are not structural values *imitated* from sculpture or architecture, but *analogous* standards in language and its structure. We use these metaphors only because we grasp the structural principles of a statue or a building more vividly, and hence more quickly. The literary forms used by the Greeks, with all their manifold variety and elaborate structure, grew organically out of the transference of the bare simple forms in which men express themselves in language, to the ideal sphere of art and style. In the art of oratory too, their ability to carry out a complex plan and create an organic whole out of many parts proceeded purely and simply from a natural perception, increasingly sharpened, of the laws which govern feeling, thought, and speech—the perception which finally (grown abstract and technical) created logic, grammar, and rhetoric. In this respect we have had much to learn from the Greeks, and what we have learnt from them is the rigid and unalterable set of forms which still govern literature, thought, and style.

This applies even to the Greek mind's most miraculous creation, the most eloquent witness to its unique structure—philosophy. In philosophy the force which produced the forms of Greek art and thought is most visibly displayed. It is the clear perception of the permanent rules which underlie all events and changes in nature and in human life. Every people has produced a code of laws; but the Greeks always sought for one Law pervading everything, and tried to make their life and thought harmonize with it. They are the philosophers of the world. The *theoria* of Greek philosophy was deeply and inherently connected with Greek art and Greek poetry; for it embodied not only rational thought, the element which we think of first, but also (as the name implies) vision, which apprehends every object as a whole, which sees the *idea* in everything—namely, the visible pattern. Even when we know the dangers of generalizing, and of interpreting the earlier stage by the later, we cannot help realizing that the Platonic idea—a unique and specifically Hellenic intellectual product—is the clue to understanding the mentality of the Greeks in many other respects. In particular, the tendency to formalize which appears throughout Greek sculpture and painting sprang from the same source as the Platonic idea. The connexion was noted even in antiquity,[3] and has often been

observed since; but the same holds good of Greek oratory, and
in fact of the basic intellectual attitude of the Greeks throughout. For instance, the earliest natural philosophers, with their
efforts to see the cosmos as a whole governed by one law, are a
complete contrast to the calculating, experimental, empirical
scientists of modern times. They did not work by summarizing
a series of separate results and systematizing them into an abstract conclusion, but went much further, and interpreted each
isolated fact from a general conception which gave it position
and meaning as part of a whole. It was this tendency, too, to
construct universal patterns which distinguished Greek music
and mathematics from those of earlier nations, so far as they are
known to-day.

The unique position of Hellenism in the history of education
depends on the same peculiar characteristic, the supreme instinct
to regard every part as subordinate and relative to an ideal
whole—for the Greeks carried that point of view into life as
well as art—and also on their philosophical sense of the universal, their perception of the profoundest laws of human nature, and of the standards based on them which govern the
spiritual life of the individual and the structure of society. For
(as was realized by Heraclitus, with his keen insight into the
nature of the mind) the universal, the *logos,* is that which is
common to all minds, as law is to all citizens in the state. In approaching the problem of education, the Greeks relied wholly on
this clear realization of the natural principles governing human
life, and the immanent laws by which man exercises his physical
and intellectual powers.[4] To use that knowledge as a formative
force in education, and by it to shape the living man as the potter
moulds clay and the sculptor carves stone into preconceived form
—that was a bold creative idea which could have been developed
only by that nation of artists and philosophers. The greatest
work of art they had to create was Man. They were the first
to recognize that education means deliberately moulding human
character in accordance with an ideal. 'In hand and foot and
mind built foursquare without a flaw'—these are the words in
which a Greek poet of the age of Marathon and Salamis describes the essence of that true virtue which is so hard to acquire.
Only this type of education deserves the name of culture, the
type for which Plato uses the physical metaphor of *moulding*

character.[5] The German word *Bildung* [6] clearly indicates the
essence of education in the Greek, the Platonic sense; for it
covers the artist's act of plastic formation as well as the guiding
pattern present to his imagination, the *idea* or *typos*. Throughout history, whenever this conception reappears, it is always inherited from the Greeks; and it always reappears when man
abandons the idea of training the young like animals to perform
certain definite external duties, and recollects the true essence
of education. But there was a special reason for the fact that the
Greeks felt the task of education to be so great and so difficult,
and were drawn to it by an impulse of unparalleled strength.
That was due neither to their aesthetic vision nor to their 'theoretic' mentality. From our first glimpse of them, we find that
Man is the centre of their thought. Their anthropomorphic
gods; their concentration on the problem of depicting the human
form in sculpture and even in painting; the logical sequence by
which their philosophy moved from the problem of the cosmos
to the problem of man, in which it culminated with Socrates,
Plato, and Aristotle; their poetry, whose inexhaustible theme
from Homer throughout all the succeeding centuries is man, his
destiny, and his gods; and finally their state, which cannot be
understood unless viewed as the force which shaped man and
man's life—all these are separate rays from one great light.
They are the expressions of an anthropocentric attitude to life,
which cannot be explained by or derived from anything else, and
which pervades everything felt, made, or thought by the Greeks.
Other nations made gods, kings, spirits: the Greeks alone made
men.

We can now define the specific character of Hellenism, in
contrast to the Orient. By discovering man, the Greeks did not
discover the subjective self, but realized the universal laws of
human nature. The intellectual principle of the Greeks is not
individualism but 'humanism', to use the word in its original
and classical sense. It comes from *humanitas*: which, since the
time of Varro and Cicero at least, possessed a nobler and severer
sense in addition to its early vulgar sense of humane behaviour,
here irrelevant. It meant the process of educating man into his
true form, the real and genuine human nature.[7] That is the
true Greek paideia, adopted by the Roman statesman as a model.

It starts from the ideal, not from the individual. Above man as a member of the horde, and man as a supposedly independent personality, stands man as an ideal; and that ideal was the pattern towards which Greek educators as well as Greek poets, artists, and philosophers always looked. But what is the ideal man? It is the universally valid model of humanity which all individuals are bound to imitate. We have pointed out that the essence of education is to make each individual in the image of the community; the Greeks started by shaping human character on that communal model, became more and more conscious of the meaning of the process, and finally, entering more deeply into the problem of education, grasped its basic principles with a surer, more philosophical comprehension than any other nation at any other period in history.

The ideal of human character which they wished to educate each individual to attain was not an empty abstract pattern, existing outside time and space. It was the living ideal which had grown up in the very soil of Greece, and changed with the changing fortunes of the race, assimilating every stage of its history and intellectual development. This was not recognized by the classicists and humanists of earlier generations than ours —they left history out of account and construed the 'humanity', the 'culture', or the 'mind' of Greece or of classical antiquity as the expression of an absolute and timeless ideal. Of course the Greek nation bequeathed to its successors a great number of imperishable and immutable discoveries in the realm of the spirit. But it would be a most dangerous misconception of what we have described as the Greek will to shape individual character on an ideal standard, if we imagined that the standard was ever fixed and final. Euclidean geometry and Aristotelian logic are even now permanent sets of principles for the operation of the mind, and cannot possibly be put aside. Yet even these intellectual laws, universally valid, and purged of all temporal content, were created by Greek science; are, when viewed with a historical eye, Greek through and through; and do not exclude the co-existence of other mathematical and logical principles of thought and observation. And this is still more true of the other works of the Greek mind, which still bear the stamp of the age and nation that made them, and are directly connected with a definite historical situation.

The Greek critics who lived at the beginning of the Roman empire were the first to describe the masterpieces of the great age of Greece as 'classical' in the timeless sense—partly as formal patterns for subsequent artists to imitate, partly as ethical models for posterity to follow. At that time, Greek history had become part of the life of the world-wide empire of Rome, the Greeks had ceased to be an independent nation, and the only higher ideal which they could still follow was the preservation and veneration of their own tradition. So they were the first to develop the classicist theology of the mind—a legitimate description of that peculiar type of humanism. Their aesthetic *vita contemplativa* was the original form of the modern humanist's and scholar's life. Both lives were based on the same principle, an abstract timeless conception of the mind as a realm of eternal truth and beauty high above the troubled destinies of any one nation. Similarly, the German humanists of Goethe's time regarded the Greeks as the perfect manifestation of true human nature in one definite and unique historical epoch—an attitude nearer to the rationalism of the 'age of enlightenment' than to the new historical outlook which their doctrines actually encouraged.

A century of historical research, waxing while classicism waned, now separates us from that point of view. If to-day we counter the opposite danger—a boundless and aimless passion for viewing everything as history, a night in which all cats are grey—by returning to the permanent values of classical antiquity, still we can never again set them up as timeless idols. They cannot display the standards implicit in their meaning, and their irresistible power to transform and mould our lives, except as forces working within a definite historical milieu—just as they did in the era when they were created. We cannot any longer read or write histories of Greek literature *in vacuo,* cut off from the society which produced it and to which it was addressed. The Greek mind owes its superior strength to the fact that it was deeply rooted in the life of the community. All the ideals made manifest in its work were drawn, by the men who created them and reduced them to aesthetic form, from that powerful suprapersonal life. The man revealed in the work of the great Greeks is a political man. Greek education is not the sum of a number of private arts and skills intended to create a perfect independent personality. No one believed that it was, until the decline of Hellenism, when the Greek state as such had vanished—the age from which modern pedagogy is directly derived. It is easy to understand why the German classicists, living in an unpolitical age, followed that belief. But our own intellectual interest in the state has opened our eyes to the fact that in the best period of Greece mind without state was as impossible as a state without minds. The greatest works of Hellenism are memorials of a unique sense of the state, which developed uninterruptedly from the heroic age of Homer's epics to Plato's educational state, in which the individual and the community fight their last duel in the territory of philosophy. Any future humanism must be built on the fundamental fact of all Greek education—the fact that for the Greeks humanity always implied the essential quality of a human being, his political character.[8] It is a mark of the close connexion between the productive artistic and intellectual life and the community that the greatest of the Greeks always felt they were its servants. This attitude is well known in the East also: it seems to be most natural in a state where life is organized by severe quasi-religious rules. Yet the great men of Greece came forward not to utter the word of God, but to teach the people what they themselves knew, and to give shape to their ideals. Even when they spoke in the form of religious inspiration, they translated their inspiration into personal knowledge and personal form. But personal as it might be in shape and purpose, they themselves felt it fully and compellingly social. The Greek trinity of poet, statesman, and sage (ποιητὴς, πολιτικὸς, σοφός) embodied the nation's highest ideal of leadership. In that atmosphere of spiritual liberty, bound by deep knowledge (as if by a divine law) to the service of the community, the Greek creative genius conceived and attained that lofty educational ideal which sets it far above the more superficial artistic and intellectual brilliance of our individualistic civilization. That is what lifts classical Greek literature out of the category of pure aesthetics, in which many have vainly tried to understand it, and gives it the immeasurable influence on human nature which it has exercised for thousands of years.

The art of the Greeks, as it was at its greatest periods and in its noblest masterpieces, plays the strongest part in that influence upon us. In fact, we need a history of Greek art, considered as a reflection of the ideals which dominated Greek life from time to time. It is true of Greek art as well as of Greek literature that until late in the fourth century it is principally the expression of the spirit of the community. Who can understand, for instance, the athletic ideal evoked by Pindar's hymns of victory, without knowing the statues of the Olympic victors, which show us its physical incarnation, or the images of the gods that embody all the Greeks felt about the physical and spiritual perfection possible to man? The Doric temple is unquestionably the mightiest monument left by the Dorian character and the Dorian ideal of severely subordinating each individual part to a rigidly compact whole. It has still a vast power to make historically present the vanished life which it eternalizes and the religious faith by which it was inspired. But the true representatives of paideia were not, the Greeks believed, the voiceless artists—sculptor, painter, architect—but the poets and musicians, orators (which means statesmen) and philosophers. They felt that the legislator was in a certain respect more akin to the poet than was the plastic artist; for both the poet and the legislator had an educational mission. The legislator alone could claim the title of sculptor, for he alone shaped living men. Often as the Greeks compared the act of education with the work of the plastic artist, they themselves despite their artistic nature hardly ever thought that a man could be educated by looking at works of art, as Winckelmann did. They considered that the only genuine forces which could form the soul were words and sounds, and—so far as they work through words or sounds or both—rhythm and harmony; for the decisive factor in all paideia is active energy, which is even more important in the culture of the mind than in the *agon* which exercises physical strength and agility. According to the Greek conception, fine art belonged to a different category. Throughout the whole classical period it kept its place in the sphere of religion, from which it had originated. Essentially, a picture or a statue was an *agalma,* an ornament. That does not apply to the heroic epic, and from the heroic epic educational energy flowed into every other type of poetry. Even where poetry was closely connected with religion, its roots were deeply sunk in the soil of social and political life; and that applies to works in prose even more than to poetry. Thus, the history of Greek culture coincides in all essentials with the history of Greek literature: for Greek literature, in the sense intended by its original creators, was the expression of the process by which the Greek ideal shaped itself. Moreover, we have practically no literary evidence but poetry to help in understanding the centuries preceding the classical period, so that even for a history of Greece in the factual sense, the only subject which can really be discussed is that process as depicted in poetry and art. It was the will of history that nothing else should survive of all the life of that age. We cannot trace the culture of the Greeks through those centuries except by studying the ideal which they shaped and cultivated.

That fact prescribes the method and defines the purpose of this book. No special justification is needed for the choice of subjects discussed in it and the standpoint adopted in each case. On the whole they must justify themselves, although individual readers will doubtless regret that this or that has been omitted. It is an old problem that is posed here in a new way: for education has from the very beginning been closely connected with the study of the ancient world. The ages which succeeded it always regarded classical antiquity as an inexhaustible treasure of knowledge and culture—first as a collection of valuable external facts and arts, and later as a world of ideals to be imitated. The rise of modern classical scholarship brought with it a fundamental alteration in the point of view. Recent historical thought has been chiefly exercised to discover what really happened at any time and how it happened. In the passionate endeavour to see the past clearly, historians have slipped into regarding classical antiquity simply as a piece of history (although a peculiarly interesting piece) and have paid little attention to its direct influence on the world of to-day. To feel or not to feel that influence has become a matter of personal perception, and it has been left to personal taste to assess its value. But as this kind of encyclopaedic and factual approach to ancient history grew more and more general (although even as practised by its greater pioneers it was much less dispassionate and objective than they believed), few observed that some sort of 'classical culture' still existed in practice while it maintained its position unassailed. The classicist historical conceptions on which it was once based had been shattered by modern research; and classical scholarship made no endeavour to re-establish its ideal on a new basis. But at this juncture, when our whole civilization, shaken by an overpowering historical experience, is beginning to examine its own values once again, classical scholarship must once more assess the educational value of the ancient world. That is its last problem, and its own existence will depend on the answer. It can be answered only by historical science, on the basis of historical fact. The duty of classical scholarship, therefore, is not to give a flattering and idealistic description of the Greeks, but to interpret their imperishable educational achievement and the directive impetus which they gave to all subsequent cultural movements, by studying their own intellectual and spiritual nature.

BOOK ONE
ARCHAIC GREECE

NOBILITY AND ARETÉ

EDUCATION is such a natural and universal function of society that many generations accept and transmit it without question or discussion: thus the first mention of it in literature is relatively late. Its content is roughly the same in every nation—it is both moral and practical. It consists partly of commandments like *Honour the gods, Honour thy father and thy mother, Respect the stranger;* partly of ancient rules of practical wisdom and prescriptions of external morality; and partly of those professional skills and traditions which (as far as they are communicable from one generation to another) the Greeks named *techné*. The several Greek states later embodied in their written laws the elementary rules of respect for gods, parents, and strangers: such legislation, of course, drew no fundamental distinction between law and morality.[1] The rich stream of popular wisdom, on the other hand, carrying with it many ancient rules of conduct and many precepts sprung from old superstition, first flowed into daylight in the gnomic poetry of Hesiod.[2] But the arts and handicrafts naturally resisted the exposure of their secrets in writing, as can be seen from the doctors' professional oath in the Hippocratic corpus.[3]

The training of the young, in the above sense, must be distinguished from cultural education, which aims at fulfilling an ideal of man as he ought to be. In such an ideal pattern, utility is neglected, or at least relegated to the background. The vital factor is τὸ καλόν, the Beautiful as a determinant ideal.[4] The contrast between these two views of education can be seen throughout history, for it is a fundamental part of human nature. It matters little in what words we choose to describe them, but we may, perhaps, use the word Education for the former, and Culture for the latter. It is obvious that culture and education have different origins. Culture is shown in the whole man—both in his external appearance and conduct, and in his inner nature. Both the outer and the inner man are deliberately pro-

3

duced, by a conscious process of selection and discipline which
Plato compares to the breeding of good dogs. At first this
process is confined to one small class within the state—the nobility. The aristocratic origin of the *kalos kagathos* in classical
Greece is as clear as that of the gentleman of England. Both
titles carry us back to the ideal of knightly aristocracy. But as
the two types were taken over by the bourgeoisie in its rise to
power, the ideals inspiring them became universal and at last
affected the whole nation.

It is a fundamental fact in the history of culture that all
higher civilisation springs from the differentiation of social
classes—a differentiation which is created by natural variations
in physical and mental capacity between man and man. Even
when such social differentiations lead to the creation of a rigid
and privileged class, the hereditary principle which rules it is
counterbalanced by the new supplies of strength which pour in
from the lower classes. And even if the ruling caste is deprived
of all its rights, or destroyed, through some violent change, the
new leaders rapidly and inevitably become an aristocracy in their
turn. The nobility is the prime mover in forming a nation's culture. The history of Greek culture—that universally important
aspect of the formation of the Greek national character—actually begins in the aristocratic world of early Greece, with the
creation of a definite ideal of human perfection, an ideal towards
which the élite of the race was constantly trained.[5] Since our
earliest literary evidence shows us an aristocratic civilization
rising above the mass of the common people, we must start our
historical survey with a sketch of that civilization. All later culture, however high an intellectual level it may reach, and however greatly its content may change, still bears the imprint of
its aristocratic origin. Culture is simply the aristocratic ideal of
a nation, increasingly intellectualized.[6]

It would seem obvious for us to use the history of the word
paideia as a clue to the origins of Greek culture. But we cannot
do so, since the word does not occur before the fifth century.[7]
That is of course merely an accident of transmission. If new
sources were discovered, we might well find evidence of its occurrence at an earlier date. But even then we should be none
the wiser; for the earliest examples of its use show that at the

beginning of the fifth century it still had the narrow meaning of 'child-rearing' and practically nothing of its later, higher sense. We can find a more natural clue to the history of Greek culture in the history of the idea of *areté,* which goes back to the earliest times. There is no complete equivalent for the word areté in modern English: its oldest meaning is a combination of proud and courtly morality with warlike valour. But the idea of areté is the quintessence of early Greek aristocratic education.

The aristocracies of early Greece are first described by Homer—if we may use that name for the two great epics, the *Iliad* and the *Odyssey*. In Homer we find both the historical evidence for the life of that epoch and the permanent poetic expression of its ideals. We must study him from both points of view. We shall first use him to build up our picture of the aristocratic world, and then examine the ideals of that world as they are embodied in his heroes. For in the great figures of the epic the ideals of aristocracy attain a cultural significance which is far wider than their first narrow sphere of validity. We cannot, in fact, follow the history of culture unless we fix our attention on the ebb and flow of historical development, and at the same time on the artistic struggle to perpetuate the ideal which is the highest expression of every creative epoch.

In Homer, as elsewhere, the word areté is frequently used in a wide sense, to describe not only human merit but the excellence of non-human things—the power of the gods, the spirit and speed of noble horses.[8] But ordinary men have no areté; and whenever slavery lays hold of the son of a noble race, Zeus takes away half of his areté—he is no longer the same man as he was.[9] Areté is the real attribute of the nobleman. The Greeks always believed that surpassing strength and prowess were the natural basis of leadership: it was impossible to dissociate leadership and areté. The root of the word is the same as that of ἄριστος, the word which shows superlative ability and superiority; and ἄριστος was constantly used in the plural to denote the nobility. It was natural for the Greeks, who ranked every man according to his ability,[10] to use the same standard for the world in general. That is why they could apply the word areté to things and beings which were not human, and that is why the content of the word grew richer in later times. For a man's ability can be appraised by different standards, varying according to the duties he has to perform. Only now and then, in later books, does Homer use areté for moral or spiritual qualities.[11] Everywhere else (in conformity with the ideas of primitive Greece) it denotes the strength and skill of a warrior or athlete, and above all his heroic valour. But such valour is not considered as a moral quality distinct from strength, in the modern sense; it is always closely bound up with physical power.

It is not probable that in living speech the word areté had only the narrow Homeric sense, at the time when the two poems came into being. The epics themselves recognise standards other than areté. The *Odyssey* constantly exalts intellectual ability—especially in its hero, whose courage is usually ranked lower than his cleverness and cunning. In Homer's time merits different from valour and strength may well have been contained in the notion of areté: apart from the above exceptions, we find such extensions elsewhere in early poetry. It is clear that the new meaning given to the word by everyday speech was then forcing its way into the language of poetry. But areté as a special description of heroic strength and courage was by then fast rooted in the traditional speech of heroic poetry, and was to remain as such for a long period. It was natural that, in the warlike age of the great migrations, men should be valued chiefly for their prowess in battle: there are analogies for this in other countries. Again, the adjective ἀγαθός, which corresponds to the noun areté though it derives from a different root, came to imply the combination of nobility and valour in war. It meant sometimes 'noble' and sometimes 'brave' or 'capable'; but it seldom meant 'good' in the later sense, any more than areté meant 'moral virtue'. This old meaning long survived, in such formalised expressions as 'he died like a brave hero'; [12] and is often found in sepulchral inscriptions and accounts of battles.

Now, although the military connotation of these words [13] predominates in Homer, they have also a more general ethical sense. Both meanings were derived from the same root: both denote the gentlemen who possess (both in war and in private life) standards which are not valid for the common people. Thus the code of the nobility had a twofold influence on Greek education. In the first place, the city-state inherited from it one of the finest elements in its ethical system—the obligation to be brave. (In the city-state courage was called manliness, a clear reminiscence of the Homeric identification of courage with manly areté.) And, secondly, the higher social standards of the polis were derived from aristocratic practice; as is shown not so much in any particular precepts of bourgeois morality as in the general ideals of liberality and a certain magnificence in the conduct of life.[14]

In Homer, the real mark of the nobleman is his sense of duty. He is judged, and is proud to be judged, by a severe standard. And the nobleman educates others by presenting to them an eternal ideal, to which they have a duty to conform. His sense of duty is *aidos*. Anyone is free to appeal to aidos; and if it is slighted the slight awakes in others the kindred emotion of *nemesis*.[15] Both aidos and nemesis are essential parts of Homer's ideal of aristocracy. The nobleman's pride in high race and ancient achievement is partnered by his knowledge that his pre-eminence can be guaranteed only by the virtues which won it. The aristoi are distinguished by that name from the mass of the common people: and though there are many aristoi, they are always striving with one another for the prize of areté. The Greek nobles believed that the real test of manly virtue was victory in battle—a victory which was not merely the physical conquest of an enemy, but the proof of hard-won areté. This idea is exactly suited by the word *aristeia,* which was later used for the single-handed adventures of an epic hero.[16] The hero's whole life and effort are a race for the first prize, an unceasing strife for supremacy over his peers. (Hence the eternal delight in poetic accounts of these aristeiai.) In peace-time too, the warriors match their aretai against one another in war-games: in the *Iliad* we see them in competition even in a brief pause in the war, at the funeral games of Patroclus. It was that chivalrous rivalry which struck out the motto of knighthood [17] throughout the centuries:

αἰὲν ἀριστεύειν καὶ ὑπείροχον ἔμμεναι ἄλλων.

(This motto, which teachers of all ages have quoted to their pupils, modern educational 'levellers' have now, for the first time, abandoned.) Into that one sentence the poet has condensed the whole educational outlook of the nobility. When Glaucus meets Diomede on the battlefield, and wishes to prove himself a worthy opponent, he first (in the Homeric manner) names his illustrious ancestors, and then continues: 'Hippolochus begat me, and I claim to be his son. He sent me to Troy, and often gave me this command, to strive always for the highest areté, and to excel all others.' It is the finest possible expression of the inspiration of heroic strife: and it was familiar to the author of the eleventh book of the *Iliad,* who makes Peleus give the same counsel to his son Achilles.[18]

There is another way in which the *Iliad* bears witness to the high educational ideals of the early Greek aristocracy. It shows that the old conception of areté as warlike prowess could not satisfy the poets of a new age: their new ideal of human perfection was that character which united nobility of action with nobility of mind. And it is important to notice that the new concept is expressed by Phoenix, who is the old counsellor and teacher of Achilles, the pattern-hero of Greece. At a crisis in the action, he reminds his pupil of the ideal on which he has been moulded: 'to be both a speaker of words and a doer of deeds'. The later Greeks were right in believing this verse to be the earliest formulation of the Greek educational ideal, of its effort to express the whole of human potentialities.[19] It was often quoted in the later ages of rhetoric and sophistication to set off the departed heroic world of action against the wordy and inactive present; but it can be interpreted in another way, for it shows the whole mental outlook of the aristocracy. They believed that mastery of words meant intellectual sovereignty. Phoenix speaks this line to Achilles when he has just received the envoys of the Greek chiefs with sullen anger. The poet presents the eloquent Odysseus and Ajax the laconic man of action as contrasts to Achilles himself. By this contrast he emphasises the highest ideal of developed humanity as personified in the greatest of the heroes—Achilles—who has been trained to it by the third envoy Phoenix. The word areté had originally meant warlike prowess; but it is clear from this passage that a later age found no difficulty in transforming the concept of nobility to suit its own higher ideals, and that the word itself was to acquire a broader meaning to suit this developing ideal.

An essential concomitant of areté is honour. In a primitive community it is inseparable from merit and ability. Aristotle [20] has well described it as a natural standard for man's half-realised efforts to attain areté. 'Men,' he says, 'seem to pursue honour in order to assure themselves of their own worth—their areté. They strive to be honoured for it, by men who know them and who are judicious. It is therefore clear that they recognise areté as superior.' The philosophy of later times then bade man obey an inner standard: it taught him to regard honour as the external image of his inner value, reflected in the criticism of his fellows. But the Homeric man estimated his own worth exclusively by the standards of the society to which he belonged. He was a creature of his class: he measured his own areté by the opinion which others held of him. Yet the philosophic man of later times could dispense with such external recognition, although (as Aristotle says) he might not be entirely indifferent to it.[21]

Homer and the aristocracy of his time believed that the denial of honour due was the greatest of human tragedies. The heroes treat one another with constant respect, since their whole social system depends on such respect. They have all an insatiable thirst for honour, a thirst which is itself a moral quality of individual heroes. It is natural for the great hero or the powerful prince to demand high and higher honour. When the Homeric man does a great deed, he never hesitates to claim the honour which is its fit reward. It is not chiefly the question of payment for services rendered which occupies him. The sources of honour and dishonour are praise and blame (ἔπαινος and ψόγος). But praise and blame were considered by the philosophic morality of later times to be the foundations of social life, the expression of objective social standards.[22] Nowadays we must find it difficult to imagine how entirely *public* was the conscience of a Greek. (In fact, the early Greeks never conceived anything like the personal conscience of modern times.)[23] Yet we must strive to recognise that fact, before we can comprehend what they meant by honour. Christian sentiment will regard any claim to honour, any self-advancement, as an expression of sinful vanity. The Greeks, however, believed such ambition to be the aspiration of the individual towards that ideal and supra-personal sphere in which alone he can have real value. Thus it is true in some sense to say that the areté of a hero is completed only in his death. Areté exists in mortal man. Areté *is* mortal man. But it survives the mortal, and lives on in his glory, in that very ideal of his areté which accompanied and directed him through-out his life.[24] The gods themselves claim their due honour. They jealously avenge any infringement of it, and pride themselves on the praise which their worshippers give to their deeds. Homer's gods are an immortal aristocracy. And the essence of Greek worship and piety lay in giving honour to godhead: to be pious is 'to honour the divinity'.[25] To honour both gods and men for their areté is a primitive instinct.

On this basis, we can comprehend the tragic conflict of Achilles in the *Iliad*. His indignation at his comrades and his refusal to help them do not spring from an exaggerated individual ambition. A great ambition is, for Greek sentiment, the quality of a great hero. When the hero's honour is offended, the very foundations of the alliance of the Achaean warriors against Troy are shaken. The man who infringes another's honour ends by losing sight of true areté itself. Such a difficulty would now be mitigated by feelings of patriotism; but patriotism is strange to the old aristocratic world.[26] Agamemnon can only make a despotic appeal to his own sovereign power; and such an appeal is equally foreign to aristocratic sentiment, which recognises the leader only as *primus inter pares*. Achilles, when he is refused the honour which he has earned, feels that he is an aristocrat confronted by a despot. But that is not the chief issue. The head and front of the offence is that a pre-eminent areté has been denied its honour.[27] The death of Ajax, the mightiest Greek hero after Achilles, is the second great tragedy of offended honour. The weapons of the dead Achilles are awarded to Odysseus, although Ajax has done more to earn them. The tragedy of Ajax ends in madness and death;[28] the wrath of Achilles brings the Greek army to the edge of the abyss. Homer can scarcely say whether it is possible to repair honour once it has been injured. Phoenix advises Achilles not to bend the bow too far, and to accept Agamemnon's gift as an atonement—for the sake of his comrades in their affliction. But it is not only from obstinacy that Achilles in the original saga refuses the offers of atonement: as is shown once more by the parallel example of Ajax, who returns no answer to the sympathetic words of his former enemy Odysseus when they meet in the underworld, but silently turns away 'to the other souls, into the dark kingdom of the dead'.[29] Thetis entreats Zeus [30] thus: 'Honour my son, who must die sooner than all others. Agamemnon has robbed him of his honour; do you honour him, Olympian!' And the highest of the gods is gracious to Achilles, by allowing the Achaeans, deprived of his help, to be defeated; so that they see how unjustly they have acted in cheating their greatest hero of his honour.

In later ages, love of honour was not considered as a merit by the Greeks: it came to correspond to ambition as we know it. But even in the age of democracy we can see that love of honour was often held to be justifiable in the intercourse of both individuals and states.[31] We can best understand the moral nobility of this idea by considering Aristotle's description of the *megalopsychos,* the proud or high-minded man.[32] In many details, the ethical doctrines of Plato and Aristotle were founded on the aristocratic morality of early Greece: in fact, there is much need for a historical investigation (from that point of view) of the origin, development, and transmission of the ideas which we know as Platonic and Aristotelian. The class limitations of the old ideals were removed when they were sublimated and universalised by philosophy: while their permanent truth and their indestructible ideality were confirmed and strengthened by that process. Of course the thought of the fourth century is more highly detailed and elaborated than that of Homeric times. We cannot expect to find its ideas, or even their exact equivalents, in Homer. But in many respects Aristotle, like the Greeks of all ages, has his gaze fixed on Homer's characters, and he develops his ideals after the heroic patterns. That is enough to show that he was far better able to understand early Greek ideas than we are.

It is initially surprising for us to find that pride or high-mindedness is considered as a virtue. And it is also notable that Aristotle does not believe it to be an independent virtue like the others, but one which presupposes them and is 'in a way an ornament to them'.[33] We cannot understand this unless we recognise that Aristotle is here trying to assign the correct place in his analysis of the moral consciousness to the high-minded areté of old aristocratic morality. In another connexion [34] he says that he considers Achilles and Ajax to be the ideal patterns of this quality. High-mindedness is in itself morally worthless, and even ridiculous, unless it is backed by full areté, the highest unity of all excellences, which neither Aristotle nor Plato shrinks from describing as *kalokagathia*.[35] The great Athenian thinkers bear witness to the aristocratic origin of their philosophy, by holding that areté cannot reach true perfection except in the high-minded man. Both Aristotle and Homer justify their belief that high-mindedness is the finest expression of spiritual and moral personality, by basing it on areté as worthy of honour.[36] 'For honour is the prize of areté; it is the tribute paid to men of ability.' Hence pride is an enhancement of areté. But it is also laid down that to attain true pride, true magnanimity is the most difficult of all human tasks.

Here, then, we can grasp the vital significance of early aristocratic morality for the shaping of the Greek character. It is immediately clear that the Greek conception of man and his areté developed along an unbroken line throughout Greek history. Although it was transformed and enriched in succeeding centuries, it retained the shape which it had taken in the moral code of the nobility. The aristocratic character of the Greek ideal of culture was always based on this conception of areté.

Under the guidance of Aristotle, we may here investigate some of its further implications. He explains that human effort after complete areté is the product of an ennobled self-love, φιλαυτία.[37] This doctrine is not a mere caprice of abstract speculation—if it were, it would be misleading to compare it with early conceptions of areté. Aristotle is defending the ideal of fully justified self-love as against the current beliefs of his own enlightened and 'altruistic' age; and in doing so he has laid bare one of the foundations of Greek ethical thought. In fact, he admires self-love, just as he prizes high-mindedness and the desire for honour, because his philosophy is deeply rooted in the old aristocratic code of morality. We must understand that the Self is not the physical self, but the ideal which inspires us, the ideal which every nobleman strives to realise in his own life. If we grasp that, we shall see that it is the highest kind of self-love which makes man reach out towards the highest areté: through which he 'takes possession of the beautiful'.[38] The last phrase is so entirely Greek that it is hard to translate. For the Greeks, beauty meant nobility also. To lay claim to the beautiful, to take possession of it, means to overlook no opportunity of winning the prize of the highest areté.

But what did Aristotle mean by the beautiful? Our thoughts turn at once to the sophisticated views of later ages—the cult of the individual, the humanism of the eighteenth century, with its aspirations towards aesthetic and spiritual self-development. But Aristotle's own words are quite clear. They show that he was thinking chiefly of acts of moral heroism. A man who loves himself will (he thought) always be ready to sacrifice himself for his friends or his country, to abandon possessions and honours in order to 'take possession of the beautiful'.[39] The strange phrase is repeated: and we can now see why Aristotle should think that the utmost sacrifice to an ideal is a proof of a highly developed self-love. 'For,' he says, 'such a man would prefer short intense pleasures to long quiet ones; would choose to live nobly for a year rather than to pass many years of ordinary life; would rather do one great and noble deed than many small ones.'

These sentences reveal the very heart of the Greek view of life—the sense of heroism through which we feel them most closely akin to ourselves. By this clue we can understand the whole of Hellenic history—it is the psychological explanation of the short but glorious aristeia of the Greek spirit. The basic motive of Greek areté is contained in the words 'to take possession of the beautiful'. The courage of a Homeric nobleman is superior to a mad berserk contempt of death in this—that he subordinates his physical self to the demands of a higher aim, the beautiful. And so the man who gives up his life to win the beautiful, will find that his natural instinct for self-assertion finds its highest expression in self-sacrifice. The speech of Diotima in Plato's *Symposium* draws a parallel between the struggles of law-giver and poet to build their spiritual monuments, and the willingness of the great heroes of antiquity to sacrifice their all and to bear hardship, struggle, and death, in order to win the prize of imperishable fame. Both these efforts are explained in the speech as examples of the powerful instinct which drives mortal man to wish for self-perpetuation. That instinct is described as the metaphysical ground of the paradoxes of human ambition.[40] Aristotle himself wrote a hymn to the immortal areté of his friend Hermias, the prince of Atarneus, who died to keep faith with his philosophical and moral ideals; and in that hymn he expressly connects his own philosophical conception of areté with that found in Homer, and with its Homeric ideals Achilles and Ajax.[41] And it is clear that many features in his description of self-love are drawn from the character of Achilles. The Homeric poems and the great Athenian philosophers are bound together by the continuing life of the old Hellenic ideal of areté.

THE CULTURE AND EDUCATION OF THE HOMERIC NOBILITY

ARETÉ was the central ideal of all Greek culture. We may complement and illustrate what we have already learnt of it by a survey of the life of the primitive Greek aristocracy, as it is depicted in the 'Homeric' poems. We shall find that this survey confirms the views we have already reached.

In considering the *Iliad* and the *Odyssey* as historical evidence for early Greek civilization, we cannot treat them as a unity, as the work of one poet. We do in practice continue to speak of 'Homer'; so did the ancients, who originally subsumed many other epics under the same name.[1] The Greeks of the classical period (when the historical sense was not yet developed) were the first to separate the *Iliad* and the *Odyssey* from the rest of the epic corpus, and to discard the other poems as unworthy of Homer. But their choice need not affect our judgment; it has not the validity of what we call historical tradition. Historically, it is clear that the *Iliad* is a work of greater antiquity than the *Odyssey,* and that the *Odyssey* portrays a later stage of civilization.

When that fact is acknowledged, it becomes vitally important to assign each of the poems to the century in which it was created. But, speaking broadly, this problem can be solved only by examination of the poems themselves; and all the intellectual labour which has been spent on such examination has led only to universal doubt and uncertainty. The excavations of the last fifty years have added much to our knowledge of Greek prehistory. In particular, they have given us a clearer view of the historical basis of the old heroic saga-tradition. But we cannot truly affirm that we have been helped to fix the dates of the *Iliad* and *Odyssey* thereby; because they were created centuries later than the sagas which are their core.

Analysis of the poems themselves, then, is our chief guide in dating them. But analysis was not originally directed to that

end. It was inspired rather by the ancient tradition that the final
recension of the epics had been made at a comparatively late
date—a tradition which provoked conjectural reconstructions of
the earlier stages during which the epics had circulated as numerous independent ballads.[2] At first, this analysis proceeded on
purely logical and aesthetic grounds. It was chiefly Wilamowitz
who brought it into relation with our historical knowledge of
primitive Greece.[3] To-day, the real problem is this: are we to
confine our historical analysis to an examination of the *Iliad* and
Odyssey as a whole (which would be equivalent to abandoning
the investigation), or are we to extend it to the inevitably hypothetical attempt to distinguish *within the epics* strata of different
ages and characters?[4] This problem does not affect the justifiable and still unsatisfied claim that the poems should be judged
above all as an artistic whole. That ideal, of course, affects any
discussion of Homer's poetic value. But—to take one example—
it is impossible to examine the *Odyssey* as a historical description
of the primitive aristocracy of Greece, if the sections which are
most relevant for that purpose were produced in the middle of
the sixth century.[5] This point of view cannot be countered by
simple scepticism. It must be met either by reasoned opposition,
or by an acceptance of all its consequences.

Naturally, I cannot produce my own analysis of the poems in
this book. However, I believe I have proved satisfactorily that
the first book of the *Odyssey* (which critics since Kirchhoff have
regarded as one of the latest insertions in the poem) was considered to be the work of Homer, not only by Solon, but very
probably by the Greeks of the age before Solon's archonship
(594). That is, it was held to be Homeric in the seventh century
at least.[6] In his latest work on the subject Wilamowitz was
forced to the belief that the great intellectual movements of the
seventh and sixth centuries had no influence on the *Odyssey*—an
assumption which is difficult to explain even by his own account
of later rhapsodic poetry as pedantic and remote from life.[7] On
the other hand, the ethical and religious rationalism which is
supreme in the present form of the *Odyssey* must date from an
earlier period in Ionia; for the beginning of the sixth century
saw the rise of Milesian natural science, a phenomenon which
harmonises neither with the society described in the *Odyssey* nor
with its geographical and political ideas.[8] I am quite convinced

that the *Odyssey* existed, virtually in its present state, before Hesiod. On the other hand, I feel certain of this: philological analysis has made certain fundamental discoveries about the origins of the epic, which will remain valid even if our logic and imagination can never solve the whole secret. The scholar always wants to know more than can be known. His ambition is pardonable, but it has often brought his work into disrepute. Nowadays, a book which refers (as this does) to 'early' and 'late' strata in the *Iliad* must contain new arguments to justify the reference. I believe that I could offer such arguments, although I shall not put them forward here. On the whole, the *Iliad* gives the impression of greater antiquity than the *Odyssey;* but that need not mean that it reached its final form much earlier than the sister poem. It was, of course, the model on which all later epics were to be constructed; yet the epic pattern itself is the creation of one particular age, and soon fitted itself to other material. It may be added that those who consider the later periods of epic to be aesthetically inferior to the earlier are suffering from a prejudice created by the Romantic age and its peculiar conception of folk-poetry. They underestimate the poetic value of the 'editorial period' which closed the development of epic poetry—nay, they deliberately disparage it, instead of trying to understand its artistic aims and methods. And this prejudice has largely created the distrust with which 'common sense' regards scholarship and scholarly criticism: a distrust based, as always, on the discrepancies between the findings of various scholars. But in investigating this weighty problem, where scholarship must constantly turn back to examine its own hypotheses, scepticism must not be allowed to have the last word —although scholars studying the subject cannot now aim so high as they did in previous generations.

In the elder epic, we see a world at war: and war, we must assume, was incessant during the great wandering of the Greek peoples. The *Iliad* tells of an age almost wholly dominated by the ancient hero-spirit of areté; and it embodies the ideal of areté in each of its heroes. It blends in an indissoluble unity the old poetic pictures of the saga-heroes and the living traditions of the contemporary aristocracy—an aristocracy which (as is shown by the description of Hector and the Trojans) already knows the organized life of the city-state. Throughout the poem, the brave man is the nobleman, the man of rank. Battle and victory are his highest distinction; they are the real meaning of his life. The *Iliad* is, of course, compelled by its material to describe the warlike type of life above all others; the *Odyssey* has few occasions for describing the prowess of heroes in battle. But if any fact about the origin of the poems is established, it is that the oldest heroic poetry was a glorification of fighting and heroic prowess, and that the *Iliad* took its material from old poems of that type.[9] The story of the *Iliad* is branded with the stamp of antiquity. Its heroes prove themselves noble not only by their love of battle and their lust for honour, but also by their general conduct, in which they remain aristocrats, with the strength and the unmistakable weaknesses of an aristocracy. We canot imagine them existing in peace: they live on the field of battle. Apart from battle, we see them only during temporary pauses in the war, at their meals, at sacrifice, in council.

The *Odyssey* presents a different picture. The *Nostos,* the tale of the Heroes' Return, made a natural pendant to the tale of the wars at Troy; and it easily led on to the description of their life in peace. The sagas of the Return were very old. But a later age found its chief interest in the human side of the heroes' lives, was repelled by the bloody fighting of the *Iliad,* and was drawn to mirror its own life in the characters and events described by the old sagas. When the *Odyssey* depicts the existence of the heroes after the war, their adventurous voyages and their home-life among their families and friends, it is inspired by the life of the aristocrats of its own day, projected with a naïve realism into a more primitive epoch. It is therefore our chief piece of evidence for the nature of early Greek aristocratic civilization. That civilization belongs to Ionia (where the *Odyssey* must have been created) but it may be regarded as typically Greek in all that interests us here. We can clearly see that the *Odyssey* portrays that life, not as an assemblage of poetic details derived from old sagas, but as something real, something recorded from contemporary observation. Epic tradition offered far fewer models for the portrayal of these domestic scenes: it had been concerned with heroes and their deeds, not with quiet descriptions of ordinary events. The new motif of peaceful life was not only introduced by the tales of the Nostos, but was chosen along with the tales themselves, by the taste of a more contemplative, hedonistic, and pacific age.

By seeing and portraying as a living whole the culture of an entire social class (that of the noblemen settled on their estates), the *Odyssey* marks a decided advance in artistic observation of life and its problems. It is an epic changing into a novel. Its world merges, at the circumference, into the fairyland of the heroic sagas and the poet's adventurous imagination; but at the centre it is illuminated by the strong light of reality. It is true that even its descriptions of home-life sometimes contain fabulous elements—the princely splendour of Menelaus' palace and the home of the rich Phaeacian king makes an abrupt contrast with the rustic simplicity of Odysseus' manor-house, and is obviously inspired by traditions of the pomp and beauty of the great Mycenaean kingdoms, perhaps also by contemporary tales of Oriental splendour.[10] Nevertheless, the picture of the nobleman's life which the *Odyssey* gives is distinguished by its vivid realism from that given by the *Iliad*. As we have shown, the *Iliad* offers a largely idealized picture of the aristocracy, an imaginative portrayal embodying many features taken straight out of old heroic poetry. It is dominated by the outlook which shaped the heroic tradition—namely, admiration of the superhuman areté of the ancient heroes. There are only a few traces of a realistic political attitude, to betray the relatively late period which saw the creation of the *Iliad* in its present form. Such is the episode of Thersites, 'the Daring': as is shown by the disrespectful tone he adopts to the nobles.[11] Thersites is the only really malicious caricature in the whole of Homer. But everything goes to show that the role of the aristocracy was still unshaken when the new age began to deliver such attacks as these upon the old régime. It is true that the *Odyssey* contains no similar traces of political innovation. The community of Ithaca is governed, in the absence of its king, by a popular assembly under the leadership of the noblemen; and the city of the Phaeacians is a faithful likeness of an Ionian city ruled by a king.[12] But the poet obviously feels that aristocracy is a social and psychological problem: he looks at it with an interest which is somehow detached.[13] He is thus enabled to depict it objectively, and completely; despite his sharp criticism of the unworthy nobles, he shows that unmistakable admiration for truly noble sentiments and aristocratic culture which has made his evidence so indispensable for students of history.

In the *Odyssey*, the aristocracy is an exclusive caste with a strong consciousness of its privileges, its commanding power, and its refinement of life and behaviour. Instead of the grandiose passions, the tragic destinies, and the colossal figures of the *Iliad*, we find in the younger poem a multitude of everyday characters. Each of them has something human, something lovable in him. Their speeches and their acts are filled with what is called *ethos* by the later rhetorical critics. They show great refinement in all their intercourse with one another: in Nausicaa's judicious treatment of Odysseus as he comes, naked and shipwrecked, to implore her protection, in Telemachus' conversation with his father's old guest-friend Mentes, and the gracious entertainment which he enjoys at the courts of Nestor and Menelaus, in the hospitable reception which Alcinous offers to his famous guest, in the noble courtesy of Odysseus' parting from Alcinous and his queen, no less than in the meeting of the old swineherd Eumaeus with his master in beggar's guise, and in his wise civility to his master's young son Telemachus. The deep spiritual refinement of these scenes complements the formal correctness shown on other occasions—the correctness that always characterizes the life of a society which admires polite speech and civil behaviour. Even the exchanges between the brutal, arrogant suitors and Telemachus are, despite the parties' mutual hatred, conducted with impeccable politeness. Every member of this society, noble or commoner, bears its one invariable stamp, the stamp of decorum and good breeding in all situations. The shameless behaviour of the suitors is constantly stigmatized as a disgrace to them and to their class. No one can witness it without indignation; and in the end it is severely punished. Nevertheless, they are called the noble suitors, the illustrious suitors, the valiant suitors quite as often as they are reproached by references to their outrageous conduct: the poet always remembers that they are gentlemen of rank and breeding. Their punishment is very hard, because their offence was doubly grave. And although their wickedness is a dark blot on the escutcheon of their rank, it is hidden by the shining courtesy of the principal characters, who are described with all conceivable charm and sympathy. The suitors do not diminish the poet's admiration for the nobility as a whole. He loves the men and women whom he portrays: we can see in every line that he admires their culture and their high refinement. It is certain that he had an educational purpose in thus exalting them. He presents the courtesy of his heroes as an absolute value; not as an unimportant background to their life, but as a real factor in their superiority. For him, the forms and formalities of their life are inseparable from their conduct. Courtesy is the bloom on their lives. It gives them a special excellence, which they justify both by their grand and noble deeds, and by their blameless conduct in happiness and misery alike. By divine ordinance they are favoured above all men; the gods protect and cherish them; and their mortal worth shines out in the nobility of their life.

The presuppositions of aristocratic civilization are fixed residence in one place, ownership of land,[14] and respect for tradition. These are the factors which allow a set form of life to be transmitted unaltered from one generation to another. But to them must be added 'good breeding'—a conscious education of the young towards the aristocratic ideal, under the severe discipline of courtly manners and morals. Although the *Odyssey* shows the same kindly courtesy extended to every commoner down to the beggar at the gate, although it assumes no sharp cleavage between the nobles and the people, although there is a patriarchal friendship and co-operation between master and servant, nevertheless there is no trace of any conscious education and culture outside the upper class. Aristocracy, in all ages and all nations, is marked by *discipline,* the deliberate formation of human character through wise direction and constant advice. It is the only class which can claim to produce the complete Man —a claim which cannot be justified without cultivating all the fundamental human qualities towards that perfect end. It is not enough for the young to grow 'as gently as a tree' into the social and moral code of their ancestors. The superior rank and worth of the aristocracy imply an obligation to shape its members during their malleable youth into the accepted ideal of nobility. In this process education becomes culture for the first time: that is, it becomes a process by which the whole personality is modelled on a fixed pattern. The Greeks always felt the importance of such a pattern in the development of any type of culture.[15] It is, in fact, essential in any aristocratic civilization, whether its ideal be the καλὸς κἀγαθός of Greece, the *cortesia* of mediæval knighthood, or the social elegance that smiles its conventional smile from the portraits of the eighteenth century.

In the *Odyssey* as in the *Iliad,* the highest standard of manly character is the traditional ideal of warlike valour. But the *Odyssey* also exalts the intellectual and social virtues. Its hero is the man who is never at a loss for an apt word or a clever plan. His chief merit is his cunning—the fertile practical insight which saves his life and wins his return to his home through lurking dangers and powerful enemies. The Greeks themselves, especially those of the mainland, did not accept this ideal without some objections. But it was not the creation of any individual poet: it was worked out through long centuries of experience—hence its frequent inconsistencies.[16] The cunning storm-tossed adventurer Odysseus is the creation of the age when Ionian sailors wandered the seas far and wide. His connexion with the Trojan saga, and above all his part in the destruction of Ilium,[17] made it necessary to glorify his character. The courtly manners which are attributed to him in the *Odyssey* were imposed by the social surroundings in which the poem places him; for it is the society of the *Odyssey* which makes the poem. In the other characters too the emphasis is laid less on their heroic than on their human qualities: their intellectual and spiritual sides usually predominate. Telemachus, for instance, is frequently called prudent, or sensible; Menelaus' wife boasts that he lacks no excellence, whether of mind or of body; it is said of Nausicaa that she did not fail of right understanding; Penelope is described as clever and prudent.

A word on the educational influence of women in this civilization. The real areté of woman is beauty—naturally enough: men are valued by their intellectual and physical excellence. The cult of feminine beauty in Greece of this period corresponds to the courtly refinement of every knightly age. However, woman is not only the goal and ideal of erotic admiration (like Helen and Penelope); she also has a constant social and legal status as mistress of the household, and as such her virtues are sober morality and domestic prudence. Penelope is highly praised for her wisdom, her chastity, and her good housekeeping. Yet the sight of Helen's beauty, which has brought such disaster on

Troy, is enough to disarm the Trojan elders: as they look on it, they decide to blame the gods alone for all their misfortune.[18] After the fall of Troy she returns to Sparta with her first husband; and in the *Odyssey* she is the pattern of all great ladies, the model of social elegance. She leads the conversation with her young guest Telemachus—even before he is presented to her she makes a graceful reference to his surprising resemblance to his father Odysseus, and shows, by her tact, her complete mastery of the social art.[19] No decent housewife ever appears without her distaff: her maids place it before her whenever she takes her seat in the men's hall. But Helen's workbox is silver, and her distaff is golden: they are only decorative attributes of the great lady.[20]

Women held a higher social position at the close of the period of Homeric chivalry than at any other time in Greek history. Arété, the wife of the Phaeacian king, is honoured like a goddess among the people. Her appearance is enough to end their disputes; her advice sways the deliberations of her husband.[21] When Odysseus needs protection and transport back to his home in Ithaca, on Nausicaa's advice he does not make his appeal to her father the king, but embraces the knees of the queen in supplication; since her good will is essential if his prayer is to be granted.[22] Penelope, husbandless and helpless, moves among the noisy suitors with perfect assurance that she will receive all the respect due to a woman.[23] The courtesy with which Homeric gentlemen treat all ladies is the product of an old civilization and a highly developed social education. The respect and honour paid to woman is not due merely to the useful work she does (as it is in the peasant life described by Hesiod[24]) nor to her position as mother of legitimate children to carry on the family name (as in later Greek city-life); although an aristocracy which takes pride in purity of descent must also respect the women who are the mothers of the next generation.[25] The Homeric nobility honours woman as the repository of high morality and old tradition. That is her true spiritual dignity; and it has its effect even on man's erotic behaviour. In the first book of the *Odyssey* (which shows a greater refinement of moral ideas than the older parts of the epic) there is one detail which illustrates the current sexual ethic. When Eurycleia, the trusted old servant of Odysseus' family, lights Telemachus on his way to bed, the poet briefly tells her life-story in the epic manner. Old Laertes, he says, had purchased her for a very high price when she was a girl. Throughout his life he kept her in his home, and honoured her as highly as his own wife, but he never lay with her because he feared his wife's anger.[26]

Far less refined ideas appear in the *Iliad*. When Agamemnon wins Chryseis as spoil of conquest, he resolves to take her back to Greece with him, and declares at an assembly of the army that he prefers her even to his wife Clytaemnestra, since she is not inferior to the queen either in beauty and stature or in wit and skill.[27] (The ancient commentators have observed that all the areté of a woman is here described in one line.) This high-handed decision may, it is true, be part of Agamemnon's personal character; but the masterful tone in which he thrusts all considerations aside is not unexampled elsewhere in the poem. Amyntor, father of Phoenix, quarrels about his mistress with his son, and leaves his wife for her sake. The wife incites her son to make love to the concubine and estrange her from Amyntor.[28] Be it noted that this happens in peace-time: it is not the behaviour of war-maddened soldiers.

The morality of the *Odyssey* is universally on a much higher plane. In the wonderful conversation of Odysseus and Nausicaa, when the experienced man speaks simply and wisely to the naïve girl, we see with what tenderness and refinement the hero treats a woman.[29] There true culture is portrayed for its own sake, just as lovingly as the beauties of Alcinous' garden, the pomp of his palace, or the melancholy loveliness of Calypso's lonely isle. The essential good-breeding of the whole scene is produced by the educative influence of woman upon a stern and warlike masculine society. Finally, the intimate relationship of the hero to his divine companion and friend, Pallas Athena, is a most beautiful expression of the feminine power of inspiration and guidance through the trials of the world.

In investigating the state of culture among the Homeric aristocracy, we need not depend entirely on the evidence offered by occasional descriptions of courtly manners and morals; the epics also contain a vivid description of the education of young noblemen. We should do best here to take the later sections of the *Iliad* in conjunction with the *Odyssey;* since a conscious interest in educational problems, like the above-mentioned emphasis on moral refinements, is confined to the newer strata of the poems. Besides the *Telemachia,* with which we shall deal presently, the chief evidence on this point is Book IX of the *Iliad.* The idea of setting the old man Phoenix beside the young hero Achilles, as his tutor and adviser, has produced one of the finest scenes in the epic—although the conception itself is certainly later than the body of the poem. It is difficult after all, to imagine the heroes of the *Iliad* except as mature warriors. Few readers ask themselves how these men grew up, and how the farseeing wisdom of their parents and instructors guided them from boyhood towards their mighty deeds and heroic maturity. There is no doubt that the original saga took little account of such questions. But the feudal spirit, which through its inexhaustible interest in the pedigrees of the great heroes created a new branch of epic poetry, managed also to construct histories of the youth and education of the great men of old.

The tutor of the heroes *par excellence* is the wise centaur Chiron, who lived among the wooded glens of Mount Pelion in Thessaly.[30] Tradition said that many famous heroes had been his pupils; and that Peleus, deserted by his wife Thetis, made him guardian of his son Achilles. In early times his name was attached to a didactic poem in the epic style (Χίρωνος ὑποθῆκαι) : it was a series of instructive aphorisms in verse, probably derived from aristocratic tradition.[31] The poem was apparently addressed to Achilles himself. It must have been full of proverbial commonplaces, to be attributed to Hesiod as it was in antiquity. The few verses which have been preserved are not enough to allow us to describe it with any certainty; but Pindar's appeal to it [32] is sufficient evidence of its aristocratic content. Pindar himself represents a new and deeper view of the relation of education to natural ability: he holds that mere teaching has little to do with the formation of heroic areté. But his pious faith in saga-tradition leads him to confess that the great men of ancient times received instruction from masters filled with a love of heroism. Sometimes he simply admits the fact, sometimes he strives to deny it; but it is certain that he found the tradition firmly established, and it is clearly older than the *Iliad.* Although the poet of Book IX substitutes Phoenix for Chiron as Achilles' instructor, yet in another passage [33] Patroclus is bidden to smear on a warrior's wound the healing remedies that he learned from

Achilles, who had been taught them by Chiron, most righteous of the centaurs. Chiron's instruction is there confined to medical matters—he was of course the instructor of Asclepios.[34] But Pindar calls him the teacher of Achilles in the hunt and in all the high arts of chivalry; it is clear that this was the original conception.[35] The poet of the Embassy to Achilles could not set the half-savage centaur beside Odysseus and Ajax in their attempt to pacify Achilles; he must have held that only a knightly hero would be a fitting instructor for the greatest of all heroes. (The poet would not abandon the saga-tradition without good reason: he must therefore have made the change at the dictates of his own experience.) As a substitute for Chiron he chose Phoenix, who was a vassal of Peleus and prince of the Dolopians.[36]

Grave doubts have been cast upon the originality of the speech of Phoenix in the Embassy scene, and in fact upon the whole character of Phoenix, who never appears again in the *Iliad*. There is unmistakable evidence that an earlier form of the scene must have existed, in which Odysseus and Ajax were the only envoys sent to Achilles by the army. But it is impossible to reconstruct this earlier form merely by excising Phoenix's great admonitory speech—as impossible as are most such reconstructions, even where the traces of revision are as obvious as they are here.[37] In the present form of the poem, the character of the old teacher stands in close relation to the two envoys. As we have shown,[38] Ajax embodies the element of action in Phoenix's educational ideal, and Odysseus the element of speech. Achilles alone unites both these elements: he fulfils the true harmony of the highest powers of both body and mind. Any interference with the speech of Phoenix is bound to affect the speeches of the other two envoys, and so to destroy the whole artistic structure of the scene.

The absurdity of such criticisms can be proved in another way. The common explanation of the insertion of Phoenix's speech entirely misconceives the poetic purpose of the scene. The speech is actually of extraordinary length: it lasts more than a hundred lines; its climax (and, to a careless reader, its chief purpose) is the tale of Meleager's wrath. Critics have therefore supposed that the poet modelled the Wrath of Achilles on an earlier tale of the Wrath of Meleager, and that in this passage he was quoting his source (making a literary allusion in the Hellenistic manner) and giving an extract from the older epic.[39] We may or may not believe that a poetic version of Meleager's saga existed at the period when *Iliad* IX was created, or that the poet took over a purely verbal tradition. In any case, Phoenix's speech is the very model of a protreptic address delivered by a teacher to his pupil, and the lengthy narrative of Meleager's wrath and its disastrous consequences is one of the mythological examples which are frequent throughout the speeches of the *Iliad* and *Odyssey*.[40] The chief characteristic of every variety of didactic speech is the introduction of an instructive example.[41] And the cautionary example of Meleager is most appropriate in the mouth of the old teacher whose selfless fidelity and devotion Achilles cannot question. Phoenix can voice a truth which Odysseus dare not utter. And, coming from him, this last attempt to bow the hero's stubborn will has a graver and deeper meaning: for its failure shows the climax of the tragedy as the grim outcome of Achilles' own wrath and obduracy.

This passage, more than any other in the *Iliad*, justifies Plato's description of Homer as the teacher and guide of tragic poets.[42] The ancients themselves felt this. For the scene gives an ethical and instructive turn to the plot of the whole poem; and the form in which the example of Meleager is couched strongly emphasizes the basic moral principle of Nemesis.[43] It compels every reader to feel the full import of Achilles' decision, upon which depends the fate of the Greek army, of his dear friend Patroclus, and ultimately of himself. Through it we are led to think of the wrath of Achilles as a universal problem. The poet who left us the *Iliad* in its present complete form evoked in this scene the mighty religious conception of Até, the madness of doom: like an ominous phantom, it rises half-seen behind the other compelling moral allegory of the Litai, the prayers, and the callous heart of man.[44]

The whole idea is of the greatest importance in the history of Greek education. It shows us the regular pattern, the underlying ideal of the old aristocratic training. When Achilles has no experience either of warfare or of the art of oratory, his father Peleus sends his most trusty vassal to be his companion on the battlefield and at court, and to mould him after the traditional pattern of manliness.[45] Phoenix is marked out for this post by his long years of faithful service to Achilles: and his service is only a continuation of the almost parental love which has always bound him to the young hero. In a touching passage he reminds Achilles of his boyhood, when he was held on Phoenix's knee at dinner in Peleus' hall, since he would not eat beside anyone else; and he tells him how he cut slices of meat for Achilles before himself, and held the wine cup for him to drink: 'often you spluttered out the wine, poor silly child, and wet the shirt on my breast'.[46] Phoenix, in fact, has always thought of Achilles as the son who was denied to him by his father's curse; and thus he looks to Achilles for filial protection in his old age. But he is not only the tutor and half-paternal friend of Achilles. He is also his guide through the deeper problems of moral self-discipline. The figures immortalized by the ancient sagas are living patterns for this type of education. Not only heroes of superhuman strength and courage, they are also men inspired and enlivened by the stream of new and daily deepening experience which flows through the noble old traditions and draws from them an ever fresh significance.

It is clear that the poet admires the lofty type of education which he has immortalized in the character of Phoenix. But, for this very reason, he finds that the fate of Achilles, the hero *sans reproche,* is a difficult problem. Against the vast irrational power of Até, the goddess Infatuation, every educational resource and every form of exhortation is vain. But the poet incarnates the ideas and the pleadings of higher reason as kindly half-divine figures, who follow slowly and haltingly behind the fleet steps of Até to repair the harm that she does.[47] They are the daughters of great Zeus. When they approach, men must respect them and listen to them: they will be friendly to those who do, and help them. But if a man refuses and stubbornly hardens his heart against the Prayers, they send Até on him, and he atones by his own ruin.[48] This vivid and concrete presentation of the unequal struggle between good and evil spirits to win the human heart expresses that internal conflict between blind passion and higher insight which is the truest and deepest problem of all education. Here we must not introduce the modern ideas of free-will, choice, and guilt. The ancient conception is far wider and far more tragic. The critical problem is not that of guilt and responsibility, as it is at the beginning of the *Odyssey.*[49] We see in fact

that the cheerfully practical educational ideas of the old aristocracy are even in the *Iliad* (where they first appear) already
merging into a grave consciousness of the limitations of every
type of education.[50]

The antitype of the relentless Achilles is the mild Telemachus.
In the first book of the *Odyssey* we are shown something of his
education. While Achilles rejects the teachings of Phoenix and
meets his doom thereby, Telemachus gives willing ear to the
counsels of the goddess Athena, disguised as his father's friend
Mentes.[51] But the advice of Mentes is the same as the prompt-
ings of Telemachus' own heart. He is in fact the pattern of the
docile youth who is led on to glory by accepting the advice of an
experienced friend. In the succeeding books Athena—the goddess who in Homeric belief inspired men to fortunate adventures—disguises herself as another old friend, Mentor,[52] and
accompanies Telemachus to Pylus and Sparta. This idea seems
to derive from the custom of sending a guardian with every
noble youth when he left his home on a journey. Mentor watches
every step his pupil takes, and helps him at every turn, with
kindly words and wise advice. He instructs him in the forms of
courtly behaviour, when he finds himself in novel and difficult
situations. He teaches him how to address old noblemen like
Nestor and Menelaus, and how to make his request of them in
such a way as to ensure its success. Ever since the publication of
Fénélon's *Télémaque,* the name of Mentor has denoted an old
and faithful guide, philosopher, and friend. His love for Telemachus embodies the love of a teacher for his pupil.

This educational motif, which runs through the whole
Telemachia,[53] deserves closer examination. It is clear that the
poet's purpose was not merely to set down a few scenes from
high life. The core of his charming narrative is, and is intended
to be, the problem of converting the young son of Odysseus into
a thoughtful man whose high purposes shall be crowned with
noble achievement. It is impossible to read the *Odyssey* without
feeling its deliberately educational outlook as a whole, although
many parts of the poem show no trace of it. That impression
derives from the universal aspect of the spiritual conflict and
development which moves parallel with the external events in

the tale of Telemachus—which is in fact their real plot and leads to their real climax.

In a critical discussion of the origins of the *Odyssey*, one notable question must be raised. Was the Telemachia at one time an independent poem, or was it written for the epic as we have it at present? We may leave the problem unsolved.[54] Even if there was at one time a separate epic of Telemachus, the independent working-out of this part of the saga can be explained only by the interest of an audience in its peculiar subject. An age which had thought much of educational problems was led to study and develop the traditional material in which they could be embodied and realized. Apart from the bare facts of Telemachus' birth and home, tradition offered no nucleus of concrete fact for creative imagination. But the poet developed the tale of Telemachus' youth on its own logical basis, and introduced it into the *Odyssey* by a fine device—bringing gradually together two separate figures: Odysseus, kept far away on the seagirt isle of Calypso, and his son, waiting idly at home for his father. Both at once start to move towards each other; and the hero returns to a home which is ready to receive him. This plot unfolds itself against a background of aristocratic life. At first, Telemachus is only a youth, helpless before the arrogant suitors of his mother. He watches their insolent conduct with resignation, and without the strength to make an independent decision to end it; a mild and incompetent young man, whose innate nobility makes it impossible for him even to oppose the men who are ruining his home, far less to justify his rights with violent action. Passive, amiably weak, hopelessly complaining, he would be useless as a comrade for Odysseus on his return to his lonely fight with the suitors, his final danger and final revenge. It is Athena, then, who trains Telemachus to be a man of strong decision and ready daring, a fit companion for that last fight.

We have tried to show that the character of Telemachus in the first four books of the *Odyssey* is so presented as to serve a deliberate educational end. To this view it has been objected that Greek poetry does not display internal developments of character.[55] The Telemachia is certainly not a novel of educational problems, and the change in Telemachus' character cannot be described as development in the modern sense. The ancients could

conceive it only as the work of divine inspiration. But to Telemachus inspiration does not come in the usual epic way, by divine
command or in a dream sent by a god. It is not a cold mecha-
nism or an obscure magic. The divine favour is shown to him in
a natural and lifelike manner, in the form of deliberate influence
upon his will and intellect, a conscious schooling of the young
man's spirit. After that schooling, nothing more is needed but
the decisive external impulse, to give him readiness and initiative
for his task. The poet has struck an exquisite balance between
the various factors which influence Telemachus: his own direc-
tionless and abortive impulses, his fine natural character, the
favour and help of the goddess, and the divine guidance which
finally moves him to action. This delicate counterpoise is proof
of the poet's deep understanding of his problem. The principles
of epic poetry made it possible for him to identify a goddess's divine intervention with the natural influence of education on
young Telemachus' character—by making Athena speak to him
in the guise of his old guest-friend Mentes. And his artifice is
rendered more plausible by the universal feeling which still con-
vinces us as we read the poem: the feeling that the act of education, releasing the powers of a young soul, breaking down the
restraints which hampered it, and leading it into a glad activity,
is itself a divine impetus, a natural miracle. When Achilles' old
teacher fails in his last and hardest task of bending the doomed
hero's will, Homer presents his failure as due to the opposition
of an evil spirit; and in the happy transformation of Telemachus
from a weak youth to a real hero he acknowledges the work of
divine grace. In every great educational ideal which the Greeks
conceived and fulfilled, we see their full consciousness of that divine imponderable. We shall see it most clearly in the two great
aristocrats, Pindar and Plato.

In Book I of the *Odyssey* Athena herself, when in the guise of
Mentes she gives advice to Telemachus, expressly describes her
advice as *education*.[56] Her speech serves to bring Telemachus'
resolution to maturity. He decides to claim his rights, to oppose
the suitors publicly by calling them to account in the assembly,
and to demand help in searching for his lost father.[57] His first
plan fails: the assembly is unsympathetic; and he resolves to take
matters into his own hands, to start secretly on that hazardous
journey which is to make him a man at last. This resolution and

this journey are the *Telemachou paideia,* the schooling of Telemachus. In it, every educational factor comes into action on his
soul. An experienced elder guides and advises him. He feels the
gentler influence of his mother's love; but she, anxious for her
only son's safety, cannot be consulted at the critical moment,
since she would not sympathize with his sudden decision, and
would only hinder him with her fears. He has before him the
memory of his great father. He leaves home, and travels to
friendly courts, seeing the world and the lives of other men. He
is encouraged and befriended by great men, whose advice and
help he seeks. He makes new friends, finds new supporters. He
is protected meanwhile, and his path is smoothed, by the kindly
influence of a deity who plans his life and stands by him in his
perils. We see his embarrassment when, reared as the simple
squire of a small estate, a little island on the borders of Greece,
he enters the unknown world, and is entertained by great princes.
And by describing the sympathy with which he is met everywhere
he goes, the poet shows that even in a strange or hazardous
situation Telemachus' sound training and discipline do not desert
him, and that his father's name can still make his hard way
easier.

We must pay closer attention to one point which is specially
important in any discussion of the intellectual principles of aristocratic culture. That is the rôle of *example* in education. In
early ages, when there is neither a code of laws nor a system of
ethics, the only standards for the conduct of life are provided by
a few practical religious injunctions and by a store of proverbial
wisdom handed down from one generation to another. Apart
from these, the most effective guidance in personal difficulties is
given by the lives of model heroes of old. We can see the immediate influence of environment and especially of parental example in the characters of Telemachus and Nausicaa.[58] But an influence no less powerful than environment was the vast number of
pattern-lives described in traditional lore. In a primitive society
such traditions serve a function corresponding to that of history
(including Biblical history) in the modern world. The sagas
contain all the spiritual wealth which is the heritage and the
inspiration of every new generation. The instructor of Achilles
in the *Iliad* refers in his great speech to the warning example of

Meleager; [59] and Telemachus in the *Odyssey* has an apt model to imitate during his training as a man. The obvious pattern for him to follow was Orestes, who revenged himself on Aegisthus and Clytaemnestra for murdering his father. That act also was one of the numerous episodes in the tragedy of the Heroes' Return. Agamemnon was struck down immediately after his return from Troy, while Odysseus had spent twenty years away from his home: the difference in time was enough to allow the poet to place Orestes' exile in Phocis and his revenge earlier than the beginning of the *Odyssey*. The act was recent; but its fame had already spread throughout Greece, and Athena holds it up to Telemachus in glowing words.[60] Most examples drawn from tradition derive their authority from their venerable antiquity—Phoenix, speaking to Achilles, claims his respect for ancient times and ancient heroes [61]—but the situation of Orestes, so recent and so similar to that of Telemachus, is for those very reasons a more compelling example for him to follow.

The poet clearly attaches the greatest possible importance to this motif. 'You ought not to live like a child,' says Athena to Telemachus; 'you are too old for that. Have you not heard of the glory which Orestes has won throughout the world for killing the treacherous murderer Aegisthus, who slew his father? You too, my friend—I see you are comely and strong—must be valiant so that coming generations may praise you'.[62] Lacking the example of Orestes, Athena's advice would have no standard to give it weight and conviction. And in the difficult decision about the use of force against the suitors it is doubly necessary for her to appeal to a famous example in order to sway Telemachus' tender heart. In the assembly of the gods at the beginning of the poem, the poet makes Zeus himself refer to the moral problem of retribution,[63] quoting the example of Aegisthus and Orestes. Thus he justifies, even to the most sensitive conscience, Athena's later reference to the case. Again and again as the plot develops, this vital example is cited to influence Telemachus and to school him for his fateful mission. For instance, Nestor, telling Telemachus of the fate of Agamemnon and his house,[64] breaks off to point out that Orestes is a model for Telemachus to copy; and Telemachus answers, 'Yes, he took full revenge, and the Achaeans will spread his glory far and wide, to be known to future generations too. If only the gods would invest me with such

strength, to take vengeance on the suitors for their sore trans-
gressions!' Again, at the end of Nestor's narrative, there is
another reference to Orestes' example.[65] Nestor mentions it
twice, at the end of each half of his long speech, with strong
emphasis and with express reference to Telemachus' own case.

This repetition is of course intentional. The poet considers
that the appeal to the example of famous heroes and traditional
instances is an integral part of all aristocratic ethics and education. We shall return to this practice later, in order to show how
it helps us to understand epic poetry, and how deeply it is rooted
among the foundations of primitive society. But the later Greeks
also held to the *paradeigma,* the *example for imitation,* as a
fundamental category in life and thought.[66] We need only mention Pindar's use of mythological examples, which are such an
essential element of his triumphal hymn.[67] The practice penetrates all Greek poetry, and some Greek prose too.[68] But it
would be wrong to explain it merely as a stylistic trick. It is part
of the very essence of old aristocratic ethics; and its educational
importance still affects its use in early poetry. Sometimes in
Pindar we can see the true meaning of the mythological example
breaking through. And if we remember that Plato's whole philosophy is built on the conception of pattern, and that he describes the Ideas as 'patterns established in the realm of Being',[69]
we can easily see the origin of the category. The Idea of the
'Good' (or more correctly the Idea of the ἀγαθόν), that universally applicable pattern,[70] is directly descended from the
models of heroic areté which were part of the old aristocratic
code. Between the educational principles of that primitive age,
and Pindar, and Plato's philosophy, we can see an unbroken,
organic, necessary line of development. It is not evolution—in
the half-scientific sense which historians often use: it is a gradual
unfolding of the essential elements in the earliest form of that
Greek spirit which throughout all the variations of its history
remains fundamentally one and the same.

HOMER THE EDUCATOR

PLATO tells us that in his time many believed that Homer was the educator of all Greece.[1] Since then, Homer's influence has spread far beyond the frontiers of Hellas. Plato's passionate philosophical criticism of the poets succeeded in showing that the educational influence of poetry was far less wide than men had believed;[2] but all his attacks did not shake the supremacy of Homer. The Greeks always felt that a poet was in the broadest and deepest sense the educator of his people.[3] Homer was only the noblest example, as it were the classic instance, of that general conception. We should be wrong not to take it seriously, to limit our understanding of Greek poetry by substituting for that ideal the modern belief in art for art's sake. That belief, although it characterizes certain types and periods of poetry and the fine arts, does not appear in the great Greek poets. We cannot therefore apply it to the study of Greek poetry.[4] In early Greek thought there was no separation between ethics and aesthetics: the distinction was comparatively late in arising. Plato himself held that the value of Homer's poetry was immediately diminished by a proof that it did not tell the truth.[5] The idea that poetry is not useful to life first appears among the ancient theorists of poetics;[6] and it was the Christians who finally taught men to appraise poetry by a purely aesthetic standard—a standard which enabled them to reject most of the moral and religious teaching of the classical poets as false and ungodly, while accepting the formal elements in their work as instructive and aesthetically delightful.[7] Many poets since then have conjured up the gods and heroes of pagan mythology; but now we think of them merely as the shadowy puppets of poetic fancy. We might easily regard Homer from the same narrow point of view; but if we did, we should never come to understand what myth and poetry really meant to the Greeks. We are naturally repelled when the philosophical critics of the Hellenistic age sum up Homer's educational influence in a bald rationalist *fabula docet,*[8] or when

they follow the sophists in making the great epics a mere encyclopaedia of art and knowledge.[9] But that scholastic idea is only
the degenerate form of a real truth—coarsened, like all beauty
and all truth, by passing through coarse hands. We are right in
feeling such bare utilitarianism to be repulsive to our aesthetic
sense; but it is none the less certain that Homer (like all the
great Greek poets) is something much more than a figure in the
parade of literary history. He is the first and the greatest creator
and shaper of Greek life and the Greek character.

At this point we must discuss the educative influence of Greek
poetry in general, with special reference to Homer. Poetry can
educate only when it expresses all the aesthetic and moral potentialities of mankind. But the relationship of the aesthetic and the
moral element in poetry is not merely that of essential form and
more or less accidental material. The educational content and
the artistic form of a work of art affect each other reciprocally,
and in fact spring from the same root. We shall show that the
aesthetic effect of style, structure, and form in every sense is conditioned and interpenetrated by its intellectual and spiritual content. It is of course impossible to lay this down as a general
aesthetic law. There is and always has been a type of art, which,
passing over the central problems of life, depends for its effect
purely on its form; and indeed some artists deliberately ridicule
every great and lofty theme, or show themselves indifferent in
their choice of subject. Such consciously frivolous art has of
course its ethical effect. It relentlessly exposes the shams of convention, and thus purifies the moral and aesthetic outlook of its
age. But poetry cannot be really educative unless it is rooted in
the depths of the human soul, unless it embodies a moral belief,
a high ardour of the spirit, a broad and compelling ideal of humanity. And the greatest of Greek poetry does more than show
a cross-section of life taken at random. It tells the truth; but it
chooses and presents its truth in accordance with a definite ideal.

On the other hand, it is usually through artistic expression
that the highest values acquire permanent significance and the
force which moves mankind. Art has a limitless power of converting the human soul—a power which the Greeks called
psychagogia. For art alone possesses the two essentials of educational influence—universal significance and immediate appeal.

By uniting these two methods of influencing the mind, it surpasses both philosophical thought and actual life. Life has immediate appeal, but the events of life lack universal significance:
they have too many accidental accompaniments to create a truly
deep and lasting impression on the soul. Philosophy and abstract
thought do attain to universal significance: they deal with the
essence of things; yet they affect none but the man who can use
his own experience to inspire them with the vividness and intensity of personal life. Thus, poetry has the advantage over
both the universal teachings of abstract reason and the accidental events of individual experience. It is more philosophical
than life (if we may use Aristotle's famous epigram in a wider
sense), but it is also, because of its concentrated spiritual actuality, more lifelike than philosophy.

These observations are far from being applicable to the
poetry of all ages. They do not even apply to the whole of Greek
poetry, although their significance is not confined to Greek
poetry alone. But, based as they are upon Greek poetry, they
bear upon it more closely than upon the literature of other
nations. In fact, they only reproduce the views developed in the
age of Plato and Aristotle, when the Greek aesthetic sense, at
last realizing its powers and its sphere, came to study the great
achievements of Hellenic poets. Despite many variations in detail, the Greeks even of a later epoch retained the same general
view of art; and since that view arose at a time when they were
still sensitive to poetry and to the specially Hellenic qualities of
their poetry, we must, to be historically correct, inquire how far
it applied to Homer.

Through the art of Homer, the ideas of the Homeric age
have achieved a far greater permanence and universality, and
thereby a wider and more lasting cultural influence, than those of
any other epoch. The two great epics show, more clearly than
any other type of poetry, the absolute uniqueness of Greek cultural ideals. Most of the literary forms created by Greek literature are unparalleled in any other language and civilization.
Tragedy, comedy, philosophical treatise, dialogue, scientific
manual, critical history, biography, forensic, political, and cere-
monial oratory, travel-notes, memoirs, collections of letters, au-
tobiographies, reminiscences, and essays—all these literary types
were created and bequeathed to us by the Greeks. But other

nations at the same stage of development resembled early Greece in their social structure, in their aristocratic ideals, and in their possession of a native heroic poetry expressing those ideals. And, like the Greeks, many other nations created epics out of their primitive ballad-poetry: the Indians, the Germans, the Romance peoples, the Finns, and many nomad tribes of Central Asia. So by comparing the epics of numerous races and civilizations we can discern the special characteristics of Greek epic poetry.

It has often been observed that all these poems, created as they were at the same stage of cultural development, have many similarities. The earliest Greek epic poetry resembles the others in its primitive features—but only in them, only in what is external and impermanent; not in its rich humanity and artistic perfection. The Greek epics express, with an incomparable depth and fulness, the eternal knowledge of truth and destiny which is the creation of the heroic age—the age that cannot be destroyed by any bourgeois 'progress'. Even the Germanic epics, with all their nobility, cannot be compared with the *Iliad* and *Odyssey* for depth and permanence. The vast difference between the historical position of mediaeval epic and that of Homer is shown by the fact that he influenced Greek civilization for a full thousand years, while the German and French epics of the middle ages were forgotten soon after the decline of chivalry. In the studious Hellenistic age, the Homeric epics still lived and produced an entire new science: the science of philology, which aimed at discovering the secrets of their origin and transmission, and drew its life from the unquenchable vigour of the poems themselves. But it was not until modern scholarship had long been at work that the mediaeval epics, *Roland, Beowulf* and *The Nibelungs,* were rescued from their dusty oblivion in old manuscripts. The only epic of the middle ages which became part of the life, not only of its own nation, but of all humanity, is Dante's *Divine Comedy*—and that for the same reason as the Homeric epics. Although it speaks in the accents of its own age, its deep humanity and its vast knowledge of life raise it to a pitch of greatness unequalled in England until Shakespeare, unequalled in Germany until Goethe. The primitive poetry of every people is and must be strongly marked by national characteristics; and it is accordingly difficult for other nations and later ages to appreciate them fully. Early native poetry cannot attain universal significance unless it reaches and incorporates the widest humanity. Greece had a unique power of discerning and reproducing the elements in human life which are real and all-embracing: for Homer, who stands on the threshold of Greek history, became the teacher of all humanity.

Homer is for us the representative of early Greek civilization. We have already discussed his value as historical evidence for the oldest society of Greece; but his immortal picture of the ancient chivalrous world is more than an involuntary reflection of reality in art. In that aristocracy, with its lofty traditions and exacting standards, the Homeric epic found an expression of the higher life of the spirit; and through that life the epics themselves live and move. The spiritual lifeblood of the *Iliad* is the pathos and the heroic doom of man's struggle; the *Odyssey* is inspired by human character, shown in aristocratic culture and morality. The society which produced that life was itself to die, leaving no trace in history; but its portrait, worked out by the art of Homer, remained to be the ideal basis of all Hellenic culture. Hölderlin has said, 'That which endures is the work of the poet', and his words express the law governing the history of Greek education. Its growing structure is built by the poets. From stage to stage, with increasing sureness of touch, Greek poetry realizes and fulfils its educational purpose. It might be asked whether the Homeric epics, entirely objective as they are, can be said to share that purpose. We have already, in the foregoing analyses of the Embassy to Achilles and the Telemachia, given concrete examples to prove the existence of a deep-rooted educational purpose in these passages. But Homer's educational value is a much more universal thing: it is not confined to deliberate discussions of this or that educational problem, or to passages which strive to produce an ethical effect. The Homeric epics are a vast and complex work of the spirit, which cannot be assessed by one single formula: they contain, besides those comparatively late sections which show a frank interest in education, passages of an entirely different nature, passages in which the poet's eye is fastened so firmly upon the object he is describing that we can admit no thought of an underlying ethical purpose. The ninth book of the *Iliad* and the Telemachia are inspired by a far less objective intellectual and spiritual attitude; they aim so

consciously at producing their effect that they closely approxi-
mate to elegiac poetry. We must distinguish these deliberately
educational passages from what may be called objective education: that is, from educational effects which are not envisaged
by the poet himself, but are implicit in the very nature of epic
poetry. Consideration of these effects will lead us back to the
very beginnings of the epic.

Homer gives us several pictures of the old bards, out of whose
work grew the epic. The bard's vocation is to keep alive among
posterity 'the deeds of men and gods'.[10] Glory, and its preservation and increase—that is the real purpose of the heroic poems;
and heroic poetry is several times described in so many words as
'the glories of men'.[11] Homer, who loves names which mean
something, calls the bard in the first book of the *Odyssey* Phem-
ius—'the man who spreads report', 'the speaker of *fame*'. And
the name of the Phaeacian bard, Demodocus, contains an allusion to the publicity which he creates. The bard, because he
speaks fame, has an established position in society. Plato counts
poetic ecstasy as one of the beautiful effects of divine madness,
and thus describes the poet's rapture: 'Possession by the Muses,
and their madness, invade a gentle and chaste soul, awaken it,
and bewitch it with songs and all kinds of poesy; and, by glorifying countless deeds of men of old, educate posterity'.[12] This is
the original Hellenic ideal of poetry. It is based on the natural
and inseparable bond between poetry and the myth (which is the
tradition of the great deeds of men of old), and thence it derives the social function of the poet—as the teacher, and in a
sense the constructor, of his community. Plato does not believe
that the poet consciously intends to influence his hearers: he educates them rather by the very act of preserving the glory of the
past in his poetry.

Here we must recall our discussion of the importance of
example in the morality of Homer's noblemen. We have pointed
out the educational significance of examples drawn from myth—
Phoenix holds them up to Achilles, and Athena to Telemachus,
to warn or to encourage.[13] The myth is a natural corrective influence, even when examples and parallels are not deliberately
chosen from it. It acts as a pattern for life—not chiefly by providing a traditional event to parallel some occurrence in daily
life, but by its own nature: for the traditions of the past are

made up of glory, of the reports of great men and lofty actions, not of casual incidents. The uncommon has a compelling force, even when it is merely described and acknowledged. But the bard does more than describe the uncommon: he praises what is praiseworthy in the world. Like the Homeric heroes, who throughout their lives insist on receiving and repaying the due meed of honour, every truly heroic action hungers after eternal glory.[14] Myth and heroic poetry are the nation's inexhaustible treasure of great examples: from them it derives its ideals and its standards for daily life. This connexion between the epic and the myth is shown by Homer's use of traditional examples in all situations in which one man advises, warns, exhorts, encourages, or commands another. It is significant that such examples are not used in narrative, but always in the speeches. The characters appeal to the myth as a collection of authoritative instances.[15] That is to say: the myth has universal application. It is not a mere congeries of facts, although it is doubtless the echo of historical events—events which, by long transmission and preservation in the imagination of posterity, have reached heroic magnitude. That is how we must interpret the close connexion of poetry and myth, which is an invariable law throughout Greek literary history. It arises from the origin of poetry in the heroic ballad, from the ideal of glory, of the praise and imitation of great heroes. The law does not hold beyond the sphere of high poetry; at the most, we find the mythical element introduced here and there in other genres (such as lyric) to ennoble and idealize ordinary material. But the epic is a wholly ideal world; and myth, for the early Greeks, was the supreme idealizing factor.

We can see its effect on the epics in every detail of style and structure. For example, the language of the epics is characterized by the use of stereotyped decorative epithets. That usage springs directly from the original spirit of the old κλέα ἀνδρῶν. In the great epics, which are the climax of the long evolution of heroic poetry, these epithets are frequently fossilized; but their use is imposed by the epic conventions. The separate epithets are not often used to convey a real and individual meaning. They are largely ornamental. Still, they are an indispensable element in the centuries-old epic tradition, which is often powerful even when it is irrelevant or actually harmful. They are part of the furniture of that ideal world into which the epic raises everything it touches. And the epic style, with its exalting, ennobling, and transfiguring power, affects more than the use of epithets: the same nobility appears in the epic descriptions and portraits. Everything low, contemptible, and ugly is banished from the world of the epic. The ancients themselves observed how Homer transports everything—even ordinary objects and common events—to a higher plane. The rhetor Dio of Prusa, who can hardly have been fully conscious of the deep and necessary connexion between the praise of merit and the noble style of the epic, contrasts Homer with the carping Archilochus, and observes that men need blame more than praise.[16] His opinion concerns us less here because it expresses a pessimistic attitude which is directly opposed to the educational principles of the old aristocracy and its cult of great examples; we shall later have occasion to study his social ideals, which were widely different from those of the Homeric nobility. But he had a delicate taste in aesthetic matters; and he has admirably described the actual nature of the epic style, and its tendency to adorn everything it touches. 'Homer', he says, 'praised almost everything—animals and plants, water and earth, weapons and horses. He passed over nothing without somehow honouring and glorifying it. Even the one man whom he abused, Thersites, he called *a clear-voiced speaker.*'

Epic poetry, then, is distinguished by its idealizing tendency (which is connected with its origin in the old heroic lays) from all other literary types; and from that tendency it derives its predominant place in the history of Greek education. All the Greek literary genera sprang from the natural forms of human self-expression. Thus, lyric poetry was born of folk-song, whose primitive forms it varies, refines, and perfects; iambic poetry arose from the ritual abuse thrown about in the festival of Dionysus; the hymn and the processional ode developed out of religious rites; the epithalamion from public marriage-ceremonies, comedy from the komos-revel, and tragedy from the dithyramb. The original patterns from which the later poetic genera developed can be divided into those which concerned the worship of the gods, those which concerned private life, and those which concerned the life of the community. Those types of poetry which sprang from private life or religious usages have, to begin with, little to do with education. Heroic poetry, on the other hand, aims naturally at the creation and perpetuation of a heroic ideal. Its educational aim and influence are far greater than that of all other types of poetry, because it gives an objective picture of life as a whole, and portrays men at hand-grips with destiny, struggling to win a noble prize. Didactic and elegiac poetry, which followed the path marked out by epic, both resemble it closely in their form. From it they inherited the educational spirit, which later passed to still other types, iambic and choral poetry. Tragedy, too, owes both its traditional material and its ethical and educational spirit to epic, not to its own Dionysiac origin. And if we consider that the types of prose literature which have the greatest educational influence—such as history and the philosophical treatise—were created by a conflict of ideas with the philosophic assumptions of epic poetry, we may feel justified in asserting that the epic is the root of all higher Greek culture.

There are two ways of approaching our next problem, which is to show the educational factor at work in the internal structure of the epic. One is to examine the epics as they stand, treating them as complete wholes and paying no attention to the results reached and problems raised by scientific criticism. The other way is almost hopelessly blocked by a mass of hypotheses about the origin of the poems. Both paths, then, are impracticable; and we must choose a middle way. We shall take good account of the historical development of the epics, but we shall not feel bound to discuss the results of critical analysis as they affect every detail of our study.[17] Even a complete agnostic is bound to recognize the obvious facts of the prehistory and origin of the epic; and therein we differ from the ancients, who when speaking of the educational value of Homer always thought of the whole *Iliad* and the whole *Odyssey* together.[18] Modern critics of the poems must of course always aim at considering them as wholes, even when analysis shows those wholes to be a later creation, wrought out by generations of poetic work on an inexhaustible mass of traditional material. But we must always accept the possibility not only that the poems in their growth assimilated and altered older versions of the saga-material, but that when complete they admitted the insertion of entire passages of later origin. And therefore we must endeavour to make the stages in their growth and completion as clear and intelligible as possible.

Our study of the development of epic will of course be influenced by our conception of the nature of primitive heroic poetry. If we assume that the epics grew out of very ancient heroic ballads—and the heroic ballad is in many nations the first type of literature—it is difficult not to suppose that the oldest form of the epic was the *aristeia,* the Tale of Prowess, in which a famous hero fights a duel with a powerful adversary and defeats him.[19] The exploits of a single champion interest us much more deeply than a general battle-scene, which soon becomes complicated and obscure, and grows really exciting only in those episodes which are dominated by great heroes. Our sympathy is sooner awakened by a duel than by a battle, because it is less impersonal, because it shows more clearly the interplay of character, and because its various incidents and motives form a far deeper unity. The description of a great champion's prowess always has a strongly protreptic effect. Similar episodes, built on the epic pattern, appear later in historical works. In the *Iliad* the aristeiai are the climaxes of the action. As they stand, they are scenes complete in themselves, and in some measure independent of the main plan of the epic—which shows that they were once entirely separate from it, or were modelled on separate and independent ballads. Thus the poet of the *Iliad* breaks up the story of the battle before Troy into the tale of Achilles' wrath and its results, and a number of important episodes—the aristeiai of Diomede (v), Agamemnon (xi), Menelaus (xvii), and the duels between Menelaus and Paris (iii) and Hector and Ajax (vii). These scenes were the glory and the delight of the race for which the heroic ballads were sung: they were the reflection of its own ideals.

The novel artistic achievement of the epic is to combine a number of these episodes into a unity of action. It surpasses the old ballad (which merely assumed knowledge of the general plot and related this or that individual episode) by showing all the famous heroes as actors in one great drama.[20] The poet has combined many of the characters and events celebrated by earlier ballads into one gigantic whole, the tale of the Trojan war. His work shows what he held that war to be: a struggle between immortal heroes for the highest areté. And not only Greek heroes: their enemy was a nation which strove mightily to save its liberty and its fatherland. 'One omen is the best—fight for your home' are the words which Homer puts in the mouth, not of a Greek, but of the greatest Trojan hero,[21] who seems all the more deeply and truly human because he dies fighting for Troy. The great Achaean champions are of a more heroic mould. Love of country, love of wife and children are for them less compelling motives. Allusions are made here and there to their purpose of revenge for the abduction of Helen; and there is an attempt to stop the general bloodshed by sane diplomatic negotiation for the return of the stolen wife to her lawful husband. But this justification has no real importance. What interests the poet in the Achaean army is not the justice of its cause, but the brilliance of its heroes.

Before the changing background of struggle, valour, and death rises one tragic destiny—that of the heroic Achilles. His story is the bond by which the poet gathers the successive battles of the war into a poetic unity. The tragedy of Achilles prevents the *Iliad* from being merely a venerable relic of ancient days and battles long ago, and makes it a deathless memorial of human life and human suffering. The epic is not only an immense advance in the art of constructing a unified poem of great scope and extreme complexity; it also contains a new and deeper view of life and its problems, a greater intensity of contemplation which raises heroic poetry far above its original sphere and gives the poet a new position as an educator in the highest sense. He is now no longer the impersonal Speaker of Fame, celebrating the past and its great deeds. He is a poet in the full sense of the word, for he creates and interprets the story which he hands on.

At bottom, artistic creation and spiritual interpretation are one and the same. It is easy to see that the immense superiority and originality of Greek epic in the art of constructing a unified whole springs from the same root as its educational effect—from its deeper consciousness of the problems of life. Increasing pleasure in the mastery of great masses of material characterizes the last stage in the development of epic poetry among other nations as well as the Greeks; but it does not necessarily lead to the art of the great epic poem. Even when a large poem is produced at that stage, it easily degenerates into rambling historical romance, beginning 'with Leda and her egg'[22] and proceeding from the birth of the heroes through a wearisome succession of old traditional tales.[23] The Homeric epic is concentrated, vivid, dramatic. It plunges *in medias res*. It keeps its main plot always on the anvil, and hammers it out with short sharp blows. With astonishing perception it chooses not to relate the history of the whole Trojan war or the entire career of Achilles. It presents only the crisis, the one representative moment which evokes the ten years' war with all its battles and varying fortunes, past, present, and future, in a short space of time. The ancient critics marked this choice and admired it. For its sake both Aristotle and Horace called Homer not only the epic poet *par excellence,* but the highest model of poetic power and mastery. Through it Homer turns away from simple history; he strips the event of its material, factual husk, creates it anew, and shows us how its problems develop by their own inner compulsion.

The *Iliad* begins at a great moment. Achilles retires in fury from the war. The Greeks are hard pressed. After years of fighting the prize of all their labours is lost just before they grasp it, lost through human folly and wrong. Deprived of their greatest champion, the other Greek heroes, fighting as they have never fought before, show themselves in the full blaze of their valour. Encouraged by the absence of Achilles, the enemy throw the full weight of their power against the Achaeans, drive them triumphantly from the battlefield, and press them ever harder until their plight moves Patroclus to come to their help. His death at the hands of Hector at last wins the intervention of Achilles, although he had been unmoved by the Greeks' entreaties and the proffered expiation. To avenge his dead friend he enters the battle again, slays Hector, saves the Greeks from ruin, buries Patroclus with savage old rites of mourning, and sees the same fate advancing on himself. When Priam grovels in the dust before him, praying for the body of his son Hector, the pitiless heart of Achilles melts at last into weeping, as he thinks of his own old father, who like Priam is bereaved of his son, even though that son still lives.

The terrifying anger of Achilles, which is the core of the whole close-knit plot, glows in the same blinding light which surrounds his figure throughout the poem. He is the young hero of superhuman strength and courage, who faces an early doom. He has deliberately chosen the short steep ascent to heroic glory rather than a long ignoble life of peace and pleasure. He is the true *megalopsychos*, the high-minded man; and for that very reason he will not yield to the mighty rival who deprives him of the only reward of his struggles, his honour as a hero.[24] As the poem begins, his bright face darkens with anger; and even its conclusion is unlike the triumphal close of the usual aristeia. Achilles has no pleasure in his victory over Hector; and the great story dies away in his inconsolable grief, in the ghastly lamentations of the Greeks for Patroclus and the Trojans for Hector, and in the victor's dark foreknowledge of his inevitable doom.

Some critics would prefer to amputate the poem of its last book, or to continue it to the death of Achilles. They believe, in fact, that the *Iliad* originally was, or ought now to be, an *Achilleid*. But they have read it from a historical rather than an aesthetic point of view, and have studied its content rather than its form and the artistic problems which it faced and solved. The *Iliad*, celebrating the glory of the greatest aristeia of the Trojan war—Achilles' victory over mighty Hector—mingles the ineluctable tragedy of the doomed heroes with the pathos of their own struggles against one another and against destiny. A true aristeia tells of the hero's victory, not of his fall. There is deep tragedy in Achilles' resolve to be revenged on Hector for the dead Patroclus, although he knows that he himself is fated to die immediately thereafter; but that tragedy is not developed to its catastrophe. It is used in the *Iliad* as a dark background to set off the brilliance of Achilles' victory. His heroism is not the simple berserk courage of the old champions, for it culminates in his deliberate choice of a great deed at the cost of his own life. All the later Greeks are agreed on this view of his character, and point to it as proving the ethical and educational value of the poem. Mark that the full tragedy of his heroic resolve does not appear until it is interwoven with his anger and with the failure of the Greek attempts at reconciliation; for it is his angry refusal which compels his friend Patroclus to enter the war and to die at the nadir of the Greek defeat.

We must therefore conclude that the *Iliad* has an ethical design. We have no space to spend on the study which would be necessary to show every detail of its plan. And even if we were to trace it throughout the poem (thereby assuming its unity as a work of art) we should not thereby solve or dismiss the old problem of the growth of the Homeric epics.[25] Yet if we demonstrate and emphasize—as in this study we must—the fact that the poem is built on one single ethical plan, we shall do much to check the tendency of scholarship towards excessive analysis and dissection. We need not ask what architect made the design. Whether it belongs to the original conception of the poem, or was imposed upon it by a later poet, it is impossible to overlook its presence in the finished work; and without understanding it, we should find it impossible to appreciate the purpose and effect of the *Iliad*.

The existence of the design can be shown here by a very few salient facts. The poet's own point of view is perfectly clear in the first book of the *Iliad,* as he tells how the strife between Achilles and Agamemnon began with the insult to Apollo's priest Chryses and the anger of the god. He takes no sides. He gives an entirely objective account of the attitude of both parties in the quarrel, but he shows plainly that both have erred in pushing their claims to excess. Between them stands the wise old Nestor —the personification of *sophrosyne,* of moderation. He has seen three generations of mortal men; and now he seems to sit high above the troublous present, and to speak from all time to soothe the violence of the moment. Nestor is the equipoise of the whole scene. The leit-motiv of Ité is heard even in this, the first episode of the poem. Agamemnon is infatuated when he commits the first offence, and in Book IX Achilles in his turn is blinded by Até.[26] He 'knows not how to yield'; [27] but clings doggedly to his anger and thus exceeds the limit allowed to mortal men. And the consequences of his anger are far greater. He himself, when it is too late, speaks repentantly of his criminal blindness, and curses the sullen rancour through which he was led to be untrue to his own heroic mission, and to sit idly by while he sent his best friend to his death.[28] In the same way Agamemnon, when he is at last reconciled with Achilles, complains in a lengthy allegorical speech of the destructive power of Até.[29] Homer presents Até, like Moira, in a wholly religious light. She is a divine force whom man's strength can scarcely escape. Yet he shows (especially in Book IX) that if man is not the master of his fate, he is in a certain sense an unconscious co-worker in shaping it. It is through a deep spiritual necessity that the Greeks, who consid-

ered man's highest self-expression to lie in heroic action, should
have felt so strongly the daemonic power of infatuation, and
seen that it lay in the eternal contradiction between man's will
and his actions, while the fatalistic wisdom of Asia, shrinking
before that power, took refuge in the glorification of divine inaction and the will to annihilation. The long process through
which the Greeks realized the problem of destiny culminated in
Heraclitus' maxim ἦθος ἀνθρώπῳ δαίμων; but it was begun by the
poet who created the character of Achilles in the *Iliad*.

The work of Homer is throughout inspired by a comprehensive philosophy of human nature and of the eternal laws of the
world-process, a philosophy which has seen and judged every
essential factor in man's life. He contemplates every event and
every character in the light of his universal knowledge of the
underlying and eternal truth. The love of Greek poetry for
gnomic utterances, its tendency to measure each event by a
general standard and to reason from the general to the particular, and its frequent use of traditional examples as universal
types and ideals—all these tendencies originate with Homer.
The finest expression of the epic view of human life is the pictures on the shield of Achilles, which are fully described in Book
XVIII (478 ff.) of the *Iliad*.

On the shield Hephaestus wrought the earth, and heaven, and
the sea, and the tireless sun, and the moon at its full, and all the
signs which crown the sky. And he made two cities of men,
beautiful to see. In one, there were marriage-rites and feasting:
a bridal procession was marching through the city by the light of
torches, while many a marriage-song rose up, and dancing-boys
whirled among them to the music of flute and lyre; and the
women stood at their doors admiring it all. The citizens were
assembled in the market-place, where a quarrel was afoot between two men, about the blood-price to be paid for a man who
had been killed. The elders were sitting upon polished stone
seats in a sacred circle, each holding a herald's staff of office: and
they stood up in turn to give their verdicts.

The other city was besieged by two armies, gleaming in
armour. They were in two minds whether to destroy the city or
to plunder it. But the citizens had not yet submitted, but marched
out to an ambush, leaving their wives and their children, along

with the old men, to guard the city wall. And when they came to the place for the ambuscade—it was by a river, at the watering-place of cattle—they took their posts, and attacked a herd which was driven down to the river. Then the enemy rushed up, and a battle broke out along the river banks. Spears flew back and forward: Eris and Kydoimos, the demons of War, moved among them as they fought, while Kér, the spirit of Death, in blood-stained garments, dragged the dead and wounded men by the feet through the mêlée.

And Hephaestus made a field, where ploughmen drove their teams up and down: at the field's edge where they turned a man came up and gave them a cup of wine. And he made a manor at reaping time. The reapers plied their sickles, while the trusses fell behind them and were bound into sheaves by the binders; the king who owned the manor stood watching in silent joy; and his squires prepared a meal under an oak tree beyond. Hephaestus made a vineyard too, with a gay vintage dance; a herd of horned cattle, with drivers and dogs; a pasture ground in a beautiful valley, with sheep, and shepherds, and sheepfolds; and a dancing place, where young men and maidens were dancing, holding one another by the hand, while a divine minstrel sang to his lyre—all these completed the vast picture of all the activities of human life. Round the rim of the shield flowed the Ocean, embracing the whole world.

That deep sense of the harmony between man and nature, which inspires the description of Achilles' shield, is dominant in Homer's conception of the world. One great rhythm penetrates the moving whole. No day is so full of human striving that the poet forgets to tell how the sun rises and sinks above the turmoil, how the toil and battle of the day is succeeded by repose, and how the night, which loosens men's limbs in sleep, embraces all mortals. Homer is neither a naturalist nor a moralist. He is neither swept away without foothold in the chaotic waves of life, nor standing, a serene observer, on the shore. Physical and spiritual forces are equally real for him. He has a keen and ob-jective insight into human passions. He knows their elemental violence, which overpowers man himself and whirls him away in their grip. But though that force may often seem to overswell its banks, it is always controlled by strong barriers beyond. For Homer, and for the Greeks in general, the ultimate ethical

boundaries are not mere rules of moral obligation, but fundamental laws of Being.[30] It is to this sense of ultimate reality,
this deeper knowledge of the meaning of the world, beside which
all mere 'realism' seems thin and partial, that the Homeric epic
owes its overpowering effect.

Homer sees life as governed by universal laws; and for that
reason he is a supreme artist in the craft of motivation. He does
not passively accept tradition: he does not relate a simple succession of events. He presents a plot which develops by its own
compulsion from stage to stage, governed by an unbreakable
connexion of cause and effect. With the first line, the dramatic
narrative of each epic begins to unfold without interruption
towards its logical end. 'Muse, sing of the anger of Achilles and
his strife with Atreus' son Agamemnon. Which of the gods set
them to strive with each other?' The question flies straight as an
arrow to the goal. Upon it follows the tale of Apollo's wrath, a
tale which gives only the essential factors which cause the tragedy: it is set at the head of the epic like the aetiology of the
Peloponnesian War at the beginning of Thucydides' history.
And the plot does not develop in a loose chronological sequence.
It is ruled throughout by the principle of sufficient reason. Every
action has its roots in character.

But Homer does not, like modern authors, see every action
from within, as a phenomenon of human consciousness. In his
world, nothing great happens without the aid of a divine power.
The poet who tells a story is necessarily omniscient. Our authors
must speak of the most secret emotions of each character as if
they themselves had entered his mind. Homer, on the other
hand, presents all human action as guided by the gods. It is not
always easy to draw the line beyond which this narrative method
becomes simply a poetic device; but it is certainly mistaken to
hold that the intervention of the gods is never more than a trick
of the epic style. For Homer does not inhabit a rationalized
world, full of the banal and the commonplace, and disguised only
by the painted scenery of poetic illusion. If we study the instances
of divine intervention in the epics, we can trace a development
from the occasional external interference of the gods (a motif
which must belong to a very early stage of the epic style) to the
constant spiritual guidance of a great man by a divinity, as
Odysseus is guided by the perpetual inspiration of Athena.[31]

Not only in poetry, but in religion and politics, the ancient East believed the gods to be the chief actors. In the royal inscriptions of Persia, Babylonia and Assyria, and in the prophecies and histories of the Jews, the gods are described as really responsible for all the actions and sufferings of men. The gods have always an interest in human life. They take sides, in order to show their favour or assert their rights. Every man holds his god responsible for the good and evil which befall him, and for every inspiration and every success. In the *Iliad,* too, the gods are divided into two camps. That is, no doubt, an ancient conception; but certain features in its working-out are late—such as the poet's endeavour to assert, above the feuds created in heaven by the Trojan war, the loyalty of the gods to one another, the unity of their power, and the reality of their divine kingdom. The ultimate cause of any event is the will of Zeus. Homer holds even the tragedy of Achilles to be the fulfilment of that will.[32] And the gods are introduced to justify every development of personal motive in the plot. This does not conflict with its normal psychological motivation. The psychological and the metaphysical aspects of any event are not mutually exclusive: on the contrary, Homer holds them to be complementary.

This gives epic poetry a strange double aspect. The audience must see every action from two points of view—for it happens both on earth and in heaven. The stage on which the drama is played has two levels, and we follow the plot in human purpose and action and in the higher purpose of the ruling gods. Naturally, this shows us the full limitations and short-sightedness of human action, with its dependence on the inscrutable decrees of a superhuman force; the actors cannot see these daemonic compulsions as the poet can. If we think of the mediaeval Christian epics written in German and in the Romance languages, and remember how they introduce no gods into their plots, and therefore present every action from the subjective side alone, as a simple human activity, we shall realize their vast distance from the deep poetic sense of reality which inspires the work of Homer. The fact that he holds the gods to be implicated in every human action and suffering obliges the Greek poet to see the eternal meaning of all man's acts and destinies, to find them their place in a general scheme of the world, and to measure them by the loftiest religious and moral standards. Thus the Greek epic has a far richer and more objective view of life than the epic of the Middle Ages. And here again only Dante can be compared with Homer for depth of vision.[33] The Homeric epics contain the germs of all Greek philosophy.[34] In them we can clearly see the anthropocentric tendency of Greek thought, that tendency which contrasts so strongly with the theomorphic philosophy of the Oriental who sees God as the sole actor and man as merely the instrument or object of that divine activity. Homer definitely places man and his fate in the foreground, although he sees them *sub specie aeternitatis,* in the perspective of the loftiest general ideals and problems.[35]

The *Odyssey* shows this characteristic of epic construction even more strongly than the *Iliad.* It is the work of an age which has systematized and rationalized its beliefs; at least the poem as we have it was completed in such an age and bears its clear imprint. When two nations are at war, and call on their gods, with prayer and sacrifice, for help, the gods are placed in a difficult situation—that is, if their worshippers believe in their omnipotence and impartiality. Thus we can trace in the *Iliad,* with its comparatively advanced moral and religious beliefs, a struggle to harmonize the ideal of one indivisible and intelligent divine power with the original conception of most of the gods as local and specialized divinities. The Greek deities were very human and very near to mankind. Their human traits led the Greek nobles (proudly conscious of their own divine descent) to imagine that the life and activity of the heavenly powers were not unlike their own life on earth. Throughout the *Iliad,* that belief—so often attacked by the abstract and idealistic philosophy of subsequent ages—is giving way to the deeply religious conception of the heavenly powers, and of the supreme deity in particular, which was the germ of the loftiest ideals of later Greek art and thought. But it is not until the *Odyssey* that we find a more logical and consistent view of the power of the gods.

The idea of the council in heaven at the beginning of Books I and v of the *Odyssey* is of course borrowed from the *Iliad;* but there is a striking contrast between the tumultuous disputes on Olympus in the *Iliad* and the majestic council of superhuman beings in the *Odyssey.* The gods of the *Iliad* are almost palpably human. Zeus asserts his supremacy by threats of physical violence;[36] and one god will use very human methods to deceive

another or to nullify his power.[37] But the Zeus who presides over
the heavenly council in the *Odyssey* personifies a high philosophical conception of the world-conscience. He opens his
speech [38] on the fate of Odysseus by a general discussion of the
problem of human suffering and the unbreakable connexion between destiny and human error. The entire poem is filled with
the same purpose—to justify the ways of God to man.[39] The
poet holds the supreme deity to be an omniscient power, far
above all the thoughts and efforts of mortal men: a spiritual
power, whose essence is thought; a power infinitely superior to
the blind passions which make men sin and entangle them in the
net of Até. This moral and religious ideal governs the whole
story of the sufferings of Odysseus and the hybris of the suitors,
that insolence which is expiated only by their death: the problem is clearly set out, and it develops under that same conception to its end.

The divine will which governs the whole story, and at last
brings it to a just and happy conclusion, naturally appears—
always consistent and always omnipotent—at the crises of the
story. For the poet systematizes all its incidents to harmonize
with his own religious beliefs. Every character is therefore
consistent and appropriate. This rigid ethical plan probably
belongs to the last stage in the development of the *Odyssey*.[40]
Homeric critics have not yet worked out the process by which
the plan was imposed on the earlier versions of the traditional
saga of Odysseus. Besides the general religious and moral structure which governs the whole of this final version, the poem contains many delightful minor motifs—idyll, heroic tale, adven-
ture-story, fairy-tale. But the power of the *Odyssey* does not depend on them; it owes the unity and directness of its central
structure, which has been admired throughout all ages, to its
broad and comprehensive development of a central moral and
religious problem.

What we have said deals with only one aspect of a phenomenon of far-reaching effect. Just as Homer allots to the destinies
of men and nations their due place within a well-defined ethical
universe, so also he sets each of his characters within its own appropriate world. He never shows us man in the abstract, man as
pure spirit. His men and women are complete and living persons.
They are not lay-figures, who move into striking groups or fall

into dramatic attitudes and then remain motionless. They have a life of their own: they are so solidly real that we can almost see and touch them; their actions are harmonious, and their life is consistent with the life of the real world. Consider Penelope. She could have been driven to express a more intense and lyrical emotion, galvanized to gestures of more violent joy and grief; but in a long poem neither the character nor the audience could have supported such excesses. Homer's characters are always natural; they express their whole nature at every moment; they are imagined in the round, and wrought with an incomparable closeness and liveliness of texture. Penelope in her room is the housewife, Penelope among the insolent suitors is the deserted wife praying for her lost husband; Penelope is the mistress of her maids both true and faithless, and the mother of a cherished only son: she has no one to help her except the honest old swineherd and Odysseus' father, bent with age, far from the city, working in his little garden; her own father is too far away to help her. It is all simple and logical; her character touches life on all sides, and thereby develops with a quiet inevitability into a true sculptural whole. The secret of Homer's sculptural power is his gift of placing every character within its own surroundings as clearly and accurately as the mathematician co-ordinates a point within a geometric system.[41]

Ultimately, it is the Greek spirit, with its native passion for clarity of form, which enables Homer to create a complete and independent cosmos, where changes and chances are always balanced by an element of order and stability. As we study him to-day, we cannot but marvel when we see all the characteristically Hellenic powers, the tendencies which develop throughout Greek history, already manifest in Homer's work. This is of course less obvious when we read the poems by themselves; but when we contemplate Homer and the later Greeks in one broad survey, we cannot help seeing the underlying identity of spirit. The deepest grounds of this identity lie in the unsolved secrets of heredity, blood and race. As we study them, we feel both that they are closely akin and that they are fundamentally alien to us; and it is the recognition of this necessary difference between members of the same species which is the real benefit of our intercourse with the Hellenic world. That factor of race and nationality, which we can feel by intuition, not by logic, continues to work with a strange immutability through all the historical variations of spirit and the varying tides of fortune; but in our thought of it we must not underestimate the immeasurable effect on later Greece of Homer's creation of a complete human world. That world was the first work of the Panhellenic spirit: it made the Greeks conscious for the first time that they were a nation; and thereby it set an ineffaceable stamp on all later Greek culture.

HESIOD: THE PEASANT'S LIFE

HESIOD OF BOEOTIA, whom the Greeks called their second greatest poet after Homer, depicts a world very different from that
of the Homeric nobility. His *Works and Days* (which is later
than his other poem—the *Theogony* or *Descent of the Gods*—
and more genuinely native to the soil), a vivid record of the
life of the peasantry in mainland Greece about the end of the
eighth century, is an indispensable complement to Homer's few
glimpses of the life of the common people in early Ionia. But
it is also a work of special importance in a study of the development of Greek culture. Homer's poetry brings out one fundamental fact: that all culture starts with the creation of an aristocratic ideal, shaped by deliberate cultivation of the qualities appropriate to a nobleman and a hero. Hesiod shows us the second
basis of civilization—work. The later Greeks recognized this
when they gave his didactic poem the title of *Works and Days*.
Heroism is shown, and virtues of lasting value are developed,
not only in the knight's duel with his enemy, but in the quiet incessant battle of the worker against the elements and the hard
earth. It is not for nothing that Greece was the cradle of a
civilization which places work high among the virtues. We must
not be deceived by the carefree life of the Homeric gentlemen
into forgetting that the land of Greece always demanded hard
and constant labour from its people. Herodotus confirms this, by
comparing it with richer lands and nations. 'Poverty,' says one
of his characters, 'is native to Greece; but manly virtue is an acquisition—for it was produced by wisdom and a severe law. By
using it Greece defends herself against poverty and tyranny.' [1]
Greece is a hilly country, with many narrow valleys and remote
districts shut off by mountains. It has hardly any of the broad,
easily cultivated plains of northern Europe; and its inhabitants
are forced to wring their bare existence out of the soil, to struggle with it for the last ounce it will yield. They always believed
that cattle-rearing and agriculture were the most real and impor-

tant type of work: it was only along the coast that seafaring later became paramount.² In early times, Greece was predominantly a land of farmers.

But Hesiod is not merely a poet of Greek peasant life. In his work we can see how an aristocratic civilization and its intellectual leaven, the Homeric epics, worked upon the lower classes of Greek society. Hellenic culture was something more than the imposition of the manners and morals of a superior caste upon other ranks. Every class contributed something to it. And even the coarse, dull peasantry was profoundly influenced by its contact with the finer culture of the nobility. At that period, the herald of the higher life was the rhapsode who recited the Homeric poems. In the famous prelude to the *Theogony,* Hesiod tells how he was called to be a poet: how, when he was a simple shepherd feeding his flock at the foot of Mount Helicon, the Muses came to inspire him, and gave him the rhapsode's staff.³ But the new rhapsode of Ascra brought to the listening crowds of villagers more than the blaze and glitter of Homeric poetry. His thought was rooted deep in the rich soil of primitive peasant life; and as his widening experience carried him beyond the simple vocation of a Homerid, and made him a poet in his own right, the Muses enabled him to create eternal poetry out of the ideals of the farmer's work and life, and to add them to the spiritual heritage of all Greece.

He shows us a clear picture of life in the plains of mainland Greece. Although one part of the nation differed so much from another that we cannot generalize freely from his account of Boeotia, it is certainly to a large extent typical of Greece in general. Power is held, and culture is transmitted, by the landowning nobles. But the peasants have a life of their own, with considerable intellectual and legal independence. They are free agriculturists and cattle-rearers, living on the produce of their own labour: we do not hear of serfdom; ⁴ and there is nothing whatever to show that the peasants were descended (like the helots of Laconia) from a race which had been conquered during the great migrations. Every day they assemble in the market-place or the λέσχη, and discuss their public and private affairs.⁵ They are quite free in criticising the conduct of their fellows, and even of the noblemen. 'What people say', φήμη, deeply affects the prestige and prosperity of the ordinary man: for he can win place and respect only by being part of the crowd.[6]

The external occasion chosen by Hesiod for writing the *Works and Days* is his lawsuit with his lazy, greedy, litigious brother Perses. Perses has wasted part of his inheritance; and, after winning a lawsuit about Hesiod's share by bribing the judges, he now comes forward with fresh demands.[7] The lawsuit was, in fact, a contest between might and right; but Hesiod does not speak of it as if it were a special instance. He voices the general feeling of most of his fellow-peasants. And even so, he is remarkably outspoken in his attacks on the greed of the 'gift-eating' nobles and their harsh misuse of their power.[8] This is obviously a different life from that governed by the patriarchal noblemen of Homer's poetry. Such aristocratic tyranny and popular discontent did exist before Hesiod: but he believes that the Homeric heroes lived in an entirely different epoch—a better time than the 'age of iron' which he paints so darkly in the *Works and Days*.[9] Nothing shows the utter pessimism of the working folk so clearly as Hesiod's account of the five ages of man, beginning with the golden reign of Kronos, and gradually degenerating to the hard present, where justice, morality, and happiness are at their nadir. Aidos and Nemesis have veiled their faces, and quitted the earth to rejoin the other gods on Olympus, leaving nothing to mankind but suffering and endless strife.[10]

Such a grim life could not create any such pure ideal of human culture as was produced by the happier world in which the Homeric nobles ruled. It is therefore important to discover what share the common people took in developing the aristocratic ideals into a cultural pattern which covered the whole nation. The answer to this question lies in the fact that the country was not yet conquered by the city. The old feudal civilization was largely rooted in the soil. Country life was not yet synonymous with intellectual underdevelopment; it was not yet measured by an urban standard. 'Peasant' had not come to mean 'uncultured'.[11] At that time even the cities (especially those of mainland Greece) were principally country-towns, and so in large part they remained. There was in the countryside a steady growth of native morality, and thought, and faith, a crop as constant as the

grass and grain which every field produced, and as truly native
to the soil.[12] The steam-roller of the city had not yet crushed flat
everything that was uncommon or individual among the beliefs
and practices of the country-folk.

In the country, it is naturally the landed gentry who are the
leaders of the higher spiritual life. As the *Iliad* and *Odyssey*
show, the Homeric epics were first sung by wandering minstrels
at the manors of the nobility. But Hesiod himself, who worked
as a farmer and grew up within the milieu of peasant life, knew
Homer's poetry from his youth, before he became a professional
rhapsode. The public for whom he writes is first and foremost
the peasantry; and yet he assumes that they will know the stylized Homeric language which he employs. The spiritual process
which began when the peasantry learnt the Homeric epics is
best shown by the structure of Hesiod's own poems, for they
reflect Hesiod's own progress towards culture. Every subject
which he treats automatically enters the already fixed Homeric
pattern. Words, phrases, fragments of lines, even whole lines are
borrowed from Homer. It is from Homer that Hesiod takes his
idealizing epic epithets. This borrowing created a remarkable
contrast between the style and the content of the new poetry.
Still, it was necessary for the prosaic earthbound farmer-folk to
adapt the strange diction and ideals of a higher social class,
before they could impart to their own half-comprehended
thoughts and aspirations that deliberate clarity and moral conviction which alone could allow them to find convincing expression. When the peasantry of Hesiod's day came to know the
poetry of Homer, they acquired an immense new stock of methods of expression. But that was not all. They also found that
Homer (despite his heroic and emotional tone, so different from
their own sober life) expressed the greatest problems of human
life with a sharpness and clarity which showed them how to rise
from the narrow struggles of daily existence into a higher and
purer spiritual atmosphere.[13]

Hesiod's poems also show us fairly clearly what other spiritual
possessions besides Homer were handed down among the Boeotian peasants. The rich lode of saga-material in the *Theogony*
contains much that is familiar to us from Homer, but also many
ancient traditions which appear nowhere else. It is of course not
always possible to distinguish between the myths which had

already been made into poetry and those which were only transmitted by word of mouth. In the *Theogony* Hesiod shows most
clearly his power as a creative thinker. The *Works and Days*
are much nearer to the real life of the peasant. But even in the
Works and Days he will suddenly interrupt his train of thought
to tell a long myth, in the certainty of pleasing his audience.[14]
The common people as well as the nobles had an enormous interest in myths: the myth stirred them to long, long thoughts and
tales; it summed up their whole philosophy of life. But Hesiod's
instinctive choice of myths reflects the peculiar outlook of the
peasant. He obviously prefers those which express the peasant's
realistic and pessimistic view of life, or describe the causes of the
social difficulties which oppress him. Such are the tale of Prometheus, in which he finds the solution to the problem of the trouble
and toil of human life; the description of the five ages of the
world, which explains the vast difference between the peasant's
existence and the brilliant life of the Homeric world, and reflects
man's perpetual nostalgia for a better world; and the myth of
Pandora, which expresses the sour prosaic belief (unknown to
the world of Homeric chivalry) that woman is the root of all
evil.[15] We can hardly be wrong in assuming that Hesiod was not
the first to spread these stories among the country-folk, although
he was doubtless the first to set them firmly in the broad social
and philosophical framework of a great poem. The manner in
which he tells the tales of Prometheus and Pandora, for instance,
presupposes that they were already known to his audience.[16] The
popular interest in these myths of religious and social purport
predominates in Hesiod over the love of the heroic sagas which
Homer preferred. A myth is the expression of a fundamental
attitude to life. For that reason, every social class has myths of
its own.

Besides their myths, the common folk have an ancient store of
practical wisdom, laid up by the experience of immemorial generations of nameless workers. It consists partly of agricultural
and vocational lore, partly of moral and social rules, all compressed into such brief maxims as stick easily in the memory.
Hesiod's *Works and Days* contains much of this rich tradition;
and, although the deep philosophical meditations in the first section of the poem have more interest for students of his character
and history and of the development of his ideas, some of its

finest poetry is found in those closely-packed proverbial phrases, many of them set down in their original form. The second part of the *Works and Days* incorporates all the traditions of peasant life—old counsels about establishing a home and taking a wife, precepts for field-work in the different seasons of the year, and a weather-guide, with advice about changing clothes and sailing the seas. And it is all prefaced and concluded by pithy moral commandments and prohibitions. We have anticipated a little in speaking of Hesiod's poetic achievement: our task at this point is only to analyse the culture of the peasants for whom he wrote. But the second part of the *Works and Days* displays that culture so plainly as to make analysis unnecessary. Its form, its content, and its structure mark it clearly as part of the heritage of the common folk. It is a complete contrast to the culture of the nobility. In thinking of education and the conduct of life, the Hesiodic peasantry envisages nothing like the chivalrous ideal of a complete human personality, harmonious in mind and body, foursquare in battle and speech, song and action.[17] Instead, it prizes the old moral code whose strength is in the slow, changeless wisdom of the farmer and his relentless daily toil. That code is more real and closer to the earth, although it lacks a high ideal.

It was Hesiod who introduced the ideal which served as a focus for all these different elements and made it possible to concentrate them into the epic form—the ideal of Justice. Out of his fight for his own rights against his brother's aggrandisement and the corruption of the judges, was born the passionate faith in justice which inspires his most personal poem, the *Works and Days*. The great novelty of this work is that its author speaks in his own person. Abandoning the traditional objectivity of epic, he himself comes forward to preach the blessings of justice and the damnation of injustice. He provides a motive for this stylistic innovation by speaking, at the very outset, of his dispute with his brother Perses. He addresses Perses immediately, and directs all his warnings to him.[18] By one method after another, he tries to convince him that Zeus preserves justice even although earthly judges spurn it, and that ill-gotten gains never prosper. Then he turns to the judges themselves, the great nobles, to tell them the story of the hawk and the nightingale or to plead with them in other ways.[19] He makes the lawsuit so real for his readers, he recreates so vividly the moment just before the verdict, that it would be easy to make the mistake of thinking that he actually wrote at that moment, and that the *Erga* is nothing but an occasional poem. Many modern editors have wrongly assumed this to be true: and their assumption appears to fit the fact that Hesiod never speaks of the result of his lawsuit. Surely he could not have left his audience in the dark, if the suit had actually been decided? Attempts were accordingly made to find within the poem evidence of the actual result and to trace some significant changes in Hesiod's own position. Believing that they had discovered such changes, scholars analysed the work—which has in fact an archaic looseness of structure, and is difficult for us to conceive as a unity—and divided it into a chronological series of 'Admonitions to Perses'.[20] In fact, they transferred, to the criticism of Hesiod's didactic poem, Lachmann's theory of the Lays which composed the Homeric epics. But it is difficult to apply this belief to those long sections of the poem which are purely didactic, and have nothing to do with the lawsuit, and yet are still addressed to Perses; for example, the sailor's and the farmer's calendars, and the two collections of moral maxims which go with them.[21] And how could the general religious and moral doctrine of Justice and Injustice in the first part of the poem affect a real lawsuit? The lawsuit was clearly an important event in Hesiod's life; but he began with the concrete fact simply in order to give his teaching artistic shape, to make it seem real and urgent. Without this, his own appearance to preach his doctrine, and the dramatic effect of the first part, would have been impossible.[22] It was, of course, an almost inevitable artistic device, for Hesiod had felt and suffered deeply in his fight for justice. But the end of the lawsuit is not described, because the actual fact is of no importance to the doctrine which inspires the poem.[23]

Just as Homer magnifies the struggles and agonies of his heroes into a drama played in heaven and on earth together, so Hesiod dramatizes his own little lawsuit into a battle between the powers of heaven and earth with justice at stake, and thereby raises an unimportant fact to the dignity and permanence of epic. He cannot show his audience the councils and actions of the gods, as Homer does; for no mortal knows the will of Zeus re-

specting himself. He can only pray to Zeus to defend the right.
So the *Works and Days* begins with a hymn and a prayer. The
poet invokes Zeus, who brings the mighty low and exalts the
humble, to make straight the verdict of the judges.[24] Meanwhile
Hesiod himself takes the active part on earth—he will tell the
truth to his erring brother Perses, and lead him away from the
ruinous path of injustice and strife. He says that Eris, Strife, is
indeed a deity, to whom men must pay homage even against
their own will. But besides the bad Eris there is a good one,
who stirs men not to strife but to rivalry.[25] Zeus gave her a
dwelling among the roots of the world.[26] The man who has nothing and sits idle is inspired by her to labour when he sees and
envies the prosperity of his hard-working and successful neighbour. Then Hesiod warns Perses of the bad Eris. Only a rich
man can spend his time on vain strife, a man who has filled his
granaries and need not worry about his livelihood: only he can
plan to take away the goods of others, and waste his time in the
law-courts. Hesiod exhorts his brother not to take this path a
second time, but to abandon the lawsuit and be reconciled with
him: for they divided their inheritance long ago, but Perses has
taken more than his fair share, by bribing the judges. 'Fools!
they do not know how much the half is larger than the whole,
and what blessings there are in the cheapest herbs man can eat,
mallow and asphodel'.[27] In this way the poet constantly widens
his exhortations to his brother from the concrete instance to
the general truth. Even from this prologue we can see how
Hesiod connects the first part of his poem—his warning against
strife and unrighteousness and his confident assertion that
heaven will protect the just cause—with the second part, in
which he describes the farmer's and sailor's work and adds
moral maxims to tell men what to do and avoid. The connecting
link is the leit-motiv of the whole work—the connexion between
righteousness and work.[28] The only earthly power who can out-
face the oppressions of jealousy and strife is the good Eris, with
her peaceful rivalry in work. Work is a hard necessity for mankind, but it is inevitable. And even the man whose work gives
him only a scanty livelihood is more blessed by it than by an un-
righteous greed for the goods of others.

Hesiod founded this philosophy of life on the eternal laws of
the universe, laws which he himself enunciates in the religious

language and setting of myths.[29] Even in Homer can be traced
the beginnings of an attempt to interpret different myths by one
universal philosophy. But it was Hesiod, in his other great work,
the *Theogony* or *Descent of the Gods,* who first ventured to ar-
range all mythology into a comprehensive philosophical system.
He could not, of course, use the heroic sagas as material fo·
cosmological and theological speculation; but he could and did
freely use the sagas of the gods. Driven by the awakening urge
to find a due cause for each event, he constructed an ingenious
genealogical tree for all the inhabitants of heaven and hell. In
his mythical description of Chaos (yawning empty space), of
Earth and Heaven (the foundation and roof of the world,
separated by Chaos), and of Eros (the cosmic force which creates life), we cannot fail to see the three essential elements of
a rational cosmogony. Earth and Heaven are inevitable elements
in any such account of the world; and Chaos, which also appears
in Nordic myths, is clearly an idea native to the Indo-Germanic
race.[30] But Hesiod's Eros is a philosophical conception of his
own: a new idea which was to have profoundly stimulating
effects on later speculation.[31] In the Battle with the Titans and
in his history of the Dynasties of the Gods, Hesiod writes as a
constructive theologian, and gives an intelligible explanation of
the development of the world, in which ethical forces take their
place beside the telluric and atmospheric forces of nature. That
is to say, he is not content to show the relationships of the
various divinities to whom men prayed and sacrificed, and to use
the traditional data of contemporary religion. He chooses rather
to weld the facts of religion in the widest sense—the facts
of cult, myth, and psychological experience—into a history,
wrought by reason and imagination together, of the origins of
the world and the beginnings of human life. And so he describes
every active force as a divine power—an attitude appropriate to
that early period in the history of thought. His philosophy is
still a system of myths and actively living divinities, as we read
it in the strikingly original poetic form which Hesiod invented
for it. But his mythical system is formed and governed by reason: for it embraces much more than the divinities known to
Homer and to cult-religion; it is not confined to the simple catalogues and family-trees of religious tradition, but contains a new
creative interpretation of the old deities, and freely introduces

fresh personifications to satisfy the new urge to abstract
thinking.[32]

These observations must suffice to describe the background of
those myths which Hesiod used in the *Works and Days* to explain the inevitability of toil and trouble in human life and the
existence of evil in the world. Hence we can see—as we saw
from the introductory description of the good and bad Erides [33]
—that the *Theogony* and the *Works and Days,* despite their difference of subject-matter, are not separated in the poet's mind.
Hesiod's theology invades the ethics of the *Works and Days,*
and his ethical beliefs colour the theology of the *Theogony.*
Both works reflect one man's consistent world-picture. The *Theogony* is filled with the idea of causation; and Hesiod uses that
same idea, in the tale of Prometheus in the *Works and Days,*
to solve the practical, moral, and social problem of work. Work
and suffering must have come into the world at some time; but
they cannot be part of God's original perfect scheme of things.
They were introduced, says Hesiod, speaking as a moralist, by
the disastrous action of Prometheus in stealing the divine fire.[34]
To punish that deed, Zeus created the first woman, the crafty
Pandora, mother of all womankind; out of Pandora's box came
the demons of sickness and old age, with ten thousand other
evils who now inhabit all the earth and all the sea.[35]

It is a bold stroke of Hesiod, to place the myth in such a
central position and to give it this new philosophical interpretation. Its use in the general scheme of the *Erga* corresponds to
the use of the myth in a Homeric speech as a paradeigma, an
encouraging or warning example from tradition.[36] Scholars have
failed to recognize this, the true reason for the two great mythical 'episodes' or 'digressions' in the *Works and Days,* although
it is vitally important if we are to understand both the style
and the content of the poem. The *Works and Days* is a huge
admonitory speech, a protreptic utterance: as such, like the
elegies of Tyrtaeus and Solon, it is directly descended, both in
style and in tone, from the speeches of the Homeric epic.[37] In
such a speech, mythical examples are highly appropriate. The
myth is like an organism which undergoes incessant transformation and renovation. The poet completes that transformation;
but he does so not simply at his own whim. For it is he who
creates a new life-pattern for his age, and he re-interprets the

myth to harmonize with his knowledge of that pattern. Only by the incessant metamorphosis of its central idea can the myth continue to live; but the newly created idea must be incorporated in the myth's own permanent body. This explains the relationship of myth and poet even in the Homeric epics. But it is much clearer in Hesiod: in his work we can clearly trace the effects of his own personality and beliefs. For in the *Theogony* and the *Erga* the poet's individuality appears without disguise, acts visibly on his material, and uses mythology as the instrument of his own intellect and will.

Hesiod's protreptic use of myth is shown even more clearly by the manner in which he introduces the second of the two myths in the *Works and Days*. Immediately after telling the tale of Prometheus, he proceeds to describe the five ages of the world, marking the transition by a brief couplet which is almost entirely lacking in style, but has a deep and characteristic meaning. 'If you are willing,' he says,[38] 'I shall briefly tell another story, with care and skill. And you must take it to heart!' Thus, in passing from the first myth to the second, he addresses Perses once more: in order to remind his audience that these two stories, apparently so remote from each other, have both the same didactic purpose. The history of the age of gold and the degeneration of mankind through the four later ages is meant to show that man was originally better off than now, and lived without toil and trouble. It serves as an explanation of the myth of Prometheus. Hesiod ignores the fact that the two myths cannot both be really true at once—which shows that he regards them merely as two different reflections of one idea. He names, as causes of the growing unhappiness of mankind, increasing hybris and folly, the disappearance of fear of the gods, war, and violence. In the fifth, the age of iron (in which he complains that he himself must live), might alone is right. Only the evildoer can maintain himself in such an age. Hesiod then tells a third tale: the fable of the hawk and the nightingale. It is addressed expressly to the judges, the powerful noblemen. The hawk carried off 'the singer', the nightingale, and as he carried her off through the air in his claws, he answered her pitiful lamentations with [39] 'Wretched creature, why are you crying? You are in the grip of one stronger than you, and you will follow me wherever I take you. And I will eat you, if I wish, or let

you go.' Hesiod calls this animal-story an *ainos*, a fable.[40] Such
fables were always popular among the common folk, and were
employed by them as the mythical examples were employed by
the speakers in epic, to embody a general truth. Homer and
Pindar call even their mythical examples by the name of ainos.
The word was not confined to animal-fables until later; it contains the sense of *advice* which we have stressed above.[41] So the
ainos is not merely the animal-fable of the hawk and the nightingale. That is only the example, which Hesiod gives to the judges.
Both the tale of Prometheus and the myth of the five ages are
true ainoi also.

The next part of the poem contains a picture of powerful
religious effect, the picture of the just city and the unjust city:
examples of the blessing which rests on righteousness and the
curse which follows unrighteousness.[42] Again Hesiod addresses
two parties—the judges and Perses.[43] Here he depicts Diké,
Justice, as an independent divinity. She is the daughter of Zeus,
and sits beside him to complain when men do wicked things, so
that he may requite their wickedness. And the eye of Zeus is on
Hesiod's own city, and on the lawsuit which is proceeding there.
He will not allow the unjust cause to triumph. Then again the
poet turns to Perses: 'Lay up all this in your heart: give ear to
justice, and wholly forget violence. This is the way that Zeus has
ordained for mankind. Fish and wild beasts and the winged birds
shall eat one another, for there is no justice among them. But to
man he has given justice, the highest good of all.'[44] This distinction between man and the beasts is obviously connected with
the simile of the hawk and the nightingale. Men, thinks Hesiod,
should never appeal to the right of the stronger, as the hawk
does against the nightingale.

All the first part of the poem is inspired by a religious faith
which sets the idea of justice at the centre of life. Obviously, this
philosophical conception was not produced by the simple peasantry. In the form in which we find it in Hesiod, it did not even
originate in Greece proper. Like the rationalistic ideals which
created the system of the *Theogony,* it presupposes city-state
civilization and the advanced thinking of Ionia. Homer is the
oldest source of such ideas known to us. In him we find the first
eulogy of justice, although in the *Iliad* that ideal is less pronounced than in the *Odyssey,* which is nearer to Hesiod in time.

In him we see the belief that the gods are guardians of justice, and that their rule would not be truly divine if they did not make justice victorious over injustice in the end. That postulate governs the whole plot of the *Odyssey*. Even in the *Iliad,* a famous simile in the *Patrocleia* contains the belief that Zeus sends storms from heaven when men distort justice upon the earth.[45] But a vast distance separates these occasional traces of an ethical conception of the gods, and even the faith which governs the *Odyssey,* from the religious passion of Hesiod, the herald of justice, the simple man of the people whose infrangible trust in Zeus' guardianship of justice makes him stand out against the men of his own time, and still, after thousands of years, strikes us to the heart with its pathos and its power. He borrows from Homer the content of his ideal of justice, and even some characteristic phrases to describe it. But the reformer's zeal with which he experiences its compelling force, and its predominant position in his conception of the rule of heaven and the meaning of man's life, these mark him out as the prophet of a new age, in which men are to build a better society, founded upon justice. When Hesiod identifies the will of Zeus with the concept of justice, when he creates a new divinity, the goddess Diké, and sets her close beside Zeus the highest of all gods,[46] he is inspired by the burning religious and moral enthusiasm with which the rising class of peasants and townsfolk hailed the new ideal of Justice the saviour.

But the Boeotian countryside had certainly never harboured such new departures in thought as the Ionian coast. Hesiod cannot therefore have been the first to formulate this ideal and to voice the emotion with which it inspired his own society. No: but, feeling it more deeply than others, he became its archprophet. He himself in the *Works and Days*[47] tells how his father, destitute, had migrated to Boeotia from the Aeolian town of Kyme in Asia Minor. We can reasonably assume that the grim and joyless character of the family's new home, so bitterly described by Hesiod, had been felt by his father before him. They had never felt at home in the wretched village of Ascra. Hesiod calls it 'bad in winter, cruel in summer, never good at any time'. It is obvious that from his youth upwards he had learnt from his parents to view Boeotian life and society with a critical eye. He was the first to bring into it the idea of

justice. Even in the *Theogony*[48] he expressly introduces Diké.
In that passage he sets the three Horai—the goddesses of morality, Diké, Eunomia, and Eiréné—beside the three Moirai
and the three Charites: a position which he must have chosen
for them purposely. Just as, in giving the genealogy of the winds
Notos, Boreas and Zephyr,[49] he expatiates on the ruin which they
bring upon sailors and landsmen alike, so he eulogizes the goddesses Justice, Order and Peace as deities who take care of 'the
works of men'. In the *Works and Days* Hesiod's conception of
justice penetrates every aspect of the peasant's life and thought.
By connecting justice with work, he succeeds in writing a poem
which orders and illuminates the peasant's work and ideals by
the light of one dominating educational conception. We must
now briefly trace that conception through the structure of the
remainder of the poem.

Directly after the warning which closes the first part of the
Works and Days—follow justice, and abandon unrighteousness
for ever—Hesiod once more addresses his brother. These famous lines,[50] which have been quoted again and again apart from
their context for thousands of years, are alone sufficient to make
the poet immortal. 'Let me tell you this from my true knowledge,
Perses, you silly child,' he begins, assuming a tone of fatherly
superiority, though he speaks warmly and winningly. 'It is easy
to reach misery even in crowds—the way is smooth, and lies not
far away. But the immortal gods have placed sweat before success. Long and steep is the path to it, and rough at first. Yet
when you have reached the top, then it is easy despite its hard-
ness.' The full meaning of the words κακότης and ἀρετή is not
given in 'misery' and 'success'; but these translations show that
the Greek words do not signify the moral qualities of vice and
virtue, as the later Greeks and Romans believed.[51] The passage
recalls the opening words of the first part of the poem, about the
good and the bad Eris.[52] In the first part Hesiod made his hearers feel the curse of strife; now he must show them the value of
work. He praises it as the only way to areté, difficult though it
is. The idea of areté embraces both personal ability and its products—welfare, success, repute.[53] It is neither the areté of the
warrior noble, nor the areté of the landowning class, built on
wealth, but the areté of the working man, expressed in the possession of a modest competence. Areté is the catchword of the

second part of the poem, the real *Erga*. The aim of work is areté
as the common man understands it. He wishes to make something of his areté, and he engages, not in the ambitious rivalry
for chivalrous prowess and praise which is commended by the
code of the aristocrat, but in the quiet strong rivalry of work.
In the sweat of his brow shall he eat bread—but that is not a
curse, it is a blessing. Only the sweat of his brow can win him
areté. From this it is obvious that Hesiod deliberately sets up
against the aristocratic training of Homer's heroes a working-
class ideal of education, based on the areté of the ordinary man.
Righteousness and Work are the foundations on which it is
built.

But can areté be learnt? That question arises at the beginning
of every ethical and educational system. Hesiod answers it as
soon as the word is mentioned. 'Best of all,' he says, 'is the man
who considers everything himself and sees what is going to be
right in the end. Good, too, is he who obeys another man who
says what is good. But the man who neither understands for
himself nor takes another's advice to heart, he is a useless fellow.' [54] It is significant that these words are spoken after Hesiod
has named the end and aim of work, areté, and immediately before he proceeds to give his separate precepts. Perses, and any
other who may hear the poet's words, must be willing to be
guided by him if he cannot see in his own heart what will harm
and help him. These words hold the real justification and the
meaning of the whole of Hesiod's teaching. They were used by
a philosopher of a later age as the first postulate of his ethical
and educational system. Aristotle quotes them in full in the
Nicomachean Ethics [55] in his prefatory discussion of the correct
basis (ἀρχή) of ethical instruction. That fact is of great assistance in comprehending their function in the general scheme of
the *Works and Days*. There, too, the question of *understanding*
is important. Perses himself does not possess the correct insight;
but the poet must assume that he is teachable and will understand when Hesiod attempts to impart his own convictions and
to influence his conduct. The first part of the poem prepares the
soil for the seed which will be sown by the second—it clears it
of the prejudices and misconceptions which would choke the
growing recognition of truth. Man cannot reach his goal by
violence, strife, and injustice. All his striving must be adapted

to the purpose which rules the world, if he is to profit from it. Once a man has understood that in his heart, another can instruct him and help him to find the right way.

These general remarks are followed by Hesiod's separate practical precepts,[56] which now fall naturally into the setting established by the introduction. They begin with a series of maxims in praise of work. 'So then, Perses, son of heaven, remember my advice, and work, so that hunger may hate you and the fair-crowned modest Demeter may love you, and fill your granary with provender . . . Gods and men hate him who lives without work. His nature is like the drones, who sit idle and eat the labour of the bees. You should wish to do a decent share of work, so that your granaries may be full of the provender that each season brings forth.' [57] 'Work is no shame,' he goes on, 'but idleness is a shame. If you work, the idle man will soon envy you when you are rich. Esteem and glory follow riches. In your position work is the best thing, if you only turn your misguided heart away from the goods of others to your own work and provide for your livelihood, as I advise.' [58] Then Hesiod speaks of the cruel shame which goes with poverty, of wealth which God has given and wealth which has been seized by wrongdoing; and passes on to a series of separate maxims about duty to the gods, piety, and property. He speaks of the correct relationship which one should have with friends, enemies, and especially with one's dear neighbours; of giving, taking and saving; of trust and mistrust, especially regarding women; and of inheritance and the right size of one's family. These separate precepts are followed by a continuous description of the duties to be done by the farmer and by the sailor: which in turn is closed by another collection of maxims. The end of all is the Days, lucky and unlucky. We need not analyse the content of these parts of the poem. In particular, the instructions to the farmer and the sailor (vocations which were less widely separate in Boeotia than in modern times) are so factual and detailed that—despite the charm of their descriptions of daily life and work—we cannot examine them here. But the whole life described by Hesiod is interpenetrated with a peculiar beauty and rhythm which it owes to its close contact with the changeless current of nature. In the first part, he justifies his demand for social justice and honesty, and his description of the ruin which follows injustice, by deriving these facts from the moral order of the world. So, in the second part, his working-man's morality is founded on the natural order of the world in which he works, and derives all its force therefrom. Hesiod makes no distinction between the two. The moral and the natural order are, in his eyes, both derived from God. And everything which man does, both in his daily work and in his relations to other men and to the gods, is part of a teleological unity.

We have already pointed out that the source of the rich stream of human experience which flows through this part of the poem lies in the depths of ancient folk-tradition. In the *Works and Days* the quiet strong river, running for centuries underground, breaks at last into the light. That is the revelation which makes the poem so profoundly moving. Thence it derives a vitality and power which far surpasses the conventional poeticizing of many parts of the *Iliad* and *Odyssey*. The *Works and Days* here reveals to us a new world, alive with a natural and human loveliness which we can glimpse only here and there in epic—in a few similes, or in a descriptive passage like the account of Achilles' shield.[59] In it we smell the rich fragrance of the earth freshly turned by the plough; from the bushes we hear the cuckoo calling the countryman to work. It is all far removed from the rococo idylls written by scholars and city-poets in the Hellenistic age. Hesiod really shows us the whole of country life. Upon that old natural peasant world of country life and country labour he bases his ideal of justice, on which in turn he founds the whole structure of society. And thereby he perpetuates and strengthens and re-creates the peasant's world, by showing him how all his monotonous and toilsome existence is transformed in the light of a higher ideal. Thenceforward the peasant need not envy the privileged aristocratic class, which had once given him all his ideals of life and culture. Now he can find in his own society and his own activities, even in his own hardships, a higher meaning and purpose.

Thus Hesiod's poetry shows us a social class, hitherto debarred from culture and education, actually realizing its own potentialities. In the process, it uses the culture of the upper class and the stylistic medium of courtly poetry; but it derives its real content and its ethos from the depths of its own life. It is because the Homeric epic is not simply the poetry of one class, but has grown from the root of an aristocratic ideal to over-shadow all humanity, that it can help the men of an entirely different class to create their own culture, discover their own purpose in life, and work out its inherent law. That is a great achievement. But this is something even greater—the peasant, by thus realizing his own powers, leaves his isolation and takes his place among the other elements in Greek society. Just as the culture of the nobility affects every class of society when its spiritual energy is intensified by Homer, so the ideals of the peasant, interpreted by Hesiod, reach far beyond the narrow frontiers of peasant life. Granted that much of the *Works and Days* is real and useful only for farmers and peasants, still the poem gives universal meaning to the fundamental ideals of peasant life. That is not to say that the pattern of Greek life was to be defined by agrarian civilization. Actually, Greek ideals did not receive their final and characteristic form until the rise of the city-state, and were relatively little influenced by the native culture of the peasant. But it is therefore all the more important that throughout Greek history Hesiod should have remained the prophet of that ideal of work and justice which was formed among the peasantry and kept its force and meaning within a widely different social framework.

Hesiod is a poet because he is a teacher. His poetic power comes neither from his command of epic style nor from the nature of his material. If we think of his didactic poetry merely as subjects which seem 'prosaic' to later generations, treated in more or less skilfully handled Homeric language, we shall begin to doubt whether it is poetry at all. (Ancient scholars felt the same doubt about later didactic poetry.[60]) Hesiod himself, however, certainly felt that his poetic mission was to be a teacher and a prophet among the Greeks. Hesiod's contemporaries viewed Homer primarily as a teacher. They could imagine no higher spiritual influence than that possessed by the poet, the Homeric rhapsode. A poet could not teach unless he used the noble language of Homer, whose educational effect every Greek felt and acknowledged. When Hesiod succeeded Homer, he defined once and for all the creative power of poetry (and not didactic poetry alone) in its socially constructive and cultural sense. That power, which is far greater than the impulse to give moral or factual instruction, springs from the poet's determination to find the true nature of things—a determination which is founded on his deep understanding of all his world, and which gives fresh life to everything it touches. Hesiod perceived that the existence of the old social order was endangered by strife and injustice. And through that perception he came to see the inviolable foundations on which the life of his society and of each of his fellow-men was built. The deep understanding which strikes through to the simple, original meaning of life—that is what makes the poet. For such a vision, no subject is in itself prosaic or poetic.

Hesiod is the first Greek poet to speak to the men of his own time in his own person.[61] By that fact he passes beyond the sphere of the rhapsode, the 'speaker of fame' and the interpreter of saga-tradition, to reach reality and the struggles of contemporary life. It is clear from his myth of the five ages of the world that he feels the heroic life of the epic to be nothing but an ideal past; for in that myth he contrasts it with the iron present.[62] In Hesiod's age the poet strives to influence life directly. He is the first to set himself up as a leader, without basing his claim to leadership on noble birth or public office. The comparison with the prophets of Israel is obvious, and has often been drawn. But when we hear the voice of Hesiod, the first Greek poet who addresses his own community with the assurance of superior insight, we can recognize the difference which signalizes Greek culture as a new epoch in social history. With Hesiod we see the beginning of that spiritual leadership which is the distinguishing mark of the Greek world. It was the spirit in its original sense—*spiritus,* the breath of God—which the poet felt when the Muses inspired him at the foot of Helicon, and whose approach he describes as an actual religious experience. The Muses themselves, when summoning Hesiod to be a poet, thus explain their inspiring power: 'We know how to tell many lies which are like truth, but we know also how to utter the truth when we wish'.[63] So they speak, in the prelude to the *Theogony.* And in the prelude to the *Works and Days,*[64] Hesiod declares to his brother that he will tell him the *truth.* That deliberate purpose of telling the truth is something new, something not found in Homer, and the personal form of Hesiod's poetry must be somehow connected with it. His own words thus nobly characterize him as the Greek poet-prophet who seeks, through his deeper insight into the plan of the world, to lead erring mankind into the right path.

STATE-EDUCATION IN SPARTA

A NEW CULTURAL PATTERN: THE POLIS AND ITS TYPES

GREEK culture first assumed its classical form in the polis, or city-state.[1] The old aristocratic society and the life of the rural peasantry were not entirely superseded by this new social pattern: many survivals of the feudal and agrarian order appear in the early polis, and some persist even in later stages of its development. But the spiritual leadership of Greece was now taken over by the culture of the cities. Even when it was partly or wholly founded on the old aristocratic and agrarian system, the polis was a new social ideal. It was a firmer and more complete type of community, which expressed the Greek ideal more fully than any other type. Nearly every European language contains the words 'politics' and 'policy,' which are derived from *polis*. They are enough to remind us that the Greek polis is the first example of what we call the state—so that we must translate the word, according to its context, by 'state' or 'city' or by the compromise 'city-state'. From the end of the feudal period to Alexander's creation of the Macedonian world-empire, the polis is practically co-extensive with the state. There were, even in classical times, some types of state which extended over a wider territory; but they were only assemblages of more or less independent city-states. The polis is the focus of Greek history in the classical era, the most important period of the nation's development, and is therefore the centre of historical interest.[2]

If we were to accept the conventional division and attempt to study the intellectual and spiritual life of the Greeks by itself, leaving politics to the constitutional lawyer and historian, we should find it impossible to understand Greek history. No doubt a history of German culture could be written without mentioning politics for many years at a time: the political life of Germany has only recently come to have a fundamental effect on its culture. That is why German scholars long studied the Greeks and their civilization from a predominantly aesthetic point of view. But that is a grave distortion of emphasis. The centre of gravity of Greek life lies in the polis. It is the polis which includes and defines every form of social and intellectual activity. In early Greek history, every branch of intellectual life grows straight from the same root, the life of the community. Or, to change the metaphor, all intellectual activities are brooks and rivers which flow into one central sea—the life of the city— which in turn feeds them all at their sources by invisible subterranean channels. Thus, to describe the Greek polis is to describe the whole of Greek life. That is an ideal which is unattainable in practice—at least by the usual method of narrating historical facts in detailed chronological sequence. But every branch of study would benefit from recognizing that essential unity in Greek life. The polis is the social framework of the whole history of Greek culture; and within that framework we shall set out the various achievements of 'literature' down to the end of the great age of Athens.[3]

We cannot of course investigate the manifold forms of Greek city-state life, or examine the numerous constitutions collected and studied by political historians during the nineteenth century. We are compelled to limit our survey by the nature of the evidence, which contains many important details of the constitutions of individual states, but seldom gives a vivid picture of their social life.[4] No less compelling is the fact that the spirit of the Greek polis was expressed finally and decisively first in poetry and then in prose literature, and thereby impressed its ideals on the spiritual life of Greece. Thus both the literary and the historical evidence leads us to concentrate on the main, the representative types of the Greek city-state. Plato himself, in the *Laws,* where he attempts to discover and record the cardinal ideals of early Greek political thought, bases his investigation on the poets. From them he finds that there are two fundamental types of state, which between them contain all the political culture of Greece. These are the constitutional state (which was in origin Ionian) and the Spartan military state. Accordingly, we shall examine these two types with particular care.[5]

These states represent spiritual ideals which are diametrical opposites. The opposition is obviously a fundamental fact in

Greek political history. More than that: it is a fundamental fact in the history of the Greek spirit. Unless we realize that the Greek political ideal was not uniform, we cannot fully comprehend the essence of Greek culture, with its violent internal conflicts which are at last reconciled in a triumphant harmony. In studying the Ionian aristocracy and the Boeotian peasantry, as depicted by Homer and Hesiod, we had no need to discuss racial characteristics; for we had no means of comparing these societies with other contemporary tribes. The language of epic, composed as it is of a mixture of several dialects, shows that the Homeric poems are the artistic achievement of a number of different races, working together to perfect the language, the metre, and the saga-material. But we should be no more successful in working back from the *Iliad* and *Odyssey* to discover the spiritual differences between the races which created them, than scholars have been in educing complete Aeolic poems from the epics as they stand. However, the political and spiritual differences between the Dorian and the Ionian types are quite clearly marked in the polis. The two types finally unite in the Athens of the fifth and fourth centuries. For in that period the political life of Athens was moulded on the Ionian pattern, while the Spartan ideal was reborn in the realm of the intellect, through the aristocratic influence of Attic philosophy, and eventually, in Plato's cultural ideal, coalesced in a higher unity with the fundamental tenets of the Ionian and Attic constitutional state, stripped of its democratic form.[6]

HISTORICAL TRADITION AND THE PHILOSOPHICAL IDEALISATION OF SPARTA

Both in the history of philosophy and in that of art, Sparta holds a subordinate position. The Ionian race, for example, led Greece in the search for philosophical and ethical truth; but no Spartan name occurs in the long roll of Greek moralists and philosophers.[7] However, Sparta has an unchallengeable place in the history of education. Her most characteristic achievement was her state; and the Spartan state is the first which can be called, in the largest sense, an educational force.

Unfortunately, the evidence on which our knowledge of that remarkable organism is based is in part rather obscure. But, by

good fortune, the central ideal which is exemplified in every detail of Spartan education is clearly revealed in the poems attributed to Tyrtaeus.[8] Had it not been voiced so powerfully, it
could never have freed itself of its local and temporal origins,
and affected posterity so deeply and lastingly. But Tyrtaeus'
elegies are only the proclamation of an ideal. They differ from
the poetry of Homer and Hesiod in that we can learn nothing
more from them than the nature of the ideal which inspires
them. We cannot use them to re-create the historical background
of that ideal; for that we must fall back on later evidence.[9]

The chief source of information is Xenophon's *State of the
Lacedaemonians*—a product of the political and philosophical
romanticism of the fourth century, which held the Spartan state
to be a sort of political revelation from heaven.[10] Aristotle's
Constitution of the Lacedaemonians, now lost, can be reconstructed only in part from the quotations of late lexicographers
who used its abundant material. Its aim was doubtless the same
as that of the critique of Sparta in the second book of Aristotle's
Politics: [11] to pass a sober judgment on Sparta which would balance the extravagant praise bestowed on it by contemporary philosophers. Xenophon at least knew Sparta well, and lived in it.
But the equally romantic Plutarch, the biographer of Lycurgus,
was only a library historian, who used old sources of widely
varying reliability. In estimating the value of Xenophon and
Plutarch, we must remember that they were both inspired by
the conscious or unconscious reaction against the new-fangled
culture of the fourth century. In their admiration of the archaic
constitution of Sparta, the *belle sauvage,* they believed (often
anachronistically) that she had conquered the vices of their own
time, and that she had solved problems which had actually never
presented themselves to 'the sage Lycurgus'. It is utterly impossible to determine how old the Spartan system was in the age of
Xenophon and Agesilaus. The only guarantee of its great antiquity is Sparta's reputation for rigid conservatism—the creed
which made her the ideal of all aristocrats and the abomination
of all democrats. But even Sparta sometimes changed; and even
in comparatively late periods we can trace innovations in her
educational system.

The belief that Spartan education was nothing but an elaborate school of military training originated in Aristotle's *Politics*

and in Plato's *Laws* where he describes the spirit of Lycurgus'
constitution.[12] We must appraise the belief by the circumstances
of the epoch in which it arose. After her victory in the Peloponnesian War, Sparta had been the undisputed leader of Greece;
but after three decades her hegemony was destroyed in the catastrophe of Leuctra. For centuries the Greeks had admired the
Spartan eunomia, but now their admiration had been rudely
shaken. They had all come to loathe Spartan oppression, now
that Sparta, conquered by the lust for power, had lost the ideals
that inspired her old discipline. Money, once almost unknown
in Sparta, flowed into the country: and an old oracle had been
'discovered' to warn her that greed, and greed alone, would ruin
her.[13] In the light of the calculating policy of aggrandisement led
by Lysander, when a tyrannous Laconian harmost occupied the
acropolis of nearly every city in Greece, when all the political
liberties of the so-called autonomous states had been destroyed,
the old Spartan discipline appeared to be simply the mainspring
of a Machiavellian conqueror's power.

We know too little of early Sparta to be able to understand its
spirit. Modern attempts to prove that the classical Spartan constitution, the 'Lycurgan' cosmos, was created by a comparatively
late generation, are no more than hypotheses. The brilliant K.
O. Müller, the first historian of Greek races and cities—a man
whose love of the moral nobility of the Dorian people led him
to champion its greatness against the traditional admiration of
Athens—held, probably rightly, that Spartan militarism was
the survival of a very ancient era in Dorian history.[14] He believed that the régime originated in the peculiar conditions set
up by the great migrations and the early occupation of Laconia,
and that it remained unchanged through the succeeding centuries. The Greeks never lost the tradition of the Dorian migration. It was the last of those population-movements from the
north of the Balkan peninsula, by which peoples probably orig-
inating in central Europe entered Greece and mingled with a
different race, the old-established Mediterranean stock, to produce the Greeks of history. The national type of the invaders
remained purest in Sparta. The Dorian race gave Pindar his
ideal of the fair-haired warrior of proud descent, which he used
to describe not only the Homeric Menelaus, but the greatest

Greek hero Achilles, and in fact all 'the fair-haired Danaans' of the heroic age.[15]

The primary fact about Sparta is that the Spartiates themselves were only a small master-class of later origin than the majority of its population. Below them were the free-born labouring peasantry, the perioikoi, and the conquered and enslaved helots, who were serfs with practically no legal rights. The old accounts of the Spartans describe them as living in a perpetual armed camp. But that way of life was due more to the peculiar composition of the community than to any desire for conquest. The two kings, of the Heraclid race, had practically no political power in the historical period, and recovered their original importance only in occasional military campaigns. The double kingship survived from the old army-kingship of the age of the Dorian migration, and perhaps originated in the balance of power between two different hordes of invaders each with its own leader. The assembly of the Spartan people was simply the old muster of the army originally.[16] It did not debate, but shouted Yes or No to proposals put before it by the council of the elders. Later, it expanded its rights and made amendments to the proposals laid before it. The council was empowered to dissolve the assembly or to withdraw its own proposals if it did not approve of the people's verdict on them.[17] The ephorate, the most powerful office in the whole state, kept the political privileges of the kings in abeyance. It solved the dilemma of a division of power between the people and the leaders by giving both a minimum of authority, and by maintaining the traditional authoritarian character of the constitution. Significantly enough, the ephorate is a part of the system which is not unanimously attributed to the legislation of Lycurgus.[18]

What the Greeks called the legislation of Lycurgus was the opposite of legislation in their usual sense. It was not a codification of separate civil and constitutional laws, but a nomos in the original sense of the word—it was current oral tradition. Only a few fundamental laws were solemnly passed and fixed in writing —the *rhétrai,* among which was the law defining the character of the popular assembly, recorded by Plutarch.[19] This fact contrasted sharply with the cacoethes of legislation which afflicted the democracies of the fourth century, and seemed to contemporary observers to be not a survival of primitive practice but an

example of the far-seeing wisdom of Lycurgus, who, like Socrates and Plato, believed the power of education and the creation
of the social sense to be more vital than any written code of
laws. That is to some extent correct; for the effect of oral tradition and of education diminishes with the growing claim of law
to regulate every detail of life by mechanical compulsion. But
the conception of Lycurgus as the schoolmaster of Sparta is
based on an idealization of Spartan life by later philosophers,
who interpreted it by contemporary cultural theories.[20]

They were misled, by comparing Sparta with the sad degeneration of later Attic democracy, into believing that the Spartan
system was deliberately created by a legislative genius. The
archaic communal life of the Spartan men, living like soldiers
in barracks and eating at common mess-tables, the predominance
of their public life over their private life, the public education
of the youth of both sexes, and the sharp cleavage between the
industrial and agrarian *canaille* and the free Spartiate master-
class, who did not work but devoted themselves to the hunt, the
practice of war, and their official duties—the whole system
seemed to be the deliberate realization of the philosopher's educational ideal, such an ideal as Plato proposed in the *Republic*.
In fact, Plato's ideal, like other theories of paideia, was largely
based on the Spartan model, although the spirit of it was quite
new.[21] The great social problem of all later Greek educators was
to determine how individualism might be repressed and the character of every citizen might be developed on one communal
model. The Spartan state, with its rigid authoritarianism, appeared to be the solution of this problem in actual practice; and
as such it occupied Plato's mind throughout his life. Plutarch
too, who was a staunch follower of Plato's educational ideals,
constantly recurred to this belief. 'Education,' he writes in his
life of Lycurgus,[22] 'extended to grown men and women. Nobody
was free to live as he wished, but as if in a camp everyone had
his way of life and his public duties fixed, and he held that he did
not belong to himself but to his country.' And in another passage [23] he says, 'In general Lycurgus made the citizens accustomed to have neither the will nor the ability to lead a private
life; but, like the bees, always to be organic parts of their community, to cling together around the leader, and, in an ecstasy of

enthusiasm and selfless ambition, to belong wholly to their country.'

It was actually very difficult for a citizen of post-Periclean Athens, with its creed of complete individualism, to understand Sparta. We can neglect the philosophical interpretations of her system which were given by Attic philosophers, but we must accept the facts as they record them. Plato and Xenophon believed that the constitution of Sparta was the work of a single educational genius, with the authority of a dictator and the foresight of a philosopher. Actually, it was the survival of an earlier, simpler stage in social life, the stage which is characterized by strong racial and communal solidarity and scant individual initiative. Sparta's system was the creation of centuries. Only here and there can we determine what part a given individual took in shaping it. For example, the names of the kings Theopompus and Polydorus are attached to certain constitutional changes.²⁴ There is practically no doubt that Lycurgus himself really existed; but we cannot now decide whether he too was originally known as the author of similar changes, or why he was later believed to be the founder of the whole system. All we can say is that the tradition of 'Lycurgus' constitution' has no early authority.²⁵

That tradition was created by an age which thought the Spartan system was deliberately created to serve an educational purpose, and which believed *a priori* that the highest end and meaning of the state was paideia—namely, a process by which the life of each citizen should be shaped to conform with some absolute norm. We hear again and again that the Delphic oracle approved of 'Lycurgus' constitution'—thereby providing an absolute, to offset the relative outlook of democracy, with its belief that every man was a law to himself. This is another example of the tendency of observers of Sparta to describe her constitution as the ideal educational system. The fourth-century Greeks believed that the problem of education was ultimately the problem of finding an absolute standard for human behaviour. But in Sparta the latter problem was solved. The Spartan constitution was founded on religious truth, for it had been sanctioned or praised by the Delphic god himself. Thus it is clear that the whole tradition of Lycurgus' constitution was built up to harmonize with a later political and educational theory,

and is therefore unhistorical. If we wish to understand it properly, we must remember that it grew up when Greek speculation
about the nature and principles of paideia was at its height, and
when educational theorists had a burning interest in Spartan
affairs. Its survival (and the preservation of Tyrtaeus' poems)
is due to the vital importance of the Spartan ideal in the later
development of Greek paideia.[26]

When we strip off the philosophical colouring, what are the
true outlines of the picture of Sparta which remains?

Xenophon's description of his ideal state, overlaid though it
is with his own theories and interpretations, contains so much
reporting of personally observed facts that from it (after ex-
punging his own historical and educational commentary) we can
reconstruct a vivid picture of contemporary Sparta, with its
unique system of military education. But, if we abandon the
belief that the system sprang fully armed from the head of
Lycurgus, we cannot determine when it was built up. Modern
scholars have questioned the very existence of Lycurgus. But
even if he was a real person, and was the author of the great
rhêtra which was known to Tyrtaeus in the seventh century, we
are still in the dark about the origin of the educational system
described by Xenophon. All Spartan citizens were subjected to
the system of military training, and therefore were a sort of
aristocracy. There are other elements in the system which remind us of the early Greek aristocracy and its training. But although we must postulate that Sparta was originally governed
by a class of noblemen, the fact that their educational system
was extended to others shows that their position had somehow
been altered. Other Greek states were ruled by a peaceful aristocratic régime. But that was not enough for Sparta. She had
conquered the Messenians, and for centuries was compelled to
hold them down by force. She could do so only by developing
the whole Spartiate citizen body into an armed and trained master-class, free from the necessity of working for a living. This
development doubtless started during the wars of the seventh
century, and may well have been encouraged by the struggles of
the demos (which are mentioned by Tyrtaeus) to extend their
political rights. A Spartan held his citizen rights in virtue of
his status as a soldier. Tyrtaeus is the first author to describe
this ideal of the citizen-soldier, which was later realized in the

whole Spartan educational system. But even he seems to have thought the ideal was practicable and necessary only in war-time. His poems clearly show that in his time the Spartan system was coming into existence, but was not yet fully developed.[27]

Again, Tyrtaeus provides the only reliable evidence for the Messenian wars, for modern critics have discarded the evidence of Hellenistic historians as wholly or predominantly imaginary. His poetic impulse was stirred by the great revolt of the Messenians, who had first been conquered by the Spartans two generations before his time.[28] 'For nineteen years,' he says, 'they fought unceasingly and relentlessly, with steadfast will—the spearmen who were our fathers' fathers. Then, in the twentieth year, the enemy left their rich fields and fled from the high mountains of Ithome.' He also mentions the national hero Theopompus, 'beloved of the gods, our king, through whom we captured broad Messenia'. These words are quoted by the late historians.[29] Another fragment gives a vivid picture of the servitude of the conquered race. Their land, the Messenian land which Tyrtaeus describes as rich and fertile, was divided among the Spartans; the former owners worked on it as serfs, 'labouring like asses under heavy loads, and forced by bitter compulsion to bring their masters half of all the produce of their fields. . . . And whenever one of their masters died, they and their wives must go to his funeral and lament for him.' [30]

These descriptions of the situation before the Messenian revolt were intended by Tyrtaeus to encourage the Spartan army by memories of their previous victory, and to terrify it by picturing their doom if they were defeated. One of the few complete poems which has survived [31] begins with the words: 'You are the race of the unconquered Heracles—take heart! Zeus has not yet turned his head away in anger. Do not fear the numbers of the enemy, do not flee from them! . . . You know the destruction wrought by woeful Ares, and have felt the spirit of grievous war: you have been in flight and in pursuit.' This is a call of encouragement to a defeated and demoralized army. And indeed, tradition described Tyrtaeus as the leader sent to the Spartans by the Delphic Apollo, to save them in their danger.[32] The late historians said that he was actually a general, and modern scholars believed them until they were corrected by a newly discovered papyrus containing large fragments of a

hitherto unknown poem by Tyrtaeus. In this poem he speaks
in the first person plural, and calls the Spartans to give obedience
to their leaders.[33] It is entirely a vision of the future, a description of a decisive battle which is imminent, done in the Homeric
manner. It mentions the old Spartan tribes—the Hylleis, the
Dymanes, and the Pamphyloi—which were obviously units of
the army at that time, although the division was later superseded
by a new organization. And it speaks of a battle for a wall and a
ditch—which looks as if a siege were in progress. Apart from
this, Tyrtaeus gives us no historical data, and even the ancients
found no more concrete facts in his poems than we.[34]

TYRTAEUS' CALL TO ARETÉ

The will which made Sparta a great nation still lives in the
elegies of Tyrtaeus. It had the power to create a great ideal—a
power which long survived historical Sparta, and is not yet ex-
hausted; and these poems are the strongest manifestation of that
power. The Spartan community, as known to history in a later
age, was in many ways an impermanent and eccentric thing. But
the ideal which inspired its citizens, and towards which, with
iron consistency, every effort of every Spartan was directed, is
imperishable because it is an expression of a fundamental human
instinct. Although the society which incorporated it appears to
us to have been partial and limited in its outlook, the ideal itself
remains true and valuable. Plato himself considered the Spartan
conception of the citizen's functions and education to be narrow-
minded, but he saw that the Spartan idea immortalized in Tyrtaeus' poems was one of the immutable bases of political life.[35]
And he was not alone in that: he merely expressed the general
Greek view of Sparta. The Greeks of his time did not give
unqualified approval to Sparta and her policy, but they all recognized the value of her ideal.[36] In every city there was a
philo-Laconian party, which idealized the constitution of Lycurgus. The majority did not share this unconditional admiration.
Still, the position which Plato allotted to Tyrtaeus in his cultural
system remained valid for the Greeks of all subsequent ages,
and was an indefeasible element of their culture. It was Plato
who arranged and systematized the spiritual inheritance of his
nation: in his synthesis, the various ideals which inspired Greece

are objectified and set in their correct relationships. Since then, no great change has been made in his system; and the Spartan ideal has for two thousand years kept the position in the history of civilization which Plato assigned to it.[37]

The elegies of Tyrtaeus are inspired by a mighty educational ideal. The demands which they make on the self-sacrifice and patriotism of the Spartans were no doubt justified by the circumstances in which they were written—Sparta was almost sinking under the burden of the Messenian War. But they would not have been admired by later ages as the supreme expression of the Spartan will to forget oneself in one's country, if they had not been a permanent and timeless utterance of that ideal. The standards they impose on every citizen's thoughts and actions were not produced by a momentary outburst of warlike patriotism; they were the foundation of the whole Spartan cosmos. Nothing in Greek poetry shows more clearly how the creative activity of the poet begins in the life of the society to which he belongs. Tyrtaeus is not an individual poetic genius, in the modern sense of the word. He is the voice of the people. He utters the faith of every right-thinking citizen. For that reason he often speaks in the first person plural: 'let us fight!' he cries, and 'let us die!' Even when he says 'I', he is not giving free expression to his own personality, nor is he speaking as a superior authority (as the ancients thought; they even called him a general [38]); he is the universal I, he is what Demosthenes [39] calls 'the general voice of the country'.

He speaks with the voice of his country; and hence his judgment of what is 'honourable' and what 'disgraceful' has a far greater weight and authority than if it were the subjective opinion of an ordinary orator. The close relationship between state and individual might, even in Sparta, be comparatively unrealized by the average citizen in time of peace. But at a time of danger, the ideal suddenly manifested itself with overpowering force. The dreadful crisis of the long and doubtful war which was then beginning was to forge the iron framework of Sparta's state. For that dark hour, she needed not only resolute leadership, both political and military, but a universally valid expression of the new virtues which were being fired in the white heat of war. The Greek poets had for centuries been the heralds of areté, and such a herald now appeared in Tyrtaeus. As we have observed, the legend said he was sent by Apollo [40]—a striking expression of the strange truth that when a spiritual leader is needed he always comes. Tyrtaeus came to express in eternal poetry the new civic virtues which were needed in the national crisis.

He was not an innovator in matters of style. He wrote in a more or less traditional form. There is no doubt that the elegiac couplet was invented before his day, although its origins are obscure, as they were even to ancient literary critics.[41] It has some connexion with the heroic metre used in epic, and, like it, could at that time be employed as a vehicle for any subject. Therefore, there is no one unvarying structure in all elegiac poems. (The ancient grammarians,[42] misled by false etymology and by the later development of the genre, attempted to derive all elegy from the song of lamentation, but that was a mistake.) Apart from the elegiac metre itself—which in the earliest times had no special name to distinguish it from the heroic metre—there is only one constant element in elegiac poetry. It is always *addressed to someone*: either to one individual or to a collection of people. The elegy expresses a latent bond between the speaker and his audience, and that bond is the distinguishing mark of all elegiac poetry. Tyrtaeus, for example, speaks either to the citizens of Sparta or to the young men of Sparta. Even the poem which begins in a more meditative tone (fragment 9) narrows at its conclusion into an exhortation: it is addressed to the members of a body which, as usual, is assumed but not described explicitly.[43] This admonitory address is a clear expression of the educational character of the elegy. It shares that character with the epic, but (like Hesiod's didactic poetry) makes its address more direct than epic, more deliberate, more definite in its object. The epic with its mythical examples is set in an imaginary world; the elegy, with its address to real concrete people, takes us into the actual situation which inspired the poet.

But although Tyrtaeus' elegies deal with the actual life of his audience, their form is fixed by the style of the Homeric epic. The poet, in fact, clothes a contemporary subject in the archaic language of Homer. But Homer's style was far more appropriate to Tyrtaeus than to Hesiod, though Hesiod too had been compelled to use it: for what is nearer to epic poetry than savage fighting and heroic prowess? Therefore Tyrtaeus not only borrowed much of Homer's language, words, phrases and fragments of lines, but found that he could model several of his poems on those battle-scenes of the *Iliad* in which a leader addresses his men at a moment of danger to encourage them to high courage and steadfast resistance.[44] He had only to separate these exhortations from the mythical background of epic and transfer them to the living present. Even in the epic, the speeches made at crises of the fighting have a strongly protreptic effect. They seem to be addressed not so much to the other characters as to Homer's audience. Certainly the Spartans felt that effect very strongly. Tyrtaeus had only to transfer the vast moral impetus of these speeches from Homer's imaginary battles to the real struggles of the Messenian war, and he had created his elegy. We shall understand that spiritual transference better if we read Homer as the age of Tyrtaeus and Hesiod read him—not as the narrator of the past, but as the teacher of the present.[45]

Without doubt, Tyrtaeus believed that he was a Homerid, and that his elegies, his addresses to the Spartan nation, were direct descendants of the *Iliad* and the *Odyssey*. But it is not his more or less effective imitations of Homer's phrases and Homer's rhetoric which makes his work really great; it is the spiritual power with which he transforms epic devices and material into something valuable for his own day. If we subtract from Tyrtaeus' work all the ideas, words, and metrical turns which he borrowed from Homer, there will seem to be little of his own left. Yet we are bound to grant his real originality as soon as we study him from the standpoint of the present investigation, and realize that his conventional scenery and his archaic ideals of heroism are revitalized by his faith in a new moral and political authority—the city-state, which transcends every individual citizen, and for which every citizen lives and dies. He has recast the Homeric ideal of the single champion's areté into the areté of the patriot, and with that new faith he strives to inspire his whole society.[46] He is endeavouring to create a nation of heroes. Death is beautiful, if it is a hero's death; and to die for one's country is a hero's death.[47] That is the only thought which can exalt a dying man, by making him feel that he is sacrificing himself for a higher good [48] than his own life.

Tyrtaeus' transvaluation of the idea of areté is clearest in the third of his extant poems.[49] This poem was until recently rejected on purely stylistic grounds; but I have elsewhere given exhaustive proof of its authenticity.[50] It certainly cannot be placed as late as the period of the sophists, in the fifth century.[51] Solon and Pindar both knew it, and as early as the sixth century Xenophanes obviously imitated and altered one of its leading ideas in a poem which is still preserved.[52] It is fairly clear what led Plato to choose that elegy out of all the then extant poetry attributed to Tyrtaeus as best representative of the Spartan spirit: it was the precision and force with which the poet works out the true nature of Spartan areté.[53]

It opens a window on the history of the development of the idea of areté since Homer, and on the crisis which confronted the old aristocratic ideals during the rise of the city-state. Tyrtaeus exalts *true* areté above the other goods which his contemporaries believed could give a man true worth and esteem. 'I would not,' he says, 'mention or take account of a man for the prowess of his feet or for his wrestling, even if he had the stature and strength of the Cyclopes and outran the Thracian Boreas.'[54] These are exaggerated instances of the athletic areté which had been admired, above all else by the aristocracy ever since Homer's day; during the previous century, because of the rise of the Olympic Games, it had come to be regarded even by the common people as the highest pinnacle of human achievement.[55] Tyrtaeus now adds other virtues admired by the old nobility. 'And were he more beautiful in face and body than Tithonus, and richer than Midas and Cinyras, and more kingly than Tantalus' son Pelops, and sweeter of tongue than Adrastus, I would not honour him for these things, even if he had every glory except warlike valour. For no one is a good man in war, unless he can bear to see bloody slaughter and can press hard on the enemy, standing face to face. That is areté!' cries Tyrtaeus in a transport of emotion, 'that is the best and fairest prize which a young man can win among men. That is a good which is common to all—to the city and the whole people—when a man takes his stand and holds his ground relentlessly among the foremost fighters and casts away all thought of shameful flight.'[56] We must not call this 'late rhetoric'. Solon speaks in the same way. The origins of rhetorical style go far back into history.[57] Tyrtaeus' excited repetitions are prompted by the deep emotion with which he asks his central question—what is true areté? The usual answers to that question are one by one rejected, in the powerful negations of the first ten or twelve lines; all the lofty ideals of the old Greek aristocracy are removed to a lower plane, although not wholly denied or superseded; and then, when the poet has raised his audience to a high pitch of excitement, he proclaims the severe new ideal of citizenship. There is only one standard of true areté—the common good of the polis. Whatever helps the community is good, whatever injures it is bad.[58]

From this, he passes naturally to eulogies of the reward which a man wins by sacrificing himself for his country, whether he falls in battle or returns home triumphant. 'But he who falls among the foremost fighters and loses his dear life in winning glory for his city and his fellow-citizens and his father—his breast and his bossed shield and his breastplate pierced with many wounds in front—he is lamented by young and old together, and the whole city mourns for him in sad grief; and his tomb and his children are honoured among men, and his children's children likewise and his whole race after him; never is his name and fair fame destroyed, but though he lies beneath the earth he becomes immortal.'[59] The glory of a Homeric hero, however widely it is disseminated by the wandering bard, is nothing to the glory of a simple Spartan warrior, as Tyrtaeus describes it, laid up for ever deep in the hearts of his people. The close community of the city-state, which seemed at the beginning of the poem to be only an obligation, now appears as a privilege and an honour: it is the source of all ideal values. The first part states the heroic ideal of areté in terms of the city-state. The second restates, in the same terms, the heroic ideal of glory. Areté and glory are inseparable in the epic.[60] Glory is now to be given, and areté to be exercised, by and in the city-state. The polis lives when the individual dies; and so it is a safe guardian of the 'name' and, with it, of the future life of a hero.

The early Greeks did not believe in the immortality of the soul. A man was dead when his body died. What Homer calls the *psyché* is a reflection or wraith of the physical body, a shadow living in Hades, a nothing.[61] But if a man crossed the frontiers of ordinary human existence and reached a higher life by sacrificing himself for his country, then the polis could give him immortality by perpetuating his ideal personality, his 'name'. This political idea of heroism became dominant with the rise of the city-state, and remained so throughout Greek history. Man as a political being reaches perfection by the perpetuation of his memory in the community for which he lived or died. It was only when the value of the state, and indeed of all earthly life, began to be questioned, and the value of the individual soul to be exalted—a process which culminated in Christianity—that philosophers came to preach the duty of despising fame.[62] Even in the political thought of Demosthenes and Cicero there is no trace of this change; while Tyrtaeus' elegies represent the first stage in the development of city-state morality.[63] It is the polis which guards and immortalizes the dead hero, and it is the polis which exalts the victorious warrior who returns alive. 'He is honoured by all, young and old together; his life brings him much happiness, and no one will offer him insult or injury. As he grows old, he is respected among the citizens, and wherever he goes all make way for him, both the youth and the elders.' [64] This is not merely rhetoric. The early Greek city-state was small, but it had something truly heroic and truly human in its nature. Greece, and in fact all the ancient world, held the hero to be the highest type of humanity.

In this poem the polis is presented as an inspiration in the life of all its citizens. But there is another [65] of Tyrtaeus' elegies which shows its power to compel, to threaten, and to terrify. The poet contrasts a glorious death on the battlefield with the miserable wandering life which is the doom of the man who has avoided his civic obligation to fight in the army, and has been forced to leave his home. He wanders about the world with his father and mother, wife and little children. In his poverty and need, he is a stranger to everyone he meets, and is regarded as an enemy by all. He dishonours his race and disgraces his noble face and form; and he is followed by outlawry and baseness. It is an incomparably vivid illustration of the relentless logic with which the state claims the life and property of its members. With the same realism as Tyrtaeus describes the honour paid to the country's heroes, he depicts the pitiless fate of the exile. It makes no difference whether we hold that he was banished by an emergency measure imposing exile on deserters, or left home voluntarily to escape military service, and was compelled to live as an alien in another polis. In these two complementary pictures, the polis appears as both an exalted ideal and a despotic power. As such, it is something very like a god; and the Greeks always felt its divinity. They did not see a purely material and utilitarian connexion between civic virtue and the safety of the commonwealth. The polis was a universal, with a religious basis. As opposed to the areté of the heroic age, the new areté of the polis is an expression of a change in Greek religious ideals. The polis has become the epitome of all things human and divine.

It is not surprising to find that in another elegy famous in antiquity, the *Eunomia*,[66] Tyrtaeus expounds the true import of the Spartan constitution. He strives to educate the Spartans in the fundamental principle of their system—the same system that is independently described in the old rhétra, which Plutarch in his *Life of Lycurgus* transcribed in its native Doric.[67] Tyrtaeus gives the leading proof of the antiquity of that valuable relic, by paraphrasing its substance in this elegy.[68] The poet obviously became more and more an educator of his country, for his poems are in fact a summary of the whole Spartan cosmos in peace and war. The variations which appear in the form of the poem raise interesting problems of literary and constitutional history, but they are less relevant here than the discussion of its content.

The thought which underlies the *Eunomia* illuminates both Tyrtaeus' own attitude and the political ideal of Ionia and Athens, to which it is fundamentally opposed. The Ionians did not feel bound by the authority of tradition and the myth, but endeavoured to distribute constitutional privileges in conformity with a more or less universal social and legal ideal. But Tyrtaeus derives the Spartan eunomia from a divine ordinance, and holds that its divine origin is its highest and surest guarantee. 'Zeus himself, the son of Kronos, the spouse of crowned Hera, gave this city to the Heraclids, with whom we quitted windy Erineos and came to the broad Isle of Pelops.' [69] When we read this fragment in conjunction with the larger passage which reproduces the old rhétra,[70] we can see the full meaning of Tyrtaeus' reversion to the mythical origin of the Spartan state in the age of the first Dorian migration.

The rhétra expressly defines the rights of the people against the power of the kings and of the elders' council. That is its fundamental law, and Tyrtaeus derives that too from divine authority: it was approved or even enjoined by the oracle of Apollo at Delphi. After Sparta's difficult victory over the Messenians, the common people began to feel their strength, and to demand political rights as a reward for their sacrifices in the war. Tyrtaeus is ready to repress their demands, should they become excessive, by reminding them that they owe their stake in the country to their kings, 'the race of Heracles'. It was to them that Zeus gave the land, according to the old legend which described the Dorian immigration into the Peloponnese as 'the return of the race of Heracles'. Therefore, the kings are the only rightful link between the present day and the divine act which founded Sparta in the remote past. The Delphic oracle has for ever established the status of the kings.

Tyrtaeus' *Eunomia* is intended to give an authentic interpretation of the legal basis of the Spartan cosmos. Partly a rational exposition, partly a mythical reminiscence, it assumes the strong kingship of the period of the Messenian wars. But Tyrtaeus, as his poem on civic virtue shows, was far from being a reactionary. In his attempt to substitute a city-state morality for an aristocratic morality, and in his advocacy of the acceptance of every citizen within the state as one of its warriors, Tyrtaeus is much more of a revolutionary. But he does not stand for democracy.[71] As the *Eunomia* shows, the popular assembly is the muster of the army: it votes Yes or No to every proposal advanced by the council, but has no right of proposing measures on its own account. It was probably difficult to maintain this system after the war ended; but the authorities obviously used the popular influence which Tyrtaeus had gained as spiritual leader in the war, to maintain the 'right order' as a bulwark against the rising demands of the common people.

Tyrtaeus of the *Eunomia* belongs to Sparta, but Tyrtaeus of the war-poems belongs to the whole of Greece. In the trials of war, among the party-struggles of a rather unheroic world, a new heroism arose to be the fresh inspiration of true poetry.

This new poetry sang of the polis in its darkest hour of crisis, and acquired thereby a sure place beside the ideal world of Homer. We have another elegiac war-poem written not long before Tyrtaeus, by the Ionic poet Callinus of Ephesus: its style and content lead naturally to comparisons between the work of the two poets. Their relationship is obscure, and they are possibly quite independent of each other. Callinus' poem is a summons to his fellow-citizens to resist their common enemy. A fragment of another poem seems to show that the enemy was the invading hordes of savage Cimmerians who had invaded Asia Minor and penetrated the kingdom of Lydia. In the same situation, with the same determining conditions, a poetic experience of the same order was created; for Callinus, like Tyrtaeus, imitates the style of Homer and interfuses the epic form with the new sense of the communal life of the city-state.

But the spirit which moved Callinus and his fellow-Ephesians to one momentary collective effort, became the permanent inspiration of Sparta and its whole educational creed. Tyrtaeus filled the Spartans with the new sense of communal life and effort, and the heroic faith which he preached lived on in Sparta throughout her history. His voice was soon heard beyond the frontiers of Laconia as the teacher of the ideal of heroism devoted to the community. In every Greek land where civic courage was practised by the citizens or imposed by the state, where the heroes who had died for their country were honoured, the poems of Tyrtaeus were prized as the classic utterance of the 'Spartan' creed—and that in non-Spartan and even in anti-Spartan states like Athens.[72] His verses are echoed in the fifth century by the epitaphs on soldiers' graves, and in the fourth by the official funeral orations which were spoken to commemorate the dead Athenian warriors. They were recited to the flute at drinking-parties. Attic orators like Lycurgus strove to impress them on the hearts of the young as deeply as the poems of Solon. To explain the position given to soldiers in his ideal state, Plato [73] copies Tyrtaeus' injunction to honour the fighter more highly than the Olympic victor. In the *Laws* [74] he tells us that fourth-century Sparta still counted Tyrtaeus' poems the highest revelation of the spirit of the Dorian state, of that spirit which trained all its citizens to display the same courage in war. All Spartans, he says, are 'crammed' with Tyrtaeus' poetry. And he

shows that even the non-Spartans who, like himself, do not accept the Spartan conception of the true nature of the state and
of the highest human excellence, must still admit the cogency of
much of Tyrtaeus' gospel.

Tyrtaeus, of course, represents only one stage in the development of the Greek community. But whenever the Greeks recast'
their conception of areté, they quoted the passionate revolutionary lines of Tyrtaeus, and set the new creed in the old form of
his poem on true virtue. That is the true Greek idea of culture.
Once the pattern is fixed, it continues to be valid even in later or
higher stages of development; and every innovation must adapt
itself to fit it. Thus, a hundred years after Tyrtaeus, the philosopher Xenophanes of Colophon adapted his poem on virtue [75]
to show that intellectual ability alone deserved the highest rank
in the state. And, later in the same process, Plato [76] set justice
above courage, in his ideal state, and ordered Tyrtaeus to be rewritten to conform to the spirit of his constitution.

Plato did not criticize Tyrtaeus so much as the excesses of
contemporary Sparta. In the fourth century, she was a harsh,
narrow-minded, militarist power, but Tyrtaeus' poems were still
her Magna Charta. Then, even her most ardent admirer could
not find in her any trace of aesthetic feeling. Xenophon's silence,
and the unsuccessful efforts of Plutarch to conceal the deficiency,
are eloquent; and we need not try to make that failing into a
Spartan virtue. Fortunately, despite the fragmentary evidence,
we can demonstrate that the real old Sparta, the heroic Sparta
of the seventh century, was less mentally restricted than its successor, and in fact lived a richer and fuller life. Though Tyrtaeus
praises, and rightly praises, the warrior more highly than the
gymnast, the list of Olympic victors in the seventh and sixth
centuries (especially after the victorious conclusion of the Messenian war) shows, by the enormous preponderance of Spartan
names, that Sparta gave of her best to these peaceful contests
as she had to her wars.[77]

Again, Sparta in that period showed none of the sour puritan
hatred of art which at a later date was considered to be truly
Spartan. Excavations have revealed that her citizens were busily
engaged in building, and that they practised an art based on
imitation of eastern Greek styles. That squares with the fact that

the elegiac form used by Tyrtaeus was imported from Ionia. About the same period, the great musician Terpander, who invented the seven-stringed lyre, was invited to come from Lesbos to Sparta in order to lead the choirs at religious festivals and to develop Spartan music in the important new style he had worked out.[78] In later ages Sparta clung stubbornly to Terpander's style, and regarded any change in it as equivalent to a revolution. But that fossilized practice still shows the strength of the conviction held by seventh-century Sparta that aesthetic culture could form the whole character of her citizens. It is easy to imagine the original power of her artistic impulses when they were still allowed to have full play.

A welcome supplement to our picture of antique Sparta is provided by the large fragments of Alcman's choric poetry which have survived. Alcman was born in Sardis, but migrated to Sparta, where he found his life's work as an artist. The language of Tyrtaeus had been entirely Homeric, but Alcman deliberately introduced Laconian dialect into his choral lyrics; the Dorian character flashes out only here and there through the mask of Homeric convention in Tyrtaeus, but the hymn which Alcman wrote for Spartan girl-choirs scintillates with the sharp humour and the realistic vigour which were native to the race. His verses, addressed to maidens who are named and eulogized, and playing delicately with their little jealousies and ambitions, set vividly before us the eager rivalry of the musical *agones* of his day, and serve to show that the spirit of competition between Spartan women was quite as keen as it was between men. In Sparta, as Alcman's poetry shows, women were much more free in both public and private life [79] than the women of Ionia (which was influenced by Asiatic ideals) and of Athens (which copied Ionia). Like many other Dorian characteristics in speech and habits this is a pure survival from the time of the conquering invaders of Greece: the vigour and freedom of that early age were felt in Sparta far longer than in any other of the Hellenic states.

THE CITY-STATE AND ITS IDEAL OF JUSTICE

SPARTA's share in forming the ideal of man as a citizen is easier to define than that of the rest of Greece, because it is impossible to name any other city in which decisive steps towards this ideal were taken. We have no reliable evidence to guide us until we reach Athens at the beginning of the sixth century: it was there and then that the new spirit which inspired the state found expression in the poetry of Solon. Yet Athens was the last of the great Greek cities to appear in history, and her constitutional ideals presuppose a long anterior development. Throughout Solon's life and work it is clear that he was deeply influenced by Ionian civilization.[1] Accordingly, we cannot doubt that these new political ideals also originated in Ionia, the intellectual and critical centre of Greece. Unfortunately, the information which we possess about the political history of the Ionian colonies is very poor: so that we must fall back on inferences *a posteriori,* based on the facts which we know to have existed at a later period, and on parallel situations in other countries.

With the exception of Callinus, mentioned above,[2] it would seem that Ionia produced no truly political poetry comparable to that of Tyrtaeus and Solon.[3] We cannot put this fact down to pure chance: it was clearly deep-rooted in the Ionian character. Like all the Greeks of Asia Minor, the Ionians lacked constructive political energy, and never succeeded in forming a permanent and historically active state. They did, indeed, pass through a heroic age at the period of their immigration into the country —the period which is reflected in the Homeric poems: and it would be wrong to believe that they were always the weak sensual people which we know in the time just before the Persian wars.[4] They fought many fierce wars with one another and with foreign foes. Their poets, Callinus, Archilochus, Alcaeus, and Mimnermus, were true warrior-bards.[5] But they never held the polis to be the supreme absolute, as Spartans and Athenians did. Their work in the development of the Greek spirit was to set the

individual free—and it was so even in political life. In general,
then, the Ionian colonies were incapable of co-ordinating the
energies of their free individual citizens, and of using them to
strengthen their own power; but it was Ionia which first released
the political forces which, in the firmer framework of the mainland Greek cities, helped to create a vitally new ideal of the
state.

The life of the Ionian polis is first known to us from the
Homeric epics. The Trojan war itself did not allow Homer to
depict a Greek state, for he considered the Trojans to be barbarians. But he involuntarily gave Troy, in its struggle to defend
itself, some of the traits of an Ionian city-state; and Hector, the
guardian of his country, was the pattern of heroism for Callinus
and Tyrtaeus. In this stage of Ionian culture, especially as reflected in Callinus (p. 96), we can trace many resemblances to
the Spartan ideal. But at an early period the Ionian city-state
began to develop in another direction, and that movement is also
shown in the epic. In the only passage where the *Iliad* depicts a
city at peace—the late description of the shield of Achilles—we
find that, in the marketplace at the centre of the city, a lawsuit
is in process: 'the elders' sit on polished stones in a holy circle
and give judgment.⁶ That means that the heads of noble families
now held an important part in the administration of justice,
which had originally been the province of the king. The famous
condemnation ⁷ of divided government argues that kings still
existed, but their position was clearly precarious. The shield of
Achilles also pictured a royal demesne, with a king admiring his
harvest; ⁸ but he was probably only a landowning nobleman, for
the epic often gives the title *basileus,* 'king' or 'prince', to members of the nobility. As in Greece proper, agrarian civilization
(which is the basis of a landed aristocracy) at first obtained
throughout Ionia. Another example of limited monarchy is Alcinous, king of the Phaeacians. Among the elders of his council, he is only the chairman, although he is the legitimate and
hereditary king. Therefore, the transition from monarchy to
aristocracy is not far off: the king is soon to become only a
high-priest or an eponymous official, with no peculiar privileges
attaching to his rank. This transition is mentioned in several
cities, but we can see it most clearly in Athens. There the royal
family of the Codridae is gradually pushed into the background

by the advancing power of the aristocracy, which is still dominant in the age of Solon. But our knowledge is insufficient to
determine how long after the migrations this characteristic development took place in Ionia.

The Ionian coastal strip, on which the constant streams of
immigrants landed, was not wide; and the hinterland, occupied
by disorganized but warlike native peoples (like the Lydians,
Phrygians, and Carians), was impossible to penetrate. Hence,
the coastal cities were more and more driven to engage in seafaring, especially as the art of navigation was developed. To
this new enterprise many rich nobles turned their energy, and
they became its leaders. The Greek colonists had always been
much less attached to the soil, after they had torn themselves
loose from their motherland. The *Odyssey* shows the vast increase in geographical knowledge and the new type of personality created by the sailors of Ionia. Odysseus himself is not so
much a knightly warrior as the embodiment of the adventurous
spirit, the explorer's energy, and the clever practical wisdom of
the Ionian: he has seen men and cities, and he is never at a loss
in any difficulty or danger. The *Odyssey* looks eastward as far
as Phoenicia and Colchis, southward to Egypt, westward to
Sicily and the westerly Ethiopians, and northward over the Black
Sea to the land of the Cimmerians. There is nothing strange or
unusual in the tale of the sailor hero's meeting with crowds of
Phoenician seafarers and merchants: [9] the Phoenicians traded all
over the Mediterranean, and were the most dangerous competi-
tors of the Greeks. Another sailor epic was the tale of the voyage
of the Argonauts, with its wonderful stories of the distant countries and nations whom they visited. Ionian trade grew with the
growing industrialization of the cities of Asia Minor, a process
which took them still further away from their early agricultural
civilization. And it made a great and decisive advance when
gold coinage was introduced from neighbouring Lydia, and when
monetary exchange replaced barter. By our standards, the
coastal towns of Ionia were small; and the surest sign that they
were over-populated is the fact that, like the cities of Greece
proper, they sent out numerous colonies in the eighth, the seventh
and the sixth centuries to the coasts of the Mediterranean, the
Sea of Marmora, and the Black Sea. Although other historical
evidence is lacking, the astounding number of colonies planted

by one city like Miletus bears witness to the enterprise, the expansive energy, and the pulsating life which filled the Greek cities of Asia Minor during those centuries.[10]

Versatility, individual initiative, and wide vision are the chief characteristics of the new men created by these new conditions. As the physical horizon expanded, their spiritual horizon had grown too, and their sense of their own powers made them capable of wider and higher thoughts and ideals. The spirit of independent criticism which we see in Ionia both in the personal poetry of Archilochus and in the theories of the Milesian philosophers must have affected public life also. We have no records of the civil conflicts which must have taken place in Ionia as they did elsewhere in the Greek world. But the long succession of Ionian epigrams and poems which extol Justice as the basis of human society runs from the later portions of the Homeric epics through Archilochus and Anaximander down to Heraclitus.[11] As we might imagine, such praise of justice by poets and philosophers did not precede the struggle to realize the ideal, but was plainly a natural repercussion of the political struggles which lasted from the eighth century to the beginning of the fifth. The poets of Greece proper, from Hesiod downwards, spoke of Justice in the same tone, and none more clearly than Solon of Athens.

Until these struggles began, the right of the nobles to administer justice—in accordance with traditional usage, not by any written code of laws—had been unchallenged. But as the economic position of the common people improved, the conflict between the freeman of low birth and the nobleman was naturally intensified. Judicial power could easily be misused for political ends. The people demanded written laws. Hesiod's complaints against the corrupt princes who turn justice askew were the necessary preliminary to this general demand.[12] They made the word Justice, *diké*, the war-cry of the class-conflict. The process of the codification of law in the various Greek cities went on for centuries, and we know little of its history.[13] But here we are concerned chiefly with the principle which inspired it. Laws which are written down mean the same law for all, high and low alike. After the laws are written, the judges may still be noblemen and not commoners; but they are now bound to administer justice in accordance with the established standards of diké.

Homer shows us the earlier situation. He usually describes

justice by another word—*themis*.[14] Zeus gave to the Homeric kings 'the sceptre and themis'.[15] Themis is the epitome of the judicial supremacy of the early kings and nobles. Etymologically, the word means 'institution'. The feudal judge gives his decisions in accordance with the institutions set up by Zeus, and derives their rules from his knowledge of customary law and from his own intuition. The etymology of diké is not clear. The word belongs to Greek legal terminology, and is no less old than themis.[16] The parties to a dispute were said to 'give and take diké', so that the word contained the ideas of determining and of paying the penalty. The guilty man 'gives diké', which originally meant 'makes compensation' for his act; the injured party, whose rights are re-established by the judgment, 'takes diké', and the judge 'allots diké'. Hence, the fundamental meaning of diké is much the same as 'due share'.[17] Besides that, it also signifies the lawsuit, the judgment, and the penalty; but these meanings are derivative, not primary. The higher significance which the word acquires in the post-Homeric city-state is developed not from these more or less technical meanings, but from the normative element which must be assumed to be behind the ancient and familiar formulæ. Diké means the due share which each man can rightly claim; and then, the principle which guarantees that claim, the principle on which one can rely when one is injured by *hybris*—which originally signifies illegal action.[18] The meaning of themis is confined rather to the *authority* of justice, to its established position and validity, while diké means the legal enforceability of justice. It is obvious how, during the struggles of a class which had always been compelled to receive justice as themis—that is, as an inevitable authority imposed on it from above—the word diké became the battle-cry. Throughout these centuries we hear the call for diké, growing constantly more widespread, more passionate, and more imperative.[19]

The word diké contained another meaning, which was to make it still more useful in these struggles—the meaning of equality. This sense must have been innate in the word: we can best understand it by thinking of the old popular ideal of justice—compensation with an eye for an eye, and a tooth for a tooth. Obviously, that sense of equality must have been derived from the use of diké in legal proceedings; the derivation is confirmed by the history of law in other nations. Throughout all Greek thought, the

word retained this original significance. Even the political philosophers of later centuries depend on it, and seek only to re-
define the concept of equality, which had been so mechanized by
the rise of democracy as to become repugnant to Plato and Aristotle, with their aristocratic belief in the natural inequality of
mankind.

Early Greece strove, above everything else, for equal justice.[20]
Every trifling dispute above *meum* and *tuum* called for a standard by which the claims of the parties could be measured. This
is the same problem in the sphere of law as that which had, in
the same age, been solved in the economic sphere by the introduction of fixed standards of weight and measure for the exchange of goods. What was needed was a correct norm to measure legal rights, and that norm was found in the concept of
equality which was implicit in the idea of diké.

Of course, that norm could be applied in far more ways than
the Greeks thought; but perhaps that made it even more suitable
for use as a political platform. It could, for instance, be taken to
mean that an unprivileged class (that is, the commons) should
be equal to the privileged class in the eyes of the judge, or before
the law where law existed. Again, it could mean that each citizen ought to have an active part in the administration of justice;
or that the votes of all citizens in affairs of state should be constitutionally equal; or, finally, that an ordinary citizen should
have equal right to hold the principal public offices which were
actually occupied by the aristocrats. This is, in fact, the beginning of a long process during which the concept of equality grew
wider and more mechanical until it came to signify extreme
democracy. Yet democracy is not a necessary consequence of the
demand for equal justice or for a written law. Both equal justice
and codified law have existed in monarchic and oligarchic states;
while it is characteristic of extreme democracy that the state is
ruled not by the law but by the mob. But hundreds of years were
to pass until the democratic type of constitution developed and
grew common in the Greek world.

Before that could happen, a long historical process was to be
completed. Its first stage is still a kind of aristocracy—but a
changed aristocracy. For now the ideal of diké is used as a
standard in public life by which both high-born and low-born
men are measured as 'equals'. The nobles were compelled to

admit the new civic ideal created by the demand for justice, and based on diké as a norm. In the struggles of the approaching social conflict, and in the violence of revolution, they themselves were often compelled to appeal to diké for help. Even the Greek language bears traces of the formation of the new ideal. For centuries it had contained words to signify concrete offences—murder, theft, adultery; but it had had no general word for the quality through which one might avoid committing these offences and escape transgression. For that quality the new age coined the word 'righteousness' or 'justice', *dikaiosyné*—just as in its enthusiasm for the athletic virtues it had coined abstract words (which have no parallel in English) to correspond to the concretes 'wrestling', 'boxing', and so forth.[21] This new word was created as the sense of justice was more and more sharply intensified, and as the ideal of justice was embodied in a special type of human character and a peculiar areté. Originally, an areté was any kind of excellence. When the areté of a man was considered equivalent to courage, areté came to mean an ethical quality to which all other human excellences were subordinate and subservient. The new dikaiosyné was a more objective quality; but it became areté *par excellence* as soon as the Greeks believed that they had found, in written law, a reliable criterion for right and wrong. After *nomos*—that is, current legal usage—was codified, the general idea of righteousness acquired a palpable content. It consisted in obedience to the laws of the state, just as Christian 'virtue' consisted in obedience to the commands of God.

So then the will to justice, which grew up in the communal life of the city-state, was a new educational force comparable to the ideal of warlike courage in the old aristocratic culture. In the elegies of Tyrtaeus, that old ideal had been taken over by the Spartan state and raised to an all-embracing ideal of citizenship.[22] In the new state, based on law and justice, which was struggling through hard conflicts into life, the warrior-ideal of Sparta could not be accepted as the sole and universal embodiment of citizenship. Yet, as is shown by the summons of the Ephesian poet Callinus to his unwarlike fellow-citizens to resist the invading barbarians, even in the Ionian cities warlike courage was still needed at moments of crisis. Courage had in fact only changed its place within the general scheme of areté. From now on the law commands the citizen to show courage in face of the enemy, to the point of dying in defence of his country; and the law punishes failure to obey that command by heavy penalties: but it is only one of many commands. In order to be *just*, in the concrete sense which justice now has in Greek political thought (that is, in order to obey the law and to mould one's conduct by its pattern [23]), the citizen must do his duty in war as he must do his duty in other matters. The old free ideal of the heroic areté of the Homeric champion now becomes a duty to the state, a duty to which all citizens alike are bound, as they are bound to observe the limits of *meum* and *tuum* in matters of property. One of the most famous poetic utterances of the sixth century is the line, often quoted by later philosophers, which says that all virtues are summed up in righteousness. The line is a close and exhaustive definition of the essence of the new constitutional city-state.[24]

The new conception that righteousness is the areté of the perfect citizen, embracing and transcending all others, naturally supplanted previous ideals. But the earlier aretai were not superseded by it: they were raised to a new power. That is what Plato means in the *Laws,* when he says [25] that in the ideal state Tyrtaeus' poem praising courage as the highest virtue must be rewritten so as to put righteousness in the place of courage. He does not exclude the Spartan warrior's virtue: he relegates it to its proper place, as subordinate to righteousness. Courage in a civil war, he says, must be estimated differently from courage exerted against a foreign enemy.[26] To show that all areté is embraced by the ideal of the righteous man, Plato gives a very enlightening example. Usually he speaks of four cardinal virtues: courage, godliness, righteousness, and prudence. (It is here irrelevant that in the *Republic* and often elsewhere he mentions philosophical wisdom instead of godliness.) As early as Aeschylus, we find this canon of the four so-called Platonic virtues mentioned as the sum of a citizen's virtue. Plato took it over *en bloc* from the ethical system of the early Greek city-state.[27] But he recognized that, although the canon mentioned four virtues, righteousness really embraced all areté.[28] The same thing happened in the case of Aristotle. He defines many more species of aretai than Plato; but when he comes to righteousness, he says that the name signifies two conceptions: there is righteousness in the narrow sense, the juristic sense, and general righteousness which includes all political and moral virtue. It is easy to see that this is the idea which was born in the early city-state. Aristotle then quotes, with considerable emphasis, the verse mentioned above, to the effect that righteousness embraces all virtue.[29] The precepts of law regulate the relations of every citizen to the gods of the polis, to its enemies, and to his fellow-citizens.

Later ages did not recognize the fact that the ethical systems of Plato and Aristotle were based on the morality of the early city-state; for they were accustomed to thinking of those systems as timeless and eternal. When Christian moralists examined them, they found it odd that Plato and Aristotle should have mentioned courage as moral virtue; but they were forced to accept this as a basic element in Greek moral feeling. Since they had no political life, no state in the ancient Greek sense of the word, and no ethics except the purely individual ethics of religion, they could not understand such an idea, and considered it a simple paradox; and they produced useless dissertations on the question whether courage was a virtue or not, and if so, why. We, however, can recognize the natural historical process by which the morality of the city-state was taken up by later philosophers and through them influenced posterity. Philosophy cannot live by pure reason: it is only the translation into abstract and ideal form of a culture which has grown up by historical stages. Certainly that is true of the philosophy of Plato and Aristotle; it cannot be understood without Greek civilization, and Greek civilization cannot be understood apart from it.

The process of assimilation which we have—in anticipation—described, the process by which the morality of the early polis and its ideal of character is taken over by fourth-century philosophy, has an exact analogy in the rise of the city-state itself. For the city-state culture also assimilated the morality of an earlier age. It took over not only Homer's heroic areté but the athletic virtues too—the whole ideal of aristocracy; the same assimilation took place in Sparta too at the age when she first appeared in history. The city-state encouraged its citizens to compete in the Olympic games and other such contests. It crowned with its highest honours the citizens who returned victorious. Victory in such a contest had once glorified only the family of the winner; but now, as the whole citizen-community felt itself to be one family, victory served *ad maiorem patriae gloriam*.[30] And the city encouraged its sons to share not only in athletic contests but in the musical and artistic heritage of the past. It created *isonomia* not only in legal matters but in the higher things of life, which had been created by aristocratic civilization and now became the common property of the citizen-family.[31]

The enormous influence of the polis upon individual life was based on the fact that it was an ideal. The state was a spiritual entity, which assimilated all the loftiest aspects of human life and gave them out as its own gifts. Nowadays, we naturally think first of the state's claim to educate all its citizens during their youth. But public education was not advocated in Greece until it became a thesis of fourth century philosophy: Sparta alone, at this early period, paid direct attention to the education of the young.[32] Nevertheless, even outside Sparta, the early city-state educated the members of its community, by utilizing the athletic and musical competitions which were held during the festivals of the gods. These competitions were the noblest reflection of the physical and spiritual culture of the age. Plato rightly calls gymnastics and music 'the old-established culture'.[33] That culture, which had originally been aristocratic, was fostered by the state through great and costly competitions; and these competitions did more than encourage musical taste and gymnastic skill. They really created the sense of community in the city. Once that sense has been established, it is easy to understand the Greek citizen's pride in membership of his state. To describe a Greek fully, not only his own name and his father's are needed, but also the name of his city. Membership in a city-state had for the Greeks the same ideal value that nationality has for men of to-day.

The polis is the sum of all its citizens and of all the aspects of their lives. It gives each citizen much, but it can demand all in return. Relentless and powerful, it imposes its way of life on each individual, and marks him for its own. From it are derived all the norms which govern the life of its citizens. Conduct that

injures it is bad, conduct that helps it is good. This is the paradoxical result of the passionate effort to obtain the rights and
equal status of each individual. All these efforts have forged the
new chains of Law, to hold together the centrifugal energies of
mankind, and to co-ordinate them far more successfully than in
the old social order. Law is the objective expression of the state,
and now Law has become king, as the Greeks later said [34]—an
invisible ruler who does not only prevent the strong from transgressing and bring the wrongdoer to justice, but issues positive
commands in all the spheres of life which had once been governed by individual will and preference. Even the most intimate
acts of the private life and the moral conduct of its citizens are
by law prescribed and limited and defined. Thus, through the
struggle to obtain law, the development of the state brings into
being new and more sharply differentiated principles of public
and private life.

And that is the significance of the new city-state in the shaping
of Greek character. Plato says, and rightly, that every type of
constitution produces its own type of man; both he and Aristotle
claim that all education should, in the perfect state, bear the imprint of the spirit of the state.[35] Again and again the great Athenian political philosophers of the fourth century formulate this
ideal in the words 'education in the spirit of the laws'.[36] The
words show that to establish a legal standard by written law was
for the Greeks an *educational* act.[37] Law is the most important
stage in the development of Greek culture from the social ideal of
aristocracy to the fundamental conception of man as an individual, as expressed by the philosophers. And the ethical and educational systems constructed by philosophers constantly recall, in
both form and content, the legislation of earlier periods. Such
systems do not come into being in the empty air of pure thought:
they are rooted in the historical life of the nation—as the ancient
philosophers themselves said—and do but translate it into the
region of abstract and general ideas. Law was the most universal
and permanent form of Greek moral and legal experience. The
culmination of Plato's work as a philosophical educator comes
in his last and greatest book, when he himself turns lawgiver;
and Aristotle closes the *Ethics* by calling for a legislator to realize the ideal he has formulated.[38] Law is the mother of philos-

ophy, for another reason—because in Greece lawmaking was
always the work of great individuals. They were rightly considered to be the educators of their people; it is typical of Greek
ideas that the lawgiver is often named beside the poet, and the
formulas which define the law are often mentioned beside the
wise utterances of the poet: the two activities were essentially
akin to each other.[39]

The rule of law was later criticized, in the epoch of degenerate democracy, when many rash and despotic laws were hurried
into existence;[40] but such criticism is meanwhile irrelevant. All
the thinkers of this early period unite in praising law. It is the
soul of the city. Heraclitus says [41] 'the people must fight for their
law as for their walls': evoking, behind the visible city defended
by its walls, the invisible polis with its sure rampart of law. But
there is an even earlier reflection of the ideal of law, in the work
of the natural philosopher Anaximander of Miletus, about the
middle of the sixth century. Transferring the concept of diké
from the social life of the city-state to the realm of nature, he
explains the causal connexion between coming-to-be and passing-
away as equivalent to a lawsuit, in which things are compelled
by the decision of Time to compensate each other for their unrighteousness.[42] This is the origin of the philosophical idea of
the *cosmos:* for the word originally signifies the *right order* in a
state or other community. The philosopher, by projecting the
idea of a political cosmos upon the whole of nature, claims that
isonomia and not pleonexia must be the leading principle not
only of human life but of the nature of things; and his claim is
a striking witness to the fact that in his age the new political
ideal of justice and law had become the centre of all thought,
the basis of existence, the real source of men's faith in the purpose and meaning of the world. Anaximander's projection of law
upon nature is an important philosophical conception of the
world, and will be studied in detail elsewhere.[43] Here we can only
show in general how clearly it illuminates the function of the
state and the new ideal of man as a citizen. At the same time
we can see the close connexion between the origins of Ionian
philosophy and the birth of the constitutional city-state. Both are
rooted in the universal idea which, starting from this point, inspires Greek civilization more and more deeply—the idea that

the world and life in all their appearances can be interpreted by one fundamental standard.[44]

In conclusion, we must trace the process by which the Ionian city-states came into being, with special reference to the development of the old aristocratic civilization into the idea of universal culture. It should be specially noted that these general remarks are not fully applicable to the early city-state: they are a preliminary diagnosis of the process whose bases we have analysed above. But it will be valuable to define the range and tendency of the process, and to keep it as a whole before our minds.

The polis gives each individual his due place in its political cosmos, and thereby gives him, besides his private life, a sort of second life, his βίος πολιτικός. Now, every citizen belongs to two orders of existence; and there is a sharp distinction in his life between what is *his own* (ἴδιον) and what is *communal* (κοινόν). Man is not only 'idiotic,' he is also 'politic.' [45] As well as his ability in his own profession or trade, he has his share of the universal ability of the citizen, πολιτικὴ ἀρετή, by which he is fitted to co-operate and sympathize with the rest of the citizens in the life of the polis. It is obvious why the new ideal of the individual as citizen cannot be based (like Hesiod's ideal of popular education) on the conception of man's daily work.[46] Hesiod's idea of areté was inspired by the facts of real life and by the vocational morality of the working-class, his audience. From the standpoint of the present time, we should be inclined to say that the new movement ought to have taken over the Hesiodic ideal *en bloc:* by doing so, we might think, it would have substituted a new concept of the people's education for the aristocratic ideal of the education of the entire personality; the new concept would have valued each individual by the work he did in the world, and would have taught that the good of the community was achieved when each individual did his work as well as possible. That was the system proposed by the aristocrat Plato when he described, in the *Republic,* a state based on legal order, governed by a few intellectually superior men. It would have been in harmony with the life and work of the people. It would have emphasized the fact that hard work is no shame, but is the sole basis of each man's citizenship. That fact was indeed recognized; but the actual development of the citizen ideal followed quite different lines.

The new factor in the development of the city-state, which at last made every man a political being, was the compulsion laid on each male citizen to take an active part in the public life of his community, and to recognize and accept his civic duties—which were quite different from his duties as a private person and a working man. Previously, it was only the nobleman who had possessed this 'universal' political ability. For centuries power had been in the hands of the aristocrats, and they had a vastly superior system of political education and experience, which was still indispensable. The new city-state could not, without injuring itself, ignore the areté of the aristocracy; but it was bound to repress its selfish and unjust misuse. That was at least the ideal of the polis, as expressed by Pericles in Thucydides.[47] Thus, in free Ionia as in authoritarian Sparta, the culture of the city-state was based on the old aristocratic culture—on the ideal of areté which embraced the whole personality and all its powers. The working-class morality of Hesiod was not abandoned; but the citizen of the polis aimed above all at the ideal which Phoenix had taught Achilles: to be a speaker of words and a doer of deeds.[48] Certainly the leading men in each state were bound to move towards that ideal, and the ordinary citizens too came to sympathize with it.

This fact had great results. Socrates, as we know, introduced his criticism of democracy by discussing the relationship of technical or professional knowledge to political ability. For Socrates, the mason's son, the simple working man, thought it was a startling paradox that the cobbler, the tailor, and the carpenter should need special knowledge to practise their own honest trades, while the politician needed only a general and rather indefinite education to engage in politics, although his 'craft' dealt with much more important things.[49] Obviously the problem could not have been posed in these terms, except in an age which held that political areté was naturally a branch of *knowledge*.[50] From that point of view, the essence of democracy was the lack of any special knowledge.[51] But as a matter of fact the early city-states had never considered the question of political ability to be a predominantly *intellectual* problem. We have seen what they considered civic virtue to mean. When the constitutional city-state came into being, the virtue of its citizens really consisted in their voluntary submission to the new authority of the law, without distinction of rank or birth.[52] In that conception of political virtue, ethos was still far more important than logos. Obedience to the laws and discipline were far more important qualifications for an ordinary citizen than knowledge of the administration and aims of the state. To co-operate was, for him, to join others in submission to the law, and not to help to govern. The early city-state was, in the eyes of its citizens, the guarantee of all the ideals which made life worth living. πολιτεύεσθαι means 'to take part in communal life'; but besides that it simply means 'to live'—for the two meanings were one and the same.[53] At no time was the state more closely identified with all human values. Aristotle calls man 'a political being', so as to differentiate him from animals by his power of living in a state: [54] he is in fact identifying *humanitas,* 'being human', with the life in a state. His definition can be understood only by studying the structure of the early polis: for its citizens held their communal existence to be the sum of all the higher things of life—in fact to be something divine. In the *Laws* Plato constructs just such an old Hellenic cosmos based on law, a city in which the polis *is* the spirit, and in which all spiritual activity is referred to the polis as its final end. There he defines the essence of all true culture, or paideia (in contrast to the specialized knowledge of tradesmen such as the shopkeeper and the travelling merchant), as 'the education in areté from youth onwards, which makes men passionately desire to become perfect citizens, knowing both how to rule and how to be ruled on a basis of justice'.[55]

Plato's words are a true description of the original meaning of 'universal' culture as conceived in the early city-state. In his conception of culture he does include the Socratic ideal of a craft of politics; but he does not think of it as a special branch of knowledge comparable to the craftsman's professional cunning. He believes that true culture is 'universal' culture, because political understanding is the understanding of universal questions. As we have shown, the contrast between the factual knowledge of the craftsman and the ideal culture of the citizen, with its reference to his entire personality and life, goes back to the aristocratic ideal of early Greece. But its deeper meaning first appears in the city-state, because there that ideal was imposed upon the whole community, and aristocratic culture became the force which formed every man as a citizen. Aristocracy is the first, and the early city-state is the second, of the vital stages in the development of the 'humanistic' ideal of a universal ethico-political culture: in fact, the historical mission of the city-state was to lead Greece towards that ideal. And although the early city-state developed into mass-rule, an extreme democracy guided by quite different forces,[56] that development does not alter the true nature of city-state culture; for throughout its political evolution that culture kept its original aristocratic character. Its value should be estimated neither by contrast with the genius of individual political leaders—who are always produced by exceptional conditions—nor by its value for the mass of mankind to whom it cannot be communicated without becoming less rich and less potent. With characteristic good sense the Greeks always shunned such comparisons. The ideal of universal political areté is indispensable because it implies the constant creation and regeneration of a governing class; and without such a governing class no nation and no state, whatever be its constitution, can long survive.

IONIAN AND AEOLIAN POETRY: THE INDIVIDUAL SHAPES HIS OWN PERSONALITY

THE revolution which rebuilt the state on the common basis of law created a new human type—the citizen—and compelled the new community to work out a universal standard for civic life. The ideals of the old Greek aristocracy had been expressed in the Homeric epics; Hesiod had wrought into poetry the practical wisdom and experience of the peasant's life and morality; and Tyrtaeus's elegies had eternalized the severe code of the Spartan state. But the new ideal of the polis seems, at first glance, to have no comparable expression in contemporary poetry. The city-state, as we have seen, eagerly assimilated the earlier stages of Greek culture, and in so doing utilized the great poetry of antiquity as a means of expressing its own ideals, just as it used the musical and athletic traditions of the era of aristocracy. But it failed to embody and express its own nature in any poetry which could bear comparison with the now classical poetry of past ages. The only attempt at such creation was the poems which told, in conventional epic style, of the founding of this or that city; and they were few in number in the early days of the city-state, and they appear never to have risen so far as to become true national epic on the plane of the last and greatest work of the type, Vergil's *Aeneid*.[1]

The first really revolutionary expression of the ethos of the new state was not poetry, but prose. For the city-state created prose, and prose was originally the medium in which law was recorded. The city-state was a new development in communal living, created by the struggle to subject all members of the community to a rigid legal code of life and conduct: it therefore persistently strove to express that code in clear and universally valid sentences. The violence of this effort occupied men's minds to the exclusion of any wish to express in poetry the character of the new community.[2] The constitutional polis was created by logical thought, and therefore had no basic kinship with poetry. Homer,

Callinus, and Tyrtaeus had already, it seemed, expressed all that poets could express of the life of the city-state; the daily existence of its citizens was not a fit subject for poets; and the heroism of life within it—the motif first developed by Solon,[3] to be the source of a new poetic revolution—did not occur as a possible theme to any Ionian or Aeolian writer.

But poetry did find a new world, and explored it eagerly: the world of purely individual experience, far narrower than the city walls, bounded in fact by the close circle of personal intimacies. This is the world opened to us by the Aeolian lyrics and the elegiac and iambic poetry of Ionia. In these poems, the energy of the individual's will to live—which we can trace less directly in the political sphere, by its transformation of the life of the community—is immediately and directly expressed, with all its most powerful impulses laid bare. If this spiritual force had not been revealed to us, we should not have known the deepest reasons for the political revolution. Even yet we can understand little of the causal connexion between the spiritual and the material motives of the revolution, especially since we possess no account of the economic conditions of the period. But in a history of culture we are more concerned with the spiritual nature of the men of this new age, and with the extraordinary contribution of the Ionian mind to the development of Greece and of humanity. And that contribution is vitally important. There, for the first time, poets spoke in their own persons, and expressed their own opinions and emotions, while the life of their community was relegated to the background of their thought. Even when they mentioned politics—as often—their theme was not a standard with a claim to universal acceptance (as in Hesiod, Callinus, Tyrtaeus, and Solon) but a frank partisanship, as in Alcaeus, or the individual's pride in *his* rights, as in Archilochus. Even when the animals quarrel in his fable, each appeals to his 'rights' in comical imitation of human society.[4] Still, when the new poets express their own sentiments, they always do so against the social background of the city-state. The individual is still a part of that community, both when he is free and when he is under its commands. Sometimes the poet's relationship to it is unexpressed; and sometimes he accepts and uses it, and addresses his fellow-citizens to tell them his own thoughts: such is Archilochus.[5]

It is very significant that this new cult of individuality is not expressed in the modern manner, as the experience of an individual wrapped up in himself (be he bound to the world or free from it), as the utterance of purely private feelings. The conscious solipsism of modern poetry may be no more than a reversion to the primitive, to the simple cries of personal emotion which we hear in many different ages and countries and which must have been uttered even in the earliest stages of civilization. Nothing could be more foolish than the assumption that there was no personal experience and thought before the Greeks. On the contrary, there is hardly any other kind of experience and thought throughout the world and throughout history. And the Greeks were not the first people, nor the only people, to give artistic expression to private sentiments—as is shown, very impressively, by the Chinese lyrics which appeal so deeply to us to-day. But the personal nature of these very lyrics shows their essential difference from the early Greek conception of individuality.

Although the Greek poet, in exploring the new world of individuality, expresses ideas and emotions which are truly personal, he is still somehow bound by universal standards, and recognizes the law which rules his fellow-men. This must be demonstrated in greater detail. It is naturally difficult to give a sharp definition of the meaning of individuality in Archilochus and poets of his type, when the idea has long been familiar to us. Certainly it was not the Christian ideal of personality, by which every soul feels its own individual value. The Greeks always thought of personality as actively related to the world (in fact, to two worlds, the world of nature and the world of human society) and not as isolated from it. Therefore Greek expressions of personal emotion and thought have nothing purely and exclusively subjective in them: it might rather be said that a poet like Archilochus has learnt how to express in his own personality the whole objective world and its laws—to represent them in himself. Personality, for the Greeks, gains its liberty and its consciousness of selfhood not by abandoning itself to subjective thought and feeling, but by making itself an objective thing; and, as it realizes that it is a separate world opposed to the external law, it discovers its own inner laws.

This process, which has a direct bearing on the development of European thought, can be illustrated by a few special examples. We have already observed a parallel to it in the rise of elegiac poetry with Tyrtaeus and Callinus. There we remarked on one important fact in the history of culture—that Sparta's civic ideal is expressed in poetry by a direct translation and adaptation to the real present of the Homeric parainesis, the speech which encourages men to heroic courage.[6] The same process of adaptation is now repeated in Archilochus; except that the Spartan army, the whole community, is now replaced by the personality of the poet himself. Again and again in his elegies Archilochus or his surroundings take on Homeric characters and destinies. In such adaptations of form and content we can clearly see the completion of Homer's great educational mission: for now the epic is taking possession of individual personality and character, and the formative influence of Homer has contributed above all else to raise the individual to a higher stage of freedom in life and thought.

When Archilochus calls himself 'the servant of lord Enyalios' and adds that he understands 'the lovely gift of the Muses',[7] we are apt to think that the real innovation in this way of thinking is the poet's keen consciousness of his own powers, the fact that he feels himself to be somehow different from other men through his strange dual profession of warrior and poet. But we must remember also that he is *shaping* his own personality by clothing it in the heroic costume of epic phraseology—as here, or as when he speaks proudly of the battles, in which he served as a soldier of fortune against 'the masters of Euboea, famed spearmen', as the 'mêlée of Ares' and the 'groanful work of the spear'.[8] He drinks his wine and eats his bread in the pose of a Homeric hero, 'leaning on the spear' which brings him his food and drink.[9] Yet, these are the words of a man who is not of noble birth: it is the epic which gives style to his life and his thought.[10]

He does not, however, always feel equal to maintaining this heroic rôle. He does not express his personality only by raising it to the dignity of a Homeric hero. The very act of measuring himself against the epic ideal allows his sharp Greek eyes to find the places where the armour of the old champions no longer fits his unheroic limbs. But even when he recognizes his own inadequacy, his good humour is still invincible: he makes his in-adequacy a new subject of self-expression and gay self-assertion, even in the face of the inaccessible ideals of the past. A Homeric hero, for instance, would have thought the loss of his shield to be the death of his honour, and would rather have died himself than suffer such disgrace.[11] On that point the modern hero of Paros differs from them, and he is sure that his own contempo-raries will think he has the laugh on his side when he says,[12] 'One of our Saian foes is now exulting over my shield, a faultless piece of armour which I left unwillingly beside a bush. But I my-self escaped the end, which is death. Let the old shield go! I shall buy a better one!' The delicious blend of modern realistic humour, the cynical assurance that even a hero has only one life to lose, with the lofty epic flourishes 'a faultless piece of armour' and 'the end, which is death', is an infallible source of comic effect. Under cover of these proud phrases, the bold runaway ventures his most impudent boast: 'I shall buy a better one!' What is a shield, after all? Only a piece of oxhide, with a metal lid!

It was a daring feat, thus to transform heroism into plain naturalism; but even here Archilochus was preceded by the later epic. Thus, at the end of the *Iliad,* when Achilles has returned to the mourning Priam the corpse of his son, he invites him to eat and drink, mentioning Niobe, who like him had mourned for her children: 'Niobe too', he says, 'gave thought to food when she had grown tired of weeping'.[13] We are only human, after all. Even heroism has its limits. In that speech the tragedy of natural humanity, and in Archilochus' poem its comedy, alike break through the severe heroic code. But always the Greek intelli-gence is bent on finding the correct norm—either to assert a higher ideal against nature, or as here to vindicate nature against the excessive demands of an ideal. These passages show that the chains of chivalrous honour and class prejudice are loosening, and have already been shaken off by the soldiers of fortune. But it is still a long way to the philosophical revolution in moral standards which set up 'nature' as the sole norm for personal conduct.[14] Still, when Archilochus boldly sets himself beyond the confines of conventional respectability—and through-out his poetry that attitude is clear and unashamed—he already feels not only that he is more audacious, but that he is more natural and more honourable than the slave of traditional honour and morality.

What seems at first to be a purely personal utterance of Archilochus, is often the expression of a change in the general view of propriety and impropriety, and of a righteous crusade against the idols of the tribe and the power of convention. The change is not merely a lazy desertion of a traditional code, it is a serious fight to impose a new one. In the earliest type of Greek society there was no more powerful judge of human conduct than Fama, public opinion. From its judgments there was no appeal. The Homeric nobleman agrees with the Hesiodic peasant and craftsman in bowing before it.[15] But Archilochus speaks for a freer world when he proclaims his independence of the demos's judgment of right and wrong, fame and shame:[16] 'If one cared for the gossip of the people one would never have much pleasure in life.' Doubtless this emancipation was aided (as the word 'pleasure' shows), by the indolence of human nature: a certain moral slackness accompanied the new natural liberty. But the opposition to the power of public opinion was not based on hedonistic grounds alone. Archilochus' criticism of it is a direct attack on its very principle. Men are told that the polis will honour and preserve the name of a citizen who serves it well, even after his death—all the poets from Homer downwards have spoken of this as the sure reward of public service; but Archilochus says that 'after his death no one is honoured or famous among the citizens: while we live, we pursue the pleasure of living, but the dead are always very badly off.'[17] Another fragment of his poetry shows his meaning even more clearly. Thinking of the slander which always creeps out when a man is dead and need be feared no longer, he says,[18] 'it is not noble to abuse the dead.' A man who sees so clearly through the psychology of public opinion, and has realized the baseness of the mass of mankind, has lost all trace of respect for the voice of the people. Homer said[19] that the mind of men is as changeable as the day which Zeus brings forth. Archilochus applies the saying to the life of his own time.[20] Can any great thing, he asks, come out of these ephemeral creatures? The old aristocratic morality worshipped public opinion as a higher power, interpreting it differently—

for the nobleman thought that public opinion meant fame for great deeds and their joyful acknowledgment by his generous peers. But that standard becomes absurd when it means the gossip of the jealous commoner who measures every great man by his own little yardmeasure. As such, public opinion is only a necessary safeguard against the new freedom of thought and action which has been produced by the new city-state spirit.

It is not for nothing that Archilochus was famous as the first and greatest representative of ψόγος in poetry, the formidable Satirist, the Scold.[21] Hasty conclusions about his personal character have been drawn from the bitter censorious nature of much of his iambic poetry—on the principle that in iambics, if in any genius of Greek poetry, one is justified in looking for purely psychological motives and in explaining each poem as the immediate reflex of its author's unpleasant personality.[22] But to reason like this is to forget that the rise of the lampoon in the early city-state is a symptom of the increased importance of the demos, the common people. Iambic 'flyting' was originally a general custom at the festivals of Dionysus, and this character it retained: it was rather the free expression of public opinion than the utterance of one man's personal enmity. Witness to this is the truest survival of the iambus in a later age, which is in the old Attic comedy, where the poet speaks as the voice of public criticism. (That is not contradicted by the equally certain fact that, like Archilochus, he sometimes opposes, instead of voicing, the opinion of the community. Both opposition and support of public opinion are part of his duties.) If it were true that the iambus was only the voice of a free individual demanding a hearing for his own views, it would be hard to explain why the same root could produce the philosophical reflections of Semonides and the political exhortations of Solon. Closer investigation shows that Archilochus' iambics have a parainetic, or hortatory, aspect which is quite as important as their critical and lampooning aspect, and which in fact is essentially akin to it.

He does not use the mythical examples and patterns which appear in the epic exhortations. Instead, he uses another kind of moral example, which shows very clearly the type of audience he is addressing. This is the fable. 'I will tell you a fable . . .' begins the story of the ape and the fox; [23] and the tale of the fox and the eagle [24] likewise begins 'There is a fable among men, which is this. . . .' He never uses fables in his elegies, with their tone of conventional heroism, but only in his iambic poetry. In discussing the *Works and Days* of Hesiod, we observed that the fable was a very old element in popular sermonising; [25] and now it is obvious that the same current has flowed into Archilochus' poetry, and reappears in his iambics, meant like Hesiod's poems to appeal to the people. There is another iambic poet whose work resembles Hesiod's, and allows us to reconstruct the original form of the public lampoon: namely, Archilochus' contemporary, the much inferior poet Semonides of Amorgos, author of a poem against women. [26] Because Hesiod also frequently dispraises women it has been thought that he was a natural misogynist, who had suffered something to make him hate the sex. [27] But bitter jests against womankind are a very old element in public lampoonery. Repeated in Semonides, they are not simply a weak imitation of Hesiod: they are an essential motif in old iambic poetry, which was certainly not confined to public attacks on unpopular individuals. Both the elements appeared in the old iambus—invective against persons, and 'flyting' of whole classes of people, such as lazy and good-for-nothing women. No doubt the women in their turn would abuse men; [28] but their abuse was not made into poetry until Aristophanes.

We must be careful in reconstructing the popular lampoon, the ψόγος, from the literary versions of it which we possess; but there is no doubt that it originally had a social function which can still be traced. It expresses neither moral disapproval nor arbitrary personal dislike for an inoffensive person: so much we can tell from its public character, for publicity was its precondition and justification. The revel of Dionysus, where all tongues were loosened, was the occasion when the bitter truths which the citizens knew about each other could be shouted from the housetops. Public opinion wisely shrank from the occasional misuse of this freedom; and, after all, purely personal rage and hatred could have little ideal or artistic value even if finely expressed. Certainly the Greeks would never have listened to the words of Archilochus at musical competitions centuries after his death, and placed him next to Homer as the educator of the Greeks, [29] if his poems had not still shown the inherent relation between iambic poetry and public opinion. Another proof of it is his habit of appealing to his fellow-citizens in his iambic poems no less than in others. In reconstructing his work from the scanty fragments, we must here utilize the iambic poetry of Catullus and Horace—for they too inveigh relentlessly against the scandals of their time, and even when they attacked one individual they still presuppose at least an ideal public as their sympathetic audience.[30] The general course of development followed by the iambic in early Greek poetry after Archilochus makes it certain that, when an iambic poet criticizes a person, an opinion, or a tendency, which has for any reason attracted public attention, he is not voicing a casual dislike of his own, but speaking as the representative and teacher of his fellow-citizens.

This new type of poetry had a powerful effect because it responded to a need of the time. It was the first appearance in Greek poetry of a novel element which contrasts strangely with the lofty style of the Homeric poems, the conventional epic dignity which appears even in Archilochus' elegies. The new departure was created by the spirit of the city-state, for the passions of its citizens could not be controlled by epainos alone— the praise which was the sanction and reward of the old aristocratic education. The ancients themselves perceived that the 'common nature' of the ordinary man is more responsive to blame than to praise.[31] When Archilochus addresses the public in a tone confident of success, we can see that as censor he is their representative. He even ventures to scold the great officials of the city—generals and demagogues—and he is always sure that his invective will be applauded.[32] Even in the story of his unsuccessful wooing of Neobule and his proud and passionate abuse of her father for rejecting him, it is clear that he thinks of the whole community as his witnesses, while he himself is both plaintiff and judge. 'Father Lycambes', he cries, 'who has upset your reason? You were sane enough before, but now you are a laughingstock to all the citizens'.[33] Even here, there is still something hortatory about the form of his invective.

Of course, writing a lampoon always offered a strong temptation to give vent to personal feelings. A fair-sized fragment of an iambic poem,[34] discovered on papyrus at the end of last century and rightly ascribed to the great hater himself, shows all the violence of private enmity in the exuberant detail with which the poet describes the sufferings which he wishes for his enemy.

Pindar, who was the greatest master of the art of educating and encouraging men through praise of noble deeds, says: [35] 'From afar off I have seen the fault-finder Archilochus often in distress, because he battened on scolding enmity.' Yet the effective conclusion shows that even this poem is dictated by a hatred which is *justified,* or which Archilochus believes to be justified: 'I should like to see all that for the man who wronged me, treading our oaths beneath his feet, after once being my friend.' [36] One line, which is preserved without its context, is a piece of abuse aimed at an unknown: 'You have no gall to burn your liver'! [37] This clearly refers to a quality which Archilochus hated—the inability to feel righteous indignation, which later appears in Peripatetic ethics as a moral deficiency. [38] The passage illuminates all Archilochus' hate-poetry. Like the close of the poem against the false friend, it shows that his iambics contain a strongly normative element. It is because he knows that he is judging the men he blames by a universal, not a personal, standard, that he can so easily abandon his own personality. This explains the easy transition from iambic lampoons to didactic or reflective iambic poetry.

Let us turn to the work which reveals Archilochus' philosophy of life, his didactic and reflective poems. Again we notice his dependence on Homer, as he encourages his friends to endure misfortune patiently or tells them to leave everything to the gods. Tyché, Fortune, and Moira, Fate, give man all he has. [39] The gods often lift up men who lie on the ground in disaster, and often cast down to the earth men who stand firm. [40] All these phrases frequently occur in later Greek thought, in discussions of the power of Tyché. Archilochus' religious thought is rooted in the problem of Tyché, and his knowledge of God is knowledge of Tyché. He has taken from Homer the content of these utterances, and some of their actual phrases, but he has transferred the battle of man against destiny from the heroic world to the world of daily life. The drama is now played out on the stage of the poet's own life; modelling its action on the epic, he sees himself as a hero, acting and suffering with epic dignity and passion, and his own career as inspired and explained by the Homeric philosophy. [41] The more freely and consciously men learn to guide their own thoughts and actions, the more inevitably they are brought face to face with the problem of destiny. The Greeks, as they learnt to understand the problem of human freedom, penetrated deeper into the mystery of Tyché. Yet in the effort to attain freedom men are compelled to forego many of the gifts of Tyché. Consequently it was Archilochus who first formulated the idea that a man could be free only in a life chosen by himself. It is a famous poem [42] in which the speaker declares that he will not strive for the wealth of Gyges, nor overstep the frontier between gods and men by ambition, nor aim at a despot's power: 'for that is far from my eyes.' Another poem, his strange address to his own heart,[43] shows the experience on which this proud renunciation is based. It is the first great monologue in Greek literature: a hortatory address, not to another person, as is usual in elegiac and iambic poetry, but to the poet himself; so that Archilochus is both the speaker who counsels and the listener who reflects and resolves.[44] There is an example of this in the *Odyssey,* and Archilochus borrows its ideas and its situation. But see what he makes of Odysseus' famous words: 'Be strong, my heart, you have borne fouler things before!' [45] He calls to his will to rise up from the whirlpool of desperate sufferings in which it is sunk, to stand firm and boldly resist the enemy. 'Neither exult openly in victory, nor lie at home lamenting in defeat; but take pleasure in what is pleasant, yield not overmuch to troubles, and understand the rhythm which holds mankind in its bonds.'

The ideal on which this proud independence is built is not the purely practical counsel of moderation as the safest course in daily existence. It is the universal conception that there is a 'rhythm' [46] in all human life. That is the foundation on which Archilochus bases his exhortation to self-control and his warning to avoid excessive joy or grief—he means, to avoid feeling excessive emotion for *externals,* for the happiness or unhappiness which comes from destiny. This sense of 'rhythm' is probably an early trace of the conception which first appears in Ionian natural philosophy and historical thinking—the idea that there is an objective law of averages in the natural course of existence. Herodotus expressly speaks of the 'cycle of human affairs',[47] thinking chiefly of the rise and fall of human fortunes.

We must not be misled by his words into thinking that Archilochus' rhythm is a *flux*—although the modern idea of rhythm is

something which flows, and some derive the word itself from
ῥέω, 'to flow.' [48] The history of the word warns us against that
interpretation. Its application to the movement of music and the
dance (from which we derive our word) was secondary, and
somewhat concealed the primary meaning. We must first inquire
what the Greeks took to be the essence of dancing and music;
and that is clearly shown by the primary meaning, which appears
in Archilochus' lines. If rhythm 'holds' [49] mankind—I translated
it 'holds in bonds'—it cannot be a flux. We must rather think of
Prometheus in Aeschylus' tragedy, who is chained immovably
in iron fetters; he says, 'I am bound here in this "rhythm" '; and
of Xerxes, of whom Aeschylus says that he chained the current
of the Hellespont, and 'changed to another form ("rhythm")'
the watery way across it: that is, he transformed the waterway
into a bridge, and bound the current in strong bonds.[50] Rhythm
then is that which imposes bonds on movement and confines the
flux of things: just as it is in Archilochus. Democritus too speaks
in the true old sense of the rhythm of the atoms, by which he
means not their movement but their pattern—or as Aristotle
perfectly translates it, their *schema*.[51] That is the interpretation
which the ancient commentators correctly give for Aeschylus'
words.[52] Obviously when the Greeks speak of the rhythm of a
building or a statue, it is not a metaphor transferred from musical language; and the original conception which lies beneath the
Greek discovery of rhythm in music and dancing is not *flow* but
pause, the steady limitation of movement.[53]

In Archilochus we see the miracle of a new, personal form of
culture, founded on the conscious realization of a natural and
final basic pattern in human life. To this pattern human thoughts
and desires can be made to conform, without the compulsion of
traditional morality. Man's thought now becomes master of his
life; and, just as it attempts to codify universal laws for the life
of the city-state community, so it strives to invade the soul and
to control within fixed frontiers the chaos of warring passions.
During the succeeding centuries this struggle is reflected in
Greek poetry, for philosophy does not enter it until much later.
Archilochus' work is an important stage on the road which
poetry travels down from Homer to the fourth century. His
poetry, and that of his age, was born of the need of the free
individual to see and solve the problem of human life outside

the mythical content of epic poetry, which had hitherto been the only sphere in which it could be posed or answered. As the poets assimilated the ideas and problems which had been set forth in the epic, and literally made them their own, they naturally created for them new poetic forms, the elegy and the iambus, and gave them a direct bearing on their own personal lives.

Of the poetry written in Ionia in the century and a half after Archilochus, enough survives to prove that it moves along the path he had explored; but none of it has the scope and power of his own work. His successors were chiefly influenced by his elegies and his reflective iambics. The existing iambic poems of Semonides are frankly didactic. The first,[54] with its direct address, clearly shows the educational trend of the iambus: 'My son,' he says, 'Zeus holds in his hand the end of all things, and arranges it as he wishes; but men have no sense. Creatures of a day, we live like animals, without knowing how God will bring everything to its conclusion. Hope and self-persuasion feed us all, and we aim at the impossible. . . . Old age, disease, death in battle or in the waves of the sea outstrip men before they have reached their goal; and others end their lives by suicide.' Like Hesiod,[55] Semonides complains that man is subject to every possible misfortune. Countless evil spirits, unexpected miseries and pains surround him. 'If you would believe me, we should not love our own unhappiness'—and there again we hear Hesiod's voice [56]—'and should not torture ourselves by setting our hearts on grievous unhappiness.'

The end of the poem is lost, but an elegy [57] on the same subject supplies the advice which Semonides must have offered to mankind. The ground of their blind pursuit of unhappiness is that they hope for immortality. 'One thing, finer than all others, was said by the man of Chios: "the generation of men is as the generation of leaves." [58] But few who heard that word put it away in their hearts; for everyone keeps the hope which grows in the hearts of the young. As long as a man has the lovely flower of youth, his mind is light and he makes many impossible plans. For he expects never to grow old nor to die, and while he is well he cares nothing for illness. Fools, to think like this, and not to know that mortal men have only a short space to be young and to live. But do you learn this and, thinking of the end of life, give your soul some pleasure.'

Here youth appears as the source of all overbold illusions and intentions, because it lacks the Homeric wisdom to think that life is short. The moral drawn by the poet is, however, a strange new one—to enjoy the pleasures of life while one may. That is not in Homer.[59] It is the conclusion of an eclectic generation, for which the lofty code of the heroic age has lost much of its deep seriousness, and which chooses from that code the part which suits its own outlook, namely the lament for the shortness of human life. When that sad truth is transposed from the world of the epic to the more natural world of the elegiac poet, it must inevitably create, not a tragic heroism, but a burning hedonism.[60]

As the city-state tightened the chains of law on its citizens, they strove more and more eagerly to complement its political rigidity by liberty in their own private life. The libertarian ideal is that expressed by Pericles in the funeral speech,[61] when he describes the free Athenian ideal as the counterpart to Spartan severity: 'We do not grudge our neighbour his private pleasures, nor do we make him repent them by our bitter looks.' It was necessary for the rigid legal code of the city-state to allow the instincts of its citizens to have some play; and if the cry for liberty changed to a cry for pleasure, that is a very human impulse. It is not true individualism, for it does not come into conflict with supra-individual forces.[62] Yet, within the boundaries which they set, there is a palpable broadening of the individual's demand for happiness; in the balance of life and duty, the individual now casts his weight more strongly on the side of life. The Athenian civilization of the Periclean age recognized the principle of this distinction between the state's demands and the individual's wishes; but a fight was needed to gain that recognition, and the fight was won in Ionia. There arose the first poetry of hedonism, passionately vindicating the individual's right to sensual happiness and beauty, and asserting the worthlessness of a life lacking these things.

Like Semonides of Amorgos, Mimnermus of Colophon writes to proclaim the joy of life. This message, which in Archilochus is merely the bye-product of strong natural instincts and expressed the mood of a moment, is in his two successors the ultimate secret of life. It becomes a crusade, an ideal of life to which they wish to convert all mankind. Without golden Aphrodite, what is life and what is pleasure? Rather would I be dead, cries Mimnermus,[63] than care no more for love. Yet it would be very wrong to call him a decadent voluptuary. (We have not enough of Semonides' work to enable us to reconstruct his character ` Mimnermus sometimes speaks in the clear voice of a statesman and a warrior, and the tense Homeric phrases of his poems vibrate with chivalrous ardour.[64] But when a poet begins to write freely of his private pleasures, it is a new step in poetry, and one which deeply influences human culture.

For now men are groaning more and more heavily under their bondage to destiny and to 'the gifts of Zeus' which must be accepted as they come,[65] and at the same time lamenting ever more keenly the shortness of life and the transitoriness of sensual pleasure; both these complaints, which are heard throughout post-Homeric poetry, bear witness to the growing tendency to see everything as it affects the individual's right to live. The more one yields to the demands of nature, and the deeper one plunges in natural delights, the more profound is the melancholy resignation that follows. Death, age, disease, misfortune, and all the other dangers which ambush man's life [66] grow to giants threatening him at every breath he draws, and even if he tries to escape in the delights of the moment, he will still find them poisoned by the sorrow of the world.

The hedonist school of poetry marks one of the most important phases in the history of the Greek spirit. To prove its importance we need only remember that Greek logic always posed the problem of the individual will in ethics and politics as a conflict between pleasure (τὸ ἡδύ) and nobility (τὸ καλόν). In the philosophy of the sophists the conflict becomes more clearly marked; [67] and the culmination of Plato's philosophy is the defeat of pleasure in its claim to be the highest good.[68] In the fifth century the opposition became sharp and definite; all the efforts of Attic philosophers from Socrates to Plato were directed to reconciling the opponents; and they met in a final harmony in Aristotle's ideal of human personality.[69] But before that could happen, the natural instinct to enjoy life and to aim at pleasure had to be affirmed as a principle, directly conflicting with the creed of τὸ καλόν which was preached directly and indirectly in epic and the early elegy. This affirmation is first made in Ionian poetry after Archilochus. The direction of this spiritual development is unmistakably centrifugal. It is as great a force in loosening the social structure of the city-state as the power of law had been in binding it together.

These new impulses could not have gained utterance and recognition except in the didactic and reflective form wrought out by the post-Archilochean iambic and elegiac poets. When they preach hedonism, it is not the chance preference of an individual; it is a universal principle, the 'right' of every individual to enjoy his own life. Every poem of Semonides and Mimnermus reminds us that it was written in the age when the Greeks began to apply logic to nature, at the birth of Milesian nature-philosophy. Greek logic did not hesitate to face the problem of human life— as we might think from the traditional treatment of this period in histories of philosophy, where the emphasis is usually laid on the cosmological problem.[70] It invaded and inspired poetry, always the medium for expressing ethical ideas, and made it discuss moral problems. The poet now offers his hearers a philosophy of life. The surviving poems of Semonides are not, like those of Archilochus, impulsive utterances of personal feeling, which occasionally take on a reflective tone: they are sermons on a definite text. And Mimnermus, though he is a far greater artist than Semonides, shows the same contemplative bias in most of his work. Thus, as poetry turns from the heroic world to the world of common humanity, it keeps its educational character.

While Ionian poetry at the turn of the seventh century concentrates on general discussion of the individual's right to live and enjoy life, the Aeolian lyric poets Sappho and Alcaeus express the individual's inner life itself. Their lyrics are a unique phenomenon in the spiritual life of Greece. The nearest approach to them is the peculiarly personal speech of Archilochus, who colours both his private experiences and his general ideas with the varied hues of personal emotion. His work is a necessary prelude to theirs; yet even his hate-poems, which are so filled with his own passions and prejudices, are oriented by a universal moral standard. The Aeolian lyric, especially in Sappho, goes far beyond that, and becomes the voice of pure emotion. It was obviously the work of Archilochus which gave individual personality such significance and variety of expression that after him the most secret motions of the spirit could be revealed and transformed into poetry; and it was his work which enabled his successors to give universally valid form to apparently formless personal feelings—so that Sappho actually translated her most intimate and subjective life into immortal humanity without robbing it of the charm of immediate experience.

The marvellous process by which the inner soul of man shapes itself in Aeolian lyric poetry is no less miraculous than the contemporary creation of philosophy and the constitutional state by the Greeks of Asia Minor. Miracle though it is, it must not blind us to the fact that the Aeolian lyric, like other forms of Greek poetry, is rooted in the life of the community. It is clear from the rich variety of poems which have been discovered in the last few decades that, just as Archilochus in every poem speaks of and to the world which surrounds him, so the poetry of Alcaeus and Sappho was always inspired by external motives and written for a definite audience. Therefore, it was written within definite conventions; and now we are learning to trace the conventional elements in it as clearly as in the work of Pindar. But for us there is a deeper and more positive significance in the fact that a drinking-song of Alcaeus presupposes a drinking-party of his comrades, and a love-song or a wedding-song of Sappho presupposes the society of young girl-musicians who were her friends.

The symposium, or drinking-party, was for Greek men— through its free friendly companionship and its fine intellectual tradition—the capital of the newly conquered realm of individual liberty.[71] Therefore we find that men express their personalities chiefly through poems written for the drinking-party. At this time the poetry of the symposium wells into a broad river, fed from many sources and bearing with it all the strong emotions a man can feel.[72] The surviving fragments of the songs of Alcaeus embrace every type of emotional expression and logical reflection. One large group of them is made up of political songs, filled with intense passion and Archilochean venom, like the savage attacks on the murdered tyrant Myrsilus.[73] The poet found a fit audience for his erotic poetry in his trusted friends: among them his anguished heart could be eased of its heavy secret. Poems which give grave and thoughtful advice to friends show the growing importance of personal relationships to steady and strengthen the lonely insecure life of the individual. Other lyrics again spring from the emotional contemplation of nature—a mood which can first be traced in Archilochus.[74] Alcaeus and his friends did not see nature as an objective or aesthetic spectacle, like the shepherd in Homer who gazes with joy from the mountain peak upon the splendour of the midnight stars;[75] they felt that the changes of sky and season, the succession of light and darkness, calm and storm, winter frost and the cheering breath of spring, reflected the changing emotions of the human soul, and that earth and sky echoed and strengthened their cries of love and grief. The gentleness, the serenity, and the resignation of Alcaeus' poems on destiny and the chances of life contrast strangely with the debauched philosophy of the drinking-songs, which call for a Dionysiac intoxication to drown the cares of the world. Thus even the personal tone of his poetry does not break its connexion with society, although that society is a circle of personal friends, where the individual can freely speak what is in his heart.

Drinking-songs are not unlike the ritual utterance of hymns and prayers; for both are primitive forms of self-expression translated into poetry. In a prayer, man stands stripped of all but his own individuality, and faces pure Being as he did at the beginning of life. While he addresses the deity as a Thou, invisible but present, his prayer becomes a medium for uttering his own thoughts or giving vent to his own emotions without a human audience; and nowhere is this shown more beautifully than in the poems of Sappho.[76]

The Greek spirit needed Sappho, to explore the last recesses of the new world of personal emotion. The Greeks themselves felt that they owed her much, for as Plato says they honoured her as the tenth among the Muses. There were other Greek women who wrote poetry, but none of them equals or approaches her. She is unique. Yet her poetry, compared with the rich variety of Alcaeus' lyrics, is limited in scope. It speaks always of the woman's world—and not of all that world, but only of the life of the poetess herself within the circle of her girl-friends. Woman is the mother, the mistress, and the wife of man; it is in these aspects that she appears most frequently in Greek poetry and is honoured by poets of every age, because she lives in these aspects in the heart of man. But in Sappho's poetry woman is seldom incarnated as mother or lover—only when a friend enters or leaves her band of maidens. Woman as such is not the subject of Sappho's inspiration. Her friends are girls who have just left their mothers' sides; protected by the unmarried woman who serves the Muses like a priestess, they are dedicated to serve beauty by their dances, games and songs.

The Greek poet was a teacher; and the two functions were never more closely identified than in Sappho's thiasos of girls consecrated to music. No doubt the beauty that they worshipped extended beyond the scope of Sappho's own poems, to embrace all the beauty inherited from the past. To the masculine heroism of tradition, Sappho's songs, quivering with the rapture of complete and harmonious friendship, added the ardour and nobility of the feminine soul. They depict an ideal third life between childhood and marriage—an age in which women were educated to attain the highest possible nobility of spirit. The very existence of Sappho's circle assumes the educational conception of poetry which was accepted by the Greeks of her time; but the novelty and greatness of it is that through it women were admitted to a man's world, and conquered that part of it to which they had a rightful claim. For it was a real conquest: it meant that women now took their part in serving the Muses and that this service blended with the process of forming their character. Yet this essential fusion which shapes the human soul is impossible without the power of Eros to release the forces of the spirit. The parallel between the Platonic and the Sapphic Eros is obvious. The feminine Eros, still charming us by his melodious and tender songs, was yet strong enough to create a true community among the souls of his worshippers. Thus he was more than mere emotion: he must have joined the souls which he inspired in some higher unity. He was present in the sensuous grace of dance and play; he was embodied in the glorious figure who was the friend and the ideal of her comrades. The great moments of Sappho's lyric poetry come when she strives to win the unripe heart of a girl, when she bids farewell to a beloved friend who is leaving her companions to return home or to follow the husband who has won her in marriage (and marriage at that time had nothing to do with love), and finally when she thinks sadly of a comrade, walking at evening in a quiet garden far away and vainly calling the name of her lost Sappho.

It would be both vain and unsuitable either to work out unprovable psychological explanations of the nature of Sappho's Eros, or to grow indignant at the blasphemy of such explanations and assert that she and her friends felt only the emotions of which bourgeois Christianity would approve.[77] From her poems it is clear that Eros was a passion which shook its victim's whole being, and held the senses no less firmly than the soul. We need not trouble to determine the existence of a sensual side in Sappho's passion; what interests us is its amazing power to grip and transform the whole personality, and the vast sweep of the emotion which it set free. No masculine love-poetry among the Greeks even approached the spiritual depth of Sappho's lyrics. For Greek men distinguished spirit and senses as two opposing poles of being—so that it was late before they came to believe that erotic passion could gain such importance as to invade their spiritual nature and interpenetrate the whole of life.

That change in the masculine attitude has been called Hellenistic effeminacy. And certainly, at this early period, only a woman was capable of the utter abandonment of soul and senses alike which we should consider worthy of the name of love. Love is woman's whole existence, and she alone welcomes it with her whole nature undivided and unfaltering. But at that time, when there were few if any marriages for love, it was hard for a woman to conceive such passion for a man; just as the highest incarnation of a man's love was not presented as love for a woman, but as the Platonic Eros. It would however be anachronistic to interpret Sappho's emotion, which never breaks away from the senses, as equivalent to the metaphysical aspiration of the Platonic soul towards the idea, the supramundane yearning which is the secret of Plato's Eros. Yet she has this in common with Plato: she too felt that true passion stirs the soul to its depths. From that feeling rises the vast sorrow which gives her poetry not only the tender charm of melancholy but the higher exaltation of true tragedy.

She soon became a figure of myth; mythologists explained the riddle of her character and her emotions by telling of her unhappy love for a handsome young man, Phaon, and converted her spiritual tragedy into a real leap from the Leucadian cliffs.

But there is no man in her world; man appears only at its gate, as the suitor of a beloved maiden, and he is met by an unfriendly gaze. When Sappho thinks that a man is happy as the gods if he can sit opposite his love and hear her sweet voice and her enchanting laughter she is remembering the emotions she herself feels when she is near her beloved. That voice and that laughter make her heart numb with longing in her breast. 'When I even see you, my voice stops, my tongue is broken, a thin flame runs beneath all my skin, my eyes are blinded, there is thunder in my ears, the sweat pours from me, I tremble through and through, I am paler than grass, and I seem almost like one dead.' [78]

Sappho's highest art is her gift in describing her inner experience with the unemotional simplicity of a folk-song, and yet with the sensuous directness of personal feeling. Is there any comparable achievement in European art before Goethe? If we may believe that the song we have quoted was written for the marriage of a pupil, and that Sappho chose that ritual form to carry her own incomparably personal language, we need no other example to prove that her deep emotion could convert conventional style and speech into the pure expression of her own personality. It is the very simplicity of the situation which seems to encourage those delicate shades of emotion which give it real significance. But it is not mere chance that such a depth of individuality was possible only for a woman, and that a woman was capable of it only through the power given her by love. As herald of the power of love, Sappho enters the kingdom of poets, which had hitherto been held by men alone. And her unique vocation is symbolized in the exordium of an ode discovered not many years ago: 'Some say the fairest thing on earth is a troop of horsemen, others a band of foot-soldiers, others a squadron of ships. But I say the fairest thing is the beloved.' [79]

SOLON: CREATOR OF ATHENIAN POLITICAL CULTURE

THE voice of Athens was heard for the first time in the choir of Hellas about the year 600. At first she seemed only to imitate and elaborate the melodies of others (and above all of her Ionian kinsmen), but soon she wove them into a nobler harmony as a background for her own clearer and more commanding tones. Her genius did not reach its full power until it created the tragedies of Aeschylus a century later; and we are fortunate to know even a little of its achievements before that. Nothing survives from the sixth century except considerable fragments of Solon's poetry. Still, it is not mere chance which has preserved them. For centuries, as long as there was an Athenian state with a free spiritual life of its own, Solon was revered as a keystone of its culture. Boys at the beginning of their schooling learned his poems by heart; and they were constantly cited as the classical expression of the soul of Athenian citizenship by advocates in the lawcourts and orators in the public assembly.[1] Their influence lived on until the power and glory of the Athenian empire passed away. Thereafter, in the inevitable nostalgia for past greatness, the historians and philologists of the new age collected and preserved their remains. They even prized Solon's poetical self-revelations as valuable records of historical fact: it is not long since they were so regarded even by modern scholars.[2]

Think for a moment what a loss we should have suffered if no fragment of his poems had survived. We should hardly be able to comprehend the noblest and strangest quality in the great Attic tragedies, and in fact in the whole spiritual life of Athens —the inspiration given to all her art and thought by the idea of the state. So fully did her citizens realize that the intellectual and artistic life of each individual had both its origin and its purpose in the community, that the Athenian state dominated the lives of its members to a degree unparalleled outside Sparta. But Sparta, for all the nobility and firm resolution of her communal life, left no room for the individual will to develop, and, showing more and more clearly her inability to change her ethos with changing times, gradually became a fossilized relic of the past.[3] The Ionian city-state, on the other hand, found in the ideal of justice the organizing principle of a new social order; and at the same time, by abolishing class privilege and establishing the liberty of all its members, gave each individual citizen room for the free development of his own potentialities.[4] Yet, while it made these concessions to ordinary human nature, it was unable to develop powers which might unite the surging new individual energies in a higher effort to serve and strengthen the community. These two moments—the educational force which is evidenced by the new supremacy of law within the state, and the untrammelled liberty of speech and thought enjoyed by the Ionian poets—were not yet linked by a single purpose. The culture of Athens was the first to strike a balance between the outward-striving energy of the individual and the unifying power of the state. Despite the great debt of political and intellectual education which Athens owed to Ionia, it is always easy to trace the fundamental difference between the libertarianism of Ionia, which is centrifugal, and the constructive genius of Athens, which is centripetal. That distinction explains why the first great expressions of the Greek spirit in the sphere of education and culture were Athenian. The mightiest achievements of Greek political thought, from Solon to Plato, Thucydides, and Demosthenes, are without exception the work of Athenian citizens. They were possible only in a state which could subordinate all spiritual activities to the life of the community and yet make them part of that life.[5]

Solon is the first embodiment of this truly Attic spirit, and at the same time the greatest of its creators. For, although the Athenian spirit was predestined, by the strange harmony of its spiritual powers, to some great accomplishment, the early appearance of a creative personality to direct these powers helped to mould its future history. Constitutional historians, who weigh a great man by his tangible work, estimate Solon chiefly by his part in moulding the Athenian constitution, the seisachtheia.[6] But in a history of Greek culture the essential thing is that Solon's work as the political teacher of his nation far outlasted his historical influence, and makes him an important figure even

to-day. And so we must consider him chiefly as a poet. His poetry
reveals the motives behind his political actions, which by the
greatness of their ethical feeling rise high above the level of
party politics. We have already observed that legislation was
one of the greatest forces in forming the new civic sense.[7] Solon's
poems are the clearest illustration of that truth. Their special
value for us is that they show us, behind the impersonal abstrac-
tions of the law, the spiritual personality of the lawgiver, a visible embodiment of that educational force of law of which the
Greeks were so vividly aware.[8]

The old Attic state into which he was born was still governed
by the landed nobility, whose power had been broken or abolished elsewhere in Greece. By the first attempt to codify the
Athenian homicide-law—the Draconian statutes,[9] which became
proverbial for their severity—the power of the aristocracy had
been strengthened, not impaired; and even the laws of Solon
himself were not intended to abolish it. It was only after the fall
of the Pisistratid tyranny that the reforms of Cleisthenes swept
it away. When we think of later Athens, restlessly seeking after
some new thing, we cannot help wondering why the waves of
social and political unrest which had flooded the Aegean broke
helplessly on the open coast of Attica. But at that time it was
still a purely agrarian country; while its citizens were not the
far-travelled, easily influenced sailor folk which Plato describes
in the fourth century.[10] They were still conservative farmers,
clinging to the soil, hard to move, rooted in their ancestral religion and morality. We must not, for all that, assume that the
lower classes were impervious to new social influences: witness
Boeotia, where, although Hesiod had voiced the complaints of
the people a century before Solon,[11] the feudal system survived
into the heyday of Greek democracy. Still, these complaints were
seldom translated into deliberate political action, unless they
were taken up by the superior intelligence of the upper classes,
and some wise or ambitious aristocrat rose up to lead the masses.
The serfs who worked the land were dominated by the compact
strength of the proud horse-loving squires who are pictured on
many an archaic vase driving their light chariots to a festival
or the funeral of a comrade. With their selfish caste-pride and
their arrogant disregard of the landless commoners, they kept a
deaf ear and a firm hand for the downtrodden populace, whose

deep despair is movingly described in Solon's great iambic poem.[12]

The culture of the Athenian nobility was Ionian through and through. Both its art and its poetry were moulded by the superior taste and convention of the kindred race. It was natural that Ionian influences should also affect its manner of life and its ideals: Solon was making a concession to the feelings of the common people when he legislated to forbid the Asiatic pomp and the women's lamentations which had until then been part of the funeral ceremony of every nobleman.[13] It was not until the terrible crisis of the Persian invasions a century later that Athenian fashions in clothes, hairdressing, and social usage abandoned the luxurious Ionian convention,[14] the ἀρχαία χλιδή. (The archaic statues lately recovered from the ruins of the Persian destruction of the Acropolis give us a lively idea of the rich Asiatic elegance of that style; and the haughty Attic ladies of Solon's own time are now represented by the standing goddess in the Berlin Museum.) No doubt the invading Ionian spirit brought much with it that seemed to be harmful; yet it was the inspiration of Ionia which first impelled Athens to her own spiritual achievement. Above all, without that inspiration, neither the political movement which drew its strength from the poor could have arisen, nor its great leader Solon, in whom the Attic and the Ionian spirit meet and mingle. For that important phase in the history of culture, Solon's poetry provides the really classical evidence, far outranking the scanty facts preserved by later historians and the remains of contemporary Athenian art. The forms of his poetry—elegy and iambus—are of Ionian origin. His close relationship to the Ionian poets of his time is shown by his poem addressed to Mimnermus of Colophon.[15] His poetic language is Ionian mixed with Attic forms, for at that time the Attic dialect could not yet be used for lofty poetry. And the thoughts expressed in his poems are partly Ionian too. But with his borrowings he has mingled much of his own, and created a great new mass of ideas which he is enabled, by borrowing the Ionian style, to work out freely and to express with some degree of ease.

His political poems [16]—the work of half a century, begun before his legislation and carried down to the conquest of Sa-

lamis, just before Pisistratus became tyrant [17]—at once resume
the high educational tone which poetry had had in the days of
Hesiod and Tyrtaeus. They are all exhortations addressed to
his fellow-citizens, and all inspired by a grave and passionate
sense of his mission to his country. There is nothing like them
in Ionian poetry from Archilochus to Mimnermus, unless it be
Callinus's appeal to the honour and patriotism of his fellow-
Ephesians in the crisis of the barbarian invasion.[18] But Solon's
political poetry is not a new appeal to the spirit of Homeric
heroism. It voices a new emotion: for every truly new age reveals to poets new realms of feeling in the human soul.

We have seen how, during the violent social and economic
revolutions of these centuries, and the universal battle for the
good things of this world, men had searched for a firm foothold
and found it in the ideal of justice. Hesiod was the first to appeal
to the divine protection of Diké, in his fight against the greed of
his brother. He extolled her power to guard society against the
curse of hybris, and gave her a place beside the throne of the
supreme ruler Zeus.[19] And with all the crude realism of a pious
imagination he pictured the effects of the curse of unrighteousness brought by one man's guilt on a whole city: failure of har-
vests, famine, pestilence, miscarriages, war, and death. Against
that he described the righteous city glorying in the sunshine of
God's blessing: the fields are fertile, the women bear children
who are like their husbands, peace and wealth fill the whole
land.[20]

Solon, too, places all his political faith in the power of Diké,
and there are Hesiodic traits in his picture of her. It is probable
that Hesiod's unshakable trust in the ideal of justice had had
some influence in the social struggles of the Ionian city-states, by
strengthening and justifying the resistance of the class which was
striving for its rights. Solon did not rediscover Hesiod's ideas—
they needed no rediscoverer: he took them over and completed
them. He, too, is convinced that justice is an inseparable part of
the divine world-order. He is never tired of proclaiming that it
is impossible to ignore the power of Diké, because it is always
victorious in the end. Sooner or later punishment comes, and
man's hybris must pay the penalty for overstepping the bounds
set by justice.[21]

In that conviction, Solon warns his fellow-citizens against

wearing themselves out in the blind and furious conflict of interests. He sees his city rushing towards the abyss, and tries to stem its ruin. 'Driven by avarice,' he cries,[22] 'the leaders of the people enrich themselves unrighteously: they spare neither the goods of the state nor the temple treasures, and they do not preserve the venerable foundations of Diké—who in her silence knows all the past and all the present, but does not fail to come in time to punish.' Yet when we examine Solon's idea of punishment we can see how his ideals differ from the religious realism of Hesiod's faith in justice. He does not imagine divine punishment to mean pestilence and famine, as Hesiod does.[23] He thinks of it as immanent in the state, for every transgression of justice is a disturbance of the social organism.[24] A state thus punished is afflicted by party feuds and civil war: its citizens gather in bands which think only of violence and injustice; great numbers of the destitute are driven from their homes, enslaved for debt, and sold into a foreign land. And even if a man tries to avoid this national curse by creeping into the most secret recesses of his home, the curse 'leaps over the high walls' and finds him there.[25]

There is no more vivid and potent description of the necessary implication of each individual in the life of his community than in this great warning, which was clearly written before Solon was summoned to be the 'peacemaker' of Athens.[26] The social evil is like an epidemic, which strikes everyone in the doomed city; and, says Solon, it comes inevitably to every city which stirs up civil strife and class-war.[27] This is not a prophetic vision, it is a statesman's diagnosis of the facts. It is the first objective statement of the universal truth that the violation of justice means the disruption of the life of the community;[28] and Solon is eager to drive home his discovery. 'My spirit commands me to teach the Athenians this'—that is the phrase which concludes his description of injustice and its social consequences;[29] and then, in a reminiscence of Hesiod's contrasting pictures of the just and the unjust cities, Solon ends his message with an inspiring description of the glories of Eunomia.[30] Eunomia, in his eyes, is a goddess like Diké—Hesiod's *Theogony* [31] calls them sisters—and her power too is immanent. She does not manifest it in external blessings, in fertility and material abundance, as in Hesiod; but in peace and harmony of the whole social cosmos.

Here and elsewhere Solon clearly grasps the conception of the inner rule of law in social life.[32] It should be remembered that at the same time in Ionia the Milesian natural philosophers, Thales and Anaximander, were moving boldly towards the conception of a permanent law in the eternal coming-to-be and passing-away of nature.[33] Solon, like them, was impelled to demonstrate the existence of an immanent order in the course of nature and human life, and with it an inherent meaning and an essential norm in reality. He is clearly presupposing a law connecting cause and effect in nature, and expressly setting forth as a parallel to it the rule of law in the social order, when he says elsewhere,[34] 'From the clouds come snow and hail, thunder follows the lightning, and by powerful men the city is brought low and the demos in its ignorance comes into the power of a despot.' [35] Tyranny—the domination of one noble family and its head, supported by the common people, over all the rest of the aristocracy—was the most dreadful danger which Solon could predict for the Attic Eupatrids, for it meant the immediate end of their centuries-old mastery of the state.[36] Significantly enough, Solon does not threaten them with the imminence of democracy. The masses were still politically inexperienced, so that democracy was far away: it could not come until the aristocracy had been brought low by the Pisistratid tyrants.

With Ionian scientific ideas as a pattern, it was easier for Solon than for anyone before him to establish the fact that the political life of a community is subject to definite laws. He had as material for this induction the history of numerous Greek cities on both sides of the Aegean, in which during more than a century the same processes had run their course with remarkable uniformity. Because the political development of Athens started late, he was enabled to use the history of other states for his own prognosis, and by that educative act he earned his lasting fame. But it is typical of human nature that, in spite of his early prediction, Athens too was compelled to pass through a stage of tyranny.

In Solon's extant poems we can still trace the growth of his conviction from his first words of warning down to the moment when his clear insight was verified, and one man, Pisistratus, seized absolute power for himself and his family. 'If you have suffered for your weakness, do not blame the gods! You yourselves allowed these men to grow great by giving them power, and therefore you have fallen into shameful servitude'.[37] These words are obviously reminiscent of the beginning of the warning elegy which is quoted above.[38] There Solon says: 'Our city will not perish by the decree of Zeus and the counsel of the blessed gods immortal, for Pallas Athene, its proud protector, has stretched out her hand above it; but the citizens themselves in their folly wish to ruin it by avarice'.[39] And in the later poem that prophecy comes true. By pointing to his early warning of the approaching disaster Solon demonstrates his own innocence, and raises the question of the real responsibility. Since he does it in practically the same words in both passages, he is clearly dealing with one of the fundamental tenets of his political creed: in modern language, it is the problem of responsibility; in Greek, it is the question of man's share in his own destiny.

This problem is first raised in Homer, at the beginning of the *Odyssey*. Zeus the father of gods and men speaks to the assembled gods of the unjust complaints of mankind, who blame heaven for every misfortune in human life. And he asserts, in almost the same words used by Solon, that men themselves, and not the gods, increase their troubles by their own folly.[40] Solon's poems are conscious reminiscences of the Homeric theodicy.[41] The earliest religion of Greece taught that all human misery, whether it came from external causes or from the will and impulse of the sufferer himself, was caused by an inevitable até, the agent of a higher power. The philosophical idea which the author of the *Odyssey* puts in the mouth of Zeus, as governor of heaven and earth, represents a later stage of ethical thought; for it distinguishes divine até, the unforeseen and inevitable doom sent by heaven, from human responsibility, which brings men greater misery than the portion allotted to them by heaven. The essential feature of the latter is foreknowledge—evil action deliberately willed.[42] That is the point where Solon's belief in the importance of justice for a healthy social life joins the Homeric theodicy and gives it a new depth of thought.

Recognition of the universal truth that every community is bound by immanent laws implies that every man is a responsible moral agent with a duty to be done. Thus in Solon's world there is far less scope for the arbitrary interference of the gods than in the world of the *Iliad;* for it is governed by law, and attributes

to the will of men many events which in the Homeric world were
the gifts or inflictions of heaven. Accordingly, the gods merely
carry into execution the effects of the moral order, which is identical with their will. The Ionian poets of Solon's time, who were
quite as deeply conscious of the problem of suffering, offered no
solution except melancholy resignation, and could only lament
man's fate and its inevitability.[43] But Solon, who called his fellow
men to act in full consciousness of their responsibility, himself
set the example by his political and moral courage, which stands
as a clear proof of the inexhaustible energy and moral earnestness of the Athenian character.

Though a busy politician, Solon was a deep thinker too. His
great elegiac prayer to the Muses, which has been preserved
entire, recurs to the problem of responsibility, and shows its
paramount importance in his thought.[44] Here it appears at the
centre of his general reflections on man's effort and his destiny:
which proves, even more clearly than the political poems, how
fundamentally religious was Solon's attitude. The elegy is inspired by the old aristocratic moral code—known to us chiefly
from Theognis and Pindar, as well as from the *Odyssey*—with
its traditional emphasis on material wealth and social prestige.
But it revises that code to harmonize with Solon's deep faith in
law and divine justice.[45] In the first section Solon limits the natural impulse to possess, by teaching that wealth must be right-
eously gained. Only the riches given by the gods, he says, will
last: riches won by injustice and violence only foster até, which
comes swiftly.

Here, as throughout his poetry, the thought recurs that injustice can maintain itself only for a brief time, and diké always
comes sooner or later. But here, the idea advanced in his political poetry, that 'divine punishment' is immanent in the social
order, is replaced by the religious image of 'the retribution of
Zeus', which falls as rapidly as a tempest in spring. 'Suddenly it
scatters the clouds, stirs the depths of the sea, rushes down on
the fields and ruins the fair work of men's hands; and then it
rises up again to heaven, the sun's rays shine out on the rich
earth, and no cloud is to be seen. Such is the retribution of Zeus,
which lets none escape. One man makes amends soon, another
late; and if the guilty man escapes punishment, his innocent children and his descendants suffer in his stead.'[46] This is the very

core of the religious doctrine which, a century later, created Attic tragedy.

Now the poet turns to the other até, the doom which can be turned aside by no man's thoughts and efforts. It is clear that, although Solon's contemporaries had largely rationalized and moralized their conception of human action and destiny, there was still a residue of disbelief in the universal justice of heaven. 'We mortals, good and bad alike, think that we shall get [47] whatever we hope for, until misfortune comes, and then we complain. The sick man hopes to become well, the poor man to become rich. Everyone strives for gold and profit, each in a different way, as merchant-sailor, farmer, or craftsman, bard or seer. But the seer himself cannot avert misfortune even if he sees it impending.' Although these ideas are set out with archaic simplicity, the central thought of the second part of the poem stands out clearly: Moira, Fate, makes all human effort fundamentally insecure,[48] however earnest and logical it may seem to be; and *this* Moira cannot be averted by foreknowledge, although (as shown in the first part of the poem) misery caused by the agent can be averted. She strikes good and bad men without distinction. The relation of our success to the acts which we will is entirely irrational. Even the man who tries his best to succeed, frequently comes to ruin, and the man who begins badly is often allowed by God to prosper and escape the consequence of his folly. There is a risk in all human action.[49]

Although Solon recognizes the irrationality of the sequence of will and action, he still considers that the agent is responsible for the effect of a bad act; and so the second part of the elegy does not seem to him to contradict the first. While he believes that even the best-willed action may not succeed, he does not preach resignation and inaction. That was the conclusion reached by the Ionian Semonides of Amorgos, who complains that mortals waste much trouble and effort in striving for unattainable and illusionary ends, and that they wear themselves out in care and sorrow instead of resigning themselves and abandoning their blind pursuit of their own ruin.[50] At the end of this elegy, Solon takes a clear stand against such apathy. Instead of viewing the world from the sentimental human side, he takes the objective view, God's view, and asks himself and his audience whether facts which humanity thinks irrational may not have an intelli-

gible justification from a higher point of view. The essence of
wealth—which is after all the object of all human effort—is that
it has neither measure nor end in itself. Even the richest of us
prove that, says Solon, for they strive to double their riches.[51]
Who could satisfy men with all their wishes? There is only one
solution, and that is beyond men's grasp. The gods give men
profit, but take it away again. For when Zeus sends as a compensation the evil spirit of infatuation,[52] now this man has it and
soon another one.

It has been necessary to analyse the thought of this poem, because it contains Solon's theory of social ethics. The poems in
which, *post factum,* he justifies his legislation [53] show how closely
his political acts were linked with his religious ideals. For instance, when divine Moira becomes the necessary balance
which abolishes the inevitable economic differences between man
and man, his moral theory is clearly a justification of his policy.[54]
All his acts and words indicate that the leading aim of his reforms was to find a just medium between excess and deficiency,
between excessive power and helplessness, between privilege and
serfdom.[55] Therefore he could wholeheartedly support neither
party in the state: yet both parties, rich and poor, really owed
to him the strength they had won or retained. He constantly
illustrates, by impressive images, his dangerous position not so
much above as between the two opponents. He recognizes that
his strength lies chiefly in the impalpable moral authority of his
severely disinterested character. He compares the selfish ambition of the busy party-leaders with skimming cream off the milk
or with pulling in a well-filled net [56]—images which would be
vividly real to the Athenian farmers and fishermen—but he describes his own attitude in stylized Homeric language, which
shows how keenly he felt his own position as a heroic champion
of his cause. Now he holds his shield over both parties alike, so
that neither can defeat the other, and now he advances fearlessly
into no-man's-land among the flying spears, or, like the wolf,
bites his way through the raging pack around him.[57] The most
effective of the poems are those in which he speaks in his own
person, because his personality is always magnificently individual,
and brightest in the great iambic poem [58] where he gives his
account 'before the tribunal of time'. The artless profusion of its
lively images, the impulsive generosity of Solon's feeling of kin-

ship with all humanity, and the strength of his sympathy make the poem the most personal of all his political utterances.[59]

No great statesman has ever risen higher above the mere lust for power than Solon. When he had completed his work as legislator, he left his country and went away on a long journey. He himself never tires of declaring that he did not use his position to make himself a rich man or a tyrant, as most men would have in his place; and he is willing to be called a fool for missing the chance.[60] Herodotus bears out his account of his independence, in the romantic story of his interview with Croesus.[61] He shows us Solon the sage, talking with the Asiatic despot among his astounding wealth without abandoning the conviction that none of the great ones of the earth was so happy as the simple Attic peasant on his farm—who, after winning his daily bread for himself and his children in the sweat of his brow, and fulfilling a lifetime of duty as father and citizen, gains the crown of honour by dying for his country at the threshold of old age. The spirit of the tale is a unique and charming blend of the conservatism of the Athenian, clinging to the soil, and the adventurous spirit of the Ionian, travelling 'for the sake of seeing sights'.[62] It is delightful to trace this invasion of the Athenian character by Ionian culture, through the extant fragments of Solon's non-political poems. They are the work of a mind so rich that its possessor was reckoned by his admiring contemporaries as one of the Seven Wise Men of Greece.

The most notable are the famous verses in which Solon answers the complaints of the poet Mimnermus about the pangs of old age, and his yearning to die when he passes sixty, without knowing illness and grief. 'If you will obey me, then strike that out, and do not grudge it to me if I have thought of something better: rewrite your poem, Ionian nightingale, and sing this: "I wish the Moira which is death would overtake me at eighty".' [63] Mimnermus' thought sprang from the free Ionian spirit which uses its own standards to value life, and is willing to reject it when it loses its worth. Solon does not accept that valuation. His healthy Athenian energy and his rich enjoyment of life are fit opponents for the supersensitive melancholy which shrinks from the sixtieth year of life because that year will deliver it over to the pains and troubles of existence. Solon cannot believe that old

age is a slow and painful extinction. His old age is a green tree,
whose irrepressible energy produces new blossoms from year to
year.[64] And so he refuses even to die in silence and unlamented:
he wants his friends to sigh and weep for him when he dies.[65]
Here again he opposes a famous Ionian poet, Semonides of
Amorgos: for Semonides taught that life was so short, and so
full of pain and grief, that we should not mourn the dead for
more than a day.[66] Solon does not believe that human life is
kinder than Semonides has said. Once he cries, 'No one is happy.
All the mortals on whom the sun gazes are wretched'.[67] And like
Archilochus and all the other Ionians he laments the insecurity
of life: 'The mind of the immortal gods is quite hidden from
men'.[68] Yet all this is outweighed by his joy in the gifts of life—
the growth of children, the strong pleasures of sport and hunt-
ing, the delights of wine and song, friendship, and the sensuous
happiness of love.[69] The power of enjoyment, in Solon's eyes,
is wealth not inferior to gold and silver, lands and horses. When
a man goes down to Hades, it does not matter how much he has
owned, but how much of its goods life has given him. His poem
of the hebdomads (which is preserved entire [70]) divides man's
life into seven-year periods, and gives each age its own special
function. It is filled with a truly Greek feeling for the rhythm
of life; for one age cannot change places with another—each
has its own meaning, and each is in accord with another, so that
the whole rises and falls with the rhythm of universal nature.[71]

Solon's attitude to the problems of ordinary life, as to political questions, is determined by this same new sense of the submission of all things to inherent laws. He expresses himself with
the curt simplicity of a Greek proverb. Natural things are always
simple, when one recognizes them. 'But the hardest thing of
all is to recognize the invisible Mean of judgment, which alone
contains the limits of all things.' These words of Solon [72] seem
designed to give us the correct standard by which to measure
his greatness. The idea of the mean and the limits—an idea of
fundamental importance in Greek ethics—indicates the problem
which was of central interest to Solon and his contemporaries:
how to gain a new rule of life by the force of inner understanding. The nature of this new rule cannot be defined: it can be
comprehended only through sympathetic study of Solon's words,

his character, and his life. For the mass of men it is enough to obey the laws which are laid down for them. But the man who makes these laws needs a higher standard, which is not written. The rare quality by which he can find it Solon calls *gnomosyné*, 'judgment', because it always suggests the *gnomé*—which is both true insight and the will to put it into action.[73]

That is the clue to understanding the unity of Solon's spiritual world. The unity was not given to him: he had to create it. We find that the conception of justice and the rule of law, which was the focal point of Solon's political and religious thought, already prevailed in Ionia: but there, as we have seen, it seems to have found no voice in poetry. The other aspect of Ionian thought, expressed all the more enthusiastically by the Ionian poets, is a shrewd practical wisdom and a hedonistic individualism. For that side too Solon has a deep sympathy. What is new in his thought is that he brings the two poles of Ionian philosophy together into a unity which is clear and perfect in his poetry. His poems reflect the rare completeness and harmony of his life and character. He put aside individualism, but he recognized the claims of the individual's personality: more, he was the first to give those claims an ethical basis. Because he brought together the state and the spirit, the community and the individual, he was the first Athenian. By creating that unity he struck out the type to which all the men of his race were to conform.

PHILOSOPHICAL SPECULATION:
THE DISCOVERY OF THE WORLD-ORDER

THE origins of philosophical speculation in Greece have usually been studied within the traditional scheme of the 'history of philosophy'. In this scheme, ever since Aristotle, the 'Presocratics' have been given their position and their label, as the first to ask the questions and develop the systems which were to be used in classical Athenian philosophy—namely, in Platonism.[1] Lately, however, scholars have tried not so much to treat them as stages in the continuous development of philosophical thought, as to appreciate them separately, as individual philosophers: and we have thus come to realize more of their true importance. Still, in a history of Greek culture the perspective must be a little altered. Although the early philosophers deserve a prominent place in it, they cannot claim the same importance in the culture of their own age as can Socrates—the educator *par excellence*—in the late fifth century, or in the fourth century Plato, who was the first to see the rôle of philosophy in the education of a new type of man.[2]

In the age of the Presocratics and society, the poet was still the undisputed leader of his people; and he was being joined by the law-giver and statesman. There was no change in this situation until the rise of the sophists. These men were really cultural innovators—and in that they differ from the early ontologists and natural philosophers. The full value of their work can be given only in a history of education. Their general contributions to philosophical theory were trifling, so that conventional histories of philosophy have never paid them much attention.[3] In this book the cases are reversed: for we cannot treat the great natural philosophers and their theories as separate contributions to the advance of philosophical thought. We must rather investigate their importance to the age in which they lived, and try to realize the searching changes which their new intellectual attitude was to make in the development of the Greek character.

Finally, we must mark the point at which pure philosophical speculation, after long neglecting the problem of the nature of human areté, set to work to solve it, and thereby grew away from individual philosophers to become a great, impersonal, cultural force within society.

It is hard to fix the point when rational thinking begins in Greece. The line should run through the Homeric epic. Yet it is hardly possible to separate 'mythical thinking' in the epic from the rational ideas with which it is interpenetrated. If we analysed the epics from this point of view we should find that logic invaded mythology quite early, and began to transform it.[4] There is no discontinuity between Ionian natural philosophy and the Homeric epics. The history of Greek thought is an organic unity, closed and complete. But, to take a contrasting example, mediaeval philosophy was not an outgrowth of the epic of chivalry, but a scholastic adaptation of ancient philosophy as studied at the universities; for centuries it had no influence, in central and western Europe, either on aristocratic civilization or on the subsequent bourgeois civilization. (The great exception is Dante, who unites theological, aristocratic, and bourgeois cultures in himself.)

Actually, it is not easy to say how the Homeric idea[5] that Ocean is the origin of everything differs from the doctrine of Thales that water is the basic principle of the universe: for Thales' theory was certainly inspired by the tangible reality of the inexhaustible sea. Hesiod's *Theogony*, again, is a rational system, deliberately built up by logical inquiry into the origin and nature of the world. Yet within that system the old force of mythological thought is still active:[6] it lives on in what we think of as 'scientific' philosophy, in the work of the Ionian 'physicists'; and without it we could not explain the astonishing ability of the early scientific age to create great new philosophical systems. Love and Hate, the two natural forces of binding and separation in the philosophy of Empedocles, have the same intellectual ancestry as Hesiod's cosmogonic Eros. Thus we cannot say that scientific thinking began either when rational thinking began or when mythical thinking ended.[7] Even in the philosophy of Plato and Aristotle we can find genuine mythologizing: for instance, the Platonic myth of the soul, or Aristotle's description of the love which all things have for the unmoved Mover of the universe.[8]

To adapt a phrase of Kant, mythical thought without the formative logos is blind, and logical theorizing without living mythical thought is empty. From that point of view we must interpret the growth of Greek philosophy as the process by which the original religious conception of the universe, the conception implicit in the myth, was increasingly rationalized. Picture this process as the gradual shading of a great circle, in smaller concentric circles from the circumference to the centre. Then it is rational thinking which invades the circle of the universe, taking possession of it more and more deeply, until in Plato and Socrates it reaches the centre, which is the human soul. From that point, the movement spreads back again until the end of ancient philosophy in Neoplatonism. The strength of Plato's myth of the soul was such that it could resist the tendency to reduce all Being to a rational system,[9] and could reconquer the already rationalized cosmos, until the Christian religion came to possess and use the newly remade world of myth.

It has often been asked why Greek philosophy begins by inquiring into nature and not into man. To explain this important fact, scholars have endeavoured to correct history and to derive the doctrines of the early natural philosophers from the spirit of religious mysticism.[10] But that is to alter the problem, not to solve it. It is solved as soon as we realize that it arises only from the mistake of narrowing our horizon to 'the history of philosophy'. We must include in our survey not only natural philosophy, but also the constructive ethical, political, and religious thought of Solon and the Ionian poets from Archilochus onwards. Then, as soon as we break down the barrier between poetry and prose, we shall have a complete view of the origins of philosophical speculation about man as well as about nature.[11] The only difference is that political theory is naturally practical, while speculation about *physis* or *genesis* (the 'origin' of the universe) is theoretical—it is carried on for the sake of *theoria*. The Greeks did not think of human nature as a theoretical problem until, by studying the external world, especially through medicine and mathematics, they had established an exact technique on which to begin a study of the inner nature of man.[12] We are reminded of Hegel's epigram: 'the mind's way is roundabout.' The soul of the Orient, weighed down by religious yearning, sinks into the abyss of emotion, and finds no firm foothold in it; but the Greek spirit, trained to think of the external cosmos as governed by fixed laws, searches for the inner laws that govern the soul, and at last discovers an objective view of the internal cosmos. It was chiefly that discovery which, at the crisis of Greek history, made it possible to follow Plato's ideal and develop human character in a new way—on the basis of philosophical knowledge.[13] Thus, in the fact that the philosophy of the soul was preceded by the philosophy of nature, there is a deep historical meaning which comes out when we study the history of culture as a whole. The lofty speculations of the early Ionians were not intended to educate Greece; yet they were, in the midst of the chaotic growth of a new society, and the collapse of the old mythical conception of the universe, a fresh attempt to solve the deepest problem of life, the problem of Being itself.[14]

The most notable feature in the character of the first philosophers—of course they did not call themselves by that Platonic name [15]—is their intellectual devotion to knowledge, their absorption in studying Existence for its own sake. Their singlemindedness was admired and yet considered paradoxical by the later Greeks, and doubtless by their contemporaries too. Their scholarly disregard for the things which others held important—money, honour, even home and family—their apparent forgetfulness of their own interests, and their indifference to popular enthusiasms, begot many famous anecdotes. These stories were carefully collected and handed down (especially in the Platonic Academy and the Peripatetic school) as examples and models of the βίος θεωρητικός, which Plato declared was the true *praxis* of the philosopher.[16] In them the philosopher is the great eccentric, an uncanny but lovable character, who deliberately isolates himself from the society of men in order to live for his studies. He is childishly naïve, awkward and impractical; he lives in eternity, not in time and space. While watching some celestial phenomenon, the wise Thales falls into a well, and his Thracian maid jeers at him for wanting to look at things in heaven when he cannot see what is at his own feet.[17] Pythagoras, asked why he lives, replies, 'To look at heaven and nature'.[18] Anaxagoras is accused of caring nothing for his kinsfolk and his country, but points to heaven and says, 'There is my country'.[19] These anecdotes all refer to the philosopher's inexplicable interest in the structure of the cosmos, in what was then called (in a deeper sense) meteorology—the knowledge of things in the heights. His behaviour and aspirations seem to the common people to be bizarre and over-ambitious: the Greeks used to think that a deep scholar was unhappy, because he was περιττός.[20] The full sense of the word is untranslatable, but it denotes a quality bordering on hybris, for the thinker overpasses the boundary between the human and the divine mind.

These ardent lonely spirits, devoted to one aim alone, could live only in Ionia, where there was an atmosphere of complete personal liberty. There they were left in peace; elsewhere their independence offended others and brought them into trouble. In Ionia, men like Thales of Miletus soon became popular; their deep sayings and anecdotes of their lives were eagerly retailed.[21] From this interest in their personalities, we can safely infer that their contemporaries vaguely understood that the philosophers and their ideas were phenomena created by the age in which they lived. As far as we know, Anaximander was the first to write down his thoughts in prose and to publish them—as a lawgiver publishes his laws. By that act, the philosopher relinquished the privacy of his thinking; he now ceased to be an ἰδιώτης, and claimed a hearing from all mankind. If we may venture to infer, from later scientific Ionian prose, what the style of Anaximander's book must have been, we may guess that he wrote in the first person to contradict the opinions current among his fellow-Greeks. Thus Hecataeus of Miletus starts his genealogical treatise with an extraordinarily naïve sentence: 'Hecataeus of Miletus speaks thus: I write such things as I think to be true; for many and foolish, it seems to me, are the accounts of the Greeks.'[22] Heraclitus begins curtly and decisively like an inscription: 'Of this logos, although it is true for ever, men have no understanding before they hear it and after they first hear it. Although everything happens according to this logos, they seem quite inexperienced when they make trial of such words and works as I tell of by explaining each thing according to its own nature and stating how it is.'[23]

The boldness with which these philosophers applied pure independent logic to the current conception of the universe is parallel to the courage of the Ionian poets in voicing their emotions and opinions on human life and their own age. Both ventures are based on the growing power of the individual. At this stage logic appears to work like an explosive. The oldest authorities shake and fall under its impact. Nothing is correct but that which *I* can explain to myself on conclusive grounds, that for which *my* thought can reasonably account. From Hecataeus, the first ethnologist and geographer, and Herodotus, the father of history, to the Ionian doctors who founded two thousand years of medical science, the whole of Ionian literature is filled with this spirit and expounds its criticisms in the characteristic first-personal form. Yet in this victory of the rational I over traditional authority, there is latent a force which is to triumph over the individual: the concept of Truth, a new universal category to which every personal preference must yield.[24]

The natural philosophers of the sixth century started by inquiring into the origin of the universe, its *physis*. Physis gave its name to the whole intellectual movement and to the type of thinking which it created; and that is not unjustified, if we only remember the original significance of the Greek word, and do not introduce the modern idea of physics.[25] For the problem of the origin of things—which we should call a *meta*physical problem —was in fact always their chief interest; and their physical theories and discoveries were subordinate to it. It is true that a rational science of nature was created by the same movement, but it was at first embedded in metaphysical speculation, and only gradually became an independent branch of research. In the Greek conception of physics two subjects are confused: the inquiry into the origin of the universe (which compels reason to move beyond phenomena observed by the senses), and the comprehension of everything which proceeds from that origin and now exists (τὰ ὄντα), by empirical investigation (ἱστορίη). It was natural that the inquisitive nature of the Ionians, the great explorers and observers, should make them push their investigations to the point where the ultimate problems arise; and equally natural that, once they had asked what the universe was and how it came into existence, they should find themselves impelled to extend their knowledge of facts and to explain individual phenomena. Since Egypt and the Near Eastern countries were neighbours of Ionia, it is highly probable (and the probability is supported by sound tradition) that these older civilizations, through constant intellectual intercourse with the Ionians, influenced them not only to adopt their technical discoveries and skills in surveying, navigation, and astronomy, but also to penetrate the deeper problems to which the Egyptian and Oriental myths of creation and divinity gave answers far different from those of the Greeks.

But it was an innovation in the very principles of thought when the Ionians, assimilating and elaborating the empirical knowledge of celestial and natural phenomena which they got from the Orient, used that knowledge independently to help them discover the origin and nature of the universe; and when they subjected the myths dealing with the real and visible world, the myths of creation, to theoretical and causal inquiry. That is the true origin of scientific thought. That is the historical achievement of the Greeks. No doubt they took some time to free themselves from the domination of the myth; but their liberation was a rational and scientific process, as is shown by the fact that it was one continuous movement, carried on by the independent but connected investigations of a number of philosophers. The birthplace of Ionian natural philosophy is held to be Miletus, the metropolis of Ionian civilization: for the lives of the first three cosmologists Thales, Anaximander, and Anaxagoras, cover the period down to the destruction of Miletus by the Persians at the beginning of the fifth century B.C. The violent interruption of three generations of high intellectual achievement by the brutal invasion of external historical fate is not more obvious than the continuity of the work done by these great philosophers, and their peculiar intellectual type—which has rather anachronistically been called 'the Milesian school'.[26] Yet they asked their questions and pursued their investigations in one definite direction; and they established the methods and the concepts which were to be used by subsequent Greek natural philosophers down to Democritus and Aristotle.

We can best study the spirit of early Ionian philosophy by taking as an example the most impressive of these three men, ANAXIMANDER. He is the only one whose conception of the universe we can more or less accurately define. In him we see the astonishing breadth and scope of Ionian thought. He was the first to create a world-picture of truly metaphysical profundity and rigorous structural unity. Yet he also made the first map of the earth and created scientific geography.[27] And Greek mathematics had its birth in the age of Milesian philosophy.[28]

Anaximander's conception of the earth and the universe is a triumph of geometrical imagination. It is a visible symbol of the idea of proportion, which is deeply rooted in the thought and life of archaic man. Anaximander's world is constructed on severely mathematical ratios. For him, the Homeric idea of the earth as a disc is merely deceitful appearance. Actually, he says, the sun after moving from east to west during the day returns under the earth at night to reach its starting-point at dawn. Therefore the universe is not a hemisphere, but a complete sphere with the earth at its centre. Not only the course of the sun but the courses of the stars and the moon are circular. The outermost circle is that of the sun, which is 27 times the diameter of the earth. The moon's course is 18 times the diameter of the earth: and since the circle of the fixed stars is the innermost—the text of the description of Anaximander's cosmos is here corrupt [29]—it is obviously 9 times the diameter of the earth. And the diameter of the earth is 3 times its height, for the earth is shaped like a cylinder with flat ends.[30] It does not rest (as mythological thought naïvely assumes) on a solid foundation; nor does it grow like a tree into the air out of invisible roots [31] reaching down into the depths. It hangs free in space. It is not borne up by the pressure of the air: it is held in equilibrium by being at an equal distance on all sides from the globe of heaven surrounding it.[32]

The same mathematical tendency underlay the construction of the Ionian map of the world. This map, which was the work of several generations of scholars, is attributed by Herodotus to 'the Ionians' collectively. Sometimes he follows it and sometimes he contradicts it, but his dependence on it is always clear. His chief authority is certainly Hecataeus of Miletus (who was nearest to him in time [33]) ; but Hecataeus—as we are expressly told [34]—took the design of his map from Anaximander; and the schematic structure of the world pictured in it is more suited to Anaximander's geometrical conception of the universe and of the earth than to the character of Hecataeus, the inquisitive traveller who had seen foreign lands and foreign nations, and who was more interested in single facts than in all-embracing schemes.[35] Herodotus could not have spoken of 'the Ionians' if he had not known that Hecataeus had had predecessors in the art of constructing such maps. Accordingly we need have no hesitation in attributing to Anaximander the fundamental scheme of the map which we know—from Herodotus, Scylax, and other authors—that Hecataeus employed. In it the surface of the earth was divided into two roughly equal parts, Europe and Asia. A section of Asia was apparently cut off and named· Libya. The frontiers of the two continents were great rivers; and over and above that Europe was almost exactly halved by the Danube, and Libya by the Nile.[36] Herodotus makes fun of the schematic structure of the old Ionian maps of the world, which showed the earth as round as if it had been turned on a lathe, and surrounded by the Ocean—which had never been seen by mortal eyes, at least on the east and north.[37] It is an apt jest at the passion for constructing maps of the earth according to *a priori* geometrical assumptions. The age of Herodotus spent much time on supplementing the lacunae in the Ionian maps by new facts, and in modifying or excising their downright assertions. It allowed nothing to remain as true unless it had been empirically established as a fact. Still, it owed nearly everything to the creative genius of Anaximander and the pioneers who preceded him: for they made the inspiring discovery that the world is built up on a system which is orderly, not chaotic, and they attempted to express this discovery in the language of mathematical proportion which they were the first to construct.[38]

A similar bold departure from the data of sense-perception was Anaximander's choice of the Infinite (ἄπειρον) as the basic principle of all things, in place of Thales' principle, Water. All the natural philosophers were impressed by the great drama of coming-to-be and passing-away which is plain to every observer of nature. What is the inexhaustible substance from which everything is born and into which everything passes? Thales believed it to be water, which evaporates into air or freezes solid as stone. Water is free to change into anything. All life on the earth comes from moisture. We do not know which of the old physicists was the first to teach that (as the Stoics too believed) the fire of the stars is fed by the vapours rising out of the sea.[39] Again, Anaximenes believed that not Water but Air was the original element: his chief doctrine was that all-pervading life

came from the air: air governs the world as the soul governs
the body, and the soul itself is air, breath, *pneuma*.[40] Anaximander chose the *apeiron*—it is not a definite element, but (in
words which seem to be his own) 'includes everything in itself,
and guides everything'.[41] Aristotle opposed him on the ground
that it would be better to say that matter is included in everything than that it includes everything.[42] But from the other epithets applied to the apeiron in Aristotle's account of the theory,
such as 'immortal' and 'indestructible', it is plain that the apeiron
is an active force.[43] Only a god can 'guide everything'. And there
is a tradition that Anaximander declared the apeiron, constantly
producing new worlds [44] and assimilating them again, was the
Divine.[45] Thus, when things are produced by the apeiron, they
leave the original unity in which all the warring contraries of
this world are brought together in peace. To this creed we must
apply the great saying—the only one which is directly stated to
be Anaximander's own:—'It is necessary that things should
pass away into that from which they are born. For things must
pay one another the penalty and compensation for their injustice
according to the ordinance of time.' [46]

Since Nietzsche and Rohde much has been written about that
saying, and many mystical interpretations of it have appeared.[47]
It has been taken to mean that the existence of individual things
is a sinful desertion of the eternal First Cause, the crime of Eden
for which all creation must atone. However, now that the correct text has been established (by the addition of ἀλλήλοις, which
is lacking in the old editions) it should be obvious that Anaximander is speaking of the pleonexia or aggrandisement of things
against one another.[48] Existence in itself is not a sin—that is a
non-Greek idea.[49] The words are a personification of the strife
between things, which is compared to a lawsuit among men. We
must picture an Ionian city-state. There is the market-place
where suits are heard and decisions are given; and the judge
sitting on the bench to ordain (τάττειν) the compensation to be
paid.[50] The judge is Time. We know him from Solon's political
poems: his power is inevitable.[51] When one of the contestants
has taken too much from the other, the judge deprives him of
his excess and gives it to the other to make up the deficiency.
Solon's idea was this: Diké does not depend on human, earthly
justice; nor does she act by sudden temporary strokes of divine

punishment, as the old religion of Hesiod's time held; her power is immanent, manifested in the process by which all inequalities compensate themselves in time; and that inevitable process is the 'punishment of Zeus', or 'divine requital'.[52] Anaximander goes much further. He holds that this eternal process of compensation is at work not only in human life but in the whole world. The immanent compensatory process in human life induces him to believe that nature too with its forces and oppositions is subject to an immanent rule of law like mankind, and that it is this rule of law which regulates coming-to-be and passing-away throughout creation.

To a modern eye this appears to be the dawn of the majestic idea that all nature is subject to universal laws. But Anaximander was not thinking of the monotonous causal series which modern scientists construct. He was formulating a moral, not a physical law of nature. There is a deeply religious meaning in his conception that natural phenomena are governed by a moral standard.[53] It is not a compendious description of events, but a justification of the nature of the universe: he shows creation to be a cosmos 'writ large'—namely a community of things under law.[54] Its meaning and its purpose is the continuous and inescapable process of coming-to-be and passing-away—the process which is hardest for simple men, with their passion for life, to bear and understand. We do not know whether Anaximander himself used the word *cosmos* in this connexion: it is used by his successor Anaximenes, if the fragment in which it occurs is correctly attributed to him.[55] But actually Anaximander's idea of the eternal power of Diké ruling natural phenomena implies the idea of a cosmos, although not exactly in the later sense of the word. Therefore we are justified in describing his conception of the universe as the spiritual discovery of the cosmos. The discovery could not be made anywhere but in the depths of the human soul. It has nothing to do with telescopes, observatories, or any kind of empirical research. It was produced by intuitive thought, the same kind of thought which created the idea (also ascribed to Anaximander [56]) of the infinite number of universes. No doubt the philosophical idea of a cosmos entails a break with current religious beliefs. But it also entails the magnificent new realization that Being is divine, despite the horror of impermanence

and annihilation which (as the poets show) saddened and per-
plexed all that generation.[57]

This great discovery opened the way to countless new philosophical explorations. The idea of a cosmos is even now one of
the most essential categories of man's understanding of the universe, although it has gradually lost its metaphysical in its scientific meaning. But it conveniently symbolizes the whole influence
of early natural philosophy upon the culture of the Greeks.
Solon's ethico-legal conception of responsibility and retribution
was derived from the epic theodicy; [58] similarly Anaximander's
doctrine of the systematic justice of the universe reminds us that
the most important idea in the new philosophy, that of Cause
(αἰτία), was originally the same as the idea of Retribution, and
was transferred from legal to physical terminology. Closely connected with this is the parallel transference of the related words
cosmos, diké, and tisis from the sphere of law to that of nature.[59]
Anaximander's fragment shows us much of the process by which
the problem of causality developed out of the problem of the
ways of God to man. His idea of diké is the first stage in the
projection of the life of the city-state upon the life of the universe.[60] But we do not find that the Milesian philosophers expressly brought the superhuman cosmos into relation to human
life.[61] It would not have occurred to them to do so, because their
investigations were concerned not with humanity but with the
eternal scheme of things. Still, they used human life as an example to help them in interpreting *physis;* therefore, their picture
of the universe could later be used to establish a harmony between eternal Being on the one side and human life and human
values on the other.

PYTHAGORAS of Samos, although he worked in south Italy,
was an Ionian philosopher too. His intellectual character is as
difficult to assess as his actual personality. The traditional accounts of his life and genius kept changing with the development
of Greek civilization, so that he is described as an inventor, or a
politician, or a teacher, or the head of a monkish order, or the
founder of a religion, or a miracle-worker.[62] Heraclitus despised
him as a polymath like Hesiod, Xenophanes, and Hecataeus; yet
he thought of him as learned in one particular sphere, like the
others mentioned.[63] Compared with the unity and completeness
of Anaximander's lofty intellect, Pythagoras' mind, with its

blend of many different qualities (however we may conceive the blend), has something freakish and accidental about it. The modern fashion of describing him as a sort of medicine-man has no claim to serious consideration. From the accusation of poly-mathy, we may infer that the later 'so-called Pythagoreans' (as Aristotle describes them [64]) were right in naming Pythagoras as the founder of their peculiar science—the science which they distinguished from Ionian 'meteorology' by the general name of *mathemata*, 'studies'. It is a very general name, and in fact con-notes very heterogeneous branches of knowledge: the science of number, the basis of acoustics and the theory of music, the ele-ments of geometry, what was then known of the movements of the stars, and, at least for Pythagoras himself, a knowledge of Milesian natural philosophy.[65] But what connexion has all this with the doctrine of transmigration (allied to the beliefs of the Orphic religion) which is without dispute attributed to Pythago-ras and which is described by Herodotus as typical of the early Pythagoreans? [66] Akin to it are the ethical precepts ascribed to the founder himself. Finally, Herodotus firmly believes that the community founded by him in Italy resembled a religious order: it survived in south Italy for more than a century, until its po-litical enemies brought about its downfall.[67]

The Pythagorean doctrine that number is the principle of all things is akin to, and is prefigured in, the rigidly geometrical symmetry of Anaximander's cosmos.[68] It must not be interpreted as an elaboration of simple arithmetical theory. According to traditional accounts, it arose from the discovery of new laws of nature, governing the relation which the length of a lyre-string bore to the height of the tone produced by it.[69] Very daringly, and no doubt under the influence of the mathematical symbolism of Milesian natural philosophy, Pythagoras universalized his newly discovered laws, and declared that the whole cosmos and human life itself was ruled by number. His doctrines have no resemblance to mathematical science in the modern sense. Num-ber meant much more to him than it does to us. For he did not use it to reduce all natural phenomena to measurable *quanti-tative* relations, but held numbers to be the *qualitative* essences of very different things, such as heaven, justice, *kairos,* and so on.[70] Contrariwise, when Aristotle says that according to the Pythagoreans numbers were the *material* of which things consisted, he is no doubt making the mistake of translating into material terms their theoretical identification of numberness and existence.[71] He must be nearer their real meaning in his explanation that the Pythagoreans believed that things *resembled* numbers in many ways, and in fact more closely than fire, water, or earth—the principles from which previous philosophers had derived all nature.[72] The most important illustration of Pythagorean doctrine is found at a subsequent stage of the development of philosophy—in Plato's strange attempt towards the end of his life to reduce his Ideas to numbers. Aristotle criticizes him for believing that quantities could express qualitative differences. The criticism may appear merely trivial to us; but it has been justly observed that the Greek conception of number originally contained a qualitative element, and that the process by which numbers were reduced to pure quantities was slow and gradual.[73]

Perhaps the Pythagorean views would be further illuminated by an investigation of the origin of the Greek words for the various numbers, and the remarkable differences in their etymologies—if we could expose the visual element which is certainly contained in each of them. We can understand at least how the Pythagoreans came to prize the power of numbers so highly, when we compare the lofty utterances of their contemporaries on the same subject. Prometheus, in Aeschylus, calls the discovery of number the masterpiece of his civilizing wisdom.[74] In fact, the age which discovered that number is the ruling principle of several important aspects of existence had made a great forward step in the search for the meaning of the universe: it had come appreciably nearer to showing that all nature is ruled by an inner law which we must study to understand her. The discovery—like all great advances in systematic knowledge—was given exaggerated importance at the time, and, like many stimulating and permanently valuable discoveries, was misused in practice. In speculations which now seem frivolous, the Pythagoreans attempted to reduce everything in the universe to manifestations of an arithmetical principle. They would not believe that anything could exist which could not be explained as being in some way a number.[75]

Mathematical science was an essentially new element in Greek culture. At first, its various branches were developed independently. It was soon recognized that each of these branches was a valuable educational discipline, but it was some time later that they began to interact, and the science to exist as a whole. The late, semi-mythical traditions about Pythagoras emphasize above all else his influence as a teacher. Plato certainly served as the model for that conception of him; it was embroidered by the Neopythagoreans and Neoplatonists; and modern accounts of his 'educational wisdom' are almost entirely based on uncritical acceptance of edifying biographies written in late antiquity.[76] Yet even in that conception of his character there is a residuum of historical truth. Plato speaking of Homer and his claim to be called the educator of Greece (a title which many contemporaries were ready to confer upon him) asked whether he could really be called a 'leader of paideia' in the sense in which, for instance, Pythagoras was entitled to this rank. Plato seems to think of Pythagoras primarily as the founder of the 'Pythagorean life' in this connexion. But the question is not only whether Pythagoras himself was a teacher: the really great teacher in that age was the spirit of the new science, which is, in the traditions we possess, represented by him. The educational influence of mathematics was due chiefly to its normative aspect. If we recall the importance of music in early Greek culture, and the close relationship of music to Pythagorean mathematics, we shall recognize that as soon as the Pythagoreans had discovered the numerical laws governing musical sound they were bound to create a philosophical theory of the educational influence of music. The connexion between music and mathematics which Pythagoras established was thenceforward a constant possession of the Greek spirit.

The connexion produced concepts which were to have far-reaching effects on the creative thinking of the Greeks. Under its influence new laws, governing all aspects of existence, were formulated and recognized. All the marvellous principles of Greek thought—principles which have come to symbolize its most essential and indefeasible quality—were created in the sixth century. They were not always in existence—they were established and developed by a regular historical process. And one of the most decisive advances in that process was the new investigation of the structure of music. The knowledge of the true nature of harmony and rhythm produced by that investigation would

alone give Greece a permanent position in the history of civilization; for it affects almost every sphere of life. The work of the
Pythagoreans created a new world ruled by inflexible laws, comparable to the rigid causality of Solon's doctrine of justice in
society. While Anaximander had believed the universe to be a
cosmos of things governed by the absolute power of justice, the
Pythagoreans conceived that the principle of the cosmos was
harmony.[77] He had established the causal *necessity* (calling it
the 'justice' of existence) of the sequence of temporal phenomena; and they in turn emphasized the *harmony,* the structural
aspect of the cosmos under its laws.

This harmony was expressed in the relation of parts to the
whole. But behind that harmony lay the mathematical conception
of proportion, which, the Greeks believed, could be visually
presented by geometrical figures. The harmony of the world is a
complex idea: it means both musical harmony, in the sense of a
beautiful concord between different sounds, and harmonious
mathematical structure on rigid geometrical rules. The subsequent influence of the conception of harmony on all aspects of
Greek life was immeasurably great. It affected not only sculpture
and architecture, but poetry and rhetoric, religion and morality;
all Greece came to realize that whatever a man made or did was
governed by a severe rule, which like the rule of justice could not
be transgressed with impunity—the rule of fitness or propriety
(πρέπον, ἁρμόττον). Unless we trace the boundless working of
this law in all spheres of Greek thought throughout classical and
post-classical times, we cannot realize the powerful educative
influence of the discovery of harmony. The conceptions of
rhythm, of relation, and of the mean are closely akin to it, or
derive from it a more definite content. It is true not only of the
idea of the cosmos, but also of harmony and rhythm, that it was
necessary for Greece to discover their existence in 'the nature of
being' before she could employ them in the spiritual world, to
find order and method in human life.

We do not know the inherent connexion between Pythagoras'
mathematical and musical theories and his doctrine of transmigration. The philosophical speculations of his age were essentially metaphysical, so that the myth of metempsychosis (which
is not founded on logic) must be an importation from outside

the field of philosophy. We shall discuss it together with the beliefs of the Orphic sect, which may well have been its source.
Later philosophers too were more or less strongly influenced
by it.

After the release won by the naturalistic movement of the
seventh century, the Greeks of the sixth century were exercised
to create a new spiritual pattern for their life; and that endeavour involved not only a serious philosophical effort but a
powerful religious revival. THE ORPHIC MOVEMENT is one of
the most impressive proofs of the new upwelling of spiritual
forces from the dim recesses of the mind of the people. In its
search for the higher meaning of life, it resembles the attempt
of logical thought to establish a philosophical foundation for the
rule of moral law throughout the cosmos. Its actual teachings
were not very important. Modern writers have exaggerated its
values, and credited it with many late Greek beliefs, in order to
make it fit their *a priori* assumption that it was a redemptionist
religion.[78] Still, its doctrine of the soul was the beginning of a
new consciousness of the self and a new feeling for human life.
It had, unlike the Homeric conception of the soul, a frankly
moral significance. Any creed which lays down that the soul
comes from God and does not perish, naturally teaches that it
must be kept pure during its earthly existence; and a believer in
such a creed feels himself responsible for all his conduct during
this life.[79] We have met the idea of responsibility before, in
Solon. There it meant the social responsibility of the individual
to the community; here it means moral responsibility, or the religious ideal of the pure life. Purity, which had at first been
only a ritual notion, gradually extended to the moral sphere.
Of course Orphic purity must not be confused with the asceti-
cism of the later spiritualist movement, which considered
'matter' to be evil in itself; yet Orphism taught certain ascetic
types of self-restraint, notably abstinence from all animal food.[80]
And the Orphic notion that the soul was a guest from heaven,
sojourning for a time in the mortal life of earth, leads straight
to the abrupt cleavage between soul and body, and so to the idea
that the body is essentially bad.

The rapid spread of the Orphic cult in Greece and the Greek
colonies can only mean that its doctrines answered a deep spiritual need which was not satisfied by the official religions. There

were other new religious movements in the sixth century, notably the powerful and growing cults of Dionysus, and the worship of the Delphic Apollo: these too responded to the craving for a more personal religion. Historians of religion find it impossible to explain why two violently contrasting deities like Apollo and Dionysus should have been worshipped together in the Delphic cult. Yet the Greeks obviously felt that these gods had something in common—which, in the age when we find them jointly revered, was their power to affect the souls of their worshippers.[81] They were the most personal of all gods. It might almost be said that Apollo's spirit of order, clarity and moderation could not have sunk so deeply into men's hearts if the wild excitement of Dionysus, sweeping away all civic *eukosmia,* had not first broken the ground. That revolution and resettlement gave the Delphic religion such authority that it came to command all the constructive energies of Greece. The 'seven wise men', the greatest kings, and the most powerful tyrants of the sixth century all extolled the oracle of the Delphic Apollo as the highest type of wise counsel. In the fifth century both Pindar and Herodotus were deeply influenced by the Delphic spirit, and testify to its power to exalt and inspire. Its influence was not—even at its heyday in the sixth century—perpetuated in the creation of any lasting records: there was no Delphic bible. But at Delphi the educational power of Greek religion reached its maximum, and spread from there far beyond the frontiers of Hellas.[82] The wise sayings of sages were dedicated to Apollo and inscribed in his temple, since their worldly wisdom was only a reflection of his divine wisdom. And at his door his worshippers saw the command *Know thyself*—the doctrine of sophrosyné, by which men learn to remember the limits of human power and ambition, expressed in the legislative form that was characteristic of the age.

It is a mistake to believe that Greek sophrosyné was produced by the naturally harmonious character of the Greek people. If it had been, why should they have been so earnestly enjoined to pursue it, at the time when they had suddenly realized the dark gulfs over which move our life and the soul of man? The moderation that Apollo preached was not the humdrum doctrine of peace and contentment. It was a strong repression of the new individualistic impulse to wantonness; for in the Apolline code the worst of outrages against heaven was 'not to think human thoughts' [83]—to aspire too high, beyond the limits fixed for man. Hybris, which had originally been a concrete legalistic idea, the opposite of diké,[84] now grew into a religious conception too: it now meant the *pleonexia* or aggrandisement of man against God. This new connotation, which became the classical expression of the religious sentiment of the age of the tyrants, is the one which has come down to us. For a long time, along with the conception of the envy of the gods, it sharply defined the essential doctrines of much of Greek religion. The fortune of mortal men is as changeable as the day: so men must not aspire too high.

But the Greeks, driven by the human need for happiness, escaped from this tragic realization into the inner world of their own souls—either in the self-forgetfulness of Dionysiac intoxication (which was therefore complementary to the severe restraint of Apollo's creed) or in the Orphic teaching that the 'soul' is the best part of man and has a higher and purer destiny than his body. The passionless search for truth had now revealed to men the ceaseless process of birth and death which is Nature, and had shown that it was governed by a mighty universal law that cared nothing for the little life of mankind, but far transcended their brief happiness with its iron 'justice'. So, to strengthen them against this awful truth, men turned to the belief in their divine destiny. The soul, whose existence in us could be proved by no scientific demonstration, was now held to be a stranger in an inhospitable world, yearning for its eternal home. Ordinary men dreamt of life beyond the grave as an eternity of sensuous delight; while a few nobler spirits strove to keep their balance within the whirling chaos by hoping for release when their journey through the world was completed. But both classes were united by their faith in their own higher destiny. They were confident that when at last the pure soul reached the other world, it would speak as its password at the gate the truth by which it had lived on this earth: 'I too am of divine descent'. These are the words [85] inscribed on the Orphic gold plates which were deposited in graves in southern Italy to serve as passports to the life beyond the grave.

The Orphic conception of the soul marks an important advance in the development of man's consciousness of selfhood. Without it Plato and Aristotle could never have developed the theory that the human spirit is divine,[86] and that man's sensual nature can be dissociated from his real self, which it is his true function to bring to perfection. The doctrines of Empedocles, inspired as they are by the Orphic conception of man's divine nature, are enough to show how closely the new religion was associated with the problems of philosophy. The connexion of the two is first manifest in Pythagoras' teaching; and he was extolled by Empedocles in his Orphic poem *The Purifications*.[87] In fact the Orphic doctrine of the soul and the natural philosophy of Ionia are mingled in the philosophy of Empedocles—a synthesis which shows very instructively how these two different ways of viewing the world could supplement and complete each other. The union of the two is symbolized in his image of the soul tossed up and down in the whirl of the elements: air, water, earth, and fire cast it out in turn and thrust it from one to another, 'and such a one am I,' he says,[88] 'a wanderer banished by God'. In the cosmos revealed by the physicists, the soul can find no home; but it redeems itself by its religious consciousness of selfhood. Only when the soul can make a place for itself in the philosophers' cosmos (as in Heraclitus [89]), can man, in his quest for religious satisfaction, be content with the theories of metaphysics.

XENOPHANES of Colophon, the second of the great Ionian thinkers who taught and worked in southern Italy, was not a systematic philosopher like his predecessors. Milesian natural philosophy was the work of pure scientific research. But Anaximander, by making his doctrines accessible in book form, was definitely addressing the public; and Pythagoras was the founder of a society devoted to putting his own doctrines into practice. Both were therefore to some extent engaged in teaching—which is an essentially different activity from philosophical research. Still, philosophy affected current beliefs so deeply by its criticisms that it was impossible to keep it entirely separate from other intellectual activities. Natural philosophy had been greatly stimulated by contemporary political and social movements; and in its turn it had a potent influence on state and society. Xenophanes was a poet: his work was an invasion of poetry by the spirit of philosophy. That is a sure sign that philosophy was becoming a cultural force, for poetry was then, as always, the true expression of national culture. In the impulse which moved philosophy to put on poetic form we can see the whole of its power over man—its claim to complete supremacy over the whole soul, with its domination of reason and emotion alike. The new Ionian medium of prose was coming into favour very slowly, and had much less influence than poetry: for while prose, written in one local dialect, commanded a narrow audience, poetry used the language of Homer and was truly Panhellenic in speech. And the influence which Xenophanes meant his poems to have was also Panhellenic. Even Empedocles, who was a physicist, and Parmenides, who was an abstract logician and metaphysician, used the Hesiodic type of didactic poem as their medium. They were possibly encouraged by the example of Xenophanes; for, although he was neither a true philosopher nor (despite frequent ascriptions) the author of a didactic poem on nature,[90] he was a pioneer in the poetic presentation of philosophical reasoning. In his elegies and his *silloi* (a new kind of satire) he attacked and thereby popularized the enlightened doctrines of the Ionian physicists [91] and took up the cudgels against the prevailing ideals of culture.

These ideals were, above all else, the teachings of Homer and Hesiod. Xenophanes himself says so: 'all have learnt from Homer since the beginning'.[92] Therefore Homer was the focus of Xenophanes' attack, in his struggle to create a new culture.[93] Philosophy had replaced Homer's conception of the universe by a natural and logical explanation of events; and it was that new explanation of the universe which fired Xenophanes' poetic imagination.[94] For him it meant the abandonment of the old, polytheistic, anthropomorphic world of gods, which was (in Herodotus' famous phrase) created for the Greeks by Homer and Hesiod.[95] They had, he cried, attributed all shameful actions to the gods, theft and adultery and deceit.[96] His own conception of God, which he presents with fervent trust in the validity of his new doctrine, is that God is the same as the whole universe. There is only one God in that sense.[97] God is like mortals neither in shape nor in mind. He is all Sight, all Thought, all Hearing.[98] He sways the universe without effort, by pure thought.[99] He does not hurry busily here and there like the gods of epic poetry, but rests unmoved.[100] Men think that the gods are born, and have clothes, voices, bodies like themselves:[101] if oxen, horses, and lions had hands and could paint like men, they would paint gods in their own images: the oxen would draw gods like oxen and the horses like horses.[102] Negroes believed in flatnosed black-faced gods, and the Thracians in gods with blue eyes and red hair.[103] All the things which happen in the external world—things which men think are the work of the gods, and which terrify them—are brought about by natural causes. The rainbow is only a coloured cloud[104]; the sea is the source of all waters, winds and clouds.[105] 'We are all born from earth and water.'[106] 'Earth and water are everything which comes into being and grows.'[107] 'Everything comes from earth and returns to it at last'.[108] Civilization was not a gift of the gods to men, as mythical tradition says, but men themselves discovered everything in time, and improved it.[109]

Not one of all these ideas was new. They were at bottom the doctrines of Anaximander and Anaximenes, who really created this naturalistic explanation of the universe. But the work of Xenophanes was to preach them with passionate conviction. He was inspired not only by their terrific power to destroy outworn beliefs, but by their creative religious and moral force. Thus, his biting jests at the inadequacy of the Homeric conception of the gods and the universe were part of his effort to drive home the new and more worthy faith of which he was the apostle. It was the power of this new truth to revolutionize the life and faith of mankind which made it the fitting basis for a new culture. So the physicists' cosmos became, by a curious retrogression in thought, the pattern of eunomia in human society,[110] the metaphysical foundation of city-state morality.

Xenophanes wrote other poems besides his philosophical satires. A restless spirit, he looked back in one poem[111] (written at the age of ninety-two) on sixty-seven years of wandering, which probably began with his emigration from Colophon to southern Italy; but in his epic The Founding of Colophon he glorified his old home.[112] He also wrote a poem on the foundation of the colony of Elea, in which he himself may have taken part.[113] In any case these poems contained more personal feeling than was usual in the treatment of objective themes. His philosophical poems were wholly inspired by his personal faith in the exciting new doctrines which he brought from Asia to his new home in Magna Graecia and Sicily. Some modern scholars describe him as a rhapsode who recited the Homeric epics in public, and read his own satires against Homer and Hesiod to his friends in private.[114] But that description misinterprets the facts: for it does not accord with the peculiar unity of his character, which has left its indelible mark on every extant line of his poetry. He wrote for all the men of his time to read, as his great poem of the Banquet [115] shows. It is a rich and imposing description of the old-fashioned symposium, filled with deep religious sentiment. Every trifling detail of the ritual is raised to a loftier significance in Xenophanes' account. The symposium is still, to him, the shrine of high traditions of the great deeds of the gods, and of ancestral examples of manly virtue. He tells the other guests to say nothing of the gods' shameful quarrels, or of the battles of Titans, Giants, and Centaurs—the inventions of earlier ages, which other poets loved to sing at banquets—but to honour the gods and keep alive the memory of true areté.[116] In other poems he tells us what he means by honouring the gods. From this sentence we learn only that the criticisms levelled against traditional accounts of the gods in his extant poetry were meant to be recited at banquets: thus they reflect the educational tendency of the archaic symposium. At the symposium areté was honoured; and Xenophanes means that along with areté the gods too should be worshipped in the new pure fashion which recognizes the eternal laws of the universe.[117] He holds that philosophical truth is the guide to true areté.

Another, and a greater, poem [118] by Xenophanes deals with the same question. In it he passionately champions his new conception of areté. It is a document of major importance for the history of culture, so that we cannot pass it over here without careful study. It shows us a world far different from Xenophanes' free Ionian home—the severely ordered and defined world of the old aristocracy, in which the highest ideal is still the Olympic victor. The ancient glories of that world and that ideal blazed forth for the last time in the choric songs of Xenophanes' contemporary Pindar, and then gradually faded to extinction. Hurled into the strange aristocratic life of the western Greek world by the Median invasion of Asia Minor and the fall of Colophon, Xenophanes spent nearly seventy years in it, but never found a home. In every Greek city which he entered, his songs were admired and his new teachings were heard with excited interest; and, as is shown by the famous anecdote of his

witty conversation with the tyrant Hiero of Syracuse,[119] he sat
at the tables of the rich and the great. But he never found the
natural appreciation and social prestige which had been his in
Ionia: he was always alone.

In his poem can be seen, more clearly than anywhere else in
the whole history of Greek civilization, the inevitable clash between the two spiritual foes—the old aristocratic culture, and
the new philosophical ideal of humanity which now sought to
eject it from its place and power in the social order. Sport or
spirit?—that is the essence of the conflict. It seemed as if the
invaders must fall back defeated from the strong walls of tradition; yet their battle cry had in it a victorious ring, and in fact
their triumph was not far off. The absolute dominance of the
athletic ideal was broken. Xenophanes could not, as Pindar
could, hold that each Olympic victory, in wrestling or boxing,
running or chariot-racing, was the revelation of the victor's divine areté.[120] The city loads the victor in the games with honours
and gifts, he cries, 'and yet he does not deserve them as I do;
for this wisdom of ours is better than the strength of men and
horses! It is a mistaken custom: and there is no justice in pre-
ferring strength to wisdom. For even if a city has among its
citizens a good boxer or a victor at wrestling or the pentathlon,
it is not any more in right order (εὐνομίη) for all that; and a
victory at Olympia gives little joy to the city, for it does not
fill its store-rooms.' [121]

That is a surprising way to defend the value of philosophical
knowledge. Still, it shows once again with the greatest clarity
that the city and its welfare are the basic standard of all values.
Therefore, Xenophanes was bound, if he wished to replace the
traditional ideal of manhood by the philosophical man, to show
that the innovation would benefit the city. It is reminiscent of
the poem in which Tyrtaeus proclaimed the unconditional superiority of the Spartan civic ideal, warlike prowess, above all
other human excellences, and especially above the athletic excellence of the Olympic victor. 'This', he said, 'is a good shared by
all the city'—and his words were the first attack of the city-state
morality on the old chivalrous ideal.[122] Later, when the constitutional state came into being, justice was exalted as the highest
virtue—still in the name of the polis.[123] And now Xenophanes
appeals to the welfare of the polis to prove the value of his new

conception of areté—intellectual culture (σοφίη). It supersedes all earlier ideals, by assimilating them and making them subordinate to itself. It is the power of the intellect which creates justice and law, right order and welfare, in the city. Xenophanes deliberately modelled his poem on the elegy of Tyrtaeus, as a suitable form for his new thought.[124] His ideal marks the last stage of the development of the political conception of areté: first came courage, then prudence and justice, and now finally wisdom—the virtues which Plato retained as the essence of the citizen's highest areté. And this elegy is the first assertion of the new 'intellectual virtue', σοφία, which was to play such an important part in philosophical morality.[125] In it, philosophy discovered its own importance for mankind—that is, for the city-state; and now the gap between the disinterested search for truth and the criticism and guidance of human life had been bridged.

Although Xenophanes was not an original thinker, he was an important factor in the intellectual life of his time. It was he who first told Greece that philosophy could be a cultural force. Even when Euripides attacked the conventional admiration for athletic prowess,[126] he used the methods and arguments developed by Xenophanes; and Plato too followed him in his criticism of the educational value of the Homeric myths.[127]

PARMENIDES of Elea, on the other hand, was one of the greatest philosophers who ever lived; his position in the history of culture cannot be assessed without a comprehensive view of the vast and fructifying influence of his intellectual discoveries. In every epoch of Greek philosophy the effect of his work can be traced, and even to-day he is a leading representative of a permanent philosophical position. For he introduced a third basic form of Greek thought, parallel to Milesian natural philosophy and the arithmetical theories of the Pythagoreans, and like them influencing the whole intellectual and spiritual life of man. This was logic.

The speculations of the early physicists were not guided by logic, but by other kinds of spiritual activity—by imagination led and controlled by reason, the characteristically Greek sense of structure and architectonic form through which they analysed and ordered the visible universe, and a strange symbolist belief that the non-human world could be interpreted through human life. Thus, the universe as conceived by Anaximander is a visible symbol of the cosmic processes of coming-to-be and passing-away, the warring opposites ruled by eternal diké; and in that conception there is little trace of abstract logical reasoning.[128] But the sentences of Parmenides are a severely logical structure sustained and controlled by the sense of necessary sequence of thought. It is not for nothing that the extant fragments of his work form the first more or less comprehensive and connected set of philosophical dogmas which exists in Greek. We cannot realize or communicate his meaning by studying his calm vision of the universe, but rather by contemplating the mental processes which produced it.[129] The energy with which he imposes his doctrines on his audience arises not from the enthusiasm of the doctrinaire, but from the logician's triumphant belief in the necessary sequence of his thoughts. He too holds that the highest aim of human thought is the realization of an absolute necessity, ananké: he also calls it diké or moira, obviously under Anaximander's influence.[130] But he tells us that diké holds all existence fast in her toils, and will not loosen them, so that that which is can neither come into being nor pass away. And by that he does not mean simply to contrast his diké with the diké of Anaximander, which is manifested in the coming-to-be and passing-away of all things. He means that his own diké, which keeps all coming-to-be and passing-away far removed from Being, and holds Being immovably in its bonds, is the necessity implicit in the conception of Being, the necessity which he metaphorically calls the 'just claim' of Being.[131] As he repeats again and again, with increasing force, Being is, and Notbeing is not.[132] That which is cannot not be: that which is not cannot be—thus Parmenides expresses the law of thought which was established by his realization that a logical contradiction cannot be resolved.

The compulsion of pure thought is the great discovery on which the philosophy of Parmenides is centred. It defines the polemic tone of his teaching. What may seem to us in his chief propositions to be the discovery of a logical law was regarded by him as an objective discovery, which put him into opposition to all the ideas of the Ionian physicists. If it is true that Being never ceases to exist and Notbeing never exists, then (Parmenides realized) coming-to-be and passing-away are impossible.[133] Yet appearances, which seem to tell us that coming-to-be and passing-away do occur, imposed on the natural philosophers so that they held that Being arose out of Notbeing and passed away into Notbeing again. They held, in fact, the belief which all men share. We trust our eyes and ears instead of our reason, which is the only guide to reliable certainty. Reason is our spiritual ears and eyes, and the man who does not use it is like the blind and the deaf [134]—he is lost in a maze of contradictions. He must at last come to believe that Being and Notbeing are the same and yet different.[135] If we assert that Being arises from Notbeing, we say that the origin of the world is unknowable; for what is not, cannot be known: real knowledge must correspond to an object.[136] So if we seek the truth, we must free ourselves from the sensory world of coming-to-be and passing-away,[137] which leads us to accept such unthinkable conclusions, and turn to true Being, which we can comprehend by reason. 'For thinking is the same as Being'.[138]

The great difficulty of pure reason always is to acquire some concrete knowledge of its object. In the extant fragments of his work Parmenides shows himself exercised to deduce, from his rigorous new conception of Being, a number of definitions which are inherent in its nature: he calls them signposts on the road of research along which pure reason takes us.[139] Being is without birth and therefore deathless; it is one; it is complete; it is immovable, eternal, ubiquitous, a unity, interconnected, indivisible, homogeneous, boundless, impenetrable. Obviously all the positive and negative qualities which Parmenides attributes to Being were coined on the model of the old natural philosophy, and worked out by careful analysis of the contradictions implicit in that philosophy.[140] Here we need not demonstrate this in detail. Unfortunately our understanding of Parmenides' doctrines is diminished by the gaps in our knowledge of earlier philosophies. But it is certain that he made constant references to Anaximander; and he may well have attacked Pythagorean theories too, although we can produce no evidence for the conjecture.[141] In this book we cannot undertake a systematic exposition of his attempt to attack, from his new point of view, and to destroy all the principles of natural philosophy, nor of the paradoxes which are the logical result of his own principles. (These paradoxes were investigated chiefly by his pupils, among whom

Zeno and Melissus deserve special mention as more or less independent thinkers.)

Parmenides held that the discovery of pure reason and of the stringent rules of logical thought meant the discovery of a new 'road' to truth—in fact, of the only practicable one.[142] In Greek philosophy the metaphor of the right road (ὁδός) of research constantly reappears; although it was only a metaphor, it has an almost technical sound about it, especially in the contrast of the right road and the wrong, where it approaches the sense of 'method'.[143] This concept, fundamental in the development of scholarship, was created by Parmenides; for he was the first thinker who deliberately endeavoured to solve the problem of philosophical method, and clearly distinguished the two chief channels in which, thenceforth, philosophical research was to run—thought and perception, the way of the senses and the way of reason. Whatever is not known by the way of reason is only 'men's opinion'.[144] Our salvation depends on our abandoning the world of opinion for the world of truth. Parmenides considered this conversion to be violent and difficult, and yet a great act of liberation. He presents his reasoning with a majestic sublimity and a deep religious emotion which makes it inspiring as well as convincing. For it is enthralling to watch him, in his search for knowledge, freeing himself and men for the first time from the appearances which impose on sense, and discovering reason to be the organ through which alone the totality and unity of Being can be apprehended. Although his discovery was troubled and distorted by many problems, it brought into action one of the fundamental forces of the Greek genius for educating humanity and comprehending the universe. Every line he wrote pulsates with his ardent faith in the newly discovered powers of pure reason.

This faith of his explains the structure of his work, divided as it is into two sharply contrasting sections, *Truth* and *Opinion;* [145] and it also solves the old question—how can Parmenides have been both a poet and a dry logician? It is oversimplification to reply that in his day any subject could be treated in Homeric and Hesiodic verse. No: Parmenides was a natural poet, because he was carried away by his conviction that he must preach his discovery, the discovery which he believed to be in part at least a revelation of the truth. This conviction is not the same as

Xenophanes' boldly personal evangelism. Parmenides' poem is charged with a proud humility. Although his presentation of the facts is uncompromisingly austere, still he feels that he is only the instrument and servant of a power far higher and more worthy than himself. In his immortal prelude [146] he avows this philosophical inspiration. If we study it, we find that the image of the 'man who knows' [147] travelling towards truth is an essentially religious symbol. The text is corrupt at the most vital point, but I believe that the original words can be reconstructed. The 'man who knows' is an initiate who is called to watch the mysteries of truth: a symbol of the new knowledge of Being.[148] The road by which he travels 'uninjured' (so I should restore the words) to his goal is the road of salvation.[149] That philosophical research could be described in the terminology of the mysteries (which were at that time growing in importance) is a very significant fact: it shows that philosophy was consciously taking the place of religion. It has been said that for Parmenides both God and emotion are meaningless compared with the rigorous laws of thought; [150] but the obverse of this fact is that Parmenides considers thought and the truth which it apprehends to be something very like religion. It was the consciousness of his high mission which led him, in the prelude to his poem, to draw the first real picture of a philosopher—the 'man who knows', led by the daughters of light, far from the paths of men, along the hard road to the house of truth.

Philosophy had come very close to life in Xenophanes' educational and evangelistic writings; in Parmenides, it seemed to have receded, even further than at first, from human life and human affairs, because in his conception of Being all concrete individual existences—and therefore man too—disappeared; but in HERACLITUS of Ephesus the return to humanity is complete. Historians of philosophy long considered Heraclitus to be a physicist and described his doctrine that fire was the origin of all things as parallel to Thales' principle of water and Anaximenes' principle of air.[151] Yet the deep significance that fills the paradoxical aphorisms of 'the Dark' (as he was called) ought to have kept scholars from confusing his painfully repressed personality with that of a scientist devoted only to the search for facts. Nowhere throughout his work is there any trace either of a purely didactic attitude or of a purely physical theory of the universe. The utterances which could be taken to mean either that he was a physicist or that he was a teacher must not be detached from their context, for they cannot stand alone. No doubt he was greatly influenced by natural philosophy. The physicists' conception of reality, the cosmos, the incessant rise and fall of coming-to-be and passing-away, the inexhaustible first principle from which everything arises and to which everything returns, the circle of changing appearances through which Being passes—these fundamentally physical ideas were the basis of his philosophy.

Yet those who had preceded him in the search for an objective conception of the universe—the Milesians, and, even more rigorously, their opponent Parmenides—had dehumanised the problem, and had eventually lost sight of human life in the vast pattern of nature. Heraclitus, on the other hand, held that the human soul with all its emotions and sufferings was the centre of all the energies of the cosmos. He could not forget himself in contemplation of the high distant procession of natural events, in which the seer at last becomes the totality of things seen. Cosmic phenomena happened through him, he held, and for him. He believed that all his acts and words were only the effect in him of nature's power, although most men did not realize that they were merely the instruments wielded by a higher order.[152] That was the great novelty in Heraclitus' doctrines. His predecessors had completed the conception of the cosmos:[153] they had brought the Greeks to realize the eternal conflict between Being and Becoming. But now they were driven to ask the awful question: 'In this universal struggle, what place is there for man?' With restless energy and childlike eagerness, his contemporaries —Hecataeus and others—devoted themselves to the Milesian passion for manysided research (historia), collecting and assimilating quantities of historical traditions and geographical and ethnological data. But Heraclitus demolished this naïve rationalism by the blunt phrase 'Learning does not teach men to have sense';[154] and he expressed the revolutionary tendency of his own philosophy in one pregnant saying, 'I sought for myself'.[155] Humanization of philosophy could not be more trenchantly expressed.

No philosopher before Socrates awakes such keen personal

sympathy as Heraclitus. He stands at the very pinnacle of the
freedom of Ionian thought, and his 'I sought for myself' expresses the highest consciousness of selfhood. A nobleman by
birth, he speaks with a proud decision which appears at first
sight to be aristocratic arrogance converted to dogma by his own
genius. But he did not seek for himself by psychological research
into his own nature. Before him, philosophers had engaged in
logical reasoning, or in intellectually ordered observation of
phenomena; but now he revealed that a new world of knowledge
could be attained if the soul were to turn to contemplate herself.
There is an underlying connexion between his claim of self-study
and another of his sayings: 'Travel over every road, you cannot
discover the frontiers of the soul—it has so deep a *logos*'.[156]
This is the first appearance in Greek of the idea that the logos
and the soul can be *deep:* and Heraclitus' entire philosophy
flowed from this new spring of knowledge.

Logos for Heraclitus was not the conceptual thinking (νοεῖν,
νόημα) of Parmenides,[157] whose pure analytical logic would not
admit the metaphorical idea that the soul is boundless. It was a
form of knowledge, the origin of both 'action and speech'.[158]
If we want an example of this special type of knowledge, we
shall not find it in thought, which teaches that what is can never
not be, but in the insight which struck out such a brilliant truth as
'Ethos is man's daemon'.[159] It is highly important and significant
that in the very first sentence [160] of his book (a sentence which is
fortunately preserved) Heraclitus lays down that knowledge has
a productive relation to life. There he speaks of the words and
actions that men attempt without grasping the logos which alone
teaches them to 'do while awake' those actions which those without it do 'while asleep'. That is, logos can give a new life of conscious knowledge. It affects every sphere of human action.
Heraclitus was the first philosopher to introduce the idea of
φρόνησις and to put it on a level with σοφία: that is, he connected
knowledge of Being with insight into human values and conduct,
and made the former include the latter.[161] The prophetic tone of
his speech derived its logical power and urgency from his claim
as a philosopher to open men's eyes to their own actions, to reveal to them the foundations of life, to awake them from
sleep.[162] Many of his sayings confirm the view that he felt himself to be an interpreter of life. Nature and life are a *griphos,* a

riddle, a Delphic oracle, a Sibylline utterance—we must learn to read their *meaning*.[163] He feels that he is the solver of the riddle, the philosophic Oedipus who robs the Sphinx of her enigma : for 'Nature loves to hide herself'.[164]

This is a new way to philosophize: a novel conception of the philosopher's calling. It can be expressed only in words and metaphors drawn from intuition. Even the logos cannot be defined except in metaphor. The universality of the logos, of its evocative influence, of the self-consciousness that it awakes in the man whom it inspires, is most clearly expressed in Heraclitus' favourite contrast of sleep and waking.[165] He also mentions an essential quality of the logos, which distinguished it from the ordinary intellectual condition of the majority of mankind : it is 'common' or 'universal' (ξυνόν).[166] That is, it is the one cosmos which exists for the 'waking' alone, while the 'sleepers' each have their own private world, a world of dreams.[167] We must not imagine that this social universality of Heraclitus' logos is merely a metaphorical expression of the universal validity of logic. Community is the highest good known to the moral code of the city-state : it takes up and transforms the private existence of each individual. Thus, what at first seemed to be an exaggerated individualism in Heraclitus, his imperative and dictatorial attitude, is now revealed as the very opposite of individualism; for it is a deliberate destruction of the weak and erring individual caprice, in which the whole of life was almost lost. Men must follow the logos. The logos is a still higher and more universal 'community' than the law of the city; and upon it men can support their lives and their thoughts, and 'strengthen' themselves with it, 'as a city strengthens itself with law'.[168] 'Men live as if each of them had a private insight of his own'.[169]

From this it is obvious that Heraclitus is not thinking of the deficiencies of some kind of theoretical knowledge, but of the whole of human existence, of men's conduct in practice and of its failure to correspond to the universal spirit of the logos. There is a law in the universe, as in the city. This uniquely Greek idea appears here for the first time in history. And it embodies the educational genius of the Greek statesman and lawgiver at its very highest. Only the logos can comprehend the law that Heraclitus calls divine, the law by which 'all human laws are nourished'.[170] The logos is the mind—the organ that perceives the meaning of the cosmos. The thought which was implicit in Anaximander's conception of the universe now becomes explicit in Heraclitus' consciousness of selfhood—the idea of the logos which knows itself and its own place and effect in the scheme of the universe. By it lives and thinks the divine 'fire' which as life and thought is infused through the entire cosmos.[171] Through its divine origin it is able to penetrate the divine heart of nature from which it was born. Thus, within the new cosmos which his predecessors had discovered, Heraclitus gave man his place as a completely cosmic being. To live as a cosmic being, man must voluntarily learn, and obey the cosmic laws. Xenophanes had extolled 'wisdom' as the highest human virtue, because it was the source of law and order in the city;[172] so Heraclitus justifies its claim to supremacy by saying that it teaches men to follow in speech and action the truth of nature and its divine law.[173]

Heraclitus expressed the power and purpose of the cosmic wisdom, unrealizable by the average intellect, in his original doctrine of the warring forces within the unity of nature. That doctrine was in some degree borrowed from the concrete physical conceptions of the Milesian physicists; but ultimately it owed its living force, not to the suggestions of the philosophers, but to Heraclitus' own direct insight into the process of human existence, by which he saw both intellectual and physical activity as a strange complex unity, a bipolar life. 'Life', however, meant for him not only human but also cosmic existence. Only if understood as life, does the existence of the cosmos lose its apparent contradictions. Anaximander had held that coming-to-be and passing-away were the balanced forces of an eternal justice, or rather of a lawsuit of things before the tribunal of time, in which they must pay one another compensation for their unrighteousness and pleonexia.[174] Heraclitus simply said that conflict was 'the father of everything'.[175] Only in conflict could diké establish herself. Here he uses Anaximander's insight to give a visual interpretation to the new Pythagorean conception of harmony. 'That which opposes, fits; different elements make the finest harmony'.[176] That is a law which obviously rules the whole cosmos. Throughout nature there are abundance and lack—the causes of war. She is full of sharp opposites: day and night, summer and winter, heat and cold, war and peace, life and death succeed each other in eternal interchange.[177] All the conflicting opposites of

cosmic life constantly replace one another and are again replaced.[178] To continue the metaphor of the lawsuit, they keep
compensating each other. The whole process of the world is a
legal process—it is an interchange (ἀνταμοιβή), for the life of
one thing is the death of another in this eternal see-saw of
existence.[179] 'It rests by changing'.[180] 'Living and dead, waking
and sleeping, young and old are at bottom one and the same.
This changes, and is that; and that changes again, and is this'.[181]
'If you have not heard me, but my logos, it is wise for you to
admit that all things are one'.[182] As symbols for the clash and
harmony of opposites in the cosmos Heraclitus uses the bow and
the lyre. Both do their work by 'counterstriving conjunction'.[183]
The general conception which was needed in philosophical terminology here is that of tension: but it is supplied by the visual
image.[184] Heraclitean unity is full of tension. This brilliant insight into the meaning of life was to give an enormous stimulus
to the thought of subsequent ages: it has not, in fact, been estimated at its true value until our own time.

If we are to grasp what is new and essential in Heraclitus'
influence on Greek culture, we must here refrain from further
philosophical analysis of his doctrine of unity in opposites, and
in particular from any discussion of the difficult problem of its
relation to the teaching of Parmenides.[185] Compared with the
philosophers who preceded him, Heraclitus was the first philosophical anthropologist. His philosophy of humanity might be
figured as the innermost of three concentric circles: the outermost his theology, the next his cosmology, and within them both
his anthropology. In reality the three circles are inseparable;
at least his anthropology cannot be dissociated from his cosmological and theological teaching. For Heraclitus, man is part
of the cosmos, and as such he is subject to the laws of the cosmos
in the same way as all its other parts. But since, by virtue of his
own intellect, he harbours within himself the eternal law of the
life of the universe, he can share the highest wisdom, from
whose counsel springs the divine law. The freedom of the Greek
lies in the fact that he subordinates himself, as one part, to the
whole which is the city-state, and to its law. That is a different
kind of freedom from the liberty of modern individualism, which
always feels that it belongs to a suprasensual and universal
world, higher than the here-and-now world of the state. But the

philosophical liberty to which Heraclitus aspires never conflicts
with the Greek's allegiance to his polis: for in it Heraclitus
teaches that man is one part of a universal 'community' of all
things, and that he is subject to the law of that community.[186]
Our religious instinct naturally seeks a personal ruler for that
community, and Heraclitus too felt that need. 'One thing, which
alone is wise, will and will not be called by the name of Zeus'.[187]
But Greek political opinion at that time held that the rule of one
was tyranny: Heraclitus could reconcile this view with the religious impulse, because he held that law was not the opinion
of the majority but the emanation of the highest knowledge.
'Law is also obedience to the will of one alone'.[188]

Heraclitus' insight into the meaning of the world was the birth
of a new and nobler religion, an intellectual realization of the
way of the highest wisdom. Living and acting by that realization
were called φρονεῖν,[189] and Heraclitus, in prophetic words,
showed how to reach it by following the way of the philosophical
logos. The earliest physicists had not expressly posed the religious problem, for their conception of the universe was a de-
humanized world of being. The Orphic cult, to fill the gap,
taught that, though natural philosophy seemed to destroy mankind too in the midst of the confusion of universal coming-to-be
and passing-away, man's soul was really akin to the divine, and
so eternal.[190] Yet natural philosophy, in its concept of a cosmos
under the rule of diké, offered a focus on which religious ideals
might centre; and Heraclitus with his doctrine that man has a
place in the cosmos at last unified the two contrasting ways of
thought. And his conception of the soul raised the Orphic religion to a higher level, for he taught that through its kinship
with the 'everliving fire' of the cosmos the philosophical soul is
capable of knowing divine wisdom and harbouring it in itself.[191]
Thus the conflict between the cosmology and the religion of the
sixth century was resolved into unity in Heraclitus, who stood
at the threshold of the new century. We have already observed
that the cosmos of the Milesians was rather a universal moral
code than a law of nature in the modern sense. Heraclitus raised
its moral character to a cosmic religion, in his 'divine nomos',
and thus based the moral code of the philosophical man upon the
moral law of the entire universe.

THE ARISTOCRACY: CONFLICT AND TRANSFORMATION

THUS far, we have traced the influence of Ionian culture on the Greeks of the mainland and the west only in the religious and political struggles of Solon's Athens and in Xenophanes' crusade against traditional religion and the athletic ideals of the old nobility. The enemies of the aristocracy described their ideas as narrow and limited, themselves as muscle-bound, old-fashioned and anti-intellectual. Still, they were a powerful social force, quite apart from their numerical influence, and they offered a stern spiritual and intellectual resistance to the innovators. It must not be forgotten that, after Solon, who was more affected by Ionian influences than any of his successors, many of the poets of Greece proper [1] were passionate reactionaries. The two leaders of the reaction towards the end of the sixth century, Pindar the Theban and Theognis the Megarian, were both filled with whole-hearted admiration for the aristocracy to which they themselves belonged. Their work was addressed to the nobles, who had nothing but repulsion and distrust for the social revolution inspired by Ionian ideas. Yet these nobles did not live in a world which was a peaceful survival from the past, but in one which was incessantly invaded by the new age, and forced to defend itself with passionate energy. It was through that struggle for spiritual and material survival that the aristocracy acquired its fundamental conviction of its own innate value. Since we meet that conviction again and again in Theognis and Pindar, we must study them together, as representatives of a common cause, although there is a vast difference between their characters and their artistic achievements. For, while Pindar's work was in the field of choral lyric, and Theognis' in that of gnomic poetry, the two poets jointly represent one and the same stage in the history of culture. They are inspired by the class-consciousness of the nobility, with its proud assurance of its own merits:

they embody the aristocratic ideal of culture, as it was towards the end of the sixth century.

Thus carefully and authoritatively stated by Pindar and Theognis, the aristocratic ideal of Greece proper was infinitely superior in educational weight and completeness to the Ionian ideal, with its various self-contradictory attempts to glorify natural life and individual personality. Not only Hesiod, Tyrtaeus, and Solon, but Pindar and Theognis too, deliberately set out to educate their hearers; and in that purpose above all they differ from the ingenuous naturalism of all Ionian art and thought. No doubt the collision between the two sets of ideals intensified the character of both: yet that collision can hardly be the sole, or even the chief, reason for the fact that all the truly great educators of Greece appear to belong to the mainland tribes. Of course, the rule of the aristocracy (from which all impulses to higher culture arose) lasted longer on the mainland than in Ionia; and it may be partly because of that survival that any new movement there was necessarily embodied in a definite new human ideal opposed to the existing type. Xenophanes, proudly aware of his own intellectual energy, attacked the old feudal ideal as outworn and fossilized; yet in Pindar and Theognis that same ideal sprang suddenly into an astonishing new moral and religious vigour. They never allow us to forget their social position and the nature of the class which they address and represent; but their poetry is rooted in the ageless depths of humanity. Yet we must not be misled by the unwavering energy with which they proclaim their faith, into forgetting that they were defending a dying world. Their poetry did not commence a renaissance of the aristocracy in political and social life; still, it eternalized the aristocratic ideal at the moment when it was most gravely endangered by new forces, and it made the socially constructive powers of that ideal into a permanent possession of the Greek nation.

We owe it to the poets alone that we have any conception of the life and social condition of the Greek nobility in the sixth and fifth centuries. The plastic arts and the scanty remains of historians who deal with the period can only serve as illustrations of the essential truths which poetry has preserved. Of course the evidence of sculpture, architecture, and vase-painting is extremely valuable, but it cannot give us reliable information unless we study it as an expression of the ideals already stated by the poets. We must therefore dispense with a comprehensive historical account of social changes in Greece during that period, although we can trace a few of the principal events which occurred in important cities. The only complete picture we can construct—although it too has serious gaps—is that of the development of the Greek mind as expressed in books. Theognis and Pindar, each in a different way, provide two highly important masses of evidence for that process. (The recently discovered choral poetry of Bacchylides, which had previously been almost unknown, merely shows that Pindar's evidence, though scanty, is sufficient.) We may deal with Theognis first: because he was probably the elder of the two poets, and because he illustrates the dangerous social situation of the aristocracy during this period, whereas Pindar rather expresses its religious beliefs and its ideal of human character.

THE TRANSMISSION OF THEOGNIS' POEMS

First of all, we must discuss the process by which the poems attributed to Theognis have come down to us. Since almost every aspect of this difficult problem is disputed, the point of view which will be adopted in this book should be explained and defended.[2] Interesting as it is, it is essentially a philological problem; and I should not here investigate it in such detail if it would not enable us, by examining the transmission of Theognis' poems, to reach a deeper understanding of the history of that peculiar phase of Greek culture which is associated with his influence on subsequent generations.

The strange collection of poems which (by pure accident) has been handed down under the name of Theognis must have existed practically in its present form as early as the fourth century. Modern scholars have spent a good deal of trouble and thought on analysing its composition. It seems not to have passed through the refining fire of Alexandrian criticism.[3] Though it had been often used at the drinking-parties in the fifth and fourth centuries, it fell gradually into obscurity as the symposia themselves (once an important feature of Greek political life) were discontinued, and it came down to subsequent ages only as a literary curiosity. It is actually an anthology of maxims and poems by various poets of all periods from the seventh to the fifth centuries, attributed to Theognis because its nucleus is a book of his poems. Selections from it were sung at banquets to the music of the flute. From the frequent alterations and bowdlerisations of the original words we can see how often even the most famous verses were deformed by singers.[4] The selection, however, contains no poems later than the fifth century: that was the time when the Greek aristocracy ceased to be a political factor. Clearly the book survived chiefly in aristocratic circles: not only the Theognidean pieces in it but many other poems too express a violent hatred for the demos, the commons, and we can best imagine them as sung by the aristocratic political clubs at Athens in Critias' time—in the circle which produced the Old Oligarch's pamphlet on the constitution of Athens, and to which Plato himself was closely allied by birth. Plato's own dialogue, *The Banquet,* depicts the connexion of Eros and the symposium in its highest form;[5] and that connexion is clearly reflected in the history of the Theognidea, for the loosely connected book of songs which appears as Book II of the collection is devoted to the praise of Eros, who was always worshipped at such gatherings.

Fortunately, we need not rely on the sense of style alone in the attempt to separate Theognis' poetry from that of other authors and other ages. Many parts of the book are instantly recognizable as poems or fragments of poems by famous poets whose work we still possess. Others can be judged by more or less certain evidence. Theognis' own book comes at the beginning, and its structure makes it fairly easy to distinguish from the loosely connected extracts from other poets which follow it. Still, it is not a connected poem, but a collection of maxims. If it had been more closely knit, the work of others could never have been associated with it. Yet, loosely as it hangs together, it does possess an internal unity. Despite the comparative independence of each of the short pieces which compose the book, a single train of thought runs through them all; and they have an introduction and an epilogue [6] which sets them clearly apart from the remainder of the collection. In enucleating the genuine work of Theognis, we can use as a criterion not only the unmistakable tone of blunt Junkerish pride, but the repeated *address to Cyrnus* at the beginning of nearly every sentence. Similar forms of address appear in Hesiod's didactic poem to Perses, in the work of the iambic poets, and in the lyrics of Sappho and Alcaeus. Since Theognis is setting forth his teaching in a series of separate maxims, he repeats the address 'Cyrnus!' or 'Son of Polypaos!' frequently throughout the book, though not at the beginning of every axiom. (Cyrnus, son of Polypaos, was a young nobleman whom Theognis loved, and to whom he directs all his advice.) The same habit characterizes early Nordic didactic poetry: the name of the person addressed recurs again and again. Thus the address to Cyrnus in Theognis is a constant leit-motif by which we can recognize the genuine work of Theognis among the rest of the collection.

The address to Cyrnus is not found only in the poems which form the original book, and close with the epilogue; it appears here and there in the rest of the collection. However, it is extremely frequent all through Theognis' own book of maxims, while elsewhere its occurrences are rare and closely grouped together. We must therefore conclude that the poems in which it appears outside the main body of Theognis' work are—provided they are not forgeries—quotations taken from what was once a more complete collection of his poems. Some of them actually appear inside as well as outside his book: such a repetition would be impossible in one single anthology. It is clear, then, that the latter part of the collection was originally an independent anthology, which contained passages from Theognis as well as from other poets. It was assembled at a period when Theognis had already become a classical poet—at latest, towards the end of the fifth century or the beginning of the fourth century. Plato [7] expressly says that anthologies of the kind were used as schoolbooks at that time; and it could also have been employed at symposia. Later still, both these books—the original *Maxims of Theognis* with its prologue and epilogue, and the anthology of *Sayings from the Poets*—were blended into the single collection which we now possess. (The blending was crudely done, as is plain from the fact that no one took the trouble to remove the repetitions, whether they were noticed or not.) Accordingly, we must form our estimate of Theognis not only from the connected book of maxims, but also from the scattered pieces which appear here and there in the anthology following it. But the maxims, the 'Sayings to Cyrnus', are the foundation on which all else depends. We must therefore study them more closely, before we enquire how much can be learnt of Theognis from the other fragments which have come down to us in the anthology.

How do we know that the 'Sayings to Cyrnus' were actually written by Theognis? Like that of so many other poets, his name could well have disappeared from this or any other general collection of poems; for the author of popular banqueting songs was seldom able to perpetuate his claim to their authorship. But Theognis used a special stylistic device to mark his own work with an unmistakable sign of copyright. He handed his own name down to posterity in the prologue to his book, and thus not only assured himself of immortality but set his stamp— or, as he called it, his *seal*—upon all his work. Here are his own words: [8] 'Cyrnus, my seal is to be artfully set on these poems, so that they will never be stolen without detection, nor will anyone take bad poetry when good is at hand. And everyone will say "These are the verses of Theognis the Megarian—he is famous among all men". Yet I cannot please all my fellow-citizens, and no wonder, son of Polypaos; for not even God pleases everyone when he sends rain or holds it back.'

These words express the artist's highly developed consciousness of his mission and his endeavour to maintain his claim to his own creations: and in that they are comparable with the signatures which then for the first time began to appear on vase-paintings and pieces of sculpture. It is particularly interesting to trace this emphasis on individual achievement in the conventional aristocratic character of Theognis, because it shows that the spirit of his age influenced him more deeply than he knew. It cannot be doubted that, by the imprint of the seal, he meant the incorporation of his name into his poems: for, in the first place, a seal bears the name or device of its owner, and, secondly, the statement of his plan to stamp his poetry with a seal is immediately followed by the statement of his own name. It was of course not an entirely new custom for an author to mention his name at the beginning of his book; but the example set by Hesiod in the introduction to the *Theogony* had not been imitated, and only Theognis' immediate predecessor, the gnomic poet Phocylides of Miletus, had marked his maxims with his own name—obviously because his peculiar type of verses could easily pass into general circulation as proverbs without the name of their creator. Yet several famous poetic utterances by Phocylides and Theognis are cited by later authors simply as anonymous proverbs. Those of Phocylides were especially subject to this danger because they were separate maxims with no continuous line of thought to knit them together: therefore he attached his name to every one of them. The first line of his couplets always begins, 'This too said Phocylides: . . .' Hipparchus, son of Pisistratus, copied him when he wrote maxims to be inscribed on the statues of Hermes which were set up on the highroads of Attica, and began each of them with the words 'Hipparchus' monument:' and then continued, 'keep faith with friends', or 'walk on in justice'.[9] Theognis did not need to go so far as this, for as we have seen his work formed a more or less connected whole which was to be handed down without dissection or disturbance: it was the inherited educational wisdom of the aristocracy. As he himself says in the prologue and in the epilogue, he expected knowledge of his book to spread 'throughout the world, over both land and sea'.[10] To safeguard his claim to it and to preserve its teaching, it was enough for him to give his own name at the beginning, as did all the authors in the then newly discovered sphere of prose literature. A modern writer need not take such precautions, because his name and the title of his book are printed on the titlepage. But in the late sixth century books had no titlepage, so that the only solution was that adopted by Hecataeus, and later by Herodotus and Thucydides, to begin a book by giving one's name and the statement of one's purpose in writing it. In the medical writings which are handed down under the name of Hippocrates there is no designation of individual authors, so that we have no means of telling who or what the author of each treatise was. In poetry the device of the seal never became as popular as in prose: apart from the instances given above, it is found only in the musical nomes of the fifth century, where we call 'seal' the section towards the end of the poem in which the poet gives his name.[11] Whether this practice was borrowed from Theognis or not, we cannot now tell.

In view of the vicissitudes which Theognis' book suffered in the centuries after it was written, scholars have recently suggested that he could not possibly have ensured his copyright to it without sealing each individual couplet. The 'seal' has therefore been considered to be simply the vocative 'Cyrnus!' [12] This is a very convenient theory; for it seems to enable us to determine the authenticity of any couplet in a quick, mechanical, and yet decently objective manner, whereas without such a criterion the whole problem will always be complex and uncertain. But Theognis could scarcely foresee the difficulties which would beset scholars nearly three thousand years after his death, when only one copy of his book survived. That is what actually happened—our text of Theognis depends on one ancient manuscript, and one alone. He hoped his book would always be in everyone's hands, though he could scarcely expect to live for thousands of years. He could not anticipate that a century after his death his book would be ruthlessly abbreviated, anthologized, and finally tacked onto the poems of many anonymous authors to make a songbook for the dinner-table. Least of all could he expect that when he incorporated his own name into the prelude to his poem, the trick would not defend him from plagiarism, but would allow all the nameless poems which were added to make up the anthology to be fathered on him. Still, we may be thankful that the seal of his name set at the beginning of his book allows us to evoke his true character from its concealment in the debris of other poets. It would be impossible so to evoke any of the other writers in the anthology: so far, therefore, Theognis did attain his purpose.

But from internal grounds it is impossible to hold that the seal is simply the form of address to Cyrnus. The more closely we study the Cyrnus-book, the more impossible we find it to separate the maxims addressed to Cyrnus from the others—for they all form part of one continuous train of thought. We are of course always in danger of accepting, among the poems which do not contain Cyrnus' name, work which is not by Theognis although it is contained in the old book of maxims: in fact, immediately before the epilogue (and therefore within the limits bounding the authentic work of Theognis) a poem by Solon appears.[13] Yet that poem disturbs the train of thought so gravely that, even if we did not know from other sources that it was by Solon, we should eject it as foreign to the Theognidean work. Neither this nor any other problem can be solved without careful study and criticism of the content and form of each poem, and it is now generally admitted that even the name Cyrnus (especially outside the limits of the book of maxims) is not an absolute guarantee of the authenticity of any poem.

We must therefore build up our picture of Theognis principally from the complete book of 'Sayings to Cyrnus', for it is in that book above all that his personality is comprehensible. A few traits can be added from the scattered Cyrnus-maxims which appear in the collection appended to the Sayings; but it must be remembered that there we are working in the dark, for we cannot recapture the original turn of thought which connected and preserved Theognis' sayings, and the value of the separate maxims is therefore gravely diminished. Those poems, outside Theognis' own book, which are not addressed to Cyrnus, cannot be used as evidence—because we cannot determine which of them are by Theognis, and which by other poets. But special mention is due to a beautiful set of verses [14] by some Megarian poet, which seem to be excerpts from the prologue to an independent poem, and are usually held to be Theognidean. They are filled with the joviality of a drinking-party, though it is oppressed and intensified by the threatening danger of the Persian invasion. If Theognis wrote them, he survived until 490 or even 480 B.C. Yet our admittedly scanty knowledge of the internal politics of Megara would lead us to place the 'Sayings to Cyrnus' considerably earlier than that: they seem to describe Megara as it was about the middle of the sixth century. Ancient scholars held that he lived and worked about 544 B.C.: though unfortunately we cannot check their statement.[15] The poems which mention the Persian invasion give us little help either way. But their spirit appears to be a little different from that of the Cyrnus-book; and from the manner in which their author uses Theognis' own work it would seem that the bold hypothesis of a second Megarian poet who followed Theognis is less improbable than it has been considered. But since the poems have only two small coincidences with Theognis' prologue, we must acknowledge that the hypothesis is at present, though not improbable, based on insufficient evidence.

THE CODIFICATION OF THE ARISTOCRATIC EDUCATIONAL
TRADITION

Structurally, Theognis' book of 'Sayings to Cyrnus' belongs
to the same species as Hesiod's *Works and Days* and the maxims
of Phocylides. It is a collection of ὑποθῆκαι, 'teachings'.[16] The
word appears at the end of the prologue, immediately before the
beginning of the maxims proper. 'I shall teach you, Cyrnus, in
friendly fashion, the things which I myself learnt from the
nobles when I was still a boy'.[17] The essence of his teaching
therefore is that it is not the ideas of Theognis himself but the
tradition of his class. An early attempt to reduce the principles
of aristocratic culture and training to poetry was the *Teachings
of Chiron*, mentioned in a previous chapter.[18] The aphorisms of
Phocylides of Miletus are meant to be general guides to the conduct of life. The new attitude of Theognis is particularly significant when contrasted with the work of Phocylides on the one
hand and of Hesiod on the other. His aim is to expound all the
principles of aristocratic education, the hallowed doctrines which
until he wrote had only been verbally transmitted from father
to son. Thus his work is a deliberate parallel and contrast to
Hesiod's codification of the principles of peasant wisdom.

Cyrnus, the young man to whom the poems are addressed, was
bound to Theognis by Eros. The poet obviously considers that
bond to be the basis of his educational relationship to him; and
it was meant to make the man and the boy a typical couple, in
the eyes of the class to which they both belonged. It is very significant that the first time we have an opportunity of studying
the Dorian aristocracy closely we should find that homosexual
love is a ruling motive in their character. We need not here discuss this phenomenon, which is at present the subject of such
keen debate; for it is not the purpose of this book to describe
society for its own sake. But we must point out the position and
the basis of homosexual love in the spiritual life of the Greek
people. It must be recognized that the love of a man for a youth
or a boy was an essential part of the aristocratic society of early
Greece, and was inextricably bound up with its moral and social
ideals. It has been called, specifically, *Dorian* boy-love;[19] and
the description is so far correct that the practice always remained

more or less foreign to Ionian and Athenian popular sentiment, as is shown by Attic comedy above all else. The customs of the ruling class naturally came to be adopted by the rich bourgeois; and among them was παιδικὸς ἔρως. But the Athenian poets and legislators who accept or praise it were chiefly aristocrats, from Solon (whose poems name boy-love as one of the best things in life,[20] comparable to sport and the love of women) to Plato.[21] And the aristocrats throughout Greece were very strongly influenced by the Dorian nobles. It is true, then, that the Greeks themselves even in the classical period had vastly different opinions of the morality of the widespread practice of homosexual love because it was connected with definite social and historical traditions. From this point of view it is much easier for us to understand why large sections of the nation despised or punished it, while in other social strata it had developed until, for men at least, it was part of the highest conceptions of moral nobility and spiritual perfection.[22]

It is, after all, easy to understand how a passionate admiration of noble bodies and balanced souls could spring up in a race which for countless years had prized physical prowess and spiritual harmony as the highest good attainable by man, and which had striven by grave and ceaseless rivalry, by exertion involving the utmost energies of mind and body alike, to bring these qualities to the greatest possible perfection. Men who loved the possessors of these enviable qualities were moved by an ideal, the love for areté. Lovers who were bound by the male Eros were guarded by a deeper sense of honour from committing any base action, and were driven by a nobler impulse in attempting any honourable deed.[23] The Spartan state deliberately made Eros a factor, and an important factor, in its ἀγωγή.[24] And the relation of the lover to his beloved had a sort of educational authority similar to that of the parent to the child; in fact, it was in many respects superior to parental authority at the age when youths began to ripen into manhood and to cast off the bonds of domestic authority and family tradition. It is impossible to doubt the numerous affirmations of the educational power of Eros, which reach their culmination in Plato's *Symposium*. Such, then, was the power which inspired the educational doctrines of the aristocrat Theognis. The erotic aspect of that power, which is easily overlooked in comparison with its passionate moral earnestness, is voiced at the end of his book [25] in accents of anguished intensity. 'I have given you wings, Cyrnus, with which you will fly over land and sea. . . . At every feast and revel you will be on the lips of many a guest; lovely youths will sing your name clearly and beautifully to the music of flutes; and when you have gone down to the dead you will still wander through the land of Greece and the islands of the sea, to be sung by men of the future as long as earth and sun shall remain. Yet I get no respect from you, for with your talk you deceive me like a little child.'

For many years the severe eukosmia of the noblemen's symposia under the rule of Eros remained unshaken. But the time of Theognis saw a change. From Solon's poetry we have seen how the aristocracy had to fight for its position either against the threat of tyranny or against the growing power of the common people. By Solon the nobles are presented as a narrow and exclusive party, whose political supremacy meant wasteful misgovernment and caused the suppressed masses to thrust huge and dangerous demands upon the state. The danger thus created had prompted Solon to construct his system of political morality, with its attempt to uphold the mean between the extremes and to guard the state from tyranny.[26] The poems of Theognis too assume that the class-war is in full fury. At the beginning of his book he sets several fairly long poems which cast an interesting light on the whole condition of society. The first elegy [27] is obviously modelled on Solon's poetry, in style, structure, and emotional tone. But there is an important difference: for Solon, though himself an aristocrat, knew the weaknesses of his class as well as its merits, and taxes it with them; while Theognis asserts that the opponents of aristocracy alone are responsible for the unrest and injustice which fill his city. Clearly the situation in Megara had developed to the disadvantage of the old landowning nobility. The leaders, he says, are distorting justice and spoiling the people: they are greedy for money and for ever greater power. He foretells that the peace which holds the city at present will end in civil war, and then in tyranny. The only remedy which he seems to know is that the state should return to the old constitution, in which the aristocracy holds its rightful privileges: and that remedy seems to be impossible of attainment.

A second poem [28] completes this gloomy picture. 'The city is still the same, but its people have changed. Men who never knew anything of justice and the law, but wore away goatskins on their ribs and laired outside the city like wild deer—these men are now the nobles, Cyrnus, and those who once were noble are now poor wretches. It is an unbearable sight! And they laugh at one another and deceive one another and know no steady standard to tell them what is noble and ignoble, because they have no tradition. Make none of these citizens your true friend, Cyrnus, for any purpose whatever. Speak to them all in friendly words, but do not associate with them in any serious purpose; for you will learn the character of these miserable fellows, and see that they cannot be trusted in anything. Treachery, deceit, and wiles are what these hopeless creatures love.'

It would be a grave error to read this poem as a document merely of hatred and contempt and not also of the most savage resentment. We must take it in conjunction with the first elegy to see the narrow class-interpretation which Theognis here gives to Solon's doctrine that justice is the basis of all social order. But it would be too much to expect the old master-class, now overthrown, to cling to Solon's ideal of universal justice throughout the state: and even a disinterested observer must acknowledge that the distressed nobleman's appeal to that ideal gives his picture of the city much of the emotional intensity of true poetry. The lofty elegiac style here derives new vigour and vividness from the invective realism which Theognis borrowed from the iambic poets. But his description of the rule of injustice, though partly modelled on Solon's great iambic poem, is perhaps even more strongly influenced by Hesiod's *Works and Days:* for it was obviously the Hesiodic pattern which led him to construct his book in two main sections held together by a prologue and an epilogue. [29] And his imitation of Hesiod was not confined to the structure of his poem, but arose from the similarity of their spiritual situation and outlook. In the *Works and Days* Hesiod was prompted to describe the whole moral code of the peasant worker, with its general doctrines as well as their particular applications, by his dispute with his brother Perses about a matter of property—the poem therefore turns on a question of justice. In the same way, Theognis was impelled to expound the morality of the aristocracy by his intellectual hatred

for the social revolution. The first section of both works is inspired by a complaint against the distortion of justice, and both
poets develop that thought in several long arguments. This striking parallel still holds when we turn to the second part of
Theognis' book, which is a collection of brief aphorisms clearly
modelled on the second part of the *Works and Days*. The analogy is not disturbed by the presence, in the latter part of Theognis' work, of several longer pieces which range from three or
four couplets to short reflective elegies. In the true archaic manner, both poets were led, by their own personal situation and the
needs of the moment, to utter eternally valid truths. And the
resulting lack of artistic balance between the two sections of the
book is for modern minds counteracted by the gain in personal
expression and emotional intensity—so much so in fact that we
might easily make the mistake of believing that this free utterance of personal emotion was a universal rule, and of interpreting the whole poem as a personal utterance, whereas it was
meant to be a statement of objective truth.

The second elegy in the first part of the book sets forth the
theme of the collection of moral aphorisms which follows it: the
injustice and perfidy of the class which now rules Megara, says
Theognis, is due to the fact that it has no standards [30] of what is
noble and ignoble. That is the fact which he wishes to impress
upon Cyrnus, so that the boy may distinguish himself from the
mob by truly noble self-discipline and behaviour. Only he who
has tradition possesses these standards. It is now time for that
tradition to be preserved for the world by a man who can couch
it in immortal phrases: and so it can show the wellbred youth
how to become a true nobleman. Theognis warns his pupil not
to associate with bad men (κακοί, δειλοί)—that is his concrete
description of everyone and everything which has not been produced by aristocratic training, as opposed to the nobles (ἀγαθοί,
ἐσθλοί) who are only found among the peers of Theognis himself. This dichotomy is one of his principal themes: he lays it
down as an axiom early in the book, when he announces his intention of handing on the ancestral doctrines of his class,[31] and
he repeats it later, at the beginning of the collection of aphorisms.[32] Between the description of his purpose and the aphorisms stands the section devoted to politics;[33] it gives the factual
ground for Theognis' command, 'Mix with the nobles, do not

associate with bad men', by picturing the degradation of those bad men in the darkest colours. His whole teaching exemplifies what he means by mixing with the nobles, for he himself puts on the authority of true nobility to teach his young fellow-noblemen the truth.

We need not follow the whole course of Theognis' thought through the collected aphorisms of the second half of his book. Every word he writes and every injunction he makes derives its peculiar force and urgency from the imminence of the danger which has been brought home by his description of social conditions in Megara. He begins with a long string of *gnomai*, maxims warning his pupil against making friends with bad ignoble men, because they are untrustworthy.[34] His advice is to have few friends—men who do not say this to your face and that behind your back, and men on whom you can count in time of trouble. Every revolution produces a violent disturbance of credit and confidence; and men who hold the same political faith are drawn closer to one another, for treachery is spread far and wide. Theognis himself says that a trustworthy man is worth much gold at times of political discord.[35] Is this still the old aristocratic code?

That code had indeed idealized the friendship of Theseus and Pirithous, and of Achilles and Patroclus: and the reverence for a great example such as these is a very old element in aristocratic education. But now, when the aristocracy has been attacked and has fallen, the old doctrine of the value of good examples and noble friendships is transformed into a party-principle: the friendship of the ancient heroes is now a model for the friendship of members of the same political *hetairia*.[36] It is impossible to avoid this conclusion from the fact that Theognis begins his teaching by insisting upon the correct choice of friends and on the necessity of well-tested loyalty as the first condition of friendship. Possibly he himself had learnt this from his parents, for the struggles of the aristocracy had lasted for many years. In any case, the social conflict had altered the nature of the old aristocratic moral code: hard times make narrow minds. Although its origin made that code fundamentally different from the new classless state-morality represented by Solon, the aristocrats were now compelled to consider themselves part and parcel of the state. No doubt they could still regard their class as a secret state within the state, lament its unjust overthrow, and plot for its restoration; but to the dispassionate observer it was only a political party struggling for power and kept from collapse by the innate feeling of class-solidarity. The old injunction to avoid evil communications now changes into a demand for political exclusiveness. This general distortion of the code resulted from the weakness of the nobility; and yet there was much true moral worth in the demand for loyalty (although it was political loyalty to one class which was meant) and for unconditional honesty as the precondition of friendship. That demand is the ultimate expression of political *esprit de corps,* the spirit which haughtily condemns its enemies thus:[37] 'the new people laugh when they betray one another'. It is not to be compared with the lofty state-ideal of Solon, and yet we cannot deny the earnestness of its chief commandment, that the ἀγαθός, the nobleman, shall be noble in conduct as well as in birth. Theognis believed that the identification of nobility with noble character was the strength of his class, and its last defence in the struggle for existence.

All Theognis' teaching is coloured by that insistence on carefully chosen friendships. The social revolution had driven him and his class to adopt this protective attitude. But although the aristocracy had developed into a party, we must not regard it as simply a political party. It had merely been compelled to close its ranks and stand on the defensive. Since meanwhile it was in a minority, and had no chance of winning back its supremacy, Theognis cautions his young friend against deliberately accepting existing conditions, and says,[38] 'Walk in the middle of the road, as I do'. By that he does not mean the heroic stand of Solon, exposed to the attacks of both extremes,[39] but a safe and cunning avoidance of any outright offensive or even defensive action. Cyrnus is to play a deep game, to vary his character with his various friends; he is to be like the octopus, which takes the colour of the stone to which it clings, and changes its hue whenever necessary.[40] In fact, Theognis recommends protective mimicry in the struggle for life against the demos. The moral difficulty of the struggle lies in the fact that it must necessarily be a secret one; but Theognis believes that even in such conditions a nobleman will always remain noble. He even holds that the nobleman is 'a citadel and a tower for the emptyheaded commons, although he gets little honour for it'.[41] This code is not a mass of contradictions: it is a necessary consequence of the position of the aristocracy. But it is certainly not the old aristocratic code of ethics.

One of the most revolutionary changes in that code was the altered conception of areté. This alteration was closely connected with the fundamental cause of the revolution—namely, the redistribution of economic power among the several classes of society. The position of the old aristocracy had been founded on its possession of landed property, and had been gravely shaken by the appearance of money as a new means of exchange. We do not know whether political factors had also affected the situation; but certainly by the time of Theognis the nobility was, at least in part, reduced to poverty, and a new class of rich plebeians was rising to political power and social influence. This economic change was a serious blow to the old aristocratic conception of areté, which had always included the possession of social prestige and the external goods of life, for without them many specific qualities of the nobleman, such as liberality and magnanimity, could not be put into action.[42] Even for simple peasants wealth had meant areté and respect, in Hesiod's words: [43] the phrase shows that the early Greek conception of areté always included a considerable degree of social prominence and influence.

That conception of areté was broken up by the impact of the new city-state morality. Whenever the aristocratic ideal of areté is attacked or altered (particular instances are Tyrtaeus and Solon), we can see how closely it was connected with wealth (ὄλβος, πλοῦτος) and how difficult it was for it to survive when the connexion was broken. Tyrtaeus had declared that the areté of the citizen—which, during Sparta's struggles with Messenia, was soldierly courage above all else—was worth more than wealth and all the goods which the noblemen prized; [44] and Solon had said the same of the highest political virtue of the constitutional state, justice.[45] Yet Solon had been nurtured in the old tradition: and he prayed to the gods to send him wealth (righteous wealth, be it said) and founded his hopes of areté and prestige upon the possession of wealth.[46] He did not believe that unequal distribution of property was contrary to the will of God, for he knew there were other forms of wealth besides gold and land—the natural riches of health and the joy of life.[47] If he had been compelled to choose between areté and wealth, he would have chosen areté.[48]

It is instructive to compare these positive, forward-looking, revolutionary ideas with the weak regrets of Theognis, who never tired of uttering complaints and curses against poverty. He declared that it had an infinite power over men's lives, and he had doubtless known poverty himself.[49] Yet, for all his hatred of being poor, he retained some standards and aspirations higher than mere wealth—standards to which he believed that wealth should be willingly sacrificed. From watching the hateful parvenus of Megara, he found how seldom money and spiritual nobility go together, and he was compelled to acknowledge the worthiness of Solon's preference for righteous poverty.[50] In Theognis' attitude to poverty and riches, we can trace with perfect clarity the transvaluation of the old aristocratic conception of virtue, under the impact of social and economic change: the ideals of Theognis were forcibly altered, while Solon's were born of the freedom of his own spirit.

All Theognis' poems reflect this keen interest in Solon's views of areté and wealth. The political elegies in the first part of his book [51] were inspired by Solon's *Eunomia,* and the poems which appear among his shorter aphorisms by Solon's great address to the Muses.[52] This latter poem is a meditation on man's efforts to win wealth and success, from the point of view of the rightness of the divine government of the universe. It falls into two parts, which express the two sides of a great contrast. Theognis took these two themes and wrote an independent poem on each of them—thereby destroying the sublime justification of the ways of God to man which in Solon's poem was the conception binding the two parts together. He was not in fact capable of working out such a deep religious truth with the sublimity and objectivity of Solon. Solon's first thought— that God's power is seen in the fact that wealth won by injustice does not prosper in the long run—stirs Theognis to comparatively subjective reflections. He agrees with Solon, of course, but he adds that men constantly forget this truth because the punishment of wickedness comes so slowly. We can trace in his words the impatience of the partisan of a defeated cause, who expects heaven's revenge to fall on his opponents, but fears that he himself may not live to see it.

In his variations on the theme stated in the second part of Solon's poem, Theognis neglects the essential problem, which is this: although the government of the universe is invariably just (as Solon has shown in the first part), why do the endeavours of the good so often fail, while the mistakes of the evildoer have no bad results? This moral dilemma awakes no interest in Theognis whatever; far less does he consider the question from God's point of view, like Solon, and thus find a suprapersonal law of compensation in the chaos of human hopes and efforts. Once more Solon's presentation of the problem awakes in Theognis only a subjective response, a mood of quiet personal resignation. He has learnt from his own experience of life that men are never responsible for their own success or failure. Nothing is left then, except to abandon oneself to the will of God, for one can contribute nothing to one's own destiny. Even wealth, prosperity, and honour, he says elsewhere, have the seeds of ruin latent within them; so that we need pray for only one thing: *tyché*, fortune.[53] What good can money do to a base man, if it falls to his lot? His mind is not 'straight,' and his money can only bring destruction to him.[54]

Accordingly, Theognis holds that areté is the quality which characterizes the true nobleman when the presence or absence of wealth is left out of account: namely, the very rare quality of spiritual nobility.[55] Some have held that he was incapable of such lofty moral sentiments; but the fact is that his respect for the impoverished aristocracy taught him to moralize in Solon's manner. And there is no real ground for denying him the authorship of the beautiful maxim: [56] 'In justice all virtue is summed up, and every just man is a nobleman.' Though he may have taken over this thought from a commoner like Phocylides,[57] he could not help adopting it as the motto of his own party; for the masses in their struggle for power had borne it on their banner, and then, as Theognis saw, they had trampled it to the ground. Now it became the rallying-cry of the old ruling class: though now unjustly oppressed, they alone had once 'known justice and law' and were still, in Theognis' eyes, the only possessors of true righteousness.[58] No doubt this view limits the scope of the supreme ideal of justice, and makes it the virtue of one party, not a virtue which can be possessed by the whole state. But Theognis would not be repelled by that limitation. Pindar too believed that justice was an essential and inseparable element of aristocratic culture, and in fact its full flower. That belief marked the conquest of the old aristocratic ideal by the new spirit of the city-state.

There was still one barrier to the complete assimilation of that spirit by the nobility—their unshakable belief in the virtues of noble blood. Theognis affirms that their highest duty is to preserve their purity of descent, and bitterly attacks the foolish and disloyal nobles who attempt to prop their fallen fortunes by marrying the daughters of rich commoners, or giving their daughters to the sons of parvenus. 'We select rams and asses and horses which are noble, and try to breed them from good stock: but a nobleman does not hesitate to marry a baseborn woman; wealth confuses breed'.[59] This sharp emphasis on the selective nature of noble birth and training is a sign that the aristocratic code has undergone a change. It is now on the defensive, in the struggle against the levelling power of money and numbers. In Athens, where the whole state had to face and solve great communal problems, the wisest men could not continue to be mere reactionaries, although they were largely aristocrats. Solon himself had risen above reaction and opposition. But wherever there was a small aristocracy fighting to preserve its existence and its peculiar way of life, it saw its own image in the educational maxims of Theognis. Many of his ideas were revived at a later stage, during the struggle of the bourgeoisie against the proletariat; and in the last resort the value of his teaching stands or falls with the existence of an aristocracy, whether it owes its position to its descent or to some other lofty tradition. The essentially aristocratic idea that a race must be preserved by inbreeding and special training was worked out in Sparta above all, and also by the great educational theorists of the fourth century; we shall study it in more detail when we discuss their work.[60] It is enough meanwhile to say that both in Sparta and in the theories of Plato and Aristotle this ideal was extended beyond the limits of one class,[61] and became part of the general Greek ideal that the city-state is the educator of all its citizens.

PINDAR, THE VOICE OF ARISTOCRACY

When we turn from Theognis to Pindar, we leave the fierce struggles of the nobility in Megara and elsewhere to defend its place in society, and mount to the summit of the calm, proud, inviolate life of early Greek aristocracy. At this height we can forget the problems and conflicts of Theognis' world, and be content to marvel at the power and beauty of that noble and distant ideal. Pindar shows us the Hellenic ideal of an aristocracy of race in the hour of its noblest transfiguration, when, after centuries of glory extending from the mythical past to the hard modernity of the fifth century, the nobility could still draw the gaze of all Greece upon its exploits at the games of Olympia and Pytho, Nemea and the Corinthian Isthmus, and could still transcend all regional or racial dissidences in the universal admiration of its triumphs. It is this aspect of Greek aristocracy that we must study if we are to see that the part it played in the shaping of the Greek character was more than the jealous preservation of inherited class-privilege and class-prejudice, and the cultivation of a relentlessly intensified code of ethics based on property.[62] It was the true creator of the lofty ideal of humanity which is manifest to this day—though more often admired than understood—in the Greek sculptures of the archaic and classical periods.[63] The athlete whom these works portray in the harmonious strength and nobility of this utmost perfection lives, feels, and speaks for us again in Pindar's poetry, and through his spiritual energy and religious gravity still affects us with the strange power which is given only to the unique and irrecoverable achievements of the human spirit.[64] For it was a uniquely precious moment when the God-intoxicated but human world of Greece saw the height of divinity in the human body and soul raised to a perfection high above earthly powers, and when in those gods in human shape the effort of man to copy that divine model through which artists had realized the law of perfection, unattainable but imperious, found its purpose and its happiness.

Pindar's poetry, though archaic, is archaic in a different sense from the works of his contemporaries and even of his predecessors. Compared with it, Solon's iambics seem thoroughly modern in language and feeling. Pindar's variety, his plenitude, his logi-

cal difficulty are only the outward and, as it were, modern guise
of his deep-seated sense of the past—a love of antiquity which
was rooted in the severe austerity of his nature and the remoteness of his actual life.[65] To pass from the 'older' civilization of Ionia to Pindar is like leaving the direct line of development which runs from the Homeric poems to the personal lyrics
and the natural philosophy of the Ionians, and entering a different world. Although Hesiod was a faithful student of Homer
and of Ionian ideas, the reader of Hesiod is often astonished by
sudden glimpses into the dark prehistory of mainland Greece,
buried far beneath the foundations of the epic. Much more so,
when we open Pindar, we are at once in a world unknown to the
Ionia of Hecataeus and Heraclitus, a world which is in many
ways older than Homer and Homer's characters, lit as they are
by the first brilliance of Ionian thought. For although Pindar's
faith in the mission of the nobility has much in common with
Homer, Homer takes it lightly, almost gaily, while the younger
poet speaks of it in deadly earnest. This is partly brought about
by the difference of purpose between epic and the Pindaric hymn:
the latter gives a solemn religious injunction, while the former
relates and adorns. Still, the grave severity of Pindar is not
simply dictated by the form and external purpose of his poems:
it springs from his deeply-felt kinship with and reverence for the
aristocracy of which he writes. It is because his own nature is
essentially aristocratic by birth and nurture that he can give the
aristocratic ideal the compelling force which we call Pindaric.[66]

In ancient times the volume of his work was considerably
greater than what we now possess. It was only recently that a
fortunate discovery in Egypt made us acquainted with his religious poetry, which had been quite lost.[67] There was much
more of it than of his hymns of victory (later called the
epinikia), but it was not essentially different from them.[68] For
the religious meaning of the athletic contest was embodied in all
his songs for the victors at the four great games; and the religious life of the nobility reached a culminating point in the incomparable energy and ambition of the contest.

Since the earliest ages of known history, Greek gymnastic
activity (in the broadest sense of the word) had been connected
with the festivals of the gods. Perhaps the Olympic games originated from funeral games held for Pelops at Olympia, like the

games which the *Iliad* describes as held for Patroclus at Troy. It is known that even funeral games could be celebrated at fixed and recurrent occasions: they were so repeated for Adrastus at Sicyon, although there they assumed a different character.[69] Old-established contests of that kind may easily have been taken over into the service of the Olympian Zeus. And from the votive images of horses discovered beneath the foundations of the earlier Olympic sanctuary, it is plain that there were chariot-races at the ancient cult-centre of Olympia long before the traditional date when Coroebus won the first victory in the footrace.[70] During the early centuries of Greek history, the three other regular Panhellenic games grew up on the model of Olympia, and by Pindar's time they were comparable with it, although they never reached its importance. The development of the various contests from the simple footrace into the multiform programme reflected in Pindar's hymns was by late chronologists arranged in accurately divided temporal stages, but the value of their evidence is disputed.[71]

But here we need concern ourselves neither with the history of the contests nor with their technical aspect. Naturally, competitive athletics was originally an aristocratic exercise: this is confirmed by poetry, and was an essential precondition of Pindar's view of it. Although in his time the gymnastic contests had long ceased to be the preserve of the nobility alone, the old families still took a leading part in them. They had enough wealth and leisure to allow them to engage in prolonged training. And among them the tradition survived by which athletic prowess was highly valued, while also the peculiar qualities of character and physique which fitted men for athletics were most easily inherited by their members—although in time members of the bourgeoisie too developed the same qualities and traditions and won victories in the games. It was not till after Pindar's day that the inflexible energy and undying tradition of centuries of aristocracy were forced to give way before professionalism, and only then did Xenophanes' attack on the overestimation of coarse unintellectual 'strength of body' call forth a late but lasting echo.[72] As soon as the Greeks began to feel that the spirit was different from or even hostile to the body, the old athletic ideal was degraded beyond hope of salvation, and at once lost its important position in Greek life, although athletics survived for centuries more as a mere sport. Originally, nothing could have been more foreign to it than the purely intellectual conception of *physical* strength or efficiency. The ideal unity of physical and spiritual which (although it is irreparably lost to us) we still admire in the masterpieces of Greek sculpture, indicates how we must understand the athletic ideal of manly prowess, even if that ideal may have been very far from reality. It is difficult to determine how far Xenophanes' complaints were justified; but the work of the great Greek sculptors is enough to show that he was a poor interpreter of the lofty ideal which the religious art of that time strove to embody in shapes worthy of the gods.

Pindar's hymns were written to celebrate the greatest moment in the athlete's life, his victory at one of the great games. Victory was the precondition of the poem, for it was usually sung by a chorus of the victor's young fellow-citizens at or shortly after his triumphant return. In Pindar, the close connexion between the hymn of victory and its external occasion had a religious significance comparable to the connexion between worship and art in the hymns to the gods. And that connexion was not an obvious one. The epic had never been a type of religious art, and in Ionia it had been followed by the personal lyric, which expressed merely the thoughts and emotions of the poet. In line with this development, even the hymn praising the gods, which had from time immemorial been a religious form of poetry parallel and equipotent to the epic, had been invaded by a freer spirit. Consequently, its old conventional form was subjected to many variations: the poet introduced his own religious ideas into the hymn and thus made it a vehicle for expressing his personality; or, like the Ionian and Aeolian lyricists, he used the hymn and the prayer as a mere form in which to communicate the most secret emotions of the human spirit to the listening deity. And there was a further development towards the end of the sixth century, which proved the increasing interest in individual personality even in Greece proper: the hymnal form was transferred from the service of the gods to the glorification of men, so that a human being became the subject of a hymn. Such exaltation was of course impossible except for men of semi-divine majesty, such as Olympic victors. Yet the increasing worldly tone of the hymn is unmistakable in that departure; and there is no doubt about the worldliness of Pindar's great contemporary, the professional

poet Simonides of Iulis on Ceos, with his 'Muse who gives herself for gold' [73] (he specialized in hymns of victory as well as
many other less religious types of occasional poetry), and of his
less important nephew and rival, Bacchylides.

Pindar was the first to make the triumphal hymn a sort of religious poem. Inspired by the old aristocratic conception of the
athletic contest, he gave a definite moral and religious significance to the spectacle of men struggling to bring their manhood
to perfection in victory; and thereby he created a new type of
lyric, which rose from a far greater depth of emotion and experience, and which seemed to look down from a sunny and triumphant peak upon the mysteries and struggles of man's destiny.
Severe, difficult, and devoutly religious as his poems are, they
still live and move with an incomparable freedom. It was only in
that religious form that Pindar could admit the possibility of a
hymn to a human victor. By transmuting the hymnal form in this
way, he had taken it over from its proud inventors, and made it
his own: his justification was his lofty conviction that he alone
knew the true meaning of the noble subject with which it dealt.
By his use of the triumphal hymn he was enabled to give a new
authority to the old aristocratic code, even in an age which
viewed it with little sympathy; and at the same time the new
lyric now at last attained its 'real nature' by being thus animated
with the true aristocratic faith. He never felt that, while he
hymned the athlete's victory, he was somehow dependent on the
athlete—that would have been dishonour to the art of poetry;
nor did he play the artisan and create to suit the wishes of his
subject. On the other hand, he never condescended. He always
stood on the same plane as the victor whose triumph he celebrated, be he a king, a nobleman, or a simple citizen. In his eyes,
the poet and the victor belonged to each other. That view of the
relationship was his own, and was strange to the Greeks of his
time, but it was a rebirth of the old, the original function of the
bard—to proclaim the glory of great deeds.[74]

So he restored to poetry the heroic spirit which was its earliest inspiration: he made it more than a simple record of events
or a decorative expression of personal emotion, for he made it
once more into praise of the prowess which is a pattern for posterity.[75] Yet the fact that his poems were each dictated by a
purely external, apparently casual occasion was his greatest

strength: for it was victory which always demanded the song.
The foundation of his poetry was this concentration upon a permanent standard. Again and again, in different phrases, he recurs to that thought, whenever he 'takes the Dorian lyre from its
peg' and strikes the strings.[76] 'One thing thirsts for another, but
victory loves song best, song the readiest companion of crowns
and virtues.' [77] He declares that it is 'the flower of justice' [78] to
praise noble men; in fact he frequently calls song 'the debt' which
the poet owes the victor.[79] Areta—we must write the word in
the severe Doric form which Pindar himself uses—areta triumphant in victory will not be 'silently hidden in the ground',[80]
but demands to be made eternal in the song of the poet. At
Pindar's magical touch everything in this dull ordinary world
at once regains the fresh vigour of creation's morning. 'The
word,' he says in his song for the Aeginetan boy Timasarchus,
'lives longer than deeds, when with success given by the Graces
the tongue draws it from the depths of the heart.' [81]

We have not enough of the Greek choral lyric poetry written
before Pindar to give his work a definite place in its development; but it seems clear that he transformed the genus into
something new, and that his own poems cannot be 'derived' directly from the choral tradition. Earlier choral poets had lyri-
cized the epic by taking its material and resetting it in a lyric
form; [82] but that is directly opposed to Pindar's method,
although his language owes much to his predecessors. It would
be truer to say that, through his work, the heroic spirit and the
praise of heroism which were the inspiration of the epic are reborn in lyric form. There could be no greater contrast to the
free expression of personal feeling in Ionian and Aeolic poetry
from Archilochus to Sappho than Pindar's subordination of his
poetry to a religious and social ideal, and his complete, almost
priestly self-dedication to the service of the last survival of
ancient chivalry.

To comprehend Pindar's conception of the nature and purpose of his poetry is also to understand its form more clearly.
Scholars who have commented on the hymns have devoted much
attention to the problem of their form. August Boeckh, in his
great edition, was the first who attempted to interpret the poet
through a full understanding of his historical situation and
through spiritual sympathy and intuition. He endeavoured to

extract a hidden unity from the difficult sequences of Pindar's thought, but he was often led to untenable views of the structure of the poems.[83] It was therefore a welcome reaction when Wilamowitz and his contemporaries abandoned Boeckh's method and strove to appreciate the manifold variety of the hymns rather than the problematical unity underlying it.[84] Their method naturally increased our understanding of details which had been left unexplained. Yet it is impossible not to try to apprehend a work of art as a whole; and in the case of Pindar, whose art is so immediately connected with his ideal purpose, it is doubly important to determine whether his poems have a structural, as well as a stylistic, unity. Certainly they have no rigid pattern; but when that fact is recognized, the question remains, on a higher level of interest. No one to-day will believe (as did critics of the Romantic age, encouraged by their own presuppositions) that they followed the free impulse of the poet's imaginative genius; and the unconscious tendency even to-day to treat the structure of Pindar's poems in that manner does scant justice to the craftsmanship which, during the present generation, we have learnt to regard as an element no less important than originality in Greek art.

If we start with what we have seen to be the unbreakable connexion between the victory and the song,[85] we can see that there were several different ways in which Pindar's poetic imagination might approach and master its subject. It could, for instance, describe the physical details of the boxing-match or the chariot-race—evoking the excitement of the spectators, the clouds of dust, the clatter of wheels, as Sophocles does in *Electra* by the messenger's dramatic description of the chariot-race at Delphi. Pindar, however, seems to have paid little attention to that aspect of the contest: he describes it only in formal allusive phrases and gives it only minor emphasis. He thinks far more of the spiritual difficulty of the games than of their physical appearance, for his gaze is fixed upon the victor.[86] He believes that victory is the manifestation of the highest human areta, and it is that belief which dictates the form of his poems. We cannot apprehend their form unless we understand his belief: for although a Greek artist was severely limited by the traditional form in which he chose to work, ultimately he chose and developed that form in accordance with the highest convictions of his soul.

Pindar's own view of his mission as a poet is the best guide to understanding him.[87] He thinks of himself as rivalling artists and sculptors, and he often borrows metaphors from their work. Remembering the rich treasurehouses of the various Greek cities in the temple-precinct at Delphi, he conceives his poetry as a *thesauros,* a treasury, of hymns.[88] Sometimes in the grandiose prelude of a poem he imagines his hymns as the pillared façades of a palace;[89] and in the introduction to the fifth Nemean he contrasts his relation to the victor with that of the sculptor to his subject. 'I am not a sculptor,' he says, 'to make statues that will stand motionless on their pedestals.'[90] The very contrast implies a comparison; the next sentence, however, shows that he feels his work to be greater than the sculptor's. 'But on every ship and in a skiff go, my sweet song, from Aegina, proclaiming that Lampon's powerful son Pytheas wins the crown of the fivefold contest at the Nemean games.' The comparison was obvious: for in Pindar's time sculptors carved only images of the gods or statues of athletic victors. But the resemblance goes deeper. Statues of that period show the same attitude as Pindar's poetry to the victor whom they depict: they do not record his personal features, but the ideal male body trained for the contest. Pindar could find no more suitable comparison, for he too does not write of the victor as an individual but as the representative of the highest areta. The attitude of both the sculptor and the poet is directly dictated by the character of an Olympian victory and the underlying Greek conception of man's nature. This comparison occurs once more—whether borrowed from Pindar we cannot say: in the *Republic* Plato compares Socrates to a sculptor when he has worked out an ideal description of the areté of the philosopher-king. And in another passage in the same work Plato describes the principle by which an ideal is created to be a pattern, with no emphasis on reality, and compares the power of philosophy to construct an ideal with the art of the painter who depicts not real men but an ideal of beauty.[91] The Greeks themselves were fully aware of this deep kinship between the principles of their fine arts—especially sculpture with its statues of gods and heroic victors—and the evocation of the highest ideal of humanity in the poetry of Pindar and later in Plato's philosophy. The visual arts on the one hand and poetry and philosophy on the other work towards the same end. Pindar is a sculptor on a higher level: he carves his victors into the true models of areta.

His complete absorption in his mission cannot be fully realized until he is compared with his contemporaries and rivals, Simonides and Bacchylides. Both these poets praised manly prowess because praise of it was a traditional part of the hymn of victory. Still, Simonides' work is full of personal utterances which are enough to show that—even apart from the question, what is the victor's areté?—the true nature of areté in general was coming to be a central problem for the men of the early fifth century. He speaks feelingly of its rarity. Areté lives, he says, on difficult peaks, surrounded by the holy choir of lightfoot nymphs; few mortals can see her unless soul-torturing sweat has been wrung out of their vitals.[92] In this sentence we meet the word ἀνδρεία for the first time: it still has the general meaning of 'manly virtue'. It is explained by the famous skolion [93] which Simonides addressed to the Thessalian Scopas—a poem which reveals a conception of areté involving both mind and body. 'Hard it is to become a man of true areté, foursquare and faultless in hand and foot and mind.' The deliberate, severe, and lofty art which underlies areté was in these words made clear to Simonides' contemporaries, who must have had a special new feeling for it. That is the best way for us to understand the problem posed by Simonides here. Destiny, he says, often casts man down into inescapable misfortune, which does not allow him to reach perfection. Only the gods are perfect, and man cannot be perfect when the finger of doom touches him. None but the man whom the gods love, to whom they send good fortune, reaches areté. Therefore Simonides praises the man who does not willingly do what is base. 'But when among us who are nourished by the earth I find a blameless man, I shall proclaim him to you.'

The evidence of Simonides is vitally important in explaining the interesting process by which the idea that man, with all his acts, is wholly or partially dependent on destiny—an idea which had been developing in complexity and significance in Ionian lyric poetry since Archilochus—entered the old aristocratic code of morality. For Simonides, like Pindar, was bound to represent the old tradition in his hymns of victory. What makes him particularly interesting is that several very different currents of tradition meet in his work. He stands, for example, in the direct line of Ionian, and Aeolian, and Dorian ways of life: he is the typical representative of the new Panhellenic culture which arose about the end of the sixth century, and he is an invaluable witness to the development of the Greek idea of areté. That is why Socrates disputes with the sophists in Plato's *Protagoras* about the true interpretation of his skolion.[94] Yet for that very reason he is not fully representative of the aristocratic moral ideal, as Pindar is. Simonides cannot be omitted from any historical survey of the idea of areté in the age of Pindar and Aeschylus; yet we cannot truthfully say that areté was more to him than an extremely interesting subject for intellectual discussion. He was the first sophist.[95] But areté is not only the root of all Pindar's faith, but the guiding structural principle of his poetry. His admission or exclusion of any thought is dictated by its bearing on his great task—to celebrate the victor as a representative of areté. More than of any other Greek poet is it true of Pindar that the form of his work can be understood only through the moral standard which it embodies. It is impossible to show the truth of this in detail, since the scope of this book does not permit us to analyse the structure of works of art for its own sake.[96] But if we pursue the investigation of Pindar's ideal of nobility, we shall learn something more of the principle on which he constructed his poems.

Since Pindar conceives of areta as an aristocratic quality, he believes it to be bound up with the great deeds of heroes of the past. He always sees the victor as the worthy heir to the proud traditions of his family, and honours the great ancestors who have bequeathed some of their glory to him. Yet he does not depreciate the achievement of the victor of to-day. Areta is divine because a god or a demigod was the first ancestor of a family which possesses it: the power descends from him, and is constantly renewed in each succeeding generation. Thus Pindar cannot consider a victor purely as an individual, since his victory was won through his divine blood. Accordingly, almost all his praise of a hero's deeds passes over into praise of the hero's descent. Praise of the victor's ancestors is a regular element in his hymns of victory: through it, the victor joins the divine company of gods and heroes. The second Olympian hymn opens: 'What god, what hero, what man shall we noise abroad?' And beside Zeus, to whom Olympia is sacred, and Heracles, who founded the games, it sets Theron, the ruler of Acragas, winner of the four-horse-chariot race, 'upholder of his city, flower of an honoured line.' Of course it is not always possible to speak of the good deeds and happy fortunes of a victor's family; and the depth of Pindar's religious feeling and the freedom of his spirit are seen at their noblest when he mentions the shadow of divinely sent suffering which falls on high virtue.[97] Who lives and acts, must suffer. That is Pindar's faith: it is the faith of Greece. Action in this sense is confined to the great, for only they can be fully said to act and suffer. Thus, says Pindar, time brought wealth and honour to the family of Theron and his father, as a reward for their native virtues, but time also involved it in guilt and suffering. 'Not even Time can undo what has been done, but forgetfulness may be brought by a favouring spirit. For malignant suffering dies mastered by noble joy, when God's fate lifts rich fortune on high.' [98]

A family derives not only its fortune but even its areta from the gods. It is therefore a difficult problem for Pindar to decide how it sometimes happens that after a long succession of famous men the areta of a family disappears. Such a cessation seems like an inexplicable interruption in the chain of evidence which proves the godlike prowess of a family, and which binds the present to the heroic past. The new age in which Pindar lived believed no longer in the areta of blood and race, and must have known several notably unworthy representatives of this or that famous line. In the sixth Nemean hymn Pindar expatiates on the transitoriness of human areta. The race of men and the race of gods are not the same, though both receive the breath of life from the same mother, earth. But our strength is different from theirs— the race of men is nothing, while heaven, the abode of the gods, is forever unshaken. Yet we resemble the immortals either in might of mind or in nature, despite the uncertainty of our fate. So now Alkimidas, victor in the boys' wrestling-match, proves the godlike strength of his family. It seemed to disappear in his father, but it returned in the steps of his father's father, Praxidamas, who was a great victor at Olympia, at the Isthmus and

Nemea. And he through his victories ended the obscurity of his father Socleides, who was of a glorious father the inglorious son. So it is with the fields, which change, and now give men their yearly life and now rest inactive. In fact, the aristocratic system depends on the constant succession of distinguished men. The failure of that crop, aphoria in one or more generations of a family, is an idea which was never hard for Greek minds to grasp. We meet it again in the Christian era, when the author of the treatise *On the Sublime* discusses the disappearance of creative genius in the age of decadence.[99]

Thus Pindar, constantly recurring to the ancestors of the victor whom he celebrates—and the ancestors of a family in Greece proper were not only remembered, but were actually present in their honoured tombs—forms an entire philosophy, rich with deep meditations on the merit, the happiness, and the suffering of different generations within one rich, brilliant, and noble family. The histories of the great houses of Greece would furnish copious examples of the splendour and decline of great tradition. But Pindar's interest in it was chiefly centred upon the educational power of great examples. Since Homer, one of the very foundations of aristocratic education had been glorification of the past and of great heroes long dead. If the praise of areta is principally the work of the poet, then he is an educator in the highest sense.[100] Pindar accepted this mission with a deep religious comprehension of his duty and his powers: and therein he differed from the impersonal Homeric bards. His heroes were men who lived and struggled in the immediate present, but he set them in the world of the myth. That is, he set them in the world of ideal heroes, whose heroism became a pattern for posterity to follow; invested by the brilliance of that world, they were to be kindled by its glory to exert their highest powers and thereby to reach the same pinnacle of achievement. This purpose gives Pindar's use of myths its peculiar value. He considered blame—which the great Archilochus had used in his poems—to be ignoble.[101] His detractors are said to have informed King Hieron of Syracuse that Pindar had disparaged him. In the dedicatory section of his second Pythian ode, Pindar, conscious of the debt of gratitude he owes to the king, refutes the charge. But although he will not desist from praising Hieron, he shows him a pattern to imitate: for he holds that by listening to scandalous

gossip he has not shown himself at his best. He cannot aspire to
be higher than he is; but he should allow the poet to show him
his true self, and below that he must not sink. In this passage
Pindar's use of the ideal pattern reaches its greatest sublimity.
The sentence 'Become what you are' seems to sum up his whole
educational message.[102] That is the meaning of all the traditional
models which he holds up to mankind: men must see in them
their own true selves, raised to a higher plane. Once more we see
the deep social and spiritual kinship of this aristocratic ideal of
paideia with the educational spirit of Plato's philosophy of ideas.
That philosophy is rooted in the aristocratic system of education, and is fundamentally alien to all the Ionian natural philosophies with which historians of philosophy almost invariably connect it. Strange, that in the introductions to standard editions of
Plato Pindar is never mentioned; while the hylozoists' primal
elements—air, fire, water, and so on—appear and reappear in
every successive edition with the persistency of an endemic
disease.[103]

The kind of praise which Pindar gives to King Hieron requires
as much candour as does criticism, and it spurs the recipient on
to far greater efforts. To realize the truth of this, we need only
consider the simplest example of educational praise in all Pindar's work: the sixth Pythian ode. It is addressed to a young
man named Thrasybulus, son of Xenocrates and nephew of the
tyrant Theron of Acragas; he has come to Delphi to drive his
father's chariot in the games, and won the race. Pindar celebrates his victory in a short hymn, and praises his filial love—for
filial love was in the old aristocratic code a duty second only to
that of reverence for the supreme Zeus.[104] The wise centaur
Chiron, the pattern teacher of heroes, had impressed it on
Achilles while he was under his care. And next to this august
name, the poet mentions Nestor's son Antilochus, who in the
Trojan war gave up his life for his old father's sake, fighting
against Memnon the leader of the Ethiops. 'But of men of
to-day Thrasybulus has come nearest to his father's standard.' [105]
The traditional model Antilochus is here interwoven in the
praise of filial devotion, and his deed is briefly eulogized. Thus
the poet enlightens and glorifies every individual case of areta
by a great example taken from the vast treasure of heroic para-
deigmata, and constantly idealizes and recreates the immediate

by transfusing it with the power of tradition. He lives and
works in a world in which the myth is more real than any
reality; [106] and whether he is glorifying the old nobility or
parvenu tyrants and fatherless bourgeois, he raises them all to
the same pinnacle of half-divine glory by the magical touch of
his deeper knowledge, his realization of the higher meaning of
their life and their struggle.

In Chiron, the wise centaur who teaches the young heroes,
Pindar finds the mythical pattern for his own educational mission. We find it elsewhere too—for instance in the third
Nemean, which is so rich in educational examples. In that poem,
he evokes the ancestors of the Aeginetan victor Aristocleides to
be the models for great prowess. They are Peleus, Telamon, and
Achilles. The poet's mind turns from Achilles to the cave of
Chiron where he was brought up.[107] But when men believe that
areta lies in the blood of a noble family, can they also believe
that education is possible? Pindar recurs to this question several
times. It had been posed, in essence, as early as Homer, for in
the ninth book of the *Iliad* [108] Achilles is confronted at the crisis
by his teacher Phoenix; and Phoenix's admonitory speech falls
unheard on the hardened heart of Achilles. There, however, the
problem is whether inborn character will respond to guidance.
Pindar is concerned with the modern question, whether the true
virtue of man can be learnt, or only inherited by blood. A question of the same type recurs again and again in Plato; [109] but
Pindar was the first to formulate it, for it was thrust on him by
the conflict of the aristocratic educational tradition with the new
rational spirit. And throughout his work it is plain that he has
thought long and deeply on it. He gives his answer in the third
Nemean ode: 'Through inborn glory a man is very mighty; but
he who learns from teaching is a twilight man, wavering in
spirit, never stepping forth on firm foot, but lipping a myriad
virtues with imperfect spirit.' [110] Achilles astonished Chiron by
showing his inborn heroism before he had been taught. So says
the saga, and according to Pindar it knows all. Therefore the
saga gave the right answer to the question. Education cannot act
unless there is inborn areta for it to act upon, as there was in
Chiron's glorious pupils, Achilles, Jason, and Asklepios, whom
he 'fostered, strengthening their hearts in all seemly matters.' [111]

That pregnant phrase contains the fruits of long thought on the problem. It shows the deliberate resolve of the aristocracy to preserve its position at a time of crisis.

Like the areta of the Olympic victor, the art of the poet cannot be learnt: and both flow from the same divine source. The poet's art is, essentially, 'wisdom'. Pindar constantly uses the word σοφία to denote poetic genius. It is impossible to find a satisfactory translation for it; each of us would translate it according to his own view of the true nature and effect of the Pindaric spirit, and there is a vast difference between the various possible views. If it is simply understanding of the craft of making good poems, then the word must be translated by an aesthetic term.[112] Homer spoke of the carpenter's σοφία, and even in the fifth century the word could still refer entirely to technical skill. But we cannot help feeling that there is greater weight in the word as Pindar uses it. By his time it had long been used of the possessor of higher knowledge, exceptional understanding, insight into subjects far above the comprehension, though not the respect, of the common herd. For instance, Xenophanes used it of his poetic understanding. In his poems, he proudly calls his revolutionary criticism of the current conceptions of the universe 'my wisdom'.[113] And it is at once apparent that the expression and the thought cannot be separated: both together, as a unity, form his σοφία. The same must surely be true of Pindar's deeply meditative art. The 'prophet of the Muses'[114] speaks 'the truth'. He 'draws it from the deep of his heart'.[115] He pronounces judgment on the true worth of man. He distinguishes the 'true tale' of mythic tradition from the stories which are ornamented with lies.[116] The poet, on his divine mission, prompted by the Muses, takes his place beside kings and the great ones of the earth, sharing their claim to the loftiest place among mankind. He has no wish to earn the approbation of the mob. 'May it be permitted to me to please and to mingle with the noble' is the sentence which closes the second Pythian ode, addressed to Hieron of Syracuse.

But even if 'the noble' are rich and powerful men, the poet is not their courtier. He is still 'the straight-tongued man who comes to the fore under any rule, in a tyranny as well as where the violent host or the wise guard the city'.[117] Wisdom, he believes, exists only among the nobility; and so his poetry is, in the deepest sense, esoteric. 'I bear beneath my arm many swift arrows within their quiver; they speak only to those who understand, and they always need interpreters. Wise is he who knows much by nature; but those who have but learnt, in the violence of their chattering, vainly croak like ravens against the divine bird of Zeus.' [118] The 'interpreters' needed by his poems (the 'arrows') are the noble souls who have by nature the higher insight which poetry demands. The image of the eagle recurs elsewhere in Pindar. Here is the close of the third Nemean hymn: 'Swift is the eagle among birds, which darts down from afar and suddenly grips the bloody prey in its claws; but the chattering daws feed low.' [119] Pindar takes the eagle as a symbol of his consciousness of his poetic mission. It is not a mere decorative image. He feels that he is describing a metaphysical quality of the spirit, when he says that its essence is to live in the unapproachable heights, and to move freely through the kingdoms of the air, far above the lower sphere where the chattering daws seek their food. The metaphor was taken over by his younger contemporary Bacchylides, and handed down until it appears at last in Euripides' magnificent line, 'All heaven is open to the eagle's flight'.[120] It was an expression of Pindar's spiritual nobility, his imperishable claim to be an aristocrat. Even here, his faith in the areta of blood still persists: it explains the immeasurable gulf which he sees between his own inborn poetic powers and the knowledge of 'those who have learnt' (μαθόντες).[121] Whatever view we may hold of the descent of areta through noble blood, we must acknowledge the gulf which Pindar points out between natural nobility born in its possessor and the knowledge and powers which have been merely acquired by learning, for the difference between these things is actual and right. Pindar set up this truth before the very gate of the age in which Greek civilization was to give to learning a hitherto undreamed-of scope, and to reason the greatest significance it has ever possessed.[122]

As we leave Pindar, we turn our backs on the aristocratic world, now sinking deeper and deeper into silence, and re-enter the great clamorous stream of history. He himself left that world behind—not in intention but in effect—in the great poems in which, as a poet whose Panhellenic function was fully recognized, he celebrated the chariot-victories of the powerful Sicilian tyrants Theron and Hieron. He ennobled the new states they had built up, and gave their work additional authority and importance, by adorning it with the splendour and majesty of the old aristocratic ideals. It may be felt that this was a historical paradox, although the parvenu despot has always loved to deck himself in the proud trappings of outworn nobility. Pindar himself, in those odes, passed far beyond the aristocratic convention, and spoke in his own voice with a clarity unparalleled elsewhere in his poetry. He felt that the education of kings was the last and highest task to which the aristocratic poet was called in the new age.[123] Like Plato, he hoped to influence them for good, to induce them to realize in a changed world his own political dreams, and to show them how to repress the growing boldness of the mob. With that mission in mind, he stood in the brilliant court of Hieron of Syracuse, a lonely apostle of 'truth' beside the greatest of those 'who had learnt', Simonides and Bacchylides: as Plato was to stand in the court of Dionysius beside the sophists Polyxenus and Aristippus.

It would be interesting to know if Pindar's path ever crossed that of one other great man who visited Hieron—Aeschylus the Athenian, who produced *The Persians* for the second time in Syracuse.[124] The army of the young Athenian democracy had driven the Persians back from Marathon; and at Salamis its fleet, its generals, and its political energy had been decisive in winning victory and freedom for all the Greeks of Europe and Asia Minor. While the Greeks fought for their national existence against Persia, Pindar's city stood aside in ignominious neutrality. If we search his poems for an echo of the heroic events which were throughout Hellas awaking a new sense of power over the future, we shall hear only the deep sigh of an anxious onlooker's divided heart. In the last of the Isthmian hymns, Pindar speaks of the 'stone of Tantalus' which has long hung over the head of Thebes, and has been removed by some god; [125] but we cannot tell whether he is thinking of the danger of Persian domination, or of the hatred of the Greek victors whose cause Thebes had betrayed, and whose revenge threatened to destroy it. Not Pindar, but his great rival, the versatile Simonides, became the classical lyric-poet of the Persian wars: it was he, with his brilliant, supple, cold, masterly style, whom the Greek cities chose to write the memorial poems for the monuments of their dead. It seems to us now to have been a tragic misfortune that Pindar should have been pushed into the background by Simonides at that time: yet perhaps it was a necessary consequence of his attitude, for he persisted in celebrating a heroism which was then outworn. Yet victorious Greece found something akin to the spirit of Salamis in his verses, and Athens loved the poet who had invoked her with dithyrambic enthusiasm: [126] 'O shining and violet crowned and famous in song, bulwark of Hellas, illustrious Athens, city divine!' Pindar's work was to survive through the new world, led by Athens, which was fundamentally alien to him; and yet he had more love for the enemy of Athens, Aegina, 'sister' of Thebes, with its rich old families of sailors and merchant-princes. But the world to which Pindar's heart belonged, the world which he had glorified, was even then passing away. It almost seems to be a spiritual law of nature, that no great historical type of society has the strength to formulate its own ideal with deep and sure knowledge until the moment when its life is over: as if then its immortal soul were shaking itself free from its transitory mortal shape. Thus in its last agony the aristocratic culture of Greece produced Pindar, the dying Greek city-state, Plato and Demosthenes, and the mediæval hierarchy of the Church, when it had passed its height, brought forth Dante.

II

THE CULTURAL POLICY OF THE TYRANTS

OUR study of aristocratic poetry has taken us into the fifth century, when it was still in its full splendour. But before this there was an intermediate stage between the rule of the nobility and the rule of the people. This was tyranny—a phenomenon no less important in the history of culture than in the development of the Greek state. It has been mentioned before, and must now be discussed at length.

As Thucydides realized, the rule of the Sicilian tyrants (for two of whom Pindar wrote his great odes) was quite unlike the usual Greek tyranny.[1] In the western outposts of Hellenism, facing the aggrandisements of the naval and commercial power of Carthage, autocracy lived far longer than in any other Greek land; but in Hellas itself, that epoch of political history was closed by the fall of the Athenian Pisistratids in 510. In Sicily, tyranny was brought about by conditions totally different from the inevitable social process which had produced it in Greece proper and its eastern colonies. It did indeed coincide with the collapse of aristocratic rule and the rise of the masses; but it was quite as much military and diplomatic expression of the commercial imperialism of powerful Sicilian cities like Acragas, Gela, and Syracuse. Even later, after half a century of democracy, the needs of Sicily produced, by inevitable logic, the tyranny of the Dionysii: and it was its very inevitability which Plato held to be its historical justification.[2]

Let us turn back to consider Athens and the rich cities of the Isthmus as they were in the middle of the sixth century, when the time was ripe for the appearance of tyranny in Greece proper. Athens represented the last stage of the movement towards tyranny. Solon had long prophesied its coming; in the poems of his old age, he spoke of it as imminent, and finally he lived to see it become a fact.[3] Although sprung from the Athenian nobility, he had broken away from the traditions of his caste. His poems had prefigured, his laws had delineated, and his life had embodied a new ideal of human character, an ideal whose attainment was independent of the privileges of birth and property. Yet when he demanded justice for the oppressed workers of Attica, he never envisaged anything like the democracy which later claimed him as its founder. He merely wished the old aristocratic state to justify itself morally and economically, and at first he had no thought of its impending downfall. But the nobles had learned nothing from history, and they learned nothing from Solon. After he retired from office, party strife broke out again with renewed fury.

We know nothing of the history of the succeeding decades; but Aristotle saw from the archon-lists that the government of Athens must have been seriously disturbed on several occasions. In some years there was, it seemed, no archon at all; and one archon attempted to hold his office for two years.[4] There were three factions, headed by the most powerful families—the nobles of the coast, the nobles of the interior, and the nobles of the Diacria, the poor highlands of Attica.[5] All three parties courted the support of the people: for the people was now becoming an important factor in politics, although (or even because) it was not an organized party with a leader to voice its deep discontent. By skilful tactics, Pisistratus, the leader of the Diacrian nobles, manœuvred his rivals into a disadvantageous position, although some—such as the Alcmaeonids—were far richer and far more powerful than he. He secured the support of the people, and made concessions to their demands. After several vain attempts to seize power, alternating with periods of exile, he succeeded at last in establishing himself, with the help of a bodyguard which was not armed with spears like soldiers, but with clubs. The power thus founded he strengthened throughout his long reign so firmly that after his death his sons inherited it without disturbance.[6]

Tyranny is of the utmost importance, both as a historical phenomenon, and as a motive force behind the far-reaching cultural revolution which begins in the sixth century with the fall of the aristocracy and the political rise of the bourgeoisie.[7] As a typical example, we shall examine the Athenian tyranny in some detail, since we know more about it than any other. But we must first review the previous development of tyranny in other Greek states.

In most of the cities where it existed, we know no more than the name and a few remarkable actions of the tyrant. How the tyranny arose, and what brought it into being, we seldom know; and still more rarely do we know the real personality of the tyrant and the character of his rule. But the surprising unanimity with which all the Greek states turned to this kind of government in and after the seventh century [8] indicates that the causes for its appearance were the same everywhere. In the sixth century, where we have more facts to guide us, we can see that the rise of tyranny was part of the great social and economic changes which are known to us chiefly from the work of Solon and Theognis.[9] The landowning nobility, which had until then held the supreme power in every state, found its position terribly shaken by the spread of money as a means of exchange to replace the old system of barter in kind. Clinging to outworn economic techniques, they were largely pushed into the background by the possessors of the new wealth gained from trade and industry. And their own ranks were split by the differences which arose when some of the old houses turned to trade also, and acquired new wealth. There were many noble families which became impoverished (as Theognis shows) and could no longer maintain their social position. Others, like the Alcmaeonids in Attica, accumulated such wealth that their power became intolerable to their fellow-nobles, and they themselves could not resist the temptation to bid for political power. By severe legislation which virtually made bankrupt peasants and tenant-farmers into serfs of the landowner,[10] the agricultural workers were driven to thoughts of revolution; and discontented noblemen could easily seize power by putting themselves at the head of the unorganized masses. The *nouveaux riches* who joined the side of the landowning nobility were not welcomed—the nobleman has never been sympathetic to the millionaire merchant—and even the accession of strength which they brought was a doubtful gain.[11] For, joined by the rich, the nobles moved further than ever away from the landless and moneyless masses, and now that the situation had narrowed to the simple conflict of rich against poor, revolution was much nearer. The rise of tyranny was aided by the fact that, without a leader, the commons could not shake off the coercion of the aristocracy, although when they had done so they were usually content to accept the domination of their leader, now the tyrant.[12] After centuries of obedience to their masters, they could not yet conceive the ideal of a free people ruling itself. They were even less capable of attaining such an ideal then, than in the era of the great demagogues: in fact, they could never have attained it even in a later age without the demagogues, and Aristotle was right to base his history of Athenian democracy in the *Constitution of the Athenians* upon the succession of these, its leaders.[13]

Tyranny seems to have appeared at the same time in Greece proper as in the cities of Ionia and the islands, where we should expect a higher stage of intellectual and political development to have produced it earlier.[14] About the year 600, Miletus, Ephesus, Lesbos and Samos were all ruled by famous tyrants, who as a rule maintained close relations with their fellow-tyrants in mainland Greece. Although, or even because, the tyrants had reached power purely through internal revolution, they were associated with one another by bonds of international solidarity, frequently strengthened by dynastic marriages. In fact, they anticipated the democratic and oligarchic party-solidarity which was so widespread in the fifth century. And thus, oddly enough, they created the first far-seeing foreign policy for their respective states, and (for instance in Corinth, Athens, and Megara) even carried it into action by founding colonies. All such foundations were bound to their metropolis by much closer ties than those acknowledged by earlier colonies. Thus, Sigeum was simply an Athenian fort on the Hellespont; Periander made similar fortress-outposts for Corinth in Potidaea, which he founded, and Corcyra, which he had to conquer. In Greece proper Corinth and Sicyon were the first cities to develop tyranny, and they were followed by Megara and Athens. The Athenian tyranny of Pisistratus was established with the help of the despot of Naxos, and he in turn was supported by Pisistratus. In Euboea too tyranny appeared very early; but in Sicily, where it was to reach its highest development, it came late. The only important Sicilian tyrant of the sixth century was Phalaris of Acragas, the founder of his city's prosperity. In Greece, much as we may admire Pisistratus, the greatest of the tyrants was undoubtedly Periander of Corinth, one of the 'seven wise men' of Hellas. After the fall of the aristocratic government of the Bacchiads, his father had founded a dynasty which retained its power for several generations, but reached its zenith in Periander. Pisistratus' part in history was to prepare for the future greatness of Athens, but Periander raised Corinth to a height from which she declined after his death and which she never reached again.

Elsewhere in Greece, aristocratic rule continued. As always, it was based on the possession of large estates, and only here and there (in Aegina, for instance, a purely commercial state) on great wealth too. A tyranny never lasted longer than two or three generations. It was usually overthrown by the aristocracy after it learned its lesson and became certain of its policy; but the aristocracy seldom held the power it had recaptured, and usually, as in Athens, had to surrender it to the common people. As Polybius explains [15] in his theory of the succession of types of government, the fall of a tyranny was chiefly caused by the inability of the tyrant's sons or grandsons (less brilliant than himself) to maintain the power which they had inherited, or by the despotic misuse of the power which they had received from the people. Tyranny became the bogey of the fallen aristocrats, and they bequeathed their terror of it to the democracies. But hatred of tyranny was only a one-sided expression of the fighting spirit in politics. As Burckhardt neatly says, in every Greek there was a hidden tyrant; to be a tyrant was such an obvious and generally accepted form of happiness that Archilochus could describe the contented carpenter no better than by saying that he did not covet a tyranny.[16] The Greeks always felt that the rule of one supremely able man was, in Aristotle's words, 'according to nature', and they tended to acquiesce in it when it appeared.[17]

The earlier tyrannies were something half-way between the patriarchal kingships of primitive Greece and the rule of the demagogues in the later democracies. Maintaining the external forms of aristocratic government, the despot endeavoured to unite all authority in his own person and in those of his adherents. He was supported by a small but effective body of troops. If a state does not produce a legal and efficient form of government for itself, backed by the will of all or most of its citizens, it can be ruled only by an armed minority. But the tyrant's armed force was always visible; and its unpopularity did not diminish with the passing of time. The tyrant was therefore compelled to counterbalance it by carefully maintaining the external forms of election to official posts, by systematically cultivating public loyalty to his person, and by pursuing an economic policy which would satisfy the majority of his subjects. Pisistratus sometimes appeared in court when he was involved in a lawsuit, in order to demonstrate that the rule of law and order was unshaken: this made a great impression on the public.[18] Every tyrant kept down the old aristocratic families with a strong hand, and banished noblemen who might become dangerous rivals, or gave them honourable duties to perform in another part of Greece: thus Pisistratus supported Miltiades in his important campaign to conquer and colonize the Chersonese. And no tyrant allowed the citizen body to flock to the cities, where it might form an organized power to endanger his rule. Both economic and political motives induced Pisistratus to favour the country people of Attica, who loved him dearly in return. Many years later, his tyranny was still called 'the reign of Kronos', the Golden Age; [19] and many sympathetic anecdotes were told of his personal visits to the country and his conversations with the simple peasants, whose hearts he won by a combination of pleasant manners and low taxes.[20] His tactics were a blend of political shrewdness and sound agrarian instinct. He even took the trouble to spare the peasants the journey into town to attend court: for he himself made regular trips round Attica to hold the assizes.[21]

Unfortunately, we cannot give such a detailed description of any other tyrant's internal policy; and even this account of Pisistratus we owe to Aristotle, who built it up from the Attic chronicles.[22] It is impossible to overlook the strong economic element in his work: compared with it, his political acts were only stopgap solutions. The really attractive thing about tyranny, especially that of Pisistratus, was its success; but that success can only be attributed to the supreme personal rule of one man, genuinely gifted, and entirely devoted to the service of his people. We may well doubt whether all tyrants were as gifted or as devoted; but we must judge the régime only by its best representatives. On the standard of success, it was a period of rapid and valuable progress.

On the spiritual side, the rule of the sixth-century tyrant may be compared with that of his political opponents, the great lawgivers and *aisymnetai*. These were temporary dictators appointed by many cities and given extraordinary powers in order to introduce permanent changes into the constitution or to restore it after a disturbance. They influenced the general standard of culture principally by creating, through their legislation, an ideal which allowed and even enjoined political activity on the part of the citizens; while the tyrant repressed all individual initiative and himself promoted every action undertaken by the state. Although, then, the tyrant did not educate the citizens towards universal political areté, he became their model in another sense. Without the responsibility which attached to their position, he was the prototype of the statesmen of later centuries. He was the first to show that a nation could be governed on a far-sighted plan involving long-term calculations of means and ends. That is, he was the first to engage in real *politics*. In political life he was the characteristic expression of the newly awakened individualism of the seventh and sixth centuries, as the poet and the philosopher were, in different but related spheres. During the fourth century, when the general interest in great individuals increased and produced the new literary form, biography, its favourite subjects were poets, philosophers, and tyrants.[23] And the seven wise men who became famous about the beginning of the sixth century included not only lawgivers and poets but tyrants like Periander and Pittacus.[24] A particularly significant fact is that nearly all the poets of that period lived at the courts of tyrants. Individualism was not yet a general rule, and there was no universal levelling-down of the intellect: individualism still meant true spiritual independence. And for that very reason the few independent souls sought one another out for mutual support.

The concentration of culture at the courts of tyrants had the effect of intensifying intellectual and aesthetic life not only in the narrow circle of artists and connoisseurs but throughout the country. Such was the result of the patronage of Polycrates at Samos, of the Pisistratids in Athens, of Periander in Corinth, and of Hieron in Syracuse—to name only the most brilliant of the despots. In Athens, we know more details of the tyranny, and we can estimate the full effect on the development of Attica which was produced by the tyrants' interest in art, poetry, and religion. Their court was the studio of Anacreon, Simonides,

Pratinas, Lasus, and Onomacritus. It fostered the beginnings of comic and tragic drama, and of Athenian music, which reached such a high development in the fifth century. It encouraged the great recitations of Homer, and incorporated them in the Panathenaea, the national festival which Pisistratus so splendidly reorganized. It planned the great festivals of Dionysus, and stimulated the practice of the fine arts, sculpture, architecture, and painting. It made Athens what she always remained— a city of the Muses. From it flowed a joyful new spirit of enterprise and a finer sense of pleasure. In a dialogue falsely attributed to Plato,[25] Pisistratus' younger son Hipparchus is described as the first aesthete, and Aristotle [26] calls him 'an amorist and a lover of the arts'. It was a real tragedy that this gay, politically harmless man should have been struck down by the tyrannicides in 514.[27] While he lived, he was a generous patron to many poets. One of them, Onomacritus, repaid his patronage by forging oracular verses in support of the Pisistratid dynasty, and writing entire epics under the name of Orpheus to suit the court's fancy for mystical religions. The thing became such a scandal that the tyrants were eventually forced to abandon him to popular feeling. He was banished, and saw his patrons no more until Hippias joined him in exile.[28]

That one scandal does not diminish the services of the dynasty to the cause of literature. Their court was the source of the inexhaustible stream of poetry and art which flowed for centuries through the symposia of Athens. They were ambitious to win victories in the chariot-race at the great national games; and they supported every form of athletic competition. They provided, in fact, a powerful stimulus to the advance of general culture in the life of their time. Some have believed that the great development of religious festivals and the encouragement of all the arts, which are typical of the Greek tyrannies, were merely stratagems to distract the restless minds of the citizens from political questions and to give them a new but safe interest. Even if these motives did play some part in the cultural policy of the tyrant, his deliberate concentration on his task shows that the development of art and intellect was meant to be a real contribution to the life of the community: it was part of his service to the public. By it he showed that he was a true *politikos;* he brought his subjects to a deeper understanding of the true greatness and value of their city. Public interest in religion and the arts was of course not a new thing, but it was suddenly increased to a vast extent when they were systematically cultivated by a rich and powerful ruler. His official encouragement of cultural activity was a proof of the tyrant's affection for the common people. That duty was later taken over by the democratic state, which merely followed his example. After the work of the tyrants, no state could afford to exist without pursuing a systematic cultural policy. At that period, however, the state's interest in culture was confined to the adornment of religion by the arts and the support of artists by the tyrant. These activities never brought the state into conflict with itself. Dissensions within the state could be created only by poetry which invaded public life and ideas more deeply than the lyric poets at the tyrant's court ever ventured to do, or by science and philosophy, which did not then exist at Athens. We never hear that the early tyrants showed any favour to famous philosophers; they concentrated rather on increasing the scope and popularity of the arts, and on improving the aesthetic and physical standards of the people.

Sometimes it seems that systematic patronage, as practised by many despots of the Renaissance and later by other enlightened princes, although immensely stimulating to contemporary intellectual life, was somehow artificial, and that the culture which they encouraged was deeply rooted neither in the aristocracy nor among the people, but was the luxurious caprice of a small society. We must not forget that the same kind of culture had already appeared in Greece. The Greek tyrants of the end of the archaic period were the first Medicis [29]—for they also enjoyed culture as something unconnected with the rest of life, as the bloom on the specially favoured existence of a few, and generously imparted it to the common people, to whom it was entirely foreign. The aristocracy had never done so; but the culture which it possessed could not be imparted in that way. And on that very fact was based the permanent importance of the aristocracy, even after its fall from power, in the culture of the nation. But it is natural for spiritual activity to cut itself off from ordinary life, to find an ivory tower a better workshop than the harsh noisy streets of everyday. Great artists and thinkers love the patronage of powerful men: in the words attributed to Simonides, the most important member of Pisistratus' circle, the wise must wait at the doors of the rich. And with the increasing refinement of perception, art and science tend to become more professional and exquisite, to address themselves to a few connoisseurs. The sense of privilege binds artist and patron together, even when they despise each other.

This was true in Greece at the end of the sixth century. In consequence of the high development of intellectual life in Ionia, poetry in the late archaic period was no longer part of the life of society. Theognis and Pindar, being apostles of the aristocratic creed, were exceptions to that rule. They were therefore ahead of their age, and less akin to their other contemporaries than to Aeschylus, the Athenian of the age of the Persian wars. Aeschylus on the one hand, and Theognis and Pindar on the other, although working on different principles, represent the overthrow of the professional art which flourished under the tyrants. Their relation to it is the same as that of Hesiod and Tyrtaeus to the epic poetry of the late rhapsodes. The artists who were patronised by Polycrates, Periander, and the Pisistratids—musicians and poets like Anacreon, Ibycus, Simonides, Lasus, and Pratinas, and the great sculptors of the same period —were in fact *artists* in the full sense of the word. They were a special class of men with astounding technical gifts, who were equal to any task and were at ease in any society, but who had no roots anywhere. When the Samian court passed away and Polycrates died on the Persian cross, Anacreon journeyed to the court of Hipparchus in Athens, in a fifty-oared galley specially sent to bring him; and when the last of the Pisistratids was banished from Athens, Simonides migrated to Thessaly, where he lived in the court of the Scopad princes until the whole clan was crushed out of existence by the fall of the roof in their banqueting-hall. There is something symbolic about the tradition that Simonides himself was the only survivor. He migrated once again, at the age of eighty, to the court of the tyrant Hieron of Syracuse. The culture which such men represented was as rootless as their lives. It could entertain a clever nation of beauty-lovers, like the Athenians, but it could not stir their souls. Just as the Athenian gentlemen of the last few years before Marathon were adorned by perfumed Ionian robes and luxurious curls and gold grasshopper hair-brooches, so the city of Athens was adorned by the graceful sculptures and the harmonious poems of the Ionians and Peloponnesians who haunted the tyrants' court. Their art sowed the Athenian air with the seeds of beauty, and infused into it a rich fertilizing light from all the rest of Greece: it was they who made Athens ready for the birth of the great Attic poet who was to fulfil the latent genius of his nation in the hour of its destiny.

BOOK TWO
THE MIND OF ATHENS

THE DRAMA OF AESCHYLUS

AESCHYLUS was only a boy when Athens was ruled by tyrants. He grew up to manhood under the new democracy which had swiftly repressed the aristocrats who strove to seize power after the fall of the Pisistratids. The tyranny had actually been over-thrown by the jealousy of the noble families which it held down; but a return to the feudal anarchy of the period before Pisistratus was unthinkable. It was Cleisthenes, one of the Alcmaeonids returning from exile, who led the common people against his fellow-nobles (just as Pisistratus had done) and finally abolished the old aristocratic system. He replaced the ancient arrangement of the Attic population into four *phylai* or tribes—which divided the whole citizen-body into rival groups of clans—by a purely regional distribution into ten *phylai*. This reform broke up the old family-loyalties, and destroyed their political power by a new democratic electoral system based on the new *phylai*. The rule of the great clans was over. However, the aristocracy still retained considerable influence in political and intellectual life. The leaders of the Athenian democracy were noblemen until the death of Pericles; and the chief poet of the new state, Aeschylus son of Euphorion, was—like the first great thinker and writer of Athens, Solon himself—a scion of the landed nobility. He came from Eleusis, where Pisistratus had lately built a new shrine for the local mystery-cult. The comic writers loved to describe him as growing up under the protection of the venerable goddess of Eleusis. It was a pretty contrast to Euripides, 'son of the garden-goddess',[1] when Aristophanes made Aeschylus open his contest against the perverter of tragedy with the solemn prayer:[2]

> 'Demeter, who hast nourishèd my soul,
> now make me worthy of thy mysteries!'

Welcker's attempt to trace Aeschylus' devout attitude towards religion to a supposed 'theology of the mysteries' has now been refuted.[3] There is probably more of the real truth in the story that he was prosecuted for revealing the holy secret of the mysteries on the stage, but was acquitted when he proved that he did so without knowing it.[4] Yet even if he was never initiated, but drew his knowledge of sacred things from his own soul, there was an imperishable truth in the manly humility and pious strength of the prayer put into his mouth by Aristophanes. We can more easily resign ourselves to the lack of any tradition about his life, when we see that even the Athenians of his own century, who appreciated him so deeply, were content with the impressive myth which surrounded his character. What they felt about him was expressed with noble simplicity in the epitaph written for his grave. To prove that he attained the highest glory possible to man, it mentions only the fact that he fought at Marathon; it says nothing of his poetry.[5] It is, of course, not authentic: being merely an idealized portrait of Aeschylus, set down with finished brevity by a later poet. But the age of Aristophanes would have described him in the same terms, for it thought of him as the 'Marathon-warrior', the spiritual representative of the first generation of the new Attic state, filled with all its high and earnest moral purpose.

Few battles in history have been fought so entirely for the sake of an ideal as Marathon and Salamis. We should have had to assume that Aeschylus had taken part in the naval battle too, even if Ion of Chios [6] had not said so in his travel-memoirs written a generation later; for the Athenians had left their city and embarked on their ships πανδημεί, 'with the entire population'. The messenger's description of Salamis in *The Persians* is the sole surviving account by an eye-witness of the historical drama in which Athens established her future power and her aspirations to the hegemony of the whole Greek nation. But that is Thucydides' view [7] of Salamis, not Aeschylus'. For Aeschylus, it was a revelation of the deep wisdom of the eternal justice which rules the world. Guided by the intelligence of an Athenian, and inspired to a new heroism by the struggle for national independence, a little army had overthrown the myriads of Xerxes, unmanned by their own slavery. *Europæ succubuit Asia*.[8] The spirit of Tyrtaeus was reborn from the ideal of freedom and justice.[9]

Since the date of Aeschylus' first play cannot be fixed within ten years or so, we cannot determine whether he was inspired even before the Persian wars with the deep religious feeling which is expressed in the majestic prayers to Zeus in *The Suppliants*.[10] The basis of his faith was the same as that of his spiritual guide Solon. But the additional tragic power with which he transfused the religion of Solon must be attributed in part to the cleansing violence of the storm through which he and the men of his time had passed, and which still rages through every line of *The Persians*. Freedom and victory were the two bonds between his Solonic faith in justice and the new democracy which grew up around him. The state was not a chance detail in the background of his dramas: it was the spiritual stage on which they were played. Aristotle truly says that the characters of early tragedy spoke politically, not rhetorically.[11] Even in his last words, the superb close of *The Eumenides,* with its solemn prayer for the prosperity of the Athenian nation and its reaffirmation of belief in the divine government of the world, Aeschylus revealed the essentially political character of his poetry.[12] That was the basis of its educational force, a force at once moral, religious, and purely human; for morality, religion, and all human life were now aspects of the all-embracing life of the polis. Though Aeschylus resembles Pindar in his educational conception of his work, there is a deep distinction between the methods of the two poets. Pindar hoped that the aristocracy in all its splendour would be reborn in the old spirit of rigid loyalty to tradition. Aeschylus showed in his tragedies how the hero could be born in the new spirit of freedom. It seems a short and inevitable journey from Pindar to Plato, from the aristocracy of race to the aristocracy of spirit and intelligence; but the transition can be made only through Aeschylus.

Once more, as in Solon's time, the good genius of the Athenian people produced, at the beginning of its career in world-history, a poet to form and strengthen its spirit for the new task. State and spirit now coalesced, and became a perfect unity: and that very rare unity gave the new type of man which appeared at this time its quality of classical uniqueness. It is difficult to say which helped the other more, the state or the spirit. We might well conclude that the state which the Athenians had made did more to further the cause of the spirit, for the state was more than its officials: it was the struggle of the entire population to escape from the chaos of the previous hundred years, by establishing a political cosmos conceived and realized through the highest effort of all their moral powers. The young democracy of Aeschylus' time is the perfect illustration of Montesquieu's words in *L'esprit des lois* that the ancient democracy in its true and original form was based on virtue. At last the state had become, in Solon's sense, the force which binds together all human endeavours. That faith in the ideal of justice [13] by which the young state was inspired now seemed to be divinely consecrated and affirmed in the victory [14] over Persia. And now, for the first time, the true culture of the Athenian people came into being.

At one stroke all the enervating refinement, all the exaggerated luxury created in Attica by years of hasty material progress was abolished. Just as the rich Ionian robes disappeared, to be replaced by the simple Dorian male costume,[15] so on the faces of the men sculptured in those years the graceful, meaningless, conventional smile of the Ionian social and physical ideal gave place to a deep, almost morose seriousness. It was the next generation, the era of Sophocles, that found the ideal of classical harmony to balance the two extremes. That which neither aristocratic culture nor the influence of a highly developed alien civilization could give to Athens was produced by her own historical destiny. Through that destiny a great poet arose, deeply conscious that he was part of the Athenian nation, to implant in his fellow-citizens the eager and devout sense of victory, and to unite classes, separated by differences of birth and culture, in a common gratitude and aspiration. For ever afterwards, the greatest historical and spiritual achievements of Athens were to belong, not to one class, but to the entire people. All the earlier greatness of the Athenians now sank into comparative insignificance: the people now became its natural inheritors. The civilization of the Athenian people in the fifth century was formed not by its new constitution nor by its new right of suffrage, but by its victory. That victory, not the older aristocratic culture, was the foundation of Periclean Athens. Sophocles, Euripides, and Socrates were sons of ordinary citizens. Sophocles came of a family of manufacturers; Euripides' parents were small farmers; the father of Socrates was a stonemason in a little suburban town. After the Areopagus, which in Aeschylus' time was the balance-wheel of the whole state, was deprived of its importance, the democratic constitution grew more and more radical,[16] and the antidemocratic tendency of aristocratic society and culture became more and more marked. But we must not interpret the age of Salamis by the age of Critias. In the days of Themistocles, Aristides, and Cimon, the commons and the nobles were bound to each other by the great tasks which they shared—rebuilding the city, constructing the long walls to the harbour, establishing the Delian league, and finishing the war on the Asiatic coast. The Athenians of those decades, to whom tragedy, the new poetic form, was addressed, had in their character something of the soaring aspiration and power, something also of the self-renunciation, humility, and reverence which characterize the spirit of Aeschylus.

Tragedy restored to Greek poetry its power of embracing all human interests. Therein it can be compared only with the Homeric epic.[17] In spite of the rich fertility of literature in the intervening centuries, tragedy was equalled only by epic in its wealth of subject-matter, its power of handling large masses of material, and its sheer magnitude of creative achievement. It seemed as if the poetic genius of Greece, once born in Ionia, had been reborn in Attica. Epic and tragedy are two huge mountain-chains, connected by an unbroken line of foothills.

If we regard the development of Greek poetry since its first great period, that of the epic, as expressing the progressive formation and definition of the great historical forces which moulded the Greek character, we shall find that the rebirth to which we have referred takes on a special meaning. The poets after Homer concentrated more and more on elaborating the intellectual content of poetry, whether by expressing their own personal beliefs or by establishing and expounding general standards to which their fellow-citizens were to conform.[18] Most post-Homeric poetry was actually developed out of epic; but after they had become completely independent of it, the mythical tradition which embodied the intellectual content of epic was either abandoned entirely (as in Tyrtaeus, Callinus, Archilochus, Semonides, Solon, Theognis, and usually in the lyric poets and Mimnermus) or introduced merely from without (as in Hesiod's *Works and Days,* the Pindaric myths, and sometimes in the lyricists), in the form of mythical examples to explain the abstract mythless ideas of the poet. Much of the work of these poets was pure preaching, *parainesis,* and consisted of general advice and instruction. Another part of it was reflection on abstract themes. Even praise, which in epic concerned only the deeds of mythical heroes, was now given to real contemporary men; and the purely emotional lyric now described the feelings of living persons. Thus post-Homeric poetry came to express, ever more completely and more directly, the actual spiritual life —social and individual alike—of the time in which it was written: and this important change in the nature of poetry was made possible only by the comparative abandonment of the heroic saga-tradition, which together with the praise of the gods, had once been the only subject which a poet could use.

Yet, from another point of view, although the post-Homeric poets endeavoured to realize the intellectual content of epic in their own age, and thereby to make poetry more and more the immediate guide and interpreter of life, the saga-tradition retained its importance, even after the epic period, as an inexhaustible source of poetic material. The poet could employ it to idealize his subject, for he ennobled the thoughts and actions of his contemporaries by referring them to mythical parallels, and thus made his poems move in a plane of higher reality: such, as we have seen, is the use of mythical examples in lyric poetry.[19] Or he could actually write poems on mythical subjects, treating them with a new emphasis and interest, far different from those of the epic, and consequently altering the form in which they were presented. Thus the cyclic poets were chiefly interested in rehandling the material provided by the saga of Troy. They did not appreciate the artistic and spiritual grandeur of the *Iliad* and the *Odyssey;* they wanted merely to narrate the events which had happened before and after. These epics—written in a sort of dictionary-epic phraseology which appears here and there even in the later books of the Homeric poems—satisfied the growing interest in history; and indeed the historical emphasis was inevitable, since primitive people treat all saga-tradition as real historical narrative. The historical attitude to the myth was even more marked in the catalogue-poems, which were ascribed to Hesiod because he was a famous poet whose style resembled theirs. They answered the demands of noblemen for genealogies tracing their descent back to gods and heroes: they were in fact the prehistory of their age. Both these types of epic poetry maintained themselves beside the mythless poetry of the seventh and sixth centuries. With none of its immediate and living significance, they still responded to certain needs of their time; for Homer and the myth were the inescapable background of all contemporary life. They were, so to speak, the scholarship of the time. They were the direct ancestors of the Ionian chronicles which rehandled traditional material with or without genealogical intentions—the books of Acusilaus, Pherecydes, and Hecataeus. Poetic form had long been merely an antiquated and pointless decoration for work of this kind, and the scanty remains of the logographers who wrote in prose seem far fresher and more modern than their poetic ancestors. They endeavoured to revive public interest in traditional history by the grace and directness of their narrative style.

At the same time as mythical traditions were thus being transferred into prose history, they were undergoing another metamorphosis in choral poetry, the new genus which appeared in Greek Sicily. The saga was in fact being transmuted from the epic to the lyric form. Still, it was not being once more taken seriously. Stesichorus of Himera is no less coolly critical in his approach to it than Hecataeus of Miletus. Choric poets before Pindar, unlike the epic writers, regarded the sagas not as an end in themselves but as good idealized subjects for their choruses and their music. *Logos, rhythmos,* and *harmonia* were all formative elements in the choric ode, but the *logos* was the least important. The music, which guided the development of the words, was the real focus of interest. The peculiar impression of vacuity and incompleteness which the remains of some of these odes, without their music, make on the modern reader is produced by the choral technique of breaking up a long saga into a number of moments of lyrical emotion and stringing them together in ballad-like narrative form, simply as a vehicle for musical expression. Even the myths told in narrative form in a simple lyric frame, as in Sappho, were intended to awake only one mood.[20] She meant them to be the substratum of her lyrical emotion; at least, that is the sole effect of myth as used in her poems, and thus enveloped by emotion its real character is lost.

Although the myth retained some of its old authority in poetry and prose—and it is important to note that it also provided subjects for most of the sixth-century vase-painters—it had ceased to be the vehicle for great and moving ideas. If it was neither an ideal setting nor a historical narrative, it was merely stylized decoration. Any large spiritual impulses of that age were expressed not through the myth but in sheerly intellectual form. We might well expect that this development would be carried further: that poetry would abandon the discussion of large abstract topics to the newly invented philosophical and narrative prose of Ionia, and that all the reflective and intellectual poetic forms of the sixth century would be replaced by prose λόγοι using *areté, tyché, nomos,* and *politeia* as subjects for prosaic instruction or investigation, as in the sophistic movement of later centuries.

But the inhabitants of Greece proper had not been able to follow the pioneering Ionian spirit so far as this, and the Athenians never chose to, since poetry, for them, was not so far rationalized that they could envisage such a transition. In the sixth century, poetry in mainland Greece had regained what it had lost in Ionia, its noble function as a guide and inspiration of life. Actually, the intellectual explorations of Ionian scientists and philosophers were no more 'philosophical' than the deep thoughts awakened in the Athenian mind by the violent efforts and victories which attended the Athenian people's entrance into history; but the new Athenian conception of life's scope and duties could be shown to the world only in sublime poetry by highly spiritualized religious symbolism. Sixth-century Greece, shaken by the fall of the old aristocratic régime and of its ancestral religious faith, and disturbed by the rise of strange and hitherto unimagined spiritual forces, yearned for a new moral standard, a new life-pattern. And nowhere was that disturbance greater or that yearning deeper than in the land of Solon; nowhere was there a richer combination of delicate sensibility with youthful energy, still unused and almost crudely immature, and a vast variety of spiritual and intellectual talent. That was the soil which brought the marvellous fruit of tragedy to ripeness. It was fed and borne up by roots in every region of the Greek spirit, but its taproot was plunged deeply into the rich subsoil of all the poetry and of all the higher life of Hellas—the myth.

Thus, in an age which seemed to be moving ever further away from heroism, and (as Ionian literature shows) exercised its greatest powers on reflective thinking and heightened emotional perception, there sprang from those roots a new and more deeply felt spirit of heroism, which was closely and fundamentally akin to the myth and to the way of life embodied in the myth. It poured new life into the old mythical forms, and gave them back their speech, as Odysseus gave life and speech to the dead—by letting them drink of the blood of sacrifice. Without that sacrifice, the miracle of the myth's resurrection could not be understood.

The attempts of modern scholars to trace the ancestry of tragedy and determine its true nature usually pass by this question. In fact, they have externalized the problem, by deriving the new creation, tragedy, from some earlier but similar literary type—by believing, for instance, that the Dionysiac dithyramb 'took serious form' when some inventive genius made it deal with subjects from the heroic sagas. According to this view, Attic tragedy is nothing but 'a heroic myth dramatized and played by a chorus of Athenian citizens'.[21] But though the mediæval literature of all civilized western nations is full of dramatizations of the lives of the saints, none of them developed into tragedy until they were influenced by the ancient models. And the dramatization of the Greek sagas would have been no more than an ephemeral innovation in choral lyric, with no interest for us and no possibility of further development, if the sagas had not been transposed to a higher plane of the heroic spirit from which they had been produced, and thereby acquired a new artistic power of creating character. Unfortunately we have no accurate description of the oldest form of tragedy, and can only estimate from the height of its development how it must have started. In its finished form, which we find in Aeschylus, it is a rebirth of myth, brought about by the new conception of man and of the universe which had been given by Solon to the Athenian people, and which in Aeschylus reached the highest and most sensitive realization of the religious and moral problems which it had to face.

It is not the purpose of this book to give a complete account of the origin and growth of tragedy; completeness in any subject is beyond its scope.[22] As far as the problem concerns us here, we shall study the earliest developments of the genus with special reference to the ideas expressed in tragedy. For tragedy was a many-sided thing, and can be approached from widely different points of view. We are attempting merely to examine it as a spiritual embodiment of the new type of human character which was growing up in the fifth century, and of the educational power which it possessed in a supreme degree. The remains of Greek tragedy are so large that we must consider the problem from an appropriate distance, if our study is not to grow into a separate book. But it is right and necessary thus to maintain perspective through distance; for tragedy can be appreciated only if we start with the conviction that it is the highest manifestation of a type of humanity for which art, religion, and philosophy still form an indissoluble unity. It is that unity which makes it such a happy experience to study the ways in which the epoch expressed itself, and which renders that study far preferable to any history of philosophy, religion, or literature alone. The periods in which the history of human culture runs not in one stream, but in a series of separate channels marked literature, philosophy, and religion, are necessarily one-sided, however deep may be the historical reasons for their one-sidedness. It seems as if poetry, which the Greeks were the first to raise to such a difficult height of technical excellence and spiritual significance, had wished to reveal all its beauty and power and wealth once more before it left this earth and journeyed back to Olympus.

The undisputed supremacy of Attic tragedy, which lasted for a hundred years, coincided chronologically and spiritually with the rise, greatness, and decline of the secular power of Athens. Within that period tragedy attained that domination over the Athenian people which we see reflected in the allusions of the comic poets. Its power over the Athenians was an essential factor in creating its far-reaching influence throughout the whole Greek world, for the Athenian empire made the Attic dialect understood almost throughout Greece. And finally, tragedy furthered the intellectual and moral degeneration which Thucydides correctly asserted to have been the ruin of Athens, just as it had given the state strength and cohesion during its rise and glorified it at the zenith of its power. If we were studying the develop-

ment of tragedy from Aeschylus through Sophocles to Euripides
(we need not here consider the many other playwrights who
were stimulated by their achievements) from a purely artistic or
psychological point of view, we should judge the whole process
far differently. But from the point of view of the history of human culture, in the deepest sense of the word, the development
of tragedy passed through the stages sketched above; and so it
was described by the contemporary Attic comedians, who mir-
rored the ideas of their time with no thought of posterity. The
men of that age never felt that the nature and influence of
tragedy were purely and simply aesthetic. Its power over them
was so vast that they held it responsible for the spirit of the
whole state; and although as historians we may believe that even
the greatest poets were the representatives, not the creators, of
national spirit, our belief cannot alter the fact that the Athenians
held them to be their spiritual leaders, with a responsibility far
greater and graver than the constitutional authority of successive political leaders. Only by keeping that in mind can we understand the attacks made on the freedom of poetry in Plato's
Republic—attacks which seem so inexplicable and repulsive to a
liberal mind. Yet the idea that the tragic poet was responsible
for the spirit of the state cannot have been the original conception of his function; for the age of Pisistratus thought of poetry
purely as a thing to be enjoyed. It was created by the tragedies
of Aeschylus: it was Aeschylus whom Aristophanes conjured up
from the lower world as the only man (in the absence of a Platonic censorship) who could recall poetry to its true function.

After the state organized the dramatic performances held at
the festival of Dionysus, tragedy more and more evoked the
interest and participation of the entire people. The dramatic
festivals of Athens were the ideal national theatre—an ideal
which many poets and producers have since striven in vain to
recapture. The subject matter of tragedy had little connexion
with the cult of the deity at whose festival it was performed.
Not many tragedians handled the myth of Dionysus, although
Aeschylus in the *Lycurgia* presented the Homeric saga of the
Thracian king Lycurgus who sinned against Dionysus, and
Euripides treated the kindred story of Pentheus in *The Bac-
chants*. The true fervour of Dionysus was more suited for the
burlesque satyric plays—the older form of the Dionysiac festi-

val-drama which survived alongside tragedy and which was demanded by the people as a pendant to every tragic trilogy.[23] But
the ecstasy of the tragic actors was truly Dionysiac. It worked
by suggestion on the audience, to make them feel the passions
portrayed on the stage as vividly as if they were their own. This
applies even more to the citizens who made up the chorus: by
rehearsing for a whole year, they grew into the rôles which they
were to portray. The chorus was the high school of early Greece,
long before there were teachers of poetry; and its influence
always went far deeper than merely learning the meaning of the
words to be sung.[24] It was not for nothing that the institution of
chorodidascalia preserved in its name the word which means
'instruction'. Since the performances were infrequent and highly
ritualized, since the state and the whole population were interested in them, since each band of performers in eager competition with others devoted themselves for a year to practising the
new 'chorus' which the poet himself prepared for the great day,[25]
and since a number of poets competed every year to win the
crown of tragedy, it is no exaggeration to say that the tragic
festival was the climax of the city's life. By the festal exaltation
with which the citizens assembled early in the morning to do
honour to Dionysus, spirit and senses alike were prepared for
the strangely solemn influence of the new art of tragedy. The
audience, sitting on plain wooden benches about the pounded
earth of the round dancing-place, was not already blasé with
literature; and the poet by his *psychagogia* could capture the
souls of an entire nation in a moment, as no rhapsode had ever
done with the poems of Homer. Thus the writer of tragedies
was an important political figure; and the state took official cog-
nizance of the art of an elder contemporary of Aeschylus,
Phrynichus, when by writing a tragedy on a recent disaster for
which the Athenians felt themselves partly responsible—the
Persian capture of Miletus—he moved the people to tears.[26]

Dramas with a mythical plot had an equally deep influence
on the audience; for the spiritual power of tragedy did not depend on its closeness to vulgar reality. Tragedy shook the com-
placent certainty of humdrum daily life by incomparably daring
and lofty imaginative language, which reached its highest emotional tension when supported by the rhythm of dance and music
in the dithyrambic ecstasy of the choruses. By deliberately avoid-

ing the vocabulary and syntax of ordinary language, it transported the audience to a world of higher reality. In this noble language, men were called 'mortals' and 'creatures of a day'— not merely by a trick of style, but because its words and images were inspired by a new and living religious feeling. 'Thou who first of the Greeks built towers of lofty language!'—so Aeschylus is addressed by a poet of a later generation.[27] And the boldness of his 'tragic bombast' (as it seemed to be in the light of common day) was felt to be the fit expression of his mighty thoughts. It is only the breath-taking power of his language which can compensate in some degree for the loss of the music and dancing which were integral parts of tragedy. An additional factor was the majesty of the spectacle,[28] which it would be idle antiquarianism to attempt to reconstruct. All we can hope to do by reviving it is to free the modern reader's imagination from the frame of the closed theatre of to-day, with its stage walled in on three sides, which is of course quite unsuitable for Greek tragedy. Even the terrifying tragic masks which appear so often in Greek art are enough to remind us of the essential difference between the drama of Greece and that of all subsequent ages. Tragedy was so far removed from ordinary reality that the Greeks, with their exquisite sense of style, found an inexhaustible source of comic effect in parodying it by transferring its language to the situations of daily life. For every tragedy was played by characters of superhuman majesty in a strange world heavy with religious awe.

The spectator felt that the powerful immediate effect of the play on his senses and emotions was also the manifestation of a deep dramatic power which interpenetrated and inspired every detail of the whole. The concentration of an entire human life into the brief but impressive plot of a tragedy, and its presentation to the eyes and ears of the audience, produced a far stronger temporary effect than the leisurely narrative of epic poetry. The vividly and directly experienced emotion of Dionysiac ecstasy justified the tragedian in concentrating the whole story of a myth into one fateful climactic event. This was quite different from the technique of epic poetry, which told the traditional story for its own sake, and until the end of its development did not envisage the myth as a single tragic whole—as is shown by the structure of the *Iliad* and the *Odyssey*. The earliest tragedy originated from the goat-choruses (of which its name still reminds us) when a poet realized that dithyrambic ecstasy provided a spiritual tension which could be translated into art. It would enable writers to present action as really and visibly happening, and singers to assume a character not their own; and to this dramatic presentation could be added the lyrical concentration of myth which appeared in earlier Sicilian choral poetry. Thus the chorus of lyrical narrators became an actor, and felt the emotions which it had hitherto only described and shared by sympathy. It was naturally impossible, then, for early tragedy to represent a realistic series of events with lifelike details. The chorus was entirely unfitted for such a task. All that it could attempt was to become a perfect instrument of the varied emotions called out by the plot, and to express them by song and dance. The poet could make full use of the limited possibilities of this instrument only by introducing several violent and sudden changes in the course of events described by the plot, so as to draw from the chorus a wide range of contrasting types of expression. This device is still obvious in Aeschylus' earliest drama, *The Suppliants,* where the chorus, composed of the daughters of Danaus, is still the only real actor.[29] This play shows why it was necessary to add a speaker to the chorus of primitve tragedy: his function was to describe to the chorus, and sometimes to initiate by his own actions, a succession of situations which would evoke the dramatically exciting ebb and flow of its lyrical emotion. Thus the chorus moved through 'the troubling passage from joy to pain and from pain to joy'.[30] Through the dance it expressed its delights, its hopes, its thankfulness; it relieved its doubt and anguish by prayer, which had long served to express every kind of intimate emotion in the personal lyric and reflective elegy.

The earliest form of tragedy, which was not action but pure passion, used the force of *sympatheia,* through which the spectators shared the emotions of the chorus, to focus their attention on the doom sent by the gods to produce the tragedy. Without the problem of *tyché* or *moira* (which had been brought home to the Greeks by the Ionian lyric poets) true tragedy would never have developed out of the early 'dithyramb on a mythical theme'.[31] We have lately discovered several interesting examples of the genuine lyric dithyramb, which expresses one single moment of the saga in terms of pure emotion; and it is very far removed from Aeschylus. No doubt an essential factor in the development of tragedy was the introduction of several speakers, so that the chorus no longer took the entire interest, and the speakers shared the action with it until finally they became the chief agents. But this technical improvement was only the means of making the plot, which remained first and foremost a description of human suffering, a fuller and nobler expression of the high idea of God's power over man's life.

Until this idea was infused into it, the new drama did not become truly 'tragic'. It is therefore useless to look for a general conception of tragedy, and the earliest tragedies at least show no trace of one. The definition of tragedy was worked out only after the greatest Greek tragedies had been written. And if we try to give an acceptable meaning to the question 'what is the tragic element in a tragedy?' we must answer it differently for each of the great tragedians.[32] A general definition would only confuse the issue. The shortest way to find a universally applicable answer is by tracing the history of the ideas expressed in tragedy. The Greeks of the sixth and fifth centuries had long been brooding on the great religious problem: why does God send suffering into the life of man?[33] The force of this question was now intensified in the presentation of human suffering to the eyes and ears of the spectators at the tragic festivals by the emotional ardours which the chorus expressed through dance and song, and which through the entrance of several speakers developed into the presentation of a complete episode of human fate. As the spectators shared in the agony of the tragic characters and chorus beneath the thunderstrokes of fate (which Solon had compared to a tempest), they felt their highest spiritual energies called out to resist the storm, and were driven by pity and terror, the immediate psychological effects of their experience,[34] to fall back on their last defence—their faith in the ultimate meaning of life itself. The specifically religious effect on the audience of sharing in the terrors of human destiny, which Aeschylus' tragedies succeeded in producing as an integral part of the action, is the essentially tragic element in his dramas.[35] To appreciate them, we must abandon all modern conceptions of the essence of drama or the essence of tragedy, and direct our attention to that element alone.

When we say that the old myths were made to live again in

tragedy, we mean that they were made actual not only to the senses, but to the minds of the spectators, and not only by the change from narrative description to dramatic action but by the renaissance of their characters and their spirit in the new medium. The traditional legends were now handled from a contemporary point of view. Aeschylus' successors, particularly Euripides, went so far in that direction that they finally vulgarized tragedy into a drama of everyday life; but the first step had been taken by Aeschylus himself in presenting traditional heroes (who were often known only by name and by the bare outlines of their deeds) in accordance with his own conception of them. King Pelasgus in *The Suppliants* is an up-to-date statesman: his acts are determined by the decisions of the popular assembly, and he appeals to it when he is called on to act in a sudden crisis.[36] In *Prometheus Bound,* Zeus is a modern tyrant as seen by the contemporaries of Harmodius and Aristogeiton. Even Agamemnon is far from being a real Homeric king; he belongs to the age of Delphic religion and morality, for he is haunted by the fear of committing any hybris in the pride of power and victory. His whole point of view is dictated by Solon's creed that abundance leads to hybris, and hybris to ruin.[37] The fact that he still does not escape ate is, even more, a perfectly Solonian idea. Prometheus is conceived as the first counsellor of the jealous and distrustful young tyrant Zeus: he has helped Zeus in establishing the new monarchy which he has seized by force; but when he attempts to use that power to carry out plans of his own for the redemption of suffering mankind, the tyrant deprives him of his share in it and banishes him to eternal torture.[38] Aeschylus makes him not only a statesman but something of a sophist, as is shown by the use of the word 'sophist' (which still had an honourable meaning) in addresses to him.[39] Palamedes too, in the lost drama of that name, was depicted as a sophist. Both Prometheus and he proudly enumerate the arts which they have discovered, to aid mankind.[40] Prometheus is equipped with the newest geographical knowledge of strange distant countries. In Aeschylus' time such knowledge was still rare and mysterious, and stirred the eager imagination of the audience; but in both *Prometheus Bound* and *Prometheus Unbound* the hero's long lists of countries, rivers, and nations are not merely poetic decorations—they demonstrate the omniscience of the wise Titan.[41]

The same general criticism applies to the construction of the speeches in Aeschylus' tragedies. As we have explained, the geographical speeches of the sophist Prometheus are intended to assist in expressing his character. Similarly, it is quite in character that much of the advice which old Oceanus gives to Prometheus, to make him surrender to Zeus, should be made up of well-known prudential clichés.[42] In *Seven against Thebes* we seem to hear a fifth-century general giving orders to his army. The prosecution of the matricide Orestes before the Areopagus in *The Eumenides* could furnish valuable historical evidence on Athenian murder-trials, for it is carried out on the regular Attic system; [43] and the hymns praying for the prosperity of Athens in the closing procession are modelled on the language and ritual of public religious ceremonies.[44] Neither post-Homeric epic nor the lyric poets modernized mythical tradition to such a degree as that, although they often altered it to suit their purpose. Aeschylus did not make needless changes in the events as described by tradition, but in rounding out a legendary name into a complete character he could not help transfusing into myth the modern idea which was to be its spiritual lifeblood.

Not only is this true of the characters and their speeches, it applies also to the tragedies as wholes. The structure of all three —characters, speeches, and tragedies alike—is dictated by the view of life which is peculiar to the poet and which he therefore rediscovers in his material. This may sound like a platitude, but it is not. Until the appearance of tragedy no type of poetry had ventured to use myth merely as the vehicle for an idea, and to choose or neglect myths in accordance with their fitness for that purpose. For it must not be thought that every part of the saga-tradition could be dramatized and automatically become a tragedy. Aristotle [45] points out that, though the art of tragedy had been more and more carefully cultivated, there were only a few subjects in the huge realm of saga which attracted poets, and these few had been treated by almost every tragedian. The legend of Oedipus, the legend of the Atridae, and the legend of the royal house of Thebes—Aristotle mentions a few more— were naturally fitted for dramatic development: they were potential tragedies. The epic poets had narrated the events of saga-tradition for their own sake; and the one idea which governs the treatment of the whole mass of material in the later sections of the *Iliad* could not maintain its mastery over the various sections of the entire epic. The lyric poets, when they dealt with legends, emphasized the lyrical moments in them. Tragedy was the first type of poetry to apply to mythical tradition a regular structural principle—the conception of the inevitable rise and fall of human destiny, with its sudden reversals and its final catastrophe.

Welcker was the first to show that Aeschylus usually composed not single tragedies but trilogies.[46] Even after Aeschylus, when poets no longer wrote trilogies on single themes, tragedies were usually presented in trios. It is not known whether the triad-form was originally the only way to treat a tragic theme, or Aeschylus, making a virtue of necessity, moulded the three dramas required by the state into a greater drama on one subject. However, we can easily tell the basic reason for his choice of the triadic form. He shared Solon's view of life, for which one of the greatest problems was the fact that a son often inherits his father's guilt and an innocent generation the guilt of its predecessors. In the *Oresteia* and in his dramas of the Argive and Theban royal houses, Aeschylus attempted to cover the entire course of fate through several generations of one family. He could use the same scheme where the fate of one hero moved to its end through several different stages, as in his *Prometheus Bound, Prometheus Unbound,* and *Prometheus the Torchbearer.*[47]

It is peculiarly fitting to begin the study of Aeschylus by a consideration of the trilogy, which clearly demonstrates that the poet is interested not in a person but in a doom, and that the doom need not fall on one individual, but can affect a whole family. In his tragedies man is not the chief problem: man is merely the vehicle of destiny, and that destiny is the real problem. From the first verse of each of his tragedies we feel the atmosphere heavy with storm, oppressed by a spirit, the incubus of the whole house. Of all the playwrights who have ever written, Aeschylus is the master in tragic exposition. In *The Suppliants, The Persians, Seven against Thebes,* and *Agamemnon,* the first words prepare the spectator for the doom which he feels hanging in the air for the few moments before, with irresistible violence, it breaks. The characters in these dramas are not men, but superhuman powers. Sometimes, as in the last play of the *Oresteia,* these powers actually take the plot out of the hands of human beings, and carry it to its conclusion; but they are always present, and their presence is always felt, whatever part they play. It is impossible to avoid comparing the tragedies with the pediments of Olympia, which are so obviously inspired by tragedy. There too a divinity stands in the full majesty of its power among struggling men, and guides their struggles and their fate.

The tragic poet's hand is clearly shown in the constant introduction of God and fate into the play. The myths did not introduce them in this manner; but Aeschylus ranges every dramatic event under the supreme problem developed by Solon out of the thought of the later epic: how to justify the ways of God to man. He is constantly striving to explore the hidden reasons for God's power over human life. Solon had been chiefly exercised to discover the original connexion of sin with misfortune. In the great elegy [48] which he devoted to this problem the thoughts which inspired Aeschylean tragedy were set forth for the first time. In epic poetry we have the idea of sinful infatuation, até, which combines the belief that God sends unhappiness with the belief that man brings it on himself: the sin which leads man to his ruin is thus the effect of a daemonic power which no man can resist. That is the power which causes Helen to leave her home and husband to flee with Paris, which makes Achilles harden his heart and reason both against the deputation from the army, which offers to repair the insult to his honour, and against the advice of his grey-headed guardian and teacher Phoenix.[49] But as man becomes increasingly conscious of his selfhood, he tends to consider his own will and reason independent of higher powers: and thereby he becomes more responsible for his own fate.

In a very late portion of the Homeric poems, Book I of the *Odyssey,* the poet attempted to delimit the responsibility of God and man for man's unhappiness, and declared that the divine government of the world cannot be blamed for misfortune which men incur against the dictates of their better judgment.[50] Solon enlarged this idea by his magnificent faith in Justice. He held that justice was the divine principle immanent in human life, and that if it were transgressed it would avenge itself inevitably and independently of human justice. As soon as men recognize this connexion between crime and punishment, they take on themselves a great part of the responsibility for their own misery. And with that recognition men come to place the gods—as the guardians of the justice which governs the world—far higher in the moral scale than before. But what man can really understand the ways of God? In this case or in that we may think that we can see God's reasons, but often and often God allows the foolish and the wicked to flourish like the green bay-tree, while a serious endeavour to do good and live justly may fail even if it is perfectly planned and rightly willed. It is impossible to deny that 'unpredictable misfortune' [51] exists in the world: it is the indissoluble remainder of the old até, in which Homer believed, and which still lives on although the existence of guilty misfortune has been recognized. In human experience it has a particularly close connexion with what men call good fortune: for good fortune very quickly changes into the deepest misery, since it leads men directly into hybris. The daemonic danger lurks in greed, which is never satisfied, but always wants twice what it already has. So good fortune and prosperity can never remain in the possession of one man or one family; by their very nature they are bound to change owners. This tragic realization was the strongest support of Solon's faith in the divine justice which governs the world; [52] and the philosophy of Aeschylus could not exist without that faith, which is not so much belief as knowledge.

The immediate dependence of Aeschylean tragedy on this faith is most simply shown by *The Persians*. It is notable that this play does not belong to a trilogy: but it therefore allows us to see the tragic action developing in complete unity on a small scale. Besides, the absence of legendary elements makes *The Persians* a special case. The poet made a tragedy out of a historical event which he himself had witnessed—thereby showing what he considered to be essentially tragic. *The Persians* is certainly not 'dramatized history'—not a cheaply patriotic melodrama written in the flush of victory. Guided by his deep sense of sophrosyné and his knowledge of the limits which it is not permitted to humanity to cross, Aeschylus made his own audience, the victorious Athenian nation, witnesses of the terrifying historical drama of Persian hybris and the divine tisis which crashed down upon the pride and confidence of a mighty nation. Here history actually becomes a tragic myth: because it has the magnitude of myth, and because the catastrophe of man so clearly displays the power of God.

Some have wondered why the Greek poets did not write more tragedies on 'historical themes'. The reason is simple: most historical events did not satisfy the conditions of Greek tragedy. *The Persians* shows how little attention the tragic poet pays to the external dramatic reality of a situation. His entire interest is in the effect of destiny upon the soul. In this respect Aeschylus' attitude to history is the same as his attitude to the myth. But even the suffering of the tragic characters is introduced to serve a deeper purpose; and in that, *The Persians* is a model Aeschylean tragedy, though in the simplest form known to the poet. *Suffering brings knowledge:* that is a piece of very ancient folk-wisdom.[53] The epic did not use it as a leading poetic theme: it was Aeschylus who gave it a deeper meaning and made it his central motif. There are other proverbial ideas which lead up to it—such as the Delphic god's command to realize the limits of human power, *Know yourself,* which Pindar with his devout admiration for Apollo constantly repeated and elaborated. Aeschylus too felt the force of that proverb, and used it as a major theme in *The Persians*. But it did not exhaust his conception of φρονεῖν, tragic knowledge acquired through suffering. In *The Persians* he embodies this idea in one of the characters, by calling up from the dead the wise old king Darius, whose legacy of power his heir Xerxes has squandered in empty arrogance. His ghost foretells that the heaps of corpses on the battlefields of Greece will be dumb warnings to posterity of the fact that mortal pride never prospers.[54] 'For when arrogance blooms it bears the fruit of doomed infatuation, whence it reaps a harvest rich in tears. Seeing how these acts are requited, bethink you of Athens and Greece, and let none despise the immediate gift of heaven and, coveting others, squander a great fortune. God stands ready to punish overweening pride: he calls men to a heavy reckoning.'

This is a revival of Solon's doctrine that even he who has most wealth always covets twice as much. But in Solon that is only a thoughtful recognition of the fact that man's reach exceeds his grasp, while in Aeschylus it grows into the pathos of watching and sharing in daemonic temptation and in the infatuation which makes men yield to that temptation until it leads them to the abyss. Like Solon, Aeschylus holds that God is holy and just, and that his eternal government of the world is faultless. But he gives a heart-rending pathos to the tragedy of man, who brings on God's punishment by his own blindness. In the first scene of *The Persians,* even while the chorus is proudly describing the might and splendour of the Persian army, which it longs to see returning, the sinister shadow of até falls across the stage. 'But what mortal man can escape the crafty deceit of the god? For Até first cozens him flatteringly and then lures him into the net out of which there is no deliverance.' And it adds that its 'sable-clad heart is torn with fear'.[55] The inescapable net of Até is mentioned again at the close of *Prometheus Bound.* Hermes, the messenger of God, warns the Oceanides that they alone are to blame if, by giving sympathy and comfort to the condemned Titan who is about to be hurled into the abyss, they knowingly and voluntarily fall to destruction with him.[56] In *Seven against Thebes* the chorus, while lamenting the two sons of Oedipus who have fallen victims to their father's sin and have killed each other in single combat before the gates of Thebes, sees an appalling vision: [57] 'But at last the Curses raised the clear battle-cry, when the whole race was routed in resistless defeat. The trophy of Até stands at the gates where the brothers were slain, and where the daemon paused after conquering them both.'

Aeschylus did not believe that destiny was simply a force which punishes the guilty man to make an example for others. So much is clear from the language of the macabre images in which he depicts the workings of até; for no poet before him had so vividly realized and expounded its daemonic nature. By Aeschylus' description, even the strongest believer in the moral power of knowledge is driven to see that até always remains até, whether (as Homer says) its foot moves over the heads of men, or (in Heraclitus' phrase) man's own character is his daemon.[58] What we call character is not an essential element in Aeschylean tragedy. His whole conception of fate is summed up in the tension between two ideas—his faith in the perfect and uninterrupted justice of God's government of the world, and his horrified realization of the daemonic cruelty and perfidiousness of até, which leads man to violate the world-order and inevitably to be punished for his violation. Solon, starting with the belief that injustice was social pleonexia, injurious aggrandisement, endeavoured to discover whether injustice was punished; and determined that it always was. Aeschylus, starting with the tragically moving experience of the power of fortune in human life, and searching for sufficient ground for its actions, was always led back to a faith in the ultimate justice of heaven. We must not overlook this difference of emphasis in the general agreement of Aeschylus' and Solon's views, if we are to understand why the same doctrine in one is so peaceful and in the other so dramatic and so moving.

The tension of Aeschylus' thought appears more clearly in the other tragedies than in *The Persians,* which is a fairly simple and straightforward development of the idea that God always punishes hybris in man. It was clearest of all in the great trilogies, as far as can be judged from the extant fragments; although we can see little of it in the earliest surviving tragedy, *The Suppliants,* since it is the first play in a trilogy of which the rest is lost. It is most easily traced in the *Oresteia,* which survives entire, and next to it in the Labdacid trilogy, since we fortunately possess its last play, *Seven against Thebes.*

In the *Oresteia* not only Aeschylus' structural art and his genius for imaginative language, but the tension of his religious and moral thought is at its highest point: it is almost incredible that he completed this gigantic work, the most powerful drama in the entire literature of the world, in his grey old age soon before his death. In the first place, we must observe that it is impossible to separate *Agamemnon* from the two tragedies which follow it. Strictly speaking, it is barbarous to treat it as an independent play—to say nothing of *The Eumenides,* which cannot be understood except as a colossal finale to the whole trilogy. *Agamemnon* is no more an independent work than *The Suppliants:* it leads straight on to the second tragedy. For the *Oresteia* is not simply a dramatic account of the curse of guilt which clings to the family of the Atridae: that would have made a trilogy of co-ordinated but semi-independent tragedies of guilt, one for each generation, with *Agamemnon* in the centre and an *Orestes* as the last play. No: *Agamemnon* states the conditions of the unique antinomy which occupies the central position, the involuntary but inevitable guilt of Orestes, acquired when he obeys Apollo's command to kill his own mother in revenge for his father. And the whole of the final tragedy shows how this knot, which no human wit could loosen, is cut by a divine miracle of grace—a miracle which brings about both the acquittal of the guilty Orestes and the abolition of the custom of revenge for blood (a horrible relic of the old supremacy of the family in law and custom) and sets up in its place the new constitutional state as universal arbiter of justice.[59] Thus in the representative poetry of the new democracy the city-state appears as the guarantor of the freedom and the human dignity and security of the individual.

The guilt of Orestes is not founded on his character. Aeschylus does not consider him to be a man whose nature destines him to commit matricide. He is merely the unfortunate son who is bound to avenge his father: at the moment when he enters manhood, he is faced by the dreadful deed which will destroy him before he even tastes life, and to which the god of Delphi constrains him again and again whenever he shrinks from the fixed end. He bears the burden of an immutable fate. None of Aeschylus' tragedies exposes the problem on which his poetry and thought were centred more clearly than the *Oresteia*. That problem is the conflict between the divine powers which, each in its own way, strive to uphold justice.[60] The living man Orestes is only the point at which, with destructive impetus, they collide; and even his final absolution is far less important than the general reconciliation between the old and new gods of justice, and the festal hymns which consecrate the founding of the new state-justice and the conversion of the Furies into Kindly Spirits.

The trilogy devoted to the fate of the Thebian kings closes with *Seven against Thebes,* a drama which actually surpasses the *Oresteia* in sombre tragic power, not least for the dreadful fratricide with which it ends. The whole Theban triad was inspired by Solon's thought that the sins of the fathers are visited on the innocent children.[61] Eteocles and Polynices, sons of Oedipus and Jocasta, fall victims to the curse which haunts their house.

Aeschylus grounded the curse upon the sin of the early Labda-cids; for, devout as he was, he would have been quite unable to write of a crime so awful as the fratricide unless it had had, in his eyes, a sufficient reason.[62] But the tragedy of the *Seven* is not the pitiless completion of an omnipotent and unerring divine punishment, which would satisfy the God-fearing moralist. The emphasis is on the fact that here the inexorable causality of ancient guilt destroys a man who deserves a better fate because of his virtuous deeds as prince and hero, a man who enlists our sympathy as soon as he speaks. Polynices is a mere shadow in the background; [63] but his brother Eteocles, the hope and guardian of his city, is very carefully drawn. In him the conflict of per-sonal areté and suprapersonal doom reaches its highest tension: so that the play is an extreme contrast to *The Persians* with its simple lapidary logic of hybris and punishment. The guilt of Eteocles' ancestors scarcely avails to balance the awful weight of suffering which lies on him. If we appreciate the sombre unre-solved tragedy of the *Seven,* we shall realize far more vividly the significance of the final reconciliation depicted in *The Eumenides.*

The boldness of *Seven against Thebes* lies in its antinomy, its moral conflict. On the one hand Aeschylus affirms the higher justice whose power we must judge not by the fate of any indi-vidual but by a general view of the whole story; and on the other he evokes pity and terror by showing the inescapable power of the daemon moving towards its cruel end and beating down the staunch resistance of the heroic Eteocles. What is new and great in this play is the tragic inevitability with which Aeschylus delib-erately guides the last descendant of the guilty family towards his certain death.[64] Thereby he creates a character which reveals its highest areté only in a tragic situation. Eteocles is to die; but before he dies he is to save his city from defeat and slavery. Behind the mournful account of his death we cannot but hear the triumphal hymn of thanksgiving for deliverance.[65] Thus the poet, for ever grappling with the problem of destiny, solves it by rec-ognizing that there can be a greatness in tragedy, an otherwise unattainable height which man can reach even at the instant of his destruction. And the hero, by sacrificing his doomed life to the salvation of his fellow-men, thereby reconciles us to what might seem, even to the devout, a senseless and needless destruc-tion of the highest areté.

Seven against Thebes is a revolutionary advance on the earlier type of tragedy, such as *The Persians* and *The Suppliants*. It is one of the first extant dramas which have a hero at the centre of their plot.[66] In earlier tragedies the chorus played the chief part and was the focus of the action. But in the *Seven* the chorus has no individuality (as the Danaids have in *The Suppliants*); it simply represents the traditional elements of lamentation and tragic terror which compose the atmosphere of tragedy. It is a crowd of women with their children, panic-stricken citizens of the besieged city. Against the background of their fears, the hero stands out all the more nobly, in the grave and thoughtful energy of his actions.[67] Greek tragedy always describes suffering rather than action, but Eteocles suffers by acting until he is struck down.

Prometheus Bound also centres on a heroic figure, who occupies the foreground not only in one tragedy (as in the *Seven*) but throughout the trilogy. We can, however, judge the trilogy only by the one play which has survived. *Prometheus Bound* is the tragedy of genius. Eteocles dies fighting like a hero, but neither his heroism nor his prowess as a warrior is the source of his tragic fate, far less his personal character. His tragedy falls on him from without by the curse of his house. But Prometheus' suffering and disaster are caused by his own nature and actions. 'By free will,' he says,[68] 'yes, by free will I sinned, I will not deny it: by helping mankind I made my own agony.' Therefore *Prometheus Bound* is in a different category from most of the other extant dramas. Still, the tragedy of Prometheus is not a purely individual one: it is the agony of all spiritual pioneers.[69] The hero was created by Aeschylus' imagination. Hesiod knew Prometheus only as the Evil One, who was punished by Zeus for stealing fire from heaven.[70] But Aeschylus, with that mighty imaginative power which we cannot sufficiently admire and honour, built up his act into an imperishable symbol of humanity. Prometheus he made the Bringer of Light to suffering mankind. The divine power of fire was for him the concrete image of civilization.[71] And Prometheus was the civilizing genius who explores the whole world, who makes it subservient to his will by organizing its forces, who reveals its treasures and establishes on a firm basis the groping insecure life of man. Both Hermes, messenger of the gods, and the spirit of sheer Force, servant of their justice, who rivets the fetters on Prometheus, address him derisively as *sophist,* master of discovery.[72] Aeschylus took the main outlines of the character of Prometheus, the hero of the intellectual world, from Ionian theories of the origin of civilization,[73] which with their triumphant faith in *progress* contrasted so sharply with the peasant Hesiod's melancholy description of the five ages of the degenerating world, and of its approaching ruin.[74] Prometheus is inventive and exploratory genius, inspired by a helpful love for suffering humanity.[75]

In this tragedy, suffering is the badge of all the human race. It is Prometheus who first brings light into man's troglodytic existence, 'poor, nasty, brutish, and short'. If further proof is needed that Aeschylus regards the god, nailed to the rocks as if in derision of his work, as an embodiment of human life, it is the fact that he suffers like mankind and multiplies human suffering in his own agony. Who can venture to say how far the poet here pushed his conscious symbolism? In Prometheus we find much less of the individuality which makes all the mythical figures of Greek tragedy as personal as if they had really lived. Men of all ages have recognized in him a representative of humankind: they have felt themselves nailed to his rock, and have joined in the shout of his powerless but unconquerable hate.[76] Aeschylus may have conceived him first and foremost as a lifelike figure of drama; but in the core of his character, his discovery of fire, there is and always was a philosophical element, a deep rich ideal of humanity which thousands of years cannot exhaust. It was reserved for the Greeks to create, in his symbol of the heroic struggles and agonies of all human genius, the greatest expression of the tragedy of their own nature. Only the ECCE HOMO— which, with its suffering for the sins of the world, arose from a different spirit—formed another eternal symbol of humanity without taking something from the truth of Prometheus. Poets and philosophers of all nations have for centuries loved *Prometheus Bound* far more than any other Greek drama, and they will always love it, as long as a spark of Prometheus' fire still burns in the human soul.

The permanent greatness of the *Prometheus* tragedies did not lie in the theogonical secrets—whatever they may have been— which according to the overt and covert threats of Prometheus were to be revealed in the second part of the trilogy,[77] but in the intellectual heroism of Prometheus himself, which reached the highest and most stimulating tragic emotion in *Prometheus Bound.* It is certain that *Prometheus Unbound* completed the picture given there, but it is equally certain that we cannot reconstruct it. We cannot say whether the violent and cruel despot of *Prometheus Bound* was transformed, later in the trilogy, into the personification of eternal wisdom and justice whom we admire in *Agamemnon* and *The Suppliants.* It would be interesting to know how Aeschylus himself regarded the character of Prometheus. Certainly he did not conceive that the Titan's sin was merely an offence against the property of the gods, consisting in the theft of their fire, but rather (in accordance with the spiritual and symbolic significance which he imparted to it) that it was connected with some deep tragic imperfection in the benefit he had done to mankind by his wonderful gift.[78]

In every age, there are enlightened spirits who dream of the victory of knowledge and art over the external and internal forces which are inimical to man. Aeschylus does not attack this faith in *Prometheus Bound;* but its hero boasts of the kindness he has done to humanity by helping it to rise out of darkness to the light of progress and civilization, and the chorus of Oceanides shyly expresses its admiration for his godlike creative genius, though they do not wholly approve of his conduct.[79] In order to make Prometheus impart his enthusiasm to us as he does, the poet must have shared in these lofty aspirations and himself admired the greatness of Prometheus' genius. But he does not imagine that the work of a civilizing pioneer can ever be crowned by one complete and glorious success. Again and again the chorus repeats that the sovereign independence of creative genius knows no bounds. Prometheus has separated himself from his brothers the Titans and realized the hopelessness of their lives: for they recognize no power but brute strength, and will not understand that the intellect alone rules the world [80] —that is how Prometheus conceives the superiority of the new Olympian world-order over the Titans whom it has hurled down to Tartarus. Yet he himself is still a Titan in the immoderate love which leads him to lift suffering mankind by main force over the barriers set for it by the ruler of the world, and in the proud impetuosity of his creative impulses. In fact, he is more Titanic in spirit, although on a higher plane, than his giant brothers; for in a fragment of *Prometheus Unbound,* they come, released from their chains and reconciled with Zeus, to visit him in his place of torture, where he is suffering agonies far more hideous than they have ever known.[81] Once more we can neither overlook the symbolism nor complete it, since the continuation of the story is missing. The sole guide to its completion is the pious resignation of the chorus in *Prometheus Bound:* [82] 'I shudder to see thee torn by a myriad torments: for without fear of Zeus, in selfwill, thou dost honour mankind overmuch, Prometheus. But how is thy boon so bootless, my friend? where, where is there any defence? where is there help from the creatures of a day? Hast thou not seen the feeble dreamlike impotence in which the blind race of man is fettered? The plans of mortals will never overstep the accord set up by Zeus.'

And thus the fate of the civilizing genius Prometheus leads the chorus through pity and terror to a tragic realization, as it says itself: [83] 'Thus I have learnt from gazing on thy ruinous fate, Prometheus.' This is a passage of the utmost importance for Aeschylus' conception of the effect of tragedy. The audience goes through the same experience as the chorus, and is meant to feel and learn the same things. The coalescence of audience and chorus marks a new stage in the development of Athenian choric art. In *The Suppliants,* as we have said,[84] the chorus of Danaids is still the only real actor: no other hero appears on the stage. That this was the original nature of the chorus was first clearly laid down by the young Nietzsche in his brilliant but unequal work, *The Birth of Tragedy.* But we must not generalize from his discovery. When one man took the place of the chorus in the centre of the plot, the function of the chorus was bound to change. It became more and more an 'ideal spectator', although attempts were still made to give it a part in the action. And one of the strongest factors in the educational power of Greek tragedy is the fact that it has a chorus to objectify the tragic experiences of the actors by its lyric cries of sympathy. The chorus of *Prometheus Bound* is nothing but pity and terror: and thereby it embodies the effects of the tragedy so perfectly that Aristotle could have found no better example to illustrate his famous definition of them.[85] Although the chorus identifies itself with Prometheus' agonies so completely that at the end of the play, despite the warnings of Hermes, it chooses to sink into the

abyss with him and share his torments, its tragic emotion is puri-
fied into tragic knowledge in the choral song quoted above. For
there the chorus raises itself above emotion to pure contemplation, and so reaches the highest aim of all tragedy.

When it says that the highest knowledge can be reached only
through suffering, it is expressing the fundamental belief on
which Aeschylus' tragic religion is based. All his works are built
upon that mighty spiritual unity of suffering and knowledge. It
is easy to trace the development of the idea through his life as a
poet: back from *Prometheus Bound* to *The Persians,* where it is
voiced by the ghost of Darius, and the deep passion and deep
thoughtfulness of the prayers in *The Suppliants,* where the Danaids in their tribulation strive to comprehend the inexplicable
ways of Zeus; and again forward to the *Oresteia,* where the
solemn prayer of the chorus in *Agamemnon* [86] gives the poet's
faith the noblest expression of all. That deeply moving faith in
the ultimate blessing of pain, which Aeschylus strove throughout
a lifetime to fortify against doubt and fear, has a vast and truly
evangelical power of reforming and guiding the human spirit. It
is prophetic, and yet more than prophetic. Its cry, 'Zeus, whoso-
ever he be!' rises before the last of the doors which conceal the
eternal secret of life—the God whose nature can be known only
by suffering in the experience of his actions, 'who has made the
road to knowledge for mortals, by laying down the law, *Learn
by Suffering.* Instead of sleep there flows into the heart the agony
of remembering guilt; so even unwillingly men come to health of
mind. But grace comes by force from the gods who sit on thrones
of majesty.' Only in this tragic knowledge can Aeschylus find
rest, after he 'casts off the burden of doubt'. And in reaching it
he is helped by the myth which changes so easily into a pure symbol: Zeus is the conqueror of the primitive world of Titans and
their challenging arrogant hybristic strength. Despite all attacks,
order constantly re-establishes itself against chaos. That is the
meaning of suffering, even when we cannot understand it.

Thus the devout soul of Aeschylus realized through the power
of suffering the splendour of God's triumph. None can truly
know that suffering and that triumph until, like the eagle in the
air, he joins fullheartedly in the cry of victory with which all
living things salute Zeus the conqueror. That is the meaning of
the 'accord set up by Zeus', in *Prometheus,* the *harmonia* which

mortal wishes never overstep, and to which even the Titan-made civilization of mankind must end by adapting itself. And from this point of view there is a deep significance in the fact that Aeschylus' life and his poetic achievement close, in the final scene of the *Oresteia,* with the picture of *cosmos,* harmonious order throughout the state, reconciling all oppositions, and itself based upon the eternal cosmos. As it takes its place in this universal order, the new figure of 'the tragic man' created by the art of tragedy displays its hidden harmony with the whole of life, and, by reaching new heroic heights of endurance, agony, and strength, rises to a far loftier humanity.

SOPHOCLES AND THE TRAGIC CHARACTER

IN any account of the educational power of Attic tragedy, Sophocles and Aeschylus must be named together. Sophocles consciously assumed the position of successor to Aeschylus, and his contemporaries, while venerating Aeschylus as the master and inspirer of the Attic theatre, readily gave Sophocles the place next to him.[1] This idea of tradition and inheritance is deeply rooted in the Greek conception of poetry, for the Greeks did not focus their attention principally on individual poets, but on poetry itself as an independent and self-perpetuating form of art, which, when bequeathed by one poet to another, continued to be a complete and authoritative standard. We can realize this by studying the history of tragedy. As soon as it reached maturity, its magnificence almost compelled artists and thinkers of the fifth and subsequent centuries to exert their highest powers in a noble rivalry.

The competitive element which was implicit in all forms of Greek poetic activity grew in proportion as art became the centre of public life and the expression of the whole political and intellectual outlook of the age. Accordingly, it reached its highest point in drama. That is the only possible explanation of the huge numbers of second- and third-rate poets who took part in the Dionysiac competitions. Nowadays we are always amazed to hear of the swarm of satellites and minor planets which accompanied during their lifetime the few great and eternal lights of Attic poetry. For all its prizes and organized festivals, the state did not stimulate the enthusiasm of the minor poets—it merely guided it and controlled it, although its very guidance was an encouragement. It was then inevitable (quite apart from the permanence of professional tradition in all art, and especially in Greek art) that the constant competition and comparison between tragedies as they were produced from year to year should create a continuous form of intellectual and social control over this new artistic type—a control which did not interfere with artistic freedom, but made public taste extraordinarily sensitive to any falling-off in the great tradition and to any diminution in the power and depth of the influence which tragedy exercised.

Hence there is some measure of justification for comparing three artists so dissimilar and in many respects so incapable of comparison as the great Attic tragedians. It is always unfair, if not actually foolish, to regard Sophocles and Euripides as successors of Aeschylus, for that view imposes standards upon them which are too high for the age in which they lived. The best successor of a great man is he who, having creative powers of his own, goes his own way unperturbed by previous greatness. The Greeks themselves were always willing to admire, not only the man who struck out a new form, but also, perhaps even more, the man who brought it to perfection. In fact, they considered the highest originality to lie not in the first but in the most perfect achievement in any field of art.[2] But since every artist develops his own art within the form which he finds ready to hand, and is therefore in some degree indebted to it, he must recognize that the traditional form which he uses is a standard for himself, and must allow his work to be judged as maintaining, diminishing, or enhancing the significance of the form which he employs. It is obvious then that the development of Attic tragedy does not run from Aeschylus to Sophocles and from Sophocles to Euripides, but that the immediate successor of Aeschylus is Euripides, quite as much as Sophocles, who actually outlived him. Both Sophocles and Euripides continued the work of their master, but there is good reason for the emphasis which modern scholars lay on the fact that there are far more points of contact between Euripides and Aeschylus than between Sophocles and either of the other two. Aristophanes and other contemporary critics were right in regarding Euripides as the corruptor, not of Sophoclean, but of Aeschylean tragedy;[3] for he took up the tradition where Aeschylus had left it, although in fact he did not curtail but vastly increased the scope of tragedy. His achievement was to admit the questionings and criticisms of his own age, and to build tragedies round up-to-date problems rather than the religious doubts which had exercised Aeschylus. But despite all the violent contrasts between the two poets, they were akin in their fondness for discussing and dramatizing large spiritual problems.

From this point of view, Sophocles once appeared to be almost outside the main stream of development. He seemed to have none of the passionate intensity and depth of personal experience which enriched the work of his two great fellow-dramatists; scholars felt that there was, in view of his perfection of form and his lucid objectivity, some historical justification but also much unnecessary prejudice in the classicists' admiration for him as the greatest of the Greek dramatists. Thus they followed the modern psychological trend in rejecting him in favour of the powerful but uncouth archaism of Aeschylus and the sophisticated subjectivism of Euripides, both of whom had been too long neglected.[4] When they at last endeavoured to give Sophocles his true place in the revised history of Greek drama, they were compelled to look elsewhere for the secret of his success. They found it either in his religious attitude or in his technical skill as a playwright; which was developed during his youth by the great rise of dramatic technique led by Aeschylus, and which aimed at one thing above all else—dramatic effect.[5] But if Sophocles' art is nothing more than dramatic craftsmanship (however important that may be), we should be compelled to ask why he was judged not only by the classicist critics but by the ancients themselves to be the perfection of tragedy. And it would be extremely difficult to assign him a worthy place in a history of Greek culture like this book, which is not fundamentally concerned with the purely aesthetic aspect of poetry.

There is no doubt that he has no religious message so powerful as that of Aeschylus. There was a deep quiet devoutness in his character, but it was not expressed with marked emphasis in his plays. What was once called the impiety of Euripides strikes us as far more religious than the unshakable but placid piety of Sophocles. We must admit that modern scholars are right in saying that his real strength did not consist in dramatizing problems, although as the successor of Aeschylus he inherited the ideas and problems with which Aeschylus had dealt. We must start by considering the effect produced by his plays on the stage —and that effect, be it noted, was not created entirely by clever technique. Of course, he was bound to be technically superior to old Aeschylus, since he belonged to the second generation, the generation which always refines and subtilizes the work of the pioneer. Yet how can we explain the fact that all attempts to satisfy the changed taste of to-day by putting Aeschylus and

Euripides on the modern stage have failed—apart from a few experimental productions before more or less specialized audiences—while Sophocles is the one Greek dramatist who keeps his place in the repertoire of the contemporary theatre? Certainly he owes his position nowadays to no classicist prejudice. The rigid undramatic effect of the choruses which dominate Aeschylus' tragedies cannot be counteracted by the depth of their thought and the richness of their language, when they stand still to speak their lines, and neither dance nor sing. The dialectic of Euripides does indeed strike a sympathetic note in troubled times like our own; but nothing is more transient than the problems of bourgeois society. We need only think how remote we are to-day from Ibsen or Zola (who are of course infinitely beneath Euripides) to realize that the great strength of Euripides in his own day is an insuperable weakness on the modern stage.

The ineffaceable impression which Sophocles makes on us to-day and his imperishable position in the literature of the world are both due to his character-drawing. If we ask which of the men and women of Greek tragedy have an independent life in the imagination apart from the stage and from the actual plot in which they appear, we must answer, 'those created by Sophocles, above all others'.[6] He was much more than a technician: for characters which *live* cannot be created by mere excellence in dramatic technique, which has at best a temporary effect. Perhaps nothing is harder for us to understand than the quiet, unpretentious, natural wisdom of Sophocles, which makes us feel that his real flesh-and-blood men and women, with violent passions and tender emotions, proudly heroic but truly human, are like ourselves and yet noble with an incomparable dignity and remoteness. There is no sophistical subtlety, no artificial exaggeration about these characters. Later ages vainly tried to achieve monumental sublimity by violence, by colossal size and startling effects. Sophocles found sublimity in the effortless calm of true proportion: for it is always simple and even obvious. Its secret lies in the abandonment of everything inessential and accidental, so that nothing is left but the perfect clarity of that inner law which is hidden from the outward eye.[7] The men created by Sophocles have none of the earthy compactness of Aeschylus' characters, who look impassive, even stiff, beside them; nor is their mobility spoilt by lack of balance, as in so many of Euripides' puppets—it is hard to call them characters, since they never grow beyond the two dimensions of the theatre, costume and declamation, and never round out into real physical presences. Sophocles stands midway between his predecessor and his successor: he surrounds himself effortlessly with the men and women he has made. Or rather, they surround him. For true characters are never created by mere caprice. They must be begotten upon life by necessity: neither by the empty universal type nor the uniquely detailed individual, but by essential law, which is opposed to the inessential accident.

Many writers have drawn parallels between poetry and sculpture, and compared each of the three tragedians with one stage in the development of plastic art.[8] There is always something trivial about such parallels—all the more when they are pedantically elaborate. In an earlier chapter of this book we drew a symbolic comparison between the central position of Zeus or Fate in archaic tragedy and the position of the deity in the middle of the Olympic pediments;[9] but that bore only upon the structural idea behind both works of art and did not refer to the sculptural quality of Aeschylus' characters. But when we call Sophocles the sculptor of tragedy, we mean that he possesses one quality unlike any other poet—a fact which makes it impossible to institute any comparison between the development of tragedy and that of sculpture. A poetic and a sculptural character both depend on the artist's knowledge of ultimate laws of proportion. And that is as far as the parallel will go; for the specific laws of spiritual life cannot be applied to the spatial structure of visual and tangible physical existence. Yet the highest aim of the sculptors of Sophocles' time was to depict men in such a way that the spirit shone through the physical form; and therein they seem to have caught a ray of light from the spiritual world which was first revealed in the poetry of Sophocles. The most moving reflection of that light shines from the memorials set up at that time on Attic graves. Although they are artistically far inferior to the richness of feeling and variety of expression which make up the work of Sophocles, yet the deep quiet humanity which breathes in them is enough to show that their art and his poetry were inspired by the same emotion. Serene and fearless, they image eternal humanity triumphant over suffering and death: and show thereby a deep and genuine religious feeling.

The tragedies of Sophocles and the sculptures of Phidias are the two imperishable monuments of the great age of the Athenian spirit. Together, they represent the art of the Periclean era. Looking backward from the work of Sophocles, one seems to see all the previous development of tragedy as merely leading up to this perfection. Even Aeschylus appears to be only a preparation for Sophocles; but Sophocles cannot be said to prepare the way for Euripides or the tragic *epigonoi* of the fourth century. Later poets are merely echoes of the greatness of the fifth century, and the true strength and promise of Euripides are most manifest when he leaves poetry and invades the new domain of philosophy. Therefore Sophocles is classical, inasmuch as he is the climax of the development of tragedy: in him tragedy 'had its nature', as Aristotle would say.[10] But there is another unique sense in which he is classical: and here that description connotes more than perfection within one literary form. His position in the development of the spirit of Greece makes him classical— and in this book we are concerned with literature chiefly as the expression of that spirit and its transformations. The work of Sophocles is the climax of the development of Greek poetry, considered as the process by which the formation of human character is increasingly objectified. From this point of view alone can our earlier discussion of his tragic characters be fully understood and even gain additional significance.[11] Their excellence is not in their form alone; it is a more deeply human excellence, for in it aesthetic and moral and religious elements interfuse and interact. Such a fusing of motives is not unique in Greek poetry, as we have seen from our study of earlier authors. But in Sophocles' tragedies form and norm are unified in a special sense, and they are unified above all in his characters. He himself said tersely but accurately that his characters were ideals, not ordinary men like those of Euripides.[12] As a creator of men, Sophocles has a place in the history of human culture essentially unlike that of any other Greek poet. In his work the fully awakened sense of culture is made manifest for the first time. It is something totally different from the educational effect of Homer or the educational purpose of Aeschylus. It assumes the existence of a society whose highest ideal is *culture,* the formation of perfect human character; and such an assumption was impossible until, after one entire generation had struggled to discover the meaning of destiny, after the sore spiritual agonies of Aeschylus, humanity itself had become the centre of life. The character-drawing of Sophocles is consciously inspired by that ideal of human conduct which was the peculiar creation of Periclean society and civilization. He assimilated that ideal so fully that he humanized tragedy, and converted it into an imperishable pattern of human culture which was entirely in the inimitable spirit of the men who created it. Sophoclean tragedy could almost be called a purely cultural art and be compared (though in far less artificial conditions of time and outlook) to *Tasso* with its unique position in Goethe's effort to discover form in life and art, were it not that the word culture has so many different associations that it inevitably tends to grow vague and colourless. We must carefully avoid certain contrasts which have become clichés of literary criticism (such as that between 'original experience' and 'cultural experience') if we are to understand the true Greek meaning of culture.[18] Culture was for the Greeks the original creation and original experience of a process of deliberate guidance and formation of human character. Understanding that, we shall also understand the power of such an ideal to inspire the imagination of a great poet. It was a moment unique in the history of the world when poetry and culture came together to create an ideal.

The unity of the Athenian nation and the Athenian state, overarched, as it were, by the spiritual cosmos of Aeschylean tragedy, and won with such toil in the Persian wars, prepared the ground for a new national culture transcending all enmities and contrasts between the aristocratic civilization and the life of the common people. The happiness of the generation which on that ground built up the Periclean state and Periclean culture is strangely imaged in the life of Sophocles. The general facts of his career are well known, but they are much more significant than the smaller personal details which careful researchers have brought to light. No doubt it is only a legend that in the flower of his youth and beauty he danced in the chorus which celebrated the victory of Salamis, where Aeschylus had fought as a soldier; but it is important to observe that his life did not really begin until the storm of war had ended. He stands, so to say, on the narrow and precipitous peak of glory from which Athens was so soon to fall. His art shines clear and bright with the cloudless, windless serenity, εὐδία and γαλήνη, of that incomparable noon which dawned on the morning of Salamis. And he died shortly before Aristophanes called upon the ghost of Aeschylus to return and redeem his city. He did not see the final catastrophe of Athens. After the last Athenian victory, at Arginusae, had once more awakened the hopes of his nation, he passed away; and now he lives beyond the grave—so Aristophanes described him soon after his death—in the same calm harmony with himself and with the world which he had maintained throughout his earthly existence.[14] It is difficult to say how much of his *eudaimonia* sprang from the favoured age in which he lived, how much from his happy nature, and how much again from his own deliberate art, from the quiet mysterious wisdom which a more showy talent can neither equal nor appreciate, and must therefore dismiss with a gesture of embarrassment. True culture is produced only by these three forces acting together, and its generation is an eternal mystery. The marvel of it is that we cannot explain it, far less create it: we can only point to it, and say 'it is here'.

Even if we knew nothing else of Periclean Athens, we could tell from the life and character of Sophocles that in his time men were for the first time engaged in deliberately forming human character in accordance with a cultural ideal. Proud of the manners of their new society, they coined for them the word ἀστεῖος, *urbane* or *polite*. Twenty years later it was current in all Attic prose writers, Xenophon, the orators, and Plato; and Aristotle described and analysed the ideal of free courteous social intercourse and cultivated behaviour which it connoted. That ideal was the basis of Athenian society in the age of Pericles. The grace of refined Attic culture—which, be it noted, was vastly different from the pedantic conception of culture—could not be more beautifully illustrated than in a witty anecdote told by a contemporary poet, Ion of Chios.[15] It describes an actual event in the life of Sophocles. Serving as a fellow-*strategos* of Pericles, he was the guest of honour in a small Ionian city. At dinner he sat next to a local teacher of literature and suffered agonies of annoyance and boredom when his neighbour criticized the poetic colouring of Phrynichus' fine old line: 'There shines on crimson cheeks the light of love.' With the ease of true sophistication and a touch of genuine personal grace, he extricated himself from the painful situation amid general applause, by convicting the pedant of incompetence in the fine art of poetic exegesis; and at the same time he proved that he understood his compulsory profession of generalship by carrying out a cunning 'stratagem' against the handsome page-boy who offered him the winecup. The charm and delicacy reflected in this story are unforgettable elements in the character, not only of Sophocles, but of the whole Athenian society of his time. The spirit and outlook of the anecdote remind us irresistibly of the bust of Sophocles in the Lateran. Beside it we may well set the sculptor Cresilas' bust of Pericles, which shows the face neither of a statesman nor (despite the helmet) of a general. As Aeschylus was, in the eyes of posterity, the Marathon-warrior, the faithful Athenian citizen, so Sophocles and Pericles, as depicted in story and bust, are the highest ideal of the *kalos kagathos,* the Athenian gentleman of the fifth century.

That ideal was inspired by a clear and delicate perception of correct and appropriate behaviour in every situation, which, despite its precise rules for speech and conduct and its perfect sense of proportion and control, was in effect a new spiritual freedom. Entirely without effort or affectation, it was an easy and unconstrained way of life, appreciated and admired by all— and, as Isocrates wrote some years later, imitable by none. It existed only in Athens. It meant an abandonment of the exaggerated violence of emotion and expression that characterized Aeschylus, for the miraculously natural poise and proportion which we feel and enjoy in the sculptured frieze of the Parthenon as well as in the language of the men and women of Sophocles. An open secret, it can only be described, not defined; but at least it is not a matter of pure form. After all, it would be too extraordinary if the same phenomenon appeared at the same time in poetry and sculpture without being created by some suprapersonal feeling common to all the men who were most characteristic of their age. It is the radiance of a life that has found the final peace and final harmony with itself which are expressed in Aristophanes' description of Sophocles: [16] a life which even the passage through death cannot affect, which re-

mains both 'there' and 'here,' εὔκολος, content. It would be trivial
and unworthy to interpret this way of life as purely aesthetic, a
complex of elegant attitudes, or as purely psychological, a harmony of consonant spiritual powers, and thereby to mistake its
symptoms for its essence. It was not only the accidents of personal character that made Sophocles the master of the rich central tones which Aeschylus could never sound successfully. In his
work more than in that of any other poet, form is the immediate and appropriate expression, in fact the full revelation of
being, and its metaphysical manifestation. To the question, 'What
is the nature and meaning of this life?' Sophocles does not reply
like Aeschylus with a theory of the universe, justifying the ways
of God to man, but simply by the form of his speech and the
characters of his men and women. This can hardly be understood
by those who have never turned to Sophocles for guidance at
moments when, in the chaos and unrest of life, all principle and
all structure seem to dissolve away, and have never restored the
balance of their own lives by contemplating the firm harmonious
repose of his poetry. The effect of its sounds and rhythms is
always one of balance and proportion; and balance and proportion are for him the principle of all existence, for they mean the
reverent recognition of that justice which is implicit in everything and which can be realized only at the fulness of spiritual
maturity. It is not for nothing that his choruses again and again
describe disproportion as the root of all evil. The pre-established
harmony of Sophocles' poetry and Phidias' sculpture is ultimately based on the quasi-religious acceptance of this law of
harmony. In fact, the universal recognition of the law in fifth-
century Greece is such a natural expression of the characteristically Greek quality of *sophrosyné*—a quality whose metaphysical basis was the Greek view of the meaning of all life—
that when Sophocles himself glorifies harmony and proportion,
we seem to hear a manifold echo of his words in every region
of the Hellenic world. It was not a new idea; but the historical
influence and the absolute significance of an idea do not depend
on its novelty, but on the depth and power with which men
understand it and live it. Sophocles' tragedies are the climax of
the development of the Greek idea that proportion is one of the
highest values in human life. The process leads up to him, and in

him it finds its classical poetic expression as the divine power which rules the world and human life.[17]

There is another way to demonstrate the close connexion between culture and the sense of proportion in the mind of fifth-century Greece. In general we are compelled to draw inferences from the works of the Greek artists to the artistic theories which they held; their works are in fact the principal evidence for their beliefs. But in trying to understand the obscure and yet fundamental principles which assisted in the creation of works of art so many in number and so various in possible interpretations, we are justified in seeking contemporary evidence to guide us. In this context, then, we possess two remarks made by Sophocles himself—which indeed owe their ultimate historical authority only to the fact that they harmonize with our intuitive judgment of his art. We have already quoted one of them,[18] in which Sophocles described his own characters as ideal figures in contrast to Euripidean realism. In the other [19] he distinguished his own work from that of Aeschylus by saying that Aeschylus wrote cor rectly without knowing why: he denied him that deliberate intention to be *right* which seems an essential element in his own work. Both remarks taken together presuppose a very special awareness of standards to be followed: Sophocles guided his work by a standard and in it presented men 'as they ought to be'. Now, such awareness of the ideal standards of character is peculiar to the period when the sophistic movement was beginning. The problem of the nature of human areté is now taken up with terrific intensity from the educational side. All the discussions of that age, and all the efforts of the sophists, were directed towards finding and producing man 'as he ought to be'. Until then, poetry alone had given reasons for the values in which men believed; but it could not remain unaffected by the new educational movement. Aeschylus and Solon had given their work far-reaching influence by making it reflect the struggles of their own souls to apprehend God and Fate. Now Sophocles, following the cultural trend of his age, turned to Man, and expressed his own moral standards in the characters he drew. The beginnings of this movement can be traced in the later plays of Aeschylus, where he enhances the tragic element by depicting a conflict between destiny and some strongly idealized figure like

Eteocles, Prometheus, Agamemnon, Orestes. In that device
Sophocles is his immediate successor: for his principal characters
embody the highest areté as envisaged by the great educators of
his own time. It is impossible, and for Sophocles needless, to
decide whether the cultural ideal or the poetic creation came first.
What is essential is that in his time poets and educators had the
same great purpose in view.

The sense of beauty that produced the men and women of
Sophocles arose from a vast new interest in the *souls* of tragic
characters. It was a manifestation of the new ideal of areté,
which for the first time emphasized the central importance of the
psyché, the 'soul', in all culture. In the course of the fifth century the word psyché acquired a new overtone, a loftier significance, which reached its fulness in the teaching of Socrates.[20]
The soul was now objectively recognized as the centre of man's
life. From the soul came all men's actions. Long before, sculptors had discovered the laws that shape and govern the body
and had studied them with the greatest enthusiasm. In the 'harmony' of the body they had rediscovered the principle of cosmos
apprehended by philosophers in the structure of the universe.[21]
With that principle in mind the Greeks now turned to the exploration of the soul. They did not see it as a chaotic flow of
inner experience, but subjected it to a system of laws, as the only
realm of being which had not yet incorporated the ideal of cosmos. Like the body, the soul obviously had rhythm and harmony.
Thus the Greeks reached the idea of a soul-structure.[22] One is
tempted to find its first clear expression in Simonides' description of areté as 'built foursquare in hand and foot and mind'.[23]
But it was a long way from that inchoate idea of the life of the
soul as analogous to the physical ideal of athletic perfection, to
the theory of culture which Plato no doubt rightly ascribes to
the sophist Protagoras.[24] That theory was a completely logical
development of the idea that the soul can be formed like the
body—an idea which has ceased to be a poetic image and become
an educational principle. Protagoras said that the soul can be
educated into true *eurhythmia* and *euharmostia*, rhythm and concord. The right rhythm and harmony are to be produced in it
by the influence of poetry embodying these standards. Even in
this theory the ideal of forming the soul is approached from a
physical point of view; but Protagoras conceives the process to

resemble sculpture, the work of a plastic artist, rather than athletic training, as Simonides had done. The standards of eurhythmia and euharmostia are likewise borrowed from the world of
visible physical existence. Only in classical Greece could the concept of culture have been inspired by the sculptor's art. Even
Sophocles' ideal of human character clearly betrays its sculptural
origin. At that period education, poetry, and sculpture affected
one another deeply—none of them could have existed without
the others. Educators and poets were inspired by the sculptor's
effort to create an ideal figure, and took the same path towards
the ἰδέα of humanity; while the sculptor or painter was led by the
example of education and poetry to look for the soul in every
model he used.[25] The focus of interest for all three was the
higher value which now attached to humanity. The Athenian
mind has now become anthropocentric; humanism has been born
—not the emotion of love for all other members of society,
called *philanthropia* by the Greeks, but intellectual search for
and interest in the true nature of man.[26] It is especially significant that now for the first time tragedy shows women as well as
men, as worthy representatives of humanity. Apart from such
subordinate feminine characters as Clytaemnestra, Ismene, and
Chrysothemis, Sophocles' power of drawing strong noble human
beings is seen at its highest in many of his tragic heroines—
Antigone, Electra, Dejanira, Tecmessa, Jocasta. After the great
discovery that man was the real object of tragedy, it was inevitable that woman also should be discovered.

We can now understand the changes which tragedy underwent
when Sophocles took it over from Aeschylus. The most obvious
external change is Sophocles' abandonment of the trilogy, which
had been Aeschylus' regular dramatic form. It was now replaced
by single dramas, centred on one principal actor. It was impossible for Aeschylus to give dramatic treatment to the connected
development of one destiny on the epic scale, often covering the
sufferings of several generations of the same family, in anything
less than a trilogy of tragedies. His chief concern was the unbroken course of the fate of a family, because it alone formed a
whole large enough to demonstrate the working-out of divine
justice, which even religious faith and moral sentiment can
hardly trace in the doom of one individual. In his plays, there-

fore, single characters are subordinated to the main theme, although they may serve to introduce the spectator to it; and the poet himself is compelled to assume a higher and less human position, making his puppets move and suffer as if he himself were the power which guides the universe. But in Sophocles the ideal of justifying God's ways to man which dominates religious thought from Solon to Theognis and Aeschylus falls into the background. The tragic element in his plays is the inevitability of suffering: the necessity of destiny, seen from the point of view of the individual sufferer. He has not, therefore, abandoned Aeschylus' religious view of the nature of the world, but has merely shifted the emphasis from universal to individual problems. This is particularly clear in an early work like *Antigone,* where his conception of the meaning of the world is still boldly marked.

Aeschylus had traced through several generations of the Labdacid house the destructive effects of the curse which the family had brought on itself by early guilt. In Sophocles too, the curse of guilt looms in the background as the final cause of all their woe. Antigone herself is its last victim, as Eteocles and Polynices are in *Seven against Thebes.*[27] Sophocles actually makes Antigone and her opponent Creon assist the curse in its work by their own violent actions, and the chorus never ceases to lament their transgression of the proper limits of action and to warn them of their partial responsibility for their own misfortune.[28] But although these motives could be considered to justify the cruelty of destiny in the Aeschylean manner, the spectator's whole attention is focussed not on the problem of destiny, but on the individual characters, so much so that he feels that they are the chief interest of the drama, and that their predominance needs no external justification. By her own nature Antigone is destined to suffer—we might almost say chosen to suffer (without introducing Christian ideas of predestinate suffering), for her deliberate acceptance of suffering becomes her own peculiar form of nobility. Her tragic destiny is apparent in the prologue, in her first conversation with her sister. Ismene's tender maidenly nature shrinks from making the deliberate choice of ruin and death, although her love for Antigone never falters, as is touchingly proved later when she falsely accuses herself before Creon and makes a despairing attempt to join her sister in death. Still, she is not a tragic figure. Her gentle character accentuates the strength of Antigone, and we must admit that Antigone has a deeper justification for rejecting Ismene's fond readiness to share her doom. Just as the tragedy of Eteocles in the *Seven* is enhanced by the heroism which he displays when he is innocently involved in the fate of his family, so here his sister Antigone surpasses all the heroic qualities of her noble race.

The second song of the chorus creates a universal background for the suffering of the heroine. It hymns the power of man, who has created all arts, mastered nature through the power of the mind, and learned the highest skill of all—the power of justice which builds the state. A contemporary of Sophocles, the sophist Protagoras, had worked out a similar theory of the origin of civilized society; [29] it was the first attempt at a rational account of man's development; and the majestic rhythms of this song have much of its Promethean pride in human progress. But with Sophocles' peculiar tragic irony, at the very moment when the chorus has extolled the power of justice and the state, and has proclaimed the banishment of the lawbreaker from all human society, Antigone is led onto the stage in chains. By obeying the unwritten law and performing the simplest duty of a sister to her dead brother, she has deliberately come into conflict with the king's command: for he had pronounced a decree which exaggerated the power of the state to the point of tyranny, by forbidding under pain of death the burial of Antigone's brother, Polynices, killed fighting against his own country. Instantly, therefore, the spectator is shown another aspect of humanity: the proud hymn dies away in the sudden tragic realization of the weakness and vanity of man.

With great penetration Hegel saw that *Antigone* dealt with the tragic conflict of two moral principles: the law of the state, and the rights of the family. [30] From this point of view, the severe though exaggerated logic of King Creon's devotion to the state makes his character easier for us to understand; while the agony and defiance of Antigone justify the eternal laws of family duty against the interference of the state, with the irresistible persuasiveness of true revolutionary passion. Still, the emphasis is not upon this general problem, though a poet in the age of the sophist might well choose to universalize the two principal characters into representatives of a conflict of ideas. And the discussions of hybris, unreason, and immoderation are not the centre of interest, as in Aeschylus, but provide the background for the tragedy. There is always an immediately intelligible reason for the sufferings of a Sophoclean hero: he is not condemned to suffer, as if by some supernatural judge, he is through his own noble nature a visible example of the inevitability of the doom into which the gods lead men. The irrationality of ate had puzzled Solon and exercised the minds of all the serious thinkers of that age, but for Sophocles it is the basis, not the central problem, of tragedy. Aeschylus had tried to solve the problem of ate: Sophocles admits its insolubility as a fact. Yet he does not passively accept the unavoidable suffering sent by God, which Greek lyric poets had from the earliest times lamented; and he has no sympathy whatever for the resignation of Simonides, who concluded that man must forfeit his areté when cast down by inescapable misfortune.[31] By making his tragic characters greatest and noblest of mankind, Sophocles cries Yes to the fateful question which no mortal mind can solve. His characters are the first who, by suffering by the absolute abandonment of their earthly happiness or of their social and physical life, reach the truest greatness attainable by man.

In their agony Sophocles draws from these characters a marvelous and delicate variety of tragical music; and he enhances its searching beauty by every device of the dramatist's imagination. Compared with those of Aeschylus, his plays are an immeasurable advance in dramatic effect. Yet he did not achieve this by abandoning the fine old choric songs and dances and telling a story for its own sake with Shakespearean realism. No doubt that view of his technique might be supported by the superrealistic power with which the tale of Oedipus is unfolded, and might even be responsible for much of the modern interest in staging that play; but it could never help us to understand the astonishing structural complexity and balance of his dramas. They were constructed not in accordance with the external sequence of physical events, but by a higher artistic logic which, in a series of contrasting scenes, each more powerful than the last, expresses the very soul of the chief character, displaying it from every possible point of view. The classical example of this device is *Electra*. With brilliant invention, Sophocles uses one bold artifice after another to retard and interrupt the simple plot, so that the heroine passes through the whole gamut of emotion until she reaches the final agony of despair. And yet, violently as the pendulum swings from one extreme to the other, its central equilibrium is maintained throughout. The finest scene of all from this point of view is that in which Electra and Orestes recognize each other once again. Orestes has returned in disguise to save his sister and redeem his family honour, but he is made to reveal himself with such torturing slowness that Electra suffers every agony between heaven and hell. Sophoclean drama is the drama of the emotions through which the soul of the chief actor must pass, following in its own rhythm the harmonious development of the plot. The source of his dramatic effect is the hero's character, to which, as to the highest and final point of interest, it always returns. Dramatic action is for Sophocles the process by which the true nature of a suffering human being is unfolded, by which he fulfils his destiny, and through it fulfils himself.

Like Aeschylus, Sophocles thinks of drama as the instrument through which men reach a sublime knowledge. But it is not τὸ φρονεῖν, which was the ultimate certainty and necessity in which Aeschylus found peace. It is rather a tragical self-knowledge, the Delphic γνῶθι σεαυτόν deepened and broadened into a comprehension of the shadowy nothingness of human strength and human happiness.[32] To know oneself is thus for Sophocles to know man's powerlessness; but it is also to know the indestructible and conquering majesty of suffering humanity. The agony of every Sophoclean character is an essential element in his nature. The strange fusion of character and fate is nowhere more movingly and mysteriously expressed than in the greatest of his heroes, to whom he returned once again at the very close of his life. It is Oedipus, a blind old man begging his way through the world, led by his daughter Antigone—another of Sophocles' most beloved figures. Nothing reveals the essence of Sophoclean tragedy more deeply than the fact that the poet grew old, as it were, along with his characters. He never forgot what Oedipus was to become. From the first, the tragic king who was to bear the weight of the whole world's sufferings was an almost symbolic figure. He was suffering humanity personified. At the climax of his career Sophocles proudly exerted all his powers to show him staggering under the tempest of ruin. He presented him at the very moment when he calls down curses on himself and in despair wishes to destroy his own life, as he has destroyed the light of his eyes with his own hand. And he snapped the thread, as he did in *Electra,* at that climactic moment when the character of the hero was tragically complete.

It is therefore highly significant that shortly before his death Sophocles took up the tale of Oedipus once again. It would be a mistake to expect the second drama to solve the problem of the first. If we were to interpret old Oedipus' passionate self-defence, his repeated claim that he acted unwittingly,[33] as an answer to the question *Why?* we should be misunderstanding Sophocles, treating him, in fact, as if he were Euripides. Neither destiny nor Oedipus is acquitted or condemned. Yet in the later play the poet seems to look on life from a greater height. *Oedipus at Colonus* is a last meeting with the restless old wanderer, just before he reaches his goal. Despite misfortune and age, his noble character is unbroken, its impetuous violence still unquenched.[34] By knowing his own strength and nobility, he has been helped to bear his own agony, the inseparable companion of his long years of exile, clinging to him until the last.[35] There is no place for sentimental pity in this harsh portrait. Yet Oedipus' agony has made him venerable. The chorus feels its terror, but its grandeur even more; and the king of Athens receives the blind beggar as an honoured and illustrious guest. An oracle has said that Oedipus will find his final repose in Attica. But his death is veiled in mystery: he goes away, without a guide, into the grove, and is never seen again. Strange and incomprehensible as the road of suffering along which the gods have led him, is the miracle of release which he finds at the end. 'The gods who struck you down now lift you up.' [36] No mortal eye may see the mystery: only he who is consecrated by suffering may take part in it. Hallowed by pain, he is in some mysterious way brought near to divinity: his agonies have set him apart from other men. Now he rests on the hill of Colonus, in the poet's own dear homeland, in the eternally green grove of the Kind Spirits where the nightingale sings from the branches. No human foot may tread in that place, but from it there goes out a blessing over all the land of Attica.

3

THE SOPHISTS

THE age of Sophocles saw the beginnings of an intellectual movement which was to have immeasurable effects on the history of mankind. This was the movement mentioned in our introductory chapter: it was *paideia,* education, or rather culture, in the narrower sense. The word paideia, which at its first appearance [1] meant 'childrearing', and which in the fourth century, the Hellenistic, and the Imperial Roman ages constantly extended its connotation, was now for the first time connected with the highest areté possible to man: it was used to denote the sumtotal of all ideal perfections of mind and body—complete *kalokagathia,* a concept which was now consciously taken to include a genuine intellectual and spiritual culture. This new comprehensive conception of the cultural ideal was firmly established by the time of Isocrates and Plato.

Areté had from the very first been closely bound up with education.[2] But, as society had changed, so also had the ideal of areté, and with it the way to achieve areté. Everywhere in Greece, therefore, attention was now focussed on the principal question: *What type of education leads to areté?* Without that question, the unique Hellenic ideal of culture could never have arisen; but for all its fundamental clarity, it presupposes the varied development which we have traced from the oldest aristocratic conception of areté to the new political ideal of citizenship in the democratic, justice-loving state. The nobles inevitably felt that areté should be maintained and transmitted by means different from those used by the Hesiodic peasants or the citizens of the polis—so far as the latter had any special means to perform that function. For, outside Sparta (where since Tyrtaeus' time there had grown up a unique system of civic education, the *agogé,* unparalleled anywhere else in Greece), there was and could be no official form of education comparable to the old aristocratic training evidenced by the *Odyssey,* Theognis, and Pindar; and private attempts at creating an educational system went forward very slowly and gradually.

In fact, the new bourgeois city-state was at a great disadvantage compared with the old aristocracy, in that—although it possessed a new ideal of manhood and citizenship [3] and believed it far superior to the old—it had no regular method of deliberately educating the young to attain that ideal. A father would give his son technical training in the rules and skills of his vocation, if he followed him in his trade or profession; but such training could not replace the physical and spiritual education of the whole personality as practised by the aristocratic καλὸς κἀγαθός and patterned on an ideal which combined the highest qualities of body and soul.[4] But the citizens of the polis must soon have begun to look for a method of educating their sons into the new citizen-ideal. Here as elsewhere the new state was compelled to imitate its predecessor. Aristocratic education had been based on the inheritance of areté through noble blood: the new areté was necessarily based on the same kind of principle. The Athenian state, for example, made every free-born citizen of Athenian descent consider himself a member of the Attic community, and qualified him to serve it. This was simply an extension of the idea of kinship through blood, but now the community was composed of the members of one city, not the members of a few noble families. That was the only possible basis for the city-state. Despite the new emphasis on individual personality, it would then have been unthinkable that education should be founded on anything but membership of the political community. In fact, that is the supreme axiom of all cultural education, and the greatest proof of its truth is the origin of Greek paideia. Its aim was to transcend the aristocratic principle of privileged education, which made it impossible for anyone to acquire areté unless he already possessed it by inheritance from his divine ancestors. It seemed easy to transcend it by the application of logical reasoning, the new instrument whose power was constantly growing. There was only one method—to apply a deliberate system of education to the mind. The fifth century, be it noted, had an almost limitless faith in the powers of the mind, and was little disturbed by Pindar's arrogant taunting of 'those who had learned'.[5] Political areté could not be allowed to depend on the inheritance of noble blood, unless the extension of state-privileges to the mass of the population (which was inevitable) was to be stultified. And if the new polis had taken over the physical areté of the nobility by the institution of gymnastic training, why could it not equally well produce the undeniable intellectual advantages of aristocratic training, the hereditary gifts of leadership, by a deliberate system of education?

Therefore the great educational movement, which distinguished the fifth and fourth centuries and which is the origin of the European idea of culture, necessarily started from and in the city-state of the fifth century. It aimed, as the Greeks understood it, entirely at political education, training to serve the polis. The essential need of the state created the ideal of education which recognized and employed the power of knowledge, the great new spiritual force, to form human character. Whether or not we approve of the Athenian democratic principle which gave rise to these problems, is irrelevant for this discussion. At any rate, unless the whole population had been given an active part in government (and that is the basis and one of the distinguishing marks of democracy), it would have been impossible for the Greeks to ask and answer the eternal questions which exercised them so deeply at that period of their history and which they left for posterity to answer in its own way. In modern times too, the same development has raised the same urgent questions once again. Only at this stage of spiritual development are such problems as those of freedom and authority, or education for citizenship and education for leadership, conceived and answered, and only at this stage do they acquire their full urgency as moulders of men's destiny. They do not arise in primitive societies, in herd-communities or family-communities where there is no conception of the powers of the individual mind. Hence their significance is not confined to the Greek city-state democracy, although they were first conceived within the democracies of the fifth century. They are problems of the state *per se*. And the proof of that is that the great Greek philosophers and educational theorists, starting from the educational experience of democracy, soon reached bold conclusions which went far beyond the existing type of constitution and which are infinitely valuable guides in any similar situation in later ages.

The educational movement which we are now to examine starts from the culture of the old aristocracy, and then after moving away in a wide curve, as it were, returns in Plato, Isocrates, and Xenophon, to the original aristocratic traditions and the aristocratic ideal of areté, now re-established on a newly intellectualized basis. But in the first part of the fifth century it is still far from its eventual return. Then the first aim of educators was to break down the old cramping views, the traditional admiration for noble descent, which could be justified only when manifested in intellectual and moral power, as σοφία and δικαιοσύνη. Xenophanes shows how closely 'power of mind' and citizenship were connected in the ideal of areté even at the beginning, and how that ideal was founded on right order in the state and the welfare of the community.[6] Likewise in Heraclitus, although in a different sense, law is based on 'knowledge', which in fact produces it; and the earthly possessor of this god-like knowledge claims a special position in the polis, or else comes into direct conflict with it.[7] The writings of these great men show the first urgency of the new problem of the connexion between state and intellect, which was to bring the sophistic movement into being: they show also how, when the aristocracy of race had been displaced by the aristocracy of intellect, a new conflict immediately appeared in place of the old. This was the problem which ceaselessly exercised all philosophers until the city-state passed away —that of the relation between a great intellectual personality and the community in which he lived. In Pericles, it found a happy if temporary solution for both the community and the individual.

The sophistic movement first gave wide publicity and influence to the claim that areté should be founded on knowledge. But perhaps such a powerful educational movement could not have been initiated by the appearance of great individual thinkers and the conflict of their personalities with the community, if the community itself had not felt that the horizon of the average individual ought to be widened by intellectual education. That feeling grew in strength after the Persian wars, when Athens entered the international sphere in economics, commerce, and politics. The state owed its salvation to one man of outstanding intellectual powers. Soon after its victory, it expelled him, because his power could not be reconciled with the archaic ideal of *isonomia*—it looked like a concealed tyranny. Yet the logic of history led to the conclusion that, if the democratic state was to maintain itself, it must have the right kind of man as its leader. That was in fact the chief, the *only* problem of democracy, for the democratic principle was bound to develop *ad absurdum* whenever the democratic state attempted to be more than a strictly regulated system of ratifying the decisions of its representatives, and really became the domination of the masses.

From its first appearance, therefore, the aim of the educational movement led by the sophists was not to educate the people, but to educate the leaders of the people. At bottom, it was only the old problem of the aristocracy in a new form. It is true that nowhere else had even the simplest citizen so many opportunities of acquiring the foundations of elementary education as he had in Athens—even without a state-directed educational system. But the sophists always addressed themselves to a select audience, and to it alone. Their pupils were the men who wished to become politicians and eventual leaders of their states. A man who had that aim in view could not fulfil the demands of his age simply by attaining the old political ideal of justice, the universal obligation of every citizen, as Aristides had done. He had not merely to obey the laws,[8] but to create laws to guide the state: and for that he needed more than the indispensable experience which could be gained only by long political practice; he needed a universal insight into the true nature of human life. The chief qualities of a statesman cannot be acquired. Presence of mind and sound foresight (the qualities which Thucydides praises above all else in Themistocles[9]) are inborn. But the talent for speaking convincingly and powerfully can be developed by training. It was the distinctive mark of leadership even in the noble elders who formed the council of state in the Homeric epics, and it maintained that position throughout subsequent ages. Hesiod held it to be a power given to the king by the Muses, through which he can guide every assembly with gentle compulsion; in fact, he put it on the same plane as the poet's inspiration.[10] Doubtless he thought of it principally as the judicial ability to utter words which establish truths and make decisions. In the democratic state, where the whole people assembled for political purposes and where any citizen might speak, a talent for oratory became indispensable to every politician: it was the rudder in the statesman's hand. In classical Greek the politician is simply called *rhétor,* an orator. The word had not yet acquired the purely formal meaning which it had in later times, but denoted the content of the orator's speeches too: it was obvious and natural at that time that every public speech would deal with the state and its interests.

Eloquence, then, was the point from which any attempt to educate a man for political leadership was bound to start. Political education logically became rhetorical education—although the *logos* which was its object might contain very various proportions of formal and material instruction. When this is understood, it is easy to see why a class of educators arose who publicly professed that in return for money they would teach 'virtue'.[11] 'Virtue' used to be the translation of *areté;* but to translate it by such a word is a false modernization, which predisposes us to dismiss as senseless arrogance the claim of the sophists—the 'teachers of knowledge', as they were called by their contemporaries and soon by themselves too. The foolish misunderstanding vanishes as soon as we interpret areté to mean political areté, its natural significance in classical Greece, and take it to denote first and foremost intellectual power and oratorical ability, which in the new conditions of the fifth century were bound to be its principal manifestations. We inevitably look back on the sophists with the sceptical eyes of Plato, who held that the beginning of all philosophical knowledge was the Socratic doubt whether 'virtue could be taught'.[12] But it is historically incorrect, and it keeps us from understanding this important epoch in the history of culture, to saddle it with problems which arose only at a later stage of philosophical thought. In the history of the human mind, the sophists are a phenomenon quite as necessary as Socrates or Plato; in fact, without them, Socrates and Plato could never have existed.

The sophists' attempt to teach political areté was a direct reflection of a deep-seated change in the structure of the state. Thucydides, with the insight of genius, saw and described the vast transformation which Athens underwent at its entry into the political arena of Greece. As it changed from the old static city-state to the dynamic imperial state of Pericles, all its energies were brought into violent action and competition, both externally and internally. The rationalization of political education was only a special case of the rationalization of all life within Athens; for now more than ever before the end of life was achievement, success. This change was bound to affect the standards by which character was judged. Ethical qualities now fell into the background, and the emphasis was laid on intellectual qualities. Scarcely fifty years before, Xenophanes had been the lonely champion of the new ideal of character; but his admiration for knowledge and reason now became universal, especially in commercial and political life. The ideal of areté assimilated all the values which Aristotelian ethics later united under the heading of intellectual excellences (διανοητικαὶ ἀρεταί) and attempted to merge with ethical value so as to form a higher unity.[13] The age of the sophists, of course, had no such problem in view. Then, for the first time, the intellectual side of man came to the fore, and thereby created the educational mission which the sophists endeavoured to fulfil. That is the only possible explanation of their belief that they could teach areté. Therefore the sophists, with their educational presuppositions, were in a sense just as correct as Socrates, with his fundamental doubts: for Socrates and the sophists were really thinking of different things.

Although they said their aim was the education of the mind, they used an extraordinary variety of different methods to achieve it. Still, we may attempt to derive all the aspects of that variety from one single intellectual aim, if we realize how numerous are the aspects under which the mind can appear. From one point of view, the mind is the organ by which man apprehends the world of objects—it is bound to things. But if we take the sophistic attitude and free the mind of its content of real objects, it is not an empty receptacle—it has a genuine internal structure, revealed for the first time. That is the mind viewed as a formal principle. Corresponding to these two concepts of the nature of the mind, there were among the sophists two fundamentally distinct methods of educating it. One was to import to it an encyclopaedic variety of *facts,* the material of knowledge, and the other to give it *formal* training of various types.[14] It is obvious that these two opposing methods could be united only in the transcendent concept of intellectual culture. Both of them have survived to the present day, though usually as a compromise rather than a complete assertion of one against the other. The same was true to a great extent in the age of the sophists. But although various sophists blended the two methods in different ways, we must not overlook the fact that they were fundamentally different answers to the same problem of educating the mind. And as well as the purely formal method of education, the sophists sometimes practised a higher type of formal education, which aimed not at explaining the structure of reason and language, but at cultivating all the powers of the soul. This method was represented by Protagoras. Besides grammar, rhetoric, and dialectic, it chiefly employed poetry and music to form the soul. The basis of this, the third type of sophistical education, was political and ethical.[15] It differed from both the formal and the encyclopaedic methods by treating man not abstractly, as a lone individual, but as a member of the community; and thereby it gave him a firm position in the world of values, and made intellectual culture one part of the great whole which was human areté. This method also was intellectual education; however, it treated the mind neither formally nor factually, but as conditioned by the social order.

It has been said [16] that what was new in the sophistic movement, and at the same time common to all its members, was the educational ideal of rhetoric, τὸ εὖ λέγειν: for they all cultivated oratory, but differed in their estimate of everything else: and there were some sophists who were rhetors pure and simple, and taught nothing else whatever: like Gorgias. But that is clearly a superficial judgment. In fact, what was common to them all was that they all taught political areté,[17] and all wished to instil it by increasing the powers of the mind through training—whatever they took the training to be. We can only stand amazed at the wealth of new and permanently valuable educational knowledge which the sophists gave to the world. They were the inventors of intellectual culture and of the art of education which aims at producing it. At the same time it is clear that whenever their new culture went beyond formal or factual education, whenever their political training attacked the deeper problems of morality and the state, it was in danger of teaching half-truths—unless it could be grounded on genuine and thorough political thought, searching for the truth for its own sake. From that point of view, Plato and Aristotle later attacked the whole system of sophistic culture and shook it to its foundations.[18]

We must now inquire what position the sophists really held in the history of Greek philosophy and science. It has in fact always been very doubtful—although we usually accept without question the traditional view which appears in most histories of Greek philosophy, that they were an organic part of the development of philosophical thought. We must not depend on Plato's account of them: for the point at which he constantly takes issue with them is not their knowledge, but their claim to teach areté, their connexion with life and conduct. There is only one exception—his criticism of Protagoras' theory of knowledge in *Theaetetus;* [19] in that passage the sophistic movement is really treated as a part of philosophy, but only in so far as represented by Protagoras. That is a small connexion between sophistry and philosophy. The history of philosophy given by Aristotle in the *Metaphysics* excludes the sophists. Modern histories of the subject regard them as the founders of philosophical subjectivism or relativism. But the fact that Protagoras outlined a philosophical theory does not justify us in generalizing about all the sophists, and it would be a fault in historical perspective to hold the teachers of areté to be comparable to great thinkers like Anaximander, Parmenides, and Heraclitus.

Historia, as practised by the Ionians, was pure and disinterested research, with no reference to human life and no practical educational aim—as is sufficiently shown by the cosmological theories of the Milesians. Starting with them, we have shown how the study of the whole cosmos gradually focussed on the study of man, as the problems of human existence came more and more to be the centre of interest.[20] Xenophanes' daring attempt to found human areté on the rational knowledge of God and the universe did actually establish an immanent connexion between cosmological science and education; for a moment, it seemed as if natural philosophy by being transformed into poetry was going to dominate the life and culture of the whole nation. But Xenophanes had no successors, although the philosophers who followed him did not abandon the problems of man's nature, value, and way to salvation, once they had been raised. Only Heraclitus was a great enough thinker to construct upon one single principle a theory of the cosmos under the government of law, which included man as an essential part of it.[21] And Heraclitus, be it noted, was not a physicist like the Milesians.

The successors of the Milesian cosmologists in the fifth century, treating the study of nature more and more as a special department of science, either omitted man from their theories altogether, or each found their own solutions according to their particular capacities for philosophical thought. In Anaxagoras of Clazomenae cosmogony was affected for the first time by the anthropocentric trend to which we have already referred: he laid down that the foundation of existence is mind, the force which arranges and guides; but apart from that axiom his interpretation of nature was wholly mechanistic, and he never succeeded in showing how nature and mind interpenetrate.[22] Empedocles of Acragas was a philosophical centaur, so to speak— a prodigious union of Ionian elemental physics and Orphic religion. He taught that man, the unredeemed creature and plaything of the eternal coming-to-be and passing-away of nature, could journey along a mystical path, out of the miserable cycle of elemental processes to which he was bound by destiny, into the pure, original, divine life of the soul.[23] Thus each of these thinkers in a different way upheld the independence of the spiritual life of man against the power of cosmic forces. Even Democritus was unable to exclude from his severely logical theory of the universe the problem of man and man's moral world. But he avoided the solutions—some of them very peculiar—which his immediate predecessors had offered, and chose to separate natural philosophy from ethics: he expounded his own ethical teaching in the old-fashioned form of *parainesis,* moral exhortation, not as a branch of theoretic knowledge. As advanced by him, it was a peculiar blend of traditional maxims and the scientific and rationalist spirit of contemporary philosophy.[24] All these attempts to connect the two worlds, the world of man and the world of nature, are clear symptoms of the growing importance of the new philosophical problem of human character and human life. Still, they did not produce the educational theories of the sophists.[25]

The increasing concentration of philosophy upon the problem of man is another proof that the existence of the sophists was historically necessary; but they came into existence in response to a practical need, not a theoretical and philosophical one. That is the basic reason why they had such a strong influence in Athens, while Ionian physical science could not strike root there.

The fact is that the sophists did not understand philosophy divorced from life. They were the heirs of the educational tradition of the *poets;* they were the successors of Homer and Hesiod, Solon and Theognis, Simonides and Pindar. We cannot grasp their historical position until we give them their proper place in the history of Greek cultural education, as the inheritors of the poetic tradition.[26] Simonides, Theognis, and Pindar had already used poetry to discuss whether areté could be taught, although before them poets had simply presented and commended their own particular ideal of human character, without discussion.[27] With them, poetry became the debating-ground of educational theorists. Simonides, for example, was a typical sophist at bottom, as Plato himself says.[28] The sophists merely took the last step along the way. They transmuted the various forms of paraenetic poetry, with its marked educational emphasis, into the new artistic prose of which they were masters; and thereby they entered into frank competition with poetry, in form as well as in content.[29] At the same time, the fact that educational theory was now transferred from poetry to prose is a sign that it was at last thoroughly rationalized. Inheriting as they did the educational function of poetry, the sophists also turned their attention to discussing its nature and purpose. They were the first to give methodical instruction in the works of the great poets, from whom they usually chose the texts of their own discourses. They did not of course *interpret* poetry, as we should understand the term. They thought of the poets as immediately and timelessly present, and naïvely discussed them as if they wrote of contemporary life.[30] The cool purposefulness which is peculiar to that epoch was most strongly marked, and most inappropriate, in the sophistic belief that poetry is meant to instruct. The sophists regarded Homer as an encyclopaedia of all human knowledge, from wagon-building to strategy, and as a mine of prudential wisdom for the conduct of life.[31] Epic and tragic poetry, which do educate by the presentation of heroic actions, were interpreted from a frankly utilitarian point of view.

Nevertheless, the sophists did not merely borrow the educational traditions of poetry: they created much of their own. Their writings and lectures dealt with new and varied problems. They were so deeply influenced both by current rationalist theories of ethics and politics and by the scientific teachings of the physicists, that they created an atmosphere of comprehensive culture far more alive and stimulating and purposeful than even that of the Pisistratean age. Their pride in their own intellectual powers was reminiscent of Xenophanes: Plato is never tired of parodying and ridiculing it in its numerous forms, from exaggeratedly self-conscious dignity to mean and trivial conceit. They strongly resemble the *literati* of the Renaissance both in their intellectual arrogance and in their independence, their untrammelled cosmopolitanism. Hippias of Elis, who was conversant with every branch of knowledge, who had learnt all trades, who wore no garment or ornament which he had not made himself, was a perfect *uomo universale*.[32] There were others too who so deftly and dazzlingly combined the functions of scholar and orator, teacher and littérateur that it is impossible to place them in any one of the traditional professions. Not only their teaching, but their intellectual and psychological charm made the sophists illustrious and favoured guests at the homes of the rich and powerful in every city where they chose to remain for a time. In that, too, they are the true successors of the touring poets whom we have seen in the sixth century at the courts of tyrants and the homes of rich noblemen.[33] They lived, literally, by their wits. Constantly wandering from city to city, they had no real nationality. The fact that it was possible for men to live in Greece at that period with such utter independence is the surest and most characteristic sign that an entirely new and fundamentally individualist type of culture was coming into being—for the sophists were individualists, however much they might talk of education to serve the community and training in the areté of a good citizen. The whole age was moving towards individualism, and they were in the van of the movement: so that their contemporaries were right to regard them as the true representatives of the spirit of their age. Another sign of the times is that the sophists lived on their culture. It was, says Plato,[34] 'imported' like a marketable commodity and put on sale. There is some truth in that malicious comparison, though we must take it not as a moral criticism but as an intellectual diagnosis of the sophists and their way of life. They provide an almost untapped mine of information on what might be called 'the sociology of knowledge'.

All in all, they are a phenomenon of the first importance in the history of culture. Through them paideia—the ideal and theory of culture, consciously formed and pursued—came into being and was established on a rational basis. Therefore, they mark a huge advance in the development of humanism, even if its highest and truest form was only worked out by Plato in successful crusade against their ideas.[35] There is something impermanent and incomplete about them. They did not represent a philosophical or scientific movement, but the invasion of philosophy and science (the old Ionian physical science and *historia*) by other interests and problems, especially the educational and social problems which were created by the changes in economic and political life. Therefore the immediate effect of their work was to supersede science and philosophy, much as they have recently been superseded by pedagogy, sociology, and journalism. Nevertheless, by transmuting the old educational tradition, which had been principally incorporated in poetry, into the language and ideology of their own rationalistic age, and by establishing the theory and purposes of culture, they extended the influence of Ionian science to ethics and politics, and helped to build them into a true philosophy parallel and superior to the science of nature.[36] Their formal innovations had a more lasting effect than the rest of their work. But their great invention, rhetoric, was to meet powerful opposition and competition in science and philosophy when they became independent of it. Thus, even in its multiplicity, the culture of the sophists contained the first symptoms of the great cultural conflict which was to rage through succeeding centuries—the conflict between philosophy and rhetoric.

THE ORIGINS OF EDUCATIONAL THEORY AND THE IDEAL OF CULTURE

The sophists have been described as the founders of educational science. They did indeed found pedagogy, and even to-day intellectual culture largely follows the path they marked out.[37] But it is still an open question whether pedagogy is a science or an art, and they themselves called their art and theory of education *techné,* an art, not a science. In Plato we have a detailed account of Protagoras' views on the subject; for although his report of the great sophist's speech and behaviour is humorously exaggerated, it must be true in essentials. Protagoras, then, called his profession 'the political techné' because it was to teach political areté.[38] And this belief that education was a special art is only another example of the general tendency of that epoch to divide life up into a number of special activities, each with its own purpose clearly in view and its theory established, and each covered by a particular body of knowledge which could be transmitted by education. There were specialists and specialized technical publications in the various branches of mathematics, in medicine, gymnastics, musical theory, dramatic technique, and so forth; even artists, such as Polyclitus, were beginning to write about the theory of their subject.

Of course, the sophists believed their own art was the crown of all other arts. In the mythical account of the origin of civilization which Plato puts into the mouth of Protagoras [39] as an exposition of the nature and position of his techné, the sophist distinguishes two stages in the development of man. (Clearly, he does not conceive them to be different temporal stages in history, but separates them to emphasize the importance and the necessity of higher education as represented by the sophists.) The first of these is technical civilization. Following Aeschylus, Protagoras calls it the gift of Prometheus, which men acquired together with fire. Despite their possession of fire and the arts, he says, they would have perished miserably, being destroyed by wild animals, helpless and alone, if Zeus had not sent them the gift of justice, which enabled them to found the state and to live in communities. It is not clear whether Protagoras borrowed that idea too from Aeschylus (from the last part of the *Prometheus* trilogy) or from Hesiod,[40] the first to extol justice as Zeus' gift to mankind distinguishing them from the animals that eat one another. At any rate, Protagoras' elaboration of the theme is all his own. He says that, while Prometheus' gift of technical knowledge was imported only to a few specialists, Zeus gave the sense of justice and the idea of law to all men, since without it the state could not exist. But there is an even higher kind of insight into the principles of justice and the state, which is taught by the political techné of the sophists. He believes that to be true culture, the intellectual bond which holds together the whole structure of human society and civilization.

Not all the sophists can have had such a lofty conception of their profession—most of them were doubtless content to sell their knowledge to the public. But to appreciate the whole movement we must study its greatest representatives. Protagoras' claim that cultural education is the centre of all human life indicates that his education was frankly aimed at *humanism*. He implies that by subordinating what we now call civilization—namely technical efficiency—to culture: the clear and fundamental distinction between technical knowledge and power on one hand, and true culture on the other, is the very basis of humanism. We ought perhaps to avoid identifying specialist knowledge with the modern conception of a vocation (κλῆσις), which is in origin Christian and which is more comprehensive than the Greek concept of a techné.[41] In our sense, the work of a statesman, which Protagoras wished to educate men to perform, is also a vocation; but in Greek it is extremely daring to call it a techné, and the only justification for doing so is that the Greek language has no other word to express the ability and knowledge which the politician acquires by training and experience. And it is quite clear that Protagoras is anxious to distinguish his own techné from the professions which are technical in a narrower sense, and to present it as something comprehensive and universal. For the same reason he sharply differentiates his idea of 'universal' culture from the education given by other sophists, which is purely factual instruction. In his opinion they 'ruin young men'. Although their pupils come to them to avoid technical instruction of the kind which an artisan gets, they ignore that wish and give them another kind of technical instruction.[42] The only true 'universal' culture in Protagoras' eyes is *political* culture.

This conception of the nature of 'universal' culture summarizes the whole history of Greek education: ethics and politics taken together are one of the essential qualities of true paideia.[43] It was not till a later age that a new aesthetic ideal was superimposed on or substituted for the old conception of humanism, because the state had lost its predominant position in human life. But the close connexion between higher education and the idea of society and the state is an essential feature of classical Greece.

We are not using the word *humanism* vaguely as a historical parallel to an earlier phenomenon, but deliberately, in its basic sense, to connote the cultural ideal which after long incubation in the mind of Greece came to birth at last in the teaching of the sophists. Nowadays it is connected, like the kindred word *humanities,* with the relation of our culture to classical antiquity. But that is simply because our ideal of 'universal' culture originated in the civilisation of Greece and Rome. In that sense, then, humanism is essentially a creation of the Greeks. It is because humanism as realized by ancient Greece has a permanent importance for the mind of man that modern education is essentially and inevitably based on the study of antiquity.[44]

Moreover, we must here observe that humanism was a living and growing idea, although its essence remained the same: Protagoras' definition of it was not final. Both Plato and Isocrates took over the sophists' conception of culture, and each altered it in a different way.[45] The most remarkable evidence of that transformation is the fact that the epigram of Protagoras which was so justly famous, and in its very many-sidedness so characteristic of his humanism, was taken up by Plato at the end of his life and work, and altered from 'Man is the measure of all things' to 'The measure of all things is God'.[46] In that connexion we shall do well to remember that Protagoras said of God that he could not assert either that He existed or that He did not exist.[47] In view of the criticism to which Plato subjects the very principles of sophistic education, we must ask this question: Are religious scepticism and indifference, and moral and metaphysical 'relativism', which Plato opposed so bitterly and which made him a fierce and lifelong opponent of the sophists, essential elements of humanism?[48] The question cannot be answered by any individual opinion or preference: it must be objectively answered by history. We shall return to it from time to time throughout this book, and describe the battle of culture to support and defend religion and philosophy—a battle which reached a climax in the history of mankind when Christianity was at last accepted by the late Greco-Roman world.[49]

We can at least say this in anticipation. Before the sophists, there was none of the modern distinction between culture and religion in ancient Greek education: it was deeply rooted in religious faith. The rift between the two first opened in the age of the sophists, which was also the period in which the ideal of culture was first consciously formulated. Protagoras' assertion that the traditional values of life were all relative, and his resigned acceptance of the insolubility of all the enigmas of religion, were without doubt intimately connected with his high ideal of culture. Probably the conscious ideal of humanism could not have been produced by the great Greek educational tradition except at a moment when the old standards which had once meant so much to education began to be questioned. In fact, it clearly implies a reversion to the narrow basis of human life *per se*. Education always needs a standard; and at that period, when the traditional standards were dissolving and passing away, it chose as its standard the *form* of man: it became formal.[50] Situations of that kind have recurred at various periods in history, and the appearance of humanism is always closely connected with them. But it is quite as essential a feature of humanism that, formal as it may be at any moment, it always looks forward and backward, beyond itself—backward to the rich religious and moral forces of historical tradition, as the true 'spirit' from which the intellectual concept of rationalism, empty to the point of abstraction, must derive its concrete and living content; and forward to the religious and philosophical problem of a concept of life which surrounds and protects humanity like a tender root, but also gives it back the fertile soil in which to grow. This is the fundamental problem of all education: our answer to it will determine our judgment of the importance of the sophists. In historical terms, the main question is whether the humanism of the sophists, the first humanism which the world had seen, was destroyed or perfected by Plato. Any answer we may give to that historical question will be a profession of faith. Yet from the point of view of simple historical fact, it seems to have been settled long ago that the ideal of human culture as put forward by the sophists had within it the germs of a great future, but was not itself a complete and mature product.[51] Through its firm grasp of the formal element in education it continues to be of inestimable importance for educational practice, even at the present day. But because of the loftiness of its claims, it needed a deeper foundation, in philosophy and religion. Basically, Plato's philosophy is a reincarnation of the religious spirit of earlier Greek education, from Homer to the tragedians: by going behind the ideal of the sophists, he went beyond it.[52]

What is distinctive about the sophists is this: they were the first to conceive the conscious ideal of culture. If we survey the long development of the Greek mind from Homer to the rise of Athens we shall realize that this idea was not a startling new departure but the necessary sequel, the historical culmination of the whole process. For it is the result of the constant effort of all the Greek poets and thinkers to find and state a standard of human character. That effort was essentially an educational activity, and, especially in a nation so philosophical as the Greeks, it brought about the foundation of the concept of culture in the higher sense, as an ideal to be understood and followed. It is therefore perfectly natural that the sophists should have considered all the art and philosophy of earlier Greece as part of their cultural ideal, as its necessary content. Greece had always realized the educational power of poetry. It was therefore inevitable that poetry should be finally accepted as the material of cultural education at the moment when the meaning of education (παιδεύειν) was extended beyond the training of children (παῖδες) to the education of young men in particular, so as to encourage the belief that education might extend throughout the whole of life. Suddenly the Greeks realized that grown men too could have paideia. Originally the concept paideia had applied only to the process of education. Now its significance grew to include the objective side, the content of paideia—just as our word *culture* or the Latin *cultura,* having once meant the *process* of education, came to mean the *state* of being educated; and then the *content* of education, and finally the whole *intellectual and spiritual world* revealed by education, into which any individual, according to his nationality or social position, is born. The historical process by which the world of culture is built up culminates when the ideal of culture is consciously formulated. Accordingly it was perfectly natural for the Greeks in and after the fourth century, when the concept finally crystallized, to use the word *paideia*—in English, *culture*—to describe all the artistic forms and the intellectual and aesthetic achievements of their race, in fact the whole content of their tradition.

From that point of view, the sophists stand at the very centre of Greek history. They made Greece conscious of her own cul-

ture; and in that consciousness the Greek spirit reached its *telos,*
and realized its own form and the aim of its development. The
fact that they helped Greece to understand the true meaning of
culture is more important than the fact that they did not give
that culture its final form. At a time when traditional standards
were breaking down, they realized, and made the Greeks realize,
that culture was the great duty which had fallen to the lot of
their nation; and thereby they discovered the true, the ultimate
aim of the development of the whole people, and the basis of
every kind of organized life. That realization was a great
climax; but (as in every nation) it was the climax of autumn,
not of summer. And that is the other aspect of the sophists'
work. Although it is needless to prove that in the period from
the sophists to Plato and Aristotle, the mind of Greece developed still further and reached still greater heights, it is still true,
as Hegel said, that Minerva's owl did not begin her flight until
the dusk had fallen. The domination which the Greek spirit was
to win, and which was first preached by the sophists, was got by
Greece at the cost of her youth. It is easy to understand why
Nietzsche and Bachofen felt that the summer of Greece was the
time before *ratio,* conscious reason, appeared—the mythical
period, the age of Homer or the great tragedians. But it is impossible to accept that romantically simple view of the early age
of Greece, because the mind of a nation, like the mind of an individual, develops in accordance with an immanent and inevitable
law, and its impression on posterity must necessarily be not
single but complex. On one hand we feel that the development
of mind in a nation means an inevitable loss, and yet we cannot
resign ourselves to sacrifice the powers achieved by that development. We know that it is only through these powers that we are
enabled to admire the earlier irrational stage so freely and so
fully. That is of course our own position to-day: our culture
has reached a very late stage of development, and in many ways
we do not begin to feel at home in Greece until the rise of the
sophists. They are nearer to us than Pindar and Aeschylus, and
for that very reason we need Pindar and Aeschylus more.
Through the sophists we begin to realize that earlier stages in
the development of culture really do live on within it; for we
cannot accept the later stages unless we admire and understand
the former too.

We do not know enough of the sophists to give a detailed and individual account of the teaching and purposes of even the greatest among them. They themselves laid great stress on the differences between them, as is shown by Plato's contrasting descriptions of the sophists in *Protagoras;* but they were not really so different as they liked to think. The reason for our ignorance is that they wrote nothing which survived them long. Protagoras, who claimed supremacy in literature as in other activities, left some separate essays which were read in late antiquity, but even they were almost forgotten by that time.[53] There were a few more philosophical and scientific treatises by various sophists which survived for some decades, but in general they were not scholars, they wanted to influence the men of their own age. In Thucydides' words, their *epideixis* was not an eternal possession, but a performance to dazzle the hearers of the moment. And, as was natural, their most serious educational work was meant for living men, not for future readers. Socrates outdid them all, for he wrote nothing whatever. It is an irreparable loss to have no real insight into their educational technique. It cannot be compensated by the few details we know of their lives and opinions, for these are after all comparatively unimportant. We shall examine them only to illustrate the theories on which their teaching was founded. From our point of view it is chiefly important to study the stages by which they came to understand the process of cultural education at the same time as they apprehended the ideal of culture. Their understanding of education proves that they knew its fundamental facts, and especially that they could analyse human character. Their psychology was simple: compared with modern psychology, it was nearly as simple as the theories of Ionian philosophers about the elemental structure of the universe, compared with modern chemistry. But modern psychologists know no more of the real nature of man than did the sophists, and chemistry knows no more of the nature of the world than Empedocles or Anaximenes. We may therefore accept and admire the pioneering educational theories of the sophists, even to-day.

About a century before them, the conflict between aristocratic education and democratic ideals—the conflict which is illustrated by Theognis and Pindar—had broken out.[54] The sophists, pursuing the issues it had raised, investigated the basis of all educa-

tion—the relation between 'nature' and deliberate educational
influence in the formation of character. It is unnecessary to
quote the numerous echoes of this discussion in contemporary
literature. They show that the sophists had made all Greece conscious of the problem. The conclusion is always the same, though
expressed in different ways—nature (φύσις) is the ground upon
which all education must build. The process of completing that
education is called learning (μάθησις), sometimes teaching
(διδασκαλία), and practice (ἄσκησις) which makes what has been
learnt into a second nature.[55] This conclusion is an attempt at a
synthesis of the old opposition between aristocratic paideia and
rationalism: it abandons the aristocratic idea that character and
morality can be inherited by blood, but not acquired.

The ethical power of divine descent was now replaced by the
general conception of *human nature,* with all its individual accidents and ambiguities, but also with a far wider scope. That was
a most momentous departure, which could never have been made
without the help of the new and progressive science of medicine.
Medicine had long been a primitive sort of first-aid mixed up
with a great deal of popular superstition, curing by spells and
sympathetic magic, until the new Ionian knowledge of natural
processes, and the establishment of a regular empiric technique,
improved it into an art, and taught doctors to take scientific
observations of the human body and its processes. The conception of human nature which we find so often in the sophists and
their contemporaries arose first among the new progressive
doctors and students of medicine.[56] The concept of *physis* was
transferred from the whole universe to a single part of it—to
mankind; and there it took on a special meaning. Man is subject
to certain rules prescribed by *his own* nature, which must be
known if he is to live correctly in health and recover properly
from illness. This was the first recognition of the fact that the
physis of man is a physical organism, with a particular structure
to be understood and treated in a particular way. From that
medical conception of physis, the Greeks soon reached a wider
application of the word, which was the basis of the educational
theories of the sophists: it now came to mean the whole man,
made up of body and soul together, and in particular man's
spiritual nature. At the same time the historian Thucydides was
using the concept of human nature, but altered it in accordance

with his subject, to connote man's social and moral nature. The idea of human nature, now formulated for the first time, should not be regarded as a simple or natural idea: it was a great and fundamental discovery of the Greek mind. Only after it had been discovered was it possible to construct a real theory of culture.[57]

The deep religious problems implicit in the word *nature* were not worked out by the sophists. They started with an optimistic belief that man's nature is usually educable, and is capable of good; men with unfortunate or evil dispositions were, they believed, the exception. Of course this is the point at which the Christian attack on humanism is always delivered. No doubt the educational optimism of the sophists is not the final answer which Greece gave to the problem; yet, if the Greeks had started with the belief that all men were naturally sinful, and not the idea that all men could be shaped towards good, they would never have created the technique of education and their own ideal of culture. We need only remember the Phoenix-scene in the *Iliad,* and Pindar's hymns, and Plato's dialogues, to realize how deeply conscious the Greeks always were of the problems of education. The aristocrats in particular doubted whether education could be universal. Pindar and Plato never fell under the illusion that reason can be meted out like a material substance in a mechanical way. Socrates, the commoner, rediscovered the old Hellenic distrust of the unlimited educability of mankind. Remember the profound resignation of Plato's seventh letter, in which he speaks sadly of the narrow limits which bound the influence of knowledge upon the human race, and of the reasons which led him to address a small audience, rather than preach the gospel to the multitude.[58] But remember also that despite their doubts it was the intellectual nobility of Greece who founded and formulated all the higher culture of the nation; and you will realize that the eternal greatness and fertility of the Greek spirit were created by that conflict between the will to educate and the disbelief in the possibility of a mechanized education. Between these two poles, there is room for both the Christian sense of sin and its pessimistic view of culture, and the educational optimism of the sophists. We must try to understand the historical situation which created and conditioned their optimism, if we are to do justice to their work. We cannot avoid criticizing it even while we appreciate it, because the purposes and the achievements of the sophists still play an indispensable part in modern life.

No one understood and described the political conditions which dictated the sophistic point of view better than its great critic Plato. His *Protagoras* is the source to which we must always return, for it envisages the ideas and the educational technique of the sophists as one comprehensive unity and reveals all their social and political presuppositions with incontrovertible truth. These presuppositions always recur, when education reaches the particular point at which the sophists took it up. Plato treats the individual differences between the methods of one sophist and another simply as material for humour. He brings three great sophists on the stage at once—Protagoras of Abdera, Hippias of Elis, and Prodicus of Ceos: they are all guests in the house of the rich Athenian Callias, who converted his home into a hotel for intellectual celebrities.[59] By this device, Plato is enabled to show that, although the sophists differ in this characteristic or in that, there is a striking family resemblance between them all.

The most important of them is Protagoras. He undertakes to give an education in political areté to a well-born young Athenian who has pressed Socrates for an introduction to him; and, in answer to Socrates' frank scepticism, he explains why he believes that men are socially educable.[60] He starts with the accepted state of society. No one is ashamed to confess that he knows nothing of any art which requires special ability to practise. Yet no one publicly confesses that he has committed crimes against the law, but at least keeps the appearance of obeying them. If a man were to drop the mask, and openly admit that he was unjust, he would be thought to be mad, not candid. For we all assume that everyone can have a share of justice and common sense. Now, the fact that political areté can be acquired follows from the current system of sanctions, by which crimes are punished and virtues rewarded. We do not reproach a man for irreparable defects in his own nature, for which he deserves neither reward nor punishment. But both reward and punishment are assigned by society to encourage the good qualities which can be learnt by conscious effort. Therefore the crimes which are punishable by law must be evitable by education, unless the whole system of society is to collapse. Protagoras draws the same conclusion from the purpose of punishment. He rejects the old Greek causal theory of punishment, as retribution to be paid *because* a man has sinned, and puts forward the obviously new final theory that punishment is ameliorative and deterrent—it improves the evildoer and frightens others.[61] This educational interpretation of punishment depends on the assumption that men can be educated. Civic virtue is the foundation of the state: without it, no community could possibly exist. Anyone who has no share of it must be educated, reproved, and punished until he improves; if he is incurable, he must be excluded from the community, or else killed. Thus not only the justice of the state but the whole state itself is, in Protagoras' opinion, a wholly educational force. More accurately, it is the contemporary city-state (like his own example Athens), with its dependence on law and justice, which speaks in this rigidly logical theory of education and seeks justification through it.

This educational conception of the state's duty in administering justice seems to assume that the state exercises a systematic influence on the education of its citizens. But, as we have said above, no Greek state did exercise such an influence, with the exception of Sparta. It is remarkable that the sophists never put forward a demand for state-supervised education, although from the standpoint of Protagoras they might very well have done so. They themselves filled the gap by giving education to numbers of private persons. Protagoras points out that the whole life of every citizen is guided by educational influence from his birth up: nurse, mother, father, pedagogue, all outdo one another in shaping the child's character by teaching and showing him the meaning of just and unjust, good and bad. With threats and punishments they try to straighten his soul out, as if it were a warping branch. Then he goes to school and learns orderly behaviour, reading and writing, and playing the lyre.

When he has passed that stage, the master makes him read poems by good poets and learn them by heart.[62] They contain much moral instruction and many narratives glorifying great men, whose examples will move the child to imitate them. Through instruction in music too he is trained to sophrosyné and kept from bad conduct. Then follows the study of lyric poets, whose works are sung to music. They make the souls of young

people familiar with rhythm and harmony, so that they can be
controlled, for the life of man needs eurhythmia and proper
harmony. Rhythm and harmony, in fact, must be expressed in all
the acts and speeches of the truly educated man.[63] Moreover, the
boy is sent to the gymnastic school, where the *paidotribés* trains
his body to be a good servant to his sound mind, so that he will
never play the coward from weakness. Protagoras makes his
speech appropriate to his distinguished audience by emphasizing
the fact that rich families educate their children longer than the
poor. The sons of the rich go to school earlier and leave it
later.[64] He wants to drive home the point that everyone tries to
educate his own children as carefully as possible: so that the
communis opinio of the entire world holds men to be educable,
and in practice every child is educated without stint or scruple.

It tells us much of the new conception of culture that Protagoras does not consider education to end when the boy leaves
school. In a certain sense, he thinks that it really begins then.
Once more his theory reflects current ideas of the nature of the
state, when he asserts that it is the laws which educate men in
political areté. The real cultural education of a citizen begins
when, after leaving school and entering active life, the state
forces him to learn the laws and to live in accordance with their
pattern and example (παράδειγμα).[65] This is a very obvious example of the transformation of the old aristocratic paideia into
the new civic education. From Homer onwards, aristocratic education was governed by the idea of following noble examples. A
great man is a physical embodiment of the norm which the pupil
must follow, and the pupil's admiration for his ideal qualities
naturally prompts him to imitate them. This personal factor in
imitation (μίμησις) disappears when the laws provide the pattern. In the graduated system of education described by Protagoras, it has not wholly disappeared, but has been relegated to a
lower place: it is now part of the elementary courses of instruction in poetry, which are devoted to explanation of the content
alone, with emphasis on the moral maxims and historical examples which it embodies rather than on the form which develops
rhythm and harmony in the spirit. But the normative element is
maintained and even strengthened in the examples provided by
the law—the highest teacher of every citizen; for law is the
most universal and final expression of current moral standards.

Protagoras compares life lived in accordance with law to elementary lessons in writing, where children learn to write inside lines drawn by the teacher. The laws themselves are lines which the citizen's life must not overrun: they were invented for that purpose by great lawgivers of old. He has already compared the process of education with the process of straightening a growing branch. Now, in legal language the punishment which makes a man return to the line he has transgressed is called *euthyné*, straightening; and there too, the sophist believes, the educational function of law is made manifest.[66]

In the Athenian state law was not only the 'king' (as Pindar put it in a verse often quoted at the time [67]) but the school of citizenship. We do not think of it in that way now. Nor do we believe that the laws are the discoveries of great law-givers of the past: they are ephemeral things, as they were to become in Athens, and not even specialists can know them all. We can hardly imagine how, when Socrates was in prison facing death, and was offered a safe opportunity for escape to freedom, the laws could appear to him in the shape of living persons and advise him to remain true to them in the hour of trial, because they had educated and protected him throughout his life and were the foundation of his whole existence. Protagoras' description of the laws as teachers reminds us of that scene in *Crito*.[68] He is simply formulating the ideal of the constitutional state of his time. We should have noted the affinity between his theory of education and the Athenian ideal even if he had not frequently referred to Athens and explained that its whole structure was based on that conception of life. It is impossible to determine whether the sophist himself really felt this kinship or whether Plato merely attributed it to him in the brilliant but artistically free imitation of his lecture in *Protagoras*. This at least is certain—Plato himself always felt that the sophistic system of education was directly derived from actual political conditions.

All Protagoras' speech is intended to prove that men can be educated in areté. But the sophists referred this question not only to the assumptions on which state and society are based, and to political and moral common sense, but to a much wider issue. The problem of the educability of human nature is a special case of another problem—the relation between nature and art in general. 'Plutarch' has an illuminating discussion of this aspect of educational theory in his essay *On the education of children*. This work was of fundamental importance in Renaissance humanism: it was published again and again, and its ideas have been taken over wholesale by modern educators. In the introduction [69] Plutarch states the obvious fact that he knew and used earlier literature on the subject. His use of it is not confined to the particular point in question but to the whole of the next chapter, in which he discusses the three basic elements of all education: nature, learning, and practice. It is perfectly clear that this is founded on earlier pedagogic theory.

Most fortunately, Plutarch has given us not only the 'educational trinity' which is otherwise known to be sophistic in origin,[70] but also a continuous discussion of it which illustrates the lasting influence of the sophistic ideal of culture. His source illustrates the relation between the three elements by the example of agriculture, which is the chief instance of the cultivation of nature by human art for a definite purpose. Successful agriculture requires, first, good soil, then a skilful farmer, and lastly good seed. In education the soil is human nature, the teacher corresponds to the farmer, and the seed is the instruction and advice imparted by the spoken word. When all these three conditions are perfectly fulfilled, the product is outstandingly good. But even when a less gifted nature gets proper care, instruction, and practice, its deficiencies can be partly compensated; and on the other hand even a richly endowed nature will go to waste if neglected. This is the fact which makes the art of education indispensable. What is produced from nature after much effort is finally stronger than nature itself. Good soil becomes unproductive if not tilled—in fact, the better it is by nature, the worse it becomes. Ground which is less good, if worked correctly and continuously, will bring forth noble crops at last. The same applies to arboriculture, the other half of the farmer's work. And both physical exercise and animal-training are good examples of the fact that physis can be educated. The essential thing is to begin work at the right moment, the most educative moment—which in the human species is childhood, when nature is still pliable, and whatever is learnt is absorbed, easily but permanently, by the soul.

Unfortunately we cannot now distinguish early and late elements in Plutarch's argument. He has obviously blended some sophistic views with the teaching of post-sophistic philosophers. Thus the image of the plasticity (εὔπλαστον) of the young soul perhaps comes from Plato; [71] and the fine idea that art compensates natural deficiencies appears in Aristotle; [72] but perhaps both were first worked out by sophists. The striking comparison of education and agriculture seems to be so closely connected with the doctrine of the educational trinity that it must be part of the sophistic theory of education.[73] It was used before Plutarch, and for that reason too it must go back to an early source. Translated into Latin, it entered European thought and helped to produce the new metaphor *cultura animi:* the culture of mankind is spiritual culture, as the cultivation of the earth is agriculture. The modern word *culture* is a clear echo of the original metaphor. In later humanistic theory these ideas were revived and helped to create the great importance which civilized or 'cultured' nations have since attached to the ideal of intellectual culture.

We have described the sophists as the first humanists, and the description agrees with the fact that they created the conception of culture, although they could not guess that their metaphor would one day grow far beyond the simple idea of education, and become the highest symbol of civilization. But there is good reason for the triumph of the cultural idea: that suggestive comparison of teaching and agriculture expresses the new universal basis of Greek culture—the highest application of the general law of improvement in natural endowments by human will and reason. It is clear from this that the connexion between pedagogy and a philosophy of civilization, which is attributed to all the sophists and chiefly to Protagoras, was inherent and necessary. They held that the ideal of culture was the climax of civilization in the broadest and most universal sense, which embraces everything between the first rude attempts of man to impose his will on elemental nature, and the highest self-education and self-shaping of the human spirit. By basing education on such a wide and deep foundation, the sophists revealed once more the true nature of the Greek spirit, its concentration on the universal, the *whole* of life. Had they not done so, neither the idea of civiliza-

tion nor the idea of cultural education would have come into
being in so plastic and fertile a form.

Still, however important it was to establish a deep philosophical basis for education, there is not a great deal of value in comparing the educational process to agriculture. Knowledge which
sinks into the soul by being learnt is not in the same relation to
it as seed to the earth. Education is not a simple automatic
process of growth which the teacher guides and encourages at
his will. We have mentioned another parallel to education, the
old and well-regulated process of educating the body by gymnastic training, which offered an obvious comparison with the
new process of shaping the soul. Just as the Greeks, thinking of
sculpture, had held the cultivation of the body to be the act of
shaping it as the sculptor shapes his stone, so now Protagoras
viewed education as the act of *shaping the soul,* and the means
by which it was carried out as formative forces.[74] We cannot say
with certainty whether the sophists used the particular concept
of formation or shaping for the process of education: in principle, their idea of education would admit it perfectly. It does not
matter therefore that Plato was perhaps the first to use the word
mould, πλάττειν, for the act.[75] The idea of shaping the soul is implicit in Protagoras' assertion that harmony and the rhythm of
poetry and music must be impressed on the soul to make it
rhythmical and harmonious.[76] In that passage he is not describing the education which he himself gives, but the education which
every Athenian enjoyed to a greater or less degree, and which
the existing private schools of Athens offered. We may assume
that the teaching of the sophists was an elaboration of it, especially in the formal subjects which were the centre of their system. Before them, we never hear of grammar, rhetoric, and
dialectic: they must therefore have invented them. The new
techné is clearly the systematic expression of the principle of
shaping the intellect, because it begins by instruction in the form
of language, the form of oratory, and the form of thought.
This educational technique is one of the greatest discoveries
which the mind of man has ever made: it was not until it explored these three of its activities that the mind apprehended
the hidden law of its own structure.

Unhappily, we know hardly anything of the great work of the sophists in these subjects. Their grammatical treatises are lost, although later grammarians (the Peripatetics and the Alexandrians) used them as the basis of their own books. Plato's parodies tell us much of Prodicus' researches into semantics, and we have a little information about Protagoras' classification of the various types of words and Hippias' theory of the meaning of letters and syllables.[77] The rhetorical works of the sophists too are lost: they were manuals not meant for publication. Anaximenes' *Rhetoric* is a sort of poor relation, living on ideas inherited from greater books; but it gives some notion of their contents. We are better informed about their dialectic. The principal work in that field, Protagoras' *Antilogies,* is lost. But we can get a glimpse of their remarkable technique of speaking 'from both sides'—that is, of attacking and then defending the same thesis—in a book called *Double Speeches* (δισσοὶ λόγοι) which was written in Doric by an unknown sophist towards the end of the fifth century.[78] Logic was first taught in the school of Plato; and the juggling eristics of many second-rate sophists, which were attacked as meaningless by serious philosophers, and caricatured in Plato's *Euthydemus,* prove that the new art of disputation was at first regarded chiefly as a weapon in the armoury of the orator. It is therefore more like rhetoric than philosophical logic.

In the absence of almost all direct accounts of the formal teaching provided by the sophists, we must judge it chiefly by its immense effect on men of their own and succeeding generations. To it their contemporaries owed their unparalleled finesse and sureness of touch in oratorical structure, in proof by argument, and in every other method of elaborating thought in speech, from terse narrative of facts to the most moving parade of emotion, through the whole gamut which the Greek orators, with the certainty of a virtuoso, commanded. Oratory, as they taught it, was 'intellectual gymnastics'—the art which we find so seldom in the speeches and books of our own contemporaries. In reading the Attic orators of that period we really feel that the logos is a wrestler stripped for the ring. The taut suppleness of a well-constructed proof is like the sinewy body of a well-trained athlete. The Greeks called a lawsuit or trial an *agon,* for they always felt that it was a fight in legalized form between two

rivals. Modern scholars have shown that in the age of the sophists Greek advocates gradually abandoned the old methods of
proof by witnesses, tortures, and oaths, for the new rhetorical
tricks of proof by logical argument.[79] But even the historian
Thucydides, that earnest seeker after truth, was obviously dominated by the formal art of the sophists, in the very details of
his oratorical technique, his sentence-structure, and even his
grammatical use of words, his *orthoepeia*.[80] Rhetoric was the
principal form of cultural education in later classical antiquity.
It suited the Greek passion for form so well that it actually
ruined the nation by overgrowing everything else like a creeping
plant. But that fact must not influence our judgment of the educational value of the new discovery. Together with grammar and
dialectic, rhetoric became the basis of formal education throughout Europe. These three were called the Trivium in late antiquity, and blended with the Quadrivium to form the system of
the seven free arts: thus formally organized into an educational
system, they outlived all the beauty and brilliance of ancient culture and ancient art. The upper classes of French schools still
bear the names of these 'disciplines', inherited from the schools
attached to the mediaeval monasteries, and thereby symbolize
the unbroken tradition of sophistic culture.[81]

The sophists themselves did not join these three formal arts
with arithmetic, geometry, music, and astronomy, to form the
later system of the seven free arts. Yet the number seven is the
least important thing in the system; and the general inclusion of
what the Greeks called the *mathemata* (which from the time of
the Pythagoreans included harmonics and astronomy) within the
system of higher culture—in fact the essential thing about the
addition of the Trivium to the Quadrivium—was really the
work of the sophists.[82] Before them only practical instruction
in music was given, as is shown by Protagoras' account of the
current system of education: it was taught by professional lyre-
players.[83] The sophists added to it the Pythagorean doctrines of
harmonic theory. And they altered the history of the world by
introducing mathematical instruction too. Among the Pythagoreans it had been a subject of scientific research. The sophist
Hippias was the first to recognize its irreplaceable value as a
means of education; and other sophists, like Antiphon, and after

him Bryson, taught and studied mathematical problems; since then it has never lost its place in higher education.

To-day, the Greek system of higher education, as built up by the sophists, dominates the entire civilized world. It has been accepted by every country, especially since it can be assimilated without a knowledge of Greek. It must never be forgotten that it was the Greeks who created and elaborated not only general ethical and political culture, in which we have traced the origin of our own humanistic culture,[84] but also what is called practical education and is sometimes a competitor, sometimes an opponent of humanistic culture. The type of education that we call humanistic in the narrow sense (which cannot possibly exist without a knowledge of Greek and Latin) could appear only in a civilization which was not itself Greek, but was deeply influenced by Greek culture: namely, in Rome. The modern system of education in Greek and Latin together was first fully worked out by the humanists of the Renaissance. We shall later study its preliminary development in the civilisation of late antiquity.

We do not know the tendency of the mathematical teaching given by the sophists. One of the chief objections raised against it was that mathematics was useless in practical life. Plato of course incorporated mathematics in his own educational system, as a preparation for philosophy.[85] That certainly cannot have been the aim of the sophists in teaching it. Still, we might not be right in believing that they held it merely to be formal training for the intellect: although Isocrates, himself a student of sophistic rhetoric, after years of opposition at last conceded that mathematics was, to a limited extent, useful for that purpose.[86] In their educational system, the *mathemata* were the substantial elements, and grammar, rhetoric, and dialectic the formal elements. The later division of the seven free arts into the Trivium and Quadrivium also indicates that their teaching was divided into two complementary groups of subjects; for it was always recognized that the two groups performed different educational functions. Those who tried to unite them were trying to attain the ideal of harmony, or, like Hippias himself,[87] the ideal of universality: not to produce a unity by simply adding one group to the other. And it is not probable on the face of it that the *mathemata,* in which astronomy (not then a severely mathematical study) was included, were taught simply as a formal exercise for the mind. The sophists do not appear to have admitted that the practical uselessness of mathematics at that period was a conclusive objection to its educational value. They must have admired mathematics and astronomy for their value as exercises in pure theory. That is certainly true of Hippias, though few of the others were productive scholars. This was, then, the first recognition of the value of a purely theoretical discipline in the cultivation of the intellect. These subjects developed abilities quite different from the technical and practical ones which grammar and rhetoric and dialectic were intended to encourage. By the acquisition of mathematical knowledge the student strengthened his constructive and analytical powers, or, in general terms, his power of pure thought. The sophists never arrived at the theory of the effect thus produced: Plato and Aristotle were the first to work out the full educational importance of pure science. But we must admire the sophists for the unerring insight which enabled them to choose the right kind of discipline for this purpose, and which was recognized and honoured by educators in later ages.

When theoretical science had once been introduced as an educational discipline, it was necessary to decide how far it should be studied. The question appears in every discussion of scientific education at that period, in Thucydides, Plato, Isocrates, and Aristotle. It was not raised by philosophers alone: everywhere we can hear echoes of a widespread opposition to the strange new subject which demanded so much time and energy for purely intellectual studies divorced from the interests of ordinary life. Before then, this mental attitude had appeared only in a few eccentric scholars: their surprising lack of interest in ordinary life, and their originality, at once ridiculous and splendid, had been regarded with toleration, kindness, even respect.[88] But it was different now. Theoretical science claimed to be the true, the 'highest' kind of culture, and to replace or dominate the current educational discipline.

Its chief opponents were not found among the working people, who were naturally unable to take any interest in it—it was 'no use', and expensive, and meant for the upper classes. It could be criticized only by the governing class, who had always possessed a higher type of education and a set of fixed standards, and whose ideal of *kalokagathia,* gentlemanly character, maintained itself even in the democratic régime. The example of passionate interest in intellectual pursuits was set by great statesmen like Pericles and social leaders like Callias, the richest man in Athens; and many distinguished families sent their sons to the sophists' lectures. But it was impossible to overlook the fact that σοφία endangered the aristocratic ideal. Fathers did not want their sons educated to be sophists. A few gifted pupils followed the sophists from city to city, with the intention of making a profession out of what they learnt from them; but the young Athenian noble who attended the same lectures did not feel that theirs was an example to be followed: on the contrary, it made him realize the social gulf between him and the sophists (all of whom came from middle-class families) and made him feel that there were limits to the influence they should exercise upon him.[89] In Pericles' funeral speech Thucydides defines the attitude of the Athenian state to the new culture: though he places much importance on the cultivation of the mind, he limits φιλοσοφοῦμεν by the warning ἄνευ μαλαχίας: the ideal is intellectual culture without effeminacy.[90]

This epigram, expressing as it does a severely limited pleasure in mental exercise, casts a clear light on the attitude of the Athenian governing class in the second half of the fifth century. It is reminiscent of the dispute in Plato's *Gorgias* between 'Socrates' (who here is simply Plato himself) and the Athenian aristocrat Callicles about the value of distinterested scholarly research for the education of the nobleman who intends to engage in politics.[91] Callicles violently attacks the idea that knowledge can be an end in itself, worthy of a life's devotion. It is, he says, useful in order to keep young men from bad habits at the dangerous age before maturity, and to train their reasoning powers. A man who has no early acquaintance with intellectual interests will never be truly free.[92] But on the other hand anyone who spends his whole life in the close atmosphere of study will never be a complete man, but will be arrested at an early stage of his development.[93] Callicles sets a limit beyond which intellectual studies must not be taken, by saying that they should be pursued 'for the sake of culture'—that is, studied for a certain period merely as a preparation for life.[94] Callicles typifies his own social class. (We need not here concern ourselves with

Plato's attitude to him.) The whole of the upper class and the bourgeoisie of Athens more or less shared his sceptical attitude to the new cult of the intellect which was attracting their sons. The only differences were between one individual and another. In a later chapter we shall discuss the attitude of Attic comedy, which is one of our most important bodies of evidence in this matter.[95]

Callicles himself is a pupil of the sophists, as is shown by every word he speaks. But in his subsequent life as a statesman he has learnt to treat his sophistic education as subordinate to the whole of his political career. He quotes Euripides, whose work reflects all the problems of his day. In his *Antiope* the poet introduced the two contemporary types who were in direct opposition to each other—the man of action and the born theoretician and dreamer; the former spoke to his brother in the same tone which Callicles now uses to Socrates. It is notable that this drama was imitated by the old Roman poet Ennius, who made the young hero Neoptolemus, Achilles' son, say the words *philosophari sed paucis*.[96] It was always felt that the attitude of the Romans, those thoroughly practical and political people, to Greek philosophy and science had been given lapidary expression in this line, as if it were a historical law. Yet this 'Roman phrase' which upsets so many modern Philhellenes was originally spoken by a Greek. It is only a translation into Roman terms of the attitude of the Athenian aristocracy to the new science and philosophy of the age of the sophists and Euripides. It expresses just the same cold dislike for pure theory which the Romans always retained. Periclean civilization was resolved to engage in philosophical study 'only for the sake of culture',[97] and only as far as it was necessary in order to attain culture: for it was wholly practical and political. It was based on the Athenian empire, which aimed at ruling all Greece. Even when Plato preached the ideal of 'the philosophic life' after the empire had fallen, he justified it by explaining that it had a practical value in building up the state.[98] Isocrates gave pure knowledge exactly the same place in his cultural ideal. Ionian science was only reborn in the Peripatetic school and in Alexandria, after the great days of Athens were over. The sophists helped to bridge this gulf between the Athenians and their cousins the Ionians. They

were predestined to give Athens the intellectual abilities which
she needed for her great and complex task, and to make Ionian
knowledge the servant of Attic culture.

EDUCATION AND THE POLITICAL CRISIS

When the sophists formulated the ideal of culture, the Greek
city-state reached a climax in its development. For centuries the
state had prescribed the form of life which its citizens were to
lead, and poets of every kind had praised its divine *cosmos;* but
never before had the duty of the state to educate its members
been formulated so authoritatively and comprehensively. Sophistic culture was not created simply to fulfil an actual political
need: it deliberately took the state as the goal and the ideal
standard of all education. In Protagoras' theory the state appeared to be the spring of all educational energy, or in fact one
huge educational organization, impressing all its laws and all its
social system with the same spirit.[99] Pericles' conception of the
state, as set forth by Thucydides in the funeral speech, culminates similarly in the declaration that the state is the great educative force, and that the communal life of Athens is a complete
and pattern fulfilment of the cultural mission of the state.[100]
Thus, the sophists' ideas penetrated the sphere of practical politics: they conquered the whole state. No other interpretation of
the facts is possible. In other respects Pericles and Thucydides
show that they were deeply influenced by sophistic opinions; so
they must have been borrowers, not creators, of this thought too.
The sophists' educational conception of the state gained additional importance when Thucydides combined it with another
new idea—the idea that the new state was compelled by its very
nature to strive for *power*. The classical city-state is held in constant tension between two poles, power and education;[101] for
there is an inevitable conflict between them, although the polis
educates its citizens exclusively for itself. When it demands that
the individual be ready to sacrifice himself to serve its purposes,
it assumes that these purposes agree with the welfare of the
whole community and of its parts, rightly understood. The welfare of the community and its parts must be measurable by an
objective standard. The Greeks had long considered that standard to be justice, diké. On justice the order and therefore the

happiness of the state are founded. Accordingly, Protagoras considered that education to serve the state was education in justice.[102] But, just as this conclusion had been reached, there arose the crisis of the state, which was also the gravest crisis of education. It is an exaggeration to blame the influence of the sophists alone for this development, as many do.[103] It is merely expressed most clearly in their teaching, because they were extraordinarily sensitive to all contemporary problems, and because education always reacts strongly to any attack on established authority.

The deep moral feeling with which Solon had preached the ideal of justice in the state still lived on in the Periclean age. The city's greatest pride was to be the defender of justice on earth and the champion of the unjustly oppressed. But even after the introduction of democracy, the old fight for power over the laws and the constitution still raged: it was now carried on with new weapons far more brutal, impious, and destructive than could have been conceived by the simple honesty of earlier generations. There was indeed one central conception, which gained strength from the Persian wars onwards, until it became predominant: that was the democratic ideal, by which the numerical majority possessed all authority and all power of decision. It had won its way through savage conflict, with constant danger of civil war; and even the long and almost unopposed leadership of Pericles, who was one of the aristocratic Alcmaeonid family, was made possible only at the cost of great new extensions in the power of the masses. But beneath the surface of Athenian democracy there smouldered the inextinguishable spark of revolution, among the politically dispossessed aristocrats, or (as their enemies called them) the oligarchs.[104]

While the foreign policy of democratic Athens, under the guidance of great statesmen and the supreme command of Pericles, continued to win success after success, the aristocrats remained sincerely loyal; or else feigned loyalty and paid lip-service to the demos—soon becoming astonishingly expert in this new art, which sometimes became grotesque and ridiculous hypocrisy. But the Peloponnesian war, which put the steadily growing power of Athens to its last fateful test, shook the authority of the government and consequently of the state itself, after the death of Pericles, and finally aggravated the struggle for political mastery to an unheard-of violence. Both parties used all the weapons of sophistical rhetoric and argument in the fight; we cannot really assert that the sophists were bound by their political convictions to support one party or the other. If Protagoras believed that the existing democracy was 'the state' which was the goal of all his educational efforts, there were opponents of democracy too who possessed and used weapons which they had acquired from training given by the sophists. They may not have been forged to use against the state, but they were dangerous. Even more dangerous than the sophists' rhetorical technique were their general theories of the nature of law and justice. These made what had been a party-struggle into a conflict of ideals, which threatened to overthrow the principles on which society and the state were based.

By earlier generations, the constitutional state had been regarded as a tremendous achievement. Diké was a powerful goddess, and no one might attack the holy foundations of her rule with impunity. Earthly justice was rooted in the justice of heaven. That view was held throughout Greece. It did not alter when the old authoritarian régime changed into the new state based on reason and the laws: only the content changed, while the divine sanction remained. The deity had in fact taken on the human attributes of reason and justice. But the authority of the new law rested as of old on its agreement with the divine order —or, as the new philosophers would have put it, on its harmony with nature. Nature had become the sum of all that was divine. In it ruled the same law and the same justice that man revered as the highest moral standard. That was the origin of the idea of the cosmos.[105] But this conception of nature changed again in the course of the fifth century. Even Heraclitus had seen the cosmos as the ceaseless conflict of opposites: 'War is the father of all.' With the gradual change in opinion, conflict alone remained. The universe was now conceived as the fortuitous product of compulsion and superior power in the mechanical interplay of forces.

At first sight it is difficult to determine whether this conception of nature came first, and was then applied to the world of men, or man universalized his new 'naturalistic' view of human life, and projected it upon nature as an eternal law. In the age of the sophists the old and new views are close together. In *The Phoenician Women* Euripides describes equality, the foundation of democracy, as the law, manifest a hundredfold in nature, which man himself cannot escape.[106] Yet at the same time there were others to attack the theory of equality as accepted by the democrats and to show that nature is never ruled by mechanical *isonomia* but by the law of the stronger. In both cases, it is clear that the universe and its structure are seen from the human point of view, and interpreted in accordance with a particular set of assumptions: they are in fact an aristocratic and a democratic conception of nature. The new aristocratic conception proves that there was an increasing number of people who, instead of admiring geometric equality, emphasized the natural inequality of mankind and made that fact the basis of their entire political and moral philosophy. Like their predecessors, they appealed for authority to the divine government of the world, and flattered themselves with having the support of the latest philosophical and scientific theories.

The new principle is perfectly embodied in the unforgettable figure of Callicles in Plato's *Gorgias*.[107] He is an earnest pupil of the sophists: his views are derived from their teaching, as is shown by the first book of *The Republic*, where the right of the stronger is supported by the sophist and rhetor Thrasymachus.[108] To generalize would be a distortion of historical truth. We could easily produce a different type of sophist, whose philosophy was quite opposed to the naturalistic theory combated by Plato—the preacher of traditional morality, merely translating into prose the maxims of gnomic poetry. But the Callicles-type is far more interesting, and, as drawn by Plato, far stronger. There must have been many men of power like him among the Athenian aristocrats: Plato clearly knew them well from his youth onwards. Critias, the unscrupulous leader of the oligarchic reaction, later a 'tyrant', is the obvious example: Plato may have borrowed some traits from him or a kindred spirit to use in the fictitious character Callicles.[109] And although Plato is fundamentally opposed to the views of Callicles, he states them with the ease and sympathy of a man who has suppressed them in himself, or has yet to suppress them. In his seventh letter, he says that he himself was thought to be a highly suitable comrade and partisan by the followers of Critias, obviously not merely because of his relationship to the oligarch, and that he sympathized with their policy for some time.[110]

Education in Protagoras' sense, namely education in the spirit of the traditional ideal of justice, is attacked by Callicles with a passionate earnestness that brings home the full force of his transvaluation of all values. What the Athenian state and its citizens hold to be the highest justice is for him the depth of injustice.[111] 'We mould,' he cries, 'the best and strongest among us to our will, catching them young like lions, and we enchant and enslave them by telling them that everyone must have equal rights, and that that is the meaning of nobility and justice. But in my opinion if a man of truly strong nature comes, he shakes all that off and bursts through it and escapes, trampling down our letters and spells and incantations and all our unnatural laws, and he our slave rises up to be our master; and then shines forth the justice of nature!' From this point of view, law is an artificial bond, a convention agreed on by the organized weaklings to repress their natural masters, the strong, and make them do their will. The law of nature is directly opposed to the justice of men. By its standard, what the equalitarian state calls law and justice is nothing but arbitrary power, pure and simple. Whether that law should be obeyed or not depends, in Callicles' eyes, on one's power of resisting it. In any case he can see no inherent moral authority in the idea of justice, conceived as equivalent to the existing laws. This, coming from an Athenian aristocrat, is the battle-cry of revolution. And actually the *coup d'état* of 403 after the defeat of Athens was inspired by the spirit of Callicles.

We must realize the full scope of the intellectual revolution to which these words of Callicles bear witness. It is impossible to do it justice from the standpoint of our own age, for although that particular attitude to the state would necessarily lead to the destruction of its authority in any period of history, the belief that in political life the stronger should rule would not to-day be equivalent to a proclamation of moral anarchy in *private* life. Rightly or wrongly, we now believe that politics and morals are two separate worlds, not necessarily ruled by the same code. No theoretical attempts to bridge the gulf between them can change the historical fact that our morality goes back to the Christian religion and our politics to the Greco-Roman conception of the state, so that they spring from different moral sources. This divided allegiance, sanctioned by custom for twenty centuries, is a necessity which modern philosophers try to convert into a virtue; but the Greeks had nothing like it. We always think of political morality as a sharp contrast to individual morality: in fact, many of us would prefer to write of political 'morality' in quotation marks. But the Greeks in the classical era—in fact, throughout the whole period of city-state civilization—thought that political morality and personal morality were practically identical: since the state was the sole source of all moral standards, and it was difficult to see what other moral code could exist apart from the code of the state, the law of the community in which the individual lived and had his being. A purely private moral code, without reference to the state, was inconceivable to the Greeks. We must forget our idea that each individual's acts are ruled by his conscience. The Greeks thought so too, but not till a later and essentially different period.[112] In the fifth century there were only two possibilities: either the law of the state was the highest standard for human life and coincided with the divine government of the universe, in which case a man was a citizen, no more and no less; or else the standards of the state conflicted with those established by nature or God, so that man could not accept them, in which case he ceased to be a member of the political community, and the very foundations of his life dissolved, unless he could find some certainty in the eternal order of nature.

When this gulf appeared between the law of the cosmos and the law of the polis, Greek thought was not far from the cosmopolitanism of Hellenistic times. Some of the sophists did in fact deduce from their criticism of nomos that the only valid law was the law of the universe. They were the first cosmopolitans. From all appearances, they were of a different type from Protagoras. Plato draws a pointed contrast between him and the universalist, Hippias of Elis.[113] 'Gentlemen,' he makes Hippias say, 'I consider you all kinsmen and friends and fellowcountrymen, not of course by law but by nature. For by nature like is akin to like, but law the tyrant of men forces many things through against nature.' This is the contrast between law and nature, nomos and physis, which Callicles uses in *Gorgias*, but Callicles and Hippias, though both criticizing the law, start from different points and move in different directions. At least both begin by attacking the current conception of equality, which is the essence of the traditional idea of justice. But Callicles opposes the actual fact, that men are unequal by nature, to the democratic ideal of equality;[114] while the sophist and philosopher Hippias feels that democratic equality is too limited, because it is valid only for free citizens of equal privileges and similar descent within one state. He would extend equality and kinship to cover all human beings. The same views were expressed by the Athenian sophist Antiphon in the rationalist essay *Truth,* of which considerable fragments were recently discovered in Egypt.[115] 'In every respect we have all the same nature, Greeks and barbarians alike.' The reasons given by Antiphon for thus abolishing all historically grounded differences between nations is an interesting contrast, with its ingenuous naturalism and rationalism, to Callicles' passionate belief in inequality. 'This,' he goes on, 'can be seen from the natural needs of all men. They can all satisfy them in the same way, and in all these matters there is no distinction between barbarians and Greeks. We all breathe the same air through mouth and nose, and all eat with our hands.' This notion of international equality was very remote indeed from the ideals of Greek democracy, and at the same time an extreme contrast to Callicles' attack on them. With relentless logic Antiphon abolishes not only national differences but social differences too. 'We honour and respect men from noble families, but those from ignoble families we do not honour and respect. In that way we are like citizens of different nations.'

As far as practical politics was concerned, these brotherhood-of-man theories were not much of a danger for the existing régime, especially since their authors neither sought nor found support among the great mass of the population, but addressed themselves to a small circle of enlightened hearers, whose beliefs were largely those of Callicles. But the régime was indirectly threatened by the frankly naturalistic tone of this philosophy, which by the rigid application of its own standard to all human life was undermining the authority of the existing moral code. As early as the Homeric poems traces of naturalism can be found, and it was always sympathetic to the Greek mind. The Greeks had a natural faculty for seeing things as wholes: which, however, was apt to affect their thought and behaviour in very various ways, for different men could see the same whole and interpret it differently. One viewed the world as the theatre of heroic action calling on the noble man to exercise his highest powers; another saw it as a vast 'natural' process. One died like a hero rather than lose his shield; another left his shield lying and bought a new one, because he loved life better than leather. The contemporary state made enormous demands on the discipline and self-sacrifice of its citizens, and its demands were sanctioned by the divinity of the state. But contemporary analysis of human conduct led to a purely casual and physical view of life, and emphasized the constant conflict between the things which men by nature like and dislike and the things which law enjoins men to like and dislike. 'Most of the prescriptions of law are hostile to nature,' wrote Antiphon,[116] and elsewhere he called law 'the chain of nature.' This view was a serious threat to the conception of justice, the ideal of the old constitutional state. 'Not to transgress the laws of the state of which one is a citizen—that is justice.' Even the varying phraseology in which laws were formulated was, it was thought, a proof that legal standards were never absolute. In every state, in every city there is a different set of laws. If you wish to live in a state, you must obey its laws; but law has no absolute compulsion. Accordingly, law was envisaged as an externally imposed control which must not be broken, not as a moral and social code which had grown into men's souls. But if law had no deep-seated spiritual compulsion, then justice was only external legality, the avoidance of punishment for transgression, and one would scarcely trouble to obey the laws in acts done without a witness, where there was no need to keep up appearances. Actually that is the point where, in Antiphon's opinion, the standard of law and the law of nature essentially differ from each other. Even without witnesses the law of nature cannot be transgressed with impunity. In dealing with it one must respect not only 'appearance' but 'truth', says the sophist in obvious allusion to the title of his book. Hence his aim is to show the relativity of the standard of law and to prove that the law of nature is the only true one.

At this period, the Greek democracies were yielding more and more to the passion for making laws to settle everything in human life. As new ones were made, existing laws had constantly

to be altered or repealed; the situation was later summed up by
Aristotle in the *Politics*,[117] where he decides that it is better for
the state to have inferior laws for a long time than laws which
constantly change, even if they are good. The mass-production
of laws and the party-struggles which created them, with all the
vices and follies which were called into action thereby, created a
most painful impression on thinking men, which made it easy for
them to accept relativism. Antiphon's disgust for legislation was
in complete harmony with public opinion at the time—we need
only think of the character in Aristophanes who comes on to sell
the latest decrees of the assembly, and is thrashed amid loud and
deserved applause [118]—and also with the general tendency of the
whole period. The ideal of most of the out-and-out democrats
was a state where 'one can live as one likes'. In his description
of the Athenian constitution, Pericles himself spoke in the same
spirit, saying that in Athens the universal respect for law hin-
dered no one from gratifying his private whims without being
frowned on by others.[119] But this pretty balance between public
severity and private toleration, human as it is and authentic as
it sounds in Pericles' speech, was not everyone's ideal. Antiphon's unqualified candour probably expressed the secret feelings
of the majority of his fellow-citizens, when he says that the
natural standard of human conduct is utility, ultimately enjoyment or pleasure.[120] That was the point which Plato later chose
to attack, in order to make a firmer foundation for the reconstructed commonwealth. Of course, not all the sophists preached
hedonism and naturalism with such frank and full acceptance of
its principles. Protagoras cannot possibly have done so, for in
Plato's dialogue when Socrates tries to tempt him out on the
thin ice, he definitely denies ever having held such a theory; and
the good old man is convinced only by the subtle dialectic skill
of Socrates that he has in fact left a loophole at which the
hedonism he has rejected can still creep in.[121]

That compromise must have been characteristic of all the
finest minds of the age. Antiphon was not one of them. But his
naturalism had the merit of being logical. His distinction between acts done with and without witnesses exposed the central
problem of contemporary morality. The time was ripe for the
discovery of a new moral basis of conduct; for only thence could
law acquire the new force it needed. The simple concept of obey-

ing the law had once, when the constitutional state was coming
into being, been a great ideal of freedom and progress; [122] but
now it was not sufficient to express the deeper moral feelings of
the Greeks. Like all legalized moralities, it was in danger of
making conduct a purely external conformity, even of inculcating
an elaborate system of social hypocrisy. Aeschylus [123] had called
the truly wise and righteous man 'him who wishes not to seem
but to be good'; and his hearers were meant to think of Aristides. The greatest of the Athenians must have understood the
danger well enough. But the current conception of justice was
nothing more than correct obedience to the laws, and the masses
who obeyed them did so principally because they were afraid of
being punished if they did not. One of the last remaining props
of the deeper morality of law was religion; but religion too was
boldly criticized by the rationalists. Critias, the future tyrant,
wrote a drama *Sisyphus,* in which a character said on the public
stage that the gods were a clever invention of politicians to get
respect for their laws.[124] To keep men from transgressing the
law unobserved, he declared, the politicians had told mankind
that the gods were invisible, ubiquitous, and omniscient; and
by fear of this invisible power they held the people in subjection.
From that point of view it is easy to see why Plato in the *Republic* invented the fable of the ring of Gyges which made its wearer
invisible.[125] That ring could distinguish the man who acts justly
because his soul is just, and the man who only puts up an outward show of justice, whose sole motive is respect for social appearances. Plato was trying to solve the problem raised by Antiphon and Critias. So was Democritus, when he attributed a new
importance to the old Greek concept of *aidos,* secret shame, and
replaced the aidos which men feel for the law—the feeling which
had been annihilated by sophistic critics like Antiphon, Critias,
and Callicles—with the wonderful idea of aidos which a man
feels for himself.[126]

But neither Hippias and Antiphon nor Callicles had any
thought of thus recreating the current ethical code. There was
no trace in them of any real attempt to solve the final problems
of religion and morality. The views of the sophists on man, the
state, and the universe had none of the seriousness and deep
metaphysical understanding which had enabled the preceding
generation to build the Athenian state, and which the generation

after them was to rediscover in philosophy. Yet it would be wrong to look for their real achievement in the field of philosophy and ethics. Their strength lay in the brilliant new system of formal education which they invented. Their weakness was in the intellectual and moral foundations of their teaching; but they share it with all the men of their time. All the splendour of contemporary art and the power of the contemporary state cannot blind us to the grave moral dangers threatening that era. It was natural and inevitable that in an age of great individualism there should have been an unparalleled demand for education, and that talented educators should have arisen to fulfil it. But it was inevitable also that that generation should come to see that, more than any other, it lacked the greatest of all educative forces: rich as it was in talents, it had not the most precious and most necessary gift, an ideal towards which to direct them.

4

EURIPIDES AND HIS AGE

THE full rigour of the crisis through which the age was passing cannot be plainly seen until we study the tragic poetry of Euripides. As we have pointed out, the great difference between him and Sophocles is that he was deeply influenced by sophistic ideas. He has often been called 'the poet of the age of enlightenment', and his extant tragedies (all written late in his career) are filled with the teachings and the rhetorical devices of the sophists.[1] But although their influence explains much of his work, it does not by any means explain it all: it would be equally true to say that their ideas only become comprehensible against the spiritual background provided by his plays. Sophistry had two Janus-faces—one like Sophocles, and the other like Euripides. The sophists had Sophocles' ideal of harmonious development in the human soul: an ideal closely connected with the sculptural principle of his art.[2] On the other hand, their educational theory, with its lack of any sound moral foundation,[3] was a true product of the world of doubt and conflict portrayed by Euripides. The two poets, with the sophists who stand between them looking towards them both, represent the same Athens at the same period; they do not speak for different ages in her history. Fifteen years or so separated their births, but even in an age of rapid development that interval was not enough to make them belong to different generations. It was the difference in their characters which made them express the same world in such widely dissimilar ways. Sophocles stood upon its heights, but Euripides moved amid the dust of conflict below, watching the tragic ruin of an age-old civilization. That accounts for his peculiar position in the history of Greek thought: he was so much a child of his age that we must read his tragedies entirely as expressions of the struggles and problems of the late fifth century.[4]

The society which they depicted, and to which they were addressed, need not be described here. Unlike that of earlier periods, it is illustrated by a great quantity of evidence, especially from literature: it would be easy to devote an entire book to a description of its manners and morals, and indeed a book of that kind must some day be written. In it we can see at last the whole field of human existence, in art, philosophy, and social and political life, from its loftiest heights to its meanest trivialities. The first impression we receive is one of overpowering richness and variety, and of a physical vigour and spiritual energy hardly ever equalled in the history of our race. Whereas even as late as the Persian wars there had been an intellectual balance of power between the principal Greek peoples, the equilibrium was destroyed in the time of Pericles, and the preponderance of Athens became more and more obvious.[5] The various branches which made up the Greek race (they did not, of course, describe themselves by the common name of Hellenes until a comparatively late period) never saw such a mighty concentration of economic, political, and spiritual energy as that which produced the immortal Parthenon to enshrine Athena, the goddess who was coming to be regarded as the divine personification of the soul of Athens. The Athenians were still inspired by memories of the victories won at Marathon and Salamis. Though the generation which won them had all but passed away, its deeds, written in every citizen's heart, were a splendid ideal for posterity to imitate. It was in proud emulation of that achievement that Athens now increased her economic and political power to such an amazing extent, working with steady perseverance, planning with irrepressible energy and wise foresight, and constantly utilizing the advantages which the young democracy and its rising sea-power had inherited from the men of Salamis. Yet Athens could not continue to impose her will on Greece for ever merely because the Greeks had recognized her historical mission as the real conqueror of Persia: that is shown clearly enough by Herodotus, who was compelled to lay special emphasis on the claims of Periclean Athens to lead Greece because the rest of the Hellenic world had ceased to recognize them. The historical facts were not disputed; but at the time when Herodotus wrote, shortly before the Peloponnesian war threw the whole of Greece into conflict, they had long been distorted into the notorious and baneful ideology of Athenian imperialistic power-politics, a movement which consciously or unconsciously sought to make every member of the Greek race into a subject of Athens.[6]

In the task which the generation of Pericles and its successors had to perform, there was little of the ecstatic religious idealism which inspired the era of Aeschylus. Rather, they felt that they were the heirs of Themistocles, and they were right, for among the heroic figures of his age he had stood out as an essentially modern man, far in advance of his time.[7] And yet those Periclean Athenians who willingly sacrificed their lives and their money for the greatness of their city found, in their own sober and practical methods of pursuing the Athenian ideal, a peculiar kind of inspiration in which patriotic self-sacrifice and cold practical calculation of means and ends were united and enhanced each other's power. The Athenian state had convinced each of its citizens that he could prosper only if his city were growing in power and wealth, and thereby had converted natural egoism into one of the strongest possible motives for communal action.[8] Obviously it could not maintain this belief unless its gains continued to outweigh its losses. In time of war, the principle became a serious danger, increasingly serious as the war continued and material profits for the national effort became smaller and smaller. The age of Euripides was characterized by a calculating, business-like, profit-and-loss way of looking at everything, from the smallest detail of private life to the greatest political problem. On the other hand, their inherited passion for outward respectability made the Athenians anxious to maintain an appearance of morality even when their actions were aimed only at securing profit or pleasure. It was not for nothing that the sophistic distinction between things which are good 'according to law or custom' and things good 'by nature' was first made in that period; [9] the men of the late fifth century needed no philosophical discussion of the distinction to encourage them in making full use of it in practice, and in seizing personal advantage wherever they could find it. The breach between the two motives, idealist and practical, which had long been artificially identified with each other, appeared in every sphere of morality in that age, from the smallest commercial transactions of individuals to the unscrupulous power-policy which the state was driven to adopt more and more every year. For all the nobility with which the age expressed itself in great public works and political enterprises, and for all the energy and determination which each citizen put into his own life and his service to the state, there is something inexpressibly sad about the hypocrisy which was the necessary price for all that brilliance, and the moral rootlessness of a world which would give anything and do anything for outward success.

Long years of war terribly accelerated the destruction of all the mental and moral principles on which the Greeks had built their life and thought. Thucydides, in his account of the tragedy of Athens, viewed the decline of Athenian power simply as a consequence of the dissolution of Athenian morale. In this connexion we need not discuss the political aspect of the Peloponnesian war, which will be dealt with later, in our study of Thucydides. But we must carefully examine Thucydides' own trenchant analysis of the collapse of society,[10] the process which became more and more obvious, widespread, and dangerous from day to day. Clinically objective, his cool diagnosis of this phenomenon is a striking companion-piece to his famous description of the plague which, in the first years of the war, undermined the health and resistance of his nation. Before he relates how the horrors of class-war broke down the moral principles of the Greeks, he increases our interest and our sympathy by asserting that these events were not unique, but will recur as long as human nature remains the same.[11] We shall give his description as nearly as possible in his own words.

In peace, he says, states and individuals obey reason more easily because they are not subject to inevitable necessities: but war increases the difficulties of life and teaches the mass of men by force to adapt their character to their circumstances. In the course of the revolutions which war brought with it, faction-wars, plots, and reprisals constantly occurred, and the memory of previous revolutions and their terrors increased the violence of every new upheaval.

In this connexion Thucydides discusses the transvaluation of all values which appeared in language as a complete change in the meaning of words. Words which had long been used as names for the highest virtues were degraded by current usage to describe contemptible ways of thinking and acting, while others which had hitherto expressed blame now worked their way up to become attributes of praise. Senseless audacity was considered to be loyal courage, and far-sighted deliberation to be cowardice disguised. Prudence was now a cloak for weakness, and complete calculation was complete inaction. Mad impulsiveness was the mark of a true man, and care in plotting was a pretty excuse for shirking. The louder a man protested, the sounder he was thought to be, and his opponent was under suspicion. To make plots successfully was considered to be politically shrewd, and to detect them was even smarter; but whoever planned to do without intrigues was accused of lacking *esprit de corps* and fearing the opposite party. The ties of blood became weaker than party affiliations, because a party-comrade was more ready to act without reflection; for such associations did not give mutual help in accordance with law, but supported self-interest against justice. Even the oaths which bound comrades together were powerful not by being sacred but by making them accomplices in crime. Trust between man and man completely disappeared. Whenever the warring parties were compelled by exhaustion or temporary lack of resources to take oaths of reconciliation, each knew that this was merely a symptom of weakness, and should not be relied upon, but must be considered simply as giving one party the opportunity, when it recovered, to deliver a safer attack on its unsuspecting opponent. The leaders, both democrats and aristocrats, constantly repeated the catchwords of their parties, but were not really fighting for any high ideal. Greed, ambition, and the lust for power were the only motives for action, and when the old political ideals were brought up they were used only as shibboleths for this or that party.

The collapse of society was only the outward and visible sign of the collapse of individual character. Even the hardships and trials of war affect a spiritually healthy nation very differently from a nation whose values are rotten with individualism. Yet aesthetic and intellectual culture never reached a higher level than it did in Athens towards the end of the fifth century. The conditions which help to produce such culture could hardly have been more favourable: for several generations the nation had developed peacefully [12] and consistently; its citizens had always been accustomed to take part in all its intellectual and aesthetic activities; and these activities had always been the centre of public interest and national life. Not only that. The Athenians were naturally an extraordinarily intelligent and sensitive people: they had a subtle appreciation of beauty, with an inexhaustible delight in the free play of intellectual energy; and, as life became more complicated, they became more percipient. It is almost impossible for modern Europeans to believe that the average Athenian could have responded to the demands which contemporary writers were constantly making on his imagination; but we have no ground for disbelieving the facts as portrayed in Attic comedy of the period. Consider Dicaeopolis, the decent working-man, as he sits in the theatre of Dionysus before daybreak, comfortably munching his garlic, and talking gravely to himself about tragic poetry: he is to see some up-to-date poet's new tragedy, frigid and exaggerated, but he yearns uncontrollably for the old-fashioned masterpieces of Aeschylus.[13] Or consider the god Dionysus in *The Frogs,* sitting in the ship which he claims to have commanded at Arginusae, reading a separate edition of Euripides' *Andromeda*[14] and thinking regretfully of the author, dead not long before: he represents what might be called a higher type of public—the passionate admirers of one poet much attacked by general criticism, who read and appreciated his plays quite independently of their performances in the theatre. If the comic poet's witty parodies of tragedy were to be understood and enjoyed in the brief moments when they flashed upon the stage, there must have been a fairly large number of real connoisseurs, to say 'There he means Telephus, Euripides' beggar-king . . . that is a scene from Agathon . . . a song from Choerilus.' And in fact the contest between Aeschylus and Euripides in *The Frogs*[15] presupposes a vast interest in literature: for there, in a comedy played before many thousands of spectators from all classes of society, dozens of prologues and other passages from the two poets are quoted and discussed as if well known to everyone in the audience. And even if the plainer folk did miss many details, it is more essential and far more amazing for us that the comedian could expect a large public to react so accurately and sensitively to delicate variations in style: for without that accuracy and sensibility the audience would have been neither interested nor amused by the prolonged comparison between the two poets. We might believe that these qualities were not universal, if *The Frogs* had been the only thing of its kind; but literary parody is one of the favourite

motifs of the comic stage. Where could such a thing be done in
the modern theatre? Of course, even then there was a difference
between the culture of the man in the street and that of the
intellectual élite: often it seems quite easy to distinguish the
literary devices which tragedians or comedians intended to affect
the ordinary spectator from those which they meant to be appreciated by superior minds. But in the second half of the fifth
century and no less in the fourth century too, the widespread and
truly native culture of Athens, which was not learnt and artificial
but was a real part of each citizen's life, was something quite
unique in history: perhaps it could not have come into being except in a small city-state, where the life of the community was
fully interpenetrated by aesthetic and intellectual activity.

The life of the Athenian townsman, concentrated in the
agora, the Pnyx, and the theatre, was almost completely cut off
from the life of the countryman of Attica: hence arose the concept of boorishness, ἀγροῖκον, as a contrast to urbanity, ἀστεῖον,
which in fact meant culture in general.[16] Here we see the whole
force of the opposition between the new culture of the city-state
and the old civilization which was largely that of the landowning
squirearchy.[17] Also, the city was the scene of the numerous symposia, the drinking-parties which were the true centres of the
new society—a society, be it said, which was entirely masculine.
There had been an enormous change in the spirit of the symposium since the days of aristocracy, for it was now celebrated in
poetry not as the occasion of drunken jollity but as the focus of
serious intellectual and spiritual life. In the ordinary society of
Athens, it was a mirror of the new culture. That is shown by the
sympotic elegies written during the late fifth century—which are
full of current problems [18] and share the general trend towards
intellectualism—and by many scenes in contemporary comedy.
Throughout the age of Euripides, the symposia were torn by the
deadly conflict between the old-fashioned ways of thinking and
the new literary and sophistic culture [19]—the conflict which
marked that age as a real epoch in the history of culture. The
defenders of modernism always rallied round the name of
Euripides.[20]

The spiritual life of Athens at that time was the sum of a
number of sharply conflicting historical and creative forces. The
power of tradition, which still dominated religion, law, and the

organization of the state, now clashed with a progressive movement aimed at liberating and educating the individual. This movement was far more serious and widespread than Ionia had ever known; for however boldly one emancipated poet or philosopher may preach to an unprogressive nation living at peace with itself, a solitary crusade cannot be compared with the general excitement which prevailed in Athens at this time. In that electric atmosphere, all the earlier criticisms of traditional standards revived; and every citizen claimed the same freedom of thought and speech in intellectual matters which was guaranteed to him in political life at the national assembly. This idea was, however, quite foreign and quite shocking to the Greek state—even the democratic state—and more than once the opposition between this new individualist unconstitutional freedom and the conservative forces fortified within the state itself came to an open outbreak of hostilities: for instance, in the prosecution of Anaxagoras for impiety, and in occasional attacks on the sophists, whose emancipated teachings were often frankly revolutionary. Still, in general, the democratic state tolerated all intellectual movements, and was even proud of the new freedom of its citizens. We must recollect that the Attic democracy of this and the subsequent periods served as Plato's model for his criticisms of the democratic system, and was described by him, from his own peculiar point of view, as being equivalent to intellectual and moral anarchy.[21] Even although a few influential politicians made no secret of their hatred for the subversive influence of the sophists, they usually kept it a strictly private matter.[22] The attack on the natural philosopher, Anaxagoras, was intended to injure his protector and adherent, Pericles, as well.[23] As a matter of fact, the unconcealed respect of the man who long governed the Athenian empire for the doctrines of the new emancipated thinkers protected them throughout its wide frontiers. The frank respect of Athens for the things of the mind (a feeling almost as rare elsewhere in classical Greece as in other places and times) attracted to it all the intellectuals in the country. That which happened under the Pisistratid tyranny now happened once again on a greater scale and more spontaneously. The foreigner, intellect, once a metic, was naturalized in Athens. But this time it was not chiefly poets who were invited to Attica, although there were some, for Athens was the undisputed metropolis of the arts. It was philosophers, scholars, and intellectuals of every kind who led the new immigration.

As well as the Ionian Anaxagoras of Clazomenae, the greatest of them all, and his pupil Archelaus the Athenian, there were the last representatives of the old type of Ionian natural philosophy: such was that rather important figure Diogenes of Apollonia, on whom Aristophanes modelled his portrait of Socrates in *The Clouds*. Just as Anaxagoras struck out a new line by attributing the origin of the world not to chance, but to the principle of active reason, so Diogenes connected the old hylozoism with a new teleological view of nature. Aristotle gave Hippon of Samos a very small place in his history of philosophy, but he had the honour of being ridiculed in Cratinus' comedy *The See-alls*.[24] Plato spent some time in his youth as a pupil of the Heraclitean Cratylus. Two mathematicians and astronomers, Meton and Euctemon, assisted in the official revision of the calendar in 432. The former was famous throughout Athens, and typified abstract scholarship in the eyes of the average Athenian, as we can see from his appearance in *The Birds*.[25] In his caricature of him Aristophanes seems to have incorporated some traits from the personality of Hippodamus of Miletus. This man was the great pioneer of town-planning: he redesigned the Piraeus in a series of square blocks, with the streets crossing one another at right angles. It was a geometrician's ideal, and resembled his equally rationalistic, equally geometrical political theories, which even Aristotle thought worthy of serious attention in the *Politics*.[26] With Meton and Euctemon, he is peculiarly typical of that period, when logic was encroaching upon life more and more. Another such rationalist was Damon the musical theorist, whose lectures Socrates attended. In *Protagoras,* Plato has portrayed with sure insight and delicate irony the feverish excitement created among educated Athenians by the arrival of the sophists. But to do justice to their excitement and admiration, we must put away the sense of superiority which Plato's generation felt for the outworn age of 'enlightenment'. Plato also described the two Eleatics, Parmenides and Zeno, as lecturing in Athens. That may simply be a detail invented to give dramatic reality to the dialogue, like many others, but it must at least have been possible, and is, therefore, true in essence. Philosophers who did not live in Athens or visit it often were not mentioned: the most remarkable proof of that is Democritus' ironical remark, 'I came to Athens, and no one knew me'.[27] Much of the Athenians' admiration for this or that sophist was dictated by fashion or caprice, so that there were many ephemeral reputations which have been revised by the verdict of history. But there were now very few great solitaries like Democritus, whose home was not Abdera but the world. It is not simple accident that the man who resisted the attractions of the intellectual metropolis should have been a pure scholar. For, throughout the next century, the great men who were to play leading parts in the education of Greece lived and worked only in Athens.

What is it that gives the great Athenians (like Thucydides, Socrates, and Euripides, the true representatives of their age) such a pre-eminent place in the history of their nation that all the subordinate intellectual activity which we have described seems like the skirmishing of outposts before the decisive battle? It is this. Through these men, the rationalist spirit which already filled the air took possession of the greatest of all cultural forces —religion, morality, political theory, and poetry. Thucydides' history is a confession of faith by the now thoroughly rationalized state: it is its last intellectual achievement, at the moment of its downfall, and through it the state eternalizes its true and ideal nature. Because of that fact Thucydides is more exclusively representative of his age than either of his great fellow-countrymen. Perhaps even his most profound wisdom means more to us than it did to the later Greeks, since he wrote it down for use in a similar historical situation, which did not recur so soon as he expected. We shall close our study of this period (which ends, intellectually as well as politically, with the collapse of the Athenian empire) by discussing his attempts to understand the meaning and the destiny of the state.[28] For Socrates is concerned more with the problem of the individual, of human life in general, than with the problem of the state, as most of the great Athenians had been until his time. He is the questioning conscience of his age, shaken to its depths by the new thoughts and problems which had invaded it. Thoroughly contemporary as he may seem, he yet belongs to the beginning of another era, in which philosophy becomes the true vehicle of culture.[29] Euripides is the last great Greek poet in the old sense of the word.

But he too stands with one foot in a world quite alien to that which produced Attic tragedy. The ancients called him the philosopher of the stage, and he does in fact belong to two worlds. We see him as part of the old world which he was born to destroy, but which shines out once more in his work with all its old magical splendour. Once more in him poetry asserts itself as the guide of life, although by doing so it opens the way for the new spirit which is to thrust it from its traditional place. That is one of the great paradoxes which history loves.

There was room beside the work of Sophocles for another kind of tragedy: a new generation had grown up and was ready to take up the old problems posed by Aeschylus, and grapple with them in a new way. In Sophocles the awareness of moral and religious problems had temporarily given place to other poetic interests, but now it revived most powerfully in Euripides. The time, it seemed, had come for the tragic conflict between man and God to be resumed. The signal was given by the development of the new rationalist doctrines, which was not completed until Sophocles had passed the prime of his life. Thoughtful men were now seriously contemplating the problem of human life, which they felt had been concealed from their fathers by the veil of traditional piety; and Euripides, applying the new critical standards to old questions, must have felt as if all that had been previously written on the subject must now be rewritten. From time immemorial, mythical tradition had been the only possible material for poetry. Aeschylus and Sophocles had breathed their very life into it, and its characters were *given* to Euripides and every other poet as the inevitable subjects of their work. Even the bold revolutionary Euripides did not think of departing from it. To expect that he should, would be to misinterpret the essential nature of ancient Greek poetry, for it was bound to the myths, and must live or die with them. But Euripides did not think and write of mythology alone.

He was cut off from it now by the realities of life as they were known by his own age. It is symbolic of the attitude of that peculiarly rational and historical age to mythology that it produced the historian Thucydides, who held that to search for truth was to do away with myths. This is the spirit which inspired medical research and scientific investigation. Euripides was the first poet who deliberately worked on the artistic principle that poetry should depict *reality* as he saw it; and since the mythical traditions were at hand, he used them as a vehicle for expressing the new realities which he saw. Had not Aeschylus already transformed the old sagas to suit the ideas and the hopes of his own generation? had not Sophocles been led by the same instinct to humanize the antique heroes? and had not the myths, which seemed to have died long ago in late epic poetry, been amazingly revived in fifth-century drama through the transfusion of living blood into the pale ghostly bodies of a vanished age?

Nevertheless, when Euripides came forward to compete for the tragedian's prize, and presented mythical dramas in what appeared to be severely conservative form, he was unable to convince his audience that his own innovations were only a further step in the current tendency to humanize and modernize the myths. He must have known that he was a true revolutionary; his contemporaries were profoundly disturbed or violently disgusted by his work. Clearly Greek sentiment was more prepared to see the myths converted into a set of etiolate aesthetic and conventional ideals, as they had almost become in late epic and in much of the elaborate choric poetry of the sixth century, than expanded and transformed to fit the categories of ordinary reality, which bore the same relation to mythology as the profane world to the world of religion and the spirit nowadays. Nothing is so characteristic of the naturalistic trend of that age as the effort made by its artists to keep mythology from becoming empty and remote, by revising its standards to suit the facts of real life viewed without illusion. Euripides attacked this strange new task, not in cold blood, but with the passionate energy of a strong artistic personality, and with unshaken perseverance in the face of many years of defeat and discouragement. It was long before the Athenian people gave him any considerable support; yet he won in the end, and dominated not only the Athenian stage but the whole Hellenic world.

We need not here describe his plays individually or analyse their artistic structure for its own sake. We must study the elements which formed the style of the new art, while neglecting its traditional features. Of course, it is impossible to appreciate every aspect of Euripides' poetic achievement without a full and careful knowledge of these features too, but here we shall assume that knowledge, and proceed to bring out the dominating tendencies which appear in all or most of his plays. In him, as in every other truly living Greek poet, literary form grows organically out of one definite material: it is inseparable from it, and is often conditioned by it even in such minor details as the formation of words and the pattern of sentences. His new material transformed not only the myths but even the poetic language he inherited and the traditional form of tragedy—for Euripides did not break up that form out of mere caprice, but rather tended to fix it in a rigid schematism. The new elements which formed his style, then, were *bourgeois realism, rhetoric* and *philosophy:* The stylistic revolution which they brought about marked a great epoch in the history of the human mind, for it prefigured the future dominance of the three great cultural forces of later Hellenism. In every scene of his plays it is evident that his work presupposed a particular cultural level and addressed a special type of society; and, on the other hand, that it was the true guide which helped the new type of human character to find itself, by showing it the ideal which it hoped to approach, and which it needed, perhaps more than in any previous era, for its own self-justification.

The encroachment of *bourgeois ideals* upon life meant to Euripides' contemporaries something the same as the encroachment of proletarian ideals to us: in fact, it often verged on proletarianization, as when Euripides brought miserable ragged beggars on the stage to represent the tragic heroes of antiquity. That was just the type of debasement which his opponents most violently attacked.[30] Even in *Medea,* which is nearest in tone and spirit to the work of his predecessors, it can be traced throughout. As the individual citizen gained more and more political and intellectual freedom, the problems of human society and of the constraints on which it depends grew more obvious; men began to claim the right to live their own lives, wherever they felt themselves held down by artificial restraints; they attempted to find mitigation or escape by the use of reason. Marriage was hotly discussed. The relation of the sexes, which had for centuries been guarded by the tabu of convention, was now dragged into the light of day, and scrutinized, and found to be a conflict like every other relation in nature. Was it not governed by the right of the stronger, like them all? So the poet found the passions of his own day in the age of Jason's desertion of Medea, and infused into it problems unknown to the original myth, embodying them in the mighty lineaments of true tragedy.

The Athenian women of Euripides' time were not Medeas: they were too cultivated to play her part or else too dull and repressed. But the poet deliberately chose to write of Medea, the wild-eyed savage who murdered her children to injure her treacherous husband: for she expressed the elemental nature of woman untrammelled by Greek conventions. He presented Jason, whom the Greeks generally felt to be a blameless hero though not perhaps an ideal husband, as a cowardly opportunist, acting not from passion but from cold calculation. But that transformation was necessary to make the mythical murderess into a truly tragic figure. Euripides gave her all his sympathy: partly because he felt that the fate of women was sad, and could not see it glorified by mythology with its splendid heroic atmosphere of masculine prowess and masculine glory; and chiefly because he wished to make her the heroine of a domestic tragedy of bourgeois life, such as must often have occurred, although not in such an extreme form, in the Athens of his own time. Euripides invented domestic drama. *Medea,* with its conflict between the boundless egoism of the husband and the boundless passion of the wife, was a completely up-to-date play. Accordingly, the disputes, the abuse, and the logic used by all its characters are essentially bourgeois. Jason is stiff with cleverness and magnanimity; while Medea philosophizes on the social position of women—the dishonourable necessity which makes a woman surrender herself in marriage to a strange man and pay a rich dowry for the privilege—and declares that bearing children is far more brave and dangerous than fighting in battle.[31] It is impossible for us to admire the play wholeheartedly; yet it was a revolution in its time, and it shows the true fertility of the new art.

Towards old age Euripides was not content with embodying everyday problems in mythical material, but often changed tragedy into something very like comedy. In *Orestes*—which is not in the least like anything in Aeschylus or Sophocles—Menelaus and Helen, united after their long separation, return from

Troy at the very moment when Orestes is desperate with re-
morse for the murder of his mother and with terror of the lynch-
ing threatened by the citizens. He implores his uncle Menelaus
to help him. Menelaus offers money, but is afraid to risk his
newly-won happiness for his nephew and his niece Electra,
although he is heartily sorry for them—especially since his
father-in-law Tyndareus, Orestes' grandfather and parent of the
murdered Clytaemnestra, rushes in wild for revenge, to complete the domestic drama. Inflamed by the speeches of agitators,
the citizens condemn Orestes and Electra to death, in the absence of suitable supporters for their cause. The faithful Pylades
now appears, and swears to help Orestes in murdering Helen to
avenge Menelaus' inaction. They fail, because the gods, who
sympathize with her, rescue her in the nick of time. Instead of
her, the two desperadoes now plan to kill her daughter Hermione, and burn down Menelaus' house. But Apollo appears, as a
deus ex machina, to stop this catastrophe, and everyone lives
happily ever after. Menelaus gets another wife to replace Helen
who is transferred to the gods on Olympus, while Orestes and
Hermione, Pylades and Electra celebrate a double wedding. The
sophisticated taste of Euripides' contemporaries particularly enjoyed mixtures of different literary styles and subtle transitions
between them. The tinge of domestic drama which appears in
this fantastic tragi-comedy is reminiscent of a remark by the
contemporary poet and politician Critias: he said that girls were
charming only when they were a little boyish, and boys only
when they were a little girlish.[32] But the big declamations of
Euripides' unheroic heroes often have something unintentionally
funny in them, and the comedians of his own day found them an
inexhaustible source of amusement. Any sensitive taste must be
offended by the contrast between the original content of the
myth and this new middle-class tone, cold, shrewd, pragmatic,
rationalist, sceptical, moralistic, and frankly sentimental.

The invasion of poetry by *rhetoric* was no less momentous
than the encroachment of bourgeois ideals. It was to end by
transforming poetry completely into oratory. Rhetorical theorists in late antiquity treated poetry merely as a subordinate division, a special function, of the art of eloquence. Greek poetry
had engendered the elements of rhetoric at a very early period,

though it was not until the age of Euripides that the Greeks discovered how to apply them to the new medium of artistic prose.[33] As prose had originally borrowed the devices of poetry, so it reacted on poetry at a later date. The language used by tragic poets now approximated to the language of ordinary life in the same way as the myths had been transformed into symbols of everyday problems. At the same time, the new devices of polished logical argument were imported from the elaborate art of forensic oratory into the dialogues and speeches of tragedy: in fact these devices marked Euripides as a pupil of the rhetoricians even more than his choice of words and of figures of speech. Throughout his plays we can trace a novel competition between tragedy and the rhetorical contests of opposing litigants which so delighted the Athenians, for now verbal duels between contrasting characters on the stage became one of the principal excitements of tragic drama.

Although we know little of the early stages in the development of rhetoric, its scanty remains clearly show the close kinship between it and Euripides' poetic eloquence. One of the regular exercises in rhetorical training was to invent speeches for mythical characters, as can be seen from Gorgias' apologia for Palamedes and his praise of Helen. Similar declamations by other famous sophists were preserved as models for students. An oratorical contest between Ajax and Odysseus before the jury of Greek chieftains was attributed to Antisthenes, and an attack by Odysseus on Palamedes, to Alcidamas. The bolder the subject, the more suitable it was to display the difficult art taught by the sophists, the art of 'making the worse cause appear the better'.[34] All the tricks and sophisms of rhetorical daring and dexterity re-appear in the defence which Helen offers when accused by Hecuba in *The Trojan Women*,[35] and in the nurse's great speech to Phaedra in *Hippolytus*,[36] which proves that a married woman is not wrong in giving her love to another man. These are deliberate displays of the art of advocacy, which with its unscrupulous fluency moved the Greeks of that time to both admiration and disgust. But they were something more than exercises in formal logic and style.

Rhetoric, as taught by the sophists, aimed at putting forward the subjective view of an accused person with every possible persuasive device. The forensic eloquence of the late fifth cen-

tury and the eloquence of Euripides' tragic heroes both originated from the incessant transformation in old Greek ideas of
guilt and responsibility, under the influence of the growing trend
towards individualism. The primitive idea of guilt was purely
objective: a man could be tainted with guilt unknowingly or unwittingly. The daemon of guilt descended on him by the will of
God, not by his own; yet that fact did not free him from the
ruinous consequences of his actions. This old religious idea still
lived on in Aeschylus and Sophocles, but they strove to mitigate
its force by making the guilt-laden man play a more active part
in his destiny, though not by attacking the objective conception
of até. Their characters were 'guilty' because they bore the taint
of guilt. With our subjective attitude, we should consider them
innocent; yet their tragedy was not, for Aeschylus and Sophocles, the tragedy of their innocence and their undeserved suffering. That kind of tragedy was invented by Euripides; but it grew
out of the attitude of his age, which was fundamentally subjective and saw all problems from the standpoint of the individual.
Towards the end of his long life, Sophocles made Oedipus on
Colonus defend himself against the decree of expulsion passed
by the inhabitants of his place of refuge, by declaring himself
innocent of the hideous crimes of parricide and incest which he
had committed without his own will or knowledge.[37] There
Sophocles had learnt something from Euripides, but what he had
learnt scarcely affected his deeper conception of the true nature
of Oedipus' tragedy. For Euripides, on the other hand, that was
a problem of capital importance, and the passionate subjective
self-vindications of his heroes are always expressed as bitter accusations of the deadly injustice of man's fate. We know that in
the age of Pericles the problem of legal responsibility in Athenian penal law and in the speeches of defendants was coming to be
viewed more and more from the subjective point of view, so that
the distinction between guilt and innocence sometimes entirely
disappeared: for example, many held that acts done under the
influence of passion were not voluntary acts at all. This attitude
went very deep in tragic poetry; thus Euripides' Helen analyses
her own adultery as an act committed under the compulsion of
sexual desire.[38] That speech, and others like it, can be described
as the invasion of tragedy by rhetoric, but it was very much
more than a stylistic device.

Lastly, *philosophy*. Every Greek poet was a true philosopher —in the sense that thought, religion, and mythology formed a unity still unbroken in poetry. So far, then, Euripides was not innovating when he made his heroes and his choruses utter philosophical apophthegms. But there was something different about his work. Philosophy, which had had a sort of subliminal existence in early Greek poetry, now emerged into the light of day as independent νοῦς: rational thought invaded every sphere of existence. Liberated from poetry, it turned to attack it and to dominate it. The speeches of Euripides' characters repeatedly strike us as being highly intellectualized: this rationalist tone must not and cannot be confused with the profound and complex religious emotion found in Aeschylus, even when that emotion is highly charged with intellectual doubt. Intellectualism is the first impression we receive from Euripidean tragedy. The characters live and breathe in a thin and lofty atmosphere of thought. Although it is vague and weak compared with the firm energy of Aeschylus, their subtle and sensitive intellectual activity is the medium of a peculiar kind of tragic art, which needed a restless dialectic to express and support its new subjective capacity for suffering. But even apart from that, the characters of Euripidean tragedy are compelled by an irresistible instinct to indulge in constant analysis and argument. This is a real innovation in the nature of tragedy, which must be thoroughly understood: it is merely a secondary consideration to decide how far Euripides is to be held responsible for the things said by his characters. Plato himself, in *The Laws*,[39] defends poets against the attacks of those who, at every period in history, charge them with believing what their own heroes say: he remarks that a poet is like a fountain, which pours out anything which flows into it—he imitates reality, and therefore makes his characters utter opinions which contradict one another, but he himself does not know which of them is true. It may then never be possible to infer from the speeches of a dramatist's characters what he himself thought about life; and yet the intellectualists whom Euripides puts on the stage have a strong family resemblance, which allows us to conclude with perfect certainty that he himself was an out-and-out intellectual.

The varied theories of nature and human life which he took over from earlier and contemporary philosophers were part of

his general culture; and it is not important to determine whether
any particular idea was borrowed from Anaxagoras, or Diogenes of Apollonia, or someone else. Did he ever have a complete
and definite philosophy of life? and if he did, was it ever more
than a temporary bond on his Protean spirit? He knew everything; no idea which ever came into a human mind, sublimely
religious or frankly frivolous, was strange to him; and he could
not chain himself to one rationalist dogma, although he made
Hecuba [40] in her agony pray to the aether:

> Thou, earth's support, enthroned on the earth,
> whoever thou mayst be, hard to discover,
> Zeus, be thou nature's law or the mind of man,
> I pray to thee: for by a noiseless course
> thou guidest human fate in righteousness.

The woman who speaks like this has ceased to believe in the old
deities. Her tormented heart, incapable in its agony of abandoning the search for some meaning in the chaos of life, prays to a
vision of the First Cause set up by philosophers in the place of
the vanished gods—as if her prayer could be heard by someone
or something in universal space. But can we conclude that Euripides himself had a cosmic religion, a faith in the ultimate justice
of the world-process? Numerous speeches in his plays bear witness, with the same or greater force, to the contrary, and it
seems absolutely clear that he could see no harmony between the
cosmic and the moral laws. Of course, that does not mean that
he set out to preach this belief, although his characters voice it
when necessary with complete conviction. Against these shriek-
ing discords, we can place the dramas in which, after violent
attacks have been made on a god, he appears, to bring the sufferings of the characters to a not intolerable conclusion. Euripides
neither defends traditional religion in that type of play nor
preaches the remoteness of the gods in the other. The relentless
criticism to which his characters subject the gods accompanies
all tragic action throughout his dramas, but it is only a subordinate motif. In that respect he is in the direct line of criticism
which starts with Xenophanes' attacks on the Homeric and
Hesiodic myths of the gods, and leads to Plato.[41] The paradox,
however, is that the same critical attitude which led both Xenophanes and Plato to denounce the myths as false and immoral

obtrudes, in Euripides, into the dramatic representation of these myths, and constantly destroys the illusion which the drama is intended to create. He denies the existence and the power of the gods, but at the same time he presents the gods as real and powerful forces in his plays. Hence the genuine ambiguity of his tragedies, which is sometimes deeply serious and sometimes almost playfully frivolous.

He criticizes not only the gods, but the whole of mythology, in so far as it was considered by the Greeks to be an ideal world which should inspire mankind to imitation and admiration. Perhaps his *Heracles* may not have been intended to destroy the old Dorian ideal of heroic self-sufficiency; [42] but certainly *The Trojan Women* is a definite and powerful attack on the glory of the Greeks who conquered Troy: it strips the glamour from their heroism, and shows it to be merely brutal ambition and a bestial joy in destruction.[43] Yet in *The Phoenician Women* the same Euripides portrays most movingly and tragically the daemonic urge to power which rules all masterful men, as embodied in Eteocles; [44] while *The Suppliants* and *Andromache* show that he could write plays for a national festival [45] with no trace of tendencious pacifism. His work has been called, with some justice, the debating-platform for every movement of his age. And there is no greater proof of the fact that his generation questioned everything and believed nothing, than the disintegration of all life and tradition into discussion and philosophizing, into the anxious arguments in which all his characters, young and old, men and women, kings and slaves, are constantly engaged.

These arguments were not intended to teach the audience anything. They simply expressed the subjective attitude of this or that character to the world-order. The rhetorical, realist, and rationalist revolution in the style of tragedy exemplified the great contemporary movement towards subjectivism, which affected poetry and philosophy as it affected everything else. The process which had reached its first climax in the lyric poetry of Ionia and Aeolia,[46] and had then been halted by the creation of tragedy and the invasion of intellectual life by political interests, was resumed with great force in Euripides, and now invaded tragedy itself. He developed the lyrical element, which had always been an essential part of drama, but to a certain extent he transferred it from the chorus to the characters. He made it express the suffering of individuals. Emotional arias now became a leading element in drama [47] and were a symptom of its increasing *lyricism*. The constant attacks delivered by Attic comedians upon the new music of Euripides prove that in losing it we have really lost an essential part of his work. In music and lyric poetry his characters voiced their elemental emotions, which were no less important a part of his poetry than their intellectual reflections. Both emotion and thought had their sources deep in the troubled subjective movement of his soul and reflect it completely in their constant interplay and coalescence.

Euripides was one of the greatest of all lyric poets. Only in song could he resolve into harmony the dissonances which he felt insoluble by reason. In time, no doubt, his arias became rather artificial, and sometimes painfully vacuous.[48] But no other poet has ever approached him in the power of elevating reality into a moment of lyrical ecstasy—as in the ardent and tender devotion offered by the shy young Hippolytus to the maiden goddess Artemis, in the scene where he crowns her image, or in the devout fervour of Ion's morning-hymn, sung as the first sunbeam strikes over Parnassus hill, while he resumes his unchanging daily task of pious service as a perpetual acolyte in the temple of Apollo. The pain and the rapture with which Phaedra's sick soul abandons itself to the loneliness of forest and mountain seem to touch a sphere of emotion quite unknown to classical Greece. In *The Bacchantes,* the work of his old age, Euripides' lyrical force, still unimpaired, reached its highest point in expressing the wild elemental fury of Dionysiac madness: his words are the only true and profound revelation in all ancient literature of the inner meaning of that strange orgiastic frenzy; and even to-day they make us shudder at the illimitable power of Dionysus over the souls captured by his ecstasy.

His new lyrical art sprang from a hitherto unknown depth of understanding, which could trace the most subtle, secret, and strange emotions to their source, and did not shrink even from those which were abnormal; and from a tender sympathy with the inexpressible charm of individuality, be it in persons, things, or places. One chorus of *Medea* distils in a few lines the perfume of the unique physical and spiritual atmosphere of Athens [49]—its venerable history stretching far into the misty ages of tradition, the peaceful serenity of its life, the purity of the bright air, and the glorious wisdom which fed the men of that city where the holy muses brought fair Harmony to birth. 'Watering the land from the Cephisus river, Aphrodite wafts mild airs abroad, and, rose-garlanded, sends to partner wisdom the loves who assist men in every excellence.' These magic lines must be quoted here, for they sum up the rapturous exaltation and spiritual ardour of Athenian culture, as it was a few weeks before the fateful outbreak of the Peloponnesian War, which rudely ended the sheltered peace of Athens and once more put her civilization at the mercy of the general destiny of the state and the nation.

Euripides was the first *psychologist*. It was he who discovered the soul, in a new sense—who revealed the troubled world of man's emotions and passions. He never tires of showing how they are expressed and how they conflict with the intellectual forces of the soul. He created the pathology of the mind. It was impossible for poetry to be written on such subjects before his time, for it was then that men first learnt to look fairly and squarely at these things, to guide themselves through the labyrinth of the human soul by the light of their conviction that all these daemonic passions and obsessions were necessary and logical processes of 'human nature'.[50] Euripides' psychology was produced by the coincidence of two new factors, the discovery of the subjective world and the rationalist approach to nature which was at that time revealing a constant succession of hidden territories. Without science, his poetry could not have existed. He was the first to put madness in all its manifestations upon the stage, with relentless realism. Believing that all things were permitted to genius, he opened up an entire new field for tragedy, by depicting the infirmities which afflict the human soul and which originate in the world of the instincts, as forces affecting human destiny.[51] In *Medea* and *Hippolytus* he revealed the tragic working-out of the pathology of sexual desire unfulfilled; while *Hecuba* shows how extreme suffering distorts the character, and presents the slow hideous degeneration of a noble lady who has lost everything into a repulsive and bestial thing.

In his poetic world, always fading into subjective emotion and subjective thought, there is no fixed point. We have observed that his criticisms of the world-order and of mythology were not dictated by a single organized philosophy. The vast resignation with which he views all human acts and thoughts flows from a deep scepticism. He makes no attempt to follow earlier poets in justifying the ways of God to man. Although his characters search incessantly for happiness and have an extreme passion for justice, their search and their passion are never fulfilled. Man is now no longer able and willing to abandon himself to any view of life which does not make *himself*, in the Protagorean sense, the ultimate standard.[52] And so this development ends with a paradox: at the moment when his claim for freedom is loudest, man realizes that he is completely unfree. 'No mortal man is free: he is the slave of money or fate; or else the mob, which rules the state, or the bonds of law keep him from living as he wishes.' These words are spoken by the aged Hecuba [53] to the victorious Agamemnon, the conqueror of her city, when he wishes to give her the favour she implores, but dares not from fear of the hot hatred of his own army. Hecuba is incarnate suffering. To Agamemnon's cry,[54] 'Alas, alas, what woman has been so accursed?' she replies, 'None, unless you mean Fortune herself.'

The accursed power of Tyché now stands in the place of the blessed gods. Its devilish reality grows more urgent for Euripides as the reality of the gods fades away. So, perfectly naturally, she takes on the attributes of a new deity, dominating Greek thought more and more, and soon crushing out the old religion. She is manifold, various, fickle. Luck changes from one day to another. Who feels the anger of Tyché to-day may be favoured to-morrow. She is incalculably capricious.[55] In some of Euripides' plays she appears as the power which rules the world and plays with men like puppets. This idea is the inevitable complement of the conception of man's weakness and unfreedom. In fact, his only liberty is to watch Fortune's acts with an ironic unconcern— as in *Ion, Helen,* or *Iphigenia among the Taurians*. It is not for nothing that these plays were all written about the same time. Euripides was clearly much exercised with the problem at that period, and chose his subjects accordingly. The plots are elaborate and complex intrigues, in which we watch with breathless excitement the race of human craft and cunning against the arrow-swift flight of Tyché. *Ion* is the purest example of this type of drama. Again and again as it develops, our attention is expressly directed to the power of Tyché. At the close, she is addressed as the deity of perpetual change; as such, the hero thanks her for saving him from doing a grave crime unwittingly, for revealing to him the marvellous secret of his own destiny, and for uniting him happily with his long-lost mother. About this period, in fact, the poet seems to have developed a peculiar passion for the miraculous. The paradoxical nature of all human happiness and misery comes out more and more strongly in his work. Comedy thrusts its way in between the scenes of tragedy. The comedies of Menander are logically the next stage in this trend.

In general, the work of Euripides is marked by infinite fertility of invention, restless questioning and experiment, and ever-increasing mastery of his medium. Finally he reverted to the old-fashioned type of tragedy. In *The Phoenician Women* he created a drama of doom, using a strongly Aeschylean plot and structure (though he may have exaggerated the Aeschylean sombreness) with colossal figures moving half-seen through a huge and terrible action. *The Bacchantes,* written in his old age and produced after his death, has sometimes been interpreted as his discovery of himself—a deliberate escape from rational self-knowledge into religious experience and mystical ecstasy. But that is reading far too much into it. To translate the Dionysiac frenzy into lyric and dramatic poetry was for Euripides an adequate end in itself, and as a psychologist he found possibilities of enormous and lasting effect in the tragic problem created by the clash of religious mass-hypnotism, awaking all the primitive instincts and energies of its victims, with ordinary society and the established state, based as it was on reason alone. But even in old age he did not reach his haven. His life ended while he was still vigorously grappling with the problem of religion. In religious matters as in others, no one has plumbed the depths of the irrational element in the human spirit so deeply as this poet of rationalism. But for that very reason his world was a world without faith. Surely it is impossible not to feel that, having understood so much and having seen so deeply and sceptically into his age and his own soul, he learnt how to praise the joy of humble faith in one of the religious truths which pass all understanding, simply because he himself had no such happy faith? The time had not yet come when that was to be the fundamental attitude of knowledge towards faith; but all its symptoms appear prophetically in *The Bacchantes*—the victory of the miraculous and of conversion [56] over reason, the alliance of individualism with religion against the state (though the state in classical times had coincided with religion), and the immediately experienced sense of liberation which comes when a soul is freed from all legalistic morality and becomes aware of God within itself.

Euripides created an independent kind of artistry which abandoned the disguise of ordinary citizenship and took on a life of its own. He was incapable of living up to the traditional vocation of an artist in the Athenian state, of being a teacher as his great predecessors had been; or at least he taught his fellow-countrymen in a different way. He had of course a certain educational purpose: yet he educated them not by constructing a complete spiritual cosmos but by his passionate interest in political and intellectual 'problems.' As a critic of his own age, and especially since his purgative criticism usually took the form of contradicting conventional views and exploding doubtful assumptions, he was bound to be a lonely man. That is how he was described by the Attic comedians,[57] and that is how his contemporaries thought of him. His loneliness is not out of accord with his own sense of living in a unique and precious spiritual atmosphere, there in Athens—the feeling which he expressed in *Medea,* when he praised the spirit of Athenian culture and Athenian life.[58] Yet it is symbolic that he ended his days in Macedonia far from his native city. That meant something far different from the death of Aeschylus on his visit to Sicily. Euripides' home was his study-chamber. The Athenians did not elect him general, as they elected Sophocles. He lived a quiet solitary life, absorbed in his books and his work, carefully guarded against intrusions from the outside world by his devoted servant and assistant, Cephisophon. Or rather, his body lived there, while his soul moved among vast remote heights and distances; and even when it returned to the earth, it addressed visitors (so the comedian says) with 'You pitiful creature!' [59] His portrait shows us a brow framed in unkempt strands of hair—the characteristic feature of a philosopher's head in Greek sculpture. More than once he described Eros and Sophia as partners. The metaphor makes us think of his own character, but we can arrive at no certain conclusion until we reach the phrase: 'Eros teaches the poet, even if he has no music in his soul'.[60] Some artists whose lives have been unhappy appear completely happy in their work. Sophocles achieved even in life the harmony which fills all his poetry. But behind the discords of Euripides' poetry there must have been discords in his life and character. In that too he embodied the individualism of his own age—more completely and deeply than all the contemporary politicians and sophists. He alone understood all its secret agonies and shared with it the dangerous privilege of boundless spiritual freedom. Desperately though he beat his wings against the bars of the social system in which he lived, he was yet free of the whole world; and in his own way he soared like the eagle of Pindar. 'To the eagle's flight,' he said,[61] 'the whole of heaven is free.' He did not, like Pindar, mount into the heights, but yearned with a strange passion for a wide frontierless flight into the distances, careless of the earth and all its barriers.

His art most strangely prefigures the future. We have pointed out that the new elements which formed his style were to be the cultural forces of succeeding centuries: bourgeois ideals (more in the social than in the political sense), rhetoric, and philosophy. These forces penetrated mythology and destroyed it. It ceased to be the body which lived and changed with the living and changing Greek spirit, as it had been from the beginning—the imperishable form for every new content. The opponents of Euripides saw this happening and strove to counter it by silencing him. But he was only bringing to completion a great stage in the development of his nation. If that is recognized, we may dismiss the romantic fashion of reproaching him, as many critics have done since K. O. Müller's *History of Greek Literature,* for sinning against the myth. In Euripides we see the birth of a new type of man, the Hellenistic Greek, from the pangs of dying poetry and the stricken city-state. His failures on the Athenian stage were compensated by his immense influence on the Greeks of subsequent generations. They held him to be the Tragedian *par excellence,* and it was principally for his plays that they built the splendid marble theatres which we still admire as monuments of Hellenistic civilization.

THE COMIC POETRY OF ARISTOPHANES

No description of Greek civilization in the last quarter of the fifth century could pass over that strange but attractive phenomenon, Attic comedy. The ancients, in calling it 'the mirror of life', meant that it reflected the eternal spectacle of human nature and its weaknesses. And yet it is also the most complete reflection of its own age, far surpassing any other type of literature or art in fullness and accuracy. If we wish to study the external appearance and habits of the Athenians, we can learn just as much from vase-painting, the epic of everyday life; but vivid, convenient, and varied as the vase-paintings are, they tell us nothing of the loftier spiritual activities which produced the greatest comic poetry now extant. One of the inestimable advantages that we owe to Attic comedy is that it shows us both philosophy and poetry and the state itself, in the heart of this living stream of activity, surrounded and inspired by it, so that they cease to look like isolated phenomena and the full power of their immediate influence can be appreciated within the frame of their own time. It is only in the period which we know through comedy that we can observe the development of the intellectual life of Athens as a continuous social process, instead of studying it as crystallized in complete and permanent works of literature, history, and philosophy. And what we observe makes it plain that the antiquarian method of writing the history of civilization by reconstructing separate periods from isolated historical details, picked up and fitted together, is a hopeless task, even when the evidence is far more copious than it is for ancient Greece. Poetry alone can make the life of its own time real and human to posterity. Hence the paradox—which is, after all, perfectly natural—that hardly any historical period, even our own immediate past, can be realized by us so vividly as the age of Attic comedy.

However, in this book we must study its artistic power (which inspired an astonishing number of authors of widely varied talents) not only as a source of evidence for the life of a vanished world, but also as one of the greatest manifestations of Greek poetic genius. More than any other art, comedy is tied to the realities of its own time and place. Although that fact makes it fascinating from a historical point of view, its sole purpose, in portraying ephemeral events and personalities, is to represent certain aspects of their eternal humanity which are overlooked by loftier types of poetry like epic and tragedy. The philosophy of poetry which was developed in the fourth century defined tragedy and comedy as fundamentally opposite and complementary expressions of the same primitive human instinct for imitation. It asserted that tragedy, and all the other types of high poetry which succeeded the epic, sprang from the inclination of noble minds to imitate great men, notable deeds and famous lives; while it explained the origin of comedy by the irresistible imitative urge of commoner natures—or, as we should put it, by the impulse of the ordinary man, with his realistic and critical outlook—to ape bad, blameworthy, and contemptible things.[1] The famous scene in the *Iliad* which holds up the vulgar and hideous agitator Thersites to the malicious laughter of the mob—a rare comedy among the many tragedies in Homeric poetry—is a true piece of popular comedy, for it caters to the instincts of the mob. So also, in the divine farce which the enamoured Ares and Aphrodite are forced to play against their will, the Olympians themselves become a laughing audience at a comedy.

If even the mighty gods could laugh and be laughed at in this frankly comic way, the Greeks obviously felt that every human being, and every being with human attributes, had not only the power of feeling heroic emotion and serious dignity, but the ability and the need to laugh. Later Greek philosophy defined man as the only animal capable of laughter,[2] though he was usually described as a talking or thinking animal; thereby they placed laughter on the same plane with thought and speech, as an expression of intellectual freedom. If we connect that philosophical conception of human nature with the laughing gods of Homer, we shall not readily believe that comedy had lower spiritual implications than tragedy, though its origin may have been meaner. Nothing shows the broad and deep humanity of Athenian culture so clearly as the differentiation and integration of the two genera, tragedy and comedy, in Attic drama. Plato was the first to point this out: at the end of *The Symposium* he makes Socrates say that the true poet must be both a tragedian and a comedian [3]—a claim which Plato himself answered by writing *Phaedo* and *The Symposium*. All Athenian culture was aimed at realizing that ideal. Not only did it pit tragedy and comedy against each other in the same theatre, but it taught the Athenians (in Plato's words [4]) to consider all human life as both a tragedy and a comedy. Its complete humanity is a mark of its classical perfection.

Modern critics were unable to apprehend the unique beauty of Aristophanic comedy until they abandoned the historical preconception that it was a crude but brilliant predecessor of the comedy of manners,[5] studied its religious origins, and realized that it was an outpouring of the ecstatic Dionysian joy of life. It was necessary in fact to return to its psychical source in order to overcome the rationalist type of aesthetic criticism, which could not see the creative energy of nature in Attic comedy.[6] But we must go a little further back if we are to see the pure spiritual heights to which the Dionysiac fervour soared in Aristophanes.

The history of comedy is the clearest possible example of the direct growth of a lofty artistic form from a root deep in the soil of Attica. Its origins were obscure—unlike those of tragedy, for the whole development of tragic poetry from the earliest dithyrambic choruses and dances to its climax in the art of Sophocles was perfectly familiar to the Greeks of that time.[7] The reasons for this were not merely technical. Tragic poetry was from the very first the centre of serious public interest. It had always been the medium in which noble thoughts were expressed. But the drunken *kōmos* which marked the rustic festival of Dionysus, with the robust obscenity of its phallic songs, was not considered to be spiritual creation, *poiésis*, poetry in the full sense of the word. When comedy became literature, as in Aristophanes, it assimilated many very diverse elements which all originated from the old Dionysiac festival.[8] It contained, of course, the spirit of the holiday revel, the kōmos, after which it was named. Another important feature was the parabasis, the procession in which the chorus gave free play to its mocking humour, taunting the audience (the gaping onlookers at the original festival) and frequently singling out individuals by name for a special shower of abuse. Equally ancient were the phallic costumes of the actors, and the disguises worn by the chorus—particularly the animal-masks of frogs, wasps, birds, and the like: for these features appeared even in the oldest comedians, who were still strongly bound to tradition and made few innovations of their own.

It is characteristic of the Athenian genius that it could blend these diverse elements into an artistic unity in comedy: the obvious parallel is Attic tragedy, which combined dance, choral song, and spoken poetry. It was that diversity in unity which made Attic comedy so much richer in scenic resources and intellectual energy than everything else of its kind produced independently of it elsewhere in the Greek world—the comedies of Epicharmus, for example, written in Dorian Sicily, and the mimes of Sophron. But the feature which had the greatest possibilities of dramatic development was its verse-form: the Ionian iambic line. It also had a Dionysiac origin, but had been raised to poetic form by Archilochus two centuries earlier. Nevertheless, the free structure of the comic trimeter proves that it did not develop from the literary iambus shaped by Archilochus, but directly from the primitive and probably improvised folkmetre of the same name, which had always been used for satiric poetry. It was only in the second generation and thereafter that the comic poets imitated the Archilochean lampoon, not in its rigid verse-structure, but in the higher craft of aiming bold satiric attacks at individuals of whom they disapproved, though they might be the greatest men in the state.[9]

This technique had little significance until the time when comedy became politically important, and the state made it a privilege and a duty for rich citizens to pay the expenses of its production; for thereby the comic festival became a public occasion,[10] and the comic 'chorus' began to compete seriously with tragedy for the interest of the citizens. Although it could not pretend to the same prestige as tragedy, it now began to imitate it. The influence of tragedy upon the comic poets is shown in the many technical devices which they borrowed, and even more in their effort to give comedy a complete dramatic structure,[11] though it was still impossible for them to trim away the luxuriant overgrowth of farcical episodes and reduce the plot to a rigid form. Similarly, the influence of tragedy was responsible for the introduction of a 'hero' into comedy, and deeply affected the composition of its lyrics. And finally, at the height of its development, it was the inspiration of tragedy which raised it to the highest point by making it conscious of its noble educational mission: that consciousness pervades Aristophanes' whole conception of comedy, and makes his work both spiritually and technically a worthy rival to all the tragic poetry of his age.

This, it seems, is the explanation of the unique and predominant position among the writers of old comedy which was unanimously given to Aristophanes by the tradition which preserved his works alone, and a relatively large number of them. It can hardly be pure chance that he alone has survived out of the triad of comedians chosen as classical models by the Alexandrians—Cratinus, Eupolis, and Aristophanes.[12] This canon, obviously meant for a parallel to the great triad of tragic poets, was only a literary historian's artificial selection, and did not reflect the true relative importance of these poets even in Hellenistic times. This is proved beyond cavil by the papyrus fragments of other comic poets which have recently been discovered. Plato was right to introduce Aristophanes in *The Symposium* as the comedian *par excellence*. Even at the time when comedies were being written by really important poets, like the dissolute genius Cratinus and the brilliantly inventive Crates, the art of comedy had nothing whatever to do with any noble cultural mission. Its only aim was to make the public laugh; like all clowns, even the most popular comedians were relentlessly hissed off the stage when they were old and lost the flowing wit which had been the real source of their effect.[13] Wilamowitz in particular has entered a strong protest against the doctrine that comedy was intended to improve the morals of the audience; and in fact nothing seems more remote from it than didacticism in general, to say nothing of moral instruction. Still, his objection does not go far enough: it does not do justice to the actual history of comedy in the period known to us.

Cratinus—the old toper whom Aristophanes [14] proposes the city should retire from the stage and keep honourably drunk in the Prytaneion till his death—seems to have excelled in relentless gibing at notoriously unpopular persons; and that was actually the essence of the old iambic, raised to the level of political satire. Eupolis and Aristophanes, the brilliant Dioscuri of the younger generation who began by writing comedies in friendly partnership and ended as bitter enemies accusing each other of plagiarism, followed him in delivering savage personal attacks on Cleon and Hyperbolus. But from the beginning of his career Aristophanes was conscious of being a higher kind of artist than others. The earliest of his extant plays, *The Acharnians,* is political lampoonery transformed into a brilliant fantasy, blending the usual coarse and vivid burlesque with the witty symbolism of an ambitious political Utopia, and enriching it by gay parodies of Euripidean tragedy. It is by combining these two primitive elements of the Dionysiac revel—grotesque fantasy and powerful realism—that Aristophanes creates the peculiar blend of actuality and unreality which was necessary before a higher form of comedy could come into being. Even in *The Acharnians* [15] he alludes ironically to the coarse and obvious jokes with which Megarian farce-writers belaboured the witless mob, and to which in his own time comic poets still had recourse. No doubt the public taste had to be suited, and Aristophanes knew how to use the indispensable tricks of old-fashioned comedy when necessary—the stale gibes at bald members of the audience, the vulgar cordax-dance, and the whipping-scenes by which the actor disguised the stupidity of his material. Such were the jokes which (as Aristophanes says with hearty insolence in *The Knights* [16]) old Crates wiped off his cabbage-eating mouth, still accustomed to the primitive Attic taste. In *The Clouds* [17] he boldly asserts that he feels himself far superior to the technique of his predecessors (and not of them alone), and that he has full confidence in his own art and his own style. He is proud (he says) of producing new subjects every year—and thereby he emphasizes the artistic inventiveness of up-to-date comedy in contrast not only with the other type but even with tragedy, which always worked on traditional material. In the terrific competition of the annual dramatic festival, originality and novelty must have been at a premium. And original ideas could be made even more attractive if spiced with the boldness of a political attack like that which Aristophanes delivered on the omnipotent Cleon. By such a challenge a comedian could excite general interest, just as a rising politician could make a striking début as prosecutor in an important state trial. All that was needed was courage, and Aristophanes believed he had done a finer thing by 'punching mighty Cleon in the belly' [18] than his colleagues in pounding away year after year at the comparatively harmless demagogue Hyperbolus and his wretched mother.

All this has nothing to do with improving public morality. The spiritual transformation of comedy was worked by different means, and accompanied by a gradual change in its conception of its own critical function.

The iambic lampoon invented by Archilochus, though very largely personal invective, became to some extent the medium of public criticism in the new liberty of the Ionian city-state.[19] But Attic comedy, the successor of the iambic, was the first critical poetry in the true and higher sense. It also had developed out of more or less harmless gibing at private individuals; but it found its true nature only when it entered the political arena. As known to us at the height of its achievement, it is a true product of democratic free speech. The Hellenistic historians of literature realized that the rise and fall of political comedy coincided with those of the Athenian democracy.[20] It never flourished again (least of all in antiquity) after the Greeks had been driven— in Plato's phrase [21]—from an excess of freedom to an excess of unfreedom. But it is not enough to consider comedy merely as an exponent of the free democratic spirit. Comedy was produced by democracy as an antidote to its own overdose of liberty, thereby outdoing its own excesses, and extending *parrhesia,* its vaunted freedom of speech, to subjects which are usually tabu even in a free political system.

More and more comedy assumed the function of expressing all kinds of public criticism.[22] Not content with passing judgment on 'political affairs' in the narrow modern sense of the phrase, it discussed politics in the full Greek sense—that is, all questions of universal interest to the community. When it chose, it censured not only individuals, not only separate political acts, but the entire governmental system, the character and the weaknesses of the whole nation. It controlled the spirit of the people, and kept a constant watch on education, philosophy, poetry, and music. Thereby, these activities were for the first time regarded as expressing the culture of the nation, and as standards of its spiritual health. They were brought to judgment in the theatre before the whole Athenian people. This was a transference of the idea of responsibility, which is inseparable from liberty and which was realized in the democracy by the institution of the *euthyné,* to these suprapersonal spiritual activities that serve or ought to serve the welfare of the community. Therefore the very democracy which so vaunted liberty was compelled by an inherent necessity to fix the limits of the liberty of the intellect.

On the other hand, it was part of the essence of Athenian democracy that this limitation should be done, not by officials, but by public opinion. Comedy was the censorship of Athens. That is what makes Aristophanes' wit so deadly serious despite its mask of outrageous laughter. Plato [23] defines the principle of comedy as malicious laughter at the harmless failings and self-deceptions of our neighbours. Perhaps that definition suits the comedy of his day better than Aristophanes, whose gaiety sometimes touches tragedy, as in *The Frogs.* But we shall discuss that later.[24] The fact that in spite of the dangers and crises of the war educational problems occupied an important, sometimes a predominant, place in comedy, shows the supreme importance which was attached to them in that period. It is only through comedy that we can study the violent passion with which the educational question was debated, and discover its causes. And comedy, by using its own peculiar powers to take over the leadership in that conflict, became one of the greatest cultural forces of its time. We shall demonstrate this in three of the principal spheres of communal life—politics, education, and art. It will not be necessary to analyse all Aristophanes' works, but each of these subjects will be discussed with reference to the plays which are particularly relevant to it.[25]

As we have seen, *political* satire, which predominates in Aristophanes' earlier plays, originally had no lofty purpose. Often its freedom could hardly be distinguished from insolence. Even in democratic Athens it often came into conflict with the authorities. Again and again they attempted to abnegate its ancient privilege of delivering slanderous attacks on individual citizens by name.[26] But the prohibitions never lasted long. They were against public sentiment; and even the spirit of the new constitutional state could not eradicate comic lampoonery, that scandalous survival of the primitive social sense. If it caricatured statesmen with anything like the nonchalant freedom of Aristophanes' portrait of Socrates in *The Clouds,* we can see why they attempted to use their power to protect themselves, while private citizens (like Socrates in Plato's account of his persecution by comic poetry) were defenceless in face of the public mockery and hatred which comedy encouraged. Cratinus did not shrink from attacking Pericles himself. In *The Thracian Women* he called him 'the squillheaded Zeus', an allusion to the oddly shaped skull which he usually hid under a helmet. But even that harmless joke betrayed the poet's underlying respect for the great statesman, 'the Olympian' who 'flashed and boomed and mixed up Greece pell-mell'.[27]

Aristophanes' political attacks on Cleon were of a different type. His jokes were not the jokes of hearty frankness. He gave his victim no half-affectionate nicknames. He fought him with all the bitterness of principle. Cratinus had felt the superiority of Pericles, and laughed at him like the jester at the king. For Attic wit did not mix up great things with small, or belittle splendid things in a familiar way: it always kept its infallible sense of proportion. But Aristophanes had to stoop to attack this enemy. The descent to Cleon after the untimely death of Pericles was too abrupt and too sudden for him and others not to feel it as a symptom of the degeneration of the entire state. Athenians who were accustomed to the magnificent manners and intellectual nobility of Pericles turned with disgust from the common tanner whose vulgarity brought discredit on the whole nation.

It was not the lack of civic courage that silenced his critics in the assembly, when his policies were objectively discussed. There his undeniable ability and the practised energy of his oratory quelled his opponents. And yet he often showed weaknesses that disgraced not himself alone but the city which he governed. It was an act of incredible boldness for Aristophanes, scarcely out of his 'teens, to attack the all-powerful favourite of the demos, in his second comedy *The Babylonians* (unfortunately lost), and to expose his brutal treatment of the other members of the Delian League, on the public stage, before the representatives of these very states. The best commentary on Cleon's policy is provided by the speeches which Thucydides [28] puts into his mouth at the time of the revolt of Mytilene, when he discusses the correct policy of Athens to the members of her alliance. Aristophanes depicted them as slaves in the treadmill. Cleon instantly prosecuted him. *The Knights* was his reply. He fell back on the support of the opposition party—the small but influential clique of feudal squires, the cavalry corps which had attained new importance since the invasion, the deadly enemies of Cleon. His chorus of knights embodied the defensive alliance of nobility and intellect against the growing power of barbarism and political terror.

It must be understood that this kind of criticism constituted a revolution in the history of comedy. It was fundamentally different from Cratinus' political jester's-tricks, just as Aristophanes' cultural persecution of Euripides and the sophists was poles apart from Cratinus' clowning parodies of the *Odyssey*. The revolution was caused by the change in the intellectual situation. At the very moment when, by the appearance of a poet of real genius, intelligence invaded comedy, intelligence was to be hunted out of Athens. The equilibrium which Pericles had established between politics and the new culture, and which he had typified in his own character, was now destroyed. If it were not restored, culture must disappear from Athens. But meanwhile intellectualism had acquired political influence. It was not the province of scholarly recluses, as in the Alexandrean era: it lived and worked in poetry, and through it had the ear of the public. So it took up the challenge. Aristophanes was not fighting against the state—he was fighting *for* the state against its temporary despot. Of course, writing comedy was not taking a regular share in political activity, and Aristophanes scarcely wished to support any particular person or party in winning power. But he could help to break the tension and to counteract the intolerable superiority of the brutal enemies of the intellect. In *The Knights* he did not support or oppose any definite policy, as he did in *The Babylonians* or *The Acharnians:* [29] he merely scourged the people and its leader, and pilloried their alliance as unworthy of the Athenian state and its illustrious past.

He put this unholy alliance on the stage by means of a fantastic allegory—not a bloodless set of symbols as allegories usually are, but a visible embodiment of an invisible fact. To symbolize the condition of that abstract thing, the Athenian state, he showed the audience an ordinary household thoroughly upset. The pater-familias, deaf old Mr. Demos, always grumbling and always being cheated, images the manyheaded mob who govern Athens. He is completely under the influence of a new slave, a coarse brutal Paphlagonian, and his two older slaves are in constant trouble. The mask of the Paphlagonian conceals the face of the terrible Cleon, and his two miserable fellow-slaves are the generals Nicias and Demosthenes. The hero of the comedy, however, is not Cleon, but his adversary the Sausage-seller. He is an even more disgusting character than the Paphlagonian, and, through his shameless conduct and total lack of culture and moral standards, always comes out on top. In the competition to see which of them can do most good to Demos, Cleon is outwitted by the Sausage-seller, who produces a pair of slippers, a warm shirt, and a cushion for the old man to sit on at the assembly. Cleon breaks down like a tragic hero at the catastrophe. The chorus shouts applause to the victor, and rather emphatically asks him to show his gratitude for their help by giving them a nice public office. The next scene is more ambitious. The victor chooses as his first official act to rejuvenate old Demos, who is therefore boiled in a huge sauasage-kettle, and emerges when the magical ceremony is complete, to be presented to the jubilant audience, reborn and crowned with garlands. Once more he looks as he did in the spacious days of Miltiades and the wars of liberation: he is the living incarnation of the violet-crowned hymn-resounding Athens of old, wearing its honest old-fashioned costume, with his hair dressed in the antique fashion; and he is hailed as king of the Greeks. He is spiritually reborn too, and sadly confesses his shame for his old errors. His corruptor Cleon is condemned to peddle the sausages made of dog-meat and donkey-dung which his victorious successor used to sell.

Thus the apotheosis of the rejuvenated nation reaches its climax: the justice of heaven is fulfilled. The wildly impossible task of squaring the circle in politics—of driving out Cleon's vices by still greater vileness—has been easily solved by the poet's imagination. Few of his audience would ask whether the sausage-seller would really make a better successor to Pericles than the tanner. Aristophanes could leave the politicians to determine what they would make out of Athens reborn. He wanted only to hold up the mirror to the nation and to its leader, almost without hoping to change them. Cleon made a marvellous comic hero—a real hero reversed, distinguished by possessing all human faults and failings. It was a brilliant idea to bring him into conjunction with the Sausage-seller, his own 'ideal', whom he never could equal or even approach, however hard he strove. The relentless savagery of Aristophanes' portrayal of Cleon makes a striking contrast to the patient tolerance with which he reveals the weaknesses of Demos, only to indulge them a little further. It would be a grave misunderstanding to imagine that he seriously believed Athens could return to the happiness of that bygone age, which he depicts with such nostalgic humour and such pure patriotic affection. In *Dichtung und Wahrheit* Goethe well describes the effect produced by that kind of poetic wishful thinking. 'A poet can create universal pleasure by skilfully reminding a nation of its own past: it admires the virtues of its ancestors, and smiles at the faults which it believes it has surmounted long ago.' The less one tries to interpret these magical fantasies, in which Aristophanes blends reality and fairyland, as straightforward political preaching, the more deeply one will understand his poetry.

Why is it that this type of comic poetry—which lives for one fleeting moment and expends all its force upon that moment— has been recognized more and more within the last century to be immortal? In Germany, the interest in Aristophanes' political comedies appeared when her political life began.[30] But it is only in the last few decades that the problems of politics have been as urgent and absorbing in Germany as they were in Athens at the end of the fifth century. The fundamental facts are always the same—the polar oppositions between the individual and the community, the mob and the intellectual, the poor and the rich, liberty and oppression, tradition and progress. But there is another factor. Despite its passionate interest in politics, Aristophanic comedy contemplates its subject from such a height and with such intellectual liberty that it abolishes the irrelevant ephemeral aspects of even the most trivial fact. What the poet describes is eternal, because it is in Nietzsche's phrase the All-too-human Humanity; and he could not describe it unless he could stand at some distance from it. Again and again his picture of temporary reality dissolves into the timeless higher reality of imaginative or allegorical truth. The most impressive example of this is *The Birds,* where the poet gaily shakes off the pressing anxieties of the present, and makes a wish-picture of an ideal state, Cloud-Cuckoo-Land, where all the burdens of earth vanish and everything is winged and free, where only human follies and weaknesses may remain and flourish harmlessly, so that the finest of all delights may not be lacking, the delight whose absence would spoil even this paradise—immortal laughter.

From the first, Aristophanes was necessarily a critic not only of politics but of *culture*. This attitude appears in his first play, *The Banqueters,* which deals with the conflict between old and new ideals in education—the theme to which he returned in *The Clouds,* and which appears many times in other Attic comedians. Here he attacks the new ideal on what might seem to be a fairly inessential point—the eccentric and ill-bred conduct of its representatives. The Athenians, however, relished this keenly, because it added a new series of faults and follies to the rather hackneyed repertoire of comic subjects. In the same spirit, Eupolis wrote *The Flatterers* to deride the sophists who toadied to rich Athenians, and their parasitism seems to have been featured in Aristophanes' own comedy *The Fryers,* which made fun of the sophist Prodicus. The same comic motif reappears in Plato's *Protagoras;* but obviously none of the comedians saw the deeper implications of sophistic culture as Plato did.[31] Still, Aristophanes in *The Banqueters* seems to have gone fairly deeply into the corrupting effects of sophistic teaching on young men. His chief characters are the two sons of an Athenian farmer, one of whom has been brought up at home in the old-fashioned way, while the other is sent to the city to enjoy the advantages of progressive education. The city-bred youth comes back completely transformed, morally corrupted, and spoilt for work on the farm, where his higher culture is useless. His father is grieved to find that he cannot sing the drinking-songs of the old poets, Alcaeus and Anacreon. Instead of the archaic words in Homer, he understands only the glosses on the text of Solon's legislation, for juristic training is now in fashion. The name of the rhetor Thrasymachus occurs in some argument about the meaning of words—a type of pedantry particularly repulsive to Athenians of the old school. But as a whole the play seems not to have passed beyond the bounds of harmless mockery.[32]

However, *The Clouds,* produced a few years later, showed how profound and sincere was Aristophanes' dislike for the new

THE COMIC POETRY OF ARISTOPHANES

371

intellectual movement, and resumed with greater vehemence the attack delivered in *The Banqueters*. He had now discovered a figure who seemed to be designed by nature for the hero of a comedy of intellectualism. This was Socrates of Alopeké, son of a stonemason and a midwife—a far more effective hero than any of the touring sophists who visited Athens at distant intervals, because he was known throughout the city and could easily be recognized on the stage. Nature herself in a fit of humour had made him a perfect comic mask, in the shape of a Silenus-face with a snub nose, protruding lips, and goggling eyes. All that was necessary was to exaggerate his character a little. Aristophanes decked his victim out with all the characteristics of the tribe to which he obviously belonged—the sophists, rhetors, and natural philosophers, or, as they were then called, meteorologists. And then—although the real Socrates spent almost the whole day walking about the market-place—Aristophanes gave this fantastically exaggerated figure a narrow mysterious Thinking-shop, where, suspended in a swing above the courtyard, he 'contemplated the sun' with his head tilted back, while his pale-faced pupils bent and scrutinized the sand, so as to fathom the underworld. Usually *The Clouds* is considered as if it were part of the history of philosophy, and is at best excused, never praised. *Summum ius, summa iniuria*. It is unfair to call the farcical Socrates of comedy to the bar of rigid historical truth. Plato himself, who reveals the important part which this caricature played in the condemnation of his master, never applies such a severe standard to it. In *The Symposium* he set his master, transfigured and glorified, beside the poet who had derided him; and he thought it no insult to the shade of Socrates to make Aristophanes play a leading part in the conversation. The comic Socrates has none of the moral energy which Plato and the other Socratics describe in their teacher. If Aristophanes knew that he really possessed this quality, he could not use it on the stage. He made his hero an eccentric and unworldly pioneer of progressive ideas, an atheistic scientist: the typical comic figure of the arrogant and oddly-behaved scholar, individualized by a few features borrowed from the character of the historical Socrates.

If we read the play with Plato's descriptions of Socrates in our mind it is impossible to find anything funny in the caricature. Real wit is the revelation of unexpected similarities; but there is

practically no resemblance between the real and the comic Socrates. However, Aristophanes was not interested in the form
and content of the Socratic conversations; and though there were
significant differences between the intellectual attitude of Socrates and that of the sophists, differences which Plato was to
work out with great care, Aristophanes ignored them and saw
only the fundamental resemblance—both the sophists and Socrates analysed everything, and thought nothing was so great or
so sacred that it was beyond discussion and did not need to be
founded on a rational basis.[33] In fact, Socrates with his passion
for abstract ideas seemed to have beaten the sophists at their
own game. We need not expect the poet, who felt that every
form of this fashionable intellectualism was injurious, to draw
any fine distinctions between one type and another. There were
many who complained of this or that evil aspect of the new culture. Aristophanes was the first to describe it as a universal
danger. He saw the destruction of all the traditions of the past,
and it moved him to passionate protest. Personally, he would
have been embarrassed if anyone had questioned him about his
own attitude to the ancient gods; but as a comedian he thought
it ludicrous for the 'meteorologists' to call the aether divine, and
he made the humour of the situation vivid and immediate by
showing Socrates praying to the Vortex which he says formed
Primal Matter, or to the Clouds, the shifting airy insubstantial
forms which are so desperately like the misty doctrines of philosophy.[34] After two hundred years of bold cosmological theorizing in which one system was constantly built on the ruins of its
predecessor, the Greeks were too sceptical of the discoveries
made by human intelligence to accept the arrogant assurance
with which the advanced intellectuals confronted the ignorant
mob. The only unshakable fact which emerged was that their
pupils often made a disgraceful misuse of the unscrupulous
verbal tricks they had learnt. So Aristophanes brought two allegorical figures on the stage to represent the Just and the Unjust
Arguments which appeared in every sophistic discussion of every
problem, and to show how the Unjust Argument conquered its
opponent, as a comic tableau of the results of progressive education.[35]

After the first skirmishes, in which these figures hurl the usual
abuse at each other, the chorus invites them to fight an exhibi-

tion match as representatives of the old-fashioned and the new-fangled types of education. It is significant that the techniques of each system are not separately compared to prove which is superior. Instead, the Just Argument describes the old educational system [36] as personified in a particular type of human character: for an educational system can prove its worth only by the complete character which it produces, not by any abstract merits. At the time when the Just Argument was still flourishing, and decent behaviour was obligatory, children were seen and not heard. They went quietly along the streets (says the Just Argument) on their way to school, wearing no overcoats even when the snow fell thick as flour. There they learnt to sing old songs to traditional melodies. If one of them put in disgusting cadenzas and flourishes like modern musicians, he was flogged. That was how to bring up a generation of Marathon-warriors. But nowadays the children are weakened by being wrapped up in big coats, and it would make you choke with rage to see the young fellows awkwardly holding their shields in front of their bellies in the war-dance at the Panathenaea.[37] The Just Argument promises to teach the young man who entrusts himself to its educational régime to hate the market-place and keep away from the baths, to be ashamed of disgraceful conduct and fire up when insulted, to rise and make room when older men come in, to keep pure the divine image of modesty, not to visit dancing-girls, and not to contradict his father. He must practise wrestling, oiled and muscular, in the gymnasium, instead of making stinging-nettle-sharp speeches in the market-place or letting himself be dragged into court to argue his head off about pettifogging trivialities. Under the olive-trees of the Academy, he will run races, crowned with reed, against decent companions, smelling of honeysuckle and poplar-leaves and gentlemanly leisure, and enjoying the spring season when the plane-tree whispers to the elm. The chorus calls these men happy who lived in the fine old days when that kind of education flourished, and admires the sweet perfume of sophrosyné which is wafted from the words of the Just Argument.

Now its opponent, the Unjust Argument, rises,[38] almost choking with rage and eager to throw everything into confusion by its dialectic. It boasts of its ominous name—which it got for being the first to discover the art of making speeches to contradict the laws. To represent the worse cause and make it win,

says the Unjust Argument, is a talent worth its weight in gold.
It then attacks its adversary with the up-to-date method of cross-
examination; and uses the new rhetorical trick of quoting noble
mythological parallels to make its case seem respectable. The
Homeric orators had always cited ancient instances to exemplify
the ideal standards which they discussed,[39] and early poets followed the same practice. The sophists had now adopted it, and
collected all the mythological examples which they could utilize
from their realistic and relativist standpoint to support them in
destroying all accepted standards. Once upon a time a man defending himself in court had been content to show that his conduct was in accordance with the laws, but now he attacked the
laws and the current morality, and tried to show that they were
in the wrong. The Just Argument had said that warm baths
weakened the physique: the Unjust Argument counters this by
referring to the national hero Heracles, for Athena had created
the warm springs at Thermopylae to refresh him. It then goes
on to praise the custom of spending one's time in the market-
place making speeches, which its opponent had condemned, and
cites the eloquent Nestor, and other Homeric heroes to prove
its point. The Just Argument now adopts the same device, when
it is cynically asked who was ever profited by sophrosyné. Once,
when his virtue had brought him into dreadful danger, the gods
sent Peleus a miraculous sword to defend himself with. But the
Unjust Argument is not impressed by this 'pretty present'. To
illustrate how much more profitable rascality is, it leaves mythology and cites a modern example, the demagogue Hyperbolus,
who acquired 'more than many talents' of gold by his underhand
tricks. The other at once reminds him that the gods gave Peleus
an even greater reward, for they married him to Thetis. The
Unjust Argument replies that Thetis left him because he was
rather poor company. And, turning to the youth for whose soul
it is fighting with the representative of old-fashioned education,
it warns him that to choose sophrosyné is to abandon all the joys
of life. Not only that: if he does so, he will be helpless when the
'necessities of nature' cause him to make a false step, for he will
be unable to defend himself. 'If you take my advice, you will give
free rein to your nature, rollick and laugh, think nothing shameful. If you are caught in adultery, deny your guilt and appeal to
Zeus, who was not strong enough to resist Eros and women.

How can you, a mere mortal, be stronger than a god?' That is the same argument Euripides makes Helen, and the nurse in *Hippolytus,* employ to justify the faults of love. The climax of the discussion is that the Unjust Argument makes the audience burst into laughter by praising their own lax morality, and then explains that anything which is the practice of the vast majority of an honourable nation cannot possibly be a vice.

This attack on the old educational standards brings out the character produced by the new system. It need not be taken as evidence for the cultural ideals of the sophists; [40] still, that is how they seemed to many contemporaries, and there must have been a number of exaggerated instances which made this kind of generalization easy. Which side did Aristophanes take in the dispute? It would be a mistake to believe that he was a whole-hearted partisan of one side or the other. He himself had enjoyed the advantages of progressive education; and it is quite impossible to imagine that his comedy could have been written in the good old days. Much as he loved them, he would have been hissed off the stage. His sweet nostalgic picture of the past, with its springtime glamour, is the same kind of gay and melancholy fantasy as the rejuvenation of old Demos at the end of *The Knights.*[41] Although he conjures up the spirit of the old paideia, he is not preaching a return to the past. In fact, he was not a rigidly dogmatic reactionary. But he was living in an age of transition, when thoughtful men shrank from being whirled along in a constant stream of innovations, seeing good old things destroyed before they were replaced by something equally good. They had none of our modern historical sense of change, still less our general belief in development, evolution, 'progress'. Thus, they could not help feeling that the historical process through which they were living meant the demolition of that firm structure of traditional values in which they had lived so long and so happily.

The Just Argument, personifying the old educational ideal, shows what the new ideal is *not*. In showing what it *is*, Aristophanes abandons his tone of hearty good humour for one of biting satire, for he considers the new system to be the complete antithesis of all that is right and healthy. His negative criticism of it is charged with the serious educational purpose which is unmistakably present throughout the play. He lays particular emphasis on the complete unscrupulousness of the clever modern intellectuals, with their abnegation of all moral standards. To us it must seem paradoxical that that point should be so stressed in a comedy whose hero is Socrates. And in the plan of the comedy as we have it there is little connexion between Socrates' character and the rivalry of the Just and Unjust Arguments: he is not even present at it.[42] But the conclusion of *The Frogs* shows that Aristophanes considered Socrates to be the perfect type of the new intellectual spirit which was infuriating him and his contemporaries with its pretentiousness and its passion for hair-splitting abstract distinctions—and which moreover was abandoning the irreplaceable values of taste and neglecting the art of tragedy.[43] With the unerring perception of a man who owed his own ideas and his own culture to these values, and now saw them endangered, Aristophanes instinctively turned away from an educational system whose greatest strength lay in cold rationalism; and his hatred for it was more than a personal matter—it was a symptom of a far-reaching historical tendency.

For this rationalist spirit had encroached on *literature* too. When Aristophanes defended tragedy against Socrates and the intellectuals, he had Euripides as an enemy at his back. It was through Euripides that the new movement had invaded high poetry. Therefore the central point of Aristophanes' fight to preserve the old cultural ideals was his defence of the old spirit of tragedy, and he showed the same uncompromising obstinacy in it as in his attack on the new education. He criticized every aspect of Euripides' poetry, including his modern music, until his criticism almost became a persecution.[44] His political convictions were far less permanent and deep-seated than his poetic faith. Even his attack on Cleon or his advocacy of peace with the Peloponnesians—which were matters of principle with him —lasted only a few years. More and more he turned his attention from politics to culture. Certainly the cultural problem was the most important of those which could still be publicly discussed. Perhaps the decline of political comedy was due to the increasing dangers and tensions of the last years of the Peloponnesian War. Absolutely free discussion of public issues presupposes a good deal of surplus energy, which at that time the Athenian state no longer possessed. Political scepticism, though growing in volume, was forced to conceal itself in clubs and private assemblies. Not long before the collapse of Athens, within the same few months, Euripides and Sophocles died. The tragic stage was deserted. A historical epoch had come to an end. The miserable successors of the great dramatists—the tragedian Meletus, the dithyrambist Cinesias, and the comedian Sannyrion—appeared a few years later in Aristophanes' comedy *Gerytadés* as ambassadors sent to the underworld to get advice from their predecessors. Thus the age mocked its own weakness. *The Frogs,* written in the brief interval between the death of the two poets and the fall of Athens, is charged with a different and more tragic emotion. As the situation of Athens became more hopeless, and the pressure on the morale of her citizens increased to the breaking-point, they grew more eager for spiritual comfort and strength. Now at last we can see what tragedy meant to the Athenian people. Only comedy could express it; and it could do so just because of its objective view of tragedy, which was made possible through the vast difference separating the comic muse from her elder sister the muse of tragedy. And only comedy still had a poet worthy of the name. With the passage of the years, she had risen to a height from which she could warn, teach, and encourage the Athenians as tragedy once had done. It was her supreme moment.

In *The Frogs* Aristophanes conjures up the ghost of tragedy, which had died with Sophocles and Euripides. The memory of these poets was the strongest bond between the Athenian hearts which had been sundered by the furious quarrels of opposing parties. To renew and strengthen it was a task worthy of a statesman. Dionysus in person descends to the underworld—to bring back Euripides! Even his greatest enemy, Aristophanes, was forced to admit that that was what the public wanted. In the god Dionysus he typified the theatre-audience, with all its comical faults and peccadilloes. But he utilized its yearning for Euripides to make his last and most comprehensive attack on his art. He abandoned his usual Euripidean jokes—which had usually been incidental and would have been unsuitable at that crisis—and looked far more deeply into the problem of the function of tragedy. Therefore, he did not criticize Euripides by Euripides' own standards, although as a great artist he had a claim to such criticism; nor did he discuss him as a representative of his age. He contrasted him with Aeschylus, the noblest representative of the religious and moral dignity of tragic poetry. In the plot of *The Frogs,* this simple but highly effective conflict between the old and new ideals of tragedy plays the same important part as the *agon* of the old and new educational systems in *The Clouds.* But while the latter does not vitally affect the plot, the former carries the whole weight of the action. A descent to the underworld was a favourite theme in comedy. In that *The Frogs* resembles *The Wards* of Eupolis, where the old Athenian statesmen and generals were brought up from hell to help the state in its despair.[45] Having connected that idea with the contest of the two great poets, Aristophanes arrives at an astonishingly apt solution: after descending to hell to bring back Euripides, Dionysus finds that his favourite is beaten by Aeschylus in a fair poetic competition, and takes back the elder poet to save the city.

It is not our task to assess the play as a work of art. We must, however, study it as the most authoritative piece of fifth-century evidence for the position of tragedy in the life of the polis. Therefore the most important scene is that section of the *agon* in which Euripides, while vaunting his own service to Athens, is asked by Aeschylus: 'Tell me, why should a poet be admired?'[46] Aeschylus' basically aesthetic criticisms of the prologues, choruses, and other elements of Euripidean tragedy, though brilliantly witty, and though so vivid and concrete that they alone can give life and reality to the whole play, do not require separate study and can therefore be neglected here. Of course, they are vitally important in dealing with the comic effect of the drama; for they serve to counterbalance the preceding discussion of the ethical purpose of all true poetry, which from time to time grows painfully, even tragically, serious, and needs some such relief. These contemporary definitions of the nature and function of poetry are specially important because we have very few direct discussions of the subject by great writers of the period.[47] Even when we recollect that the theories of the name and nature of poetry which Aristophanes attributes to Aeschylus and Euripides had already been debated and formulated by contemporary sophists, they are invaluable as corroborating the impression which we receive from their extant tragedies.

Tell me, then, why should a poet be admired? Euripides gives the same answer as Aeschylus, though his phraseology would admit an interpretation peculiar to himself. 'For cleverness and for the ability to teach others, because we make men better in the state.' [48] And if you have not done that, if you have taken decent men with noble natures and made them into rascals, what do you deserve? 'Death!' interrupts Dionysus, 'you need not ask him.' And now, with a comical affectation of real emotion, Aeschylus describes how noble and martial the Athenians were until Euripides took them over from him. They coveted nothing, he says, except to beat the enemy. From the very beginning that has been the sole function of noble poets—to write what would benefit men. Orpheus showed them the mysteries, and taught them to abstain from murder; Musaeus explained how to cure the sick and foretell the future; Hesiod taught how to till the soil and know the seasons for ploughing and cropping; and the divine Homer won honour and glory by teaching men virtues like strategy, courage, and the equipment of warriors. Aeschylus says he has moulded many true heroes on that pattern—lion-hearted champions like Patroclus and Teucer—in order to inspire the citizens to emulate them when they hear the bugle sound the charge.

And yet I made no whores, no Stheneboeas and Phaedras:
no one can say that I ever wrote of a woman in love. [49]

(By these gentle transitions from the minor to the major mode, Aristophanes often re-establishes the marvellous objectivity and balance which characterize his poetry.)
Euripides now appeals to the fact that the subjects of his feminine dramas were drawn straight from mythology. But Aeschylus asserts that a poet ought to conceal evil things rather than display them publicly as a lesson to others.

For just as children
have teachers to explain things, men are taught by poets—
so our words must be noble. [50]

Euripides accuses Aeschylus' mountainous words of lacking that very quality of nobility, because his style has ceased to be human. But his rival explains that a poet who has great thoughts and emotions must also use great language, and that demigods spoke in noble words just as they wore magnificent clothes. [51] 'But you have spoilt that, by making kings wear rags to look pathetic, and by teaching the rich Athenians to dress in rags too and to swear that they are poor, to avoid the expense of fitting out a warship. You have taught men to chatter and prate, and so emptied the gymnasiums, and incited sailors to mutiny against their officers.' [52] These words bring us back to the miserable state of Athenian politics, for which Euripides is made responsible, as he is for so many other Athenian misfortunes.

The wild comedy of Aeschylus' inverted homage to Euripides really comes out when we remember that the play was not performed to a theatre full of classical scholars taking every word literally and expecting to be infuriated by it, but to the Athenian public which adored Euripides like a god. Imperceptibly Aristophanes' subtle criticisms slide into fantastic caricatures, and the caricatures into outrageous exaggerations, so that the master of tragedy finally stands revealed as the incarnation of all the evils of the unhappy present day—the age of folly to which Aristophanes addresses words of encouragement and warning in the patriotic parabasis. But in every line we can hear his real inspiration—his dreadful anxiety for the future of Athens. He always thinks of the future of his city when he speaks of true and false poetry. Even though he knows very well that Euripides was not a charlatan, but an immortal genius, to whom he himself owes an immense debt, and with whom he really sympathizes more deeply than with his ideal Aeschylus, nevertheless he feels that the art of Euripides could not give Athens what Aeschylus had given to his fellow-countrymen in their sore need. And nothing else could save Athens at that critical moment. Therefore Dionysus is finally compelled to choose Aeschylus, and the king of the underworld dispatches the great poet to the light of day with these parting words: [53]

> Farewell, then, Aeschylus: ascend,
> and save our country by your art.
> Give good advice, and educate
> the fools whose name is Legion.

Not for many years had tragedy dared to speak in such bold words as comedy now used. After all, comedy still lived by publicity and the oxygen of public discussion, whereas tragedy had quitted the open air and concentrated its interest on intimate psychological questions. Still, the public had never been compelled to pay such earnest attention to its spiritual problems as now; its political implications had never been realized so vividly as when Aristophanes stressed them by his lament for the disappearance of classical tragedy. At this critical juncture, the greatest of all comic poets once more emphasized the intimate connexion between the spirit and the future of the state, and the vast responsibility of creative genius to the community: and thereby comedy attained the climax of its great educational mission.

THUCYDIDES: POLITICAL PHILOSOPHER

THUCYDIDES was not the first Greek historian. In order to understand him, therefore, we must discover how far the historical sense had developed in his predecessors. It is clear that no previous historian can possibly be compared with him; nor did any of his successors follow the lines he struck out, for each of them took his form and his standards from the prevailing intellectual tendency of his own age. Still, Thucydides has one point of contact with earlier historical writers. The oldest type of history was created in Ionia during the beginnings of natural science: the word ἱστορίη shows its Ionian origin, and always connoted physical research too, which was originally its true meaning.[1] As far as we know, Hecataeus (who came like the first great physicists from Miletus, the cultural capital of Ionia) was the first to transfer his 'investigation' from the whole of nature to one special field, the inhabited earth—which had hitherto been considered simply as a part of the cosmos, while the character and structure of its surface had been described only in general terms.[2] His account of the countries and peoples of the world, a remarkable blend of empirical knowledge and logical hypothesis, if taken together with his genealogical studies and his rationalist criticism of mythology, falls into its proper place in the development of Greek thought and becomes comprehensible. It was an important stage in the critical and rational destruction of the old epic tradition. It was also an essential precondition for the rise of history,[3] which, working on the same critical principle, collects and surveys traditional information about the nations inhabiting the known earth, so far as it can be checked by investigation.

This step was taken by Herodotus, who followed Hecataeus in treating geography and ethnology together as a unity, but whose chief interest was mankind. He travelled over the entire civilized world of his time—the Near East, Egypt, Asia Minor, and Greece; he studied and recorded on the spot all sorts of strange manners and customs and the wonderful wisdom of nations older than Greece; he described the splendour of their palaces and temples; and he related the histories of their royal families and of many interesting and important men, showing how the power of the gods and the rise and fall of transient human fortune was manifested in them. He gave unity to this medley, as various and intricate as an antique tapestry, by basing it upon one great central theme: the conflict of East and West, from the first historically certain clash, the war between the Greeks and the neighbouring kingdom of Lydia under Croesus, to the Persian invasion of Greece. With a Homeric pleasure and skill in telling stories, Herodotus recorded for posterity the glory of the deeds of Greeks and barbarians—for that, he says in the first sentence, was the purpose of his book [4]—and set them down in a prose style which is only at first glance unassuming and naïve, and which was meant to be enjoyed by his contemporaries as their fathers had enjoyed the style of epic poetry. His work was, so to speak, a resurrection, in the age of scientific research and sophistic logic, of the epic tradition which had been struck down by Hecataeus' rationalist criticisms; or rather it was a new growth from the old epic root. Blending the cool, dispassionate, empirical attitude of the scientist with the rhapsode's love of praising famous men, he subordinated all that he had seen and heard to his description of the power of destiny over individuals and nations. His history was typical of the rich, ancient, and highly complex civilization of the Asiatic Greeks, who, centuries after their heroic age and decades after their subjection to a foreign monarch, were once more drawn into the strong stream of history by the unexpected victory of their motherland at Salamis and Plataea, yet without losing the resigned scepticism which they had cultivated for so long.

Thucydides created political history. Although the Persian wars are the climax of Herodotus' book, he was not a political historian, for like many others he wrote political history in a non-political spirit. In the quiet city of Halicarnassus where he was born, he had seen little of political life; and when he first met it in full swing in post-war Athens, he took no part in it, but looked on from outside as an admiring spectator. Thucydides on the other hand was a true citizen of Periclean Athens, and the breath of life to Periclean Athens was political activity. Since the social upheavals of the sixth century, when Solon had laid the foundation for the sound political sense which early distinguished the Athenians from their Ionian kinsmen, every leading citizen of Athens had taken part in politics, and the Athenians had thereby acquired a vast body of political experience and well-marked political ideas. Its working appeared only in a few penetrating observations on the state of society, thrown out by the great Attic poets, and, during the Persian invasion, in the unity and determination of the Athenian people, so lately freed from the Pisistratid tyranny—until, through the growth of Themistocles' imperialist policy after Salamis, the little state became the Athenian empire.

The astonishing concentration of political thought and will revealed in the creation of the empire found full intellectual expression in the history of Thucydides. His mental horizon is limited in comparison with the encyclopaedic knowledge of Herodotus, who calmly surveys the whole known world, its countries, its men, and its gods. He never moves far beyond the sphere of influence of the Greek city-state.[5] But, though his subject is much narrower, it is charged with deeper problems, far more intensely experienced and profoundly understood. The central problem is the nature of the state—as was almost inevitable in a book written in Athens at that time. However, it is far less easy to understand why the study of this problem should have tended to encourage the historical outlook. Herodotus' history of the nations would not in itself have prompted anyone to write a political history.[6] But Athens, while concentrated earnestly and exclusively on the present, had suddenly reached a crisis in which serious political thinkers were compelled to develop a historical consciousness, although now in a new sense and with a different content. They were forced, in fact, to discover the *historical* necessity of the crisis to which the nation's development had led. This is the real nature of the intellectual revolution reflected in Thucydides' history—historical writing had not become political, but political thinking had become historical.[7]

This being so, the most recently proposed view of the process by which Thucydides became a historian is untenable.[8] It is far too confidently assumed that he and his contemporaries had a preconception of the nature and function of a historian, just as modern scholars have. Here and there, Thucydides digresses from his main theme to deal with a few separate problems of earlier history which interest him; but his chief concern is the Peloponnesian War—namely, the history of his own times. In the first sentence of his book he says only that he began work on it at the outbreak of the war, because he was convinced of the importance of the subject. But the question at once arises—where did he learn the technique of historical research, and what is the source of his knowledge of the past? The modern explanation is that he had already been studying the history of Greece, and, interrupted by the outbreak of war, recognized that the war itself was the great subject on which he must now employ his skill; but that rather than waste the material he had gathered from his previous researches, now abandoned, he inserted a scholarly excursus here and there in his book to embody it. This explanation appears to me to suit a modern scholar better than the creator of political history, the statesman and admiral who played a personal part in the war and who could conceive of no higher interest than the political problem of his own times. It was the war that made Thucydides a historian. No one could learn by mere book-work what he had learnt by practical experience: and least of all could one learn the truth from what he held to be a fundamentally different past era, about which he thought it was hardly possible to know the exact truth. Therefore he was something quite different from our usual conception of a historian; and his occasional digressions on problems of early history, however valuable the critical judgment which they display, are either incidental or else written to explain the present by the past.[9]

The chief example of this is the archaeological excursus at the beginning of the first book.[10] It was written principally to show that the past was unimportant in comparison with the present described by Thucydides—at least as far as it could be reconstructed by inference, since nothing could be really known of it. Nevertheless, his brief account of the past shows us—all the more clearly for being so summary—the standards by which he judged historical fact, and the criteria of importance which he applied to the events of his own day.

He believes that the past history of the Greek people was

unimportant—even its greatest and most famous exploits—because its life would not allow the creation of any political organization and the development of power on a large scale. There was, he says, no trade and commerce in the modern sense. Because of the migrations, in which one race constantly displaced another so that none had any fixed home, there was no security; and apart from technical knowledge security is the first condition of stable political life. The most fertile parts of the country, according to Thucydides, were naturally most often fought for, and therefore changed their population most frequently. Thus neither systematic agriculture nor accumulations of capital could come into existence, and there were no large cities, nor any of the other elements of modern civilization. It is extraordinarily instructive to see how Thucydides sets aside the whole of ancient historical tradition because it gives no answer to his questions,[11] and replaces it with his own hypotheses, a set of bold inferences based on his own clear insight into the logical connexion between cultural, political, and economic development. The intellectual character of these inferences resembles that of the sophists' hypothetical reconstructions of the life of primitive man, but their point of view is different. Thucydides is looking at the past with the eyes of a fifth-century politician: he thinks only of *power*. Technical knowledge, economic development, and intellectual culture he tends to ignore, except as necessary conditions for the development of power. Power means for him first of all the possession of great capital resources and wide territory, supported by a strong navy. This is obviously the ideal of a fifth-century Athenian. Thucydides weighed the civilization of earlier centuries by the standard of Athenian imperialism, and found it wanting.[12]

He is quite as independent in applying this principle to early history as he is in choosing it. He examines Homer with the unprejudiced unromantic eye of a modern statesman. The empire of Agamemnon he considers to be the first great power in Greek history for which there is historical evidence.[13] With inexorable logic, he deduces from a single verse of Homer, heavily overemphasized, that Agamemnon's rule must have extended to the sea as well as the land, and that it must therefore have been supported by a large navy. He is chiefly interested in the Homeric catalogue of ships, and (though usually sceptical of poetic tradition) is prepared to accept its detailed account of the strength of individual Greek contingents to the Trojan war, because it confirms his belief that the resources of primitive Greece were unimportant.[14] And he uses the same evidence to prove that naval architecture was then undeveloped. The Trojan war was the first large-scale overseas expedition, conducted by a league of allies, which is known to Greek history. There was nothing before it except Minos' Cretan naval empire, which brought to an end the piratical life of the warring half-barbaric tribes of early Greece. Thucydides conceives that Minos' fleet was engaged in policing the seas as consistently and as severely as the Athenian fleet of his own day. And thus, using the criteria of capital-accumulation, fleet-construction, and sea-power, he passes quickly over the whole of Greek history down to the Peloponnesian war, punctuating it by separate technical inventions in naval architecture, and utterly neglecting the rich intellectual and aesthetic heritage of the past. Athens, he believes, first became politically important after Persia's defeat. The accession of the islands and the Greek cities of Asia Minor to the Athenian league made her a rival to Sparta, which had hitherto been the dominant power. The subsequent history of Greece was a competition between these two power-systems, marked by occasional incidents and constant friction—until the final struggle, which made all previous struggles for power look like child's play.

This account of early Greek history, which has been so much admired, expresses Thucydides' historical outlook with unsurpassable clarity, although far from exhaustively.[15] By sketching the past in bold economic and political lines, he reveals his attitude to the events of his own time. It is for that reason that I have started by discussing his account of prehistory, not because it occurs at the beginning of his book. In his description of the war, the same principles appear at much closer quarters and far less obviously, because they are applied on a much larger scale; but here they have almost the purity of abstraction. The catchwords of realistic fifth-century politics are repeated with something like stereotyped regularity in this excursus, and make such a deep impression on the reader that he approaches Thucydides' account of the war itself with the firm belief that it describes the greatest display of power and the greatest political crisis which ever occurred in the history of Greece.

The more actual his subject, and the more active his interest in it, the harder it was for Thucydides to take up an objective attitude to it. His *purpose* as a historian must be understood from his endeavour to achieve a dispassionate point of view towards the enormous event which divided his world into two hostile armies. If he were not such a notable politician, his effort to be objective would have been less surprising, but also less great. His intention was to tell the plain truth, unaffected by partisanship and as accurately as possible—in contrast to the picturesque accounts of the heroic past given by the poets.[16] In itself, that purpose was inspired not by a political but by a scientific attitude like that of the Ionian physicists. But Thucydides won his great intellectual victory by transferring that scientific attitude from timeless nature to the political struggle of his own age, darkened and confused by passions and party-interests. His contemporary Euripides [17] had described nature and the drama which we now call history as separated by an unbridgeable gulf. There was, he said, no *historia,* calm 'investigation' of an 'unchanging' object, except natural history—physical science. Whoever entered political life was beset by hate and conflict.[18] But Thucydides, by transferring *historia* to the sphere of politics, gave a new and deeper sense to this ideal of the search for truth.[19] To understand the great innovation which he made, we must remember the peculiar Greek conception of action. According to Greek ideas, it was knowledge that moved men to act. So Thucydides' search for truth had a practical end in view, and thereby differed from the disinterested *theoria,* contemplation, practised by the Ionian scientists. No Athenian ever believed that knowledge could exist for any other purpose than to lead to right action. That is the great distinction between the Ionians on the one hand, and Plato and Thucydides on the other, although the two Athenians moved in such different worlds. Many a historian has been called 'an eye without a heart', but it cannot be said that Thucydides was naturally fitted to take an objective view of facts because of some innate lack of passion. What gave him the strength to shake off his passions, and what he held to be the advantage of the objective knowledge which he sought, he himself states, in the passage [20] where he defines the purpose of his book more accurately. 'It will perhaps be found that the absence of mythology in my work makes it unattractive to listen to; but it will suffice if it is judged useful by all who wish to study the plain truth of the events which have happened, and which will according to human nature recur in much the same way. It was written to be kept for ever, rather than to be admired for a moment.'

Several times he expresses the opinion that the history of individuals and nations repeats itself because human nature does not change.[21] This idea is the absolute opposite of what we usually call the historical attitude nowadays. A true historian, we think, believes that history never repeats itself. Every historical event is entirely individual. There is no repetition even in the events of one man's life. And yet men do acquire experience; and painful experience makes one clever, says the old proverb which Hesiod [22] quotes. Greek thought always aimed at obtaining that kind of knowledge, by reaching general conclusions. Therefore Thucydides' axiom that the history of individuals and nations repeats itself does *not* signalize the birth of the historical consciousness, in the one-sided modern sense. Though his work has the modern historical interest in separate events for their own sake, it tries to pass beyond them and to transcend what is strange and different so as to reach the universal and permanent law which they embody. It is that intellectual attitude which gives his history the charm of its imperishable actuality.[23] It is an essential element in his political outlook; for politicians cannot think ahead and act according to plan unless, in like situations, like causes are always followed by like effects: that kind of sequence makes experience possible, and therefore allows some sort of foresight of things to come, however limited it may be.

With Solon's statement of this fact, the political thought of Greece began.[24] He was concerned, of course, with the pathology of the social organism, which suffers definite morbid degenerations in consequence of anti-social excesses. With his religious outlook, he saw in this the punishment of divine justice, although according to his own conception of society as an organism the injurious effects of anti-social actions were brought about by a natural reaction. Since his time Athens had become a great

power, and there was a huge new field of political experience—
the mutual relations of various independent states, or what we
term foreign politics. The first Athenian to make use of it
was Themistocles, whom Thucydides, in a few memorable sentences,[25] describes as being virtually a new type of man. Essential elements in his description of his character are foresight and
clear judgment—the qualities which Thucydides intended his
own book to inspire in posterity. His repeated emphasis on the
same principles throughout his work proves that he took this
purpose very seriously: so far from its being merely a superficial
layer of sophistic rationalism,[26] which we must cut away in order
to recover the historian's true self, his effort to reach political
knowledge by experience constitutes his real greatness. The true
nature of history, he believed, was that it furnished political experience, not that it embodied any religious, ethical, or philosophical idea.[27] For him, politics form a world governed by its
own immanent laws, which are understood only by examining
historical facts not in isolation but as parts of a continuous
process. His far-reaching insight into the nature and laws of political events makes Thucydides far superior to all other ancient
historians. It could be achieved only by an Athenian of the great
age of Athens—the age which produced, to name two essentially
different creations of the same intellectual type, the art of
Phidias and the Platonic *idea*. His conception of the knowledge
which understands political events cannot be better described
than in the famous words of the *Novum Organum* [28] in which
Bacon contrasts his new scientific ideal with scholasticism:
*Scientia et potentia humana in idem coincidunt, quia ignoratio
causae destituit effectum. Natura enim non nisi parendo vincitur.
Et quod in contemplatione instar causae est, id in operatione
instar regulae est.*

The peculiarity of Thucydides' political philosophy, in contrast to that of the sophists or Plato on the one hand and to
Solon's religious conception of the state on the other, is that he
preaches no general doctrine: there is no *fabula docet* in his
work. He brings home the logic of politics by the direct narrative of events. He could do so only because he was treating a
very special subject: the Peloponnesian War displayed with
unique clarity and compression the connexion between real cause

and real effect in politics. It would be impossible to apply his conception of history to any series of events chosen at random: it would be the same as expecting any period to produce something like Attic tragedy or the philosophy of Plato. Even the bare factual description of a great event, however important it might be, would not satisfy his purpose as a political philosopher. He needed a special opportunity to disclose the intellectual, the universal aspect of events. The numerous speeches which punctuate his book are particularly characteristic of his narrative method: for they are above all else the medium through which he expresses his political ideas. In his explanation of the principles he follows in writing history, we should naturally expect him to say that he reproduces the speeches of important personalities as exactly as he records external facts. But he states that he does not copy them word by word: so the reader must not apply the same standard of exactitude to them as to the account of actual events. He simply means to reproduce their general sense (ξύμπασα γνώμη), but in details he makes each character say what *Thucydides himself* believes the situation demanded.[29] This is a very important device, explicable not by a historian's passion for exactitude but by a politician's wish to penetrate to the ultimate political ground for every event.

In the literal sense, that wish would be impossible to fulfil. In analysing any situation, one could never keep to what people had actually said of it, for that would often be simply a disguise for reality; one would always be bound to disclose their thoughts, which is impossible. But Thucydides certainly believed that one could recognize the motives followed by each party, and record them; and therefore he determined to make men explain their deepest motives and beliefs in a public speech to the assembly, or between four walls as in the Melian dialogue, exactly as he judged each party was bound to speak in accordance with its political attitude. So he addresses his readers as a Spartan, a Corinthian, an Athenian, or a Syracusan, now as Pericles, now as Alcibiades. This technique of constructing speeches to suit various characters may have been externally modelled on the Homeric epics, and to some slight extent on Herodotus.[30] But Thucydides used it on a grand scale, and to it we owe the fact that the Peloponnesian War, which was fought in the heyday of the intellectual life of Greece and was accompanied by a series of debates which plumbed the deepest problems of human life, appears to us to have been primarily a war of ideas and only secondarily a war of military forces. To do as some have done, and search these speeches for the relics of what was actually said on any occasion, is a task as hopeless as to try to recognize the features of particular models in the gods sculptured by Phidias. And even though Thucydides tried to obtain true information about the course of each debate he described, it is certain that many of the speeches in his book were never delivered, and that most of them were substantially different from his version of them. His belief that, after considering the peculiar circumstances of each case, he could set down what was demanded by the situation (τὰ δέοντα) was based on his conviction that every standpoint in such a conflict had its own inevitable logic, and that a man who watched the conflict from above could develop that logic adequately. Subjective as that may appear, it was what Thucydides held to be the objective truth of his speeches. And we cannot possibly appreciate it without doing justice to the political thinker concealed in the historian. As a language for these imaginary speeches he constructed a style which was the same for them all, which was always far loftier than the spoken Greek of his time, filled with antitheses that seem artificial to modern taste.[31] With their excessively difficult language striving to express equally difficult thoughts, contrasting strangely with a figurative style borrowed from sophistical rhetoricians, these speeches are the most direct expression of Thucydides' thought, which rivals the work of the greatest Greek philosophers both in obscurity and in profundity.

One of the finest examples of political thinking, in the sense implied by Thucydides in stating his own principles, occurs at the beginning of the History in his account of the causes of the war. Herodotus had begun his work with the causes of the conflict between Europe and Asia: he saw the problem as a question of war-guilt. The opposing parties in the Peloponnesian War were equally deeply exercised by the problem of war-guilt. But after the outbreak of the war had been discussed a hundred times in all its details, with no hope of fixing the responsibility for the conflict, and with reciprocal accusations by each party, Thucydides posed the problem in an entirely new way.[32] He distinguished between the 'true cause' of the war and the disputed points which were its occasion; and he concluded that the true cause was the incessantly growing power of Athens, which threatened Sparta. The conception of *cause* is borrowed from the language of medicine, as is clear from the word πρόφασις which Thucydides uses; for it was medical science which first made the scientific distinction between the real causes of an illness and its symptoms.[33] To transfer, as Thucydides did, a distinction made in organic science to the problem of the origins of the Peloponnesian War, was not merely a formal act. It meant that the problem had been fully objectified, by being taken out of the sphere of moral law. And thereby politics were marked off as an independent field of natural causality. According to Thucydides' description, the secret conflict between opposing forces finally led to an open crisis in Greek politics. It is somehow a relief to recognize objective causality as Thucydides does, for it raises the observer above the hateful conflict of parties and the ugly problem of guilt and innocence. And yet it is also rather oppressive, because it makes events which had once seemed to be voluntary actions, subject to moral judgment, appear to be the results of a long, continuous, inevitable process conditioned by a higher necessity.

Thucydides describes that phase of the process which preceded the outbreak of war—the growth of the Athenian power during the fifty years after the defeat of Persia—in a famous excursus [34] which he embodies in his account of the immediate preliminaries to the conflict. He is justified in adopting this peculiar structural device by the fact that here he was *compelled* to go beyond the chronological limits of his book. Besides, as he himself says, his short sketch of the rise of the Athenian empire is valuable in itself, since before his time there was no adequate description of that important period.[35] Not only that. One has the impression that this excursus on the pentecontaetia, and everything that Thucydides says of the true causes of the war, were inserted in his account of the preliminaries of the war after it was written, and that he had originally confined himself to describing the diplomatic and military events which directly preceded the outbreak. The impression is created not only by the remarkable structure of this section, but also by the fact that Thucydides must have described the beginning of the war in his very first draft, whereas the excursus on the growth of the Athenian empire mentions the destruction of the walls (404), and cannot therefore have assumed its present form till after the war was over.[36] And his description of the true causes of the war, which is supported by the excursus, is obviously the result of lifelong reflection on the problem: it is the work of Thucydides' maturity. In early life he dealt much more with simple facts; later he became more and more a political philosopher, and more and more boldly grasped the problem as a whole, with all its inherent connexions and its own logical necessity.[37] The effect of the book in the form which we have essentially depends on the fact that it presents one single political thesis of very large scope, which is clearly expressed at the very beginning in Thucydides' account of the true causes of the war.

It would be an unhistorical *petitio principii* to assume that a 'real historian' would have clearly grasped the true causes of the war at its outset, recognizing it in the Thucydidean sense as a long-developed higher necessity. The most remarkable analogy to this is Leopold von Ranke's *History of Prussia*. In the second edition, published after the Franco-Prussian war of 1870, he saw the historical significance of Prussia's development in an entirely new light. He himself stated that it was not till then that he worked out his far-reaching general ideas—which, in the preface to the second edition, he apologizes to his fellow-scholars for expounding, since they deal not with facts but with the political interpretation of history. These new generalizations chiefly affected his account of the genesis of the Prussian state, which he entirely rewrote and made essentially broader and more profound. It was in the same way, then, that Thucydides, after the war ended, rehandled the beginning of his work which described the origins of the war.

After realizing that the power of Athens was the true cause of the war, he attempted to discuss its inner implications. In his account of the preliminaries of the war it is notable that he added the excursus on the *external* development of Athens merely as an appendix to his marvellous description of the conference in Sparta at which the Spartans, passionately urged on by their confederates, decided to declare war. It is true that war was not actually declared until a later general assembly of the Peloponnesian league: but Thucydides with unerring insight observed that the first unofficial meeting, attended only by a few Lacedaemonian allies complaining against Athens, was supremely important: he marked it out as the decisive moment, and signalized it by reporting not less than four speeches made by participants [38]—a greater number than occurs at one time anywhere else in the book. The meeting was chiefly concerned with the complaints of the Lacedaemonian allies against Athens; yet, according to Thucydides, the Spartans were not chiefly impelled to declare war by their allies' arguments, but by their own fear of a still greater extension of Athenian power in Greece.[39] In a real debate, this could not have been stated so openly, but Thucydides boldly passes over the problems of international law which must have been the chief subject of discussion, and, out of all the speeches delivered by the allies, records only the closing speech of the Corinthian delegation.[40] They are the deadliest enemies of the Athenians, because they are the second greatest commercial power in Greece, and therefore their natural rivals. They see Athens with the clear vision of hatred; and Thucydides makes them persuade the hesitating Spartans to a final decision by making a comparison between Sparta and the energetic adventurous Athenians. They describe the Athenian national character more impressively than any Athenian orator at a public festival—than even Thucydides himself in Pericles' funeral speech, which is a free composition of his own, and from which he borrowed a number of points for the Corinthian speech.[41] No one can seriously doubt that the latter was not really delivered by the Corinthian embassy in Sparta, but was essentially an invention of Thucydides himself. To write a speech in which Athens is praised by one enemy before another was a feat of the highest rhetorical skill.[42] But also it had a double historical purpose: its immediate aim was to describe the agitation which led to the war, and its higher aim was to analyse the *psychological basis* of the rise of Athens. Against the background of Spartan dullness and indolence, old-fashioned respectability and narrow-minded conservatism, the Corinthians describe the Athenian temperament with mingled envy, hate and admiration: restless energy, marvellous *élan* in planning and in acting, elastic versatility, capable of meeting any situation and not quelled but encouraged to new activity by failures—with these qualities the Athenian nation takes over and transforms everything that

comes within its range. Of course, this is not moral praise of
Athenian virtues: it is a description of the psychical energy
which explains the amazing progress of Athens in the last half-
century or so before the war.

Thucydides now boldly counterbalances this description by
another speech of the same kind: it is delivered by an Athenian
embassy while the Spartans are deliberating whether or not to
declare war; and the scene is naturally changed from a diplomatic conference to a special public assembly called to hear the
Athenians.[43] The external motive given by Thucydides for the
delivery of the speech is, perhaps intentionally, rather obscure.
Speech and counterspeech are not addressed to the Spartan government but to the public, and they combine to make a powerfully effective unity. To the psychological analysis made by the
Corinthians the Athenians now add a *historical analysis* of the
rise of Athens from the beginning to the present day. But they
do not describe the external stages of her triumphant progress—
that is done in the excursus a little later.[44] They analyse the internal development of the motives which impelled Athens to develop her power so fully and so logically.

Thus Thucydides gives three different views of the same problem, all leading to the same result. The Athenian ambassador's
speech on the historical necessity which compelled Athens to
develop her power is a justification of that power, on the grand
scale of which Thucydides alone is capable. They are Thucydides' own ideas, and he could not have worked them out till after
the fall of Athens, when he reached the painful height of his
political experience; but here he puts them in the mouth of the
anonymous Athenian envoy, before the beginning of the war, as
a kind of prophetic knowledge. In Thucydides' opinion, then, the
power of Athens was based on the unforgettable part she played
in preserving the political existence and liberty of the Greek
people by her prowess in the victories of Marathon and Salamis.[45] After the will of her allies had converted this distinction
into a real hegemony, she was compelled by fear of the envy of
Sparta, now thrust from her traditional supremacy, to establish
more firmly and permanently the strength she had won, to guard
against the defection of her allies by centralizing the control of
the league more and more, and thus gradually to thrust her

originally independent allies into subjection. As well as the motive of fear, she was governed by ambition and self-interest.[46]

That was the course along which the power of Athens was compelled [47] to develop, by the immutable laws of human nature. The Spartans now believed they were representing justice against selfishness and aggrandisement, but if they ever managed to destroy Athens and take over her power, the sympathy of Greece would soon swing away from them, and prove that power may change its owners, but not its political character, its methods, and its effect.[48] From the first day of the war, public opinion held Athens to be the embodiment of tyranny, and Sparta the protector of liberty.[49] Thucydides thinks this perfectly natural in the circumstances; but he sees that the parts of tyrant and liberator did not correspond with any permanent moral quality in these states, but were simply masks which would one day be interchanged, to the astonishment of the beholder, when the balance of power was altered. This is unmistakably the voice of experience—the experience which Greece was to acquire from the tyrannical rule of Sparta, the 'liberator', after the fall of Athens.[50]

But Xenophon, the continuator of Thucydides' work, shows how far most of the men of that age were from understanding the law which is immanent in all political power. With a simple faith in moral justice, he held that both the fall of the Spartan hegemony and the fall of Athens were the vengeance of God upon the hybris of man.[51] To contrast that with Thucydides' analysis of the facts is to appreciate his vast intellectual superiority. It was only by penetrating to the immanent necessity of the events which led to the outbreak of war that he reached the fully objective view which he had striven to attain. That applies to his judgment of Sparta as well as to his judgment of Athens. For, just as he considered that the Athenian progress to power was necessary and inevitable,[52] so he saw, with a counter-emphasis which can hardly be overestimated, that Sparta was *compelled* [53] by fear of Athens to declare war. Neither here nor anywhere else in Thucydides are we justified in saying that his phraseology 'happens to be vague'. I believe it has not yet been observed that he uses the same word of the second outbreak of war after the interruption of a few years' uneasy peace: after a period of latent hostility, he says, the opponents were *compelled* to resume fighting.[54] The word occurs in what is called his second preface, where, after describing the Archidamian war, he proposes the revolutionary idea that both wars were to be regarded as one great war. This idea forms a great unity with his conception of the inevitable necessity of the war which is expressed in the aetiological section. Together, they are the work of his political insight at its last and highest stage of development.

With the discussion of the unity of the conflict, we pass from its causes to the war itself. His description of it shows the same intensive penetration of facts by political thought. Greek tragedy of the fifth century is distinguished from later drama by its possession of a chorus whose thoughts and emotions constantly reflect the development of the plot and emphasize its importance. In the same way Thucydides' historical narrative is distinguished from that of his successors by the fact that all his facts are accompanied and clarified by constant intellectual activity: which, however, does not appear as a tedious running commentary, but is usually translated into intellectual events, by the speeches,[55] and is thus put directly and vividly before the thoughtful reader. These speeches are an inexhaustible mine of instruction, but here we cannot even attempt to describe their wealth of political ideas. Thucydides puts these ideas partly as epigrams, partly as logical inferences or subtle distinctions; and he is very fond of placing together two or more opposing speeches on the same topic—the device of 'antilogy' used by the sophists. Thus he exposes, through the speeches of King Archidamus and the ephor Sthenelaidas, the two leading trends in Spartan policy just before the outbreak of war—the conservatives, anxious for peace, and their opponents, the war-party. Similarly he embodies the two attitudes of the Athenian people to the proposed Sicilian expedition in the speeches of Nicias and Alcibiades, who were to be its joint leaders, but were diametrically opposed in their views of its wisdom. In describing the revolt of Mytilene Thucydides uses the opportunity to explain the league-policies held by the moderate and the extreme parties in Athens, by reporting the opposing speeches of Cleon and Diodotus before the assembly, and thereby to illustrate the terrible difficulties involved in treating the allies decently in time of war. And in the speeches delivered after the fall of Plataea by the Plataeans and the Thebans before the Spartan executive commission (which pretended for the sake of impressing the world that the Plataeans had a fair trial, though the judges were the allies of the accusers), he demonstrates the fact that war and justice cannot coexist.

Thucydides' work provides many illustrations of the problem provided by party shibboleths—the problem of the relation between ideology and fact in politics. The Spartans, as champions of Liberty and Justice, are bound to play up their rôle by uttering streams of sanctimonious moral sentiment, which usually harmonizes with their own interest so neatly that they need not ask themselves where one ends and the other begins. The position of the Athenians is more difficult; so they are forced to appeal to National Honour. Cynical as that appeal may seem, it is often a good deal more sympathetic than the cant uttered by the 'Liberators', of whom Brasidas is the most amiable and the least hypocritical.

The problem of the neutrality of weaker states during a war between great powers is dealt with from two different points of view—from that of justice and from that of political realism—in the speeches delivered at Melos and at Camarina. The Sicilians, torn between their fear of foreign enemies and their hatred of the hegemony of the greatest Sicilian state, and really praying for a plague on both their houses, embody the problem of uniting in a common danger states which are separated by opposing interests. The choice between a victorious peace and a peace of mutual agreement is raised after Sparta's misadventure at Pylos, which makes her suddenly anxious for peace, while the Athenians, long sick of war, immediately refuse any offers of conciliation. The psychical problems of war which affect strategy are discussed in the addresses delivered by various generals to their armies, and those which affect political life are treated in several great speeches by leading statesmen: for example, Pericles discusses the war-weariness and pessimism of the Athenians.[56] Thucydides also describes the immense political effect of the elemental experience of the plague, which broke down morale and inflicted incalculable loss on Athens; and after picturing the horrors of revolution in Corcyra, he explains the moral collapse of society and the transvaluation of all social standards by the long war and the furious class-conflict.[57] Obviously his description is meant to be a parallel to that of the plague, and the paral-

lelism is strengthened by his coldly analytical treatment of both
phenomena: just as in discussing the origins of the war, he does
not preach like a moralist, but examines, probes, and diagnoses
like a doctor. He believes that his account of the collapse of
public morality is a contribution to his description of the pathology of war.

This brief summary is enough to show that Thucydides covers
all the great political problems which arise during a war. The
occasions he chooses for discussing them are selected with the
greatest care, and are certainly not always suggested by the
normal flow of events. He treats similar facts in very different
ways—sometimes deliberately placing the cruelties and agonies
of war in the foreground, and sometimes passing over even
greater horrors with a dispassionate mention, because it is
enough to illustrate that side of war by a few examples.[58]

In his actual narrative of the war, as in his account of its
origins, the problem of the rise and maintenance of political
power is central—in fact, most of the separate questions mentioned above are connected with it. Thucydides does not treat
it from the standpoint of an ordinary power-mad statesman:
naturally enough, considering his political insight. He regards
it expressly as a part of all human life, which is not wholly governed by the lust for power; and it is significant that the
Athenians themselves, the most blatant and ruthless lovers of
power, recognize justice as the highest standard within their
own empire, and are proud of being a modern constitutional
state based on justice instead of an oriental despotism. This is
stated in the speech in which the Athenian envoy defends the
foreign policy of imperial Athens before the Spartan assembly.[59]
Thucydides considers that the degeneration of class-conflict
within the state into a universal struggle of all against all is a
grave sickness in the body politic.[60] But in the relation of one
state to another it is different. For, although there too there are
compacts governed by justice, the final arbiter is might, not
right. If the opponents are roughly equal in strength, their relationship is called war; if one of them is vastly superior to the
other, it is called domination. Thucydides illustrates the latter
situation by the example [61] of the little neutral island Melos,
which was overpowered by Athens with her command of the sea.

In itself the event was unimportant; yet it was in the minds of the Greeks as much as a century later, and still made them hate Athens,[62] whereas during the war it utterly destroyed what scant sympathy the Athenian cause had once inspired.[63]

This is a classical example of Thucydides' technique: quite independently of the factual importance of the event, he uses it to symbolize a general problem and expands his narrative into a masterpiece of political thinking. Here he uses the dialogue-form—a sophistic device which occurs nowhere else in his book—to show the two opponents parrying argument by argument, question by answer, and to eternalize the painful conflict of might and right in all its inescapable necessity.[64] It is impossible to doubt that he composed this debate (which is ostensibly held behind closed doors, in the Melian council offices) with entire freedom of invention, to express the conflict of two irreconcilable principles. The brave Melians soon see that they cannot appeal to the Athenians' sense of justice, because the Athenians recognize no standard but their own political advantage.[65] They therefore try to prove that it is advantageous for Athens to observe some moderation in using her superior power, because the day may come when even Athens will have to appeal to the sense of human decency.[66] The Athenians, however, unterrified by this warning, explain that their interests compel them to annex the little island, because the world will interpret its continued neutrality as a sign of the weakness of the Athenian empire.[67] They observe that they have no interest in destroying the Melians, and warn them not to assume the inappropriate rôle of heroes: the old chivalrous code has no validity in modern imperialist policy. They caution the Melians not to trust blindly in God and the Spartans. God is always on the side of the big battalions, as nature constantly shows; and even the Spartans do not eschew what men call 'disgraceful' unless it suits their interest to do so.[68]

By making the Athenians justify the right of the stronger through the law of nature, and transform God from the guardian of justice into the pattern of all earthly authority and force, Thucydides gives the realistic policy of Athens the depth and validity of a philosophical doctrine. The Athenians are endeavouring to abolish the conflict between their policy and the forces of religion and morality—the forces which their weaker opponents hope to use to conquer them. Here Thucydides shows the power-policy of Athens logically developed to its utmost extreme and fully understood by its defenders. The very nature of the form he chooses to expound the conflict shows that it can never reach a final decision, for the strength of the sophistic debates (which the Melian dialogue imitates) lay not in finding the solution to a problem but in stating both sides as clearly as possible. But his attitude throughout the book makes it impossible that he should here be playing the moralist in disguise. What is really new about the Melian episode is this: it is the first frank statement of the principle that might is right—a principle which was strange to Greek thought in earlier ages and was first exploited in the fifth century. The right of the strong is now opposed, as a sort of natural right or natural law, to the current moral code, τὸ νόμῳ δίκαιον: which means that now the principle of force forms a realm of its own, with laws of its own, neither abolishing the traditional *nomos* nor admitting its superiority, but simply distinct and separate from it. We must not assume Plato's philosophical attitude when discussing Thucydides' discovery of this problem in the fifth-century conception of the state, and expect him to apply the standards of the Idea of the Good to the hostile Greek nations. In his highest intellectual achievements, such as the Melian dialogue, Thucydides remained a pupil of the sophists; [69] but by using their theoretical antinomies to describe historical fact he gave his description such tenseness and such conflict that it seems to embody all the *aporiai* of Plato. [70]

Now we must turn to the actual course taken by Athenian imperialist policy during the war. We need not deal with all its variations and fluctuations; we shall choose the critical moment when it reached its zenith, the expedition against Sicily in 415. Thucydides' description of the expedition is without dispute the masterpiece of all his narrative, but it is also a palmary instance of his political insight. From the very first book of his History, the expedition is foreshadowed. The Athenians are recommended to accept the alliance of the strong Corcyraean fleet, before the war begins, by an emphatic hint that whoever holds Corcyra is master of the sea-route to Sicily. [71] The first Athenian mission, to Sicily, with a few ships, appears to be unimportant;

yet shortly after it (424) Thucydides makes the great Syracusan statesman, Hermocrates, at a conference in Gela, attempt
to smooth over the disputes between the various Sicilian states,
so as to unite them under Syracusan leadership in order to meet
a future attack by Athens. The arguments he adduces are those
which he later brings forward at Camarina during the invasion
of Sicily.[72] There is no doubt that Thucydides added these preliminary hints after the end of the Sicilian expedition, when he
was composing his account of it. He thought the only Sicilian
politician with any real foresight was Hermocrates, who saw
long beforehand that the danger would come because it *must*
come. The Athenians, he realized, could not help extending their
power to Sicily, and no one could blame them if some Sicilian
state invited them to intervene. (This shows that even outside
Athens people had learnt to think in terms of practical politics.)
But although he saw the attractions of the Sicilian adventure
from the Athenian point of view, much was to happen before
the Athenians could even consider the idea.

The idea was seriously taken up in the years after the peace
of Nicias, which was so unexpectedly favourable to Athens.
Having scarcely recovered from the Archidamian war, the
Athenians received a request from Segesta for help in its war
with Selinus. It is the most dramatic moment in Thucydides'
whole story—the moment in the Athenian assembly when Alcibiades, in face of all the warnings of the conservative and pacific
Nicias, expounds his staggering plan for the conquest of Sicily
and the mastery of all Greece, and explains that the expansion
of a great empire like that of Athens cannot be 'rationed out';
its possessors can maintain it only by extending it further, because every pause means the danger of collapsing.[73] Thucydides
means us to remember all that was said before the war, about
the necessity of extending Athenian power without cessation,[74]
and about the restless, fearless, limitless optimism and enterprise
of the Athenian character.[75] Alcibiades is a brilliant incarnation
of that national quality. That explains why he had the power to
charm and to persuade the masses, though he was hated for his
arrogant and domineering behaviour in private life. In this singular concatenation of circumstances, in the fact that the only
leader who could bring Athens safely through the ambitious
enterprise was one who was hated and envied by the Athenian

people, Thucydides sees one of the chief reasons for the fall of Athens.[76] For she could not carry out Alcibiades' Sicilian adventure successfully, when the man who inspired and directed it was banished shortly after the expedition set out. Thus, the reader feels that the greatest effort ever made by Athens, which through the loss of fleet and army and generals shook the state to its foundations, was a fateful peripeteia, although it did not determine the final catastrophe.[77]

Thucydides' description of the Sicilian expedition has been called a tragedy. Yet it certainly does not pretend, like the Hellenistic histories, to rival tragedy in its aesthetic and emotional effects, and move the reader to pity and terror.[78] It would be safer to point to the fact that Thucydides himself once mentions the hybris which inspires the mob to bold enterprises,[79] and is clearly thinking there of adventures like the expedition. But even then he is less interested in the moral or religious aspects of the fact than in the political problem involved. It is absolutely wrong to imagine that he thought the Sicilian disaster was God's punishment for Athenian aggrandisement, for he was very far from believing that power is a bad thing in itself. From his point of view the Sicilian expedition was worse than a sin. Its failure was due to a political mistake—or rather a chain of mistakes. As a political philosopher, he held that the mob was always inevitably inclined to hybris: that is, to making illusionary plans unsupported by facts. It was, he thought, the duty of its leaders to guide that impulse correctly.[80] Neither in the outcome of the Sicilian expedition nor in the final defeat of Athens did he see the working of a dark historical necessity. We can imagine a type of pure historical reasoning which would object to interpret these two disasters as merely the results of false calculation, or tricks of chance, rather than the end of a necessary logical process. Hegel has sharply reproved the pettiness and assurance of the armchair historians who see every mistake after the event, and who could always have done much better themselves. He would probably have said that the defeat of Athens in the Peloponnesian war was due not to separate mistakes but a profound historical necessity, because the generation of Alcibiades, in which both the mob and its leader were ruled by the individualism which overleaps itself, was both spiritually and materially incapable of surmounting the difficulties of the war. Thucydides thought differently. As a statesman, he viewed the Peloponnesian war as a definite problem for the intelligence to solve. In solving it, Athens made a number of vitally important mistakes, which he now observed and diagnosed from a lofty critical standpoint. He believed that mistakes could and should be recognized after the event, and that to reject the possibility of doing so would be to deny the existence of political experience. His task was made easier by an important fact: he did not simply use his own feeling of *knowing better,* as a standard, but took his standard from the great statesman who persuaded Athens to undertake the war and who (Thucydides firmly believed) would have won it— Pericles himself.[81]

Thucydides believed that the outcome of the Peloponnesian War was almost entirely dependent on the leaders of the conflicting peoples, and that the generalship of both armies and navies was far less important. This is shown by the famous passage in the second book,[82] where, after recording the speech with which Pericles consoled the nation, depressed by the war and the plague, and heartened it for further resistance, he contrasts the great statesman's career with those of all who succeeded him as leaders of the Athenian people. In peace and war, he writes, Pericles kept Athens safe as long as he was at its head, and guided it along the narrow line of moderation between the two radical extremes. He alone correctly understood the task which Athens faced in her war with the Peloponnesian alliance. His policy was to undertake no great enterprises, to look after the navy, not to attempt to extend the empire during the war, and not to burden the state with any unnecessary risk. But his successors (says Thucydides bitterly) did the exact opposite of all this. From personal ambition and personal greed, they made enormous plans that had nothing to do with the war, and which would bring them glory if they succeeded, but would weaken the country's resistance if they failed.[83] This is obviously an indictment of Alcibiades, who is described in the same way by his cautious and incorruptible opponent Nicias during the debate on the Sicilian expedition.[84] But that debate is meant to show the reader that it is not enough to possess correct insight and high principles. If it were, Nicias (whom Thucydides describes with warm personal sympathy) would have been an ideal leader. But,

as a matter of fact, Alcibiades had far more real leadership than
Nicias, though he guided Athens into danger and did nothing
which would not profit himself. Yet he was able to 'control the
people', as Thucydides says on a subsequent occasion,[85] when he
eulogizes Alcibiades' service to Athens at the moment when civil
war was threatening.

Similarly, in his character-sketch of Pericles, Thucydides emphasizes his influence on the people and his ability to 'lead it
rather than be led by it'.[86] What made him superior to Alcibiades and all the rest was the additional fact that he was finan-
cially incorruptible, for that gave him the authority to tell the
truth instead of saying what the public wanted to hear. He
always kept the reins in his own hands: when the mob tried to
kick over the traces he could frighten them and control them,
and when they were discouraged he heartened them. Therefore
Athens under Pericles was 'nominally a democracy, but actually
a monarchy under the foremost man': [87] it was the monarchy of
superior political ability. After the death of Pericles, Athens
never had another such ruler. All his successors tried to imitate
him, but none of them could acquire so much influence as he had,
even temporarily, without flattering the mob and pandering to
its passions. According to Thucydides, it was because there was
no other man who could eliminate the influence of the people and
its mob-instincts, surmount the democratic constitution, and
govern like a king, that the Sicilian expedition failed [88]—quite
apart from the fact that Pericles would never have undertaken it
in the first place because it was directly opposed to his defensive
strategy. For, in itself, the power of Athens was quite adequate
to defeat Syracuse (so far Alcibiades' estimate was correct) if
only party-jealousies within the state had not overthrown its brilliant leader. Even after the loss of the Sicilian war, Athens maintained itself for ten years more, until it was so enfeebled by con-
tinual dissension that it could resist no longer.[89] The quintessence of Thucydides' belief is, in so many words, that under the
leadership of Pericles Athens would easily have won the Peloponnesian War.[90]

The picture of Pericles which he here displays in such a clear
light, by contrast with later politicians, is more than the portrait
of a much-admired personality. All his rivals and successors
faced the same task of guiding Athens in the fight for its life,

and only he was equal to it. Thucydides has not the least intention of describing whatever happened to be Pericles' personal character—as the Attic comedians did, at least by caricaturing it. His Pericles is the model leader and statesman, with only the traits which are appropriate to a political figure. If *we* realize that fact only in the last stages of the war, then the summary of Pericles' career after his last appearance in Thucydides' history is enough to show that Thucydides himself realized it in the same way, and after the same experience.[91] He saw Pericles from the distance which enables us to recognize greatness. It is difficult to determine whether the policy he attributes to him was formulated in exactly the same way by Pericles himself, or (for instance) Thucydides made Pericles advise the Athenians to refrain from extending their territory because he knew Pericles' actual policy in that respect and had seen the evil effects of its reversal by his successors. But it seems quite clear that it was only after the end of the war that he could have looked back and described Pericles' political wisdom almost entirely by pointing out that he did *not* make the mistakes of his successors. That applies even to his rather remarkable praise of Pericles for taking no money and making no profit out of politics.[92] Thucydides does make him deliver a speech at the outbreak of war, and say, 'No annexations! no unnecessary risks!' [93] But even in that passage we can hear the voice of the historian who had seen the final defeat, for Pericles says, 'I fear our own mistakes far more than the strategy of our enemies.' When Thucydides says that Pericles' sound foreign policy was based on his firm position in the internal government of Athens, he is thinking exclusively of the comparative insecurity of Alcibiades. For though he assessed internal policy chiefly by its effect on foreign policy, he was led to recognize that sound internal government, of the old type described by Solon, was enormously important for the successful prosecution of a war, by observing the fatal effects which ensued when the Athenians rejected Alcibiades' authority at the moment when he was about to lead them to great successes abroad.

Other features in this portrait of Pericles as the ideal statesman—which we have approached through Thucydides' concluding character-sketch of him—are provided by his speeches. The first [94] expounds the strategy of the war, and the last [95] shows us the leader who still controls the nation even at the most critical juncture. The close connexion between these two speeches and the summary of Pericles' character allows us to assume that the entire portrait of Pericles, speeches and all, was worked up as a unity late in Thucydides' career as a historian; indeed that is generally admitted in the case of the third and greatest speech,[96] the funeral oration over the bodies of the Athenians who fell in the first year of the war.

The funeral speech, more than any other speech in Thucydides, is a free composition by the historian himself. It has been interpreted as Thucydides' own epitaph on the past glories of Athens—rightly, inasmuch as death alone has the power to display the pure ideal of that which has passed away. In the conventional funerary orations over fallen Athenian soldiers, it was customary to give a brilliant account of their prowess. Thucydides carries this further, and makes the speech an idealized picture of the entire Athenian state. He could not allow anyone but Pericles to deliver it, for he was the only statesman who had the lofty intellect and character that made him worthy to expound the spirit of Athens. In the age of Thucydides, politics was fast becoming a specialty of careerists and climbers, thirsting for power and success. That is exactly what made Pericles superior to Cleon, and to Alcibiades too, in Thucydides' eyes—he had conceived an ideal of the state and of personal character, which gave all his work a real purpose. No translation can rival Thucydides' masterly ease in coping with his difficult task: abandoning all the trivialities of formal oratory, he describes the contemporary city-state, with the superb practical energy of its imperialist policy and the indescribable variety of its spiritual and vital force, so as to weld it all into one great unity.

A man like Thucydides, who understood the more recent developments of the city-state, must have seen many complexities in the social structure that did not enter into political ideals (such as Solon's *eunomia* and Cleisthenes' *isonomia*) which were created in an age of greater simplicity and still honoured in a later epoch. Before he wrote, there had been no language adequate to express the concepts which were part of the nature of the new state. But he was accustomed to envisage the relation of one state to another as the natural and necessary conflict of opposing principles; and he discovered that the same conflict was the basic principle which governed the hidden structure of Athenian society. This is well exemplified in his view of the character of the Athenian constitution. He considers it to be an original creation, copied from nothing else, but rather worthy of imitation by other countries. This view anticipates the later philosophical theory that the best possible constitution was a mixed one.[97] In his opinion, the Athenian democracy is not the realization of the mechanical ideal of external equality, which some worship as the height of justice and others condemn as the depth of injustice. That is shown by his description of Pericles as the 'first citizen', who really ruled the state.[98] His remark, in that connexion, that Athens under Pericles was 'nominally a democracy' is converted into a generalization in the funeral speech, in the mouth of the foremost man himself. In Athens, says he, every man is alike before the law, but in politics the aristocracy of talent is supreme.[99] Logically, that implies the principle that if one man is supremely valuable and important he will be recognized as the ruler of the state.[100] This conception would, on the one hand, allow that the political activity of each individual has some value for the community; yet it also admits the fact—recognized in Thucydides even by the radical demagogue Cleon—that the people alone cannot possibly govern a large and difficult empire.[101] Thucydides considers that Periclean Athens was a happy solution of a problem which was becoming acute under the complete mob-rule [102] of the decades following the death of Pericles—the problem of the relationship which ought to exist between a superior individual and the political community.

History has shown that this solution depends on the appearance of a genius to lead the state—an accident as uncommon in a democracy as in other types of state—and that even a democracy is not safe from the dangers of being leaderless. Nevertheless, the Athenian democracy offered a leader like Pericles infinite opportunities to organize the energies of the individual citizens (which he so splendidly eulogizes [103]) and to employ them as active forces in politics. That is what ruined the tyrannies of the fourth century—they did not manage to find any solutions for that problem since they did not want to accept that which the Periclean democracy had furnished for its leader. The despot Dionysius did not really succeed in inducing the citizens of Syracuse to co-operate in governing it, in such a way that (as Pericles advised) every individual should divide his life between his private vocation and his public duties; that was impossible in the absence of some active interest and true insight into the life of the state.

Politeia means not only the constitution of the state but the entire life of the state as far as it is conditioned by the constitution. Even though the constitution of Athens was not like the Spartan discipline, which regulated every detail of the citizen's daily existence, the influence of the state was an all-pervading spirit which deeply affected the life of every Athenian. In modern Greek, *politeuma* means *culture*—perhaps the last vestige of the ancient conjunction of life and politics. Therefore, Pericles' description of the Athenian politeia covers the entire content of private and public life: economics, morals, culture and education. Only when we conceive it with such fullness and concreteness do we realize that Thucydides' ideal of the state is no mere power-machine, but something rich in colour, shape, reality. It springs from Pericles' own ideal of the Athenian politeia, and without that living content it would be imperfect. The power of which Thucydides speaks is never simply *pleonexia,* mechanical and spiritless greed. The remarkable composite character which marks all the expressions of the Athenian spirit—literary, artistic, philosophical and moral—reappears in Pericles' conception of the state: he deliberately praises a synthesis of the rigidly communal outlook of the Spartan armed camp, and the Ionian principle of the economic and intellectual freedom of each individual citizen. Thucydides does not conceive the new type of state as a static thing, the rigid legal structure idolized in the early *eunomia*. But constitutionally and economically and spiritually he holds it to be a sort of Heraclitean harmony of radical and inevitable opposites, maintaining itself through its tension and its equilibrium. He therefore makes Pericles describe it as the interaction of delicately balanced opposites—self-support and enjoyment of the world's products, labour and recreation, business and holiday, spirit and ethos, thought and energy.[104]

That was the ideal which the great leader of the Athenians expounded, with the full majesty of language, in order to make them at the critical juncture fully aware of the supreme values for which they were fighting, and to turn them into passionate 'lovers' of their country. But Thucydides did not mean it to be valid for the Athenians alone. Spiritually as well as politically, he envisaged Athens as the centre of a historical sphere of influence. He saw it as exercising a vast intellectual stimulus, not only on itself but on the entire Greek world. 'To sum up, I call the whole city of Athens the school of Greek culture,' τῆς Ἑλλάδος παίδευσιν.[105] In this realization of the spiritual hegemony of Athens—a realization fully worthy of the greatest Greek historian—Thucydides' creative insight first recognized the fact that Attic culture was to have a far-reaching historical influence, and the problems which that fact involved. Thereby the Greek ideal of culture, which had attained a new breadth and sublimity in the age of Pericles, was charged with the utmost possible historical life and meaning. It became the complete expression of the noble influence which the Athenian people and the Athenian state exercised through their intellectual and spiritual life upon the rest of their world, and which led other nations to live and to create as they had done. The highest justification of the political ambitions of Athens, even after their defeat, was the ideal of paideia, through which the Athenian spirit found its greatest consolation—the assurance of its own immortality.

NOTES

INTRODUCTION

1. See my introductory essay in the collection *Altertum und Gegenwart* (2nd ed., Leipzig 1920), 11 (reprinted in *Humanistische Reden und Vortraege*, Berlin 1937).

2. On the following discussion, see my essay *Platos Stellung im Aufbau der griechischen Bildung* (Berlin 1928), and especially the exposition of principles in the first part: *Kulturidee und Griechentum*, p. 7 ff. in *Die Antike* IV, 1 (reprinted in *Humanistische Reden und Vortraege*, 1937).

3. The classical passage is Cicero, *De oratore* 7-10, which derives from a Hellenistic source.

4. See my essay *Antike und Humanismus* (Leipzig 1925), 13 (reprinted in *Humanistische Reden und Vortraege*, 1937).

5. πλάττειν, Plato, *Rep.* 377b, *Laws* 671c, and elsewhere.

6. For the English word *culture*, see *infra* Book II, chap. 3, pp. 303, 313. See especially notes 5 and 6 of the chapter Nobility and Areté.

7. See Gellius, *Noct. Att.* XIII, 17.

8. See my *Die griechische Staatsethik im Zeitalter des Plato;* also my lectures *Die geistige Gegenwart der Antike* (Berlin 1929), 38 ff. (*Die Antike* v, 185 ff.)

BOOK ONE

CHAPTER I

NOBILITY AND ARETÉ

1. There are many passages in Homer indicating the existence of these rules of respect for the gods, for parents, and for strangers. Although they do not seem to occur there as a unified tripartite code, Homer often mentions or illustrates one or another of these commandments. Hesiod, *Works and Days* 183 ff., lists among other symptoms the violation of the rights of the stranger and of family ties, together with disrespect for the gods, as characteristic signs of the advent of the iron age. Aeschylus, *Suppl.* 698-709, in the long and solemn prayer of the Danaids to Zeus Xenios to bless their benefactors, the people of Argos, incorporates at the end a prayer for the maintenance of the threefold respect for gods, parents, and strangers. This addition appears as something distinctly individual, whereas the rest of the prayer is rather typical in form, as can be shown by comparing it with the analogous prayer of the Eumenides (*Eum.* 916 ff.) for the city of Athens, or the old Roman prayer at the offering of the Suovetaurilia in Cato's *De Agri Cultura,* in which the prayer for respect of gods, parents, and strangers is missing. In the *Eumenides* the same threefold commandment is referred to in the solemn protest of the Erinyes against the violation of their rights, 490 ff. and particularly 534-549. There it is respect for parents (τοκέων σέβας) which is threatened by Orestes' matricide, whereas in the *Suppliants* the right of the stranger is at stake. In both passages respect for gods, parents, and strangers is regarded as the sum total of the θεσμοί of Diké. (See *Suppl.* 708, *Eum.* 491, 511, 539.) Paley's commentary to the *Suppliants* provides still further

parallels. Euripides knows the same tripartite code, for he gives (*Antiope* frg. 38) only a more modernized and more rational form of the old rule to honour the stranger when he adds to the respect for gods and parents that for the 'common Hellenic nomos', i.e. the unwritten law concerning the treatment of citizens of other Greek cities (for the same term, cf. Eur. *Suppl.* 311, 526, 671). Pindar, *Pyth.* VI, 33, omits the stranger, since he is unimportant for the purpose of that poem, and so do Aristotle (*Eth. Nic.* VIII, 14, 1163b16) and other authors who refer to the same precept of honouring gods and parents. Pindar traces this rule back to the teachings of Chiron the Centaur, the tutor of Achilles and other great mythical heroes; in other words, it represents for him the nucleus of an aboriginal educational tradition. Perhaps he read it in the didactic epic Χίρωνος ὑποθῆκαι (see pp. 193 and 217), to which he refers elsewhere. Aeschylus, *Suppl.* 708-709, proves that the precept, in some form or other, had been incorporated even in written legislation (ἐν θεσμίοις Δίκας γέγραπται), and indeed we are told by Aelian, *Var. Hist.* VIII, 10, that with some modification it formed part of the laws of Draco, which were called θεσμοί. This may have been the case in other Greek states.

2. See the chapter on Hesiod, p. 61.

3. See *Paideia* III, 10.

4. From the poems of Homer down to the philosophical works of Plato and Aristotle, the word καλόν, 'the beautiful', denotes one of the most significant categories of personal value. In contradistinction to words like ἡδύ or συμφέρον, the pleasant or the useful, καλόν means the ideal. Friendship based not on pleasure or profit but on τὸ καλόν is the product of an admiration for the value of the human personality as such and is mostly founded on a common ideal. An action is done διὰ τὸ καλόν whenever it simply expresses a human ideal for its own sake, not when it serves another purpose. The term καλὸς κἀγαθός does not occur in Homer, but it must be very old. The oldest passage preserved to us in which it is presupposed as an ideal would be Solon, frg. 1, 39-40, if the distich is genuine. When used of a person, the word καλός refers to handsome stature rather than to personal value (areté), as is clear from this passage and many others; therefore the addition κἀγαθός was necessary in order to express the complete ideal of human personality as conceived by early Greek society. It comprehended both a fine stature (ἀγλαὸν εἶδος, cf. Tyrt. frg. 7, 9) and true areté, which was felt to correspond to it. Whoever spoils his areté by some mean action 'belies his handsome form', just as he 'shames his lineage' (Tyrt., loc. cit.). The coincidence of these things is supposed to be normal and natural. The εἶδος or beauty of outward form is accepted and honoured as the visible manifestation of the entire personality and its ideal value. Thersites has no areté and therefore is pictured by Homer as a ridiculously ugly figure (*Iliad* II, 216, αἴσχιστος δὲ ἀνὴρ ὑπὸ Ἴλιον ἦλθεν).

5. See the distinction made on p. v *supra* (with note 2) between culture in the sense of a merely *anthropological* concept, which means the entire way of life or character of a particular nation, and culture as the conscious ideal of human perfection. It is in this latter, humanistic sense that the word is used in the following passage. This 'ideal of culture' (in Greek, *areté* and *paideia*) is a specific creation of the Greek mind. The anthropological concept of culture is a modern extension of this original concept; but it has been made out of a concept of value a mere descriptive category which can be applied to any nation, even to the 'culture of the primitive', because it has entirely lost its true obligatory sense. Even in Matthew Arnold's definition of culture as 'the best that has been thought and said in all ages', the original (paideutic) sense of the word (as the ideal of

man's perfection) is obscured. It tends to make culture into a kind of museum, i.e. 'paideia' in the sense of the Alexandrian period when it came to designate *learning*.

6. This sentence must not be taken as a dogma which we impose on history or which may be inspired by a political ideal. It is a bare statement of the facts presented by our documents of early Greek tradition and is confirmed by the example of many other nations which had a long and organic cultural development. Of course, no truly 'representative' class ever exists in isolation from the rest of the people, and the culture of such a group as the early Greek nobility is the flowering of a broader, unconscious, age-old tradition of form in worship, institutions, and customs common to the whole social organism. (See the distinction made in note 5 between culture in the humanistic sense as a conscious ideal of man's perfection (areté) and culture in a broader, anthropological sense.) The connexion of the one with the other has been justly stressed by T. S. Eliot in *Notes Toward a Definition of Culture,* reprinted in the *Partisan Review,* No. 2, 1944. In early Greek literature, culture in this more anthropological sense comes to the light first in the *Works and Days* of the Boeotian peasant poet Hesiod (see chap. 4). Nevertheless, what we call Greek culture in the specific sense of a conscious ideal of man's perfection—the culture reflected in the Homeric epos— was still the possession of a limited group of the people, the aristocracy.

This fact is by no means in hopeless logical conflict with the noble idea of later centuries that all men are born equal, for that axiom does not pretend to be a historical statement; rather, it gives expression to a metaphysical faith which, when accepted, has important practical consequences but does not alter the past. Nor has the fact that culture in the humanistic sense was originally restricted to a special class ever prevented later generations from asking that more men might share its benefits. The democratic culture of Periclean Athens was the final product of a long and gradual transformation and extension of the early aristocratic tradition. It is one of the most important tasks of this book to describe this unique and universally significant development of the fifth and fourth centuries B.C.

The significance of this process lies in the enormous broadening of the realm of culture that made it accessible to the whole city or nation; and the spirit of the new unity, both political and cultural, left its stamp on every important product of the Greek genius during that period. The metamorphosis of the old aristocratic form of life into Periclean democracy cannot be understood merely in terms of the extension of political rights to the mass of the people. As Greek culture grew from its original and more exclusive form into something more universal and humane, it followed at the same time its own inherent tendency. For the very form of this culture implied, from the beginning, a powerful element of universality and rationality which enabled and predestined it to develop beyond class limitations into the culture of the entire Greek nation and finally into a world-civilization. Thus it conquered and penetrated the world by adapting its form to the changing situation, but without surrendering its essence.

The humanistic idea underlying this transformation was the assumption that, if culture be conceived as a 'privilege' due to 'noble birth,' there can be no higher claim to such a privilege than that inherent in the nature of man as a rational being. Thus instead of vulgarizing that which was noble, the cultural development of Greece ennobled the whole human race by offering it a programme for a higher form of life, the life of reason. And more than that. The new self-ruled society of later centuries became increasingly aware of the fact that the realization of this programme depended not merely on the broader extension of culture

but also on the constant maintenance of a high qualitative level of human activity.
No form of society can survive long without a careful and conscious education
of its ablest and most valuable members, even when it is no longer taken for
granted that they belong to a privileged class of landed nobility. On a rational
plane, the only alternative to rule by a hereditary class is government by the
ablest citizens, selected and trained by education for the service of the common
good. But when we see the philosophy of the classical period of Greece so earnestly
concerned with that task of selection and education, is it not the same problem
which we meet at the beginning of Greek culture, only in a different form? That,
at least, was the way in which those later educators and cultural leaders looked
at the problem. They did not think in terms of privileges but of areté, and thereby
reduced 'nobility' to its true meaning. When the humanists of the Renaissance
revived the spiritual heritage of classical antiquity, they adopted along with the
classical cultural ideal this conception of the nobility or dignity of man. And
this humanistic idea which inspired the Renaissance was one of the roots of
modern civilization. Assuredly this concept of nobility implied in the Greek ideal
of culture has interesting implications for the problems of modern democracy;
but it is not the purpose of such a historical study as this to explore them.

7. The first appearance is in Aeschylus, *Sept.* 18, where it still means τροφή,
upbringing or child-rearing. See the chapter on the Sophists, p. 475, Note 1.

8. The areté of horses is mentioned in *Iliad* XXIII, 276 and 374. Plato (*Rep.*
335b) speaks of the areté of dogs and horses, and (353b) of the areté of the eye;
the areté of the gods is found in *Iliad* IX, 498.

9. *Odyssey* XVII, 322.

10. The Greeks felt that areté was above everything else a power, an ability
to do something. Strength and health are the areté of the body, cleverness and
insight the areté of the mind. It is difficult in view of this to accept the modern
subjective explanation which derives the word from ἀρέσκω, 'to please' (cf. M.
Hoffmann, *Die ethische Terminologie bei Homer, Hesiod, und den alten Elegikern
und Iambographen,* Tübingen 1914, p. 92). It is true that areté often contains an
element of social recognition—its meaning then alters to 'esteem', 'respect'. But
that is a secondary sense, created by the highly social character of all human
values in early times. The word must originally have been an objective description of the worth of its possessor, of a power peculiar to him, which makes him
a complete man.

11. This occurs in *Iliad* XV, 641 ff., where intelligence is mentioned along with
physical strength and warlike prowess, under the collective term 'all sorts of
aretai'. It is significant that the word should be used now and then in this wider
sense in the *Odyssey,* which is the later poem.

12. ἀνὴρ ἀγαθὸς γενόμενος ἀπέθανε.

13. Besides ἀγαθός, ἐσθλός is chiefly used in this connexion: their opposite is
κακός. In the vocabulary of Theognis and Pindar we can see how these words
kept their connexion with the nobility, although they changed their meaning as
Greek civilization developed. It was natural that areté should be confined to the
nobility in Homer's day, but such a limitation could not be valid in later times—
especially since the old ideals were revised from a wholly different point of view.

14. The development of the Homeric virtues of liberality and magnificence up
to the time of Pindar under the influence of changing economic conditions is the
subject of a Radcliffe doctoral dissertation by Miss Cora Mason, 1944. See also
a dissertation by J. Himelrijk, Πενία *en* πλοῦτος (Utrecht 1925). These ideals
of an early aristocratic society still live on in Aristotle's philosophical treatment,
Eth. Nic. IV, 1-6. The Aristotelian liberality (ἐλευθεριότης) and magnificence

(μεγαλοπρέπεια) do not spring from a feeling of pity or social sympathy with the poor, as do the φιλανθρωπία and φιλοξενία, which play such a great part in early Christian life and literature. This does not prove, however, that the older ideal is lacking in social feeling, but only that that feeling is entirely different. It is completely objectified, and where it results in action it metes out its gifts according to the criterion of τιμή in proper gradation.

15. For αἰδώς and νέμεσις, see the book by M. Hoffmann quoted in note 10, and especially the monograph by C. E. von Erffa, ΑΙΔΩΣ *und verwandte Begriffe in ihrer Entwicklung von Homer bis Demokrit* (Beihefte zum *Philologus*, Suppl. Bd. 30, 2), which I advised the author to undertake. Cf. the enlightening remarks of Aristotle on αἰδώς and νέμεσις, *Eth. Nic.* II, 7, 1108a31 ff., and the more accurate treatment of αἰδώς IV, 15. That of νέμεσις does not exist in our version of the *Ethics* and may have been lost at the end of Book IV.

16. The Alexandrian grammarians used the word *aristeia* often, combined with the name of a special hero, as a title of Homeric songs.

17. *Iliad* VI, 208.

18. *Iliad* XI, 784. The precept is no doubt secondary in this passage and is repeated in the same words from *Iliad* VI, 208, the scene of the encounter of Glaucus and Diomede.

19. This was the view of the Greek author from whom Cicero derived the section of his *De Oratore* (III, 57) where the verse (*Iliad* IX, 443) is quoted. The whole passage is interesting as an early attempt to write a history of education.

20. *Eth. Nic.* I, 5, 1095b26.

21. See the passage in Aristotle's letter to Antipater (frg. 666, Rose) regarding his reaction to the hostile attitude of the Delphians who, after Alexander's death, invalidated the honours which they had conferred upon the great scholar for his work on the chronicle of the victors in the Delphic games; obviously this work had been made possible by the assistance of the Macedonian king.

22. Arist. *Eth. Nic.* III, 1, 1109b30.

23. See F. Zucker, *Syneidesis-Conscientia* (Jena 1928). (Cf. p. 326.) We may say that what took the place of a personal conscience in Homeric times was that feeling of *aidos* and *nemesis* referred to on p. 7. (Cf. von Erffa's book on *Aidos* quoted above, note 15.) But it depended entirely on an objective social code always present in the mind of the individual; and to that ideal code he had to conform.

24. This is especially manifest in the Greek system of proper names. They frequently were taken from the realm of social ideals and therefore often refer to such concepts as glory, reputation, fame, etc., and in addition were combined with some other word that expressed the degree of or reason for such fame or reputation (such as Pericles, Themistocles, etc.). The name was an anticipation of the future areté of its bearer; it set, as it were, the ideal pattern for his whole life. This distinguishes Greek names from Hebrew or Egyptian names, for the nature of which see Hermann Ranke, *Grundsaetzliches z. Verstaendnis d. aegyptischen Personennamen* (*Sitz. d. Heidelberger Akad.* XXVII, 3. Abh., 1937).

25. τὸ θεῖον = τὸ τίμιον *par excellence,* Arist. *Eth. Nic.* I, 12, esp. 1102a4. When the Greek-speaking and thinking world was Christianized, this fundamental attitude of the Greek religious mind began in its turn to exercise a deep influence on Christian thought and custom, as is shown by the Greek-Christian literature and worship of the first centuries. The history of liturgy, sermon, and the Christian hymn will reveal much about it.

26. Nevertheless, a survey of the historical development of the Greek concept of 'fatherland' (πατρίς, πάτρα) would have to start with Homer. But, character-

420 NOBILITY AND ARETÉ

istically, it is not the famous Greek heroes of the *Iliad* who give the first impressive example of this political feeling. It is rather embodied in the Trojan Hector, darling of the people and defender of his city (cf. his famous words, *Iliad* XII, 243, εἷς οἰωνὸς ἄριστος ἀμύνεσθαι περὶ πάτρης). The passion of patriotism did not arise in the great ancient empires or in the Homeric aristocracy, but was a result of the rise of the city state, which is first reflected in such passages of the epic as previously quoted. This feeling was quite different from the idea of being a chosen people, which modern secular nationalism has inherited from the religious nationalism of the ancient Israelites. That form of patriotism is either a religion or a substitute for it.

27. *Iliad* I, 412; II, 239-240; IX, 110 and 116; XVI, 59; and above all IX, 315-322. When asked by the delegates of the Greek army to return to the battlefield and to accept Agamemnon's terms for a reconciliation with his offender, Achilles bluntly rejects the offer: 'Agamemnon will persuade neither me nor any other Greek, I think, since there is obviously no public recognition for a man who fights the enemy relentlessly. He who keeps away from battle earns a share [μοῖρα] equal to that of a man who fights with all his strength; and coward and brave man are held in one and the same honour.' Honour (τιμή) here is the objective social manifestation of a public gratitude (χάρις) due to the man of outstanding deeds done for the sake of the whole community and for which there exists no material compensation.

28. The death of Ajax was described in one of the cyclical epic poems, the 'Little Iliad', from which Sophocles took the plot of his *Ajax*.

29. *Odyssey* XI, 543 ff.

30. *Iliad* I, 505 ff.

31. Aristotle, *Eth. Nic.* IV, 4, tries to differentiate φιλοτιμία into a good and a bad sense. Xenophon, *Mem.* II, 3, 16, *Hipp.* 2, 2, and other passages, uses the word in a good sense, and so does Isocrates, 9, 3.

32. *Eth. Nic.* IV, 7-9. Cf. my essay *Der Grossgesinnte* in *Die Antike* VII, 97 ff.

33. Arist. *Eth. Nic.* IV, 7, 1124a1.

34. *Analyt. Post.* II, 13, 97b15.

35. For the origin and meaning of *kalokagathia*, see note 4. Aristotle, *Eth. Nic.* IV, 7, 1124a4, connects it closely with high-mindedness, which ought to be based on the full possession of areté. The word *kalokagathia* (as a term for what Plato calls πᾶσα ἀρετή) is not discussed or used otherwise in the *Nicomachean Ethics* (but see the brief mention in x, 10, 1179b10). In the earlier form of this treatise, the *Eudemian Ethics,* Book VIII, 15, the word is still used in the Platonic sense, as the sum total of all the special virtues (αἱ κατὰ μέρος ἀρεταί). In Plato's time οἱ καλοὶ κἀγαθοί generally meant the rich (cf. *Rep.* 569a). But Plato tried to revive its older meaning by freeing the word from the connotation of class privilege.

36. *Eth. Nic.* IV, 7, 1123b35.

37. Ib. IX, 8.

38. Ib. IX, 8, 1168b27.

39. Ib. IX, 8, 1169a18 ff.

40. *Symposium* 208-209.

41. See my *Aristotle* (tr. Robinson, Oxford 1934), 118.

CHAPTER 2

THE CULTURE AND EDUCATION OF THE HOMERIC NOBILITY

1. This fact was stressed first by F. G. Welcker, *Der epische Cyclus* (Bonn 1835), who tried to reconstruct the early epic literature of the Greeks in its entirety.

2. This controversy started on a large scale with the publication of F. A. Wolf's famous *Prolegomena ad Homerum* in 1795. This work followed almost immediately upon the rediscovery of the ancient Alexandrian theories of the epos and the later critical tradition that has come down to modern times through the scholia found in the oldest Venice manuscripts of Homer, first published by the Marquis de Villoison in 1788.

3. All the contributions to the Homeric problem made by Wilamowitz, from his early book *Homerische Untersuchungen* to his great work *Homer und die Ilias* and the late monograph *Die Heimkehr des Odysseus*, show this new historical trend. He tried throughout to compare the development of the epic to the archaeological monuments and to what little we know about the historical background of early Greek poetry. See also his lecture *Das homerische Epos* in *Reden und Vortraege*, Bd. I. The books on Homer by E. Bethe and Ed. Schwartz follow the same path. But the same tendency prevailed also among contemporary archaeologists, Schliemann, Doerpfeld, Evans, and their successors, who tried to throw light on the problem of the epic through the new evidence afforded by the excavations.

4. A distinct tendency to abandon analysis of the Homeric poems is shown in such modern works as Dornseiff's *Archäische Mythenerzählung* (Berlin 1933), and Jacoby's *Die geistige Physiognomie der Odyssee* (in *Die Antike* IX, 159). Among the scholars of the English-speaking world this tendency has always been very strong. It has been more recently represented by the Americans J. A. Scott and S. E. Bassett, whose well-known books in the Sather Classical Series oppose on principle the analytical spirit of the Homeric scholarship of the last century. The articles of G. M. Calhoun must also be added to them.

5. This opinion is held by leading modern scholars, such as E. Schwartz in *Die Odyssee* (Munich 1924), 294, and Wilamowitz in *Die Heimkehr des Odysseus* (Berlin 1927)—where he remarks (p. 171 ff.): 'Anyone who makes no distinctions within the Homeric poems in matters of language or religion or morality, anyone who follows Aristarchus in drawing a sharp line between them and the νεώτερον which is the rest of all literature, has forfeited all claim to serious consideration.'

6. See my essay *Solons Eunomie* (*Sitz. Berl. Akad.* 1926), 73 ff. There I have demonstrated, as I think beyond all doubt, that Solon in his elegy Ἡμετέρα δὲ πόλις reflects the speech of Zeus in the assembly of the gods in the first book of the *Odyssey*. (See also p. 143.) This elegy of Solon's was connected with the social unrest in Athens which he attempted to settle by his reforms (594 B.C.). It must be referred to the period preceding them, and therefore represents a most valuable clue to the form of our *Odyssey* about the turn of the seventh century. Thus the *Odyssey* known in Solon's age contained the parts of the epic which a critic like Adolf Kirchhoff has distinguished as the most recent: the *Telemachia* and with it the first book. Kirchhoff's analysis of the *Odyssey* seemed logically so conclusive to modern scholars like Wilamowitz and Schwartz that they based their own analytical efforts largely on his results. They supposed that the first

book of the *Odyssey* belonged to a much later time than it would now appear from its imitation in Solon's elegy. Their conclusions must be revised in the light of the facts mentioned above, as has been promptly recognized by Rudolf Pfeiffer in his penetrating review of the books of Wilamowitz and Schwartz on the *Odyssey* in *Deutsche Literaturzeitung* 1928, pp. 2364 and 2366. F. Jacoby, in *Die Antike* IX, 160, adds reasons for believing in an even earlier *terminus ante quem* for the *Odyssey*.

7. Wilamowitz, op. cit. p. 178.

8. Wilamowitz, op. cit. p. 182, assumes that the *Telemachia* was created in mainland Greece (a view which contradicts his arguments in *Homerische Unter-suchungen*, p. 26), and speaks of a 'Corinthian cultural circle'. I am not convinced by his reasoning. Jacoby also argues against him: op. cit. p. 161.

9. The phrase κλέα ἀνδρῶν (literally 'the fame of men'), which is used in *Iliad* IX, 189 for 'songs' as they were transmitted by the minstrels, indicates that origin of all epic song clearly enough. See G. W. Nitzsch, *Sagenpoesie der Griechen* (Braunschweig 1852), 110.

10. For Prehomeric features of absolute kingship reflected in the Homeric poems, see M. P. Nilsson, *Das homerische Koenigtum* (*Sitz. Berl. Akad.* 1927), 23 ff. The reminiscences of Prehomeric Mycenaean art in the Homeric poems are discussed in the archaeological literature; see also G. Finsler, *Homer* (2nd ed. Leipzig, 1914-18), p. 130 f.

11. *Iliad* II, 211 ff.

12. On Ithaca, see *Odyssey* II; the Phaeacian city, *Odyssey* VI-VIII.

13. The rhapsodes themselves can hardly ever have been of noble birth: but there were quite a number of aristocratic poets in the fields of iambic, lyric, and elegiac poetry (Wilamowitz, op. cit. p. 175).

14. In the first edition I said in a note to this passage that there was room for a special study of the development of the relation between property and areté in the world of Homer. Since then a student of mine at Radcliffe College, Cambridge, Massachusetts, Miss Cora Mason, has undertaken this task in her dissertation entitled *The Ethics of Wealth* (1944). She has pursued the development of the relation between areté and material possessions in early Greek poetry through the Homeric epics and in Posthomeric poetry up to and including Pindar. See also the existing literature on the problem quoted in her monograph.

15. Later Greek reflection on the nature of education lays great stress on the concepts of τύπος and τυποῦν, even when the spontaneous individual factor in this process is strongly felt, as by the sophists or by Plato. This concept is the heritage of the early aristocratic ideal of education. (See p. 20 ff.) Needless to say, the content of the later Platonic ideal type of human personality differed greatly from that of the early aristocratic world; but the educational process as such was still visualized in the same terms of moulding.

16. Pindar disliked the character of Odysseus. Sophocles' *Ajax* and *Philoctetes* both reflect clearly the less favourable opinion of that great hero which always existed along with the official admiration. In Plato's *Hippias Minor* the sophist expresses the same doubt about the character of Odysseus, but Plato makes us realize that in this regard Hippias simply follows a general trend; for Socrates remembers that he had heard the same criticism from Apemantos, the father of one of the lesser-known younger interlocutors of the dialogue, i.e. from the older generation. In the last analysis this attitude towards Odysseus goes back to the *Iliad,* which contrasts the πολύτροπος with Achilles' straightforward character. Even the *Odyssey* (VIII, 75) reflects the old tradition about this contrast of the two great heroes in Demodocus' song of the quarrel between Odysseus and Achilles.

17. In the *Odyssey* (VIII, 487-498), Odysseus himself likes this aspect of his own reputation better than any other, and asks the minstrel at the court of the Phaeacians to sing the story of the Trojan horse rather than some other.

18. *Iliad* III, 164.

19. *Odyssey* IV, 120 ff. See especially her words at 138 ff.

20. *Odyssey* IV, 131.

21. *Odyssey* VII, 71-74.

22. For Nausicaa's advice see *Odyssey* VI, 310-315. Cf. VII, 142 ff. Athena also tells Odysseus about the honour which Alcinous and his children pay to Areté, *Odyssey* VII, 66-70.

23. *Odyssey* I, 330 ff.; XVI, 409-451; XVIII, 158; XXI, 63 ff.

24. A house, an ox, and a wife are the three basic elements of the farmer's life in Hesiod's *Works and Days*, 405 (quoted by Aristotle, *Pol.* I, 2, 1252b10, in his famous economic discussion). Throughout his work Hesiod sees the existence of women from an economic point of view, not only in his version of the story of Pandora, which he tells in order to explain the origin of labour and toil among mortals, but also in his precepts about love, courtship, and marriage (ib. 373, 695 ff., *Theog.* 590-612).

25. The Greek 'Middle Ages' show their interest in this side of the problem most strikingly in the large poetic production in catalogue form dedicated to the heroic genealogies of the old families, most of all the catalogues of famous heroines from whom they derived, such as the 'Ἡοῖαι, which were preserved under the name of Hesiod.

26. See G. Pasquali, 'La Scoperta dei Concetti Etici nella Grecia Antica', *Civiltà Mod.* I (1929), 343 ff.

27. *Iliad* I, 113 ff.

28. *Iliad* IX, 447-453.

29. *Odyssey* VI, 149 ff.

30. Many editors follow the orthography of the Byzantine manuscripts and spell the centaur's name Cheiron. I prefer the form of the name preserved by an old vase inscription; see Kretschmer, *Die griechischen Vaseninschriften*, 131 ff., and A. Rzach, Hesiodus, ad *Theog.* v. 1001.

31. The remnants of the poem were collected, together with the fragments of other works, by A. Rzach in his smaller edition of Hesiod (3rd ed., Leipzig 1913), 196 ff.

32. Pindar, *Pyth.* VI, 19 ff.

33. *Iliad* XI, 830-832.

34. Pindar, *Pyth.* III, 5 ff.

35. Pindar, *Nem.* III, 43 ff., 58.

36. *Iliad* IX, 480-484.

37. The much discussed dual forms (*Iliad* IX, 182 ff.) in the description of the Embassy on its way to Achilles' tent have been explained away a hundred times since Aristarchus quieted his grammatical conscience with the resigned remark that, as this passage showed, the dual could sometimes be used instead of the plural. Another explanation is based on the parallelism of this scene in Book IX with Book I of the *Iliad,* v. 320 ff., where Agamemnon's messengers follow the same path to Achilles' tent, in order to take Briseis away from him. This parallel is too obvious to be overlooked and is expressly hinted at in Nestor's speech, *Iliad* IX, 106. In Book I, 320 ff., the same dual forms are certainly the genuine dual and do not stand for the plural. To the two heralds who were sent to Achilles in Book I correspond the ambassadors in Book IX who are to offer Achilles the return of Briseis. Yet there are three ambassadors in spite of the dual, and two heralds in addition to them. Franz Boll in *Zeitschrift f. österr.*

Gymn. (1917 and 1920) argued some decades ago that the conscious parallel might excuse the use of the dual forms for the three ambassadors in Book IX: the poet used the dual deliberately, in order to remind us of the scene in Book I. But I cannot see that the repetition of the dual forms was suited to produce this effect if there were in reality not two but three or more persons. It seems to me far more plausible that the duals which were preserved in the text of our manuscripts stem from another and older variant—a still older epic tradition, either oral or written—which presented only two ambassadors. These can have been only Odysseus and Ajax, Phoenix being an otherwise unknown, secondary figure, obviously invented for this purpose and of an altogether different character. He was the teacher, and the author chose him to convey to Achilles the moral lesson contained in his disproportionately extended diatribe. But it would be much too simple to try to 'restore' the original form of the epic narrative by excising the passage containing Phoenix's long speech and the few other references to him. Theoretically we have to recognize the existence of two parallel versions of the Embassy which in our text of the *Iliad* are blended in such a way that it is no longer possible to separate them. The invention of Phoenix the educator and his admonitory speech contribute more than anything to the unification of the poem as we now have it; it is therefore practically impossible to go back beyond this latest transformation of the poem without destroying its composition.

38. P. 9.

39. Cf. Ernst Howald, *Rheinisches Museum* LXXIII (1924), 405.

40. See pp. 33 and 41. Even the ancient commentators pointed this out. In modern times Erich Bethe, *Rhein. Mus.* LXXIV (1925), 129, rightly stressed the character of Phoenix's narration of the wrath of Meleager as an *exemplum* and connected it with the admonitory purpose of his speech.

41. See note 40.

42. Plato, *Rep.* 595c.

43. *Iliad* IX, 523.

44. *Iliad* IX, 502 ff.

45. *Iliad* IX, 438.

46. *Iliad* IX, 490 ff.

47. See what is said about this type of education in general and about the hortatory use of the mythical example (παράδειγμα) in the speeches of the Homeric poems on pp. 33-35.

48. *Iliad* IX, 502-512.

49. See pp. 33 ff., 53 and elsewhere in this book. Cf. the indexes of *Paideia* I-III, 'examples'.

50. It should not be forgotten, however, what we have proved in note 37. There it has been shown that the present form of the ninth book of the *Iliad* is not the original version but is of a more recent origin. In it the great educational problem involved in Achilles' decision is presented to him impressively and with a high degree of insight into the moral psychology of the situation by his teacher Phoenix. Originally the poet conceived of the Embassy as a strategic move on the part of the highest representatives of the Greek army, Odysseus and Ajax, who conveyed to Achilles the formal offer of King Agamemnon. The problem was only that of a difficult diplomatic mission which resulted in complete failure. It is characteristic of the poet who introduced the figure of Phoenix, Achilles' teacher, that he saw the situation entirely in the light of the educational problem which he has worked out in such an admirable way.

51. *Odyssey* I, 105 and 180.

52. *Odyssey* II, 401.

53. Eduard Schwartz, in *Die Odyssee* (Munich 1924), 253, has recently laid special emphasis on the educational element in the tale of Telemachus.

54. That the part of the *Odyssey* called the *Telemachia* (Books I-IV) was originally a separate epic poem was the thesis of Adolf Kirchhoff's *Die homerische Odyssee und ihre Entstehung* (Berlin 1859) (see especially p. viii and p. 136 ff.), and *Die Composition der Odyssee* (Berlin 1869). In these two books the analysis of the Homeric poetry shifted to the *Odyssey,* after it had centered about the *Iliad* during the first eventful stage of its development, from F. A. Wolf's *Prolegomena* (1795) to the middle of the nineteenth century. The results of Kirchhoff's analysis with regard to the *Telemachia* were accepted as definitely proved by such modern critics as Wilamowitz in *Homerische Untersuchungen* (Berlin 1884) and *Die Heimkehr des Odysseus* (Berlin 1927), Eduard Schwartz in *Die Odyssee* (Munich 1924), and R. Jebb in *Homer* (1st ed., 1886). The issue turns on the question whether the long admonitory speech of Athena to Telemachus in Book I, 252-305, in which she advises him to undertake the journey to Pylos and Sparta described in Books II-IV, is really the work of the same poet who wrote Books II-IV, or must be considered as a secondary and very imperfect addition by the hand of a redactor who wanted to incorporate the younger and independent epic of the *Telemachia* in an older and larger epic poem about the return of Odysseus.

55. Thus Wilamowitz, op. cit. But see R. Pfeiffer in the *Deutsche Literatur Zeitung,* 1928, pp. 2, 368. I must however object to his view that in the transformation of Telemachus there is much more emphasis on divine guidance than on the divine origin of the standards of aristocratic education. On the other hand, Athena's specially *educative* function cannot be denied merely by pointing out that she constantly interferes with the plot of the whole *Odyssey* and 'therefore' is merely a convenient property used by the epic poet: as Jacoby, *Die Antike,* IX, 169, avers in contradicting Pfeiffer. The influence of the divine on human life appears in many different forms.

56. I, 279, ὑποτίθεσθαι, the verb of ὑποθῆκαι, which is the exact translation of 'teaching'; see P. Friedlaender in *Hermes* XLVIII (1913), 571.

57. The assembly of the people of Ithaca in which Telemachus publicly states his case and makes his last appeal to the suitors for fair play, in Book II, has a definite purpose within the composition of the *Odyssey:* it puts the blame for the tragic outcome of the story, the slaughter of the suitors, entirely on the victims themselves. The poet who wrote Book II and the speech of Athena in which she advises Telemachus to call the assembly (Book I, 252 ff.) wanted to give the old saga, which ended in the *mnesterophonia,* a moral and juridical justification acceptable to his modern and rational mind. It seems to me that he deliberately put into Athena's mouth the advice to call the assembly first, before Telemachus left Ithaca for his exploratory journey. That feature gives Telemachus' action its divine sanction and stresses the character of the calling of the assembly as a solemn act of warning, which puts on the suitors the full responsibility for the consequences of their refusal to adopt a more reasonable course henceforth. The speech of Athena (*Odyssey* I, 252) receives even greater prominence by the fact that she announced her intention to give Telemachus this advice, to call an assembly and denounce the suitors in the presence of all the people, beforehand in the council of the gods on Olympus (*Odyssey* I, 90). This procedure makes it clear that she acted in behalf of all the gods and of Zeus himself, who approved not only of her plan as a whole but also of her method in carrying it out. When Athena warned the suitors of the consequences of their own deeds in this way, she applied what Zeus himself had declared in his speech

(*Odyssey* I, 32) on the responsibility of mortal man for his own sufferings; the example of Aegisthus to which he referred stressed the fact that Aegisthus had been punished rightly because he acted wrongly in spite of divine warning. I must admit that the observation of these facts has always been the greatest obstacle to my mind in accepting Kirchhoff's fundamental thesis that the speech of Athena to Telemachus in Book I was written not by the same poet who later in Books II-IV describes how Telemachus carried out her advice, but by some secondary hand which wanted to incorporate the already existing separate poem of the *Telemachia*. This view implies that the calling of the assembly originally had no real purpose whatever but received its present purpose, which we have defined above (the warning of the suitors), only when the redactor of Book I incorporated the *Telemachia* into our *Odyssey*. Kirchhoff seems to see only the fact that the calling of the assembly is entirely inconsequential for the time being, since the suitors do not, of course, follow Telemachus' proposal to go home. But the sagacious critic overlooks first, the function of the speech as a moral motivation for the final punishment of the suitors, and second, the emphasis laid by the author of Book I on the distinction between god-sent evil and self-caused human suffering. The assembly and the journey of Telemachus in Books II-IV take on their full importance only in the present framework of the whole poem set up in Book I. Without it they remain mere episodes in a vacuum. This seems to recommend the explanation that they were written as an exposition of the moral and legal situation of the whole *Odyssey* from the very beginning.

58. On Odysseus as an example for Telemachus, see *Odyssey* I, 255 and many other passages. In the case of Nausicaa it is not expressly stated that her mother is an example to her, but this is taken for granted in the Homeric world. See *Odyssey* VII, 69-70. In *Odyssey* VI, 25, Athena wonders ironically how Nausicaa's mother could have borne a daughter so careless of her own clothes.

59. *Iliad* IX, 524 ff. Phoenix refers to the authority of the old κλέα ἀνδρῶν which, he says, we have received from former generations. He refers to them for the special case of wrath (μῆνις) in order to find a parallel to Achilles' situation and a norm of right action which he might hold out to him. This is the example of Meleager, of which he makes a long story.

60. *Odyssey* I, 298-302.

61. See note 59.

62. *Odyssey* I, 296 ff.

63. *Odyssey* I, 32-47.

64. *Odyssey* III, 195-200.

65. *Odyssey* III, 306-316.

66. I intend to make a separate investigation of the historical development of the paradeigma in Greek literature.

67. See pp. 216-218.

68. It has been traced in early Greek poetry by R. Oehler in his dissertation, *Mythologische Exempla in der aelteren griechischen Dichtung* (Basle 1925). He works on a suggestion dropped by Nitzsch in *Sagenpoesie der Griechen* (1852), but he pays too little attention to the connexion of this stylistic practice with the old aristocratic reverence for ethical models.

69. Plato, *Theaet.* 176e.

70. For Plato's Idea of the Good as paradeigma in the soul of the philosopher king, see *Rep.* 472c, 484c, 500e, 540a, and *Paideia* II, 279-280.

CHAPTER 3

HOMER THE EDUCATOR

1. He is speaking (*Rep.* 606e) of the 'eulogists of Homer', who read him not only for aesthetic pleasure but also for guidance in the conduct of life. The same notion appears in Xenophanes (frg. 10, Diehl).

2. See *Paideia* II, 211 ff. and 358 ff.

3. Of all the modern interpreters of Greek poetry, U. v. Wilamowitz-Moellendorff has recognized most clearly this exalted position and character of the Greek poets during the early and classical periods, and has stressed this important fact over and again.

4. This is true, of course, only for the great period of Greek poetry. The poets of the Hellenistic age, such as Callimachus and Theocritus, no longer claimed to be the teachers of the whole nation. They were artists in the modern sense, living in a purely aesthetic world of their own. Culture to them was literary refinement. It is true they would still claim the rank of supreme arbiters of contemporary paideia, but for them this meant first and foremost literary taste and critical judgment. Thus they had retired definitely to the realm to which Plato's criticism of poetry had relegated them.

5. Plato's criticism of poetry was directed against its lack of philosophical truth, for its dignity and value as paideia seemed to depend on its truth. But in denying this claim of poetry, Plato did more than anyone in classical Greece to circumscribe the exact limits of the phenomenon which we call aesthetic value. The philosopher does not question poetry's competence within those limits. He wants to restrict our relationship to it to mere aesthetic enjoyment. It is therefore not accurate to say that Plato measured poetry by moral or philosophic standards alone. What he measured by this standard was not poetry but the traditional title of poetry as the true paideia. We learn from trustworthy tradition that Plato secured among other poets (such as Sophron the mimographer) the complete works of the most modern of them all, Antimachus of Colophon, with whom we now begin the Hellenistic period of Greek literature. See the report of Plato's pupil Heraclides Ponticus, and B. Wyss, *Antimachi Colophonii Reliquiae* (Berlin 1936), lxiv.

6. See especially the discussion in the Epicurean school of the problem of whether or not all great poetry ought to combine the effects of *utile* and *dulce: Philodemos ueber die Gedichte fuenftes Buch,* by Christian Jensen (Berlin 1923), 110 ff. Poetry is the 'fortress of human passions', as the Epicureans called it according to Sextus Empiricus, *Adv. Math.* I, 298 (p. 668, Bekker). 'Much in the works of the poets is not only useless but detrimental in the highest degree.' The nature of poetry cannot be judged by the moral or scientific benefits which it offers.

7. See, e.g., the famous treatise of Basil the Great dedicated to the Christian youth, concerning the use of classical Greek literature.

8. What the Stoics and Peripatetics taught about the 'paideutic' value of poetry is based mostly on the Homeric poems. See Philodemus' book Περὶ ποιημάτων quoted in note 6, in which he lists and criticizes the views of his predecessors in poetics.

9. The sophists thought of Homer as a source of all branches of technical knowledge (τέχναι). Ps. Plutarch, *De vita et poesi Homeri* represents the same view, which we know for earlier times only indirectly from Plato's polemic against it

in the *Republic* or in the *Ion*. But in Plutarch we find the idea worked out in all its details. See *Paideia* II, 360.

10. *Odyssey* I, 338: ἔργ' ἀνδρῶν τε θεῶν τε, τά τε κλείουσιν ἀοιδοί.

11. *Iliad* IX, 189, 524. *Odyssey* VIII, 73.

12. Plato, *Phaedrus* 245a. This passage firmly establishes the relation between poetry and areté as shown in the glory of the great deeds of men.

13. See p. 33 ff.

14. For Pindar's lofty conception of the essence of true poetry which followed this tradition, see p. 209 ff.

15. See R. Oehler, *Mythologische Exempla in der aelteren griechischen Dichtung* (Basle 1925), who collected the mythical examples in early Greek poetry but perhaps did not emphasize sufficiently the normative character of these references to the myth in Homeric speeches. In later centuries the mythological example becomes a mere decorative element of style, especially when used in epideictic rhetoric. But the use of examples as a point of reference for argumentative purposes can be traced down through all periods of Greek literature. The rhetorical precepts about it and even more the practice of the authors show clearly that, because of the more rational character of thought in those later ages, the mythical example is more and more replaced by the historical example, i.e. the ideal example yields to the empirical. See *Paideia* III, 369 s. Paradeigma.

16. Dio Prusensis, *or.* XXXIII, 11.

17. We may refer briefly to some of the outstanding modern books on the Homeric problem, such as U. v. Wilamowitz-Moellendorff, *Die Ilias und Homer* (Berlin 1916), Erich Bethe, *Homer, Dichtung und Sage* (2 vols., Leipzig 1914), Gilbert Murray, *The Rise of the Greek Epic* (2nd ed., Oxford 1911). Of unitarian writers we quote J. A. Scott, *The Unity of Homer* (Berkeley 1921), S. E. Bassett, *The Poetry of Homer* (Berkeley 1938). Sir Richard Jebb gives an introduction to the Homeric question and its development in the nineteenth century in his book *Homer* (1st ed., 1886). Georg Finsler, *Homer* (2. Aufl., Leipzig 1914-18), contains a good chapter on the history of the problem. On the analysis of the *Odyssey* see the books listed in note 54 of the previous chapter of this book. See also C. M. Bowra, *Tradition and Design in the Iliad* (Oxford 1930).

18. We do not consider at the moment those later ancient critics of the Alexandrian school who were the first to apply analytical methods to the epics and eliminated from them what they thought were later interpolations, the so-called χωρίζοντες (e.g. Book X of the *Iliad*, the Δολώνεια). Others denied that Homer was the author of both the *Iliad* and the *Odyssey*. See F. A. Wolf's *Prolegomena ad Homerum* (Halle 1795), clviii. On the methods of the Alexandrian school in their work on Homeric tradition, see also K. Lehrs' masterpiece, *De Aristarchi Studiis Homericis*.

19. This view was laid down by one of the older critics who in general took a sceptical attitude toward modern analytical efforts, G. W. Nitzsch, in his book *Beitraege zur Geschichte der epischen Poesie der Griechen* (Leipzig 1862), pp. 57, 356.

20. The old ballad or οἴμη used to set out after a prelude from a chosen starting point: ἔνθεν ἑλὼν ὡς οἱ μὲν ἐϋσσέλμων ἐπὶ νηῶν βάντες ἀπέπλειον (*Odyssey* VIII, 500). But not only the bard of the Phaeacians, Demodocus, starts his song in this manner. Even the poet of the proem of the *Odyssey* still follows that old technique when he asks the Muse to sing of Odysseus' return and the fate of his comrades, starting from any point she likes: τῶν ἁμόθεν γε, θεά, θύγατερ Διός, εἰπὲ καὶ ἡμῖν (ἁμόθεν γε corresponds to ἔνθεν ἑλών). Another form of indicating the starting point was ἐξ οὗ, as in the proem of the *Iliad* (I, 6): Μῆνιν ἄειδε, θεά, Πηληϊάδεω Ἀχιλῆος . . . ἐξ οὗ δὴ τὰ πρῶτα διαστήτην ἐρίσαντε . . .

21. *Iliad* XII, 243.

22. Hor. *Ars Poet.* 147.

23. This was the manner of the cyclical epic as described by Aristotle and Horace in their poetics. The beginning of the *Nibelungs* is very much the same: it starts by telling the youth of its greatest heroes, Siegfried and Kriemhild.

24. According to Aristotle, *Nic. Eth.* IV, 7, the μεγαλόψυχος is ὁ μεγάλων ἑαυτὸν ἀξιῶν ἄξιος ὤν, 'he who thinks himself worthy of great things and really is'; and that is in the first place honour deserved by true areté. For Achilles as Aristotle's pattern of megalopsychia, see note 34 of the chapter Nobility and Areté, p. 420.

25. Roland Herkenrath, *Der ethische Aufbau der Ilias und Odyssee* (Paderborn 1928), has given a full analysis of both poems from the ethical point of view, which he thinks is the approach most fitted for a true appreciation of their unified composition and art. The book contains much valuable observation, but has carried its thesis too far, overrating its importance for the question of the origin of the epic.

26. See *Iliad* I, 411-412 for Agamemnon's Até; Agamemnon himself admits his Até in IX, 116; Achilles is warned of Até by Phoenix in IX, 510-512.

27. Hor. *Od.* I, VI, 6.

28. *Iliad* XIX, 56 ff.

29. *Iliad* XIX, 86 ff., 137.

30. The consciousness of moral obligation in the form of αἰδώς, νέμεσις, καλόν, αἰσχρόν, etc., exists of course in Homer too. It is the subjective aspect of morality. But at the same time the nature of human morality appears as conformity with the inherent structure of objective reality, in the epic as well as in later poetical reflection about this problem. For Solon's concept of *diké*, see p. 142 ff.; the diké in Anaximander's philosophy of nature, p. 159; the morality of the sophists and its relation to the 'law of nature', pp. 323, 326; Sophocles' harmony, p. 277.

31. It certainly cannot be said that the divine motivation as used by the poets of the *Iliad* and *Odyssey* either was from the start or gradually becomes a mere mechanical device of epic technique. There are, of course, passages in which divine motivation operates like a *deus ex machina* (e.g. when Athena transforms Odysseus into a young man or into a beggar for the purpose of dissimulation); but on the whole the *Odyssey* shows a conscious effort to give this conventional epic apparatus a new religious meaning. Thus the principle of divine guidance is employed throughout the *Odyssey* even more completely than in the *Iliad*.

32. *Iliad* I, 5, Διὸς δ' ἐτελείετο βουλή. Here the will of Zeus is stressed as the ultimate cause at the very outset of the poem.

33. See p. 38.

34. What Homer's epic has in common with Greek philosophy is the fact that they both present the structure of reality in its entirety, though philosophy presents it in the rational form where the epos shows it in mythical form. In Homer the theme of 'the position of man in the universe', which is the classical theme of Greek philosophy, is already present at every moment, and Homer never loses sight of it. See the description of the shield of Achilles, p. 49, which is a perfect illustration of this universality and completeness of Homer's view of human life and areté.

35. Seen against the background of the Oriental conception of life, Homer's view is anthropocentric and humanistic in that sense of the term. But, on the other hand, it must be stressed that it is by no means one-sidedly human, and when we compare it with the anthropocentric view of reality of later subjectivism, e.g. the sophists of the fifth century, it appears decidedly theocentric. Everything

human in Homer is referred to an omnipresent divine force and norm. Plato realized this and restored the disturbed balance of the two elements in his philosophy. See my *Humanism and Theology* (Aquinas Lecture 1943, Marquette University Press, Milwaukee, Wis.), pp. 46 ff., 54 ff., and the whole second volume of *Paideia*.

36. The most baffling example of this is Zeus' threat in *Iliad* VIII, 5-27.

37. The most famous example is the Διὸς ἀπάτη, *Iliad* XIV.

38. *Odyssey* I, 32 ff.

39. See also p. 143, and my interpretation of the Homeric lines, *Odyssey*, I, 32 ff., in my essay *Solons Eunomie* quoted there.

40. Compare what has been said on p. 30 ff., especially in the footnotes, about the plan of the *Odyssey* and its origin, in the present form of the epic.

41. It occurs to me particularly in this context that a book like Richard Heinze's *Vergils epische Technik* or H. W. Prescott's fine book on *Vergil's Art*—which was inspired by Heinze—has not been written about Homer yet. But S. E. Bassett's *The Poetry of Homer* (Berkeley 1938) contains valuable observations of this kind.

CHAPTER 4

HESIOD: THE PEASANT'S LIFE

1. Herodotus VII, 102.

2. Horace's famous *Illi robur et aes triplex circa pectus erat* is a belated echo (reflected by other Latin authors) of the early Greek feeling about the dangers of the sea. Horace apparently follows a Greek lyric poem which is lost to us. Even in the age of Hesiod, maritime trade and seafaring were still considered as against the will of the gods. It is true we find inserted in the *Works and Days* a whole section dedicated to precepts for seafaring (ναυτιλίη), v. 618-694, which states, nevertheless, that it ought to be restricted to the season of the year most suitable for this purpose, i.e. late summer and early fall. The risk of storm and shipwreck is not too great at this time. But the sailor is warned not to stay away from his homeland until the young grapes ripen and the late autumn rainstorms begin. Spring is still another season for the sailor, but even though many people do go to sea in springtime, the poet does not approve of it. The text of the manuscripts must be corrupt in the *Erga* at v. 682, for εἰαρινός is a weak repetition of the same word in v. 678, where it belongs. ἀργαλέος was conjectured instead in 682 by Heyer and, as a guess, seems quite satisfactory. The poet does not like the πλόος in spring because it is ἁρπακτός, another difficult but evidently genuine epithet which must mean that men snatch that early but risky chance of sailing from the hands of the gods: ἁρπάζουσι πλόον (cf. v. 320). See my article about ἁρπάζειν and ἁρπαγμός in St. Paul's *Epistle to the Philippians* in *Hermes* L, 1915, pp. 537-553. It should be noted that the inhabitants of Hesiod's just city do not go aboard ships at all; cf. *Works and Days* 236 and *Theog.* 869-877.

3. Hes. *Theog.* 22-34. The proem begins with the praise of the Heliconian Muses, v. 1-21, and then goes on: 'They once taught Hesiod beautiful song while he was shepherding his lambs in the foothills of sacred Helicon, and this word the goddesses said to me'; and he quotes the words of the Muses, telling how they plucked and gave him ('me') a rod and inspired him with the gift of song. From the sudden transition from the third person to the first person singular it has been concluded that Hesiod must be a different person from him who speaks of himself as 'I' in the next lines. This would lead us to consider Hesiod as a famous poet prior in time to the author of the *Theogony;* and that conclusion

has been drawn, e.g. by Hugh G. Evelyn-White in his edition of Hesiod in the Loeb Classical Library (London 1936), p. xv. He has had some predecessors in classical antiquity, since Pausanias IX, 31, 4, remarks that some scholars assumed that the *Erga* was Hesiod's only poem. I cannot follow this interpretation, which in my opinion involves a misunderstanding of the rather natural change of the speaker from the third to the first person in the proem of a book where the name had to be given. Of course he could not say, 'I am Hesiod.' Even in the fifth century an author would give his name in the third person in a full sentence: 'Thucydides of Athens has written the history, etc.', but after that he would go on, 'As for the older times, *I* do not think they were very important . . .' (οὐ μεγάλα νομίζω γενέσθαι).

4. The peasants themselves have servants (δμῶας); cf. *Works and Days* 597, etc. But in v. 602, Hesiod also speaks of labourers who are hired for the harvest only, and dismissed later. See Wilamowitz, *Hesiodos Erga* (Berlin 1928), 110.

5. See Hesiod's *Works and Days* vv. 493 and 501, where it is said that the 'crowded lounge' (ἐπαλὴς λέσχη) is the favourite place for idlers, particularly in winter, when the cold keeps them from field work.

6. See the various proverbial sayings about the importance of 'what people say' (φήμη), *Works and Days* 760, 761, 763.

7. *Works and Days* 27-39, 213 ff., 248, 262.

8. *Works and Days* 39, 221, 264.

9. The tradition that Hesiod followed distinguished a golden, silver, bronze, and an iron age, but between the bronze and the iron age Hesiod inserted the heroic, which is the age described by Homer. He thought of it as immediately preceding his own age, i.e. the iron. It is obvious that this is a secondary invention in order to bring into the picture the Homeric world, which was for Hesiod as real as his own time. It does not fit into the construction of the metals gradually degenerating in successive ages. Hesiod often blends variants of the myth or makes additions himself.

10. *Works and Days* 197-201.

11. This was the meaning the Greek word ἀγροῖκος took on later. See the type of man described under that name in Theophrastus' *Characters* IV.

12. In *Paideia* III, 173 ff., it has been shown that even at the time when the city thought that country life and lack of culture were one and the same thing, Xenophon in his writings, most of all in his *Oeconomicus,* gave expression to an entirely different point of view. But the squire's idea of the country is not that of the plain farmer and shepherd, which Hesiod reveals in his *Works and Days*. What Xenophon and Hesiod have in common and what separates them both from the bucolic idyll of later Hellenistic poetry is the quite unromantic reality which that way of life has for them both.

13. Cf. the parallel phenomenon of Homer's influence on the form and language of the elegiac and lyric poets, pp. 89 ff., 118, 123-124.

14. Those who think of the *Theogony* and the *Works and Days* as products of two different poets (see note 3) must close their eyes to the fact that the *Works and Days* can be understood only against the background of a living mythical thought like that of the *Theogony,* which no longer expresses the purely objective attitude of Homer toward the mythical tradition but permeates it with a new, almost philosophical spirit.

15. Hesiod, *Works and Days* 81 ff. Cf. *Theog.* 585 ff. and 591 ff.

16. Cf. the loose manner in which the story of Pandora's jar (πίθος) is introduced. Hesiod does not really tell it but takes it for granted that his audience knows the details. Former critics used to conclude from such indications that the

whole section about the πίθος must be a later interpolation made by a rhapsode
who missed this part of the story. But I hope they no longer find followers
nowadays. Similarly, the cause of Zeus' wrath, the betrayal of the gods by
Prometheus at the sacrificial meal at Mekone, is not told in the *Works and Days*
v. 48, but only briefly hinted at. In *Theog.* 535 ff. this part of the story is fully
elaborated; so the hint in the other poem refers to the *Theogony,* as do other
passages of the *Works and Days.* See note 25.

17. Cf. pp. 7-8. For Hesiod's own conception of areté, see p. 70.

18. *Works and Days* 27 ff.

19. *Works and Days* 202 ff.

20. This was the title of Adolf Kirchhoff's noted book (*Hesiodos' Mahnlieder
an Perses,* Berlin 1889), in which he applied the same method to the work of
Hesiod as in his analytical treatment of the *Odyssey* mentioned before.

21. This part of the poem begins v. 298, after the famous words on areté and
the best way of attaining it (286-297). They form a sort of second proem or
transition to the merely didactic second part of the *Erga.*

22. We find the same form of archaic composition in the collection of Theognis'
poems, which starts with the general description of the political situation in
Megara at the time of the poet and adds to this brief first part the long series
of moral precepts that constitute the bulk of the work. Cf. pp. 197 ff.

23. An important step towards the understanding of the structure of the *Works
and Days* and its consideration as a unity was made by P. Friedlaender, in
Hermes XLVIII, 558. His subsequent analysis in *Gött. Gel. Anz.,* 1931, did not
appear until this chapter had been completed.

24. Pausanias, IX, 31, 4, tells us that he saw on Mount Helicon an old lead
plate near the spring, on which Hesiod's *Works and Days* was engraved, but
from which the proem with the invocation of Zeus was missing. That form of the
text may have been taken from some Hellenistic edition; the Peripatetic pupil
of Theophrastus, Praxiphanes, and the critics Aristarchus and Crates held this
view of the proem, that it was an addition. See the testimonia in Rzach's *editio
maior,* p. 127. In modern times some critics have joined them. Konrat Ziegler, in
Archiv für Relig. XIV (1911), 392 ff., even tried to prove that the proem of the
Erga is written in the characteristic style of fifth-century rhetoric, with all the
figures of speech whose use in combination is usually ascribed to Gorgias:
antithesis, isokolon, and isoteleuton. But this argument should be reversed, for
what we have in the proem of Hesiod is a regular hymn of truly archaic
structure. The similarity to the style of Gorgianic rhetoric only confirms the tradition that rhetoric in the beginning tried to compete with poetry in matters of
form. See Arist., *Rhet.* III, 1, 9. More accurately we may say that Gorgianic
rhetoric closely followed the old poetic form of the hymn. Hesiod's proem is one
of the few old documents of this genre we possess. As I have shown in *Solons
Eunomie* (*Sitz. Berl. Akad.* 1926, p. 83), this form was copied by Solon at the
beginning of the sixth century in his political poem ἡμετέρα δὲ πόλις, for in its
second part that elegy reaches its climax in a genuine hymn on Εὐνομία, who is
obviously to be regarded as a powerful goddess, just as is Δίκη in the first part
of the poem. Both are sisters in Hesiod's *Theogony,* v. 902. The proem of the
Erga is a praise of Diké and of Zeus, her protector. It is essential at the place
where it stands, as Lisco and Leo proved convincingly long ago.

25. The introduction of a second (good) Eris in contradistinction to the bad
Eris of tradition can only be interpreted as a self-correction of the poet, a sort
of palinode like the famous one of Stesichorus. Hesiod refers apparently to *Theog.*
226, where he knew only of the bad Eris. The form of the beginning οὐκ ἄρα
μοῦνον ἔην Ἐρίδων γένος expressly connects the new realization of the existence

of a good Eris with a preceding stage of thought which must now be changed. In this sense ἄρα with the imperfect is used frequently in Homer.

26. On the interpretation of the roots of the earth in the *Works and Days* v. 19, see p. 157, note 31.

27. *Works and Days* 40.

28. The praise of work (ἔργον, ἐργάζεσθαι) opens the second part of the *Works and Days*, v. 298-316.

29. On the harmony of human life with the laws of the universe in Homer, see pp. 50, 52.

30. The Greek *Chaos* is the *gingargap* of Nordic saga. *Chaos* is derived from χάσκω, which corresponds to German *gapen*.

31. The speculation of Hesiod on Eros was taken up by Aeschylus (*Danaides,* frg. 44) and by Presocratic philosophers such as Parmenides and Empedocles. The latter calls the same power φιλία and ᾿Αφροδίτη. Plato too, in his *Symposium,* makes the physician and scientist Eryximachus state the existence of a cosmogonic principle, to which he gives the name and nature of Eros. In Aristotle's *Metaphysics* there appears an Eros of the materialized forms to realize in themselves the immaterial form which he calls God. In a more naturalistic sense Lucretius, in the proem to Book I of the *De Rerum Natura,* uses the principle under the Empedoclean name of Venus (= ᾿Αφροδίτη). From the Platonic and Aristotelian concept of Eros a straight line leads to the Neoplatonists and to the Christian Pseudo-Dionysius the Areopagite, who tries to reconcile the pagan Eros with the Christian Agape, interpreting them both as a divine and cosmic power. The theories of the cosmic Eros pass from these thinkers through Dante and the scholastic philosophers to the poets of the nineteenth century, by whom this idea is revived.

32. The thought of Hesiod deserves a new and more coherent interpretation than it has received thus far. His own share in the presentation of the mythical tradition as it appears in his works must be defined more clearly. Aristotle, *Met.* B 4, 1000a18, calls him one of those who σοφίζονται μυθικῶς, and that is still the best characterization of Hesiod which has been given to date.

33. See p. 64.

34. *Works and Days* 41 ff.

35. On the plan of making the first woman and its execution, see *Works and Days* 56-105. On the world without labour and evil, which preceded the deed of Prometheus, see ib. 90-92.

36. Cf. pp. 27 and 32 ff. and notes.

37. Editors have not noticed that the beginning of the *Works and Days* (after the preliminary prayer to Zeus, which closes with the words 'but I will tell the truth to Perses') shows, by its characteristic opening, οὐκ ἄρα μοῦνον ἔην, that it is modelled on the beginning of a Homeric speech. Yet to understand this is to understand the plan of the whole poem. It is an independent 'speech' of admonition, enlarged to epic dimensions. The long admonitory speech of Phoenix in *Iliad* IX resembles it closely.

38. *Works and Days* 106.

39. Ib. 207.

40. Ib. 202.

41. αἶνος meaning 'praise' (= ἔπαινος) appears in Homer and Pindar. Aeschylus, *Ag.* 1547, and Sophocles, *O.C.* 707, also use it in this sense in lyrical parts of their tragedies. From this the meaning 'story, tale' is usually distinguished— a meaning which also occurs in Homer and the tragic poets. In reality, as we have proved before (see p. 40), the original meaning of the 'tales' told by the poet or bard was 'praise of great deeds of men and gods'. And this must be

extended even to the ordinary tale of the people: its purpose is praise, often with a moral; therefore they could call it αἶνος. The people liked fables as much as mythical stories, or even better. They too were called αἶνος, because it was 'praise' in that wider sense that they had in common with the myths: they both contained a paradigm.

42. *Works and Days* 219 ff. The just city, 225 ff., the unjust city, 238 ff.

43. Perses is addressed at *Works and Days* 213, the kings at 248. In the same way Perses had been addressed in the preceding part of the poem, first at 27, and the whole Prometheus story and the myth of the five ages of the world (see 106) were directed to him; then the judges were briefly addressed in the fable of the hawk and the nightingale. So Hesiod speaks to both parties alternately throughout the first part of the poem. In the second part this is no longer possible, for there the question of right is dismissed and precepts for work are given, which are properly addressed to Perses alone; for work is to redeem him from his injustice.

44. *Works and Days* 274. Here in 276 νόμος does not yet have the meaning of 'law', which it takes on later. See Wilamowitz, *Hesiods Erga* 73. That concept is here rather expressed by δίκη. Even the oldest ·Ionian philosophers who discovered the 'law of nature', as we should say, speak of δίκη, not νόμος. Hesiod's sharp distinction between the life of the beasts and the life of man was abandoned later in the age of the sophists by those who expressly put man and beast on one and the same level and thought them both subject to the same law: the 'struggle for life', the supreme norm of which is that might makes right. Then all law appeared as an artificial convention, whereas the struggle of the animals against each other was called φύσει δίκαιον. Cf. pp. 326, 401; II, 138.

45. *Iliad* XVI, 384-393. Note that the conception of Zeus as an ethical force defending justice is more clearly expressed in this simile than anywhere else in the *Iliad*. It has long been observed that Homer's similes, in contrast to the rigidly stylized heroic narrative, often show traces of the real life of the poet's own time.

46. See *Works and Days* 256-260. Closely connected with that central position of Diké in the divine realm is Hesiod's idea of the thirty thousand guardians of Zeus who watch over the maintenance of justice on earth as a sort of heavenly police force (*Works and Days* 252). This realism makes the Homeric idea of 'Zeus who sees and hears everything' much more tangible. Hesiod the theologian is naturally interested in the problem, who are the immortal spirits selected for this service by Zeus? He tells in the story of the five ages of the world that the men of the golden age, who were similar to the gods even during their lifetime, after death became 'good daemons' and live on earth as guardians of mortal men (*Works and Days* 122 ff.). There is a remarkable contrast between this religious realism of Hesiod's belief in divine justice and Solon's idealistic concept of diké as a principle inherent in the social world of man as such and working automatically and organically. See pp. 140-141. From Hesiod's idea of the guardian daemons the later daemonology of the Greeks developed, which was finally blended with the angelology of the Christian religion. Hesiod's view is obviously the old popular belief in spirits, interpreted in his theological and moral way.

47. *Works and Days* 633 ff.

48. *Theog.* 902.

49. *Theog.* 869 ff.

50. *Works and Days* 286 ff.

51. U. v. Wilamowitz-Moellendorff, *Sappho und Simonides* (Berlin 1913), p. 169. This view has been questioned in vain by some critics. This passage is decisive

(*Works and Days* 312-313): if thou workest, the idle will soon envy thee when thou art rich: for prosperity is followed by areté and reputation (πλούτῳ δ' ἀρετὴ καὶ κῦδος ὀπηδεῖ). All the special precepts which Hesiod gives for the farmer's work from *Works and Days* 383 on are expressly subordinated to the general idea: If thy heart desireth *wealth* (πλοῦτος), do these things and work with work upon work (381-382). The Hesiodic order of things is this: work—wealth—areté.

52. *Works and Days* 63.

53. See note 51. Areté, social position, and reputation belong together in Hesiod's opinion. Κῦδος here is the same as δόξα, which is used instead in prose. See Solon's correlation of ὄλβος and δόξα, frg. 1, 34, *supra* p. 144.

54. *Works and Days* 293.

55. Arist. *Eth. Nic.* 1, 2, 1095b10.

56. On this form of composition of Hesiod's *Erga* and the parallel structure of Theognis' didactic poem, see above note 22.

57. *Works and Days* 298-307.

58. *Works and Days* 311 ff. See note 51.

59. See above, p. 49.

60. *Anecdota Bekkeri* 733, 13.

61. *Works and Days* 174, 633-640, 654-662, *Theogony* 22-35.

62. *Works and Days* 174.

63. *Theogony* 27.

64. *Works and Days* 10. Cf. Wilhelm Luther, *Wahrheit und Luege im aeltesten Griechentum* (Borna-Leipzig 1935).

CHAPTER 5

STATE-EDUCATION IN SPARTA

1. See Alfred Zimmern, *The Greek Commonwealth* (5th ed., Oxford 1931), and Matthias Gelzer in *Das Problem des Klassischen*, Acht Vortraege gehalten auf der Fachtagung der Klass. Altertumswissenschaft zu Naumburg, hrsg. v. Werner Jaeger (Leipzig 1931). In support of the thesis that the polis was the primary form of the state in classical Hellas, it may be said that the philosophers of the classical period do not seriously take into account any other political form. Even the attempts of the Greeks during this period to form larger groups or confederacies presupposed the existence of the city-state as the normal collective unit.

2. See Fustel de Coulanges, *La cité antique* (16th ed., Paris 1898), Gustave Glotz, *The Greek City and its Institutions* (London 1929), Jacob Burckhardt, *Griechische Kulturgeschichte*, Bd. I (Berlin 1898).

3. One of the first modern minds to realize the full importance of the polis for Greek spiritual life was Hegel. This idea, however, did not come from his own philosophy and the position which he gave the state in it; on the contrary it was his true historical understanding of the Greek polis which influenced his philosophy. Hegel admired the harmony and wholeness of Greek life which centred about the life of the community. Other great humanists of the nineteenth century, such as Fustel de Coulanges and Jacob Burckhardt, viewed the omnipotence of the polis in Greek antiquity with the distrustful eyes of the liberal nineteenth-century individualist. But they agreed with Hegel on the historical fact that the ancient Greek city-state dominated all of Greek life, and they stressed that fact all the more clearly in their picture of Greek civilization precisely because they were afraid of it. Hegel, on the other hand, tried to incorporate

STATE-EDUCATION IN SPARTA

the ancient concept of man as a political being into the humanistic ideal of the eighteenth century, when culture in general had been separated from politics and kept within the limits of an aesthetic and moral ideal. Hegel went back to those humanists of the Italian Renaissance who, like Machiavelli, saw the *respublica* as the centre of human life. But he tried also to give back to this idea the ethical dignity which it had in Plato's and Aristotle's philosophy, by giving the state the Absolute as its spiritual anchor. Burckhardt, the sceptic, tried to save the liberty of the individual (to him the supreme humanistic value), which he saw endangered by the collective forces behind the powerful modern state. He thought that even the general movement for political liberty would finally result in the tyranny of the masses over all real spiritual freedom. He therefore passionately rejected Hegel's faith in the ideal of the polis and his acceptance of the entire Greek way of life. Therefore, paradoxically, while Burckhardt worshipped Greek art and thought, he painted the political reality of Greek life, even in its most liberal forms, in the darkest colours. Whatever the truth of these views, it remains a historical fact that the polis penetrated all the rest of Greek life; and whoever wants to describe its real structure must take this into account, particularly throughout the early and classical periods of Greek history. Individualism, in the over-refined sense in which Jacob Burckhardt and nineteenth-century humanism conceived it, was the final product of the dissolution of the classical harmony of man and polis, and it must be understood as such. The attitude of the present book with regard to this problem is not a dogmatic one, either in the sense of Hegel or of Burckhardt. I have called that classical harmony 'political humanism' because this term designates the Greek ideals of culture in their close connexion with the social life of the time. But I mean to show this relation not in its favourable aspects alone; for this book pursues the development of that idea through all its historical phases and ends with the grave antinomies involved in it with which later centuries of antiquity saw themselves confronted, and which led to the final separation between Greek cultural and political life. See the analysis of this historical process in the second and third volumes of *Paideia*.

4. The greatest loss in this respect was the destruction of the gigantic work of the Aristotelian school, the *Constitutions* or *Politeiai* of 158 states, Greek and barbarian, of which the rediscovered *Constitution of Athens* is the outstanding example. The fragments of the other books of this great collection were published in Valentin Rose's *Aristotelis Fragmenta* (Leipzig 1886).

5. Cf. Plato, *Laws,* Books I-III. In taking these two types as the basis of his philosophical analysis, Plato followed the actual historical development of Greece. Ever since the time when Athens emerged after the Persian Wars as the leading democratic power, Greece had been split into two camps, Athens and Sparta. So she is represented for the first time by Thucydides under the impression of the Peloponnesian War. The political picture of Greece in Herodotus is more variegated, but posterity has acquiesced in Thucydides' simplified view rather than in that of Herodotus or in Aristotle's detailed picture of the various Greek states and their constitutional forms.

6. See *Paideia* II and III, particularly the passages dealing with the problem of Plato's attitude towards the Spartan ideal (see 'Sparta' and 'Plato' in the indexes to vols. II and III). See also the funeral oration of Pericles in Thucydides' *History* and its complex idea of the Athenian state and of the opposites reconciled in it (*infra,* p. 410).

7. Plato ironically makes Socrates say (*Prot.* 342 B) that all Spartans (and Cretans) are philosophers and that the characteristic form of their philosophic nature is the so-called Laconic manner of speech; but the Spartans pretend to be uncultured.

8. Plato in *Laws* 629a and 660e chooses Tyrtaeus as the outstanding representative of the Spartan spirit and its ideal of areté, and he illustrates this by quoting from his poems. In Plato's time Tyrtaeus was generally accepted as the herald of Spartan virtue, and in Sparta everyone was impregnated with the ideals of his poetry (*Laws* 629b). See also *Paideia* III, 220 ff., and notes.

9. The fact that the poems of Tyrtaeus contain only scanty references to the actual conditions of his time has been used by modern scholars to question their authenticity; so by Eduard Schwartz in his noted article 'Tyrtaios,' *Hermes* XXXIV (1899), 428 ff. See also Verrall, *Classical Review* XI (1897), 269, and XII (1898), 185 ff.; U. v. Wilamowitz-Moellendorff, *Textgeschichte der griechischen Lyriker, Abh. d. Goett. Ges. d. Wiss.,* N. F. IV (1900), 97 ff.

10. See the treatment of that book in *Paideia* III, 166-171.

11. Arist. *Pol.* II, 9.

12. Arist. *Pol.* II, 9, 1271b1 ff. He quotes Plato's *Laws* 625c ff. for this statement. Indeed, he takes this part of his criticism from Plato's work.

13. The oracle ἁ φιλοχρηματία Σπάρταν ὀλεῖ, ἄλλο δὲ οὐδέν was mentioned by Aristotle in his lost *Constitution of the Lacedaemonians,* see Valentin Rose, *Aristotelis Fragmenta,* n. 544. The authenticity of the oracle has been questioned by Eduard Meyer and other modern scholars.

14. Karl Otfried Mueller, *Die Dorier* (1824).

15. Pindar, *Nem.* VII, 28, ξανθὸς Μενέλαος, *Nem.* III, 43, ξανθὸς Ἀχιλεύς, *Nem.* IX, 17, ξανθοκομᾶν Δανάων μέγιστοι λαγέται. Even Athena, *Nem.* X, 7, and the Graces, *Nem.* V, 54, are fair-haired in Pindar's imagination.

16. The word στρατός, which means 'the army', also has in earlier times (and in poetry, frequently even in the fifth century) the meaning 'the people', thereby preserving a valuable trace of the origin of what we call free institutions: the political rights of the citizen of an ancient polis originally derived from the part which he took in the defence of his country. For decisions of great importance, the στρατός had to be consulted. See the not infrequent examples of this usage of the word στρατός in Pindar and Aeschylus.

17. This is the state of things presupposed in the rhétra of the kings Polydorus and Theopompus: αἱ δὲ σκολιὰν ὁ δᾶμος ἕλοιτο, τοὺς πρεσβυγενέας καὶ ἀρχαγέτας ἀποστατῆρας ἦμεν; see Plut. *Lyc.* 6. It was said before by Plutarch that the demos of Sparta had the right of examining and criticizing (ἐπικρίνειν) the laws proposed by the council, and that the people used to add to or veto the measures proposed.

18. The institution of the ephorate is ascribed to King Theopompus by Plutarch, *Lyc.* 7, but Tyrtaeus, who describes the various elements of the Spartan polity in his poem called *Eunomia,* written two generations after the time of Theopompus, and who has a great admiration for that king, does not mention the ephors. Another version, the earliest witness for which is Herodotus (I, 65), says that the ephorate was founded by Lycurgus. That is no specific tradition, of course, but the institution of the ephors was ascribed to the famous lawgiver simply because everything in Sparta was considered to be his creation. See the passages of ancient authors on the various chronological traditions in F. Jacoby, *Apollodors Chronik,* 140 ff. According to Sosicrates (Diog. L. I, 68) there existed a tradition that dated the first ephors as late as the archonship of Euthydemus (556).

19. See Plut. *Lyc.* 6 and 13. In the latter chapter Plutarch quotes a rhétra of Lycurgus, μὴ χρῆσθαι νόμοις ἐγγράφοις. Accordingly we have to think of a rhétra as not originally fixed in written form; but the fact that Plutarch quotes some of them in the Laconian dialect proves that eventually they were preserved

in writing. The writer from whom Plutarch takes the text of the rhétrai in
Lyc. 6 must have found it somewhere in Sparta.

20. The absence of written laws is explained by Plutarch, *Lyc.* 13 ff., by the
fact that education was all-important in Sparta. The function of legislation was
completely taken over by paideia: τὸ γὰρ ὅλον καὶ πᾶν τῆς νομοθεσίας ἔργον εἰς
τὴν παιδείαν ἀνῆψε (scil. Lycurgus). Plutarch obviously took this interpretation
of the historical facts from Plato's *Republic;* see *Paideia* II, 237-239.

21. For Plato's relationship to Sparta, see *Paideia* III, 219 ff. (His extensive discussion of this subject is found in *Laws,* Books I-III.)

22. Plut. *Lyc.* 24.

23. Ib. 25.

24. See above, notes 17 and 18.

25. It occurs in extant Greek literature for the first time in Herodotus, I,
65-66. There the famous Spartan eunomia and the entire cosmos of the Spartiates
is derived from 'Lycurgus', who appears as a historical personality contemporary
to King Leobotes. Herodotus mentions that after Lycurgus' death he was worshipped as a god in Sparta and received a temple which was still in existence
in Herodotus' time. See V. Ehrenberg, *Neugruender des Staates* (Munich 1925),
28-54.

26. More accurately speaking, we can trace back the tradition about Lycurgus
to two different periods in the spiritual history of Greece. It first originated in
the time when rational speculation about the best form of the state (εὐνομία)
started, i.e. the sixth-fifth centuries. This speculation is reflected in the report
of Herodotus I, 65 ff. The second impulse came from the pedagogical and philosophic discussion of the time during and after the Peloponnesian War. This
phase is represented by men like Critias, Plato, and Xenophon. The first phase
stressed the religious (Delphic) origin and authorization of the Spartan cosmos.
The second elaborated on the paideutic structure of the Spartan system.

27. The principal features of Xenophon's picture of the *agogé*, the Spartan educational system, are treated in *Paideia* III, 170. It is not necessary to discuss the
matter here, because it represents more the ideal of the philo-Laconian educational movement of the fourth century than the historical reality of seventh-
century Sparta, even though scholars like to project it back into the beginning
of Spartan history, of which it is the final product.

28. Eduard Schwartz, 'Tyrtaios', *Hermes* XXXIV (1899), rejected not only the
authenticity of Tyrtaeus' poems but also the historical novels about the Messenian
Wars of later Hellenistic authors, such as the epic poet Rhianus of Bene in Crete
and the rhetorician Myron of Priene. (Both these lost works were used as sources
by Pausanias in the fourth Book of his *Perihegesis.*) Since I re-established the
authenticity of Tyrtaeus' poems in my essay *Tyrtaios ueber die wahre Areté*
(*Sitz. Berl. Akad.* 1932), a former student of mine has given a new analysis of
the Hellenistic historical tradition and successfully defended against Eduard
Schwartz's hyper-criticism the historical reality of the Messenian Wars. See
Juergen Kroymann, 'Sparta und Messenien' (in *Neue Philologische Untersuchungen,* hrsg. v. Werner Jaeger, Heft XI, Berlin 1937).

29. Tyrtaeus frg. 4.

30. Tyrtaeus frg. 5.

31. Tyrtaeus frg. 8.

32. Plato, *Laws* 629a with the scholia *ad loc.* (p. 301 Greene), and Philochorus
and Callisthenes apud Strabo, 362.

33. Tyrtaeus was allegedly a Spartan general (στρατηγός), see Strabo 362.
Several modern scholars have accepted this so-called tradition, even though it

is founded only on the legend that he was sent to the Spartans by the Athenians as a leader during the second Messenian War. In ancient times Philochorus and Callisthenes recorded this story (Strabo, loc. cit.), but even Strabo reminded his readers of the *Eunomia* of Tyrtaeus. There (frg. 2) he says of the Spartan nation: we came to this country from Erineos, when first we took possession of it. Strabo rightly infers from this that Tyrtaeus must have been a native Spartan, but strangely enough he still maintains the other part of the legendary tradition, namely that he was a leader of the Spartans during the Messenian Wars, even if he was not sent to them by the Athenians. This is refuted now by the passage quoted in the text from the new elegy found on papyrus, which is now frg. 1 in Diehl's anthology.

34. It was said in note 9 that this absence of historical allusion made the poems of Tyrtaeus suspect in the eyes of some modern scholars such as Schwartz and Wilamowitz. But the new elegy, frg. 1, proves that such allusions, even though they could not prevail in this kind of poetical exhortation, were not altogether lacking from it.

35. See Plato, *Laws* 629a-630 and 660e-661a.

36. See p. 96 and notes.

37. This admiration for Spartan valour and its expression in Tyrtaeus' poems should not be confused with the philo-Laconism of political reaction in later centuries. The spirit of Leonidas, who died with his Spartans at Thermopylae for the liberty of Greece after the soldiers of other cities had abandoned their positions, remains the genuine monument of that ideal.

38. See note 32.

39. Demosth. *Cor.* 170.

40. See p. 86.

41. Aristotle, who speaks of the origin of tragedy and comedy, does not pronounce a theory of his own about the beginnings of elegy in his *Poetics*. This gap was obviously felt in the Aristotelian school during the next generation, but no agreement was reached among scholars, as Horace (*Ars Poet.* 77) says, following the Peripatetic Neoptolemus of Parium as his source, according to the commentary of Porphyrio. The tradition concerning the inventor of elegy contained in the scattered testimonia of later ancient grammarians confirms this statement: some name Tyrtaeus or Callinus, others Archilochus or Mimnermus as the founder of this poetic genre, and all reflect the lack of real knowledge.

42. A collection of the most important testimonia of the ancient grammarians on the elegy as a poetical genre and on its origin is found in J. M. Edmonds' *Greek Elegy and Iambus*, vol. 1 (Loeb Classical Library). See the article 'Elegie' in Pauly-Wissowa, *Realencyclopaedie* v, 2260, by Crusius; C. M. Bowra, *Early Greek Elegists* (Cambridge, Mass. 1938).

43. See the interpretation of that elegy, p. 91.

44. See Felix Jacoby, 'Studien zu den aelteren griechischen Elegikern' in *Hermes* LIII (1918), p. 1 ff.

45. Hesiod's creation of the didactic epic and the hortatory nature of the earliest elegiac poetry both prove beyond doubt that the impression which the Homeric epic made on the mind of the audience at that time must have been to a great extent protreptic. It is this hortatory power of the epos to which they try to give a more concentrated and actual form in the new genre.

46. Hector, the Trojan hero and brave defender of his city, comes closest to this ideal of all Homeric characters. See the famous verse (*Iliad* XII, 243) εἷς οἰωνὸς ἄριστος ἀμύνεσθαι περὶ πάτρης. But the Greek heroes are fighting not for a fatherland but for their own name and glory.

47. Tyrtaeus frg. 6, 1-2.

48. Cf. p. 92.

49. Tyrtaeus frg. 9, Diehl.

50. See my essay *Tyrtaios ueber die wahre Areté* (*Sitz. Berl. Akad.* 1932), which provides a thorough foundation for the views put forward in this chapter.

51. This was the age to which critics such as Eduard Schwartz and Wilamowitz were inclined to attribute the poem, mostly because of what they called its harmonious and logical composition and its rhetorical form of expression. See their works quoted above in note 9.

52. This I have proved in my essay referred to in note 50, pp. 557-559.

53. See Plato, *Laws* 629a, 660e.

54. Tyrtaeus frg. 9, 1 ff.

55. The list of the Olympian victors started with Coroebus in 776 B.C., only a few decades before the second Messenian War, during which Tyrtaeus wrote his poems. On Spartan victors, see p. 97; Xenophanes' criticism of the exaggerated evaluation of the victory in the national games, pp. 97 and 173; on Pindar's hymns, p. 208.

56. Tyrtaeus frg. 9, 5-17. The Ionian words ξυνὸν ἐσλόν mean the same as κοινὸν ἀγαθόν, the *common good*. With them Tyrtaeus introduces a new criterion of true virtue.

57. Cf. Solon frg. 14 (Diehl's ed. alt.), 7, ταῦτ' ἄφενος θνητοῖσι, and Tyrtaeus frg. 9, 13, ἥδ' ἀρετή, τόδ' ἄεθλον ἐν ἀνθρώποισιν ἄριστον. For this early rhetoric, see my essay on Tyrtaeus (quoted in note 50), p. 549.

58. See note 56.

59. Tyrtaeus frg. 9, 23-32.

60. On the Homeric idea of areté and glory, see above, p. 8 ff., 40. On the *political* reinterpretation of these fundamental concepts by Tyrtaeus, see my essay on Tyrtaeus (quoted in note 50), pp. 551-552.

61. See Erwin Rohde, *Psyche*, 8th ed., first chapter: 'Seelenglaube und Seelencult in den homerischen Gedichten'.

62. The turning point in this development was Socrates. Plato, in his *Republic,* rewards his 'truly just man' by granting him the traditional honours which the polis used to give its sons; but the radical change in the relation of the individual to the polis reveals itself in the fact that the highest reward that Plato grants the just man is the immortality of his soul, the guarantee of his eternal value as a human personality. See *Paideia* II, 367.

63. One might say that Cicero in his *Somnium Scipionis* incorporates Plato's transcendental concept of human virtue and immortality into his Republic, but his is a Roman heaven, an Elysium for the great patriots and historical figures in leading political positions. So Cicero bears witness once more to the power of the old idea of the polis.

64. Tyrtaeus frg. 9, 37-42.

65. Tyrtaeus frg. 6, 7 (Diehl). Modern scholars have occasionally maintained that this long and famous elegy, which is quoted by the Attic orator Lycurgus (*Leocr.* 107) as a model of true areté for the Attic youth, represents in reality two poems. A full statement of my reasons for disagreeing with such a division must be left for another occasion; but see my essay on Tyrtaeus, loc. cit. p. 565, note 1.

66. Tyrtaeus frg. 2, 3ab (Diehl).

67. Plut. *Lyc.* 6.

68. This seems to me to be the true relationship of Tyrtaeus' *Eunomia* to the old rhétra quoted in note 67. Eduard Meyer, in *Forschungen zur alten Geschichte,* I, 229, has doubted the authenticity of this poem; but his suspicions appear to me to be groundless.

69. Tyrtaeus frg. 2.

70. Tyrtaeus frg. 3ab.

71. At least so his attitude appears when we see it retrospectively in the light of later political developments. From the standpoint of Tyrtaeus' own time, the seventh century, the redefinition of civic virtue and its reduction to the simple standard of the valour which every citizen-soldier should possess appears rather democratic, especially when we see this criterion against the background of those old aristocratic standards which, as we tried to show (p. 91), Tyrtaeus rejected as insufficient (frg. 9). The democratic element in the Spartan constitution is indeed recognized by most ancient authors. But comparing it with the point later reached by Athens, one might say that the development of the democratic tendency in Sparta, which we see still in flux in Tyrtaeus' time, was afterwards arrested.

72. See the account of Tyrtaeus' influence in the history of Greek thought and literature on pp. 556-568 of my essay quoted in note 50. To this long list of testimonia witnessing his lasting effect on later times, including the age of democratic Athens, we must now add another important one from the Hellenistic age: the epigram published by G. Klaffenbach in his report on his epigraphic travels in Aetolia and Acarnania (Sitz. Berl. Akad. 1935, p. 719). See also Paideia III, 220 and 338, note 32.

73. Plato, Rep. 465d-466a.

74. Plato, Laws 629b.

75. Xenophanes frg. 2 (Diehl). When we compare the first part of Xenophanes' elegy on true areté with frg. 9 of Tyrtaeus, it is obvious that the former's protest against overrating the value of the Olympian victor is not only an incidental agreement with Tyrtaeus' famous poem, but that it follows that model and varies it skilfully. The fundamental idea of both poems is the same: that there is a higher virtue than that of the overpraised victors in the great Hellenic games. They both want to reassert the superiority of that new idea of areté which they praise. But they differ in their conception of the highest virtue. For Tyrtaeus it is valour, but the philosophical mind of Xenophanes puts wisdom (σοφία) highest. See p. 173. Xenophanes has worked his new idea into the old poetical form of Tyrtaeus' elegy, as has 'Theognis', in a slightly different way, v. 699 ff.

76. Plato, Laws 660e.

77. See O. Brinkmann, 'Die Olympische Chronik', Rheinisches Museum, N.F. LXX (1915), 634.

78. Plut. De Mus. 4. On the time of Terpander (source: Glauco of Rhegium), Terpander and the πρώτη κατάστασις of music in Sparta, ib. 9, cf. De Mus. 42.

79. Later Aristotle (Pol. II, 9, 1269b17 ff.) criticized the Lacedaemonian women because of their licentiousness (ἄνεσις). In 1270a he traces their freedom back to the very beginning of Spartan history. He even speaks of the rule of women (γυναικοκρατεῖσθαι) in Sparta, which he thinks to be typical of military states.

CHAPTER 6

THE CITY-STATE AND ITS IDEAL OF JUSTICE

1. See the chapter on Solon, pp. 136-137, for Ionian influence on the mind of Solon.

2. See p. 96.

3. Some modern scholars have postulated its existence, but there is really no trace of such an earlier political poetry.

4. Even Xenophanes (frg. 3, Diehl) accused the Ionians of the 'useless luxury' (ἁβροσύνη ἀνωφελής) they learned from the Lydians, which caused their political downfall. He refers in particular to the inhabitants of his native city Colophon. But ἁβρόβιοι and ἁβροδίαιτοι seem to have been the standing descriptive terms for the Lydians and Ionians and their luxurious living in Aeschylus' time; see Aesch. *Pers.* 41 and *Bacchyl.* 17, 2.

5. Even Mimnermus, the poet best known for his sentimental praise of the sensual pleasures of love, celebrated in his poems the conquest of Colophon and Smyrna by the first settlers. In one elegy he described with great admiration a Colophonian hero's fight in the cavalry battles with the Lydians in the valley of the Hermos river. See frg. 12 and 13, Diehl.

6. *Iliad* XVIII, 503; see p. 49 ff.

7. *Iliad* II, 204.

8. *Iliad* XVIII, 556.

9. *Odyssey* XIII, 272.

10. See F. Bilabel, *Die ionische Kolonisation* (Leipzig 1920).

11. See Archilochus frg. 94, which shows how in his poems even the animals of the fable insist on their rights and attack injustice. On Anaximander's concept of a cosmic justice (δίκη), see pp. 159-160; on Parmenides, p. 175; on Heraclitus, cf. p. 182 ff.

12. See p. 65 ff.

13. In addition to the legislation of Lycurgus and Solon, the Greeks used to praise the laws of Draco, Zaleucus, Charondas, Androdamas, Pittacus, Philolaus, and others. Aristotle *Pol.* II, 13, mentions them as the outstanding codifications. The laws of Gortyna in Crete became known with the discovery of the famous inscription, published with a commentary by Buecheler and Zitelmann.

14. *Iliad* XI, 779, XVI, 796; *Odyssey* XIV, 56, etc. Θέμις is what is laid down by custom and, in this sense, is right.

15. *Iliad* II, 206.

16. R. Hirzel's book *Themis, Diké, und Verwandtes* (Leipzig 1907) was an excellent study at the time it was written, but today it seems unhistorical. It is now in many respects antiquated, but still contains much valuable material. There is a useful sketch of the historical development of the idea in V. Ehrenberg's *Die Rechtsidee im frühen Griechentum* (Leipzig 1921). The attempt to derive δίκη from δικεῖν, 'to throw', seems to me to be mistaken.

17. Perhaps something of that meaning was still alive in the adverbial use of the word—in reality an old accusative—as in κυνὸς δίκην, where we translate it simply 'like a dog'. See also the Homeric 'ἣ ἀνθρώπων δίκη ἐστί (i.e. 'as it is appropriate for men') and the like. ἔχει δίκην means 'he has his share'.

18. Diké and hybris are opposites in Greek. Hybris in earlier Greek authors means any concrete violation of the nomos, e.g. stealing horses. That hybris of which modern poets speak so often as something particularly Greek, i.e. transcending the limits of human nature and tempting the gods, is a special use of the word, concerning which see p. 167.

19. See V. Ehrenberg, loc. cit. p. 54 ff.

20. Cf. Solon frg. 24, 18-19. The same ideal is implicit in Hesiod's use of diké. Solon's thought is clearly inspired by Ionia. The early origin of the demand for equal rights before the judge or before the law would justify the assumption that the ideal of *isonomia* (which is first commonly advocated in the fifth century and always means democratic equality) is older than our scanty evidence would prove, and originally had the other sense of equality before the law. Ehrenberg, op. cit. p. 124, opposes this assumption: Hirzel's idea that isonomia meant 'equal distri-

bution of property', p. 240, seems to me to be unhistorical, and is quite unlike
the views of even the extreme democrats.

21. The adjective δίκαιος, which represents a preliminary stage in this development, appears in the *Odyssey* and in some late passages of the *Iliad;* but
the noun δικαιοσύνη does not occur in Homer. Παλαισμοσύνη or παλαιμοσύνη is
used by Homer, Tyrtaeus, and Xenophanes; πυκτοσύνη seems to have been invented by Xenophanes.

22. P. 91.

23. The idea that justice or righteousness is obedience to the law is universal
in the fifth and fourth centuries B.C.; cf. the newly discovered passage of Antiphon
(*Pap. Oxy.* XI, 1364, col. I (1-33), Hunt; Diels, *Vorsokratiker* II, 346); and the
passages quoted in Hirzel, op. cit. 199, note 1, especially Plato, *Crito* 54b.

24. Phocylides frg. 10 = Theogn. 147.

25. Plato, *Laws* 660e.

26. Plato, *Laws* 629c ff.

27. Aesch. *Sept.* 610. Wilamowitz called the verse spurious, and deleted it
from his edition of Aeschylus because he thought the canon of virtue dated from
Plato; but he restored it later. See my lectures *Platos Stellung im Aufbau der
griechischen Bildung,* in *Die Antike* IV (1928), 163, and *Die griechische Staatsethik
im Zeitalter des Plato* (1924), 5 (reprinted in *Humanistische Reden und Vorträge*).

28. Plato, *Rep.* 433b.

29. Arist., *Eth. Nic.* V, 3, 1129b27.

30. See what Tyrtaeus and Xenophanes say (*supra* pp. 91 and 173) about
the public recognition and outstanding social position granted by the entire polis
to the Olympic victor in their day, i.e. from the middle of the seventh to the
first third of the fifth century. With Xenophanes we reach the time of Pindar,
Simonides, and Bacchylides, whose poetry was to a great extent devoted to the
praise of the victors in the Hellenic games (see p. 206 ff.).

31. See Plato's *Laws* 654b on choral poetry as the high school for Greek youth
in the early polis state. The philosopher complains that this fine tradition no
longer exercises its educational influence in his own lifetime and proposes to
restore it in his ideal state. See *Paideia* III, 228 ff. See also on the public performances of Greek dramas *supra* p. 247.

32. See Arist. *Eth. Nic.* X, 10, 1180a24 ff.

33. Plato, *Rep.* II, 376e2.

34. The epigram comes from Pindar (frg. 152), and had a long history in
Greek literature, traced by E. Stier in his dissertation *Nomos Basileus* (Berlin
1927).

35. Plato, *Rep.* 544d, Arist. *Pol.* III, 1, 1275b3.

36. Plato, *Laws* 625a, 751c, *ep.* 335d; Isocr. *Paneg.* 82, *De Pace* 102; and cf.
Arist. *Pol.* VIII, 1, 1337a14.

37. See the chapter on Plato's *Laws* in *Paideia* III, 213-262, especially the sections on 'The Lawgiver as Educator', p. 213 ff., and 'The Spirit of the Laws';
see also M. Mühl, *Die hellenischen Gesetzgeber als Erzieher* in *Neue Jahrbuecher*
(1939), Heft 7.

38. This was the reason which led Plato finally to epitomize his philosophical
ideas on individual conduct and the communal life of men in a work significantly
entitled *The Laws,* in which the educator appears as a lawgiver to mankind.
Aristotle also, in his *Ethics,* feels in the end the need of the legislator; see *Eth.
Nic.* X, 10, 1180a15 ff. Both Plato and Aristotle refer again and again to the
existing legal tradition of the Greek people, and even to that of non-Greek
nations. Their concepts of human will, of voluntary and involuntary actions, of

justice and the various degrees of transgression of the law, are all developed
from accurate study of the positive law of their nation. Legislation thus became the
first important step towards the formulation of fixed general rules and norms of
life, a process which was to end in philosophy.

39. See my essay *Solons Eunomie* (*Sitz. Berl. Akad.* 1926), 70. The lawgiver
appears as 'author' in Plato, *Phaedr.* 257d ff., and as parallel to the poet in 278c.

40. I do not speak here of the sophists and their followers among practical
politicians, who critically contrasted *nomos* with *physis*, but of such critics as Plato,
Isocrates, and others who were in favour of strict norms of human conduct but
no longer believed that good laws were the panacea. See Plato, *Statesman* 294a-b,
Isocr. *Areop.* 40 ff.

41. Heraclitus frg. 44 (Diels).

42. Anaximander frg. 9 (Diels, *Vorsokratiker* 1).

43. See p. 159 ff.

44. In earlier centuries the Greeks conceived that universal standard as Diké,
later as the Good or as Reason (Logos). Heraclitus' philosophy combines both.
What earlier thinkers called the diké in the universe, he traces back to the logos
as its source. See *supra* p. 182 ff.

45. The Greek word ἰδιώτης means the opposite of πολίτης, even though the
same individual is both a private person and a member of the political community
(τὰ ἴδια opp. τὰ δημόσια). The contrast is intensified when the ἰδιώτης is compared with the actual politician (πολιτικός) or with any person whose life is
devoted to some kind of public service (δημιουργός), such as craftsmen. In that
connexion, ἰδιώτης comes to mean a layman. In Plato's language, e.g. in the
Republic, ἰδιώτης means the individual, so far as he has no influence on public
opinion and life. But as early as Heraclitus, a century before Plato's *Republic*,
we find the distinction between the common element (ξυνόν = κοινόν) of human
life and that which is private or individual (ἴδιον); see Diels, *Vorsokratiker* 1,
Heracl. frg. 2.

46. See *supra* p. 72 ff.

47. Thuc. II, c. 37.

48. The Greek word which in the new political order came more and more to
signify that old ideal was 'kaloskagathos'. It was no doubt of aristocratic origin,
but had expanded gradually and thus became the ideal of every citizen aspiring
to higher culture, finally coming to mean simply 'civic virtue'.

49. See *Paideia* II, 112 ff.

50. See p. 291 ff.

51. See *Paideia* II, 113.

52. Cf. p. 106.

53. Πολιτεύεσθαι = 'to live' is still to be found in the Greek language of the
New Testament; see Acts 23. 1, and Phil. 1. 27: ἀξίως τοῦ εὐαγγελίου τοῦ Χριστοῦ
πολιτεύεσθε. And so πολίτευμα means simply 'life', Phil. 3. 20: ἡμῶν γὰρ τὸ
πολίτευμα ἐν οὐρανοῖς ὑπάρχει.

54. Arist. *Pol.* I, 2, 1253a3, ὅτι ἄνθρωπος φύσει πολιτικὸν ζῷον.

55. Plato, *Laws* 643e. Cf. *Paideia* III, 224.

56. Cf. *Paideia* III, 106 ff., 237 ff.

CHAPTER 7

IONIAN AND AEOLIAN POETRY:
THE INDIVIDUAL SHAPES HIS OWN PERSONALITY

1. The κτίσις-form of epic poetry was apparently a late branch of the epic which originated in the age of the early Greek city-state, since it celebrated the mythical or myth-historical origin of the polis with which it was concerned. Xenophanes of Colophon, for example, wrote (Diog. L. IX, 20) a κτίσις of Colophon, but only after he had left the city and after it had lost its political independence. His εἰς Ἐλέαν ἀποικισμός (Diog. L., loc. cit.) was concerned with a contemporary event, the foundation of Elea in South Italy, which he had witnessed himself.

2. In his *Symposium* (209d), Plato compares the lawgivers of early Greece— Lycurgus, Solon, and many others who wrote laws for their cities—to the poets, Homer, Hesiod, and others; and likens the productions of the former to those of the latter. In the *Phaedrus* (257e), moreover, Plato points to the statesmen's practice of the art of prose in their habit of writing their laws and decrees in order to bequeath them to posterity. See his description of the great Greek and barbarian lawgivers as λογογράφοι in *Phaedrus* 258c. Obviously Plato considers them as the very founders of prose writing. The politician is also a kind of ποιητής; the assembly is his theatre, and in his followers he has his ἐπαινέται like every great poet (*Phaedr.* 258b). Similarly, Plato considers his own work as a lawgiver as something to be compared with great poetry (*Laws* 811c; see *Paideia* III, 255). In *Gorg.* 451b, the politicians who write *psephismata* in the assembly of the demos are said to be writers (συγγραφόμενοι); and the forensic speeches of the logographoi (Plat. *Euthyd.* 272a) are only another form of this early legal prose. And is not the Law (Thorah), the so-called books of Moses, the oldest and most important part of Hebrew literature? Analogies may be found in other oriental literatures.

3. See the chapter on Solon, p. 136 ff.

4. Archilochus frg. 94 (Diehl).

5. Cf. Archilochus frg. 7, 1-2; 9; 52; 54; 60; 64; 85; 88, 4; 109; all these passages refer to the fellow citizens or to the city and its public affairs.

6. See pp. 89-90 on Tyrtaeus' imitation of Homer; p. 96 on that of Callinus.

7. Archilochus frg. 1 (Diehl).

8. Frg. 3. Note also the epic colour of the names by which he addresses his friends: Κηρυκίδης, Αἰσιμίδης, Αἰσχυλίδης.

9. Frg. 2.

10. See what Critias (frg. 44, Diels, *Vorsokratiker* II, 1) says about the descent of Archilochus, that his mother was a slave.

11. Even Critias, loc. cit. (note 10), calls the loss of his shield the worst of all the shameful deeds of Archilochus. In Athens the ῥίψασπις was severely punished and lost his civic rights.

12. Archilochus frg. 6b (Diehl).

13. *Iliad* XXIV, 602 ff.

14. See p. 326 on the distinction by the sophists between 'law' and 'nature'.

15. In the moral code of the Homeric nobleman, fame is the prize and shame the penalty. Respect for the talk of the demos, as in *Odyssey* XVI, 75; XIX, 527; XXIV, 200, is part of the city-state morality, which influences the later parts of the epics. Hesiod, *Works and Days* 763, actually makes Pheme, Report, a goddess.

16. Frg. 9.

17. Frg. 64 (see note 18).

18. Frg. 65. This and the lines referred to in the preceding note must be taken together. Archilochus' criticism of the ignoble abuse of the dead by his fellow-men must have been famous among Greeks in all parts of the country. This is shown by the recent discovery of a fine archaic inscription in poetical form on the grave of a physician named Charon among the ruins of the ancient Teithronion (Phocis), published by G. Klaffenbach in *Reise durch Mittelgriechenland und die Ionischen Inseln (Sitz. Berl. Akad.* 1935, p. 702). The inscription goes back to the early period of the sixth century B.C. It is therefore not much later than half a century after Archilochus. Here is the text of the epigram: χαῖρε Χάρον · οὐδίς τυ κακὸς λέγει οὐδὲ θανόντα, πολὸς ἀνθρόπον λυσάμενος καμάτο. The editor rightly remarks that λυσάμενος should be λυσάμενον, obviously a mere mistake of the stone-mason. But what is more important is the allusion to Archilochus' frg. 64 and 65, which has escaped Klaffenbach's notice. Charon was the exception to Archilochus' rule: he was criticized *not even after his death*, since he had freed many people from their diseases. We know from Heraclitus (frg. 42, Diels) that Archilochus, like Homer, was recited at the public festivals of the Greeks, and the new epigram proves that he was known as early as the sixth century B.C., even in the remote agrarian district of Phocis, certainly not a centre of literary culture.

19. *Odyssey* XVIII, 136.

20. Frg. 68.

21. Dio Prus., or. XXXIII, 12.

22. See Pindar's criticism, *Pyth.* II, 55.

23. Frg. 81.

24. Frg. 89.

25. See p. 68.

26. Sem. frg. 7; cf. Hes. *Theog.* 590, *Works and Days* 83, 373.

27. E. Schwartz, *Sitz. Berl. Akad.* 1915, p. 144.

28. Reciprocal abuse between men and women took place at the festival of Demeter in Pellene (Paus. VII, 27, 10) and the festival of Apollo at Anaphe (Ap. Rhod. IV, 1726).

29. Heraclitus (frg. 42, Diels) proves that they did so regard Archilochus.

30. But Callimachus, in imitating Archilochus' iambics, does not seem to address such an audience. A further example of the iambic lampoon has lately been discovered. The careful editors of the Florentine papyrus, G. Vitelli and M. Norsa (*Atene e Roma*, Serie III, vol. I), believe that the poem is by Archilochus himself, but the scholarly quotations from Archilochus' other poems, the metre, and the witty piquancy of the language seem to me to suit no one but Callimachus. (Cf. also G. Pasquali, *Studi Italiani*, 1933.) In ll. 7 ff. I believe the poet has borrowed the Platonic comparison of the soul with a team of horses from the *Phaedrus* to depict violent passion.

31. See note 21.

32. Frg. 60.

33. Frg. 88.

34. Frg. 79. See R. Reitzenstein, *Sitz. Berl. Akad.* 1899, p. 857 ff., and *Hermes* XXXV, 621 ff. On more literature about the poem, see Diehl, *Anthologia Lyrica Graeca*, Vol. I, ad loc.

35. Pindar, *Pyth.* II, 55.

36. Frg. 79, 12 ff. See the similar outburst of hatred in Theognis, v. 349, τῶν εἴη μέλαν αἷμα πιεῖν.

37. I have freely paraphrased the purely anatomical image of the poem, frg. 96, in accordance with Hor. *Serm.* I, 9, 66 (cf. the similar passage in *Od.* I, 13, 4).

38. See Aristotle frg. 80 (Rose), where the passages proving this view for Aristotle are collected from Seneca, Philodemus, and Cicero. There are of course no grounds for attributing them to the lost dialogue *Politikos*, as does Rose, *Arist. Pseudep.* 114.

39. Frg. 7 and 8.

40. Frg. 58.

41. Here is a good example of this (frg. 68): 'Such is the mind of men, Glaucus, son of Leptines, as is the day which Zeus sends them.' Even the ancient rhetorician Theo, in his *Progymnasmata* (*Rhet. Graec.* I, 153W), remarked rightly that Archilochus is here paraphrasing Homer (*Odyssey* XVIII, 136 ff.). Another example: when he confesses to have failed (frg. 73) but adds that Até has led others before him astray, he seems to be thinking of some famous instances in epic poetry.

42. Frg. 22. The speaker is not the poet himself but the carpenter Charon (see Arist. *Rhet.* III, 17, 1418b28), who voices his philosophy of life.

43. Frg. 67a. The words of the third line of this great poem must be corrupt in our manuscript tradition of Stobaeus' *Anthology,* to which we owe the preservation of the poem. ἐν δοκοῖσιν ἐχθρῶν is usually understood to mean 'in ambushes of thine enemies', which makes good sense, but δοκός can hardly mean ambush. Hesychius' gloss ἔνδοκος · ἐνέδρα seems to be derived from this passage, but whether the explanation ἐνέδρα gives the proper meaning of the noun ἔνδοκος is doubtful. Hesychius' interpretation probably derived from a text with marginal glosses in which the word that was to be explained by the gloss ἐνέδρα was corrupted into ΕΝΔΟΚΟΙϹΙΝ. The normal way of expressing the idea of ambush (ἐνέδρα) in Homeric language would be ΕΝΛΟΧΟΙϹΙΝ. I suspect that ἐν λόχοισιν ἐχθρῶν is what Archilochus really wrote.

44. This form of dialogue with a person's own soul is the germ cell of the *Soliloquia* of later ages, such as the famous work of St. Augustine. The Platonic distinction of soul and reason made this kind of conversation even more natural, for it split the individual into these two elements.

45. *Odyssey* XX, 18.

46. For the sake of simplicity, I have translated Archilochus' Ionic word ῥυσμός (frg. 67a, 7) by our 'rhythm', which comes from the Attic form.

47. Hdt. I, 207 (cf. I, 5).

48. This etymological explanation is so common that I need not give specific references.

49. Archilochus' words (frg. 67a, 7) are: γίνωσκε δ' οἷος ῥυσμὸς ἀνθρώπους ἔχει.

50. Aesch. *P.V.* 241: ὧδ' ἐρρύθμισμαι. *Pers.* 747 πόρον μετερρύθμιζε.

51. Arist. *Met.* I, 4, 985b16.

52. Cf. *Scholia in Aeschylum, ad Prom.* 241. They explain ἐρρύθμισμαι as meaning ἐσταύρωμαι, ἐκτέταμαι.

53. The late Wilhelm Schulze, the great linguist to whom I long ago presented my material and the conclusions to which it had led me, was perfectly willing to look for a better etymology for ῥυθμός than the traditional derivation from ῥέω, because this one obviously does not fit the facts. He thought of ὀρθός as possibly going back to the same root.

54. Semon. frg. 1 (Diehl).

55. Hes. *Works and Days* 100.

56. Hes. *Works and Days* 58. Another reminiscence of Hesiod is frg. 29, *Works and Days* 40.

57. Frg. 29. One of the most certain results of philological research is Bergk's attribution of this poem to Semonides: it is copied by Stobaeus with the name of the more famous Simonides of Ceos.

58. This is a fine example of that adaptation of Homeric thought and form by the lyric poets which was discussed on p. 118. See notes 6 and 41.

59. Homer's Achilles concludes (*Iliad* I, 352) from the fact that his life will be shorter than that of other mortals not that he should seek to enjoy its pleasures more intensely, but that honour is the only compensation which it has to offer him for his heroic sacrifice.

60. Interesting enough is the use of the word ψυχή in the phrase (Semon. frg. 29, 13) ψυχῇ τῶν ἀγαθῶν τλῆθι χαριζόμενος, where it obviously means the individual soul and its desires. A similar use occurs in Xen. *Cyrop.* I, 3, 18, where Cyrus' mother tells the boy that his father was a free Persian who was accustomed to following the law and not his 'soul'.

61. Thuc. II, 37, 2.

62. It comes into conflict with supra-individual norms only when pleasure is made the basic criterion of human life and action. This was done later by the sophists; see p. 129.

63. Mimnermus frg. 1 (Diehl).

64. Frg. 12-14.

65. Everything destined for man in life comes from Zeus and the gods, and their gifts must be accepted. See Archil. frg. 8, 58, 68; Semonides frg. 1, 1 ff.; Solon frg. 1, 64; Theognis, v. 134, 142, 157, etc.

66. Cf. Mimnerm. frg. 2; 5; 6.

67. Cf. p. 328.

68. Cf. *Paideia* II, 118-121, 142-143, 349-353.

69. The decisive statements of Aristotle about the place of ἡδονή in the culture of human personality and its relationship to ἀρετή are to be found in *Eth. Nic.* Book X, 1-5, and in Book VII.

70. By a convention which seems hard to overcome, most of the books dealing with the history of Greek philosophy do not pay attention to the moral and political or religious poetry of the early centuries, but only to poetry concerned with nature or being, like that of Parmenides and Empedocles. A notable exception is L. Robin, *La Pensée grecque* (in *L'Évolution de l'humanité*, ed. by H. Berr). See also Max Wundt, *Geschichte der Griechischen Ethik*, vol. I, who has rightly treated Greek poetry as one of the main sources of earlier times for his subject.

71. On the importance of the ancient Greek symposium, see *Paideia* I, 170; II, 176, 186 ff.; and III, 222 ff.

72. On the connexion of early Greek poetry and symposia, see R. Reitzenstein, *Epigramm und Skolion* (1893).

73. Alcaeus and his brother Antimenidas were both leading members of the aristocratic party in Mytilene which opposed the rule of the tyrant Myrsilus and of Pittacus, the *aisymnetes*. Cf. Arist. *Pol.* III, 14, 1285a37.

74. Alc. frg. 30. Cf. Archilochus, frg. 56.

75. *Iliad* VIII, 555-559.

76. The most brilliant example of this use of the prayer-form in Sappho is frg. 1, the prayer to Aphrodite. See Solon's frg. 1, the prayer to the Muses, which is made into a sort of personal expression of his thoughts on God and the world. Later in Greek tragedy the prayer becomes a frequent form of expression for the emotions of the chorus.

77. See, for instance, Wilamowitz-Moellendorff, *Sappho und Simonides* (Berlin 1913), 71 ff., who follows in the footsteps of Welcker's noted apology for Sappho.

Wilamowitz' whole indignation turns against P. L(ouys), *Les Chansons de Bilitis* (Paris 1895), but he does almost too much honour to this publication.

78. Sappho frg. 2 (Diehl).

79. Frg. 27a.

CHAPTER 8

SOLON: CREATOR OF ATHENIAN POLITICAL CULTURE

1. See my essay, *Solons Eunomie* (*Sitz. Berl. Akad.* 1926), 69-71; the whole essay provides a basis for the views advanced in this chapter.

2. U. v. Wilamowitz-Moellendorff, *Aristoteles und Athen* (Berlin 1893), II, 304, has interpreted Solon's poems in the spirit in which they were approached by Aristotle himself in his Ἀθηναίων Πολιτεία, as the primary documents for an important phase of Athenian constitutional history and as the personal utterances of the man who was the leading figure of that age. See also I. Linforth, *Solon the Athenian* (Berkeley 1919).

3. See the chapter on Sparta, p. 98.

4. See the chapter on the Constitutional State, p. 102 ff.

5. To trace the historical development of the Greek and in particular the Attic spirit which leads up to this synthesis is one of the primary concerns of this work. That development culminates in the funeral oration of Pericles in Thucydides' *History,* so far as the reality of political life is concerned. (See *supra,* p. 408.) But we can trace it even in Plato's philosophical attempt to build up 'in theory' (λόγῳ) an ideal state which combines an ideal order with a high level of spiritual freedom for the individual to do his own work.

6. See Arist. *Ath. Const.* c. VI, XIII; Plut., *Solon* c. XV.

7. See p. 108 ff.

8. See *Paideia* III, 213 ff.

9. See Arist. *Ath. Const.* c. IV; Plut. *Solon* c. XVII.

10. See Plato, *Laws,* 706b ff.

11. See p. 68 ff. *Paideia* III, 239 ff.

12. Solon frg. 24 (Diehl).

13. Plut. *Solon* c. XXI.

14. Cf. Thuc. I, 6.

15. Solon frg. 22. See also frg. 20, which recalls Mimnermus.

16. See *Solons Eunomie* (*Sitz. Berl. Akad.* 1926) 71 ff., for Solon's relation to Homer, Hesiod, and tragedy, and for an interpretation of his political poetry.

17. Plut. *Solon* c. VIII.

18. See p. 96.

19. See p. 67.

20. See p. 68 and Hesiod's *Works and Days* 213 ff., particularly the picture of the just city, 225 ff., and the unjust city, 238 ff.

21. Solon frg. 1, 8, πάντως ὕστερον ἦλθε δίκη. 1, 13, ταχέως δ' ἀναμίσγεται ἄτη. 1, 25-28, πάντως δ' ἐς τέλος ἐξεφάνη. 1, 31, ἤλυθε πάντως αὖτις (scil. θεῶν μοῖρα). 3, 16, τῷ δὲ χρόνῳ πάντως ἦλθ' ἀποτεισομένη (cf. 1, 76). 24, 3 presupposes the same view, for ἐν δίκῃ χρόνου makes time itself the judge.

22. Solon frg. 3, 6 ff.

23. See p. 140 and *supra,* note 20, on the just and the unjust city in Hesiod.

24. Solon frg. 3, 17 ff. See my interpretation of this passage in *Solons Eunomie,* loc. cit. p. 79.

25. Solon frg. 3, 28.

26. διαλλακτής. See Arist. *Ath. Const.* c. VI, Plut. *Solon* c. XIV.

27. Frg. 3, 17. Linforth, loc. cit. pp. 141 and 201, understands πᾶσα πόλις as the whole city, which is of course possible; but I would rather interpret it here in the general sense of 'every city', as Edmonds does in *Elegy and Iambus* I, 119. The relative clause ἣ στάσιν ἔμφυλον . . . ἐπεγείρει seems to me to belong to πάσῃ πόλει, as I have translated it in the text, and not to δουλοσύνην, which immediately precedes. The words ἐς δὲ κακὴν . . . δουλοσύνην interrupt the sentence in paratactic form, as is usual in this archaic style (= ὥστε ἐς κακὴν ἐλθεῖν δουλοσύνην). δουλοσύνη is not the cause but the effect of στάσις, cf. frg. 8, 4. ἐπεγείρειν πόλεμον, διωγμόν, etc. requires a person or group of persons as subject.

28. The sentence is repeated by Theognis, v. 51.

29. Solon frg. 3, 30.

30. Frg. 3, 32 ff.

31. Hesiod, *Theog.* 902.

32. See my *Solons Eunomie,* loc. cit. p. 80.

33. See Anaximander 9 (Diels, *Vorsokratiker*). There the relation of cause and effect in nature is interpreted as a retribution (δίκη or τίσις) which things pay to each other; see *supra,* p. 157 ff.

34. Solon frg. 10. Plutarch, who quotes these lines, speaks of them even in his time as containing Solon's 'physics'.

35. The same view that the concentration of political power in the hands of one man is usually the cause of tyranny occurs in Solon frg. 8, which was referred to the time of the tyranny of Pisistratus by ancient critics; see Diog. L. I, 51 ff.

36. Cf. the fear of tyranny in Theognis, vv. 40 and 52. This poet was a member of the aristocracy of Megara. Alcaeus belonged to one of the old families of Mytilene on Lesbos; he fought first the tyranny of Myrsilus and later the one-man rule of Pittacus; see *supra* p. 131 and note 73 of that chapter.

37. See note 35.

38. See pp. 140-141.

39. Frg. 3, 1 ff.

40. *Odyssey* I, 32 ff.

41. On this subject see my arguments in *Solons Eunomie* loc. cit. p. 73 ff.

42. In Homer (*Odyssey* I, 37), Aegisthus, forewarned by Hermes that he would have to pay penalty for his deed, suffers ὑπὲρ μόρον.

43. See the previous chapter, pp. 128-129, with note 65.

44. Solon frg. 1. See Linforth's *Solon the Athenian,* 104 ff. and 227 ff. Karl Reinhardt's article 'Solons Elegie εἰς ἑαυτόν' in *Rheinisches Museum,* N.F. LXXI (1916), 128 ff., has contributed greatly to the right interpretation of the poem. Wilamowitz has commented on this elegy in *Sappho und Simonides,* 257 ff.

45. See frg. 1, 7 ff. Χρήματα δ' ἱμείρω μὲν ἔχειν, ἀδίκως δὲ πεπᾶσθαι οὐκ ἐθέλω · πάντως ὕστερον ἦλθε δίκη. Similarly Theognis, 145 ff., and Pindar, *Ol.* II, 53: ὁ πλοῦτος ἀρεταῖς δεδαιδαλμένος is Pindar's ideal. See also *Nem.* IX, 45, ἅμα κτεάνοις πολλοῖς ἐπίδοξον . . . κῦδος or *Pyth.* III, 110.

46. Frg. 1, 17-32.

47. Frg. 1, 33, marks the transition from the first to the second part of the poem. In the preceding part Solon had dealt only with the até which is caused by human injustice, but in line 34 he drops the distinction between good and bad men and begins to talk of an até which they both have in common. The words at the beginning of line 34, ἐν δηνην, are corrupt (therefore in the text I have given only a rough paraphrase of the sense), and it has not yet seemed possible to emend the line convincingly. The attempt of Reinhardt, who writes σπεύδειν ἥν, is not satisfactory. Buecheler's εὖ δεινὴν is palaeographically very tempting, and Diehl has taken it into his text in the *Anthologia Lyrica;* but it is hardly

what Solon would have said in his Greek. The conjectures of others seem to me
still less acceptable. Thus we are still far from the solution, although it should
be easy to find, because the corruption can be only a quite mechanical mistake
on the part of the scribe. It must be caused in part by itacism, as Reinhardt has
seen, since there are several *etas* in the senseless complex of letters which has
been preserved: ΕΝΔΗΝΗΝ. If Reinhardt is correct in thinking that the last
syllable must be the relative pronoun ἥν, which is to be connected with αὐτὸς
δόξαν ἕκαστος ἔχει, a present active infinitive—δειν must be hidden in ΕΝΔΗΝ.
It cannot be σπεύδειν, but rather, I think, ἔρδειν (cf. 67 and 69): he who hopes
εὖ ἔρδειν fails against expectation, and he who κακῶς ἔρδει unexpectedly succeeds. The expectation is expressed in line 33 by νοεῦμεν, which is synonymous
with ἐλπίς in 36 and with κτήσεσθαι . . . δοκεῖ in 42. In ἔρδειν ἥν δόξαν
ἕκαστος ἔχει the relative clause is adverbial and is equivalent to ἔρδειν ὡς
ἕκαστος δοκεῖ (= ὡς ἐλπίζει); and ἔρδειν ὡς ἕκαστος δοκεῖ means 'to succeed',
'to do well' (cf. 67 and 69).

48. Frg. 1, 63.
49. Frg. 1, 67-70.
50. Cf. p. 125.
51. Frg. 1, 71 ff.
52. The words at the end of the elegy, frg. 1, 75, ἄτη δ' ἐξ αὐτῶν ἀναφαίνεται,
ἥν ὁπότε Ζεὺς πέμψῃ τεισομένην, ἄλλοτε ἄλλος ἔχει, must mean 'when Zeus
sends the até which springs from too large fortunes, now this man has it [the
até] and now that one'. Solon quotes, it seems, Archilochus, frg. 7, 7, ἄλλοτε τ'
ἄλλος ἔχει τάδε · νῦν μὲν ἐς ἡμέας ἐτράπεθ' . . . ἐξαῦτις δ' ἑτέρους ἐπαμείψεται,
as does Aesch. *Prom.* 276 (πάντα τοι πλανωμένη πρὸς ἄλλοτ' ἄλλον πημονὴ
προσιζάνει), and other poets of this time. Cf. Theogn. 351. But *ipso facto* with
the changing até, money changes hands. Solon does not say this expressly in this
poem, but it is the logical implication of his last words; and in frg. 4, 11-12, he
declares, in fact, that only areté is of lasting value, whereas money (χρήματα)
is continually changing hands (ἄλλοτε ἄλλος ἔχει). The almost identical phrasing
shows that both things—até and changing fortune—are closely connected in Solon's
mind. Seen from the point of view of the poor man, this means that soon his
poverty may be knocking at another door, as Theogn. loc. cit. shows. The ῥυσμός
of Archilochus to which Solon refers has its good as well as its bad aspect.

53. So, for instance, frg. 5, 8, 10, probably 16, and particularly 23, 24, 25.
They all must belong to the time after Solon's archonship. Frg. 3 and 4 are
clearly connected with the years of heated political dispute which preceded the
appointment of Solon as διαλλακτής, i.e. before the year 594. Whether or not
the great elegy, the prayer to the Muses, also belongs to that earlier period is an
open question.

54. In Solon's opinion it is a fact that money changes hands continually; see
frg. 4, 12, and note 52. There it has been shown how this fact is connected with
Solon's view of Moira and her part in man's changing fortunes, as stated in
the great poem, frg. 1.

55. Frg. 4, 7; 5; 23, 13 ff.; 24, 22-25; 25.
56. Frg. 23, 3; and 25, 7.
57. Frg. 5, 5; 24, 26-27; 25, 8. For the restoration of the text of frg. 25, 9, see
my article in *Hermes* LXIV (1929), 30 ff. Instead of ἐγὼ δὲ τούτων . . . ἐν
μεταιχμίῳ ὅρος κατέστην (ὅρος in Solon's language means, as usual, a mortgage
stone [see frg. 24, 6], not a fitting metaphor for his dangerous position between
the two fighting fronts of the rich and the poor), I propose to restore ἐν μεταιχμίῳ
δορός. That preserves the metaphor (which is taken from the heroic world of
the Homeric epos) unmixed, as required by the prose-like style of the iambus.

In Pindar's lyric style the mixture of two metaphors would be accepted. ἐν μεταιχμίῳ δορός is a phrase which occurs later in the iambic parts of tragedy. There it goes back to Solon's obviously famous line, as is clear now.

58. Frg. 24, 3.

59. The first two lines of this poem (frg. 24) seem not yet to be rightly understood by the interpreters: ἐγὼ δὲ τῶν μὲν οὕνεκα ξυνήγαγον δῆμον, τί τούτων πρὶν τυχεῖν ἐπαυσάμην; τί is taken by modern scholars (Sandys, Edmonds, Linforth) as meaning 'why', and so they make Solon ask, Why did I stop before I achieved these things (scil. the things for the sake of which I gathered the demos)? This seems hardly to agree with what he tells us in the whole poem about the greatness of his achievements in the rôle of statesman which he had assumed. And in another poem, apparently belonging to the same period of his life, frg. 23, 21, in which he defends his actions in a quite similar way, he says: 'they should not look at me so defiantly, as if I were their enemy, for what I promised to do I have achieved with the help of the gods (ἃ μὲν γὰρ εἶπα, σὺν θεοῖσιν ἤνυσα). The words of frg. 24, 2, must therefore mean something like this: τί τούτων πρὶν τυχεῖν ἐπαυσάμην; 'Did I stop before I achieved them all? No, I did not'. This is expressed in Greek, as often, by the elegant partitive construction: 'Before achieving which of them did I stop? None'. Interpreters have obviously hesitated to take τούτων as a partitive genitive, because τυχεῖν in Attic normally requires a genitive as object; therefore they have connected τί with ἐπαυσάμην. But in Attic τυχεῖν is often construed with the accusative of a neuter pronoun; cf., e.g. the famous epigram πάντων ἥδιστον δ' οὗ τις ἐρᾷ, τὸ τυχεῖν (where τὸ is not the article but the accusative of the demonstrative pronoun). It would be very important if Solon really had felt that he had to stop before he carried out his entire programme, but what he said seems to me just the contrary.

60. Frg. 23.

61. Herod. I, 29 ff.

62. Herod. I, 30, τῆς θεωρίης ἐκδημήσας εἵνεκεν.

63. Frg. 22. The witty nickname λιγυαιστάδης is untranslatable. I have attempted to coin a name of the same general intention. See Mimnermus frg. 6.

64. Frg. 22, 7.

65. Frg. 22, 5.

66. Semonides frg. 1 and 2 (Diehl).

67. Solon frg. 15.

68. Frg. 17.

69. Frg. 12-14.

70. Frg. 19. See the interpretation of this poem by W. Schadewaldt in *Die Antike* IX, 282, 'Lebensalter und Greisenalter im fruehen Griechentum'.

71. Concerning hebdomads and other periods in Greek medicine and natural philosophy, see W. H. Roscher, *Die enneadischen und hebdomadischen Fristen und Wochen der aeltesten Griechen* (Leipzig 1903), and W. Jaeger in *Abh. d. Berl. Ak.* 1938, Nr. 3, p. 28 ff., especially p. 34 ff.

72. Frg. 16.

73. The words of the distich (frg. 16) themselves do not reveal whether or not Clement of Alexandria (*Strom.* v, 81, 1) was right in referring them to God. Those who know this author may be somewhat sceptical, since he finds hidden allusions to the problem of God everywhere in Greek classical literature for his apologetic purpose. But if he is correct and Solon is speaking of the gnomé of the immortals as the invisible measure 'which alone holds the end of all things', then it becomes man's difficult task (χαλεπώτατόν ἐστι νοῆσαι) to recognize this measure in the nature of the world and to realize it in all things which he

undertakes. What makes one hesitate to accept this interpretation, which might appear to be recommended by the words of the second line (πάντων πείρατα ἔχει), is the new word γνωμοσύνη. It is formed like other abstracts, such as δικαιοσύνη, πυκτοσύνη, παλαιμοσύνη, and seems to refer to a human rather than a divine quality. It consists in the right intuition of the invisible measure in all things, which, as Solon says, is so hard to obtain. Similar is Theognis, 694, γνῶναι γὰρ χαλεπὸν μέτρον, ὅτ' ἐσθλὰ παρῇ, who is speaking of man, not of God.

CHAPTER 9

PHILOSOPHICAL SPECULATION:
THE DISCOVERY OF THE WORLD-ORDER

1. The interest in early Greek philosophy which is so obvious in Aristotle's *Metaphysics* and *Physics* and in all his pragmatic works had its roots in the Platonic Academy; see *Paideia* III, 321, note 122. But Aristotle, as he gradually became a philosopher in his own right independent of Plato, adapted the ideas of the Presocratics to the categories of his own thought. Harold Cherniss, *Aristotle's Criticism of Presocratic Philosophy* (Baltimore 1935), has traced with great sagacity the influence which that perspective exercised on Aristotle's view of the philosophy of his predecessors.

2. The word 'philosophy', which originally meant 'culture' (*Bildung*) and not a rational science or discipline, came to be taken in the latter sense only in the circle of Socrates and Plato, who, starting from the investigation of the problem of human virtue (areté) and education, developed a new rational method of education from that discussion. Philosophy, this perfect identity of culture and intellectual discipline, did not exist in the time of the Presocratics, who called their activity ἱστορίη or wisdom (σοφίη).

3. See the chapter on the Sophists, p. 286. It is true that some modern scholars have tried to do justice to the sophists and have incorporated them into the history of Greek philosophy; but Aristotle hardly does so, because philosophy to him is a science concerned with the investigation of reality. The sophists were educators and 'teachers of virtue'. It is only logical that they should have played a much more important (though negative) part in Plato's dialogues, since Plato and Socrates took the educational problem as their point of departure. The rehabilitation of the sophists started with Hegel. But only in the circles of modern pragmatists have they assumed the rôle of the true originators of philosophy, because of their practical agnosticism. See my *Humanism and Theology* (Marquette Univ. Press, Milwaukee 1943), 38 ff.

4. A book on rationalism in Homer could and perhaps should be written some day.

5. *Iliad* XIV, 201 (302), 246. Aristotle quotes this line, *Metaph.* A 3, 983b30, as an anticipation of Thales' theory.

6. Arist. *Metaph.* B 4, 1000a18, aptly speaks of the Hesiodic type as μυθικῶς σοφίζεσθαι.

7. There was, in other words, already much rational thought in what we call 'the mythical age', and there was still a large mythical element in what we call 'rational thought'.

8. See my *Aristotle* (tr. Robinson, Oxford 1934), 50, 51-52, 150, and elsewhere.

9. That was Plato's own tendency.

10. The question was asked and the answer was given by Karl Joël, *Der Ursprung der Naturphilosophie aus dem Geiste der Mystik* (Jena 1906).

11. This has been done, e.g. by Léon Robin, *La pensée grecque* (Paris 1923), in *L'Evolution de l'humanité,* dirigée par Henri Berr.

12. We should remember that Plato, when he approached the problem of the laws of the world within man, turned to his use the methods of medicine and mathematics. See *Paideia* II, 166 ff., 301, on mathematics; and III, 21 on medicine.

13. That crisis is described in this volume, Book II, especially in the chapters on Euripides, Aristophanes, the Sophists, and Thucydides. Volume II is dedicated to Plato and the discovery of the cosmos within man.

14. The fundamental importance of the contribution of the Presocratics to the humanistic problem with which Plato and his age were concerned is obvious when we remember that they were primarily interested in the problem of Being; for true human liberty, in the Platonic sense, is related to Being.

15. See note 2.

16. See my essay, *Ueber Ursprung und Kreislauf des philosophischen Lebens-ideals* (in *Sitz. Berl. Akad.* 1928), 390 ff. See also Franz Boll, *Vita Contemplativa* (*Ber. Heidelberg. Akad.* 1920).

17. Plato, *Theaet.* 174a (Diels, *Vorsokratiker* I A9).

18. Iamblichus, *Protrept.* 51, 8. See my *Aristotle,* 92. The dictum of Anaxagoras (Iambl. loc. cit. 51, 13) is a variant of this.

19. Diog. L. II, 7 (Diels, *Vorsokratiker* I A1).

20. See Aristotle, *Metaph.* A 2, 983a1.

21. Cf. the other anecdotes about Thales, besides the one quoted in note 17 above, in Diels' *Vorsokratiker* I A1, 26 (cf. Arist., *Pol.* I, 11, 1259a6) and the Ionian tradition preserved by Herodotus, I, 74, I, 170.

22. Hecataeus frg. 1a (Jacoby, *F. Gr. Hist.* I, 7-8).

23. Heraclitus frg. 1 (Diels, *Vorsokratiker* I).

24. See Wilhelm Luther, *Wahrheit und Luege im aeltesten Griechentum* (Borna, Leipzig 1935). In this monograph the origins of the Greek concept of ἀλήθεια and the whole group of words akin to it have been carefully examined within the context in which they are found.

25. John Burnet, *Early Greek Philosophy* (4th ed., London 1930), 10 ff.

26. Hermann Diels, *Ueber die aeltesten Philosophenschulen der Griechen,* in *Philos. Aufs. Ed. Zeller gewidm.* (Leipzig 1887), 239-260.

27. See Anaximander 6 (Diels, *Vorsokratiker* I). The report preserved by Agathemerus and Strabo goes back to Eratosthenes.

28. F. Enriques and G. Santillana, *Storia del pensiero scientifico,* vol. I (Milan 1932); T. L. Heath, *A Manuel of Greek Mathematics* (Oxford 1931); A. Heidel, 'The Pythagoreans and Greek Mathematics', *Am. Jour. of Philol.* 61 (1940), 1-33.

29. See Paul Tannery, *Pour l'histoire de la science hellène* (Paris 1887), 91.

30. On the numerical proportions of Anaximander's cosmos and their most probable reconstruction, see H. Diels, *Archiv f. Gesch. d. Phil.* X. See also the ancient passages quoted therein.

31. The earth's roots appear in Hesiod's *Works and Days* 19; Wilamowitz, *Hesiods Erga* 43, believes that Hesiod means simply the depths of the earth, but see *Theogony* 728, 812. In the Orphic cosmogony of Pherecydes (frg. 2, Diels), which is partly based on very old mythical conceptions, we hear of a 'winged oak'—a combination of Anaximander's idea that the world is hanging free with the conception of a tree rooted in infinity (see H. Diels, *Archiv f. Gesch. d. Phil.* X). In Parmenides, frg. 15a, the earth is said to be 'rooted in water'.

32. Anaximander 11 (Diels, *Vorsokratiker* I).

33. See F. Jacoby in Pauly-Wissowa *RE* VII, 2702 ff.

34. Anaximander 6 (Diels).

35. Hugo Berger, *Geschichte der wissenschaftlichen Erdkunde der Griechen,* 38 ff.; W. A. Heidel, *The Frame of the Ancient Greek Maps,* 21.

36. Herodotus II, 33; IV, 49.

37. Herodotus IV, 36.

38. Cf. Karl Joël, 'Zur Geschichte der Zahlenprinzipien in der griechischen Philosophie', in *Ztschf. f. Phil. u. philos. Kritik* 97 (1890), 161-228.

39. Arist. *Metaph.* A 3, 983b6 ff. gives as a possible reason for Thales' assumption that water is the principle of all things the fact that the warm is fed by the moist. But he did not have a book of Thales, and so his explanation is his own improvisation.

40. Anaximenes frg. 2 (Diels).

41. Anaximander 15 (Diels).

42. Arist. *Phys.* III, 7, 207b35.

43. Anaximander 15.

44. Anaximander 10 and 11.

45. Anaximander 15.

46. Anaximander 9: διδόναι γὰρ αὐτὰ (i.e. τὰ ὄντα) δίκην καὶ τίσιν ἀλλήλοις τῆς ἀδικίας κατὰ τὴν τοῦ χρόνου τάξιν.

47. Burnet in *Early Greek Philosophy* (4th ed., 1930), 53 ff., gives a more prosaic interpretation of it, but seems to me to have done less than justice to the nobility of Anaximander's idea and its philosophical significance.

48. See Diels, *Vorsokratiker* I, Anax. frg. 9.

49. Even the Orphic myth in Arist. frg. 60 (Rose) does not mean that existence is a sin. See A. Diès, *Le cycle mystique* (Paris 1909).

50. τάξις is not *Ordnung* (order), as Diels translates it, but is obviously used here in an active sense. A price or penalty or tribute was fixed (τάττειν), Andoc. 4, 11; Thuc. I, 19; Herod. III, 97. τάξις in this active sense means ordinance. See Plato, *Legg.* 925b and *Pol.* 305c, παρὰ τὴν τοῦ νομοθέτου τάξιν.

51. See p. 144.

52. Solon frg. 1, 25; 30.

53. I have justified this interpretation more fully in an unpublished lecture on the fragment of Anaximander (see *Sitz. Berl. Akad.* 1924, p. 227).

54. As in Plato's *Republic* the state is the structure of the human soul 'writ large', so in Anaximander's view of the world the universe tends to be a social order (κόσμος) 'writ large'. This was only a tendency, however, because it was Heraclitus who saw this parallel in the philosophy of his predecessor with full clarity and worked it out systematically. See Heracl. frg. 114 (Diels) on human and divine law (i.e. the law that rules the universe).

55. Anaximenes frg. 2. K. Reinhardt doubts its authenticity.

56. In the first edition of this book I questioned, with M. A. Cornford, the truth of this ascription; but the arguments of R. Mondolfo, *L'infinito nel pensiero dei Greci* (Florence 1934), 45 ff., have convinced me.

57. See Anaximander 15 (Diels). For this I must refer in advance to a book of mine not yet published, *The Theology of the Early Greek Philosophers* (The Gifford Lectures, 1936, St. Andrews), which will contain a special chapter on the theological aspect of the philosophy of the Milesian school.

58. See *Solons Eunomie* (*Sitz. Berl. Akad.* 1926), 73.

59. This transference of the concept of retribution from the legal and political sphere to that of the physical universe was not a single act of one philosopher, but was long basic in Greek thought on the problem of causality, as is shown by the medical literature of classical Greece, the so-called *Corpus Hippocraticum.* There causation appears throughout as compensation and retribution in the sense

of Anaximander and Heraclitus. See the chapter on medicine in *Paideia* III, 6, with the notes.

60. Heraclitus took the next step; see note 54 and p. 181 ff.

61. It was Heraclitus who tried to show how human life must be conceived against the background of the new Ionian philosophy of nature and how all of life is changed by it. See p. 182.

62. On the various ancient views of Pythagoras' personality and intellectual character, see J. Burnet, *Early Greek Philosophy*, 4th ed., pp. 86-87.

63. Heraclitus frg. 40. The word πολυμαθίη in Heraclitus is opposed to νοῦς, 'mind, reason'.

64. See Erich Frank's book, *Plato und die sogenannten Pythagoreer* (Halle 1923); J. Burnet, loc. cit. 86.

65. Cf. Arist. *Metaph.* A 5, 985b23. The *mathemata* which Plato introduced in his *Republic*, Book VII, as propaideia for his guards consisted of arithmetic, geometry, stereometry, astronomy, and music. He connected them with the tradition of the Pythagorean school as it then existed in south Italy (see *Paideia* II, 303), and it is very probable that that tradition goes back to Pythagoras himself. Cosmology also formed part of the Pythagorean system, as is clear not only from the much-debated fragments which bear the Pythagorean names of Philolaus and Archytas, but also from the fact that Plato chose a Pythagorean of south Italy, Timaeus of Locri, as the representative figure in his cosmological work, the *Timaeus*.

66. Herodotus IV, 95; cf. II, 81.

67. J. Burnet, loc. cit. 90 ff.

68. See p. 157.

69. See the discussion of the entire source material in Eduard Zeller, *Philosophie der Griechen* I, 1, 401-403 (5th ed.).

70. Arist. *Metaph.* A 5, 985b27.

71. Arist. *Metaph.* A 5, 986a15 ff.

72. Arist. *Metaph.* A 5, 985b27 ff. Cf. ibid. 985b23, where these 'Pythagoreans' are declared to have lived at the same time as, or before, Leucippus, Democritus, and Anaxagoras. That brings them near the age of Pythagoras himself (the sixth century). Aristotle deliberately refrains from mentioning him—the exception in *Metaph.* A 5, 986a30, is an interpolation.

73. J. Stenzel, *Zahl und Gestalt bei Platon und Aristoteles* (2nd ed., Leipzig 1933), who, however, pays no attention to the Pythagoreans.

74. Aesch. *P.V.* 459, ἀριθμὸς ἔξοχον σοφισμάτων.

75. See Arist. *Metaph.* A 5, 986a1 ff.

76. The Neopythagorean sources from which we derive this detailed but legendary picture of Pythagoras' life and teaching are his two late biographers, Porphyry and Iamblichus. Some modern essays on Pythagoras as an educator, such as O. Willmann's *Pythagoreische Erziehungsweisheit*, suffer from the mistake of taking as historical truth too much of what these late ancient authors tell us of Pythagoras.

77. Arist. *Metaph.* A 5, 986a2 ff.

78. So after Macchioro and others, e.g. O. Kern, *Die Religion der Griechen* (Berlin 1926-38). See the critical reaction against the exaggerations of these scholars, who tried to give a hypothetical reconstruction of the Orphic religion of this early period, in Wilamowitz's *Der Glaube der Hellenen* II (1932), 199, and in Ivan Linforth's more recent *The Arts of Orpheus* (1941). The objections of these scholars have had a sobering effect but seem to me to go too far in their negative attitude. More moderate is W. R. Guthrie's *Orpheus and Greek Religion* (London 1935). If we accept only what can be traced back by reliable tradition

to an early sect which called itself Orphic, this is indeed not very much; but perhaps the name Orphic does not matter greatly, for it is the specific religious type and its characteristics, the βίος and the mystic conception of the soul-daemon, that interests us here, regardless of what it was called.

79. See E. Rohde, *Psyche* II, the chapter 'Die Orphiker'; W. F. Otto, *Die Manen* (Berlin 1923), 3.

80. Abstinence from all animal food is called a feature of the Orphic βίος by Plato, *Laws* 782c; Eur. *Hipp.* 952 ff.; Aristoph. *Frogs* 1032 ff. Later ancient authors ascribe the same rule to Pythagoras, and many modern scholars follow them. But this tradition is by no means certain, even though the rituals of Orphic and Pythagorean 'orgia' were compared with each other in some respects by Herodotus, II, 81. See G. Rathmann, *Quaestiones Pythagoreae Orphicae Empedocleae* (Halis Saxonum 1933), 14 ff. Aristoxenus (Diog. L. VIII, 20) denied the authenticity of the tradition of Pythagoras' abstinence from animal food. In this he was obviously opposing the general opinion of his age. The Pythagoristae, practitioners of the Pythagorean rule whose abstinent life was laughed at by the writers of the 'new comedy', pretended to be genuine followers of Pythagoras. But that is just what the scientific branch of Pythagoreanism represented by Aristoxenus questioned. See J. Burnet, *Early Greek Philosophy* (chapter on Pythagoras), who believes in the tradition of Pythagorean abstinence.

81. Dionysus moves hearts through the power of his ecstatic cult, Apollo through his moral teaching and wisdom.

82. On the moral influence of the religious propaganda of the Delphic Apollo, see Wilamowitz *Der Glaube der Hellenen* II, 34 ff. This scholar speaks on p. 38 of the Delphic god as educator, because of his precepts on the rites of purification and the rules of life connected with it.

83. Pindar *Isth.* IV, 16, *Nem.* IX, 47; *Epicharm.* B 20 (Diels, *Vorsokratiker* I), etc.

84. It has this meaning throughout in Homer and Hesiod.

85. Diels, *Vorsokratiker* (ed. 5) I, 15; Orpheus frg. 17 ff. It is true that these gold plates are of a much later date; but south Italy, the place where they were unearthed, was the seat of this religious faith for centuries. Moreover it is probable that there was a continuous tradition from the sixth century B.C. down to the third, the period to which the gold plates of Petelia are assigned, since we must consider both the conservatism of religious ritual and belief and the identity of the type of religion which these 'passports of the soul' presuppose with the old Orphic belief in the divine origin of the soul-daemon and its return to heaven.

86. Plato's *Phaedo* and *Republic* show that belief most clearly; for Aristotle, see the fragments of his lost dialogue *Eudemus* and Περὶ φιλοσοφίας, and my *Aristotle*, 40 ff., 45, 159.

87. Emped. frg. 129 (Diels).

88. Emped. frg. 115, 23.

89. See p. 184.

90. On the question of the didactic poem attributed to Xenophanes, see Burnet, *Early Greek Philosophy*, 115. Since I wrote these words, K. Deichgraeber has published his article *Xenophanes* Περὶ φύσεως in *Rhein. Mus.* 87, in which he tries to prove the existence of a didactic poem on natural philosophy by Xenophanes. I have dealt with the question more accurately in my not yet published Gifford Lectures for 1936, *The Theology of the Early Greek Philosophers,* to which I must refer the reader. Deichgraeber himself, p. 13 of his article, admits that Aristotle and Theophrastus, i.e. the two men who in classical times were most eager to study the history of earlier thinkers, did not count Xenophanes among the physicists at all, but saw in him the theologian. It is true that two later grammarians, Crates of Mallos and Pollux, quote a poem of Xenophanes in hexa-

metric form which they called Περὶ φύσεως. But it need not be a poem of the nature and proportions of Empedocles' or Lucretius' epics *On Nature,* especially since the ancients seem to have been rather free with the use of this title. This view is confirmed by the surviving fragments. The fragments of Xenophanes listed by Diels, *Vorsokratiker* I, under the title Περὶ φύσεως belong partly, as it appears to me, to the *Silloi* and have little to do with a poem on physics.

91. The *silloi* were directed against all the philosophers and poets; see Xenophanes A 22, 25. I shall not here discuss the relationship of Xenophanes to Parmenides; I intend shortly to deal with it elsewhere. K. Reinhardt, in *Parmenides* (Bonn 1916), refutes the accepted opinion that Xenophanes was the founder of the Eleatic system; but he is not in my belief justified in making him a follower of Parmenides. In fact, Xenophanes' popularized philosophy does not seem to me to be based on any definite system, and that applies even to his doctrine of the divinity of all nature.

92. Xenophanes frg. 10 (Diels).

93. Xenophanes, A 1 (Diog. L. IX, 18); A 22.

94. This is obvious from his very arguments; it does not exclude the fact mentioned in note 91 that he also attacked contemporary philosophers (Pythagoras?).

95. Herodotus II, 53. According to him, Homer and Hesiod created the theogony of the Greeks, because they had given the gods their names (ἐπωνυμίαι), honours, arts, and had indicated their forms (εἴδεα).

96. Xenophanes frg. 11 and 12 (Diels).

97. Arist. *Metaph.* A 5, 986b21-24; Xenoph. frg. 23 (Diels).

98. Xenoph. frg. 23; 24.

99. Xenoph. frg. 25.

100. Xenoph. frg. 26.

101. Frg. 14.

102. Frg. 15.

103. Frg. 16.

104. Frg. 32.

105. Frg. 30.

106. Frg. 33.

107. Frg. 29.

108. Frg. 27.

109. Frg. 18. The version told in the *Prometheus* of Aeschylus (v. 506), that he was the inventor of all the arts (τέχναι), presupposes Xenophanes' idea that man invented civilization quite by himself. Prometheus was always rightly understood by the philosophical reader as the creative genius of humanity, even though he is really a god in Aeschylus' drama. Aeschylus' version of the myth is halfway between the old legend, which conceived a special god as inventor of every craft, and the sober, rational idea that man himself created everything without divine help. For Aeschylus, Prometheus became the divine hypostatization of that creative and autarchic conception of man.

110. This is shown by the two larger elegies, Xenophanes, frg. 1 and 2. See particularly 2, 19 on the εὐνομίη of the polis and its connexion with his own σοφίη.

111. Xenoph. frg. 8.

112. Diog. L. IX, 20 (Xenoph. A 1, Diels).

113. See note 112.

114. Th. Gomperz, *Griechische Denker* I (4. Aufl.), p. 129, has pictured Xenophanes as a wandering Homeric rhapsode who in his leisure hours also recited his own poetry. This idea goes back to Diog. L. IX, 18 (Diels, *Vorsokratiker* I, Xenoph. A 1), who writes ἀλλὰ καὶ αὐτὸς ἐρραψῴδει τὰ ἑαυτοῦ.

But these words are not contrasted to the recitation of Homer, which is not mentioned at all. They are preceded by an enumeration of the various forms of poetry he wrote, and Diogenes means to say that Xenophanes not only *wrote* these poems but also *recited* them himself, on his wanderings through Greece; for that was indeed unusual. The word ῥαψῳδεῖν does not mean more than 'recite'. It need not imply, least of all in the trivialized Greek of the second century A.D., the activity of a Homeric rhapsode.

115. Xenoph. frg. 1 (Diels).

116. Frg. 1, 20.

117. To hold the right view about the dignity and greatness of the gods is part of piety, and therefore part of areté. That is how we must understand frg. 1, 20-24.

118. Frg. 2.

119. Xenoph. A 11 (Diels).

120. See the chapter on Pindar, p. 205 ff.

121. Frg. 2, 11-22.

122. See p. 91.

123. See p. 105 ff.

124. See my *Tyrtaios* (*Sitz. Berl. Akad.* 1932), 557.

125. The virtue of wisdom (σοφία) occurs in Plato's philosophy of the state as the highest areté. It is the virtue of the rulers of his *Republic*. In Aristotle's *Ethics*, it is the most important of the so-called intellectual virtues (διανοητικαὶ ἀρεταί) treated in Book VI.

126. Euripides repeated the attacks of Xenophanes against the athletes in his lost tragedy *Autolycus*, frg. 282 Nauck (Diels, *Vorsokratiker* I, Xenoph. C 2).

127. *Paideia* II, 213-214.

128. Perhaps, however, K. Reinhardt, to whose book I owe much, is right in saying (*Parmenides*, 253) that Anaximander's deduction of the predicates 'immortal' and 'imperishable' from the nature of the *apeiron* was the first step towards Parmenides' purely logical extraction of the predicates of the absolute Being from its essence. I have traced this problem further in my Gifford Lectures for 1936 (see note 57). The mixture of the empirical and speculative elements in early Greek thought deserves our attention.

129. Parm. frg. 8, 12, talks of the *power of certainty* (πίστιος ἰσχύς). The heart of Truth is unshaken (ἀτρεμές, frg. 1, 29), mere δόξα is without true power of conviction (1, 30).

130. Ananké, frg. 8, 16 (Diels), diké, 8, 14, moira, 8, 37; cf. also the frequent use of χρή, χρεών, etc.

131. Frg. 8, 14.

132. Frg. 4; 6; 7.

133. Frg. 8, 3; 8, 13 ff.; 8, 38.

134. Frg. 6.

135. Frg. 6, 8.

136. Frg. 8, 7 ff.

137. Frg. 8, 14.

138. Frg. 5.

139. Frg. 8.

140. See K. Riezler, *Parmenides*, 10 ff.

141. This has been the common view of almost all modern scholars. It rests partly on the concepts of πέρας and ἄπειρον, partly on the opinions assailed in the part of Parmenides' poem that deals with δόξα.

142. Frg. 1, 2; 4; 6; 8, 1.

143. See Otfried Becker, *Das Bild des Weges . . . im fruehgriechischen Denken* (Einzelschrift z. *Hermes*, Heft 4, 1937).

144. Frg. 8, 51.

145. In lines 50-52 (frg. 8), Parmenides makes the transition from the first part of his work, which is concerned only with Truth (ἀλήθεια), to the second, which deals with Opinion (δόξα).

146. Frg. 1.

147. Frg. 1, 3.

148. On knowledge compared with the initiation into the mysteries, see the Hippocratic Law, *Paideia* III, 11. Later Plato, in the *Symposium* 210a and 210e, uses the metaphor of the mysteries for the way of knowledge and the initiation into the cult of the true Eros; see *Paideia* II, 192.

149. Frg. 1, 3. It has often been pointed out that the accepted reading involves an impossible metaphor, describing as it does the road which leads the man to truth 'through all cities' (κατὰ πάντ' ἄστη φέρει εἰδότα φῶτα). Wilamowitz' conjecture κατὰ πάντα τατὴ is not happy. After making the conjecture κατὰ πάντ' ἀσινῆ I find that it has already been suggested by Meineke, which is a good recommendation.

150. K. Reinhardt, *Parmenides*, 256.

151. This interpretation goes back to Aristotle, who in his *Metaphysics* and *Physics* looks upon Heraclitus as one of the old monists. It is represented in modern times by Eduard Zeller, Th. Gomperz, J. Burnet.

152. See Heracl. frg. 1 (Diels), second sentence, frg. 2. On Heraclitus, see O. Gigon, *Untersuchungen zu Heraklit* (Leipzig 1935).

153. Heraclitus (frg. 30, 75, 89) regularly uses the word *cosmos* in such a way as to show that he took the concept over from his predecessors. K. Reinhardt, op. cit. 50, differs from this view.

154. Frg. 40. Representatives of that type of πολυμαθίη are for Heraclitus Hesiod, Xenophanes, Hecataeus, and Pythagoras.

155. Frg. 101: ἐδιζησάμην ἐμεωυτόν.

156. Frg. 45.

157. On νοεῖν and νόημα in Parmenides, see W. Kranz' index to Diels' *Vorsokratiker* s.v.

158. Heracl. frgs. 1, 73, and 112; ἔπη καὶ ἔργα, ποιεῖν καὶ λέγειν. It is important to notice that knowledge for Heraclitus implies both 'speech and action'; ποιεῖν does not have the Aristotelian sense in Heraclitus but is close to πράττειν; see ἔργα frg. 1, and on Heraclitus' concept of φρονεῖν note 161. The explanation of ἔπη καὶ ἔργα given by Gigon, op. cit. p. 8, does not satisfy me.

159. Frg. 119.

160. Frg. 1, cf. note 158.

161. Φρόνησις is knowledge related to action. Heraclitus' knowledge involves that relation throughout (see note 158). Therefore it is called not only νοεῖν, νοῦς (cf. frg. 114), but also φρόνησις, φρονεῖν; see frg. 2, 112, 113, 114, 116. On that concept, see my *Aristotle* 65 ff., 77, 81-84; σοφίη, frg. 112.

162. The metaphor of 'awakening those who are asleep' belongs to prophetic language. Cf. Heracl. frg. 1, 73, 75. On the language of Heraclitus in general see B. Snell in *Hermes* LXI, 353, also Wilamowitz, *Hermes* LXII, 276. Other elements of prophetic language are the comparison with the 'deaf' or with the 'absent', frg. 34.

163. See frg. 92 on the Sibylla; frg. 93 on the language of the Delphic oracle; frg. 56, the riddle propounded by boys, which Homer was unable to solve.

164. Frg. 123.

165. See note 162.

166. ξυνόν, cf. frg. 2, 113, 114.

167. Frg. 89.

168. Frg. 114.
169. Frg. 2.
170. Frg. 114.
171. Cf. frg. 30, 31, 64, 65.
172. Xenoph. frg. 2, 12.
173. Heracl. frg. 1, 32, 112, 114.
174. Anaximander 9 (Diels). See p. 159.
175. Heracl. frg. 53; cf. frg. 67.
176. Frg. 8.
177. Frg. 67.
178. Frg. 31, 62.
179. Frg. 90
180. Frg. 84.
181. Frg. 88.
182. Frg. 50.
183. Frg. 51; cf. frg. 10.
184. See frg. 51, the examples of the lyre and the bow, which have this tension in common.

185. Much depends on the interpretation of Parmenides frg. 6, 4 ff. (Diels), which formerly was generally referred to Heraclitus' doctrine of παλίντροπος ἁρμονίη. The words παλίντροπος κέλευθος, Parm. frg. 6, 9, seemed to contain an allusion to Heraclitus' famous frg. 51. K. Reinhardt in his book *Parmenides* questioned that interpretation and thereby the chronological order of the Presocratic thinkers followed by Diels in his *Fragmente der Vorsokratiker*. But there remains the difficult problem, even if we do not refer Parm. frg. 6 to Heraclitus (see *supra*, p. 175), of whether or not it is necessary to reverse the relationship of both thinkers with Reinhardt and to admit that Heraclitus' doctrine of the harmony of the opposites was intended as the solution to Parmenides' problem of their irreconcilability.

186. Frg. 114.
187. Frg. 32.
188. Frg. 33.
189. See note 161. It may be remembered that in Aeschylus' tragedy, too, the word φρονεῖν indicates (*Agam.* 176) the supreme religious wisdom which man may attain. In tragedy he attains it through suffering.
190. See *Paideia* I, 164.
191. Cf. frg. 36, 77, 117, 118.

CHAPTER 10

THE ARISTOCRACY: CONFLICT AND TRANSFORMATION

1. This was the case not only within Greece proper but also outside, as the example of Alcaeus of Mytilene proves; see chap. VII, note 73.
2. In the following discussion I have been compelled to criticize some of the views expressed by R. Reitzenstein in *Epigramm und Skolion* (1893) and F. Jacoby in *Theognis* (*Sitz. Berl. Akad.* 1931). See now Josef Kroll, *Theognisinterpretationen* (Leipzig 1936).
3. See Wilamowitz, *Textgeschichte der griechischen Lyriker* (Berlin 1900), 58.
4. This can be shown, of course, only by such verses of other poets as have

been incorporated in the Theognidean collection and which have also been preserved independently of it in their own contexts.

5. See *Paideia* II, 176 ff.

6. The book of Theognis begins with the hymns on Apollo and Artemis and the invocation of the Muses and Graces (v. 1-18). The epilogue comes at v. 237-254: the poet promises his friend Cyrnus that his poem will make him immortal, carrying his name over land and sea.

7. *Laws* 811a.

8. Theognis, v. 19-26.

9. 'Plato', *Hipparchus* 228c.

10. See prologue v. 23 and epilogue v. 245-252.

11. See the *Persians* of Timotheus, v. 241 ff., and the remarks of Wilamowitz, pp. 65 and 100 of his commentary.

12. This is the view of Jacoby, op. cit. 31; cf. M. Pohlenz's essay in *Gött. gel. Nachr.* 1933, which I did not see until the composition of this chapter was completed.

13. v. 227-232. These verses correspond to Solon frg. 1, 71-76 (Diehl).

14. v. 757-792.

15. Eusebius and Suidas place Theognis' *floruit* in Olympiad 59 (544-541 B.C.). But see W. Schmid, *Geschichte der griechischen Literatur* I, 1 (Munich 1929), 381 ff., who rejects the tradition and prefers the time shortly before and after 500, since he ascribes the lines about the Persian War (see note 14) to our Theognis.

16. Isocrates was the first to compare Hesiod's didactic poetry with Theognis and Phocylides and to classify the works of all three under the common heading of ὑποθῆκαι (*ad Nicoclem* 43). See *Paideia* III, 104, and P. Friedlaender, Ὑποθῆκαι in *Hermes* XLVIII (1931), 572. Isocrates' speech *Ad Nicoclem* and the pseudo-Isocratean *Ad Demonicum* are the legitimate successors of these didactic poems in classical prose.

17. Theognis, 27.

18. See p. 25.

19. See Erich Bethe, *Die dorische Knabenliebe* in *Rhein. Mus.* N.F. LXII (1907), 438-475.

20. One might have doubts about the meaning of παῖδες φίλοι in Solon frg. 13, where some take it as 'children of his own' (as in Mimnermus 2, 13), and not as 'boys'; but in frg. 12 the concept of παιδοφιλεῖν is defined by Solon himself in an unmistakable manner. The word παῖς is used in the same sense in frg. 14, 5, and in Mimn. 1, 9. Both passages conjoin the love of women and that of boys as the two generally recognized forms of love prevailing at that time.

21. See *Paideia* II, chap. 8, Plato's *Symposium*. But on Plato's later verdict in his *Laws* against the Dorian *eros*, see *Paideia* III, 222.

22. On Plato's erotic philosophy see Rolf Lagerborg, *Platonische Liebe* (Leipzig 1926). See also the speeches on *eros* in Plato's *Symposium*, especially those by Phaedrus and Pausanias, *Paideia* II, 179 ff., which reflect the traditional views on this subject.

23. See Plato, *Symp.* 178d.

24. Xen. *Resp. Lac.* II, 12, ἔστι γάρ τι καὶ τοῦτο πρὸς παιδείαν. See the whole section 12-14.

25. Theognis, 237 ff.

26. See p. 146.

27. Theognis, 39-52.

28. Theognis, 53-68.

29. See p. 71.

30. γνῶμαι (60), which are really authoritative judgments: compare the epigrammatic γνῶμαι which appear in the latter part of the book.

31. Theognis, 31-38. M. Hoffmann, *Die ethische Terminologie bei Homer, Hesiod, und den alten Elegikern und Iambographen* (Tuebingen 1914), 131 ff., has traced the concepts of ἀγαθός and κακός, ἐσθλός and δειλός in Theognis most accurately and has examined their meaning.

32. Theognis, 69-72.

33. v. 39-68. This part consists of the two elegiac poems Κύρνε, κύει πόλις ἥδε (39-52) and Κύρνε, πόλις μὲν ἔθ' ἥδε πόλις (53-68).

34. Theognis, 69 ff.

35. Theognis, 77 ff.

36. In times of στάσις party, not kinship, determines friendship, as Thuc. III, 82, 6, says. Originally φίλοι meant the members of the clan; in Theognis it means adherents to a party, but party in the sense of a social class.

37. Theognis, 59 ff.

38. Theognis, 220.

39. See p. 146.

40. Theognis, 213 ff.

41. v. 233.

42. See *supra*, p. 21, on Homer; on Solon, p. 144. Pindar's ideal of πλοῦτος ἀρεταῖς δεδαιδαλμένος is the same. Even Aristotle, in his ethical code, stresses the importance of external goods for the 'good life' and the development of certain moral virtues, such as μεγαλοπρέπεια and ἐλευθεριότης, *Eth. Nic.* IV, 1 and IV, 4. These virtues were inherited from the old aristocratic way of life.

43. Hesiod, *Works and Days* 313, πλούτῳ δ' ἀρετὴ καὶ κῦδος ὀπηδεῖ.

44. Tyrtaeus frg. 9, 6. Cf. *Paideia* I, 91.

45. Solon frg. 3, 5 ff.

46. Solon frg. 1, 7 ff.

47. Solon frg. 14.

48. Solon frg. 4, 9-12.

49. Of the many passages in the *Sayings to Cyrnus* which are concerned with the problem of money and poverty, I cite Theognis, 149 ff., especially 173-182. The *Sayings from the Poets*, which now form the second part of the Theognidean collection, also contain much about poverty, e.g. 267, 351, 383, 393, 619, 621, 649, 659, 667. But which of these distichs are really Theognidean is impossible to tell. The cynical elegy (699-718) which praises wealth as the only areté is an imitation and transformation of Tyrtaeus' famous poem (frg. 9), as I have shown in *Tyrtaios ueber die wahre Areté* (*Sitz. Berl. Akad.* 1932), 559 ff. The poem, though incorporated into the Theognidean collection, seems to be a product of the fifth century.

50. The Solonian passages about areté and wealth (*plutos*) were incorporated into our collection of Theognidea (cf. 227, 315, 585, 719) because they resembled so much Theognis' own utterances. In reality they were Theognis' model and source. Cf. Theognis himself on areté and wealth, v. 149, 153, 155, 161, 165, 319, 683.

51. See p. 196 ff.

52. Solon frg. 1 (Diehl): the first part is echoed in Theognis 197-208, the second in Theognis, 133-142.

53. Theognis, 129.

54. Theognis, 153.

55. Theognis, 149-150.

56. Theognis, 147-148: ἐν δὲ δικαιοσύνῃ συλλήβδην πᾶσ' ἀρετή ἐστιν, πᾶς δέ τ' ἀνὴρ ἀγαθός, Κύρνε, δίκαιος ἐών.

57. The one line ἐν δὲ δικαιοσύνῃ συλλήβδην πᾶσ’ ἀρετή ἐστιν (Theogn. 147) was quoted by Theophrastus in the first book of Περὶ ἠθῶν as belonging to Theognis, but the same author quoted it again in the first book of his *Ethics* as belonging to Phocylides. Michael Ephesius, *Comm. ad Arist. Eth. Nic.* v, 2, 1129b27 (p. 8, Wendland), notes this contradiction but sees no difficulty in supposing that the line occurred in both authors. Since this is not likely to be a mere improvisation by Michael, it is probable that he took it from a learned and much earlier source.

58. Theognis, 54, speaks of the λαοί who formerly οὔτε δίκας ᾔδεσαν οὔτε νόμους, but now are ἀγαθοί, whereas the former ἐσθλοί are now δειλοί.

59. Theognis, 183 ff.

60. See *Paideia* II, 246 ff.; III, 246 ff.

61. On Plato see the preceding note. Arist. *Pol.* VII, 16 ff.

62. On the economic aspect of the aristocratic society of early Greece, see the literature quoted on p. 422, note 14.

63. Hegel rightly remarks in his *Philosophy of History* (*Werke*, Vollst. Ausg., Berlin 1848, Bd. IX, 295 ff.) that the objective work of art, the ideal of the athlete created by Greek sculpture, was preceded by the subjective work of art that was living man, the trained body of the Olympian victor. In other words, the 'beautiful individuality' which is the law of early Greek art was determined and shaped by Greek paideia and its gymnastic ideal.

64. Several great original thinkers of the eighteenth century, men such as J. G. Herder and W. v. Humboldt, gifted with an extraordinary historical knowledge and poetic imagination, rediscovered the actual social background of Pindar's poetry. See Gleason Archer, *The Reception of Pindar in Eighteenth-Century German Literature* (Harvard dissertation, 1944), who also traces the influence of Pindar on the French and English mind since the Renaissance and cites much valuable material.

65. On Pindar's poetical language, cf. F. Dornseiff, *Pindars Stil* (Berlin 1921), which contains excellent observations, and of earlier books A. Croiset, *La poésie de Pindare* (Paris 1895).

66. On this whole section see the *Nachwort* to Rudolf Borchardt's *Pindarische Gedichte.*

67. In the sands of Egypt have been discovered papyri with several paeans, a parthenion, and a part of a dithyramb of Pindar, along with poems of Bacchylides, Corinna, and Alcman.

68. On the history of text tradition and exegesis of the four Books of Pindar's *epinikia,* cf. Wilamowitz, *Pindaros* (Berlin 1922).

69. Herod. V, 67.

70. On the Olympian games, see E. N. Gardiner, *Greek Athletic Sports and Festivals* (London 1910) and *Athletics of the Ancient World* (Oxford 1930); Franz Mezö, *Geschichte der olympischen Spiele* (Munich 1930).

71. On the order in which the various kinds of games developed at Olympia see Mahaffy, *JHS* II, 164 ff.; A. Koerte, *Hermes* XXXIX (1904), 224 ff.; O. Brinkmann, *Rhein. Mus.* N.F. LXX (1915), 623; see also E. N. Gardiner, *Greek Athletic Sports and Festivals.*

72. See Xenophanes frg. 2, 11 (Diels, *Vorsokratiker* I) and *supra,* pp. 171-172. A long fragment of Euripides' lost play *Autolycus,* preserved by Athen. X, 413c, takes up and elaborates the invective of Xenophanes against the athletes. He attacks them quite in the spirit of his predecessor on the grounds of their uselessness to society in times of war. Plato, too, in his *Republic* measures athletic prowess by the criterion of military usefulness (see *Paideia* II, 231).

73. See Pind. *Isth.* II, 6, ἁ Μοῖσα γὰρ οὐ φιλοκερδής πω τότ' ἦν οὐδ' ἐργάτις. The scholiast *ad loc.* refers this polemic allusion to Simonides. But see also *Pyth.* XI, 41. On Simonides' φιλοκέρδεια see Wilamowitz, *Pindaros*, p. 312.

74. See p. 40 on the Homeric and Platonic conception of the bard. The same idea is found in Hesiod, *Theog.* 99 ff.

75. On the *exemplum* or pattern in early Greek poetry, see p. 33.

76. Pind. *Ol.* I, 18.

77. Pind. *Nem.* III, 6.

78. *Nem.* III, 29, δίκας ἄωτος.

79. The Greek word is χρέος. Cf. *Ol.* III, 7; *Pyth.* IX, 10, etc.

80. *Nem.* IX, 7.

81. *Nem.* IV, 7.

82. This had been done in Magna Grecia by Xenocritus of Locri (end of seventh century) and in Sicily by the more famous choral poems of Stesichorus of Himera (sixth century). Both poets made their lyrics out of the heroic myth of the epos and thereby created a ballad form. Some of these poems were of considerable length, filling whole books, and thus recalled their origin from the epic.

83. On Boeckh's conception of poetic form and his approach to the problem in Pindar, see Wolfgang Schadewaldt, *Der Aufbau des Pindarischen Epinikion* in *Schriften d. Koenigsberger Gelehrten Gesellschaft* (Halle 1928), 262.

84. The turning point was marked by the work of the Danish scholar A. B. Drachmann, *Moderne Pindarfortolkning* (Copenhagen 1891).

85. See also W. Schadewaldt, loc. cit. p. 298.

86. Wilamowitz in *Pindaros* (Berlin 1922), 118, clearly saw this distinction, but alluded to it only in passing. Yet it must be the starting-point of any attempt to understand Pindar's work—not only its moral aspect, as a vehicle of the aristocratic creed, but its structure too; and Wilamowitz did not draw the logical conclusions from his discovery which would have illuminated the structure of the *epinikia*.

87. Cf. Hermann Gundert, *Pindar und sein Dichterberuf* (Frankfurt 1935).

88. Pind. *Pyth.* VI, 8.

89. *Ol.* VI, 1.

90. *Nem.* V, 1.

91. 'Socrates' is compared with a sculptor in *Rep.* 540c, and cf. 361d; theorizing compared with the painter of ideal figures (παραδείγματα) in 472d.

92. Simon. frg. 37 (Diehl). Areté is visualized in this poem as a goddess, and the final aim of mortals is to climb her sacred mountain and see her face to face. But this goal is reserved for only a few, though all are free to make the attempt.

93. Simon. frg. 4 (Diehl). See the interpretation of the poem by Wilamowitz, *Sappho und Simonides* (Berlin 1913), 159. On Simonides' concept of areté, see Wilamowitz, op. cit. p. 175.

94. Plato, *Protag.* 338e. See *Paideia* II, 118.

95. This is why the sophist in Plato's *Protagoras* chose his poem as starting-point for the discussion of areté. In Simonides' time, the poet was the wise man who was able to answer difficult questions. See Wilamowitz, op. cit. p. 169.

96. The views put forward in this chapter have long been advanced in my lectures on paideia, which encouraged W. Schadewaldt to use them in analysing the structure of Pindar's odes (*Der Aufbau des pindarischen Epinikion*, see note 83). He did not discuss Pindar's use of myths, but his book led L. Illig to do so in a dissertation offered at Kiel, *Zur Form der pindarischen Erzaehlung* (Berlin 1932).

97. Hermann Fraenkel, *Pindar's Religion* (*Die Antike* III, 39).

98. *Ol.* II, 15 ff.

99. The author of *On the Sublime* c. 44, 1, speaks of the κοσμικὴ ἀφορία in the entire field of the spirit during the Roman Empire.

100. See notes 74 and 75 and the chapter Homer the Educator.

101. *Pyth.* II, 54-58.

102. *Pyth.* II, 72, γένοι' οἷος ἐσσὶ μαθών. In quoting this passage authors often omitted the μαθών; the omission occurs as early as Eustathius (see the testimonia in A. Turyn's learned edition of Pindar, *ad loc.*). The addition of μαθών makes it clear that Hieron ought to become his own true self now that Pindar has revealed it to him.

103. This, if true, would make the present book a more natural and appropriate introduction to Plato's philosophy.

104. *Pyth.* VI, 19 ff. The precepts to honour gods and parents often appear connected, in early Greek tradition, with the commandment to respect the stranger. But this last precept is omitted by Pindar in this ode as less relevant in the present case; see *supra*, chap. I, note 1.

105. *Pyth.* VI, 44.

106. This prompts Pindar to incorporate a myth in every poem and make it the centre of his eulogy and interpretation of the present event. See Karl Fehr, *Die Mythen bei Pindar* (Zuerich 1936), and L. Illig's monograph quoted in note 96.

107. *Nem.* III, 50 ff.

108. See chap. II.

109. See *Paideia* II, 161.

110. *Nem.* III, 38.

111. *Nem.* III, 56. I have accepted Hecker's conjecture ἐν ἁρμένοισι πᾶσι (instead of πάντα) θυμὸν αὔξων · ἐν was supplemented by Erhard Schmid.

112. This view is held, e.g. by Franz Dornseiff. There are passages which can be interpreted in both ways, but cf. Theognis 770, where σοφίη is the poet's higher wisdom that distinguishes him from other mortals and makes it his mission and duty to teach them. There are three aspects of it are distinguished: thinking or searching (μῶσθαι), showing (δεικνύεν), and writing (ποιεῖν). Apparently this is the same as the ἀρετὴ σοφίη of Theogn. 790.

113. Xenophanes frg. 2, 11 ff. (Diels). See p. 173.

114. *Paean* VI, 6.

115. *Nem.* IV, 8.

116. *Ol.* I, 28b.

117. *Pyth.* II, 86.

118. *Ol.* II, 83.

119. *Nem.* III, 77.

120. *Fragmenta Tragicorum,* frg. 1047 Nauck.

121. *Ol.* II, 94.

122. See the chapter on the sophists, p. 286 ff.

123. After Theognis had created the *Ritterspiegel* in his poems, Pindar made his last great odes addressed to the Sicilian kings a *Fuerstenspiegel.* Isocrates later imitated this kind of paideia in his *To Nicocles* (see *Paideia* III, 85), in the introduction (4) in which he calls the education of the rulers the most urgent need of his time.

124. *Schol. ad Aristoph. Ran.* 1028 (from Eratosthenes' Περὶ κωμῳδίας).

125. *Isth.* VIII, 9 ff.

126. *Dith.* frg. 64.

CHAPTER 11

THE CULTURAL POLICY OF THE TYRANTS

1. Thucydides I, 17 evaluates the period of the so-called tyrants in Greek history mainly from the point of view of the greatness of their enterprises in war and power politics, and comes to the conclusion that in this respect they cannot compete with the modern Athenian democracy of the Periclean era, for they engaged only in local actions against their neighbours. Among them the tyrants of Sicily developed the greatest power. Thucydides states (I, 18, 1) that after the rule of tyrants in Athens and everywhere else in Hellas had been broken by the political or military intervention of Sparta, that form of government continued to exist only in Sicily. On the tyrants in general, see H. G. Plass, *Die Tyrannis in ihren beiden Perioden bei den alten Griechen* (Bremen 1852), and P. N. Ure, *The Origin of Tyranny* (Cambridge 1922).

2. Plato, *Ep.* VIII, 353a ff.

3. Solon frg. 3, 18; 8, 4; 10, 3-6. In a similar way Theognis (40 and 52) prophesies that the rule of a tyrant will be the outcome in the strife of the sixth century between the old aristocracy and the rising masses in Megara.

4. Arist. *Resp. Ath.* 13, 1.

5. Arist. *Resp. Ath.* 13, 4-5.

6. Herod. I, 59; Arist. op. cit. 14.

7. Like the word sophist, which came to be used at the same time, the names *tyrannos* or *monarchos* did not yet have, in that period, the negative connotation which characterized them later. The names distinguished these new men from the kings of bygone ages. They tried to maintain as far as possible the republican forms. See K. J. Beloch, *Griechische Geschichte* I, 1 (2. Aufl., Berlin 1924), 355 ff.

8. The first mention of the *tyrannis* is to be found in the middle of the seventh century in a famous poem of Archilochus (frg. 22, Diehl).

9. See the respective chapters in this book, p. 138 ff. and p. 185 ff.

10. Arist. *Resp. Ath.* 2, 2. Cf. Solon, frg. 24, 7-15 (Diehl).

11. On Theognis' warnings against intermarriage of the impoverished nobles with the *nouveaux riches,* see pp. 204-205.

12. Pisistratus is described as the enemy of the rich and of the old nobility but a friend of the common man, Arist. *Resp. Ath.* c. 16. He administered the state more πολιτικῶς ἢ τυραννικῶς, Arist. op. cit. 14, 3, and 16, 2.

13. Cf. Arist. op. cit. c. 28 *et passim.*

14. See note 8.

15. Polyb. *Hist.* VI, 7. The degeneration of the sons is seen by Polybius- as the cause of the downfall not only of the tyranny and monarchy but also of the aristocracy (VI, 8, 6). This trait is obviously taken over from Plato's *Republic.*

16. See note 8.

17. Arist. *Pol.* III, 17, 1288a28. But tyrannic rule is 'against nature', 1287b39.

18. Arist. *Resp. Ath.* c. 16.

19. Ib. 16, 7.

20. Ib. 16, 6.

21. Ib. 16, 5.

22. Aristotle's immediate source for the history of the Pisistratidae in the *Constitution of the Athenians* seems to have been the *Atthis* of an older contemporary, Androtion, a pupil of Isocrates. See Wilamowitz, *Aristoteles und Athen* I (Berlin 1893), 260 ff.

23. This has been shown by F. Leo, *Die griechisch-roemische Biographie* (Leipzig 1901), cf. p. 109 ff.

24. Pittacus was appointed *aisymnetes* of Mytilene by an overwhelming majority of the people (Arist., *Pol.* III, 14, 1285b1), but the aristocratic opposition led by Antimenidas and his brother, the lyric poet Alcaeus, called him a tyrant just the same.

25. *Hipparchus* 228b ff.

26. Arist. *Resp. Ath.* 18, 1.

27. Thucydides VI, 54, in a famous excursus proves that the popular tradition was wrong in assuming that the slain Hipparchus was the ruler and that Harmodius and Aristogiton liberated Athens from his tyranny.

28. Herod. VII, 6. Arist. frg. 7 (Rose).

29. The analogy of the Greek tyrants of the sixth and early fifth centuries with the Medicis in Renaissance Florence is correct not only in the glorification of the new régime in the art of the times but also politically; for they were both exponents of the democratic tendencies of a new form of city-state. This form was opposed to the more aristocratic and conservative type of the polis which in sixth century Hellas was represented by Sparta, in the Italy of the Renaissance by Venice.

BOOK TWO

CHAPTER I

THE DRAMA OF AESCHYLUS

1. Aeschylus addresses Euripides in Aristophanes' *Frogs* 840 as ὦ παῖ τῆς ἀρουραίου θεοῦ.

2. Aristoph. *Frogs* 886-887.

3. F. G. Welcker, *Die aeschylische Trilogie Prometheus und die Kabirenweihe zu Lemnos* (Darmstadt 1824).

4. Arist. *Eth. Nic.* III, 2, 1111a10; cf. Anonym. *comm. in Eth. Nic.* 145 (Heylbut); Clemens *Strom.* II, 60, 3.

5. See *Vita Aeschyli* 11 (Aesch. ed. Wilamowitz, ed. maior p. 5).

6. Schol. Aesch. *Pers.* 432.

7. See Thuc. I, 74, the speech of the Athenian ambassador in Sparta on Athens' ascent to power after the Persian wars.

8. Corn. Nepos, *Them.* 5.

9. This is literally true, since we trace the Tyrtaean spirit and its influence on the morale of the Athenian citizens throughout the fifth century in the language of the numerous epigrams on the graves of Athenian warriors who died in the many wars of their country, and in the funeral orations delivered publicly in their honour. See my *Tyrtaios* in *Sitz. Berl. Akad.* 1932, pp. 561-565.

10. See Aesch. *Suppl.* 86 ff. and 524 ff.

11. Arist. *Poet.* c. 6, 1450b7.

12. Aesch. *Eum.* 916 ff.

13. Montesquieu, *L'esprit des lois* III, chap. 3.

14. See the emphasis laid on diké in the great speech of Agamemnon on his return home, Aesch. *Ag.* 810 ff.; similarly the chorus in *Ag.* 249 and throughout. The *Eumenides* is entirely concerned with this problem and its importance for the polis. Diké is the highest norm of conduct which the goddess Athena herself

established for her polis, *Eum.* 691. On the fear of the law as the foundation of the Athenian democracy, see *Eum.* 698. Cf. Pericles in Thuc. II, 37, 3, and note 59.

15. Thuc. I, 6, 3-4.

16. Arist. *Resp. Ath.* c. 25-26.

17. Aristotle has seen this clearly, for in his *Poetics* he concentrates on two forms of Greek poetry only, epic and drama.

18. See the chapters of this book on post-Homeric poetry, Hesiod, Tyrtaeus, the lyric, iambic, and elegiac poets.

19. Cf. R. Oehler's monograph quoted in chap. II, note 68, and the studies of L. Illig and Fehr on the myths in Pindar referred to in the chapter on Pindar, note 106.

20. Such is the poem on the wedding of Hector and Andromache, discovered some decades ago (frg. 55a, Diehl).

21. Wilamowitz, *Einleitung in die attische Tragoedie* (Berlin 1907), 107.

22. It is for the same reason beyond the scope of this book to survey the modern literature on the problem of the origin of Greek tragedy, from Friedrich Nietzsche's *Birth of Tragedy* to the fanciful theories of modern historians of religion. The whole mass of material is discussed with balanced judgment and great completeness by A. W. Pickard-Cambridge in *Dithyramb, Tragedy and Comedy* (Oxford 1927). Cf. W. Kranz, *Stasimon* (Berlin 1933).

23. The greatest genius in the field of the satyr-play was Pratinas of Phlius in the Peloponnesus, later of Athens, whom ancient tradition called the king of satyrs. We had no real knowledge of Aeschylus' own art of satyric drama until large papyrus fragments of some of his satyr-plays were recently discovered in Egypt. These were published in volume 18 of the *Oxyrhynchus Papyri*. See the first appreciation of these memorable discoveries: Ed. Fraenkel, *Aeschylus: New Texts and Old Problems,* in *Proceedings of the British Academy* XXVIII.

24. Plato saw this clearly when in the *Laws* he tried to revive the earlier form of Greek culture (paideia) by re-introducing into the life of his own time the choric poetry and dances of the archaic period. See *Paideia* III, 228 ff.

25. The proper word for 'tragedy' or 'comedy' was χορός in Greek. ἐν ἐκείνῳ τῷ χορῷ (Plat. *Prot.* 327d) does not mean 'in that chorus' but 'in that drama'. Indeed, the persons referred to by Plato in this passage cannot have belonged to the chorus but were the actors. This signification of the word proves that even after the classical drama had taken on its definite shape the memory of a former stage of its development was still alive, when the drama and the chorus were one and the same. Even in Aristophanes' time, at the beginning of a tragic performance the herald says, 'Theognis, introduce your chorus' (*Ach.* 11, εἴσαγ' ὦ Θέογνι τὸν χορόν).

26. Herod. VI, 21. The archon in Athens decreed, after its first performance, that no one should present the drama, the Μιλήτου ἅλωσις of Phrynichus, again.

27. Aristoph. *Frogs* 1004.

28. *Vita Aeschyli* 2. It is what Aristotle, *Poet.* 6, 1450a10, calls ὄψις.

29. On the development of the chorus in Greek tragedy from the main actor into the ideal spectator, see p. 265.

30. Goethe, *Iphigenie in Tauris.*

31. See the work of W. C. Greene, *Moira: Fate, Good, and Evil in Greek Thought* (Cambridge, Mass. 1944), in which the history of the problem is traced throughout Greek literature.

32. A brilliant attempt at answering the question, What is the tragic in Greek tragedy? was made by P. Friedlaender in *Die Antike* I and II. But the question

remains whether the catagories in which the author tries to describe the phæ-nomenon would have satisfied the Greek mind as they do the modern. M. Pohlenz wanted to answer the same question in his *Die griechische Tragoedie* (Leipzig Berlin, 1930 ff.

33. The discussion of this problem by Hesiod, Archilochus, Semonides, Solon, Theognis, Simonides, and Pindar has been mentioned above in the respective treatments of these authors. They form the correct point of departure for any analysis of the problem in Greek tragedy.

34. Aristotle's famous definition of tragedy and its effect on the audience names these two effects, ἔλεος and φόβος, as the most important παθήματα which are aroused by tragedy and are subject to the tragic κάθαρσις. If they are referred to in the text in the same sense, it is not because I am an orthodox Aristotelian but simply because by long and detailed concentration on the drama of Aeschylus I have arrived at the conclusion that these categories do indeed fit the facts better than any other. Aristotle must have adopted them on the basis of an entirely empirical approach to the tragedies themselves and not by any kind of abstract speculation. Any modern attempt at approaching the Greek drama with-out preconceptions must come to the same or similar conclusions and should be undertaken in the spirit in which, for example, Bruno Snell in his monograph *Aischylos und das Handeln im Drama* (*Philologus*, Supplementband xx, 1928) has discussed the factor of tragic fear for the structure of Greek tragedy.

35. In dealing concretely with single works of Greek tragedy, it is of course impossible to separate their purely artistic aspect from their religious and human function (some would say 'moral teaching', which unduly narrows this side of it). Euripides and Aeschylus, in the comedy of Aristophanes, speak of their τέχνη as well as of their σοφία. H. D. F. Kitto's recent book *Greek Tragedy* (London 1939) is a valuable contribution to the first aspect. Ernst Howald, *Die griechische Tragoedie* (Munich Berlin, 1930), also lays stress on the poetic effect of Greek tragedy. But I would prefer to see included in the concept of 'art' the approach of what Kitto calls 'historical scholarship', so far as it helps us to understand the all-inclusive spiritual character of Greek art (σοφία) which made its great masters the πλάσται of Hellas, not only incidentally but essentially, as I think. In a book like the present it is inevitable that in its brief survey of tragedy the details of artistic analysis must be overshadowed by the consideration of the creative function of that great art in shaping Greek culture. Similarly, it cannot deal in detail with the dialectical structure of Plato's philosophy but only with its claims to being the true fulfilment of the educational mission of classical Greek poetry. That mission was acknowledged by the first Greek literary critics, who were poets themselves; see Alfonso Reyes, *La critica en la edad Ateniense* (México 1940), 111 ff.

36. Aesch. *Suppl.* 368 ff., 517, 600 ff.

37. Cf. Aesch. *Ag.* 921 ff., the carpet scene.

38. *Prom.* 197-241.

39. *Prom.* 62, 944, 1039. Aeschylus here uses the words σοφιστής and σοφός; σόφισμα is used in 459, 470, 1011.

40. Nauck, *Fragm. Trag.²*, Aeschylus under *Palamedes;* cf. frg. adesp. 470.

41. Prometheus' tale of the toilsome stages of Io's wanderings. 790 ff. tells of distant countries, mountains, rivers, and tribes of men; similarly *Prom. Lib.,* frg. 192-199 (Nauck). The poet takes his information from a learned source, pre-sumably the Περίοδος γῆς of Hecataeus of Miletus.

42. In the diatribe-like speech of Oceanus, *Prom.* 307 ff., Aeschylus is obviously drawing upon the tradition of the old *Spruchpoesie*.

43. This was shown for the first time in K. O. Müller's monumental edition of Aeschylus' *Eumenides* (1833), in which the drama was projected against the background of Attic criminal law and the aboriginal religious tradition on which it rested. Cf. also Thomson's great edition of the *Oresteia* (Cambridge 1938).

44. The choruses in Aesch. *Eum.* 916 and *Suppl.* 625, both of which are solemn prayers for the welfare of the city (Athens and Argos respectively), reveal to us, in the absence of direct tradition of the form and nature of that sort of religious speech, the ritual forms used in public prayer.

45. *Poet.* 13, 1453a18.

46. See his book quoted above in note 3. See also the most recent attempt at reconstructing Aeschylus' trilogies, Franz Stoessl's *Die Trilogie des Aischylos* (Baden-Wien 1937).

47. In the reconstruction of the order which the three plays whose titles we know held in the lost trilogy of Aeschylus, I follow Westphal's *Prolegomena zu Aeschylus Tragoedien* (Leipzig 1869), in which it is proved that the Πυρφόρος came last, not first.

48. Solon frg. 1 (Diehl); see p. 142 ff.

49. See p. 25 ff.

50. See p. 54.

51. ἀπρόοπτον κακόν and similar expressions were often used to define what the Greek language understood by até.

52. See pp. 141 ff. and 144 ff.

53. Hesiod, *Works and Days* 218, παθὼν δέ τε νήπιος ἔγνω.

54. Aesch. *Pers.* 818.

55. *Pers.* 107-116.

56. *Prom.* 1071; cf. *Solons Eunomie* (*Sitz. Berl. Akad.* 1926), 75.

57. *Sept.* 953.

58. *Iliad* XIX, 93; Heracl. frg. 119.

59. The rôle of the polis in Aeschylus' drama is of supreme importance, as its glorification at the end of the *Oresteia* reveals. The polis appears there as an indispensable part of the divine order of the world, the idea of the cosmos, of which, as we have seen before (p. 160), it had been the earthly prototype. The new freedom of the individual meant for the time of Aeschylus freedom from the power of the clan and clan justice. A strong centralized city-state founded on a strict social order and written laws was the guarantee of that freedom for the generations whose living ideals were reflected in Aeschylus' art. From the point of view of modern liberalism, which on the whole sees the freedom of the individual threatened by the very same power of the state which at first was its strongest protector, it is hard to understand the moral feeling with which the young Attic democracy speaks of the state in Aeschylus' tragedy. But in Sophocles' *Antigone* a different aspect appears, and the possibility of grave conflict between state and individual is visualized. This time it is the state which interferes with the sacred obligations of the individual towards clan and family; the state itself appears as a tyrannic power. The problem was anticipated in the last scene of Aeschylus' *Seven against Thebes,* if it is genuine. Even in the scene of the *Seven* where the political authority of the king clashes with the religious fervour of the women, which threatens to upset the order of the state in a moment of extreme danger, we have a similar conflict. That conflict must have played a part in the Dionysiac trilogy of Aeschylus, the lost *Lycurgeia,* as it does in its Euripidean counterpart, the *Bacchae.*

60. There is a similar conflict in the Danaid trilogy, of which we possess the *Suppliants,* in the Prometheus trilogy, and perhaps also in the *Lycurgeia.*

61. Solon frg. 1, 29-32 (Diehl). Cf. p. 144.

62. On the hypothetical reconstruction of the two plays which preceded the *Seven against Thebes* in the Theban trilogy, see Carl Robert, *Oidipus; Geschichte eines poetischen Stoffs* (Berlin 1915), 252, and F. Stoessl, op. cit. (note 46).

63. Euripides' sharp eye perceived the chance which this fact offered him. In his *Phoenician Maidens* he gave Polynices a lovable character, much more attractive than the gloomy and tyrannous Eteocles, who is described by the later poet as ambitious and daemonic, burning with the lust for power, shrinking not even from criminal acts to attain his supreme desire. Cf. Eur. *Phoen.* 521-525. Aeschylus' Eteocles is the true patriot and unselfish defender of his country.

64. Sophocles' *Antigone* has a famous chorus (582 ff.), which reads in part like a reflection of the Aeschylean tragedy of Eteocles. There the heroic maiden and not her brother, who had preceded her in death, appears as the last victim of the curse of the Labdacid house. Verses like *Ant.* 593 ff. strike truly Aeschylean notes.

65. See the triumphant words at the beginning of the messenger's speech, *Sept.* 792 ff., in which Aeschylus states Eteocles' undying merits for Thebes.

66. The *Prometheus* is the other drama which must be referred to in this connexion, but the chronological order of both tragedies is not quite clear. There are reasons, however, for favouring the priority of the *Prometheus*.

67. Concerning the figure of Eteocles as a ruler, see the study made at my suggestion by Virginia Woods, *Types of Rulers in the Tragedies of Aeschylus* (University of Chicago dissertation, 1941), chap. IV.

68. *Prom.* 266.

69. Prometheus is the ideal representative of creative techné throughout the drama of Aeschylus; see *Prom.* 254, 441 ff., particularly 506.

70. Hes. *Theog.* 521, 616. As we read the story now, the punishment is alleviated by Heracles, who frees Prometheus from the eagle; but this episode of the *Theogony* is evidently a later rhapsodic interpolation prompted by the different conception of Heracles set forth in the epic tradition. In *Theog.* 616 the punishment is not limited in time but is still going on (cf. the present ἐρύκει).

71. Cf. note 69.

72. Cf. note 39.

73. Hom. *Hymn* xx, 4 (*in Hephaestum*), if this is not already a reflection of Aeschylus' Prometheus. See also Xenophanes frg. 18 (Diels).

74. Hes., *Works and Days* 90 ff.

75. On Prometheus' 'philanthropy', v. 28, 235 ff., 442 ff., 542, 507.

76. So did Goethe and Shelley.

77. *Prom.* 515-525.

78. *Prom.* 514, τέχνη δ' ἀνάγκης ἀσθενεστέρα μακρῷ.

79. *Prom.* 510, but cf. 526 ff. and 550-552.

80. *Prom.* 212-213.

81. Cf. frg. 191, 192 (Nauck).

82. *Prom.* 540.

83. *Prom.* 553.

84. See note 29.

85. Cf. *Prom.* 553 ff.

86. *Ag.* 160.

CHAPTER 2

SOPHOCLES AND THE TRAGIC CHARACTER

1. Cf. Aristoph. *Frogs* 790.

2. See Isocr. *Paneg.* 10. The different merits of the first inventor (πρῶτος εὑρών) and the master who brings an art to perfection (ὁ ἐξακριβώσας) were always recognized by the Greeks.

3. See p. 377.

4. The revival of Greek tragedy which resulted from the life-work of the great historical scholar, U. v. Wilamowitz-Möllendorff, took Aeschylus and Euripides as points of departure; until his very last years Wilamowitz consciously neglected Sophocles. On this point, see also the remarks of K. Reinhardt, *Sophokles* (Frankfurt 1933), 11, and G. Perotta, *Sofocle* (Messina 1935), 623.

5. Tycho v. Wilamowitz's book *Die dramatische Technik des Sophokles* (Berlin 1917), the greatest contribution to this subject made in the last thirty years, first laid down the basis on which Sophocles must be studied from this point of view. And it must not be forgotten that it was Goethe who first directed the attention of critics to the superior craftsmanship of this ancient dramatist as one of the essential causes of his artistic effect. But against the one-sided approach from this angle which was the merit as well as the limitation of Tycho v. Wilamowitz's book there has been a marked reaction in the more recent literature on Sophocles, which must be taken as an indication of the strongly revived interest in that poet. Turolla has stressed Sophocles' peculiar religiosity as a proper starting point for understanding him. Reinhardt, in his brilliant book quoted in note 4, has made a most interesting special study of the 'situation' in Sophoclean tragedy, the relation of man to man and particularly that of man to god. Here we should refer also to H. Weinstock's valuable book *Sophokles* (Leipzig, Berlin 1931), which likewise represents a reaction against the formalism of mere dramatic technique. A more many-sided reinterpretation of Sophocles which tries to avoid the opposite extremes of both parties and to correct some of their too subjective speculations on particular problems is found in Gennaro Perotta's excellent work quoted in note 4. See also C. M. Bowra's new book *Sophoclean Tragedy* (Oxford 1944).

6. On Sophocles' characters and their effect on the literatures of later centuries, see J. T. Sheppard's *Aeschylus and Sophocles* (New York 1927), which deals mainly with English literature, and K. Heinemann's *Die tragischen Gestalten der Griechen in der Weltliteratur* (Leipzig 1920), which also includes Aeschylus, Euripides, and Seneca in its wide survey. But Sophocles' characters possess plastic qualities of their own which distinguish them from the rest. They cannot be grasped, of course, by mere *Motivgeschichte*.

7. The monumental quality of Sophoclean dramatic figures has its roots in the principle of representing in them the human areté which they embody (see p. 268). Cf. the article by W. Schadewaldt quoted below in note 10, and J. A. Moore's *Sophocles and Areté* (Cambridge, Mass. 1938).

8. These comparisons started early with the Greek writers on literary criticism. They are frequent in Dionysius of Halicarnassus, the anonymous *On the Sublime*, Cicero, and other authors who represent this tradition. Painting and poetry also were compared (cf. Horace's famous *ut pictura poesis*).

9. Cf. pp. 254-255. The comparison between Greek poetry and the fine arts has been worked out more systematically by Franz Winter in the chapter 'Parallelerscheinungen in der griechischen Dichtkunst und bildenden Kunst' in Gerke-

Norden's *Einleitung in die Altertumswissenschaft* (Leipzig, Berlin 1910), vol. II, p. 161; cf. on Aeschylus and Sophocles, p. 176 ff.

10. On Sophocles' art as the classical form of Greek tragedy, see W. Schade-waldt in *Das Problem des Klassischen und die Antike,* Acht Vortraege hrsg. v. Werner Jaeger (Leipzig, Berlin 1931), 25 ff.

11. See p. 271.

12. Arist. *Poet.* 25, 1460b34.

13. I have tried to introduce into the text here the polar terms *Ur-Erlebnis* and *Bildungs-Erlebnis* as they were used by Friedrich Gundolf in his literary criticism. *Bildungs-Erlebnis* means an experience which comes to us not through immediate contact with life itself but by way of literary impressions or through learning alone. The terminology of this contrast does not fit classical Greek poetry.

14. Aristoph. *Frogs* 82.

15. Athen. XIII, 603e.

16. See note 14.

17. For the spiritual relationship of the poet to his city see W. Schadewaldt, *Sophokles und Athen* (Frankfurt 1935).

18. See pp. 273-274.

19. Athen. I, 22a-b.

20. On the concept of soul and its importance for Socrates, see *Paideia* II, 38-44.

21. Polyclitus, in an extant fragment of his work on sculpture, defines the perfect form of the human body as a certain proportion of numbers, i.e. measures.

22. Plato speaks literally of κατασκευή ψυχῆς in this sense and distinguishes different forms of that structure; cf. *Paideia* II, 323 and 424. His new consciousness of these things was prepared by the age of Sophocles.

23. Simonides, frg. 4, 2 (Diehl). Notice the co-ordination of gymnastic and mental training.

24. Plato, *Prot.* 326b.

25. See the conversation of Socrates with the painter Parrhasius about the expression of the soul in the representation of the physical appearance, most of all the face, in Xen. *Mem.* III, 10, 1-5; cf. *Paideia* II, 45. There the educator who knows the human soul points towards a new consciousness of the laws of physiognomic expression of the 'ethos', while the artist seems to be baffled by Socrates' bold demand.

26. On the concept of philanthropy and its relation to that of *humanitas,* see *Paideia* III, 310, note 75.

27. See the chorus, *Ant.* 583 ff.

28. This has been established beyond doubt by August Boeckh in his analysis of the play in the appendix to his edition of Sophocles' *Antigone* (Berlin 1843).

29. In his myth of the origin of civilization (Plato, *Prot.* 322a) 'Protagoras' also distinguishes expressly between the level of the technical arts and the higher stage of development marked by the political arts of the state. Behind Plato's picture there is some tangible reality; the historical Protagoras wrote a book with the title Περὶ τ. ἐν ἀρχῇ καταστάσιος, which was obviously concerned with the earliest stage of human civilization. See Graf W. von Uxkull-Gyllenband, *Griechische Kulturentstehungslehren* (Berlin 1924). See also *supra,* p. 299.

30. Hegel, *Aesthetik,* Bd. II (Jubilaeumsausgabe, Stuttgart, 1928), 51-52.

31. Simonides frg. 4, 7-9; cf. p. 213 ff. *supra.* ἄνδρα δ' οὐκ ἔστι μὴ οὐ κακὸν ἔμμεναι, ὃν ἂν ἀμήχανος συμφορὰ καθέλῃ was the quintessence of Simonides' wisdom with regard to the relationship of misfortune and areté. Sophocles' heroes are unfortunate by their destiny, but not κακοί. See Ajax's words to his son,

which reflect his proud feeling of his own worth, *Aj.* 550-551: ὦ παῖ, γένοιο πατρὸς εὐτυχέστερος, τὰ δ' ἄλλ' ὁμοῖος · καὶ γένοι' ἂν οὐ κακός. Oedipus is conscious (*O.C.* 8) in the midst of all his misery, of his nobility, τὸ γενναῖον. See also 270, καίτοι πῶς ἐγὼ κακὸς φύσιν; 75, ἐπείπερ εἶ γενναῖος, ὡς ἰδόντι, πλὴν τοῦ δαίμονος.

32. Cf. the words of Odysseus, who in the tragic suffering of his enemy Ajax sees the nothingness of man, *Aj.* 125-126; see also *O.C.* 608, and most of all *O.T.* 1186 ff.

33. Cf. *O.C.* 203 ff., especially the long rhesis, 258 ff.

34. *O.C.* 8.

35. Oedipus, when he appears at Colonus as a wandering old beggar at the beginning of Sophocles' last play, seems perfectly reconciled with his long suffering and with his destiny; cf. *O.C.* 7, στέργειν γὰρ αἱ πάθαι με χὠ χρόνος ξυνὼν μακρὸς διδάσκει καὶ τὸ γενναῖον τρίτον.

36. *O.C.* 394.

CHAPTER 3

THE SOPHISTS

1. Aesch. *Sept.* 18. But see Pindar frg. 198, οὔτοι με ξένον οὐδ' ἀδαήμονα Μοισᾶν ἐπαίδευσαν κλυταὶ Θῆβαι. This fragment is an important proof of the fact that in the time of Pindar and Aeschylus even in Boeotia the word παιδεύω already implied the musical (and, of course, also the gymnastic) culture which constituted its principal content for the Periclean period. On a third passage concerning paideia in the contemporary Sicilian poet Epicharmus, if it is authentic, see *Paideia* III, 298, note 71.

2. See chap. II of Book One.

3. See chap. VI of Book One.

4. Cf. p. 3 ff. *supra.*

5. Cf. p. 220.

6. Cf. p. 173.

7. See p. 182.

8. Cf. p. 106, note 23.

9. Thuc. I, 138, 3.

10. Hes. *Theog.* 81 ff.

11. On the profession or *epangelma* of the sophists, see *Paideia* II, 111.

12. See *Paideia* II, 59, 114, etc.

13. See especially Arist. *Eth. Nic.* VI.

14. The more encyclopaedic ideal of education was embodied in Hippias of Elis. Prodicus of Ceus seems to have cultivated grammatical and linguistic studies such as his famous synonymics, which is praised and at the same time parodied by Socrates in Plato's *Protagoras* 339e-341e, 358a. Prodicus shared these formal interests with Protagoras.

15. Plato, *Prot.* 325e ff. In 318e Plato makes Protagoras himself draw a sharp distinction between his ethical and political ideal of education and the mathematical encyclopædism of Hippias of Elis.

16. H. Gomperz, *Sophistik und Rhetorik: das Bildungsideal des* εὖ λέγειν *in seinem Verhaeltnis zur Philosophie des fuenften Jahrhunderts* (Leipzig 1912).

17. Plato, *Prot.* 318e ff., *Meno* 91a ff., and elsewhere.

18. See the chapters, 'Sophistic or Socratic Paideia?', *Paideia* II, 107; 'The Educator as Statesman', ib. p. 126 ff.; '*The Republic*', ib. p. 269 and *passim*.

19. Plato, *Theaet.* 152a.

20. See chap. IX, 'Philosophical Speculation.'

21. Cf. p. 182 ff.

22. For that characterization of Anaxagoras' position between the earlier physicists and Socrates, see Plato's *Phaedo* 97b.

23. Even in the poem *On Nature* Empedocles, who was himself a physician, gave more attention to the structure of the human body than previous thinkers had done (cf. Ettore Bignone, *Empedocle,* Torino 1916, p. 242). But the other poem, the *Purifications,* shows that this is not the whole Empedocles and that he was much more deeply concerned with the problem of the human mind than with the body and its physical constitution. Cf. Bignone, op. cit. p. 113 ff.

24. Cf. Paul Natorp, *Die Ethika des Demokrit* (Marburg 1893); Hermann Langerbeck, ΔΟΞΙΣ ΕΠΙΡΥΣΜΙΗ in *Neue Philologische Untersuchungen* hrsg. v. W. Jaeger (vol. X, Berlin 1935).

25. Only Democritus is an exception in this respect; see Langerbeck, op. cit. p. 67 ff. He comes nearest to the theoretical approach of the sophists to the problem of paideia and human nature.

26. Plato, *Prot.* 316d, represents the great sophist as one who is perfectly aware of this continuity. Protagoras, of course, there exaggerates and speaks of the poets of the past as merely a group of earlier sophists, predecessors of himself. But no doubt there is some historical truth in representing the sophists as the heirs of that great educational tradition. Isocrates, too, who was a genuine pupil of the sophists, calls (*Ad Nic.* 43) Hesiod, Phocylides, and Theognis his predecessors in the art of the paraenetic logos.

27. See p. 203 ff., p. 213 ff.

28. Plato, *Prot.* 339a.

29. Cf. my *Tyrtaios* (*Sitz. Berl. Akad.* 1932), p. 564. See also *Paideia* III, 85, 104.

30. There is a delightful example of this attitude in Plato's *Protagoras,* 339a ff. Socrates gives another example of it in the *Republic,* 331e ff.

31. Plato, *Rep.* 598d, describes this type of sophistic explanation of Homer, clearly with some specific instance in mind. See *Paideia* II, 360, with the notes.

32. Plato, *Hipp. min.* 368b.

33. See p. 229 ff. On the sophists and their relation to society and the rich, see *Paideia* II, 110.

34. Plato, *Prot.* 313c.

35. There are many scholars who think that the sophists not only were the founders of humanism but also brought it to perfection, who, in other words, would set them up as a pattern for us. Our opinion in these matters depends on our attitude to philosophy as it actually grew out of a conflict with the sophistic type of education, especially the philosophy of Socrates, Plato, and Aristotle. The conflict arose over the problem of supreme values, on which, according to Greek 'philosophy', human education depends. See my *Humanism and Theology* (Aquinas Lecture 1943, Marquette Univ. Press), 38 ff., in which I have distinguished two fundamental forms of humanism opposed to each other—that of the sophists and that of the philosophers (Socrates, Plato, Aristotle). On Protagoras' humanism see *supra,* p. 300.

36. Plato, *Hipp. mai.* 218c, brings out the distinction between the practical aims of the sophists and the unrealistic tendencies of the old philosophers and sages.

37. Cf. A. Busse, *Die Anfaenge der Erziehungswissenschaft* (*Neue Jahrbuecher* XXVI, 1910), 469 ff.; C. P. Gunning, *De sophistis Graeciae praeceptoribus* (Amsterdam 1915).

38. Plato, *Prot.* 319a.

39. Ib. 320c ff.

40. Hes. *Works and Days* 276.

41. See Karl Holl, *Die Geschichte des Worts Beruf (Sitz. Berl. Akad.* 1924), XXIX.

42. Plato, *Prot.* 318d. Protagoras includes arithmetic, astronomy, geometry, music (which here means musical theory) among the *technai,* with special reference to Hippias of Elis.

43. Cf. p. 111 ff.

44. See *Humanism and Theology* (cf. note 35), 20 ff. Cf. also the essays 'Antike und Humanismus' and 'Kulturidee und Griechentum' in my *Humanistische Reden und Vortraege* (Berlin 1937), 110 and 125 ff.

45. See note 35 and *Paideia* II and III, in which this process of development of the older paideia is described.

46. Plato, *Laws* 716c; cf. Protagoras frg. 1 (Diels). See *Paideia* II, In Search of the Divine Centre.

47. Protagoras frg. 4 (Diels).

48. Cf. *Humanism and Theology,* 36 ff.

49. For the time being, see *Humanism and Theology,* 58 ff. I hope to treat in a separate volume the late ancient period in which the classical Greek paideia was blended with the new religion of Christianity.

50. Cf. *Humanism and Theology,* 39 ff.

51. Ib. p. 42 ff., 53 ff.

52. See ib. pp. 47-54.

53. Porphyry provides valuable evidence about a copy of Protagoras' treatise on Being; see Prot. frg. 2 (Diels).

54. See chap. X.

55. See the fragment from Protagoras' *Great Logos,* Prot. B 3 (Diels). Similar distinctions can be found in Plato, Democritus, Isocrates, Aristotle.

56. There is a pressing need for a new study of the conception of human natùre in the medical literature of the Hippocratic corpus. See the chapter Greek Medicine as Paideia in *Paideia* III, *passim.*

57. There was a parallel development of the scientific mind in the seventeenth and eighteenth centuries centred about the concept of human nature. See W. Dilthey, 'Zur Weltanschauung und Analyse des Menschen' (*Schriften,* Bd. II).

58. Plato, *ep.* VII, 341d.

59. See *Paideia* II, chap. V.

60. Plato, *Prot.* 323a ff.

61. Ib. 324a-b.

62. Ib. 325e.

63. Ib. 326a-b.

64. Ib. 326c.

65. Ib. 326c-d.

66. Ib. 326d.

67. See p. 109.

68. Plato, *Crito* 50a; cf. *Prot.* 326c.

69. 'Plutarch' *de lib. educ.* 1d.

70. See p. 306.

71. Plato, *Rep.* 377b.

72. That section of the lost *Protrepticus* in which Aristotle developed this idea is reconstructed from the *Protrepticus* of Iamblichus the Neoplatonist in my *Aristotle,* 74 ff., of the English translation (Robinson, Oxford 1934).

73. The comparison of education with agriculture appears also in the 'Hippocratic' *Law* 3. But since the date of its origin is unknown, it does not help

much chronologically. The *Law* seems to be a product of the time of the sophists, or not much later.

74. See p. 310 and note 63.

75. *Paideia* II, 212.

76. Plato, *Prot.* 326a-b.

77. The scanty evidence is collected in Diels, *Vorsokratiker:* Prodicus A 13 ff., Protagoras A 24-28, Hippias A 11-12.

78. *Dialexeis* 8 refers to the victory of the Lacedaemonians over the Athenians and their allies and its consequences for both sides, i.e. the end of the Peloponnesian War.

79. See F. Solmsen, *Antiphonstudien (Neue Philologische Untersuchungen,* hrsg. v. W. Jaeger, Bd. VIII), 7.

80. J. H. Finley, *Thucydides* (Cambridge, Mass. 1942), 250 ff.

81. The ancient *artes* still live on in the *ordo studiorum* of the Jesuits. The term 'liberal arts' is quite alive and is used to designate a 'general education' in the United States, although the content has been modernized, and the 'liberal arts college' is a definite type of school opposed to pedagogical utilitarianism and professionalism.

82. See Hippias, A 11-12 (Diels).

83. Plato, *Prot.* 326a.

84. See p. 300 ff.

85. Plato, *Rep.* 536d.

86. Isocr. *Antid.* 265, *Panath.* 26.

87. Plato, *Hipp. mai.* 285b ff., shows only the encyclopaedic variety of Hippias' knowledge, but in *Hipp. min.* 368b, he describes his deliberate effort to be universal—he had the ambition to be master of all crafts as well as all kinds of knowledge.

88. See p. 153 ff.

89. Plato, *Prot.* 312a, 315a.

90. Thuc. II, 40, 1.

91. Plato, *Gorg.* 484c ff.

92. Ib. 485c.

93. Ib. 485d.

94. Ib. 485a: ὅσον παιδείας χάριν. Similarly Plato, *Prot.* 312b, and later Isocrates; cf. *Paideia* III, 148.

95. See p. 370 ff.

96. *Ennianae Poesis Reliquiae,* ed. Vahlen, 2nd ed., p. 191: I quote the line in the epigrammatic form in which Cicero gives it.

97. See note 94.

98. See my *Ueber Ursprung und Kreislauf des philosophischen Lebensideals (Sitz. Berl. Akad.* 1928), 394-397.

99. Cf. Plato, *Prot.* 321d, 322b ff., 324d ff., 326c-d.

100. Thuc. II, 41, 1.

101. This is already evident in Pericles' ideal of democracy as set forth in his funeral oration. There it is still the tension of two different aspects of the state which are kept in strict equilibrium. But it has turned into a sharp antinomy in Plato's *Gorgias;* see *Paideia* II, 133.

102. Cf. the passages in note 99.

103. Plato, *Rep.* 492a-b (see *Paideia* II, 269) rightly stated that the sophists were more the products of public opinion and morality than its leaders and originators.

104. The most interesting document of these feelings and of the criticism which originated from these circles within the state of Athens is the oldest prose book

which we possess in the Attic dialect, the *State of the Athenians* of an anonymous author. The book was preserved among the works of Xenophon, presumably because the manuscript was found among his papers. Now it is generally quoted as the 'Old Oligarch'. See the thorough analysis of it by Karl Gelzer, *Die Schrift vom Staate der Athener* (*Hermes, Einzelschriften* Heft 3, Berlin 1937).

105. Cf. p. 160. On what follows, see my lecture *Die griechische Staatsethik* in *Humanistische Reden und Vortraege* (Berlin 1937), 93.

106. Eur. *Phoen.* 535 ff.; cf. *Suppl.* 399-408.

107. Plato, *Gorg.* 482c ff., especially 483d.

108. Plato, *Rep.* 338c.

109. See *Paideia* II, 137 ff.

110. Plato, *ep.* VII, 324d.

111. Plato, *Gorg.* 483e. See *Paideia* II, 136 ff.

112. See F. Zucker, *Syneidesis-Conscientia* (Jena 1928).

113. Plato, *Prot.* 337c.

114. See p. 324 ff.

115. *Pap. Oxyrh.* 1364 (Hunt): now published in Diels, *Vorsokratiker* II (5th ed.), 346 ff., frg. B44, col. 2, 10 ff.

116. Antiphon frg. A, col. 2, 26, and col. 4, 5; cf. 1, 6.

117. Arist. *Pol.* II, 8, 1268b26 ff.

118. Aristoph. *Birds* 1035.

119. Thuc. II, 37, 2.

120. Frg. A, col. 4, 9 ff.

121. Plato, *Prot.* 358a ff.

122. See p. 106, note 23.

123. Aesch. *Sept.* 592; on the reading see Wilamowitz, *Aristoteles und Athen* I, 160.

124. Crit. frg. 25 (Diels).

125. Plato, *Rep.* 359d.

126. Dem. frg. 264 (Diels).

CHAPTER 4

EURIPIDES AND HIS AGE

1. Paul Masquerai, *Euripide et ses idées* (Paris 1908); Wilhelm Nestle, *Euripides, der Dichter der griechischen Aufklaerung* (Stuttgart 1901).

2. See pp. 279 and 310.

3. See pp. 321-331.

4. It would not be correct to derive Euripides' ideas from the use of sophistic 'sources', even though he knew the literature of his time. He is of such tremendous importance for the history of his time because he shows how those sophistic ideas grew out of real life and how they changed it.

5. See Thuc. II, 41, 1, on the Athens of Pericles' time as the school of Greek culture (cf. p. 411). In the fourth century Isocrates' *Panegyricus* worked out that theme; cf. *Paideia* III, 76 ff.

6. Cf. pp. 393-396.

7. See the famous characterization of Themistocles, Thuc. I, 138, 3.

8. See Thuc. II, 60, 3 (speech of Pericles).

9. Cf. p. 326 ff.

10. Thuc. III, 82.

11. Thuc. III, 82, 2.

12. For the minor wars which were going on during the fifty years between the Persian and the Peloponnesian wars, see Thucydides' extensive digression on that period, I, 89-118.

13. Aristoph. *Ach.* 10.

14. Aristoph. *Frogs* 52 ff.

15. Aristoph. *Frogs* 830 ff.

16. The dramatic poets, Plato, Xenophon, Isocrates, and Aristotle, frequently used the word ἀγροῖκος in the sense of 'uncultured', a meaning which it obviously had quite commonly at their time. See the famous description of the ἀγροῖκος as a human type in Theophrastus' *Characters*.

17. We read of the literary and social reaction of the country against the domination of urban civilization during the fourth century B.C. in Xenophon's *Oeconomicus*, a highly interesting product of the country's endeavour not to capitulate before the city but to maintain its own values (see *Paideia* III, 172 ff.). Xenophon made an obvious objection to the city's exaggeration of its own cultural importance, that all culture started with agriculture, as the sophists themselves had pointed out. Cf. p. 312 ff.

18. One thinks of the elegies written by such men as Ion of Chios, Euenos of Paros, Critias the tyrant, and others.

19. The heated disputes of the new age over the old and the new culture (paideia) are reflected in Aristophanes' comedy. See p. 370 ff.

20. For the attacks of contemporary comedy on Euripides, see p. 376.

21. Cf. *Paideia* II, 340; see the whole section, pp. 334-341.

22. Plato, *Meno* 91c. But the same Anytus, who in this passage displays by private criticism his antipathy to sophistic education, later became one of the public accusers of Socrates. For other private critics of sophistic and philosophic paideia in the political circles of Athens, see *Paideia* II, 137 (especially note 60).

23. Plut. *Pericl.* 32.

24. For the eclectic philosophers of nature, Diogenes, Archelaus, Hippon, and Cratylus, see J. Burnet, *Early Greek Philosophy* (4th ed.), 352-361. On Hippon, cf. Arist. *Metaph.* A3, 984a3. For Cratinus' *Panoptae* and the tendency of that play, cf. Kock, *Comicorum Attic. Fragm.* vol. I, p. 60 ff.

25. Aristoph. *Birds,* 992 ff.

26. Arist. *Pol.* II, 8.

27. Democr. frg. 116 (Diels).

28. See the chapter Thucydides, p. 382 ff.

29. See the chapter Socrates in *Paideia* II, 13-76.

30. The attacks which contemporary Attic comedy made on him stressed this feature. Cf., for instance, the parody of Euripides in Aristoph. *Ach.* 411-479.

31. Cf. the reflections of Medea on the miserable lot of women, Eur. *Med.* 230 ff.

32. Critias frg. 48 (Diels, *Vorsokratiker* II).

33. See Eduard Norden, *Antike Kunstprosa*, vol. I, p. 52 ff. On the rhetorical element in early Greek poetry, see *Paideia* I, 88. Cf. also my analysis of selected rhetorical passages in Tyrtaeus' and Solon's elegies, *Sitz. Berl. Akad.* 1926, p. 83 ff. and ib. 1931, p. 549 ff.

34. τὸν ἥττω λόγον κρείττω ποιεῖν; cf. Aristoph. *Clouds* 893.

35. Eur. *Troad.* 914.

36. Eur. *Hipp.* 433.

37. Soph. *Oed. Col.* 266 ff., 537-538, 545-548.

38. Eur. *Troad.* 948. In the same way, Helen is defended by Gorgias, *Hel.* 15. According to this thesis, acting under the sway of passion (Eros) excludes the exercise of free will.

39. Plato, *Laws* 719c.

40. Eur. *Troad.* 884.

41. For Xenophanes' criticism of the Homeric gods, see p. 170 ff. On Plato, cf. *Paideia* II, 217 ff.

42. This was the profound but somewhat speculative interpretation that Wilamowitz gave to this drama in his famous commentary.

43. This was shown by Franz Werfel's free translation—or rather transformation—of Euripides' *Trojan Women,* which by overemphasizing the radically critical element in the play heightened its dramatic effect.

44. Cf. the lines expressing the daemonic passion of the true tyrant in Eur. *Phoen.* 521-525.

45. The *Suppliants* is a play of clearly patriotic tendency written during the Peloponnesian War. The *Andromache,* according to the scholia, was not mentioned in the didascalic documents preserved in the archives of the Athenian archon whose function it was to make arrangements for the performance of the drama. It must therefore have been written for another occasion than the Athenian Dionysiac festival. The eloquent praise of the dynasty of the philathenian King of Epirus at the end of the play and the connexion of the whole plot with that dynasty and its mythical origin reveal Euripides' purpose: he wrote for a national festival at the court of that king and admirer of Athens during the Peloponnesian War.

46. See the chapter on Ionian and Aeolian Poetry and the rise of the individual, p. 112 ff.

47. Cf. Wolfgang Schadewaldt, 'Der Monolog im Drama' in *Neue Philologische Untersuchungen,* hrsg. v. W. Jaeger, Bd. II, p. 143 ff.

48. This was criticized by Aristophanes in his parodies of Euripidean arias. See, e.g., *Frogs* 1309 ff.

49. *Medea* 824. The description of the pure atmosphere of Attica and its effect on the harmonious Athenian mind has a definite Hippocratic flavour. It recalls the book *On Airs, Waters and Places,* the source of all similar speculations in Greek philosophy and ethnography.

50. On the concept of 'human nature' in contemporary Greek medicine and thought, see *Paideia* III, 6, 20, and *passim.*

51. In Euripides' time there existed 'doctors of the human soul'. Such was Antiphon the sophist, who also taught and wrote about the interpretation of dreams.

52. See p. 301.

53. *Hec.* 864.

54. *Hec.* 785.

55. See *Hermes* XLVIII (1913), 442.

56. See Arthur D. Nock, *Conversion,* 25 ff.

57. See the scene in Aristoph. *Ach.* 395 ff.

58. See p. 352 ff.

59. Aristoph. *Ach.* 454.

60. Eur. frg. 663 (Nauck).

61. Eur. frg. 1047 (Nauck).

CHAPTER 5

THE COMIC POETRY OF ARISTOPHANES

1. Arist. *Poet.* 2, 1448a1; 4, 1448b24.
2. Arist. *Part. An.* III, 10, 673a8, 28.

3. Plato, *Symp.* 223d.

4. Plato, *Phileb.* 50b.

5. This was the natural way of looking at Aristophanic comedy for the later centuries of classical antiquity, which preferred to it the 'new comedy' of Menander, a poetry much closer to their own social conditions and intellectual culture. Plutarch's *Comparison of Aristophanes and Menander* is an eloquent expression of this critical verdict, which appears unhistorical to us, but which has prevailed through the ages up to the nineteenth century. This attitude was rooted in the system of late Greek paideia and its moral and cultural standards.

6. See P. Friedlaender, *Aristophanes in Deutschland* in *Die Antike* VIII (1932), 233ff., on the origins of the true understanding of Aristophanic comedy, especially by Hamann, Lessing, and Goethe.

7. Arist. *Poet.* 5, 1449a37 ff.

8. See A. W. Pickard-Cambridge, *Dithyramb, Tragedy and Comedy* (Oxford 1927), 225 ff.

9. The old comedian Cratinus was famous for his political lampoons on Pericles. The title Ἀρχίλοχοι of one of his comedies proves that he followed consciously in the footsteps of that great master of satire.

10. In the year 487. See E. Capps, *The Introduction of Comedy into the City Dionysia* in *Decennial Publications of the University of Chicago,* 1st Series, vol. VI (Chicago 1904), 261 ff.

11. This does not prevent us, of course, from acknowledging the independent origin of the primary formal elements of comedy as it has been studied by T. Zielinski, *Die Gliederung der altattischen Komoedie* (Leipzig 1885).

12. See Hor. *Sat.* I, 4; Quint. X, I, 66; *De diff. com.* 3 (p. 4, Kaibel).

13. See the parabasis of Aristophanes' *Knights,* 507 ff., especially 525 ff.

14. *Knights* 535.

15. *Ach.* 738.

16. *Knights* 539.

17. *Clouds* 537 ff.

18. *Clouds* 549.

19. See p. 121 ff.

20. *De diff. com.* 3 (p. 4, Kaibel).

21. Plato, *Rep.* 564a.

22. See Alfonso Reyes, *La critica en la edad Ateniense* (Mexico 1941).

23. Plato, *Phileb.* 49c.

24. See p. 377.

25. See Gilbert Murray, *Aristophanes* (Oxford 1933), who treats the single plays.

26. See A. Meineke, *Fragm. Com. Graec.* I, 40 ff.; Th. Bergk, *Kleine philologische Schriften* II (Halle 1886), 444 ff.

27. Aristoph. *Ach.* 530-531.

28. Thuc. III, 37 ff.

29. In the *Babylonians* the very actual problem of the despotic treatment which Athens gave her less powerful allies was under attack. The *Acharnians* made an ardent plea for peace, directed against the official policy of Athens, as did the *Peace* a few years later.

30. A true understanding of the political spirit that animated Attic comedy was shown for the first time in Germany in the ancient historian Johann Gustav Droysen's famous translation of Aristophanes' comedies, particularly in his brilliant introductions to the single plays, in which he gave them their place in the intellectual and political situation of their time. Droysen's translation has lately been reprinted (Winter, Heidelberg, without date).

31. The comic element in Plato's *Protagoras* is so strong that no doubt is left of Plato's intention of vying with the comic poets who had treated the same subject before him.

32. See the fragments of the Δαιταλῆς collected by Kock, *Frag. Com. Att.* I, 438 ff.

33. The resemblance between the Socrates portrayed on the comic stage and the typical sophists of the time was brought out by Plato in his *Apology.*

34. Modern scholars have been able to prove that some of the features of the Aristophanic Socrates in the *Clouds,* especially his deification of air as the first principle, were borrowed from the teaching of a contemporary natural philosopher, Diogenes of Apollonia. See H. Diels in *Sitz. Berl. Akad.* 1891.

35. *Clouds* 889 ff.

36. *Clouds* 961 ff. Here begins the praise of the ἀρχαία παιδεία.

37. Later Plato proposed (*Laws* 796b) to renew the ancient dances, including the war-dances such as those of the Curetes in Crete, of the Dioscuri in Sparta, and of Demeter and Kore in Athens; see *Paideia* III, 249. This recalls Aristophanes' criticism in the *Clouds,* which seems to be more than an expression of personal feeling and may reflect a broader trend of his time.

38. *Clouds* 1036 ff.

39. See p. 33 ff.

40. Aristophanes makes full use of his poetic liberty in representing the modern education of the sophists as consciously wicked.

41. See p. 368.

42. Socrates leaves the stage (*Clouds* 887) in order to make room for the *agon* of the Just and the Unjust Logos, which follows immediately. The whole invention of this *agon* seems to belong to the second performance of the *Clouds* and was obviously written for it in order to enrich the play, which had not succeeded the first time it was given. The VI hypothesis of the *Clouds* lists this scene expressly among the parts added by Aristophanes for the second performance.

43. *Frogs* 1491 ff.

44. One of the main aspects of the problem of the decay of poetry was the decline of music, which is discussed more than once. It is interesting to observe the close resemblance between the attacks of Aristophanes and the other comic poets of his time on modern music and Plato's famous criticism of it in the *Laws* (see *Paideia* III, 237 ff.). Cf. this resemblance with other features of Aristophanes' criticism of modern paideia which he shares with Plato (see note 37). The most impressive passage in comedy on the decline of musical culture is the long fragment of a comedy by Pherecrates in which Lady Music is introduced in torn garments and with her beautiful body disgraced. She complains to Δικαιοσύνη about what has happened to her and makes grave accusations against some of the musical modernists, such as Melanippides, Cinesias, Phrynis, and Timotheus. See Ps. Plut. *De mus.* 30. There it is said that Aristophanes attacked the musician Philoxenus in a similar way. His attacks on Cinesias and others are well known. The agreement between the comic poets and Plato in their repeated criticism does not favour the view that all this was mere fun and had no serious objective. It is the continuous tradition of the criticism of the *kaloi kagathoi* in Athens. Plato, too, in *Laws* 700d, calls the musical modernists ἀγνώμονες περὶ τὸ δίκαιον τῆς Μούσης, which recalls the Δικαιοσύνη in Pherecrates' musical fragment (see above).

45. Large fragments of Eupolis' Δῆμοι were discovered on papyrus some decades ago. They have thrown new light on the Hades scene in Aristophanes' *Frogs,* for which Eupolis' play was obviously the literary model.

46. *Frogs* 1008.

47. The history of ancient literary criticism centres mainly about the theories of the philosophers Plato and Aristotle. But its origin goes back to the fifth century: Aristophanes' *Frogs* marks its first appearance in what we have of Greek literature. Behind it lies, of course, the thought of the sophists on the problems of poetry, which is almost entirely lost to us. See Alfonso Reyes, *La critica en la edad Ateniense* (Mexico 1941), who has treated Aristophanes explicitly, pp. 111-56.

48. *Frogs* 1009.
49. Ib. 1043.
50. Ib. 1053-1055.
51. Ib. 1060 ff.
52. Ib. 1069 ff.
53. Ib. 1500.

CHAPTER 6

THUCYDIDES: POLITICAL PHILOSOPHER

1. On ἱστορίη as the name for the earliest natural philosophy, see p. 155. Even Aristotle called his zoology the Περὶ τὰ ζῷα ἱστορία, which we wrongly translate 'the history of the animals', *historia animalium*. Similarly Theophrastus called his botanical work a ἱστορία of the plants. They follow in this respect the old Ionian tradition.

2. See F. Jacoby, *Hekataios,* in Pauly-Wissowa, *Realencyklopaedie.* See also F. Jacoby, *Griechische Geschichtschreibung* in *Die Antike* II (1926), 1 ff.

3. F. Jacoby would confer Herodotus' traditional title of 'father of history' on Hecataeus. Something can be said in favour of this revaluation, in so far as we take the scientific and rational approach to the facts of human life as the essence of history. But the religious and dramatic element of history developed only with Herodotus' new view of it, and to this extent he really deserves his traditional title.

4. The very words of the proem of Herodotus' work remind the reader of the style and tone of the Homeric epos; ἔργα and κλέος in particular are the essence of epic song, as has often been observed.

5. Thucydides in his first chapter (I, 1, 2) mentions as the subject of his work both Greeks and barbarians. This may be attributed not only to imitation of Herodotus, who rightly defined his work in this comprehensive way, but also to the growing effect of the war on large parts of the non-Greek world. The Persian empire especially became more and more involved in the war during its later phase, as Xenophon's *Hellenica* shows. If Thucydides wrote his proem not at the start of the war but during that later period or shortly after, as I am convinced he did, the reference to the barbarians makes much better sense than if it were applied only to countries such as Epirus, Thrace, and Macedonia.

6. In Herodotus' view of the world, political events are always a part of his theological conception of life, which comprises the totality of things human and divine. In Thucydides the political element predominates, and nothing is left of Herodotus' theological framework.

7. In other words, the historical thought of Herodotus and of the rest of Thucydides' so-called predecessors did not in itself contain the germs of the constructive political history of Thucydides.

8. Cf. Konrat Ziegler, *Thukydides und die Weltgeschichte* (Rektoratsrede, Greifswald 1928).

9. Such excursuses are the so-called 'archaeology' at the beginning of the first book, with its rich material on early Greek history, and the digression on the

legendary character of the Athenian local tradition about the 'tyrannicides' Harmodius and Aristogiton, VI, 54, 1 ff. Ziegler sees in these digressions the root of Thucydides' historical research, which then turned to the present time when the war broke out. But they seem rather to be applications of Thucydides' own political experience, gained in the present age, to the problems of the past.

10. Thuc. I, 2-19.

11. In reading Thucydides' record of the past centuries of Greek history one feels reminded of the attitude taken by a modern historian of Rome, Theodore Mommsen. Concerning our main literary source for the Roman imperial period, Tacitus, Mommsen remarked that he is useless, because while he does tell us what is without importance for a true historian, he writes nothing about the problems 'which really matter'. That is exactly how Thucydides felt about all the so-called tradition, poetical and historical, which he inherited.

12. See I, 2, 2; I, 7, 1; I, 8, 3; I, 9; I, 11, 1, etc., throughout the so-called 'archaeology'.

13. I, 9.

14. I, 10, 3-4.

15. I cannot accept the view of W. Schadewaldt (*Die Geschichtschreibung des Thukydides*, Berlin 1929), who follows E. Schwartz (*Das Geschichtswerk des Thukydides*, Bonn 1919) in holding that the archaeological digression is a very old part of Thucydides' work, and reconstructing the earlier intellectual attitude of Thucydides ('pupil of the sophists') from it. I shall give elsewhere more detailed reasons for my dissent. (Since the first edition of this work, F. Bizer has re-examined this problem in his dissertation *Untersuchungen zur Archaeologie des Thukydides*, Tübingen 1937, and has taken sides with me.) See E. Taeubler's book, *Die Archaeologie des Thukydides* (Leipzig 1927).

16. I, 21, 1; I, 22, 4.

17. Eur. frg. 910 (Nauck).

18. The 'history' which Euripides praises as the supreme happiness of the human mind is, in other words, not that of Thucydides but rather that of Lucretius, which later Vergil praised in the famous line, *Felix qui potuit rerum cognoscere causas* (*Georgica* II, 490).

19. See C. N. Cochrane, *Thucydides and the Science of History* (Oxford 1929), who discusses in particular the relationship of Thucydides' methodical attitude in his history to contemporary Greek medicine. This relation has its perfect parallel in the methodical influence of medicine on contemporary philosophy and educational theory (Socrates, Plato, Aristotle); see *Paideia* III, chap. 1, Greek Medicine as Paideia. This fact proves that medicine could be understood and used as a pattern in very different ways.

20. I, 22, 4. This is the famous chapter of Thucydides' First Book, which deals with the problem of historical method.

21. This opinion is stated at the very beginning of the work in the discussion of the method adopted by the author and of the purpose which he pursues with it, I, 22, 4. The events which have occurred in the present war will occur again in the same or in a similar way in later ages, because of the unchanging nature of man. This idea, that the nature of man remains essentially the same in spite of all historical change, is expressed again in Thucydides' classical discussion of the nature of political crises, III, 82, 2; and on it is based his realistic conception of the usefulness of historical knowledge. For the same reason he gives his famous description of the symptoms of the plague, II, 48, 3 ff.; he foresees that the same disease will appear again and that the knowledge of its nature which his work attempts to provide will enable men of future ages to recognize it by its symptoms. This seems to go beyond what we consider the limits of the political

historian's task; but it has in common with his analysis of the political phenomena the conception of the task of the scientific mind and its relation to the physical as well as psychical nature of man. What is most important for Thucydides' concept of the unchangeable nature of man becomes evident in certain other passages of his work, e.g. I, 76, 2-3; IV, 61, 5; V, 105, 2. There it is said to be in accordance with human nature that the stronger always wants to rule the weaker. Human nature, then, in Thucydides' sense, is to a large degree the unchanging ascendance of passion in general, and in particular the will-to-power over the intellect. This axiom of Thucydides' historical thought is in agreement with the ideas of the sophistic age and is shared expressly by all political parties and warring nations as he represents them in his work. It is against this axiom that Plato launched his criticism of the moral foundations of what people then as now used to understand by politics. See *Paideia* II, 145, 154 ff., 157.

22. Hes. *Works and Days* 218.

23. One may call this attitude of Thucydides 'classical' as compared with the prevailing interest of modern historiography in the individual character of times, conditions, personalities, and ideas. This individualizing view of history is a product of the romantic spirit of the late eighteenth and early nineteenth centuries. See Friedrich Meinecke, *Die Entstehung des Historismus* (2 vols., Munich and Berlin 1936).

24. See p. 142.

25. Thuc. I, 138, 3.

26. See p. 387, with note 15.

27. Such ideas are expressed by Herodotus and Xenophon in their historical works.

28. Bacon, *Novum Organum* I, 3 (Fowler, 2nd ed., Oxford 1889).

29. Thuc. I, 22, 1. On the interpretation of this programme of Thucydides' work see A. Grosskinsky, *Das Programm des Thukydides* (*Neue deutsche Forschungen*, Abt. Klass. Phil., Berlin 1936), and the dissertation of my pupil H. Patzer, *Das Problem der Geschichtsschreibung des Thukydides und die thukydideische Frage* (ib. 1937).

30. See A. Deffner, *Die Rede bei Herodot und ihre Weiterbildung bei Thukydides* (Munich, diss., 1933).

31. That the style of the speeches in Thucydides' work, as I have characterized it, corresponds, at least to a certain degree, to the language of the political rhetoric of his day, is the thesis of one of the chapters of John Finley's *Thucydides* (Cambridge, Mass. 1942), 250 ff. See the same author's 'The Origins of Thucydides' Style' in *Harvard Studies in Classical Philology* 50 (1939), 35 ff., and also his 'Euripides and Thucydides', ib. 49 (1938), 23 ff.

32. Thuc. I, 23, 6.

33. The medical origin of πρόφασις was recognized and briefly stated by some of the earlier critics, Eduard Schwartz (see note 15) and others. It has been made the subject of a more extensive inquiry by Cochrane in the book quoted in note 19.

34. I, 89-118.

35. I, 97, 2. The previous treatment of this period to which he expressly refers is that in Hellanicus' Ἀττικὴ ξυγγραφή. Thucydides criticizes it as inadequate and chronologically inaccurate.

36. I, 93, 5. This sentence about the width of the long walls of Athens around the Piraeus, which could still be seen even after the systematic destruction of Athens' fortifications by the enemy, does not look like a later addition that can easily be removed from its syntactical context. Probably the whole excursus on the pentecontaetia was written after the war (see note 41).

37. The work was evidently planned as a matter-of-fact record (ξυγγραφή) from the beginning, and Thucydides kept the word even later (I, I, .I); he uses the term also to signify the type of narrative which Hellanicus had written on the history of Athens before the war (I, 97, 2). But in the course of time this 'record' absorbed all of Thucydides' political reflections, which give the distinctive mark to the finished part of the history as we read it now. This finished work is no longer a mere ξυγγραφή.

38. Thuc. I, 66-88.

39. I, 88.

40. I, 68-71.

41. This cannot be demonstrated here in detail, of course (see also note 42). But if we may take it for granted here (and I hope to prove it on some other occasion), and if, moreover, it is evident that the funeral oration of Pericles was written by the historian only after the tragic end of the war, the writing of the speech of the Corinthians must also belong to the same period. The same dating, I think, must also hold for the other three speeches delivered on the same occasion at Sparta, especially the speech of the Athenian envoy (I, 73-78). It has been stated before (note 36) that the excursus on the pentecontaetia (I, 89-118) shows traces of the same late origin. All this would favour the explanation that the whole part of Book I on the 'true cause' (ἀληθεστάτη πρόφασις) of the war, which now follows the diplomatic disputes (αἰτίαι, cf. I, 66, I), that is, the evaluation of the historical events from a profounder and more general point of view, was added only when Thucydides gave his work its final form in his latest period.

42. Cf. Plato, *Menex.* 235d. It was thought much more difficult, from a rhetorical point of view, to celebrate a city before its enemies than to praise it at home. Thucydides therefore seems to have conceived his task in the double sense of praising Athens both at home, in the funeral oration of Pericles, and abroad, among the Spartans and their allies, through the mouth of the Corinthians. Both speeches are only different parts of one and the same plan, and the idea of combining them is typical of Thucydides' objectivity. Without the speech of the Corinthians the funeral oration would approach the panegyric *eidos* of Isocrates, which is essentially subjective.

43. Thuc. I, 73-78.

44. See the excursus on the pentecontaetia, I, 89-118. Cf. above p. 393 ff.

45. In this respect he could only take over the thesis which his predecessor Herodotus had adopted in his work. But this thesis was obviously the formula of the Athenian policy itself, by which Athens justified the gradual expansion of her powers during the fifty years following the Persian War.

46. Thuc. I, 75, 3; I, 76, 2. The three motives are thus brought home to the reader's mind twice.

47. See the words ἐξ αὐτοῦ δὲ τοῦ ἔργου πατηναγκάσθημεν, I, 75, 3. Cf. also I, 76, I, where the word 'compelled' is repeated deliberately. If the Spartans had taken the rôle which the Athenians were offered by their allies during the Persian Wars, they would have been *compelled* to develop their hegemony in exactly the same way as the Athenians. The concept of political necessity or compulsion applied here is then traced back to the concept of human nature in I, 76, 2-3.

48. I, 77, 6.

49. II, 8, 4-5. Thucydides, although an Athenian himself, does not conceal the fact that the sympathy of most people in Hellas was on the Spartan side and that Athens was generally hated as the imperialistic power. No personal resentment whatever on the part of the historian is involved in this frank admission. He thought that every imperialistic power had to face this animosity and that it should not deter Athens from her task.

50. The words (I, 77, 6) 'if you defeated us and ruled in our stead you would soon lose the sympathies which you owe only to the fact that we are feared' refer to what really happened after the end of the war, as it seems to me. The mention of Pausanias and his rôle after the Persian War is an obvious allusion to the parallel case of Lysander's tyrannical power politics after the Peloponnesian War. This fixes the date of the writing of the speech of the Athenian envoy (I, 73-78) in the same period as that of the Corinthians (I, 68-71); see notes 41 and 42.

51. See *Paideia* III, 171-72, and note 71.

52. Cf. note 47.

53. See I, 23, 6, where this political necessity, the mere mathematics of power politics, is defined as the true cause (ἀληθεστάτη πρόφασις) of the war.

54. V, 25, 3. Cf. also I, 118, 2; there Thucydides states that the Spartans were never quick to go to war if they were not compelled to do so. But although at first they thought they were not so compelled, they eventually saw the unavoidable necessity of it (note 53).

55. See A. W. Gomme, *Essays in Greek History and Literature* (Oxford 1937), who discusses the speeches in Thucydides.

56. II, 60-64.

57. III, 82-84.

58. This method of Thucydides in distributing the highlights of his description of the war is critically appreciated by Dionysius of Halicarnassus in his essay *On Thucydides* (as a writer), c. 10 ff.; see especially c. 15, p. 347, 15 ff. (Usener-Radermacher).

59. I, 77, 1.

60. III, 82-84.

61. V, 84-116.

62. Cf. Isocr. *Paneg.* 100; 110. *Panath.* 63; 89.

63. See Thuc. II 8, 4, on the sympathies of Greece during the war. Cf. p. 397.

64. It is this necessity which Thucydides keeps emphasizing throughout his work. Cf. notes 53 and 54.

65. V, 89.

66. V, 90.

67. V, 97.

68. V, 105.

69. Cf. p. 324 ff.

70. See *Paideia* II, chap. on Plato's *Gorgias*.

71. I, 36, 2.

72. IV, 59; VI, 76.

73. VI, 18, 3.

74. I, 75, 3, and 76, 2.

75. I, 70.

76. See Thucydides' comments on Alcibiades' social position and private conduct, VI, 15. Cf. on his qualities as a leader VIII, 86, 4-5, the most important comprehensive characterization of Alcibiades in Thucydides' work.

77. See Thucydides' judgment on the prospects of the Sicilian expedition and the importance of its failure for the outcome of the war, II, 65, 11-12.

78. For a real tragedy in the classical Greek sense of the word Thucydides' emphasis on the ethical issues and on the atè implied in the venture of the aggressive war against Syracuse is not strong enough, even though the rhetorical art of the historian does not refrain, in telling of the catastrophe, from what ancient aesthetic theory called ἐκτραγῳδεῖν (cf., e.g. VIII, 1). And it must not be forgotten that Thucydides expressly denies what we might expect in a real tragedy,

the existence of a γνώμης ἁμάρτημα in the project of the Sicilian expedition as such (II, 65, 11). According to him, it failed only because the people were too short-sighted to choose the right means for the end which they hoped to attain. In a wider sense, of course, Thucydides' strictly pragmatic exposition of the greatness of the Athenian military enterprise and its political shortcomings has a very tragic effect on the reader, even if it lacks the religious ethos of Aeschylus; but one might ask whether this effect does not go beyond what Thucydides intended.

79. II, 65, 9.

80. According to Thucydides the Sicilian catastrophe was the result of the specific difficulties with which leadership in a great democracy is involved. See note 78. He thought that the defeat was due not to false leadership but to failure to follow the true leader.

81. II, 65, 13.

82. II, 65.

83. II, 65, 7.

84. VI, 12-13. Cf. VI, 17, 1.

85. VIII, 86, 5. This ability of κατασχεῖν ὄχλον is part of the old Solonian idea of political leadership; cf. Solon, frg. 24, 22; 25, 6 (Diehl). See note 86.

86. II, 65, 8. In this characterization of Pericles as a leader the same phrase κατεῖχε τὸ πλῆθος recurs, which Thucydides uses in describing Alcibiades as a born leader. Cf. note 85.

87. II, 65, 9.

88. II, 65, 11.

89. II, 65, 12.

90. II, 65, 13.

91. II, 65, 6. Cf. 65, 12.

92. II, 65, 7.

93. I, 144, 1.

94. I, 140-144.

95. II, 60-64.

96. II, 35-46.

97. This I hope to prove in greater detail in a special study on the idea of the mixed constitution and its history in the ancient world.

98. II, 65, 9.

99. II, 37, 1.

100. Pericles' own regime and the Athenian democracy under him are called ὑπὸ τοῦ πρώτου ἀνδρὸς ἀρχή by Thucydides, II, 65, 9. In Plato's *Menexenus,* Aspasia, the wife of Pericles, delivers in her literary salon a model funeral speech which is of course intended to be a witty companion piece to the famous funeral oration of Pericles in Thucydides' history. In this speech (238c) Aspasia calls the Athenian polity under Pericles an aristocracy and tries to prove that it is and always was 'the rule of the best with the consent of the people' (μετ' εὐδοξίας πλήθους ἀριστοκρατία). But see note 102.

101. III, 37.

102. For the general reader it may be well to recall that the democracy of Athens was 'government by the people' in a literal sense; it was not only 'representative government' as in the modern democracies, where the main function of the people is merely to elect delegates for the legislative body. Rather, the assembled mass of the people was itself the legislature, as it was also the judiciary. This was possible only in the ancient city-state. Modern democracy has gone one important step beyond its ancient predecessor in abolishing slavery; but it is only

indirectly democratic, in so far as the people to-day exercise their legislative and judicial rights only through elected representatives.

103. II, 40, 2.

104. If I am right in assuming that Thucydides' conception of the original character of the Athenian polity (II, 37, 1) rests on the idea of a mixed constitution (see p. 409), the same 'synthetic' principle of structure underlies not only the cultural but also the political life of Periclean Athens. On the latter principle, as it is manifest in Athenian culture, see the famous words of Pericles (II, 40, 1), φιλοκαλοῦμεν μετ' εὐτελείας καὶ φιλοσοφοῦμεν ἄνευ μαλακίας, which strike the perfect balance of opposite ideals. That Thucydides thought a similar balance of opposites the most desirable form of political life is stated expressly in VIII, 97, 2, a very important passage of his work, though it is as much neglected by most interpreters as the whole eighth Book to which it belongs.

105. Thuc. II, 41, 1.

INDEX

The following Index refers primarily to the text (problems, authors, and works found therein). It does not include a list of the exact passages quoted in the footnotes, but it does include the notes in so far as they discuss problems. At the end has been added a list of selected words and passages emended or interpreted in the book.

A

Academy, the Grove, 373
Achilles, 8, 10, 11, 14, 25, 26, 27, 28, 29,
   31, 32, 33, 39, 45, 46, 47, 48, 51, 52,
   73, 100, 112, 119, 199, 217, 218, 255
Acropolis, 139
Acusilaus, 243
Adrastus of Sicyon, 207
Aegina, 222, 227
Aegisthus, 33
Aeolian poets, 79, 115f. *passim*, 130f.,
   208, 210, 351
Aeschylus, 126, 136, 163, 214, 221, 232,
   237-267 *passim*, 268f., 273, 275, 304,
   330, 334, 337, 348f., 355f., 378f.,
   415n.1; *see also* Tragedy
  and Athenian democracy, 239f.
  as modernizing interpreter of myth,
   252f.
  as writer of trilogy, 254
  and inherited guilt, 254, 281
  master of exposition, 254
  superhuman character of, 255
  God and fate in, 255f., 266, 278
  and Solon, 254f.
  God and evil, 258f., 281, 283
  guilt and free will in, 262
  Persians, 256-7
  Oresteia, 259-60, 266f.
  Seven against Thebes, 260-62
  Prometheus Bound, 262-6
  Suppliants, 250, 252, 262
  idea of progress in, 262-3, 282
  knowledge and suffering in, 251, 257,
   265f., 284
  the Marathon-warrior, 276
  picture of in comedy, 378f.
  as educator, 380
  pity and fear in drama of, 470n.34
  polis in, 471n.59
Agalma, xxvii
Agamemnon, 10, 11, 24, 33, 48, 51, 259,
   279, 354, 386
Agathon, 337

ἀγαθόν, 34 (*see also* Idea of the Good)
ἀγαθός, 6
  meaning of in Theognis, 198f.
  opp. κακός, 418n.13
Agesilaus, 80
Agôn, xvii, 315, 347
  musical, 98
  agonistic virtues, 105
  in *Frogs,* 378
Agrarianism, 100, 431n.12; *see also*
  Hesiod, Aristocracy
ἀγροῖκος, 338, 431n.11, 480n.16
Aidôs, 7, 59, 72, 330, 419n.15
αἶνος, *see* Fable
  early meaning of, 68
  in Archilochus, 121f.
  in early Greek poetry, 433n.41
Aisymnetai, 229
Ajax, 8, 10f., 14, 26, 44, 347
Alcaeus, 99, 116, 130f., 189, 370
Alcibiades, 391, 398, 403f., 408
Alcidamas, 347
Alcinous, 20, 24, 100
Alcmaeonids, 224f., 237, 322
Alcman, 98
Alexandrine school, 315, 320, 362, 364
Amyntor, 24
Anacreon, 229, 232, 370
Ananké, 175; *see also* Necessity
Anaxagoras, 153, 156, 295, 339f., 350
Anaximander, 102, 110, 142, 154, 156f.,
   162, 165, 171, 175, 182; *see also*
  Causality, Retribution
  cosmology of, 157
  ἄπειρον, 158f.
  fragment of, 159f.
  δίκη in, 160f.
Anaximenes, 158, 160, 171, 178
Anaximenes rhetor, 315
ἀνδρεία, 7, 213
Androtion, *Atthis* of, 467n.22
Anonymus de sublimitate, 216
Anthologies, earliest, 189
Anthropomorphism, 170f.
Antigone, 280f.

491

Education (Cont.)
value of mathematics in, 164
Pythagoras as educator, 164
educational ethos of Delphic religion,
167
aristocratic tradition of, in Theognis,
191f.
ὑποθῆκαι, 194
Spartan ἀγωγή, 195
of kings (see Pindar), 221f.
as shaping of soul, πλάττειν, xxiif.,
279, 314, 415n.5
educator inspired by sculptor, 280
as vocational training, 3, 287
problem of, in democratic Athens,
287f.
encyclopaedic and formal training,
292f.
political and ethical education, 293f.,
300
liberal arts in, 293, 314f.
becomes a techné, 298f.
origin of educational theory, 298f.
higher education, 299f. (See Liberal
arts)
political vs. technical, 300
as universal culture, 300
aims at form of man, xiii, xxiif., 302,
314
and culture, 303f.
the 'educational trinity', 306, 312
and human nature, 306
educational optimism, 307
possibility of, assured by society,
308f.
state education unusual in Greece,
309
typical Greek, 309f.
as imitation, 310
law as educator, 310
of children, 312
theoretical, see Sophists
state as education vs. state as power,
321
in political crisis, 321f., 334f.
public discussion of, 365
attacked by comedy 370f.
choral poetry as paideia, 443n.31
Egypt, xivf., xvii, xix, 101, 155f.
Elea, 171
Electra, 283f., 346
Elegy, Greek, 88f.; see Literature
addressed to someone, 89
hortative character of, 89f.
as expression of the individual, 116f.
reflective, 116, 127
political, 139
gnomic, 185-204
origin of, 439n.41

Eleusis, 237
Eliot, T. S., 417n. 6
Empedocles, 151, 169f., 295, 433n.31
Enlightenment, 330, 340
Ennius, 320
Epic poetry, Greek, chs. I-III passim,
15-19, 25, 34, 37f.
educational factor in structure of,
43f.
origin of, in heroic ballad, 16, 38,
41, 43, 63
use of epithets in, 41f.
idealization in, 41f.
critical analysis of, 43f.
the Grossepos, 44, 45
general battle scenes in, 44, 90
art of, 45f.
mediaeval, 38, 52f.
gods and human action in, 51f.
and origin of philosophy, 53, 151
ethical plan of, 48f., 54f.
characterization in, 54f.
nostos, 18
geographic knowledge in, 101, 157
and tragedy, 241
cyclic poets, 242
catalogue poetry, 242
technique of proem, 428n.20
ἔπαινος, 9, 68, 121f.
Epicharmus of Syracuse, 361, 475n.1
Epitaphs, 96
Equality
meaning of, 103f.
criticized by Callicles, 324f.
criticized by Antiphon, 327f.
Eris, 50, 64, 70, 432n.25
Eros
cosmogonic, 65, 151
Platonic, 133f.
Sapphic, 133f.
in Theognis, 194
Dorian, 194f.
and sophia in Euripides, 357
speculation on, 433n.31
Eteocles, 260f., 279, 281, 351, 472n.63
Ethics, see Aristocrats, City-State,
Dikaiosyné, Diké, Eunomia, Phi-
losophy, etc.
Ethos, 20, 49
Eucosmia, 167
Euctemon, 340
Eunomia, 70, 94f., 141, 171, 173, 408,
410
Eupatrids, see Aristocrats
Eupolis, 362f., 370, 378
Euripides, 174, 220, 237, 240, 247, 269,
273, 285, 320, 323f., 332-57 passim,
375
subjectivism of, 270, 348

SELECTED WORDS AND PASSAGES
EMENDATIONS AND INTERPRETATIONS